Beginning Databases with MySQL

D0534096

Neil Matthew
Richard Stones

Wrox Press Ltd. ®

Beginning Databases with MySQL

First Published   February 2002

Published by Wrox Press Ltd
Arden House, 1102 Warwick Road, Acocks Green, Birmingham B27 6BH, UK
Printed in USA
ISBN 1-861006-92-6

Trademark Acknowledgements

Wrox has endeavored to provide trademark information about all the companies and products mentioned in this book by the appropriate use of capitals. However, Wrox cannot guarantee the accuracy of this information.

Credits

Authors
Neil Matthew
Richard Stones

Contributing Authors
Meeraj Kunnumpurath
Aalhad Saraf

Technical Reviewers
David Hudson
Jon Stephens

Technical Editors
Dipali Chittar
Shivanand Nadkarni
Girish Sharangpani

Index
Bill Johncocks

Production Manager
Liz Toy

Production Coordinator
Pip Wonson

Production Assistant
Dawn Chellingworth

Illustrations
Santosh Haware

Cover Design
Dawn Chellingworth

Proofreader
Agnes Wiggers

About the Authors

Neil Matthew

Neil has been programming computers of one sort or another since 1974, but doesn't feel that old. Keen on programming languages and the ways they can be used to solve different problems, he has written his fair share of emulators, interpreters, and translators, including ones for Basic, BCPL, FP (Functional Programming), Lisp, Prolog and the 6502 microprocessor hardware at the heart of the BBC Microcomputer. He graduated from the University of Nottingham with a degree in Mathematics, but got stuck into computers straight away.

He has used UNIX since 1978, including most academic and commercial variants, some now long forgotten. Highlights include UNIX versions 6 and 7 on PDP 11/34 and 11/70, Xenix on PDP 11/23 and Intel 286 and 386, BSD 4.2 on DEC VAX 11/750, UNIX System V on MicroVAX and Intel 386, Sun SunOS4 on Sparc, Solaris on Sparc and Intel, and AIX on IBM. He now collects Linux distributions to run on his home network of many PCs.

Neil's first Linux was a 0.99.11 kernel-based SLS system that was shipped across the Atlantic in boxes and boxes of floppy disks in August 1993. He has been using Linux ever since, both at home and at work, programming mainly in C, C++, and Perl. He uses and recommends Linux for Internet connections, usually as a proxy caching server for Windows LANs and also as a file and print server to Windows using SAMBA. He's sold a number of Internet firewall systems to UK companies (including to Wrox in their early days!).

Neil says that Linux combined with a free database like MySQL and a web server like Apache is a great development environment, as it offers all of the flexibility and power of traditional UNIX systems. It manages to combine the strengths of just about all of the disparate UNIX variants (such as System V and BSD). Programs written for just about any UNIX will port to Linux with little or no effort. You can also "get under the hood" with Linux as the source code is freely available.

As Head of Software and Principal Engineer at Camtec Electronics in the 1980s Neil programmed in C and C++ for real-time embedded systems. Since then he's worked on software development techniques and quality assurance both as a consultant in communications software development with Scientific Generics, and as a Systems Architect specialist with GEHE UK. Linux and other Open Source software like MySQL has played an increasing role in the work that he has undertaken over the years, from file servers, through Internet gateways, to forming the platform for a distributed radio communications system.

Neil is married to Christine and has two children, Alexandra and Adrian. He lives in a converted barn in Northamptonshire. His interests include computers, music, science fiction, chess, motor sport, and not doing it yourself.

Richard Stones

Richard started programming in the early days, when a BBC with 32k on RAM was a serious home computer. He graduated from Nottingham University, England, with an Electronics degree, but decided that software was more fun.

He has worked for a variety of companies over the years, from the very small with just two dozen employees, to the American multinational EDS. Along the way he has worked on a wide variety of interesting projects. These have ranged from communications network management systems, embedded real time systems, and multi-gigabyte help desk and user management systems, through to more mundane accountancy systems. He currently works as a Systems Architect, striving for consistency across different development projects. He has always done his best to get Linux running as part of his projects, and usually finds a niche for Linux somewhere. He has also installed Linux as file and print servers and Internet gateways, including one many years ago for Wrox themselves.

He first met UNIX-style operating systems on a PDP 11/23+. He has used many of the various commercial UNIX offerings, and bemoans the unnecessary differences between them. He first discovered Linux when Slackware CDs of the 0.99 kernel became available, and was amazed at how much quicker it ran than the commercial versions of UNIX he had previously worked on, without compromising functionality. He hopes that Linux distributions will agree on consistency of approach in a way the commercial offerings did.

He programs mainly in C, Java, and SQL, but has also worked in C++, PHP, Perl, and a little Python, as well as some proprietary real-time languages, and under duress will admit that he's quite familiar with Visual Basic, but claims he only used it because it was a lesser evil than the alternatives available at the time.

Rick is currently employed as a Systems Architect by GEHE, who are the UK's largest pharmaceutical wholesaler and retailer, as well as the largest pharmaceutical wholesaler in both France and Germany, and active in many other European countries.

Rick lives in a Leicestershire village, in England, with his wife Ann, children Jenny and Andrew, and two cats. Outside computers his passion is for classical music, especially early church music. He tries to find time to practice the piano, but it always seems to be last on the list of things to do.

Rick and Neil spoke at the first Bang!inux conference in Bangalore in February 2000, and have also given talks to their local Linux user groups.

Authors' Acknowledgments

We, Richard and Neil, would like to thank our families:

Rick's wife Ann, and children, Jenny and Andrew, for their patience during the many evenings and weekends while the book was written. Rick would also like to thank them for being so understanding about the decision to do more writing.

Neil's wife Christine for her unfailing support and understanding, and his children Alexandra and Adrian for thinking that it's cool to have a Dad who can write books.

We would also like to thank the many people who made this book possible.

Firstly, all the people who enjoyed our previous books Beginning Linux Programming, Professional Linux Programming, and Beginning Databases with PostgreSQL, making them the success they have been, providing useful feedback and spurring us on to write again.

We would like to thank the team at Wrox for their hard work on the book, especially Dan M, who helped us considerably with the initial specification of the Beginning Databases with PostgreSQL book, John F for smoothing troubled waters, and the team in Mumbai, especially Dipali, Girish, and Vijay. Thanks also to Clive Jones for his contribution of notes about some older database technologies.

We would also like to thank the people who have contributed additional material to the book; they did some excellent work.

Special thanks are also due to the team of reviewers who worked on our chapters. They provided comments and suggestions of the highest quality, and went to efforts above-and-beyond the call of duty to improve the book. Thank you very much one and all. Any errors that have slipped through are, of course, entirely our own fault.

We would also like to thank our employers, GEHE, for their support while we were writing this book.

We would like to thank the many people who have given their time and effort into MySQL and wish them every success in the future with this excellent product.

We would also like to pay homage to Linus for the Linux platform, RMS for the excellent set of GNU tools and the GPL, and the ever-expanding throng of unsung heroes who choose to make their software freely available, not forgetting those who continue to promote the cause of open source and GPLed software in other ways.

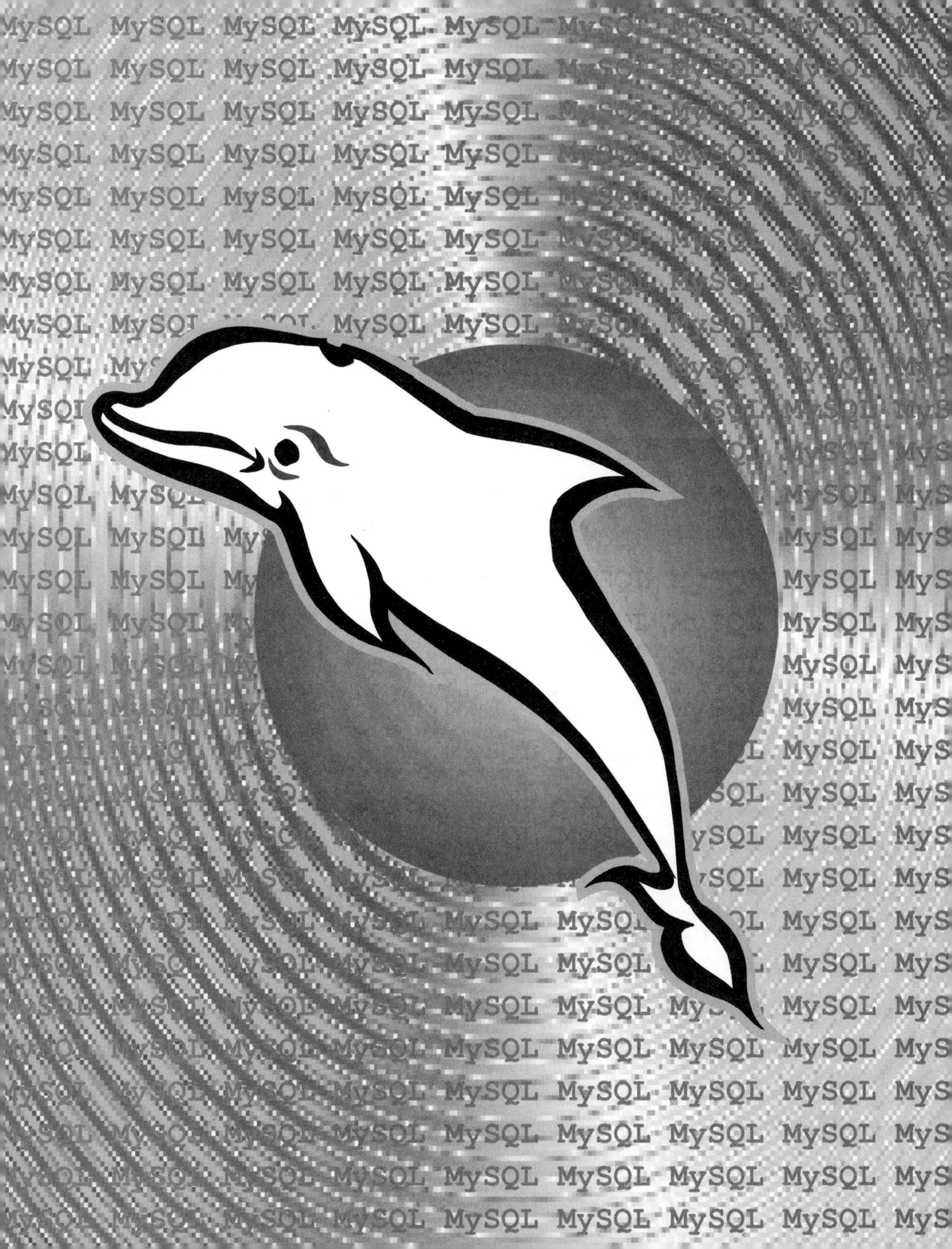

Table of Contents

Table of Contents

Table of Contents

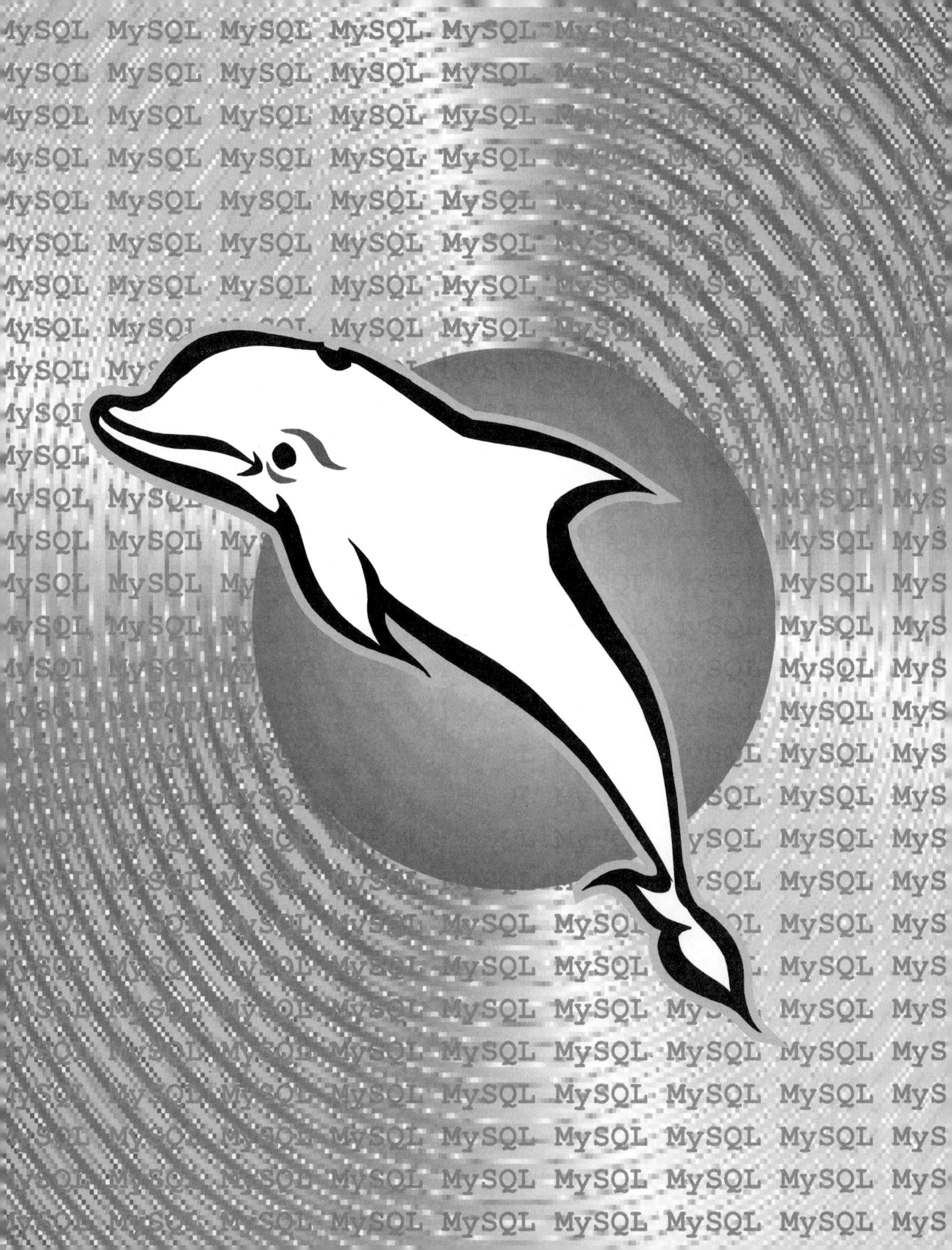

Introduction

MySQL (pronounced "my ess cue el," not "my sequel") is an Open Source relational database management system (RDBMS) that uses Structured Query Language (SQL), the most popular language for adding, accessing, and processing data in a database. Since it is open source, anyone can download MySQL, and tailor it to their needs in accordance with the General Public License (GPL). MySQL is noted mainly for its speed, reliability, and flexibility. Most users agree, however, that it works best when managing content and not executing transactions.

The MySQL relational database system was first released in January 1998 though its roots began way back in 1979, with the UNIREG database tool created by Michael 'Monty' Widenius for the Swedish company TcX. In 1994, TcX began looking around for a SQL server for use in developing web applications, and in 1995 David Axmark of Detron HB began to push for TcX to release MySQL on the Internet. MySQL is fully multi-threaded using kernel threads and provides application program interfaces (APIs) for C, C++, Eiffel, Java, Perl, PHP, Python, and TcL. MySQL allows for many column types, and offers full operator and function support in the SELECT and WHERE parts of queries.

The development team working on MySQL has already released the 'Alpha 4.0' version in September 2001, which covers features like transactions and locking. Features like stored procedures, triggers, and views are expected to be included in the subsequent versions of MySQL. By the time this book hits the market, the Alpha version of MySQL 4.1 will probably be released.

We have included in this book some useful information on some of these existing features and also on some of the expected ones. These features will include a new table definition file format, enhanced replication, and more functions for a full-text search. Later, MySQL developers hope to add fail-safe replication, a port of MySQL to BeOS, and an option to periodically flush key pages for tables with delayed keys. Over the time, MySQL plans to be fully ANSI 92/ANSI 99-compliant.

MySQL currently runs on UNIX-like platforms as well as Windows platforms. Many Internet startups have been especially interested in MySQL as an alternative to the proprietary database systems from Oracle, IBM, and Informix. NASA, Texas Instruments, Motorola, Silicon Graphics, and Yahoo's news site are some of the prominent names already hooked on to MySQL, with more to follow.

What's Covered in This Book

By reading this book, you will learn how to use MySQL effectively so that you can get your work done more productively. It consists of 16 chapters, which combine to give you an introduction to MySQL as a beginner, and take you a step towards a full understanding of databases, in particular MySQL.

Chapter 1 introduces you to the world of databases and explains why they are so useful. It also gives a general introduction to the MySQL database in particular.

Chapter 2 talks in depth about relational database principles, and how, even with a relatively straightforward database, we can take advantage of useful features of MySQL. The chapter then moves on to creating a simple database, and explains how to use some of the basic data types in it.

Chapter 3 walks you through the steps of installing MySQL from binaries and source code, both on UNIX-like environments (this chapter covers the installation on Linux) and Windows. It also covers the basics of creating and populating tables.

Chapter 4 takes a formal look at the SELECT statement, which is the heart of the SQL language. It covers various options to configure MySQL's behaviour in interpreting your data and displaying exactly the information you are looking for.

Chapter 5 introduces you to some of the graphical tools which are alternatives to the command-line tool mysql for accessing MySQL databases. It briefly covers the basic administration functions that general users and client application programs can perform.

Chapter 6 delves into other aspects of data manipulation, from adding data to the database with the INSERT command to deleting all rows from a table with the TRUNCATE command.

Chapter 7 builds on Chapter 4 by covering some of the more advanced features of the SELECT statement – aggregate functions and joins.

Chapter 8 takes a formal look at manipulating data and some advanced features like implementing constraints.

Chapter 9 talks about transactions, the 'ACID' rules, the ANSI isolation levels, and the implementation of locks.

Chapter 10 focuses on database administration. It covers issues like server control, database maintenance, backup, and recovery.

Chapter 11 discusses designing a database. It details the various stages of generating a schema and the conventional design patterns.

Chapter 12 looks at accessing MySQL from C and C++. Here you will learn to create your own client applications using these languages.

Chapter 13 looks at adding MySQL support to PHP and ways in which the MySQL database can be accessed by the PHP scripting language. It also introduces the PEAR database abstraction interface.

Chapter 14 examines accessing MySQL from Perl. It discusses the powerful string manipulation capabilities of Perl, the Perl DBI and DBIx modules, to make programming simpler.

Chapter 15 looks into Java programs, using JDBC to access relational data in a MySQL database. It also takes a peek into the features of the JDBC API.

Chapter 16 talks about non-relational storage, and other database jargons like OLTP and OLAP. To help you on your way, it gives some useful pointers to the reference material available for MySQL.

Conventions Used

You will encounter various styles of text and layout as you browse through the book. These have been used deliberately in order to make important information stand out. These styles are:

Try It Out – An Example

'Try It Out' is our way of presenting a practical example. Whenever something important is being discussed, you will find this section. This will help you understand the problem better.

How It Works

This actually gives you a step-by-step explanation of the example discussed in the 'Try It Out' section. It will tell you exactly what is going on.

> **Important information, key points, and additional information are displayed like this to make them stand out. Don't ignore them!**

If you see something like `windows.ini`, you will know that it's a file name, an object name or a function name.

Words that appear on the user interface or menu names are written are written in a different font, like Control Panel.

Code in this book has several fonts. If it is a word that we are talking about in the text, it's a distinctive font (for example, when discussing the command line tool `mysql`). If it is a command or a block of code that you can type in as a program and run, then it's in a gray box like this:

```
SELECT * FROM item;
```

Sometimes you will see the code in a mixture of styles, like this:

```
try {
    Connection con = DriverManager.getConnection(url,prop);
    Statement stmt = con.createStatement();
    ResultSet res = stmt.executeQuery("select * from MyTable");
    }catch(SQLException e) {
        //Handle exception
}
```

This is meant to draw your attention to code that is new, or relevant to the surrounding discussion (in the gray box), whilst showing it in the context of the code you have seen before (on the white background).

Where we show an output of a command we use a font type as follows:

```
+---------+---------------+------------+------------+
| item_id | description   | cost_price | sell_price |
+---------+---------------+------------+------------+
|       1 | Wood Puzzle   |      15.23 |      21.95 |
|       2 | Rubik Cube    |       7.45 |      11.49 |
|       3 | Linux CD      |       1.99 |       2.49 |
|       4 | Tissues       |       2.11 |       3.99 |
|       5 | Picture Frame |       7.54 |       9.95 |
|       6 | Fan Small     |       9.23 |      15.75 |
|       7 | Fan Large     |      13.36 |      19.95 |
|       8 | Toothbrush    |       0.75 |       1.45 |
|       9 | Roman Coin    |       2.34 |       2.45 |
|      10 | Carrier Bag   |       0.01 |       0.00 |
|      11 | Speakers      |      19.73 |      25.32 |
+---------+---------------+------------+------------+
11 rows in set (0.01 sec)
```

Downloading the Source Code

As you work through the examples in this book, you might decide that you prefer to type all the code in by hand. Many readers do prefer this, because it's a good way of getting familiar with the coding techniques that are used.

If you are one of those readers who like to type in the code, you can use our files to check the results you will be getting. They should be your first stop if you think you have typed in an error. If you don't like typing, then downloading the source code from our web site is a must! Either way it will help you with updates and debugging.

Whether you want to type in the code or not, we have made all the source code for this book available at our web site http://www.wrox.com.

Errata

We have made sincere efforts to minimize the errors in the text or in the code. However, no one is perfect and mistakes do occur. If you find an error in one of our books, like a spelling mistake or a faulty piece of code, we would be very grateful for feedback. By sending the errata you may save another reader hours of frustration, and of course, you will be helping us provide even higher quality information. Simply e-mail the information to Support@wrox.com. Your information will be checked and, if correct, posted to the errata page for that title, or used in subsequent editions of the book.

To find errata on the web site, go to http://www.wrox.com/, and simply locate the title through our Advanced Search or title list. Click on the Book Errata link, which is below the cover graphic on the book's detail page.

Technical Support

We have said in the above section that you can send your queries to the support staff, who are the first people to read them, by using the e-mail id mentioned above but please remember to write the specific book title and the last four numbers of the ISBN in the subject line. We have files on the most frequently asked questions and will answer anything general immediately. We also answer general queries about the book and the web site.

Deeper queries are forwarded to the technical editors responsible for each book. They have experience with the general programming language or particular product and are able to answer detailed technical questions on the subject. Once an issue has been resolved, the editor can post on the errata sheet on the web site.

Finally, in the unlikely event that the editors can't answer your problem, they will forward the request to an author. We try to protect our authors from any distraction from their main job. However, we are quite happy to forward specific book-related queries to them. All Wrox authors help with the support on their books. They will either mail the reader directly with their answer, or will send their response to the editor or the support department who will then pass it on to the reader.

Online Forums At p2p.wrox.com

P2P (**Programmer to Programmer**™) is a community of programmers sharing their problems and expertise. A variety of mailing lists cover all modern programming and Internet technologies. Links, resources, and an archive provide a comprehensive knowledge base. Whether you are an experienced professional or a web novice you'll find something of interest here. You could have author as well as peer support on these mailing lists. The mailing lists are moderated to ensure that messages are relevant and reasonable, which means that postings do not appear on the list until they have been read and approved.

Be confident that your query to p2p is not just being examined by a support professional, but by the many Wrox authors and other industry experts present on our mailing list.

How To Tell Us Exactly What You Think

Our commitment to readers doesn't stop when you walk out of the bookstore. We understand that errors can destroy the enjoyment of a book and can cause many wasted and frustrated hours, so we seek to minimize the distress they can cause.

Let us know how much you liked or loathed the book, and what you think we can do better next time. You can send your comments, either by returning the reply card in the back of this book, or by e-mail to feedback@wrox.com. Please be sure to mention the book title in your message.

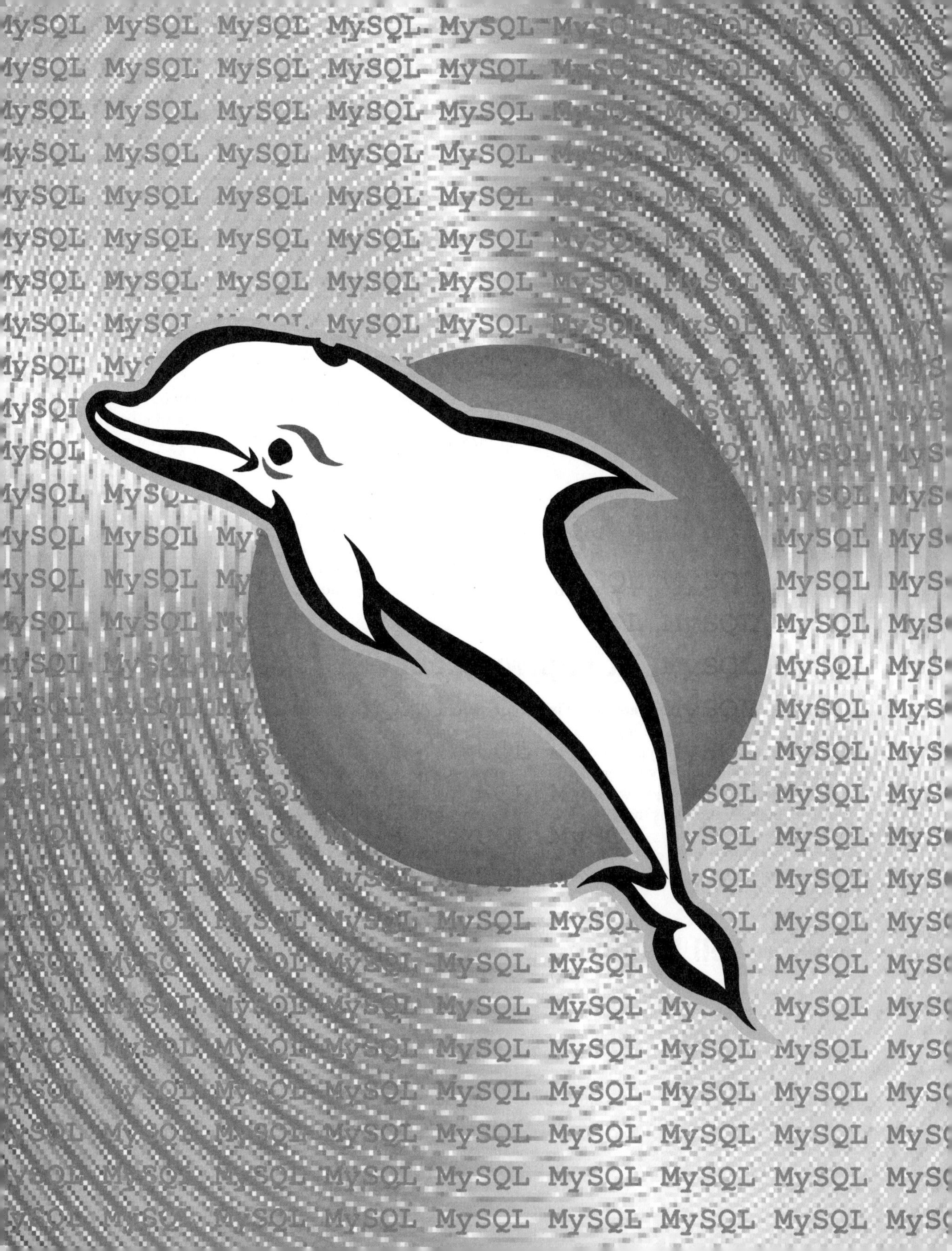
MySQL

Introduction To MySQL

This book is all about one of the most popular open source software products of recent times, a relational database called MySQL. This database is finding an eager audience among web site developers and application programmers alike. Anyone who is creating an application with non-trivial amounts of data can benefit from using a database, and MySQL is an excellent implementation of a relational database; fast, portable, open source, and free to use.

MySQL is particularly suited to web-based applications but can also be used from a wide range of programming languages including C, C++, PHP, Perl, and Java. It closely follows the industry standard for query languages – SQL92. MySQL also won the year 2000 and 2001 Linux Magazine Editor's Choice awards for top Linux Database.

We are perhaps getting a little ahead of ourselves here. You may be wondering what exactly MySQL is and why you might want to use it.

In this chapter, we will try to set the scene for the rest of the book and provide some background information on databases in general. We will cover the different types of databases, why they are useful, and where MySQL fits into this picture.

Programming with Data

Nearly all non-trivial computer applications manipulate large amounts of data and a lot of applications are written primarily to deal with data, rather than to perform calculations.

Much of recent application development is connected in some way to complex data stored in a database, so databases are a very important foundation for many applications. Resources for programming with data abound. Most good programming books will contain chapters on creating, storing, and manipulating data. You can refer to books on open source that contain information about programming with data, for example:

❏   *Beginning Linux Programming* by Neil Matthew and Richard Stones, Wrox Press (ISBN 1-861002-97-1), covers the DBM library.

❑   *Professional Linux Programming* by Neil Matthew and Richard Stones, Wrox Press (ISBN 1-861003-01-3), contains chapters on the MySQL and PostgreSQL relational database systems.

❑   *Beginning Databases with PostgreSQL* by Richard Stones and Neil Matthew, Wrox Press (ISBN 1-861005-15-6) which covers PostgreSQL database.

Data comes in all shapes and sizes and the ways that we deal with it will vary according to its nature. In some cases the data is simple, perhaps a single number such as the value of π, which might be built into a program that draws circles. The application itself may have this as a 'hard-coded' value for the ratio of the circumference of a circle to its diameter. We may call this data 'constant' as it will never change.

Another example of constant data would be the currency exchange rates used between the currencies of some European countries. In so-called 'Euro Land', the countries that are participating in the Single European Currency (Euro) have fixed the exchange rates between their national currencies to six decimal places. As a consequence, a Euro Land currency converter application could have a hard-coded table of currency names and base exchange rate (the number of national units to the Euro). These rates are never likely to change.

It is quite possible for this table of currencies to grow. As countries sign up for the Euro, their national currency exchange rates will be fixed and they would need to be added to the table.

If this happens our currency converter would need to be changed, its built-in table changed, and the application rebuilt. This will have to be done every time the currency table changes.

A better method would be to have the application read a file containing some simple currency data, maybe the name of the currency, its international symbol, and exchange rate. Then we simply alter the file when the table needs to be changed and leave the application alone.

The data file that we use has no special structure; it's just some lines of text that mean something to the particular application that reads it. Since it has no inherent structure we call it a 'flat file'. Here's what our currency file might contain:

Country	Currency	Base Exchange Rate
France	FRF	6.559570
Germany	DEM	1.955830
Italy	ITL	1936.270020
Belgium	BEF	40.339901

Although we show the data here as a table, a flat file will probably consist of lines of data with separators such as tabs or commas between the fields like this:

```
France,FRF,6.559570
Germany,DEM,1.955830
Italy,ITL,1936.270020
Belgium,BEF,40.339901
```

Flat File Databases

Flat files are extremely useful for many application types. As long as the size of the file remains manageable enough for us to be able to make changes easily and we do not need to handle too many users accessing the file at the same time, a flat file scheme may be sufficient for our needs.

Many systems and applications, particularly on UNIX, use flat files for their data storage or data interchange. The UNIX password file is an ideal example.

Here is a typical extract from a password file from a Linux system. Notice that in this case colons separate the fields:

```
root:x:0:0:root:/root:/bin/bash
bin:x:1:1:bin:/bin:/bin/bash
firewall:x:41:31:firewall account:/var/lib/firewall:/bin/false
mysql:x:60:2:MySQL Database User:/var/mysql:/bin/false
```

The flat file example we've just looked at consists of a number of elements of information or attributes, together making up what we might term a record. The records are arranged so that each line in the file represents a single record and the whole file acts to keep the related records together. Sometimes this scheme is not quite good enough and we have to add extra features to support the job the application has to do.

Returning to the foreign currency example we saw earlier, suppose we decide to extend the application to record the language spoken in each country, its population, and area. In a flat file we essentially have one record per line, each made up of several attributes. Each individual attribute in a record is always in the same place, for example the currency short name indicator is always the second attribute so we could think of looking at the data by column, where a column always contains the same type of information. Hence, to add the language spoken in a particular country we might think that we just need to add a new column to each of our lines.

We hit a snag with this as soon as we realize that some countries have more than one official language. So, in our record for Belgium we would have to cater for both Flemish and French. In Switzerland, we normally have to cater for four languages.

This problem is known as **repeating groups**. We now have a situation where a perfectly valid item (language) will be repeated in a record. Not only does the record (row) repeat but the data in that row as well. Flat files do not cope with this, as it is impossible to determine where data elements of one type (in this case, languages) stop and the rest of the record starts. Just about the only way round this (without creating further tables in more flat files) is to add some structure to the file, but then it would not be 'flat' any more.

The 'repeating groups' problem is very common and is the issue that really started the drive towards more sophisticated database management systems. We can attempt to resolve this problem by using ordinary text files with a little more structure. These are still often referred to as flat files but are probably better described as structured text files. Here's another example.

An application that stores the details of DVDs might need to record the year of production, director, genre, and cast list. We could design a file that looks a little like a `Windows.ini` file to store this information:

```
[2001: A Space Odyssey]
year=1968
director=Stanley Kubrick
genre=science fiction
starring=Keir Dullea
starring=Leonard Rossiter
...
[Toy Story]
...
```

We have solved the repeating groups problem by introducing some tags like `year` and `director` to indicate the type of each element in the record. Now our application has to read and interpret a more complex file, just to get at its data. Updating a record and searching in this kind of structure can be quite difficult. How can we make sure that the descriptions for genre or classification are chosen from a specific subset? How can we easily produce a sorted list of Kubrick films?

As data requirements get more and more complex, we are forced to write more and more application code for reading and storing our data. If we extend our DVD application to include functions that make it useful to a DVD rental storeowner with membership details and rentals, returns and reservations, the prospect of maintaining all of that information in flat files becomes very unappealing.

A third, and all too common problem, is simply that of size. Although the above structure could be scanned by 'brute force' to answer complex searching with queries such as 'tell me the addresses of all my members who have rented more than one comedy movie in the last three months'; not only will it be very difficult to code, but the performance will be dire. This is because the application has no choice but to process the whole file to look for any piece of information, even if the question relates to just a single entry such as 'How many films were produced in 1968?'

What we need is a general-purpose way of handling data, not a solution invented many times to fit slightly different, but very similar problems. We should not need to reinvent the wheel (of data storage/retrieval) each time we write a new application module.

Over the years there has been a lot of research, extending the basic flat file technique into ever more complex forms. Special techniques such as index files, record hashing, and linked files were developed until at last the solution we use today appeared.

What we need is a database.

What Is a Database?

The Merriam-Webster online dictionary (http://www.m-w.com) defines a database as a usually large collection of data organized especially for rapid search and retrieval (as by a computer).

A database management system (DBMS) is usually a suite of libraries, applications, and utilities that relieve an application developer from the burden of worrying about the details of storing and managing data. It will also provide facilities for searching and updating records.

Database management systems come in a number of flavors, developed over the years to solve particular kinds of data storage problems.

Database Types

During the 1960s and 1970s, databases were developed which solved the repeating groups problem in several different ways. This development resulted in what are termed **models** for database systems. Research performed at IBM provided much of the basis for these models that are still in use today.

One of the main drivers in early database system designs was efficiency. It is much easier to deal with database records that are of fixed length or at least have a fixed number of elements per record (columns per row). This essentially avoids the 'repeating groups' problem. If you are a programmer in just about any procedural language, you will readily see that in this case you can read each record of a database into a data record or structure in that language. Real life is rarely that accommodating. We often have to deal with inconveniently structured data.

The three models for database systems are:

- ❑ Hierarchical Database Model
- ❑ Network Database Model
- ❑ Relational Database Model

Hierarchical Database Model

The IMS database system from IBM in the 1960s introduced the hierarchical model for databases. In this model, data records are considered to be composed of collections of others. This solves the repeating groups problem.

The model can be best described using an extended parent-child structure. For example, a car is composed of (say) major components such as the chassis, a body, and running gear. Each of these components can be broken down into subcomponents. For example, the running gear could be broken down into engine, gearbox, and suspension. These subcomponents could be broken down further, until we get to the nuts and bolts and other individual components that make up every automobile.

Hierarchical model databases are still in use today. A hierarchical database system is able to optimize the data storage to make it more efficient in answering particular questions (or queries in database parlance), for example to determine which automobile uses a particular part.

Network Database Model

The network database model overcomes some of the problems associated with hierarchical models, particularly in representing many-to-many relationships.

This model introduces the idea of pointers within the database. Records can contain direct references to other records. So, for example, we may keep a record for each customer we deal with. Each customer has placed many orders with us over time (a repeating group). The data is arranged so that the customer record contains a pointer to the first order record. Each order record contains both the order data for that specific record and a pointer to the next order record. The pointer for the last order will reference the customer record, signifying the end of the group.

In our currency application we might end up with record structures that resemble this:

Once the data is loaded, we end up with a linked (or networked, hence the name network model) list used for the languages, as shown in the figure below:

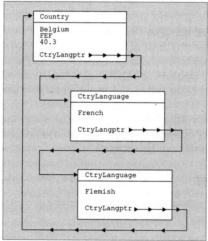

The two record types we see here would be stored in the same area of the database, with the CtryLanguage records being placed on the same database page as the Country record, not in separate tables or files as in other database models. A record key would determine the database page for the Country records, which in our case would be the country name.

A network model database has some strong advantages. If you need to discover all of the records of one record type that are related to a specific record of another type (like languages spoken in a country in our example) you can find them extremely quickly by following the pointers.

A network database can also be used for complicated data structures as each record can contain pointers to many other record types, as well as keys. In our example, a country may contain a repeating group of languages. This could also be meaningfully represented as a language containing a group of countries. This is an example of a many-to-many relationship mentioned earlier. A better database design would be to have a separate language record, which could be accessed by using a key or by the addition of a pointer in the CtryLanguage record. This would be more efficient in terms of storage.

The main disadvantage of the network model is that, once a database has been designed and is populated with data, it becomes difficult to change the design of the database or even the area sizes. For a general-purpose database this is just too inflexible. Writing applications that use a network model database can also be very tiresome, as the application typically has to take responsibility for setting up and maintaining the pointers as records are updated and deleted.

Relational Database Model

The theory of database management systems took a gigantic leap forward in 1970 with the publication of '*A Relational Model of Data for Large Shared Data Banks*', a paper by E. F. Codd (see http://www.acm.org/classics/nov95/toc.html). This revolutionary paper introduced the idea of **relations** and showed how tables could be used to represent facts that relate to 'real world' objects and hold data about them. By this time, it had also become clear one of the initial driving forces behind database design, efficiency, was often less important than another concern, that of data structure. The relational database model emphasizes data structure and the relationships between data elements much more than either of the earlier models.

There are several important rules that define a relational database management system (RDBMS). We will discuss a few of them here:

❑ Records in Tables are known as tuples

❑ Each attribute in a record must be atomic

❑ Referential Integrity

Firstly, records in a table are known as **tuples**. A tuple is an ordered group of components or attributes, each of which has a defined type. All tuples within a set of data or table should follow the same pattern, in that they all have the same number and types of components. Here is an example of a set of tuples:

```
{"France", "FRF", 6.56}
{"Belgium", "BEF", 40.1}
```

Each of these tuples has three attributes: a country name (string), a currency (string), and an exchange rate (a floating point number). In a relational database, all records that are added to this set or table must follow the same form, so the following are disallowed:

```
{"Germany", "DEM"}
- too few attributes

{"Switzerland", "CHF", "French", "German", "Italian", "Romansch"}
- too many attributes
{1936.27, "ITL", "Italy"}
- incorrect attribute types (wrong order)
```

Furthermore, in any table of tuples there can be no duplicates. This means that in any table in a relational database there cannot be any identical rows or records.

This might seem to be a rather draconian restriction since, in a system that records orders placed by customers, it would appear to disallow the same customer from ordering the same product from us twice. We will see in the next chapter that in practice there is an easy way to work around this requirement, by adding an additional attribute.

Secondly, each attribute in a record must be **atomic**, that is, a single piece of data, not another record or a list of other attributes. Also, the type of corresponding attributes in every record in the table must be the same, as we've seen. In practical terms this means they will all be either strings, integers, floating point values, or some other type supported by the database system. For example, all entries in the exchange rate column will be floating point numbers. Also note that no strings are allowed.

> **An attribute that we use to distinguish otherwise identical records, is called a key. Sometimes a combination of more than one attribute can be used as a key.**

The attribute or attributes that we use to distinguish a particular record in a table from all the other records in a table, in other words what makes this record unique, is called a **primary key**. In a relational database, each relation or table must have a primary key, something that makes each record different from all the others in that table.

One last rule that influences the structure of a relational database is **referential integrity**. This is a desire that all of the records in the database make sense at all times. The database application programmer often has to be careful to make sure that the code does not break the integrity of the database. Consider what happens when we delete a customer. If we try to remove the customer from the customer table (tables will be defined in later chapters) that contains data about customers, we also need to delete all of his orders from another table that could contain data on his orders, for example an order table (once again, defined in later chapters). Otherwise, we will be left with records about orders that have no valid customer.

We will see much more on the theory and practice of relational databases in later chapters. For now, it is enough to know that the relational model for databases is based on some mathematical concepts of sets and relations. There are however, some rules that need to be observed by systems that are built to this model.

Query Languages

Relational database management systems offer ways to add and update data, of course. However, their power stems more from their ability to allow users to ask questions about the data stored, in the form of queries. Unlike many earlier database designs, which were often structured around the type of query that the data needed to answer, relational databases are much more flexible at answering questions that were not envisaged at the time the database was designed.

Codd's proposals for the relational model use the fact that relations define sets and sets can be manipulated mathematically. He suggested that queries might use a branch of theoretical logic called the predicate calculus and that query languages would use this as their base. This would bring unprecedented power for searching and selecting data sets.

One of the first implementations of a query language was QUEL, used in the **Ingres** database developed in the late 1970s. Another query language that takes a different approach is QBE (Query By Example). At around the same time a team at IBM's research center developed SQL (Structured Query Language), usually pronounced 'sequel'.

SQL is a standardized language, the most commonly used definition is **ISO/IEC 9075:1992**, **'Information Technology --- Database Languages --- SQL'**. This is more simply referred to as SQL92 or sometimes ANSI X3.135-1992, which is an identical US standard, differing only in some cover pages. These standards replaced an earlier standard, SQL89. In fact, there is also a later standard, SQL99, but that is not yet in common usage and the updates generally don't affect the core SQL language.

There are three levels of conformance to SQL92: Entry SQL, Intermediate SQL, and Full SQL. By far, the most common conformance level is 'Entry', and MySQL implements many of the SQL features needed for this level of conformance, but there are some significant omissions. These missing features do not prevent MySQL from being a useful database system; in many cases there are workarounds that can be used to achieve similar effects. We will cover MySQL's SQL conformance in more detail in the subsequent chapters.

The SQL language comprises three types of commands. They are related to data manipulation, data definition, and data controlling:

❑ **Data Manipulation Language (DML)**
    This is the part of SQL that you will use 90% of the time. It is made up of the commands for inserting, deleting, updating, and most importantly selecting data from the database.

❑ **Data Definition Language (DDL)**
    These are the commands for creating tables and controlling other aspects of the database that are more structural than data related.

❑ **Data Control Language (DCL)**
    This is a set of commands that generally control permissions on the data, such as defining access rights. Many database users will never use these commands because they work in larger company environments where a database administrator is employed, or even several, specifically to manage the database; usually one of the roles of an administrator is to control permissions.

As you read through this book, you will be learning SQL at length. By the time you get to the end, you will be comfortable with a wide range of SQL statements and their usage. SQL has become very widely adopted as a standard for database query languages and, as we have mentioned, is defined in a series of international standards. Today, just about every useful relational database system supports SQL to a greater or lesser extent. It has become a great unifier since it means that a database application written to use SQL as the interface, can be ported to use another database at little cost in terms of time and effort.

Commercial pressures, however, dictate that database manufacturers distinguish their products from one another. This has led to SQL variations, not helped by the fact that the standard for SQL does not define commands for many of the database administration tasks that are an essential part of using a database in the real world. So, there are differences between the SQL used by (for example) Oracle, SQL Server, and MySQL.

We will see a lot more of SQL during the rest of the book. At this point, we will take a very brief look at some examples to show what SQL looks like. You will see that we do not need to worry about the formal basis of SQL to be able to use it.

Here is some SQL for creating a new table in a database. This example creates a table for items that are offered for sale and will be part of an order:

```
CREATE TABLE item
(
    item_id                 integer,
    description             char(64)          not null,
    cost_price              numeric(7,2),
    sell_price              numeric(7,2)
);
```

We state that the table requires an integer identifier, which will act as a primary key. Each item will have a unique identifier so that we can tell items apart. The description is a text attribute of 64 characters. The cost and sell prices are defined to be floating point numbers specified to two decimal places.

> **As an exercise, try to write down some SQL for creating a table suitable for holding the foreign currency data we considered earlier.**

Next, we have some SQL that can be used to populate the table we have just created. This is very straightforward:

```
INSERT INTO item(item_id, description, cost_price, sell_price)
values(1, "Fan Small", 9.23, 15.75);
INSERT INTO item(item_id, description, cost_price, sell_price)
values(2, "Fan Large", 13.36, 19.95);
INSERT INTO item(item_id, description, cost_price, sell_price)
values(3, "Toothbrush", 0.75, 1.45);
```

We will see later that we can arrange for the item_id to be generated automatically by the database system. In standard SQL it would have type serial, which means that every time an item is added, a new, unique, item_id will be created in sequence. In MySQL we use the type integer auto_increment, which has a similar behavior.

The heart of SQL is the SELECT statement. It is used to create what are widely known in SQL circles as result sets. These are groups of records (or attributes from records) that match a particular criterion. The criteria can be quite complex if required. These result sets can then be used as the targets for changes with an UPDATE statement or delete with DELETE.

Here are some examples of SELECT statements:

```
SELECT * FROM customer, orderinfo
    WHERE orderinfo.customer_id = customer.customer_id GROUP BY customer_id

SELECT customer.title, customer.fname, customer.lname,
    COUNT(orderinfo.orderinfo_id) AS "Number of orders"
    FROM customer, orderinfo
    WHERE customer.customer_id = orderinfo.customer_id
    GROUP BY customer.title, customer.fname, customer.lname
```

These SELECT statements respectively list all customer orders and count the orders each customer has made. We will see the results of these SQL statements in Chapter 2, *Relational Database Principles,* and learn much more about SELECT in Chapter 4, *Accessing Your Data.*

With MySQL, we can access our data in several ways. We can:

❑   Use a command line application to execute SQL statements.

❑   Use function calls (APIs) to prepare and execute SQL statements, scan result sets, and perform updates from a large variety of different programming languages.

❑   Access the data indirectly, using a driver, such as the ODBC (Open Database Connectivity) or the JDBC (Java Database Connectivity) standard used by Java programs or a standard library, such as Perl's DBI, to access our MySQL database.

Database Management Systems

A DBMS, as mentioned above, is a suite of programs that allows the construction of databases and applications that use them. The responsibilities of a DBMS include:

❑   **Creating the database**
Some systems will manage one large file and create one or more databases inside it, others may use many operating system files or utilize a raw disk partition directly. Users need not worry about the low-level structure of these files, as the DBMS provides all of the access developers and users need.

❑   **Providing query and update facilities**
A DBMS will have a method of asking for data that matches certain criteria, such as all orders made by a particular customer that have not yet been delivered. Before the widespread introduction of the SQL standard, the way that queries like this were expressed varied from system to system.

❑ **Multi-tasking**
If a database is used by several applications or is accessed concurrently by several users at the same time, then the DBMS will make sure that each user's request is processed without impacting the others. This means that users only need to wait in line if someone else is writing to the precise item of data that they wish to read (or write). It is possible to have many simultaneous reads of data going on at the same time. In practice, different database systems support different degrees of multi-tasking and may even have configurable levels, as we will see in Chapter 9, *Transactions and Locking.*

❑ **Keeping an audit trail**
A DBMS will keep a log of all the changes to the data for a period of time. This can be used to investigate errors, but perhaps even more importantly, can be used to reconstruct data in the event of a fault in the system, perhaps an unscheduled power down. Typically, this will include a data backup and log of transactions since the backup can be used to restore the database in case of disk failure.

❑ **Managing the security of the database**
A DBMS will provide access controls so that only authorized users can manipulate the data held in the database and the structure of the database itself (the attributes, tables, and indexes). Typically, there will be a hierarchy of users defined for any particular database, from a 'superuser' who can change anything, through users with permission, to add or delete data, down to users able only to read specific data. The DBMS will have facilities to add and delete users and specify which features of the database system they are able to use.

❑ **Maintaining referential integrity**
Many database systems provide features that help to maintain referential integrity, the 'correctness of the data', as mentioned earlier. Typically, they will disallow a data change and report an error when an insert or update will break the relational model rules.

What Is MySQL?

Now we are in a position to say what MySQL actually is. It is a database management system that incorporates the relational model for its databases and supports the SQL standard query language.

MySQL also happens to be pretty capable, very reliable, and has good performance characteristics. It runs on just about any UNIX platform, including UNIX-like systems, such as Solaris, AIX, FreeBSD, and Linux. It can also be run on Mac OS X and Windows NT/2000 servers or even Microsoft workstation systems such as 9x/ME/XP for development. Oh, and it's free for most uses and you can have the source code.

Since release 3.23 MySQL has been very stable, with each component of the system given a rating from 'stable' through 'gamma' and 'beta' to 'alpha', in order of decreasing stability. The current state can be found in the MySQL Reference Manual, part of the online documentation shipped with MySQL.

MySQL has proven to be very reliable in use, if you stick to the 'stable' components. Each release is carefully controlled and, given the large user community and universal access to the source code, bugs can get fixed very quickly.

The performance of MySQL has always been impressive and in some circumstances it compares well with commercial products. Some less fully featured database systems will outperform it at the cost of lower overall functionality. Then again, for simple enough applications, so will a flat file database.

A Short History of MySQL

MySQL started life in the mid-1990s. Michael 'Monty' Widenius at TcX DataKonsultAB in Sweden initially developed it. The first public release came in May 1995.

At first, MySQL was an attempt to overcome some of the limitations in another freely available database system, 'mSQL'. Since then progress has been very rapid, especially since contributors from the Internet community saw the potential of MySQL in providing a robust database platform for web sites.

Today a team of developers led by Michael Widenius at MySQL AB continues to develop MySQL. According to MySQL AB there are over two million installations of MySQL worldwide. Users have access to the source code and contribute fixes, enhancements, and suggestions for new features. The official MySQL releases are made via http://www.MySQL.org.

Commercial support is available from MySQL AB. See the *Resources* section at the end of the chapter for more details.

The MySQL Architecture

One of MySQL's strengths derives from its architecture. In common with commercial database systems, MySQL can be used in a client-server environment. This has many benefits for both users and developers.

The heart of a MySQL installation is the database server process. It runs on a single server (MySQL does not yet have the high availability features of a few enterprise-class commercial database systems that can spread the load across several servers giving additional scalability and resilience). However, MySQL will happily take advantage of multiple CPUs in a server.

Applications that need to access the data stored in the database are required to do so via the database process. These client programs cannot access the data directly, even if they are running on the same computer as the server process.

This separation into client and server allows applications to be distributed. We can use a network to separate clients from our server and develop client applications in an environment that suits the users. For example, we might implement the database on UNIX and create client programs that run on Microsoft Windows.

The diagram below shows a typical distributed MySQL application:

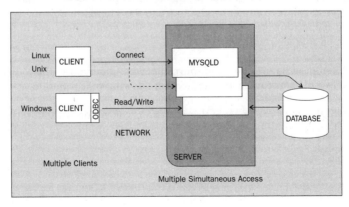

Here we can see two clients connecting to the server across a network. For MySQL, this needs to be a TCP/IP network – a local area network or possibly even the Internet. Each client connects to the main database server process (shown here as MYSQLD), which creates a new server process specifically for servicing access requests for this client.

Concentrating on the data handling in a server program, rather than attempting to control many clients accessing the same data stored in a shared directory on a server, allows MySQL to efficiently maintain the data's integrity even with many simultaneous users.

The client programs connect using a message protocol specific to MySQL. It is possible however, to install software on the client that provides a standard interface for the application to work to, for example, the ODBC standard or the JDBC standard. The availability of an ODBC driver allows many existing applications to use MySQL as a database, including Microsoft Office products such as Excel and Access. We will see more MySQL connectivity in later chapters.

The client-server architecture for MySQL allows a division of labor. A server machine well suited to the storage and access of large amounts of data can be used as a secure data repository. Sophisticated graphical applications can be developed for the clients. Alternatively, a web-based front end can be created to access the data and return results as web pages to a standard web browser with no additional client software at all. Again, we will return to these ideas in a later chapter.

Open source Licensing

As we start the 21st century, much is being made of open source software, of which MySQL is a good example. But what does this mean exactly?

The term 'open source' has a very specific meaning when applied to software. It means that the software is supplied with the source code included. It does not necessarily mean that there are no conditions applied to the software's use. It is still licensed, in that you are given permission to use the software in certain ways.

An open source license will grant you permission to use the software, modify it, and redistribute it without paying license fees. This means that you may use MySQL in your organization as you see fit.

Since you have the source code, if you have problems with open source software, you can either fix them yourself or give the code to someone else to try to fix. There are now many commercial companies offering support for open source products so that you do not have to feel isolated if you choose to use an open source product.

There are many different variations on open source licenses, some more liberal than others. All of them adhere to the principle of source code availability and allowing redistribution.

The license for MySQL allows use of MySQL within an organization without restriction. You may need a license if you wish to incorporate MySQL into a commercial application for sale to others.

The MySQL manual says:

'MySQL is Open Source Software. open source means that it is possible for anyone to use and modify. Anybody can download MySQL from the Internet and use it without paying anything. Anybody so inclined can study the source code and change it to fit their needs. MySQL uses the GPL (GNU General Public License) to define what you may and may not do with the software in different situations. If you feel uncomfortable with the GPL or need to embed MySQL into a commercial application, you can buy a commercially licensed version'.

Resources

There are many sources of further information about databases in general and MySQL, both in print and in online documentation.

For more on the theory of databases check out the Tech Talk section of David Frick's site at http://www.frick-cpa.com.

The official MySQL site is http://www.MySQL.com where you can find more information about MySQL; download copies of MySQL; browse the official documentation, additional contributed software such as management tools, GUI interfaces, and much more.

Commercial support for MySQL is also available from MySQL AB, again at http://www.MySQL.com. A commercial version of MySQL is available from NuSphere Inc. at http://www.NuSphere.com.

For more information on open source software and the principle of freedom in software, take a few moments to visit these two sites:

- ❏   http://www.gnu.org
- ❏   http://www.opensource.org

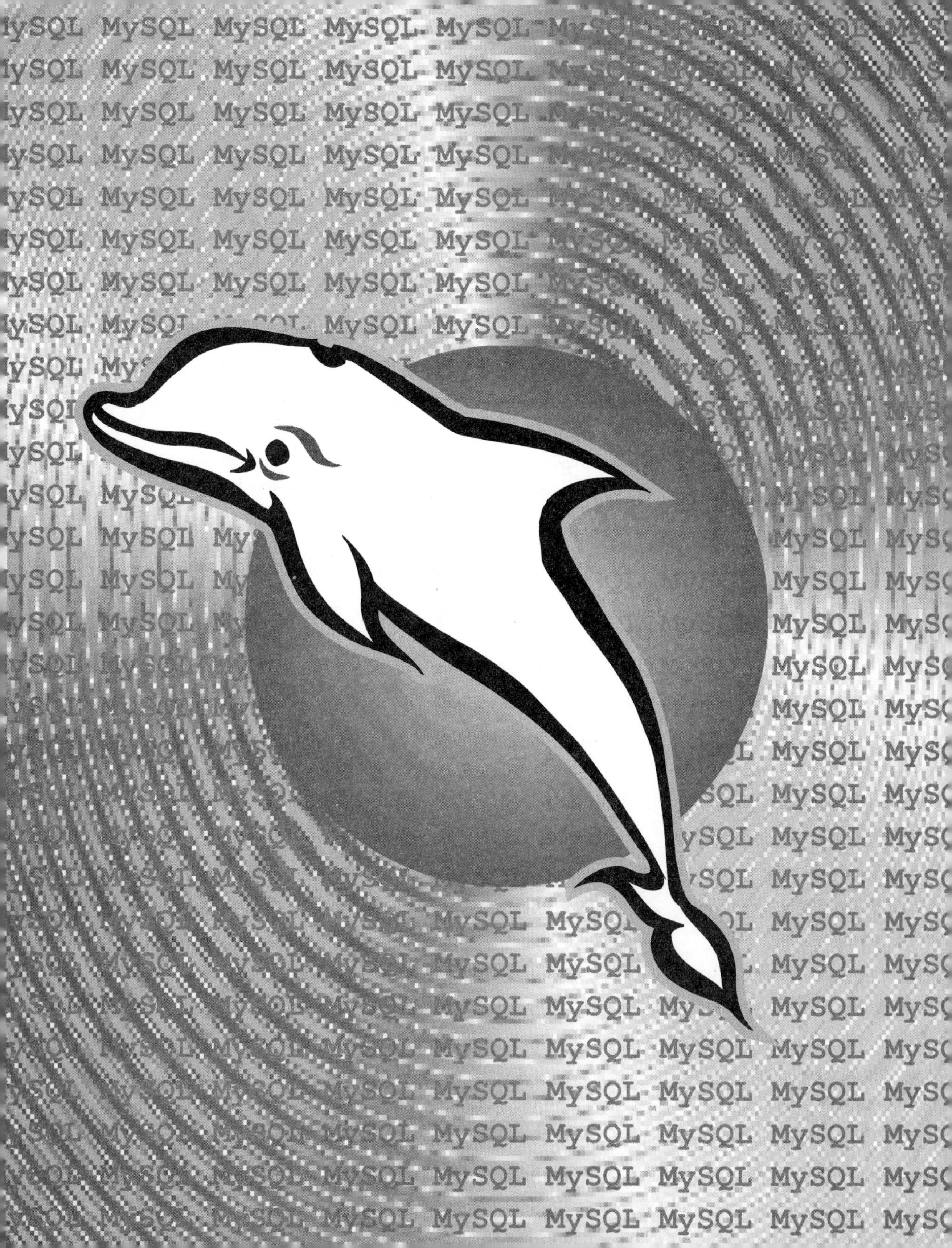
MySQL

Relational Database Principles

In this chapter we are going to look at what makes a database system, particularly a relational one like MySQL, so useful for real world data. We will start by looking at spreadsheets, which have much in common with relational databases, but also have significant limitations.

We will see how a relational database has many advantages over spreadsheets and how, even with a relatively straightforward database, we can take advantage of useful features of MySQL. Along the way we will continue with our introduction to the SQL language.

We will be taking a look at the following topics in this chapter:

- ❑ Spreadsheets and their limitations
- ❑ What's different about a database?
- ❑ Putting data into a database
- ❑ A basic database design with multiple tables
- ❑ Establishing relationships between tables
- ❑ Designing tables
- ❑ The Customer/Order database
- ❑ Some basic data types including NULL

Spreadsheets

Spreadsheet applications, such as Microsoft Excel, are widely used as a way of storing and inspecting data. Indeed, we often use a spreadsheet as an effective way of taking a set of data and looking at it in many different ways. It's easy to sort the data in different columns and see its features just by looking at it, provided your data is not too large.

Unfortunately, people often mistake a tool that is good for inspecting and manipulating data as a tool suitable for storing and sharing complex data between multiple users. The two needs are often very different.

Most people will be familiar with one or more spreadsheets, and quite at home with the data being arranged in a set of rows and columns, as we see below in a StarOffice spreadsheet holding a set of customer details:

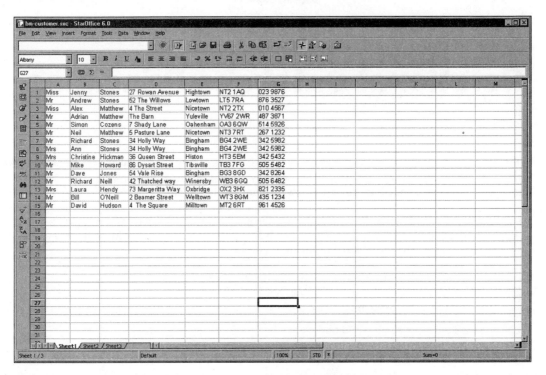

Certainly, such information is easy to see and modify. Probably without even thinking about it, we have designed this spreadsheet to incorporate several features that will be handy to remember when we start designing databases. Each customer has a separate row, and each piece of information about the customer is held in a separate column. For example, their first and last names are held in separate columns, which makes it easy to sort the data by last or first name, should we need to. The exact way we break data down into columns will depend on our needs; what is reasonable in one case may be less than ideal in another. For example, in this sample data we have not attempted to separate the house number or name from the street name. In some applications it may be desirable to separate them.

Some Terminology

Before we move on, let's just ensure we have our terminology straight by labeling a small section of the data. Surely, you all know about rows and columns, but here's a refresher:

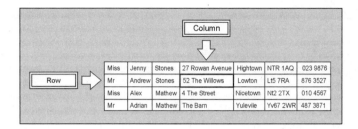

The intersection of a column and a row is a cell. In the diagram above, the arrows, showing the address line '52 The Willows', indicate a single cell.

Limitations of Spreadsheets

What is wrong with storing our customer information in a spreadsheet? The answer may be "absolutely nothing", provided you don't have a large number of customers and you don't have a large number of details for each customer. It also helps if you don't need to store any other information such as the orders each customer has placed, and there are not too many people who want to update the information at once. That might sound like a long list of possible problems, but it just depends on whether any of them are applicable for your circumstances.

There are a lot of very good uses of spreadsheets that make them a great tool for solving many problems. Just like you wouldn't (or at least shouldn't!) try to hammer in a nail with a screwdriver, sometimes spreadsheets are just not the right tool for the job.

Just imagine what it would be like if a large company, with many thousands of customers, kept the master copy of their customer list in a simple spreadsheet. In a big company, it's likely that several people would need to update the list, probably at the same time. Although file locking can ensure that only one person updates the list at any one time, as the number of people trying to edit the list grow, they will spend longer and longer waiting for their turn. In reality, what we would like is to allow many people to simultaneously read, update, add, and delete data, and merely ensure that updates are consistent. Clearly, simple file locking is going to be totally inadequate to efficiently handle this problem.

Suppose, we also wanted to store details of each order a customer placed. We could start putting order information next to each customer, but as the number of orders per customer grew, the spreadsheet would get more and more complex. Look what happens when we start trying to add some basic order information against each customer:

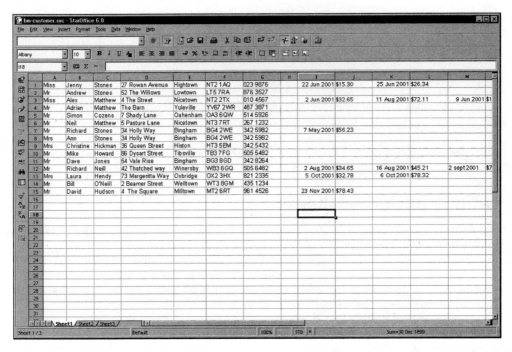

Unfortunately, it's not looking quite so elegant anymore. We now have rows of arbitrary length, which is not a nice way to store the value of each order, and will make life difficult when we want to calculate how much each customer has spent with us. Eventually, we will exceed the number of columns allowed in each row. It's the repeating groups problem we saw in the last chapter.

Here is an example of how easily you can exceed the capabilities of a spreadsheet. An acquaintance was trying to set up a spreadsheet as a favor for a friend who runs a small business. This small business makes leather items, and the price of the item depends not only on the time to make the item, but also on the unit cost of the leather used in its manufacture. The owner would buy leather in batches, whose unit prices varied significantly. Then they would use their stock on a 'first in, first used' basis as they made items for sale, normally many per batch. The challenge was to create a spreadsheet to:

❑   Track the stock

❑   Track how many batches of each type of leather were left

❑   Track how much had been paid for the batch currently being used

❑   Also, to make matters more complex, track the number of grades of leather in stock

After several days of effort, they discovered that this apparently straightforward stock-keeping requirement is a surprisingly difficult problem to transfer to a spreadsheet. The variable nature of the number of stock records does not fit well with the spreadsheet philosophy.

The point we are making here is that spreadsheets are great in their place, but there are limits to their usefulness.

What's Different About a Database?

When you look at it superficially, a relational database such as MySQL has many similarities to a spreadsheet but, as we will soon see, it is much more flexible. It can efficiently store much more complex data than a spreadsheet, and it also has many other features that make it a better choice as a data store, such as managing multiple simultaneous users across a network.

Let's first look at storing our simple single sheet customer list in a database, and see what benefits this might have. Later in the chapter, we will extend this and see how MySQL can help us solve our customer orders problem.

As we saw in the previous chapter, databases are made up of tables, or in more formal terminology, 'relations'. We will stick to using the term 'tables' in this book. First, we need to design a table to hold our customer information. The good news is that a spreadsheet of data is often an almost ready-made solution, since it holds the data in a number of rows and columns. To get started with a basic database table, we need to decide on three things:

❑ How many columns we need to store the attributes associated with each item

❑ What type of data each attribute (column) needs to store

❑ How to distinguish different rows from each other

Choosing Columns

If you look back at our original spreadsheet for our customer information, you can see that we have already decided on what seems a sensible set of columns for each customer, the first name, last name, zip code, and so on. The first criterion is already met.

Choosing a Data Type for Each Column

The second criterion is to determine what type of data goes in each column. While spreadsheets allow each cell to have a different type, in a database table each column must have the same type. Just like most programming languages, database columns have types. Most of the time the most basic types are all you need to know; the main choice is between integer numbers, floating point numbers, fixed length text, variable length text, and date and time information. We will come back to MySQL data types later in this chapter, and in more detail in Chapter 8, *Data Definition and Manipulation*. Often the easiest way to decide the appropriate data type is simply to look at some sample data.

In our customer data, we might decide to use text for all the columns, even though the phone numbers are numbers. Storing the phone number as a literal number could easily result in the loss of leading zeros, preventing us from storing international dial codes (+), using brackets around area codes, and so on. It doesn't take very much thought to determine that a phone number can often be much more than a simple integer.

Using a character string to store the telephone number might not be the best decision, since we could also accidentally store all sorts of strange characters, but it is generally a better starting point than a number type. We can always refine our initial design later. We can see that the length of the title (Mr., Mrs., Dr.) is always very short, and is unlikely to ever be longer than four characters, though of course there are some longer titles, such as 'Reverend' normally having standard abbreviations. Similarly, zip codes also have a fixed maximum length. Therefore, we will make both of these columns fixed length fields, but leave all the other columns as variable length, since, for example, we have no easy way of knowing how long a person's last name might be.

Another important difference between spreadsheet rows and database rows is that the number of columns in a database table must be the same for all the rows. That's how it was in our original version of the spreadsheet that just stored the customer name and address details.

Identifying Rows Uniquely

Our last problem in changing our spreadsheet into a database table is a little subtle, as it comes from the way databases manage relations between tables. We have to decide on what makes each row of customer data different from any other customer row in the database.

In other words, how do we tell our customers apart? In a spreadsheet, we tend not to worry about the exact details of what distinguishes customers, but in database design this is a key question, since relational database rules require each row to be unique in some way. When data is put into a spreadsheet it will be assigned a row number, but this is not permanently associated with the data, it is just a convenience. If we were to sort the data in the spreadsheet, the row numbers assigned to each customer details might change.

The obvious answer to distinguishing customers might seem to be 'by name', but unfortunately that's not quite good enough. It is possible that we could have two customers with the same name. Another item you might choose is phone number, but that fails when two customers share a phone. At this point you might try and apply some imagination, and suggest using a combination of name and phone number.

Certainly, it's unlikely that two customers will have both the same name and the same phone number, but quite apart from that being inelegant, another problem is lurking. What happens if a customer changes phone provider, or moves house, and so changes their phone number? By our definition, the customer must then be a different customer, because they are 'different' from the customer we had previously in the identifying fields. Of course we, as humans, know that they are the same customer with a new phone number, but computers are not noted for their ability to reason; they just apply rules.

This problem of identifying uniqueness turns up frequently in database design. What we have been doing is looking for a primary key – an easy way to distinguish one row of customer data in a table from all the other rows in that table. Unfortunately we have not yet succeeded, but all is not lost. The standard solution, where no obvious alternative exists, is to assign a unique number to each customer, stored in an additional column added to the table.

If we simply give each customer in turn a unique number then we have a unique way to tell customers apart, regardless of their changing their phone number, moving house, or even changing their name. This is such a common problem that most databases support a special SQL data type, the **serial** data type, for helping to solve the problem. We will discover more about this type later in the chapter, which although not a standard SQL type, is often referred to generically as though it was. MySQL does not have a built-in type 'serial', but it provides the facility to solve the primary key problem by allowing you to use a number column that is set to automatically increment as rows are added, using the AUTO_INCREMENT attribute.

Order of Rows

There is one other important difference between the data held in a spreadsheet and the same data held in a database table, that we must mention before we continue. In a spreadsheet the order of the rows is normally very important, but in a database table there is no order. That's right; when you ask to look at the data in a database table, the database is free to give you the rows of data in any order it chooses, unless you specifically ask for it ordered in a particular way.

Putting Data into a Database

Now that we have decided on a database design for our initial table, we can go ahead and store our data in it. We will come back shortly to the mechanics of defining a database table, storing, and accessing the data, but rest assured it's not difficult. Here is our data sitting in a MySQL database, being viewed using a simple command line tool, `mysql`, on a Linux machine:

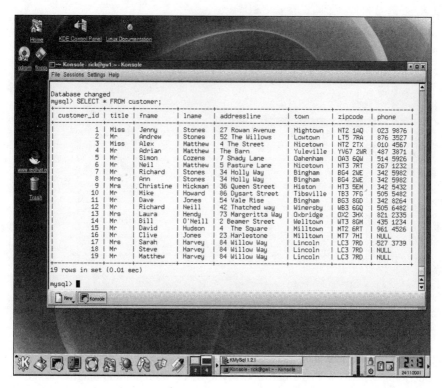

Notice that we have added an extra column, `customer_id`, as our unique way of referencing a customer. It is our primary key for the table. As you can see, the data looks much like it did in a spreadsheet, laid out in rows and columns.

MySQL is not restricted to command line use as we will see in Chapter 5, *MySQL Graphical Tools*, when we look at GUI tools; we will also see later in the book how you can build your own interfaces, including web-based ones using PHP.

Access Across a Network

Of course, if we could only access our data on the machine it was held on, we wouldn't have moved a long way forward from the situation we had with a single file being shared between different people.

MySQL is a server-based database, and as described in the previous chapter, once configured, will accept requests from multiple simultaneous clients across a network. Of course, the client can also be on the same machine as the database server is running on, but for multi-user access this isn't normally going to be the case. For Microsoft Windows users, an ODBC (Open Database Connectivity) driver is available, so we can arrange to connect any Windows desktop application that supports ODBC across a network to a server holding our data. We will see the technical details in Chapter 4, *Accessing your Data*.

The following screenshot shows Microsoft Access with a database containing linked external tables via ODBC to access the data in our MySQL database, which again is running on a Linux machine:

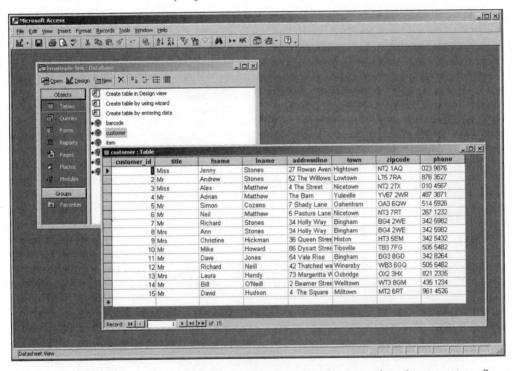

Now we can access the same data from many machines across the network at the same time. So now we have one copy of the data, securely held on a central server, accessible to multiple desktops running different operating systems, across a network. MySQL, like all relational databases, can automatically ensure that conflicting updates to the database are managed in a controlled way. It looks to the users as though they all have unrestricted access to all the information at the same time, but behind the scenes MySQL is monitoring updates and preventing conflicts.

This ability to apparently allow many people access to the data while ensuring it is always consistent, is a very important feature of relational databases. When a user changes a column, you either see it before it changes or afterwards, but never during the update.

A classic example is a bank database transferring money between two accounts. If, while the money was being transferred, someone were to run a report on the amount of money in all the accounts, it's very important that the total should be correct. It may not matter to the report's reader which account the money was in at the instant the report was run, but it is important that the report doesn't 'see' the in-between point, where one account has been debited, but the other not credited.

Relational databases like MySQL hide any intermediate states, so they can't be 'seen' by other users. This is termed **isolation**. The report is isolated from the money transfer operation, so it appears to happen either before or after, but never during the transfer. We will come back to this concept of isolation in Chapter 9, *Transactions and Locking*.

Slicing and Dicing Data

Now that we have seen how easy it is to access the data once it is in a database table, let's have a first look at how we might actually access that data. There are two very basic operations we frequently need to perform on big sets of data.

First, selecting the rows that match a particular set of values, and second, selecting a subset of the columns from the data. In database terminology, these are called **selection** and **projection** respectively, which sounds very clever, but is actually nice and easy.

Let's look at selecting a subset of the rows. Suppose we want to see all our customers who live in the town 'Bingham'. We will go back to MySQL's standard command line tool, mysql, to see how we can use the SQL language to ask MySQL to get the data we want.

The SQL command we need is very simple:

```
SELECT * FROM customer WHERE town = 'Bingham'
```

If you are typing this into the mysql client, then you also need to add a semicolon, which tells mysql that this is the end of a command, since longer commands might extend over more than one line. Generally in this book, we will use the semicolon, and if you are trying the examples as you go along using a command line tool, you will need to type it in. If you get the typing wrong, just clear the input line by typing \c.

MySQL responds by returning all the rows in the customer table, where the town column is 'Bingham':

```
 xterm                                                                    _ □ ✕
mysql> SELECT * FROM customer WHERE town = 'Bingham';
+-------------+-------+---------+--------+-------------+---------+---------+-----------+
| customer_id | title | fname   | lname  | addressline | town    | zipcode | phone     |
+-------------+-------+---------+--------+-------------+---------+---------+-----------+
|           7 | Mr    | Richard | Stones | 34 Holly Way| Bingham | BG4 2WE | 342 5982  |
|           8 | Mrs   | Ann     | Stones | 34 Holly Way| Bingham | BG4 2WE | 342 5982  |
|          11 | Mr    | Dave    | Jones  | 54 Vale Rise| Bingham | BG3 8GD | 342 8264  |
+-------------+-------+---------+--------+-------------+---------+---------+-----------+
3 rows in set (0.01 sec)

mysql>
```

As you can see, that was pretty easy. Don't worry about the details of the SQL statement yet; we will come back to that more formally in Chapter 5. Notice the `customer_id` column that we added. We will be using it later, when we come to store orders in the database. We have also stuck to the convention of typing SQL keywords in upper-case. The SQL language keywords are not case-sensitive, so you could have written:

```
select * FroM customer WHERE town = 'Bingham'
```

and got an identical result. We stick to the capitalization of SQL keywords simply for visual effect.

The case sensitivity in MySQL depends on the system you are running the server on. Generally names in relational databases are not case-sensitive. But we strongly urge you stick to a consistent case for table names, and not use 'camel' (mixed) case names for tables.

Now let's look at projection, selecting particular columns from a table.

Suppose we wanted to select just the first names and last names from our `customer` table. You will remember we called those columns fname and lname. The command to retrieve the names is also quite simple:

```
SELECT fname, lname FROM customer;
```

MySQL responds by returning the appropriate columns:

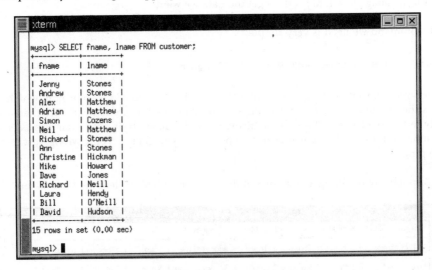

You might reasonably suppose that sometimes we want to do both operations on the data at the same time, that is, select particular column values (selection), but only from particular rows (projection). That's pretty easy in SQL as well. For example, suppose we only wanted to know the first names and last names of all our customers who live in 'Bingham'. We can simply combine our two SQL statements into a single command:

```
SELECT fname, lname FROM customer WHERE town = 'Bingham';
```

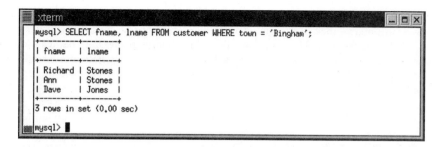

```
xterm                                                    _ □ ×
mysql> SELECT fname, lname FROM customer WHERE town = 'Bingham';
+---------+--------+
| fname   | lname  |
+---------+--------+
| Richard | Stones |
| Ann     | Stones |
| Dave    | Jones  |
+---------+--------+
3 rows in set (0.00 sec)

mysql>
```

There is one very important point to notice here. In many traditional programming languages, such as C or Java, we would have written some code to look through all the rows in the tables, stop when we found one with the right town, and print out the names we require. Although it might be possible to squeeze that onto a single line of code, it would be a very long and complex line. This is because C, Java, and similar languages are essentially procedural languages. In these languages you need to specify how the computer should behave. In SQL, which is termed a declarative language, you tell the computer what you are trying to achieve, and the internal magic of MySQL works out the difficult 'how' for you.

This might seem a little strange if you have never used a declarative language before, but once you get used to the idea it seems so obvious that it's a much better idea to tell the computer what you want to achieve, rather than how to achieve it. You will wonder how you have managed without such languages till now.

Adding Additional Information

If what we have seen so far were all that relational databases could do for us, there would not be any great incentive to use databases in preference to spreadsheets. As we will see in this book however, relational databases such as MySQL are very rich with useful features.

Database Design with Multiple Tables

We will talk about the basic database design with multiple tables in this section. For this the next feature we will look at is our 'order' problem, where our simple customer spreadsheet suddenly became very untidy once we tried to store order information against each customer. How do we store information about orders from customers, when we don't know in advance how many orders a customer might make?

As you can probably guess from the title of this section, the way to solve this problem with a relational database is to add another table to store this additional information. Just like when we designed our customer table, we start by deciding what information we want to store about each order.

For now we will assume that we want to store the name of the customer who placed the order, the date they placed the order, the date we shipped it, and how much we charged for delivery. Just like in our customer table, we will also add a unique reference number, so we know we have a unique reference for each order, rather than make any assumptions about what might be unique. There is obviously no need to store details of the customer again. We already know that, given a customer_id, we can find all the details of that customer from the customer table.

You might be wondering about the details of what was ordered. After all that is an important aspect of orders to most customers – they like to get what they ordered! For reasons that will become clear later, we will leave this aside for now. Those on the ball will probably be guessing that it's a similar problem to not knowing in advance how many orders a customer will place. We have no idea how many items will be on each order. The repeating groups problem is never far away. They are quite right, but one thing at a time!

Here is our order information table, with some sample data, being viewed in a linked MS Access table:

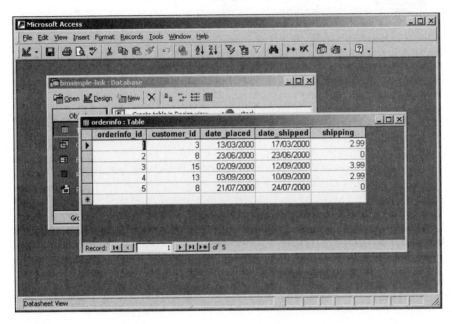

We have not put too much data in the table, as it is easier to experiment on smaller amounts of data.

Relationships Between Tables

In this section we will try and establish relations between tables. Now we have details of our customers, and at least summary details of their orders, stored in our database. In many ways, this is no different from using a pair of spreadsheets, one for our customer details and one for their order details. It's time to look at what we can do using these tables in combination. We do this by 'selecting' data from both tables at the same time. This is called a **join**, and after selection and projection from a single table, this is the third most common SQL data retrieval operation.

Suppose we want to list all the orders and the customers who placed them. In a procedural language, such as C, we would have to write code to scan one of the tables, perhaps starting with the customer table, and then for each customer we look for and print out any orders they have placed. This is not difficult, but certainly a bit time consuming and tedious to code. In SQL, I'm sure you will be pleased to know, we find the answer much more easily using a join operation. All we have to do is tell SQL three things:

❑ The columns we want

❑ The tables we want the data retrieved from

❑ How the two tables relate to each other

Don't worry too much about the SQL for now. The command we need is the example we saw in the previous chapter:

```
SELECT * FROM customer, orderinfo WHERE customer.customer_id =
orderinfo.customer_id;
```

As you can probably guess, this asks for all columns from our two tables, and tells SQL that the column customer_id in the table customer (note the *table.column* notation, which enables us to specify both a table name and a column from within that table) holds the same information as the column customer_id in the orderinfo table, using the equal (=) operator. In database terminology, we say we join the tables using the two columns customer.customer_id and orderinfo.customer_id.

Let's try out our query, which is accessing the data across a network, this time using a DOS-based version of the mysql client program. Why change? Just to show that it really makes very little difference which client machine you would like to use:

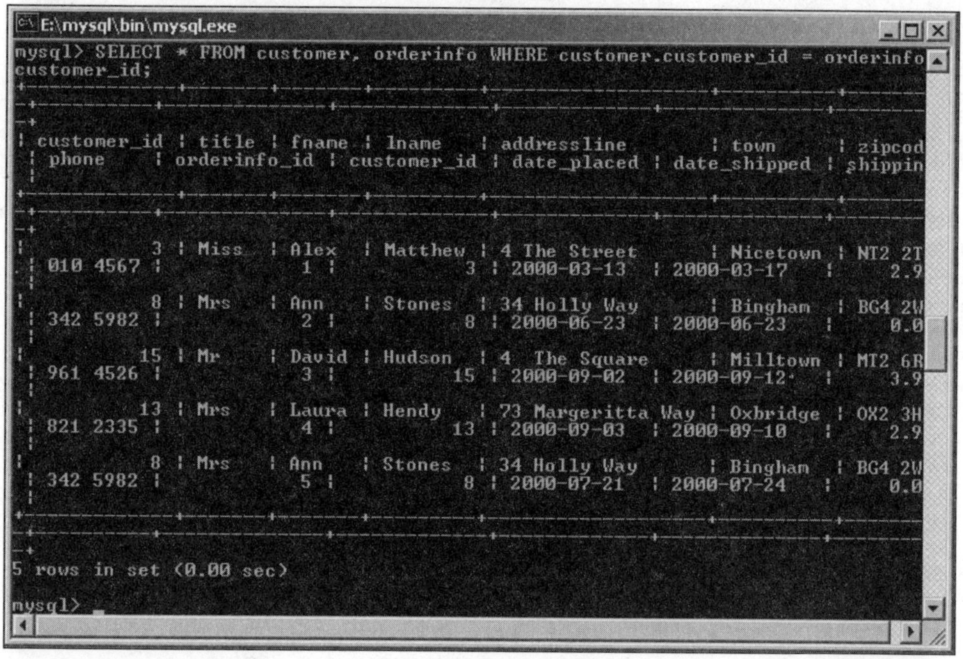

This is a touch untidy, since the rows wrap to fit in the window, but you can see how MySQL has answered our query, without us having to specify exactly how to solve the problem. Of course, we could replace the '*' with named columns to select more specific data if we just wanted, for example, names and amounts.

Let's leap ahead briefly, and see a much more complex query we could perform using SQL on these two tables. Suppose we wanted to see how frequently different customers had ordered from us. The actual command is:

```
SELECT customer.title, customer.fname, customer.lname,
       count(orderinfo.orderinfo_id) AS "Number of orders"
       FROM customer, orderinfo
       WHERE customer.customer_id = orderinfo.customer_id
       GROUP BY customer.title, customer.fname, customer.lname;
```

Without going into the details you can see that we have still not told SQL how to answer the question, just specified the question in a very precise way using SQL. We also managed it all in a single statement. For the record, this is how MySQL responds:

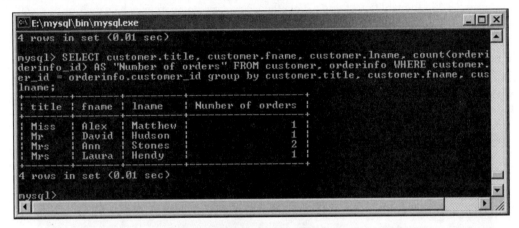

Now while many database fanatics may quite like typing SQL directly in a window to a command line tool, we have to admit it's not everyone's preference. If users prefer a Windows GUI, with a query builder for example, that's not a problem; they can simply access the database via an ODBC driver, and build their queries graphically.

Here are the screenshots of the same query being designed and executed in Microsoft Access:

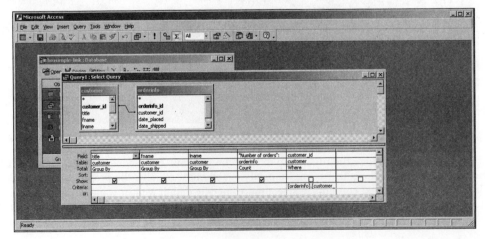

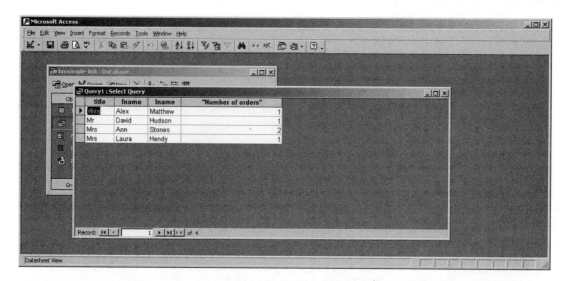

The data is still stored on a Linux machine, but the user hardly needs to be aware of the technical details. Generally in this book, we will use the command line for learning SQL, because that way you will learn the basics before moving on to more complex SQL commands, where the GUI tools are not always the most appropriate solution. Of course, you are welcome to use a GUI tool to type in your SQL, rather than the command line. It's your choice.

Designing Tables

So far we have only two tables in our database, and have not really talked about how we decide what goes in each table, except in the very informal way of doing what looked 'reasonable'. This design, which includes tables, columns, and relationships, is more correctly called a **schema**. Designing a database schema can be quite difficult to get right. We will cover the principal steps and rules in Chapter 11, *Database Design*.

Designing a high quality database schema with more than a couple of dozen tables is often a serious undertaking. Database designers earn their money by being good at this frequently challenging task.

Some Basic Rules of Thumb

Fortunately for reasonably simple databases, with up to perhaps ten tables, design is usually not that difficult, and with some practice you will usually go a long way towards a sensible design with just some good guidelines and a little practice. A good database mentor can also be a great help, if you can find one to help you review your initial designs.

In this section, we are going to look at the simple example database we are starting to build, and figure out a way to decide what tables we need.

When a database is designed, it is often 'normalized', that is, a set of rules are applied to ensure that data is broken down in an appropriate fashion. In Chapter 11, we will come back to database design in a more formal way. To get started, all we require are some simple ground rules. We strongly suggest that you don't just read these rules and then dash off to design a database with twenty tables – work your way through the book at least until Chapter 11.

These rules are just to help you understand the initial database, which we will be using to explore SQL in general, and MySQL in particular as the book progresses.

Rule One – Break Down the Data into Columns

The first rule is only to put one piece of information, or attribute, in each column. This comes naturally to most people provided they consciously think about it. In our original spreadsheet, we had already quite naturally broken down the information for each customer into different columns, so the name was separate from the zip code for example.

In a spreadsheet, this rule just makes it simpler to work on the data, for example to sort by the zip code. In a database however, it is essential that the data be correctly broken down into attributes. Why is this so important in databases? From a practical point of view, it is difficult to specify that you want the data between the 29th and 35th characters from an address column, because that happens to be where the zip code lives. If you have enough data, there is bound to be some data where the rule does not hold true, and you get the wrong piece of data. Another reason for the data to be correctly broken down is that, as we said before, in a database all records in a column must have the same type, so it is good to ensure data is broken down into its component parts and stored as the most appropriate type.

Rule Two – Have a Unique Way of Identifying Each Row

You will remember that when we tried to decide how to identify each row in our spreadsheet, we had a problem of not being sure as to what would be unique. We had no primary key. In general, it doesn't have to be a single column that is unique; it could be a pair of columns taken together, or even the combination of three columns that uniquely identifies a row.

In any case there has to be a way of saying with absolute certainty if I look at 'X' in this row, I know it will have a value, different from all other rows in this table. If you can't find a column, or at most a combination of three columns that uniquely identifies each row, it's probably time to add an extra column, just to fulfill that purpose. In our customer table, we added an extra column, customer_id, to fulfill the purpose of identifying each row.

Rule Three – Remove Repeating Information

Do you remember earlier, when we tried to store order information in the customer table, it looked rather untidy because of the repeating groups? For each customer, we repeated order information as many times as was required. This meant that we could never know how many columns were needed for orders. In a database, the number of columns in a table is effectively fixed by the design. So we must decide in advance how many columns we need, what type they are, and name each column before we can store any data. Never try and store repeating groups of data in a single row.

The way round this restriction is to do exactly what we did with our orders and customers data. We split the data into two tables, and used the column customer_id to join the two tables together when we needed data from both.

More formally, what we had was a many-to-one relationship, that is, there could be many orders received from a single customer.

Rule Four – Get the Naming Right

This is occasionally the hardest rule to get right. What do we call a table or column? If you can't decide what to call something, it's often a clue that all is not well in your table and column design.

In addition to the basic question, 'what should this be called?' most database designers have their own personal 'rules of thumb' that they like to use to ensure the naming of tables and columns in a database is consistent. However there isn't a universally agreed set of rules. It's almost as bad as 'camel case' or 'underscore' arguments for combining names in variables. What everybody does agree on is that consistency is very important. Don't have some table names singular and some plural, for example 'office' and 'departments'. Instead use 'office' and 'department'.

If you decide on a naming rule for an 'id' type column, perhaps `tablename_id`, then always stick to that rule. If you use abbreviations, always use them consistently. If a column in one table is a key to another table (see Chapter 11), then try and give them the same base name in the different tables, so it's obvious they relate to the same information.

The goal here is very simple – tables and columns should have short meaningful names, and the naming within the database should be very consistent. Achieving this apparently simple goal is often surprisingly challenging, but the rewards in simplified maintenance and ease of use are considerable.

The Customer/Order Database

We can draw our database design or schema, the way it is, using an entity relationship diagram. For our two-table database, such a diagram might look like this:

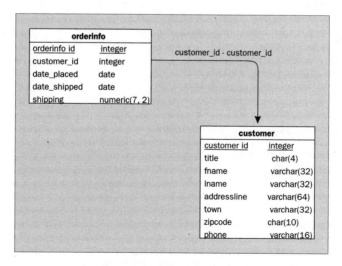

This shows our two tables, the columns, data types, and sizes in each column, and also tells us that `customer_id` is the column that joins the two tables together. Notice that the arrow goes from the `orderinfo` table to the `customer` table. This is a hint that for each `orderinfo` entry, there is at most a single entry in the `customer` table, but that for each customer there may be many orders. The underlined columns, for example `customer_id`, are our unique identifiers for each table. The data stored in the columns that are underlined must be unique in their respective tables.

It's important that you remember which way round an one-to-many relationship is; getting it confused can cause a lot of problems. You should also notice that we have been very careful to name the column we want to use to join the two tables the same way in each table, `customer_id`. This is not essential; we could have called the two columns `foo` and `bar` if we had wanted to, but you will find consistent naming a great help.

In a complex database it can get very annoying when names are not quite consistent, for example `customer_id` and `customer_ident`, or `cust_id`, or `cust_no`. It's always worth investing time in getting the naming consistent; it will make life much easier in the longer run.

Extending Beyond Two Tables

Now clearly, the information we have so far is incomplete, in that we don't know what items were in each order. You may remember that we deliberately omitted the actual items from each order, promising to come back to that problem? It's time to sort out the actual items in each order.

The problem we have with the items in each order is that we don't know in advance how many items there will be in each order. It's almost exactly the same problem as not knowing in advance how many orders a customer might place. Each order might have one, two, three, or a hundred items in it. We have to separate the information that a customer placed an order, from the details of what was in that order. Basically what we might try and do is this:

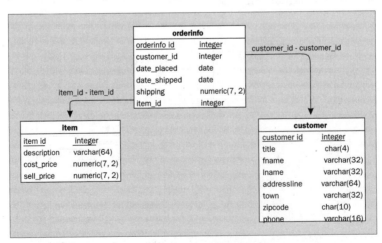

Much like the `customer` and `orderinfo` tables, we separate the information into two tables and then join them together. We have however created a subtle problem here.

If you think carefully about the relationship between an order and an item that may be ordered, you will realize that not only could each `orderinfo` entry relate to many items, but each item could also appear in many orders, if different customers order the same item. If we try and draw this using an entity relationship diagram, with just these two tables, we would draw this:

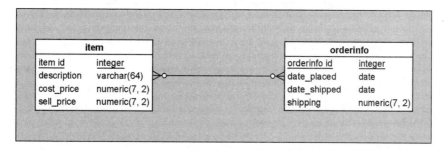

What we have here is actually a many-to-many relationship – each order can refer many items, and each item can appear in many orders. This breaks some of the underlying principles of relational database. We don't wish to go into detail here, but suffice it to say you can never have two tables in a relational database that participate directly in a many-to-many relationship.

We could try and get round this by having a different entry in each row in the `item` table for each order, but then we would have to repeat the description and price information of the item many times. This would break our rule of thumb three.

We will consider these types of relationship further in Chapter 11, but for now you will be pleased to know that there is a standard solution to this difficulty. You create a third table between the two tables that implements a many-to-many relationship. This is actually easier to do than it is to explain, so let's just go ahead and create a table, `orderline`, to link the orders with the items:

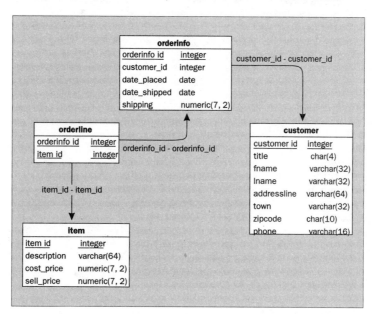

What we have done here is created a table that has rows corresponding to each line of an order. For any single line, we can determine the details of the order placed using the `orderinfo_id` column, and the item referenced using the `item_id` column.

A single item can appear in many order lines, and a single order can contain many order lines. Each orderline refers to only a single item however, and can appear in only a single order. You will also notice that on this occasion we have not had to add a unique id to identify each row. That is because the combination of `orderinfo_id` and `item_id` is always unique. However, there is another very subtle problem lurking. What happens if a customer orders two of an item in a single order?

We can't just enter another row in `orderline` table, because we just said that the combination of `orderinfo_id` and `item_id` is always unique. Are we about to have to add yet another special table to cater for orders that contain more than one of any item? Fortunately not; there is a much simpler approach. We just need to add a `quantity` field to the `orderline` table, and all will be well. You can see this in the next diagram.

Completing the Initial Design

We have just two pieces of information we need to store before we have the main structure of the first cut of our database design in place. We want to store the barcode that goes with each product, and we also want to store the quantity we have in stock for each item.

It's possible that each product will have more than one barcode, because when manufacturers significantly change the packaging of a product, they often also change the barcode. For example, you have probably seen packs that offer '20% extra for free', where the price of, for example, a bottle of soft drink has not been changed, but there is a promotion pack which contains more liquid than the standard pack. These are often referred to as 'overfill packs'. Manufacturers will generally change the barcode, so the different packaging can be identified, but essentially the product is unchanged. Therefore, we have a 'many barcodes-to-one item' relationship. We add one more table to hold the barcodes, like this:

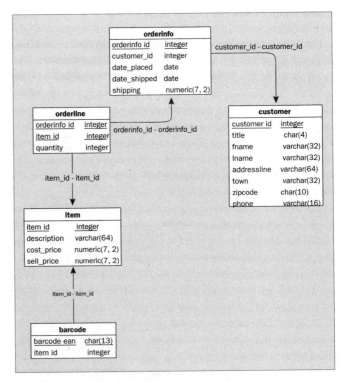

Notice that the arrow points from the `barcode` table to the `item` table, because there may be many barcodes for each item. Also notice that the `barcode_ean` is the primary key, since there must be a unique row for each barcode, and that a single item could have several barcodes but no barcode can ever belong to more than one item.

The last addition we need to make to our database design is to make provision to hold the stock quantity for each item. Now there are two ways we could do this. In a situation where most items are in stock, and the stock information is fairly basic, we would simple store a stock quantity directly in the `item` table.

There are circumstances where we might have a lot of items, but where only a few are normally in stock, and the amount of information we need to hold for stocked items is quite large. For example, in a warehouse operation we may need to store location information, batch numbers, and expiry dates. If we had an item file with 500,000 items in it, but only held the top 1000 items in stock, this would be very wasteful. There is a standard way of resolving this problem, using what is called a **supplementary table**.

What you do is create a new table to store the 'supplementary' information, such as storage information, and then create only the rows that are required for items that are in stock, linking the information back to the main table. Actually, it's much easier than it sounds. Here is our final 'first cut' design of the database that we will be using as the book progresses:

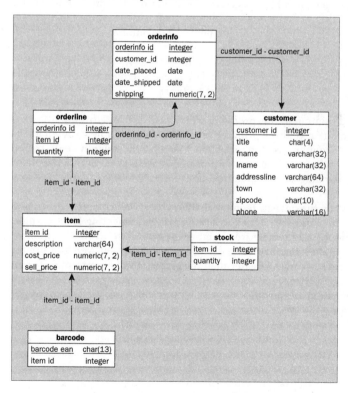

Notice the `stock` table uses `item_id` as a unique key, and holds information that relates directly to items, using `item_id` to join to the relevant row in the `item` table. The arrow points to the `item` table because that is the master table, even though it is not a many-to-one relationship in this case.

As it stands, the design is clearly complex though the additional information we are keeping is so small. We will leave the schema design the way it is to show how it is done, and later in the book we will be showing how to access data where there may be additional information in supplementary tables like this one. For those who like sneaking a look ahead, we will be using what's called an **outer join**.

Some Basic Data Types

When we started talking about data types, we kept the discussion very general. In our schema we have used a generic set of basic data types, which are not a complete set of MySQL types, but can be translated into actual MySQL types when you create the real tables.

One minor difficulty we have not tackled so far is generating our unique keys – the fields like `customer_id` and `item_id`. You will remember we said that each row in a table has to be uniquely identifiable and, where there is no clear set of columns that can be used, we add a unique 'id' column. Obviously, what we could do is make this an integer, or character field, and each time we add a new row into the database generate a new unique value for the column.

However, since the need to add a special unique column is so common in databases, many databases have a built-in solution. Usually this special type is effectively an integer that automatically increments as rows are added to the table, assigning a new unique number as each row is added. The actual implementation differs between databases, though it is often referred to as a serial field. In PostgreSQL and Sybase for example, there is a database-defined `SERIAL` data type, which is actually an automatically incrementing integer. In Oracle you use a sequence, which is also the underlying mechanism PostgreSQL uses to create `SERIAL` types.

MySQL also has a solution to this problem, which is to add an attribute `AUTO_INCREMENT` to an integer type column that is also a primary key. When we add a new row to a table that has an `AUTO_INCREMENT` column, we don't specify a value for the column at all, but allow the database to automatically assign the next number. This provides users of MySQL a simple but effective solution to the problem of generating unique column values for each row in a table.

Most databases, when they assign sequential values to 'serial' columns, don't take account of any rows that are deleted. The number assigned will just go on incrementing for each new row. Earlier versions of MySQL would simply use the next free number for `AUTO_INCREMENT` columns, which could result in values being reused after data had been deleted, but more recent versions use an always increasing number, even if that's currently greater than the largest number currently stored in the column.

The design tool we used to draw the above diagrams still shows such fields as `INTEGER`, because that's the underlying type.

To summarize the types we have used in this schema, we have:

Data Type	Description
INTEGER	A whole number.
CHAR	A character array of fixed size, with the size shown in parentheses after the type. For these column types, MySQL will always store exactly the specified number of characters. If we use a CHAR(256) to store just 1 character, there will still be (at least) 256 bytes held in the database, and returned when the data is retrieved, since the data will be padded with blanks.
VARCHAR	This is also a character array, but as its name suggests it is of variable length, and generally the space used in the database will be much the same as the actual size of the data stored. When you ask for a VARCHAR field to be returned, it returns just the number of characters you stored. The maximum length is given in the parentheses after the type. You might reasonably ask why we bother with CHAR types at all; why not just use the VARCHAR? The answer is efficiency. The database can handle fixed size records much more easily than it can handle variable sized records, so if we know that a title is at most four characters long, we may as well always store four characters, rather than ask the database to track the size each time, since the space we would save is insignificant, but the performance with the fixed length will usually be better.
DATE	This allows us to store year, month, and day information. There are of course other related types that allow us to store time information as well as data information. We will meet these later.
NUMERIC	This allows us to store numbers with a specified number of digits (the first number in the parentheses) and using a fixed number of decimal places (the second number in the parentheses). Hence, NUMERIC(7, 2) would store exactly seven digits, two of them after the decimal place.

In Chapter 8, we will look at these, and MySQL's other data types, in more detail.

NULL

One topic that often confuses newcomers to databases is the idea of NULL, used where data is missing from a column.

All relational database systems have a very special column value called NULL, which is usually defined to mean 'unknown at this time'. Notice that it doesn't mean zero, or empty string, or anything that can be represented in the type of the column. Unknown is very different from zero or an empty string. NULL can also have one or two additional and rather subtle variations on that meaning, usually dependent on the design of a particular database. We will see more of NULL values in Chapter 6, *Changing Your Data*.

Since it is important that NULL in a column could never be mistaken for 'real' data, databases usually hold a special flag, or reserve a value for NULL that can never be created by real data. For example, databases can distinguish between an empty string and a NULL. The former is simply the absence of characters, and the latter an absence of information. Let's look at an example in our sample database:

If you look at the orderinfo table you will see that we have both a date_placed and a date_shipped column, both of type DATE. What do we do when an order has been received, but not yet shipped? What should we store in the date shipped column? We could store a special date, a **sentinel value**, which lets us know that we have not yet shipped the order.

On UNIX systems we might well use Jan 1, 1970, which is traditionally the date UNIX systems count from. That date is well before the date we designed this system, therefore we will always know that this special date means 'not yet shipped'.

This is, however, clearly not ideal. Having special values scattered in our tables shows poor design, and is rather error prone. For example, if a new programmer starts on the project and doesn't realize there is a special date, they might try calculating the average time between order and shipping date, and come up with some very strange answers indeed, if there are a few shipped dates set before the order was placed.

It's very important to take care of NULL values because they can pop out at odd times and cause you surprises, usually unpleasant ones. An example is if you inadvertently attempt to use a column that holds NULL in a calculation you will always get a result of NULL, which may not be a value you were expecting.

In our orderinfo table we could set date_shipped to NULL before an order is shipped, where the meaning 'unknown at this time' is exactly what we require.

There is another subtly different use for NULL (not so common), which is 'not relevant' for this row. Suppose you were doing a survey of people, and one of the questions was about the color of spectacles. For people who don't wear spectacles, this is clearly an irrelevant question. This is a case however, where we might use NULL in the column to record that the information is not relevant for this particular row.

Testing for NULLs

One feature of the NULL value is that if you compare two NULL values the answer is always that they are different. This sometimes catches people out, but if you think about the meaning of NULL as 'unknown', it's perfectly logical that testing for equality on two unknowns gives the answer 'not equal'. MySQL has a special operator, NULL SAFE EQUAL, which can be used to make comparisons involving NULL behave in a slightly different way, as we will see in Chapter 4.

SQL has a way of checking for NULL values by asking 'IS NULL', which allows us to find and test NULL values should we need to.

NULL values do behave in a slightly odd way; therefore it is possible to specify when we design a table that some columns cannot hold NULL values. It is normally a good idea to specify the columns as 'NOT NULL' where you are sure the NULL value should never be accepted, for example in primary key columns. Some database designers advocate an almost complete ban on NULL values, but the values do have their uses. So we normally advocate allowing NULL values on specific columns, where there is a genuine possibility that 'unknown' values may be required.

The Sample Database

In this chapter, we have been designing, in a rather ad-hoc manner, a simple database to look after customers, orders, and items, such as might be used in a small shop. As the book progresses, we will be using this database to demonstrate SQL and other MySQL features. We will also be discovering the limitations of our existing design, and looking at how it can be improved in some areas.

The simplified database we are using has many elements of what a real retail database might look like. However, it also omits some complications, for example, an item might have a full description, a description that appears on the till when it is sold, and yet another description that appears on shelf edge labels.

We have another more complex problem that we have chosen to ignore so far. Suppose the price elements of an item change after an order has been shipped, then the order information is incorrect in respect to the price paid, because we only ever store the current price of an item.

The address information we are storing for customers is actually simplified. We can't cope with long addresses where there is a village name or a state, nor can we cope with overseas orders. It is often more feasible to start with a reasonably solid base and expand however, rather than try and cater for every possible requirement in your initial design. This database is adequate for our initial needs.

In the next chapter, we will be looking at installing MySQL, creating the tables for our sample database, and populating them with some sample data.

Summary

In this chapter, we looked at how a database table is much like a single spreadsheet, with four important differences:

- ❑ All items in a column must have the same type
- ❑ The number of columns must be the same for all rows in a table
- ❑ It must be possible to uniquely identify each row
- ❑ There is no implied row order in a database table, as there would be in a spreadsheet

We have seen how we can extend our database to multiple tables, which lets us manage many-to-one relationships in a simple way. We gave some informal rules of thumb to help you understand how a database design needs to be structured, though we will come back to this in a much more rigorous fashion in later chapters.

We have also seen how to work around many-to-many relationships that turn up in the real world, by breaking them down into a pair of one-to-many relationships by adding an extra table.

Finally, we worked on extending our initial database design so we have a demonstration database design, or schema, to work with as the book progresses.

In the next chapter, we'll see how to get MySQL up and running on various platforms.

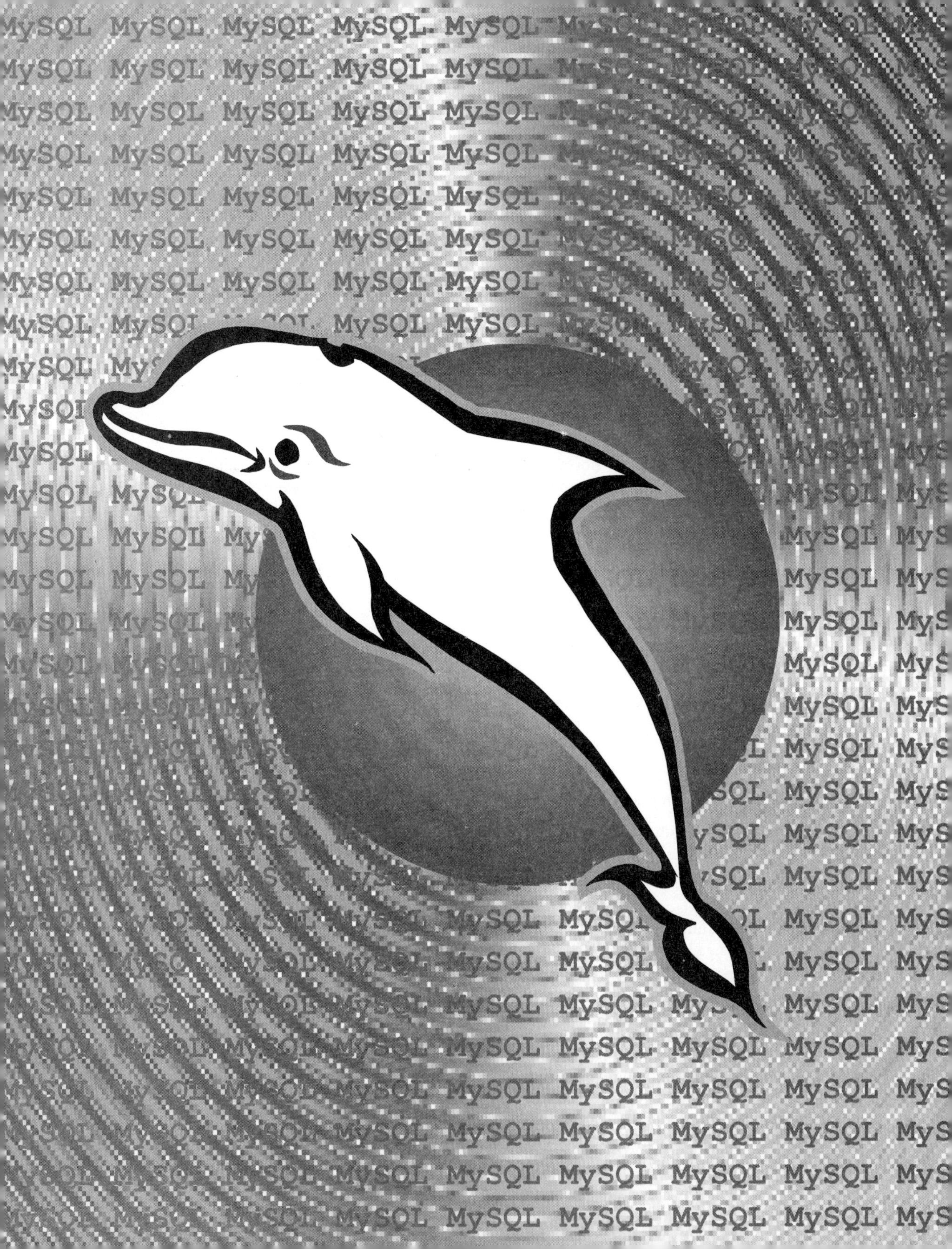
MySQL

Installing and Getting Started with MySQL

In this chapter, we will walk through the steps of installing MySQL on two operating systems. If you are running a Linux system installed from a recent distribution you may already have MySQL installed or available to you on the installation disks. We'll see how to compile the source code for the UNIX platform, using Linux as our example. We'll also see how to install MySQL on Windows platforms, for which we will use a precompiled binary package.

Along the way we'll work through the following:

- ❑ Install or upgrade?
- ❑ Installing MySQL from the Linux/UNIX binaries.
- ❑ Installing MySQL from the source code.
- ❑ Working with MySQL.
- ❑ Installing MySQL on Windows.

Install or Upgrade?

As MySQL continues to develop, you are faced time and again with the question of whether to upgrade your installation or not.

If you have a recent Linux distribution, then in all probability you should have the recent MySQL release bundled along with it. If you already have installed a Linux distribution that has an older release, then you have the option to upgrade to the latest release by downloading the appropriate packages from the MySQL web site http://www.mysql.com.

When a new version of MySQL is released, you have a choice of whether to upgrade your installation to the new version. Although it is a good idea to keep up-to-date with bug fix releases, we would urge caution about trying to live at the 'bleeding edge'. Always check out the release notes for any new release before attempting to upgrade.

MySQL releases fall into two categories, 'current stable' and 'development'. The stable versions will contain fixes for bugs in the latest version of the last major release. At the time of writing, MySQL version 3 was the last major release, and version 3.2.3 was the current stable version. It is usually safe to upgrade to the current stable version. Similarly, at the time of writing, Release 4.0 was a development release, which added many new features. It has only been in use for a short time, and so might be expected to contain a larger number of bugs than the current stable version, which has been in use for a number of years.

Two of the key questions to ask before upgrading or installing a major release are:

❑   What problems do I have with the version I am using?

❑   What features in the new release do I need?

If the answer to both of these is none, consider sticking with what you have!

There are two main ways of upgrading your installation of MySQL. You can essentially delete the entire installation, including data stored in databases, and start all over with the new version. To preserve data, you will need to back it up and restore it after the installation of the new version of MySQL. Alternatively, you can attempt to upgrade the components and leave the data intact.

An upgrade can only succeed if the two versions of MySQL are compatible. The release notes will indicate whether or not an upgrade will be possible.

> **We strongly advise backing up your existing data in the database before performing an upgrade. The details of performing an upgrade to the latest release are available at the MySQL web site.**

The backup and recovery of your existing MySQL installation is discussed in detail in Chapter 10, *MySQL Administration.*

In the following sections, we describe the installation (rather than an upgrade) of MySQL on UNIX-like platforms and on Microsoft Windows. First, we will discuss the installation for Linux platforms. The installation procedure on various Linux distributions or UNIX flavors is very similar.

There are two ways of installing MySQL:

❑   Installing MySQL using Linux/UNIX binaries

❑   Installing MySQL from the source code

We'll begin the process by learning to install MySQL from Linux binaries.

Installing MySQL from Linux/Unix Binaries

Probably the easiest way of installing on UNIX or Linux is by using precompiled binary packages. The binaries for MySQL are available for download as generic binaries (suitable for all various UNIX flavors) or as RPM (RedHat Package Manager) packages for Linux distributions that support the RPM format. At the time of writing this book, binary packages had been made available for:

- ❑   Linux (RPMs and binary tarballs)
- ❑   Solaris - Sparc and Intel
- ❑   HP-UX
- ❑   FreeBSD
- ❑   AIX
- ❑   SGI Irix
- ❑   Digital OSF/1
- ❑   Mac OS X

For a fully functional installation, you need to download and install at least the base server package from the packages listed in this table:

Package	Description
MySQL	The base server package.
MySQL-bench	MySQL benchmarks and test suite.
MySQL-client	MySQL client applications.
MySQL-devel	Header files and libraries for development.
MySQL-shared	MySQL client shared libraries.
MySQL-Max	The mysqld-max server version (includes InnoDB tables).

The exact file names may have version numbers appended with the package. It is advisable to install a matching set of packages, all with the same revision level. In a package with the version number 4.x.y, x.y determines the revision level.

To install the generic binary packages we decompress and unpack the tarball as root in the root directory:

```
# cd /
# gunzip package.tar.gz
# tar xv package.tar
```

Be sure to read any README or INSTALL files that are included in the package for further details of completing the steps needed for installation. In general, RPM packages are preferred to binaries, as they can complete all of the installation steps for you. We will use RPM packages in this chapter.

To install the RPM packages, we use the RPM Package Manager application. Make sure that you have logged on as the superuser (`root`) to perform the installation. You could use the graphical package manager of your choice, such as `GnoRPM` or `kpackage` to install the RPMs. Alternatively, you could place all the RPM files in a single directory and as superuser (`root`) execute:

```
$ rpm -i *.rpm
```

You will notice that we have used a `-i` option here which stands for 'install'. This will unpack the packages and install all the files they contain into their correct places for your distribution.

> **If you have a version of MySQL already installed from RPM packages and you get an error installing it, you may need to uninstall the packages first, using `rpm -e packagename`.**

Installing from RPM packages 'by hand' has the distinct advantage that you can upgrade to the current stable version, by repeating the procedure. To do that, just let the RPM know that you are performing an upgrade rather than a first time install by specifying the `-u` option (for upgrade) instead of the `-i` option:

```
$ rpm -u *.rpm
```

You could also install from the MySQL package that is bundled along with your Linux distribution, such as Red Hat or SuSE. For example, on SuSE 7.x you can install a version of MySQL by running the `YaST` installation tool and selecting the packages listed in the table below. We have listed below all of the packages associated, in some way, with MySQL. We need to install those whose names begin with MySQL:

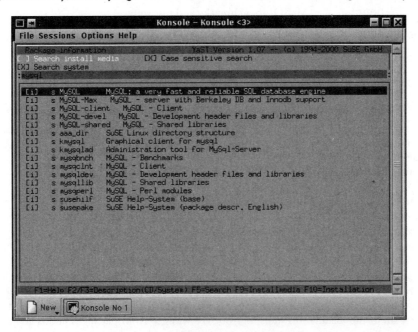

Anatomy of a MySQL Installation

A MySQL installation consists of a number of applications, utilities, and data directories. The main MySQL server application (`mysqld` or `mysqld-max`) contains the server code that services client requests to access data. A script, `mysqld_safe`, is used to start the server process, and to automatically restart it if it fails. Utilities, such as `mysqladmin`, are used to perform some administrative tasks on the server. More information on these utilities is given later in the chapter. A `data` directory is used by MySQL to store all of the files needed for a database. This is used not only for storing the tables and records, but also information about the currently running server process.

A typical installation might store the components of a MySQL system in several locations, as shown in the table below, together with some additional subdirectories, although the directory names may vary for different installations:

Directory	Description
`/usr/bin`	Client applications and utilities such as `mysql` and `mysqladmin`.
`/usr/sbin`	Server processes such as `mysqld` and `mysqld-max`.
`/var/lib/mysql`	The database itself, each database in a sub directory.
`/usr/doc`	Documentation in HTML format.
`/usr/include/mysql`	Header files for use in developing MySQL applications.
`/usr/lib/mysql`	Libraries for use in developing MySQL applications.
`/usr/man`	Manual pages for MySQL tools.
`/usr/share/mysql`	Sample configuration files.

The files that MySQL uses fall into different categories. The applications are fixed and they are not modified while MySQL is running. The data files are the heart of the system, storing all the information of all of our databases.

For efficiency and easy administration, we might wish to store the different categories of files in a different location. MySQL has the flexibility to store the applications and data in different locations, a feature that has been fully utilized by MySQL installations.

For example, as shown in the table above, MySQL applications are stored with other applications in `/usr/bin`. The data is stored in `/var/lib/mysql/data`. This means that it is easy to arrange backups of the critical data separately from the not-so-critical application files, which can be easily obtained and reinstalled.

Other binary distributions may have their own scheme for file locations. Sometimes you will find (for example, when installing from tarballs) that all of MySQL files are stored in one place, typically `/usr/local/mysql`.

With RPM packages you can use the `rpm` tool to list the files that have been installed by a particular package. To do this, use the query option, `-q` like this:

```
$ rpm -q -l MySQL
/etc/logrotate/mysql
...
/usr/share/mysql/ukrainian/errmsg.txt
$
```

To see where all the files have been installed, you will need to run rpm for all of the packages that make up the complete MySQL set:

```
$ rpm -q -l MySQL-client
/usr/bin/msql2mysql
...
/usr/man/man1/safe_mysqld.1.gz
$
```

Different distributions may also call the packages by different names, but it should be fairly obvious which one is which. The screenshot that follows shows the different RPM packages on the kpackage graphical manager tool:

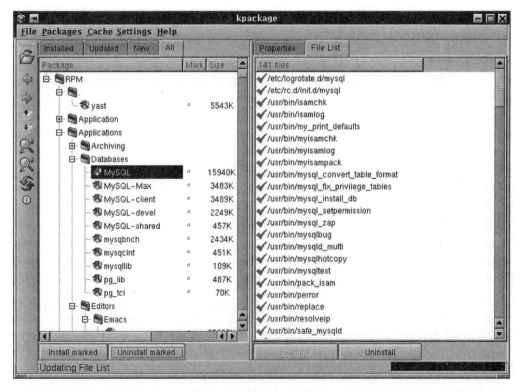

The disadvantage of installing from a Linux distribution is that it is not always clear where everything is located. So if you wish to upgrade to the most recent release, it can be tricky to ensure that you have completely removed the original installation. It is important to remember that the RPM package manager should always be used to uninstall RPM packages as it keeps track of where everything lives.

Sometimes we might need to install MySQL from the source code (for example, if you wish to build a version of the server that is optimized for your precise processor type, or includes support for non-default extensions). If you have no intention of installing from source, you might like to skip the next section and pick up again with *Starting MySQL*.

Installing MySQL from Source Code

Though RPM packages could be used to install MySQL on many Linux distributions or flavors, you can build and install MySQL from the source on just about any UNIX compatible system.

The source code for MySQL is available at http://www.mysql.com. Here you will find code for the latest release, and often the source code for beta test releases of the next release. Unless you like to live on the edge, it is probably a good idea to stick to the most recent stable release, as we discussed earlier.

The entire MySQL source code can be found in a single gzipped 'tarball' file that will have a name similar to:

```
mysql-4.0.0.tar.gz
```

Compiling MySQL is in fact a relatively simple affair. If you are familiar with compiling open source products, there will be no surprises for you here and even if this is your first attempt in compiling and installing an Open Source product, you should have no real difficulty. To perform the source code compilation, you will need a Linux or UNIX system with a development environment installed, including a C compiler, and the GNU version of the make utility that is needed to build the database system.

> The MySQL build scripts will give an error if you are missing any of the required development utilities. If this happens, you will need to install the missing development tools and try again.

Linux distributions generally ship with a suitable development environment containing the GNU tools from the Free Software Foundation. These include the excellent GNU C compiler (GCC), which is the standard compiler for Linux. The GNU tools are available for most other UNIX platforms too, and we generally recommend them for compiling MySQL. You can download the latest tools from http://www.gnu.org. Once you have a development environment installed, the compilation of MySQL is straightforward.

> At the time of writing there were some issues with compiling certain versions of the GNU C/C++ compiler, especially versions 2.96 and 3.0. Version 2.95.2 is fine. Check the MySQL AB web site for the latest news on compiler compatibility and also read the release notes of the tarball downloaded.

Transfer the source code 'tarball' to the target machine and place it in an appropriate directory for compiling. This does not have to be, and in fact ought not to be, the final resting place of your MySQL installation. One possible choice is a subdirectory in your home directory. This is very practical as you only need superuser permissions to install the source code once built; compilation doesn't need a superuser permission.

Unpack the 'tarball' to extract the source code:

```
$ tar zxvf mysql-4.0.0.tar.gz
```

Here we are using the GNU version of the `tar` utility. On systems without GNU `tar`, you may need a two-step extraction to decompress with `gunzip`, followed by a `tar` extraction:

```
$ gunzip mysql-4.0.0.tar.gz
$ tar xvf mysql-4.0.0.tar
```

> **On Solaris we recommend installing GNU `tar` as there are some problems with compatibility with Sun's version of `tar`.**

We generally prefer to unpack source code into a directory, `/usr/src`, specifically created for maintaining source code products. However, you can unpack anywhere you have sufficient disk space (around 100MB or so) for the compilation.

The extraction process will have made a new directory, related to the version of MySQL you are building. Move into that directory:

```
$ cd mysql-4.0.0
```

In this directory, you will find a file, `INSTALL-SOURCE` that contains detailed manual build instructions. This can be useful in the unlikely event that the automated method outlined here fails for some reason.

The build process makes use of a configuration script, `configure`, to tailor the build parameters to your specific environment. To accept all defaults you can simply run `configure` without arguments:

```
$ ./configure
creating cache ./config.cache
checking host system type... i686-pc-linux-gnu
checking which template to use... linux
...
Thank You for choosing MySQL!
$
```

The configuration script can take a number of parameters that alter the features built into MySQL. One of these features is the ability to use different implementations for its database tables. We can choose table types optimized for speed, or features such as transactions. We will learn more about table types in future chapters. In this book we are going to use the `InnoDB` table type, so we need to tell the configuration script to include support for this table type. We do this by specifying the `--with-innodb` argument to `configure`:

```
$ ./configure --with-innodb
```

> From MySQL version 4.0, `InnoDB` table support is the default configuration. Use –`without-innodb` to exclude it from the build.

The `configure` script automatically sets variables that control the way the MySQL software is built, for example, taking into account the type of platform and processor type you are compiling on and the features of your C compiler. Normally we do not have to override these.

> Overriding variables in the `configure` script is beyond the scope of this book. Nevertheless, if you need to set the variables before configuring, check the **man** pages for `configure`.

The `configure` script will automatically set locations for the installation. The default locations for MySQL to be compiled to use are `/usr/local/mysql` as the main directory for its operation, with subdirectories for applications and data.

You can use arguments to configure to change the default location settings. The options most often used are:

Option	Description
`--prefix=PREFIX`	Install in directories under `PREFIX`. For MySQL, this defaults to `/usr/local`.
`--localstatedir=DIR`	Install logs and databases in `DIR`. Defaults to `PREFIX/var`.
`--with-innodb`	Compile support for `InnoDB` table type.
`--enable-assembler`	Use fast versions of string functions written in assembler.
`--with-mysqld-ldflags`	Set options for the way the server program is linked.

For a full list of options to configure, you can use the `--help` argument to get a list:

```
$ ./configure --help
Usage: configure [options] [host]
Options: [defaults in brackets after descriptions]
Configuration:
--cache-file=FILE cache test results in FILE
...
$
```

We do not have to settle on final locations for the database files and the log file at this stage. We can always specify these locations to the server process, when we start it after installation.

Here we will configure MySQL to run from `/usr/local/mysql` to keep it out of the way of other applications on our system, and include support for `InnoDB` tables. Before we do so, we need to ensure that our system has a special user for MySQL, one that will own all of the files used by MySQL. The user is called `mysql` and belongs to a group also called `mysql`. To create them we need to execute the following commands as the `root`:

57

```
# groupadd mysql
# useradd -g mysql mysql
```

An error to the effect that the user mysql already exists is harmless because many Linux distributions come with such a user and group preconfigured.

Finally we need to decide the options to be passed to the C/C++ compiler for building our MySQL. These options control the level of optimization that the compiler will perform, and also control some of the run-time behavior. The documentation, especially the file INSTALL-SOURCE, describes a number of recommended options for the compiler. In particular, it notes that it is important to use the C++ option -fno-exceptions with GCC versions 2.95.2 or later. The recommended values of compiler flags for Linux and GCC are:

```
CFLAGS=-O3
CXX=gcc
CXXFLAGS=-O3 -felide-constructors -fno-exceptions -fno-rtti
```

These flags tell GCC to optimize the code in a particular way. These options are recommended by the MySQL developers as they create the fastest and most stable server.

Finally, the configure options are:

```
--enable-assembler
--with-mysqld-ldflags=-all-static
```

Now you can proceed to configuring the source distribution of MySQL:

```
$ CFLAGS="-O3" CXX="gcc" CXXFLAGS="-O3 -felide-constructors -fno-exceptions
-fno-rtti" ./configure -prefix=/usr/local/mysql --with-innodb --enable-assembler -
-with-mysqld-ldflags=-all-static
```

Once the compilation is configured, you can build the software, using make.

> The MySQL build process uses a sophisticated set of **Makefiles** to control the compilation process. Due to this, it is recommended that a version of GNU **make** be used for the build. This is the default on Linux. On other UNIX platforms, you may need to install GNU **make** separately. Often this will be given the name **gmake** to distinguish it from the version of **make** supplied with the operating system. In the instructions below **make** refers to GNU **make**.

Compile the software:

```
$ make
```

If all goes well, you should see a large number of compilations proceeding.

When make has finished you need to copy the programs to their final resting places. Use the make install command to do this, but you need to be the superuser first:

```
$ su
# make install
```

> If you wish to test out the server you have built, you can run a set of test programs before you install. To do this execute make test.

Now you have a complete, but empty installation of MySQL in the directory /usr/local/mysql and its subdirectories.

We have another couple of steps to take before we are ready to use MySQL. The initial database does not contain any user definitions, or privileges that MySQL will use to control access to our data. To create the privilege tables we need to run a script provided for this purpose. Again, this must be run as root after moving into directory /usr/local/mysql:

```
# scripts/mysql_install_db
preparing db table
...
#
```

The MySQL files need to have the correct ownership set that is to be owned by the MySQL user. After using make install, all the files are owned by root. We want root to own everything except the /var subdirectory, and we do this by using the recursive form, -R of commands chmod and chgrp:

```
# chown -R root  /usr/local/mysql
# chown -R mysql /usr/local/mysql/var
# chgrp -R mysql /usr/local/mysql
```

We are now in much the same situation as we would have been had we installed from packages. Now it's time to turn our attention to setting up MySQL to run.

Starting MySQL

The main database process for MySQL, mysqld, is quite a special program. It is responsible for dealing with all data access, from all users, to all databases. It must allow users to access their data, and not allow access to others' data, unless authorized. To do this, it needs to own all of the data files and control access by checking permissions granted to the users that request access. No normal user can access any of the files directly.

MySQL uses the concept of a **pseudo** user to manage data access. A user, called mysql, is created for the sole purpose of owning the data files. Nobody can log in as the mysql user and gain illicit access. This user identity is used by the mysqld program to access the database files on behalf of others.

The first step in establishing a working MySQL system is, therefore, to create this mysql user, as we saw in the section on compiling MySQL from source. If you skipped that section, refer to where we created a user and a group called mysql specifically for MySQL to use.

Other UNIX systems may require you to create a home directory, edit the configuration files, or run the appropriate administration tool on the system. Refer to your operating system documentation for details about these tools.

Now we are almost ready to start the MySQL server process itself. Before we do so, let's take a quick look at how the server can be configured.

When MySQL starts up, it will read a configuration file /etc/my.cnf that sets options for its behavior. It is not a problem if the file does not exist, as MySQL will simply use its defaults. In fact, the RPM binary packages ship without such a file. The source code package contains a number of sample configuration files suitable for various server setups. One of them should be installed as /etc/my.cnf. We suggest support-files/my-medium.cnf as a good starting point. Here's what sections of it look like:

```
# The following options will be passed to all MySQL clients
[client]
#password = your_password
port       = 3306
socket     = /tmp/mysql.sock

# The MySQL server
[mysqld]
port       = 3306
socket     = /tmp/mysql.sock
skip-locking
set-variable    = key_buffer=16M
set-variable    = max_allowed_packet=1M
set-variable    = table_cache=64
set-variable    = sort_buffer=512K
set-variable    = net_buffer_length=8K
set-variable    = myisam_sort_buffer_size=8M
log-bin
server-id  = 1
default-table-type = innodb

# Point the following paths to different dedicated disks
#tmpdir     = /tmp/
#log-update = /path-to-dedicated-directory/hostname

# Uncomment the following if you are using Innobase tables
innodb_data_file_path = ibdata1:400M
innodb_data_home_dir = /usr/local/mysql/var/
innodb_log_group_home_dir = /usr/local/mysql/var/
innodb_log_arch_dir = /usr/local/mysql/var/
set-variable = innodb_mirrored_log_groups=1
set-variable = innodb_log_files_in_group=3
set-variable = innodb_log_file_size=5M
set-variable = innodb_log_buffer_size=8M
innodb_flush_log_at_trx_commit=1
innodb_log_archive=0
set-variable = innodb_buffer_pool_size=16M
set-variable = innodb_additional_mem_pool_size=2M
set-variable = innodb_file_io_threads=4
set-variable = innodb_lock_wait_timeout=50
```

Here we have changed the defaults in two respects, indicated by the highlighted lines in the code. We defined the default table type to be InnoDB tables, and uncomment the lines that set options for those tables. If we wish, we can change the location of the data for our tables in this file, before we start using the database. Other options that can be set in this configuration file are covered in the online documentation.

Now we can start the database server process.

If we have installed packages from a Linux distribution, MySQL may be started automatically every time the machine is rebooted. Typically an init script runs at startup and at shutdown. Refer to your UNIX or Linux documentation for details of startup scripts. The RPMs provided by MySQL AB also contain a suitable script.

If we are installing from source code we can find a version of the init script as support-files/mysql.server, which we need to install in the correct place for our system, typically /etc/rc.d/init.d/mysql and set execute permission.

```
# cp support-files/mysql.server /etc/rc.d/init.d/mysql
# chmod +x /etc/rc.d/init.d/mysql
```

To start the MySQL server we execute:

```
# /etc/rc.d/init.d/mysql start
```

And to stop the server we run:

```
# /etc/rc.d/init.d/mysql stop
```

By default MySQL does not allow general access to data. The initial database contains permission for a user called root to perform any action on the database. To start with, this user has no password, so it should be set as soon as possible after MySQL is installed. To do this use mysqladmin:

```
$ /usr/local/mysql/bin/mysqladmin -u root password newpasswordoul
```

Note that the MySQL users are not necessarily the same as UNIX or Linux login names.

We will cover privileges in more detail in Chapter 10.

Now we can check whether the database is functioning by trying to connect to it. The mysql utility is used to interact with the database system and perform simple administration tasks such as granting privileges, creating databases, and creating tables. We will use it to create and populate the sample database later in the chapter. For now, we can simply try to connect to a database. The response we get will show that we have mysqld successfully running:

```
$ /usr/local/mysql/bin/mysql -u root
Welcome to the MySQL monitor.  Commands end with ; or \g.
Your MySQL connection id is 1 to server version: 4.0.0-alpha-log

Type 'help;' or '\h' for help. Type '\c' to clear the buffer.

mysql>
```

By default, `mysql` connects to the database on the local machine. Here we have specified the MySQL user `root` to use for the connection. The default user will be one with the same name as the current login name. To specify a particular server (host) to connect to we must specify the -h option to `mysql`.

To allow users access to our database we can use `mysql` to grant privileges. The following command grants the user `neil` access to all of the tables in a database called `bmsimple` when connecting from any host:

```
mysql> grant all on bmsimple.* to neil@'%';
```

The syntax `bmsimple.*` indicates all tables within the `bmsimple` database. To grant access to a single table we can use instead `bmsimple.tablename`. The user being granted privileges has the form `user@hostname` where the host name may be replaced by '%' to indicate all hosts, as in this case.

To check network connectivity, we can connect from another MySQL installation on another machine on the network. We specify the host (either by a name or an IP address) with a -h option:

```
remote$ mysql -h 192.168.0.66
Welcome to the MySQL monitor.  Commands end with ; or \g.
Your MySQL connection id is 2 to server version: 4.0.0-alpha-log

Type 'help;' or '\h' for help. Type '\c' to clear the buffer.

mysql>
```

The final step we need to take is to arrange for the `mysqld` server process to be started automatically every time the machine is rebooted.

For systems (such as many Linux distributions) that use System V type `init` scripting, you can place the `init` script in the appropriate place. For SuSE Linux, for example, we would place the script in `/etc/rc.d/init.d/mysql`, and make symbolic links to it from the following places to automatically start and stop MySQL as the server enters and leaves a multi-user mode:

```
ln -s /etc/rc.d/init.d/mysql /etc/rc.d/rc2.d/S25mysql
ln -s /etc/rc.d/init.d/mysql /etc/rc.d/rc2.d/K25mysql
ln -s /etc/rc.d/init.d/mysql /etc/rc.d/rc3.d/S25mysql
ln -s /etc/rc.d/init.d/mysql /etc/rc.d/rc3.d/K25mysql
```

Refer to your systems' documentation on startup scripts for more specific details.

Now it's time to create a database.

Creating the Database

We will be coming back to database administration in more detail later in the book but, for now, here is a very brief 'jump start' now that we have MySQL up and running. We are going to create a simple database, which we will call `bmsimple`, to support our database examples that we would be using throughout this book to demonstrate MySQL.

Before we start, one simple way to check if MySQL is running on your system is to look for the mysqld process:

```
$ ps -el | grep mysqld
```

If there are processes running called mysqld (the name might get abbreviated in the display), then you are running a MySQL server.

Given the appropriate permissions, each user of a MySQL database system can create databases of their own, and control access to the data they hold. We recommend that the administration user creates databases for users and that the users then create tables within the database as required. MySQL is happy to serve many databases at the same time. Let's create our sample database:

```
$ mysql -u root
Welcome to the MySQL monitor.  Commands end with ; or \g.
Your MySQL connection id is 19 to server version: 4.0.0-alpha-log

Type 'help;' or '\h' for help. Type '\c' to clear the buffer.

mysql> create database bmsimple;
Query OK, 1 row affected (0.00 sec)

mysql> \q
Bye
$
```

Now we can grant permissions on this database for existing and new users. Let's allow the user neil to have access to this database. MySQL has a Perl script that can help us manipulate MySQL's **privilege tables** to create the user and set permissions. It is called mysql_setpermission, and effectively performs the appropriate GRANT command for us (we will look at the GRANT command more in detail in Chapter 10, *MySQL Administration*). Let's see how to use it instead of GRANT to create the user and set permissions:

```
$ mysql_setpermission -u root
Password for user root to connect to MySQL:
######################################################################
## Welcome to the permission setter 1.2 for MySQL.
## made by Luuk de Boer
######################################################################
What would you like to do:
  1. Set password for a user.
  2. Add a database + user privilege for that database.
     - user can do all except all admin functions
  3. Add user privilege for an existing database.
     - user can do all except all admin functions
  4. Add user privilege for an existing database.
     - user can do all except all admin functions + no create/drop
  5. Add user privilege for an existing database.
     - user can do only selects (no update/delete/insert etc.)

  0. exit this program
```

63

```
Make your choice [1,2,3,4,5,0]: 3

Which database would you like to select:
You can choose from:
  - bmsimple
  - mysql
  - test
Which database will it be (case sensitive): bmsimple
The database bmsimple will be used.

What username is to be created: neil
Username = neil

Would you like to set a password for  [y/n]: n
We won't set a password so the user doesn't have to use it
We now need to know from what host(s) the user will connect.
Keep in mind that % means 'from any host' ...

The host please: %

Would you like to add another host [yes/no]: no
Okay we keep it with this ...
The following host(s) will be used: %.
###################################################################

That was it ... here is an overview of what you gave to me:
The database name       : bmsimple
The username            : neil
The host(s)             : %
###################################################################

Are you pretty sure you would like to implement this [yes/no]: yes
Okay ... let's go then ...

Everything is inserted and mysql privileges have been reloaded.
...
$
```

The script created the user and added entries to the privileges table as we requested.

Creating the Tables

You can create the tables in your bmsimple database by typing in the SQL commands below at the mysql command prompt. However, it's probably much easier to download the code bundle from the Wrox web site, unpack it, and then execute the commands using source <filename>, which executes commands read from a file. The commands are just plain text, so you can always edit them with your preferred text editor if you wish to:

```
$ /usr/local/mysql/bin/mysql -u neil
Welcome to the MySQL monitor.  Commands end with ; or \g.
Your MySQL connection id is 2 to server version: 4.0.0-alpha-log

Type 'help;' or '\h' for help. Type '\c' to clear the buffer.

mysql> use bmsimple;
```

```
Database changed
mysql> source create_tables.sql
Query OK, 0 rows affected (0.03 sec)

Query OK, 0 rows affected (0.02 sec)

Query OK, 0 rows affected (0.02 sec)

Query OK, 0 rows affected (0.03 sec)

Query OK, 0 rows affected (0.02 sec)

Query OK, 0 rows affected (0.02 sec)

mysql>
```

It is very good practice to script all database schema (tables, indexes, procedures) statements. That way, if the database needs to be recreated, then it can be done from the script. Scripts should also be used whenever the schema needs to be updated.

Here is the SQL for creating our tables, which you will find in create_tables.sql in the code bundle:

```
CREATE TABLE customer
(
    customer_id     int AUTO_INCREMENT NOT NULL PRIMARY KEY,
    title           char(4)                     ,
    fname           varchar(32)                 ,
    lname           varchar(32)         NOT NULL,
    addressline     varchar(64)                 ,
    town            varchar(32)                 ,
    zipcode         char(10)            NOT NULL,
    phone           varchar(16)
);

CREATE TABLE item
(
    item_id         int AUTO_INCREMENT NOT NULL PRIMARY KEY,
    description     varchar(64)         NOT NULL,
    cost_price      numeric(7,2)                ,
    sell_price      numeric(7,2)
);

CREATE TABLE orderinfo
(
    orderinfo_id    int AUTO_INCREMENT NOT NULL PRIMARY KEY,
    customer_id     integer             NOT NULL,
    date_placed     date                NOT NULL,
    date_shipped    date                        ,
    shipping        numeric(7,2)
);
```

```
CREATE TABLE stock
(
    item_id            integer NOT NULL AUTO_INCREMENT PRIMARY KEY,
    quantity           integer          NOT NULL
);

CREATE TABLE orderline
(
    orderinfo_id       integer          NOT NULL,
    item_id            integer          NOT NULL,
    quantity           integer          NOT NULL,
    PRIMARY KEY(orderinfo_id, item_id)
);

CREATE TABLE barcode
(
    barcode_ean        char(13)         NOT NULL PRIMARY KEY,
    item_id            integer          NOT NULL
);
```

Removing the Tables

If at some later date you wish to delete all the tables (also known as dropping the tables), and start again, you can. The command set is in `drop_tables.sql`, and looks like this:

```
DROP TABLE barcode;

DROP TABLE orderline;

DROP TABLE stock;

DROP TABLE orderinfo;

DROP TABLE item;

DROP TABLE customer;
```

> **Be warned, if you drop the tables, you also lose any data in them!**

If you run this script after creating the tables, then run the `create_tables.sql` again before attempting to populate the tables with data.

Populating the Tables

Last, but not least, we need to add some data to the tables or populate the tables.

These samples are all in the code bundle (see **www.wrox.com**), as `pop_tablename.sql`. You can, of course, use your own data except that your results will be different from the ones presented in the book. Until you are confident, it's probably best to stick with our sample data.

You can type each command on a single line (the line wraps are simply a requirement of the printed page). You can add spaces, tabs and blank lines to your commands if it makes them clearer to see and type. However, you do need to note the terminating semicolon, which tells mysql where each SQL command ends.

Customer Table

```
INSERT INTO customer(title, fname, lname, addressline, town, zipcode, phone)
    VALUES('Miss','Jenny','Stones','27 Rowan Avenue','Hightown','NT2
    1AQ','023 9876');
INSERT INTO customer(title, fname, lname, addressline, town, zipcode, phone)
    VALUES ('Mr','Andrew','Stones','52 The Willows','Lowtown','LT5
    7RA','876 3527');
INSERT INTO customer(title, fname, lname, addressline, town, zipcode, phone)
    VALUES ('Miss','Alex','Matthew','4 The Street','Nicetown','NT2
    2TX','010 4567');
INSERT INTO customer(title, fname, lname, addressline, town, zipcode, phone)
    VALUES ('Mr','Adrian','Matthew','The Barn','Yuleville','YV67
    2WR','487 3871');
INSERT INTO customer(title, fname, lname, addressline, town, zipcode, phone)
    VALUES ('Mr','Simon','Cozens','7 Shady Lane','Oahenham','OA3
    6QW','514 5926');
INSERT INTO customer(title, fname, lname, addressline, town, zipcode, phone)
    VALUES ('Mr','Neil','Matthew','5 Pasture Lane','Nicetown','NT3
    7RT','267 1232');
INSERT INTO customer(title, fname, lname, addressline, town, zipcode, phone)
    VALUES ('Mr','Richard','Stones','34 Holly Way','Bingham','BG4
    2WE','342 5982');
INSERT INTO customer(title, fname, lname, addressline, town, zipcode, phone)
    VALUES ('Mrs','Ann','Stones','34 Holly Way','Bingham','BG4 2WE','342
    5982');
INSERT INTO customer(title, fname, lname, addressline, town, zipcode, phone)
    VALUES ('Mrs','Christine','Hickman','36 Queen Street','Histon','HT3
    5EM','342 5432');
INSERT INTO customer(title, fname, lname, addressline, town, zipcode, phone)
    VALUES ('Mr','Mike','Howard','86 Dysart Street','Tibsville','TB3
    7FG','505 5482');
INSERT INTO customer(title, fname, lname, addressline, town, zipcode, phone)
    VALUES ('Mr','Dave','Jones','54 Vale Rise','Bingham','BG3 8GD','342
    8264');
INSERT INTO customer(title, fname, lname, addressline, town, zipcode, phone)
    VALUES ('Mr','Richard','Neill','42 Thached way','Winersby','WB3
    6GQ','505 6482');
INSERT INTO customer(title, fname, lname, addressline, town, zipcode, phone)
    VALUES ('Mrs','Laura','Hendy','73 Margeritta Way','Oxbridge','OX2
    3HX','821 2335');
INSERT INTO customer(title, fname, lname, addressline, town, zipcode, phone)
    VALUES ('Mr','Bill','O\'Neill','2 Beamer Street','Welltown','WT3
    8GM','435 1234');
INSERT INTO customer(title, fname, lname, addressline, town, zipcode, phone)
    VALUES ('Mr','David','Hudson','4  The Square','Milltown','MT2
    6RT','961 4526');
```

Item Table

```
INSERT INTO item(description, cost_price, sell_price)
     VALUES('Wood Puzzle', 15.23, 21.95);
INSERT INTO item(description, cost_price, sell_price)
     VALUES ('Rubik Cube', 7.45, 11.49);
INSERT INTO item(description, cost_price, sell_price)
     VALUES ('Linux CD', 1.99, 2.49);
INSERT INTO item(description, cost_price, sell_price)
     VALUES ('Tissues', 2.11, 3.99);
INSERT INTO item(description, cost_price, sell_price)
     VALUES ('Picture Frame', 7.54, 9.95);
INSERT INTO item(description, cost_price, sell_price)
     VALUES ('Fan Small', 9.23, 15.75);
INSERT INTO item(description, cost_price, sell_price)
     VALUES ('Fan Large', 13.36, 19.95);
INSERT INTO item(description, cost_price, sell_price)
     VALUES ('Toothbrush', 0.75, 1.45);
INSERT INTO item(description, cost_price, sell_price)
     VALUES ('Roman Coin', 2.34, 2.45);
INSERT INTO item(description, cost_price, sell_price)
     VALUES ('Carrier Bag', 0.01, 0.0);
INSERT INTO item(description, cost_price, sell_price)
     VALUES ('Speakers', 19.73, 25.32);
```

Barcode Table

```
INSERT INTO barcode(barcode_ean, item_id) VALUES('6241527836173', 1);
INSERT INTO barcode(barcode_ean, item_id) VALUES('6241574635234', 2);
INSERT INTO barcode(barcode_ean, item_id) VALUES('6264537836173', 3);
INSERT INTO barcode(barcode_ean, item_id) VALUES('6241527746363', 3);
INSERT INTO barcode(barcode_ean, item_id) VALUES('7465743843764', 4);
INSERT INTO barcode(barcode_ean, item_id) VALUES('3453458677628', 5);
INSERT INTO barcode(barcode_ean, item_id) VALUES('6434564564544', 6);
INSERT INTO barcode(barcode_ean, item_id) VALUES('8476736836876', 7);
INSERT INTO barcode(barcode_ean, item_id) VALUES('6241234586487', 8);
INSERT INTO barcode(barcode_ean, item_id) VALUES('9473625532534', 8);
INSERT INTO barcode(barcode_ean, item_id) VALUES('9473627464543', 8);
INSERT INTO barcode(barcode_ean, item_id) VALUES('4587263646878', 9);
INSERT INTO barcode(barcode_ean, item_id) VALUES('9879879837489', 11);
INSERT INTO barcode(barcode_ean, item_id) VALUES('2239872376872', 11);
```

Orderinfo Table

```
INSERT INTO orderinfo(customer_id, date_placed, date_shipped, shipping)
     VALUES(3,  '2000-03-13', '2000-03-17', 2.99);
INSERT INTO orderinfo(customer_id, date_placed, date_shipped, shipping)
     VALUES(8,  '2000-06-23', '2000-06-23', 0.00);
INSERT INTO orderinfo(customer_id, date_placed, date_shipped, shipping)
     VALUES(15, '2000-09-02', '2000-09-12', 3.99);
INSERT INTO orderinfo(customer_id, date_placed, date_shipped, shipping)
     VALUES(13, '2000-09-03', '2000-09-10', 2.99);
INSERT INTO orderinfo(customer_id, date_placed, date_shipped, shipping)
     VALUES(8,  '2000-07-21', '2000-07-24', 0.00);
```

Orderline Table

```
INSERT INTO orderline(orderinfo_id, item_id, quantity) VALUES(1, 4, 1);
INSERT INTO orderline(orderinfo_id, item_id, quantity) VALUES(1, 7, 1);
INSERT INTO orderline(orderinfo_id, item_id, quantity) VALUES(1, 9, 1);
INSERT INTO orderline(orderinfo_id, item_id, quantity) VALUES(2, 1, 1);
INSERT INTO orderline(orderinfo_id, item_id, quantity) VALUES(2, 10, 1);
INSERT INTO orderline(orderinfo_id, item_id, quantity) VALUES(2, 7, 2);
INSERT INTO orderline(orderinfo_id, item_id, quantity) VALUES(2, 4, 2);
INSERT INTO orderline(orderinfo_id, item_id, quantity) VALUES(3, 2, 1);
INSERT INTO orderline(orderinfo_id, item_id, quantity) VALUES(3, 1, 1);
INSERT INTO orderline(orderinfo_id, item_id, quantity) VALUES(4, 5, 2);
INSERT INTO orderline(orderinfo_id, item_id, quantity) VALUES(5, 1, 1);
INSERT INTO orderline(orderinfo_id, item_id, quantity) VALUES(5, 3, 1);
```

Stock Table

```
INSERT INTO stock(item_id, quantity) VALUES(1,12);
INSERT INTO stock(item_id, quantity) VALUES(2,2);
INSERT INTO stock(item_id, quantity) VALUES(4,8);
INSERT INTO stock(item_id, quantity) VALUES(5,3);
INSERT INTO stock(item_id, quantity) VALUES(7,8);
INSERT INTO stock(item_id, quantity) VALUES(8,18);
INSERT INTO stock(item_id, quantity) VALUES(10,1);
```

With the MySQL system running, the database created, the tables made and populated, we are ready to continue our exploration of MySQL features.

Stopping MySQL

It is important that the MySQL server process is shut down in an orderly fashion. This will allow it to write any outstanding data to the database and free up any shared memory resources it is using.

To cleanly shut down the database, use the `mysqladmin` utility as `root` like this:

```
# /usr/local/mysql/bin/mysqladmin shutdown
```

If startup scripts are in place you can of course use those:

```
# /etc/rc.d/init.d/mysql stop
```

The scripts also make sure that the database is shut down properly when the machine is halted or rebooted.

Resources

You can get more information on the utilities `mysql`, `mysqldmin`, and `mysql_setpermissions` by referring to the manual (man) pages, and other documentation provided with MySQL. To make life a little easier when dealing with MySQL it is useful to add the MySQL applications directory to your execution path, and similarly to the man pages. To do this for the standard UNIX shell, place the following commands in your shell startup file (`.profile` or `.bashrc`):

```
PATH=$PATH:/usr/local/mysql/bin
MANPATH=$MANPATH:/usr/local/mysql/man
export PATH MANPATH
```

As mentioned above, the source code for the current and latest test releases of MySQL can be found at http://www.mysql.com. More information on the resources for MySQL is provided in Chapter 16, *Further Information and Resources.*

Installing MySQL On Windows

Let's begin this section with some good news for Windows users. Although MySQL is mostly run on UNIX-like platforms, it has been written to be portable. It has been possible for some time now to install and run a MySQL server on Windows from pre compiled binary packages as we have seen with UNIX and Linux. You can also create Windows client applications that access the MySQL server either through a native interface, or the ODBC standard.

Clients running on Windows can be compiled either with a Windows compiler, such as Microsoft Visual C++, or the GNU C/C++ compiler using an UNIX-like environment for Windows called **Cygwin**.

Here we will concentrate simply on installing the MySQL server on Windows from a binary package.

Installing MySQL from Windows Binaries

The MySQL web site provides pre compiled versions of MySQL for many of the supported platforms, including Microsoft Windows 95/98/NT/2000/XP. The install package is available from http://www.mysql.com/downloads/.

Packages are generally available for both stable releases and development releases. Unless you truly need to use a MySQL feature only available in a development release, we would recommend that you choose the stable version.

The install package is present in the form of a `zip` file and will have a name similar to `mysql-4.0.0.zip`.

Sometimes pre release versions will have 'alpha' or 'beta' in their file names. It should be fairly easy to spot the latest version available for download.

Download this file and unzip its contents into a temporary directory. You should then have a collection of files ready to install, and a `Setup.exe` program that will perform the installation:

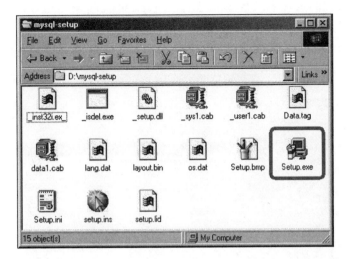

Double-click on the Setup.exe icon to begin the installation process, and follow the instructions on the screen.

> MySQL likes to be installed in a folder on your C drive, specifically C:\MYSQL. If you chose to install the setup process you in another folder on another drive you will need to carry out some configuration of MySQL when the installation is completed. We will return to configuration in a later section.

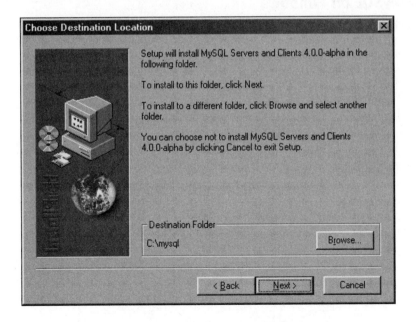

The Setup program allows you to choose between a Typical, Compact and Custom installation that vary in the features they install and the amount of hard disk space the installation will take. A full installation of MySQL 4.0 takes about 27MB of disk space. If you have sufficient space we would recommend that you perform a full install by clicking on the Custom option, and then selecting all of the components.

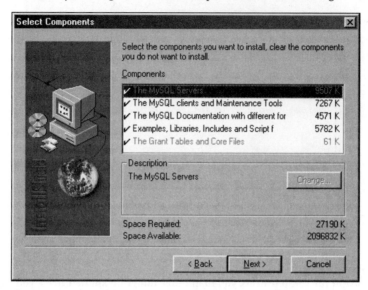

Clicking on the Setup tab copies the MySQL files to the chosen destination and finishes.

Compiling MySQL on Windows

MySQL can be compiled natively on Microsoft Windows using Microsoft's Visual C++ compiler version 6.0 updated with service pack 4 or above. You will need the Windows source distribution package from http://www.msql.com.

The steps needed to compile MySQL on Windows can be found at http://www.mysql.com/doc/W/i/Windows_source_build.html.

Configuring MySQL for Windows

MySQL can be configured and controlled using the WinMySQLadmin tool that is installed in the bin folder of the installation location. Double-click on the WinMySQLadmin.exe icon to start the program:

If this is the first time MySQL has been started, or if the MySQL configuration files cannot be found, `WinMySQLadmin` offers the option of creating a new MySQL configuration file, `my.ini`. This will be necessary if you have chosen to install MySQL in a location other than `C:\MYSQL`.

Enter a name and a password in the text boxes shown here. This will be entered into the MySQL database as a valid user account that we can use for further work with MySQL.

Click on **OK** to create the `my.ini` configuration file.

While `WinMySQLadmin` is running, it uses a 'traffic light' icon to indicate the state of the MySQL server. The icon usually resides in the Windows System Tray at the bottom right corner of the Windows desktop:

When the traffic light shows green, MySQL server is running. When the server is stopped the light shows red. To show the `WinMySQLadmin` application in full, right-click on the icon and select **Show me**, which will bring up the complete application:

The main window for `WinMySQLadmin` is a tabbed dialog box. Each tab contains a page of information used for configuring different aspects of the MySQL installation. The **Environment** page shows information about the host computer and the MySQL server:

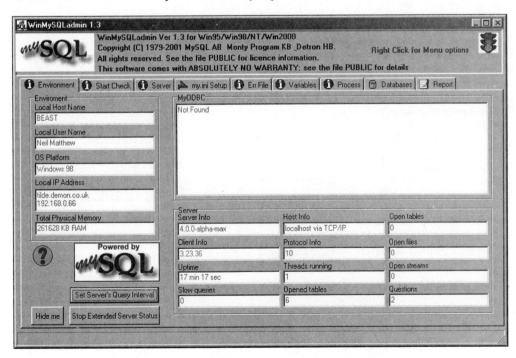

We will not spend a great deal of time here covering all of the options available in WinMySQLadmin, but instead we will concentrate on actions getting started with MySQL. In the screenshot below, we can see that the MySQL server being run is a -max version. This contains support for InnoDB tables, a MySQL table type that supports advanced features, which we will be using throughout this book.

> To return **WinMySQLadmin** to running as an icon in the System Tray click on the **Hide Me** button on the **Environment** page.

MySQL ships with a number of different 'server builds' that are useful in different environments. The -opt version is the one optimized for speed and does not include any advanced features such as support for all table types. The standard version (with no suffix) is the default choice and the -max version is rich in features. We can change the version of the server that is started by WinMySQLadmin by selecting the my.ini Setup tab:

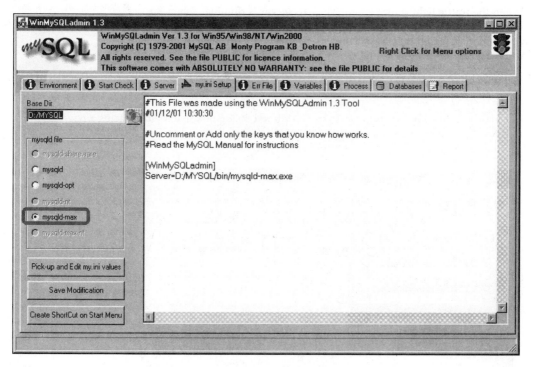

As we will be using InnoDB tables throughout the book, we can set this table type as the default by using WinMySQLadmin to edit the configuration file my.ini for us. To do this, type the following lines into the my.ini Setup window:

```
[mysqld]
default-table-type=innodb
```

Click on Save Modification:

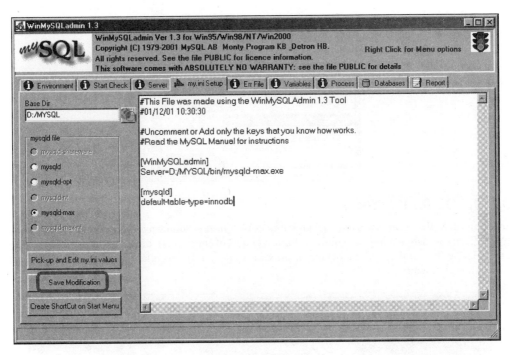

Now all we need to do is stop and restart the MySQL server to enact the change. Do this by right-clicking on the traffic light icon and selecting Shutdown the Server and then Start the Server.

> **On Windows NT and 2000 you may need to remove the MySQL service and install the service between stopping and starting the server for the change to take effect.**

Starting MySQL Automatically

The WinMySQLadmin program automatically starts the MySQL server when it is run. You can arrange to have WinMySQLadmin start when Windows is booted by adding a shortcut to the Program Menu in the Startup group. In fact, WinMySQLadmin can do this for you if you select Create ShortCut on Start Menu on the my,ini Setup tab dialog window of WinMySQLadmin.

For Windows NT and 2000 you can run the MySQL server as a service, independently of any logged-in user. To do this with WinMySQLadmin we need to first install a service for MySQL, and then start or stop it as required. Both of these actions are performed by right-clicking on the traffic lights icon and selecting WinNT:

Using MySQL On Windows

Once the MySQL server is started we can connect to it in the same way as we did under Linux or UNIX. There is also a Windows command-line version of the `mysql` program for connecting to and manipulating the databases. It is located in the `bin` folder of the installation and works in the same way as on other platforms:

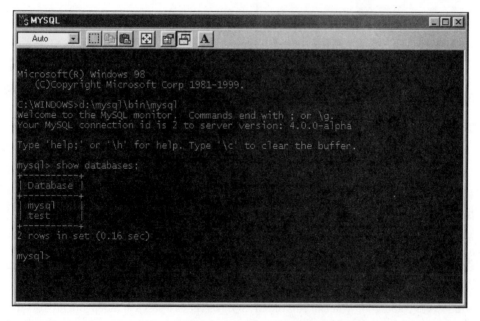

We can also use the Windows `mysql` client to connect to MySQL servers on other platforms.

Summary

In this chapter, we have taken a look at some of the options for installing MySQL. MySQL distributions come in binary, RPM, and source format. The easiest way to install is usually from pre compiled binary and RPM packages. As MySQL is an open source product we can choose to use the source code, which can be compiled on a wide range of Linux and UNIX-like systems.

We have seen the step-by-step process for compiling, installing, and confirming a working installation of MySQL on Linux and Microsoft Windows from packages. We have seen the method to compile and install MySQL on Linux from source. We have also created a sample database `bmsimple` that we will be using in database examples in the subsequent chapters of this book.

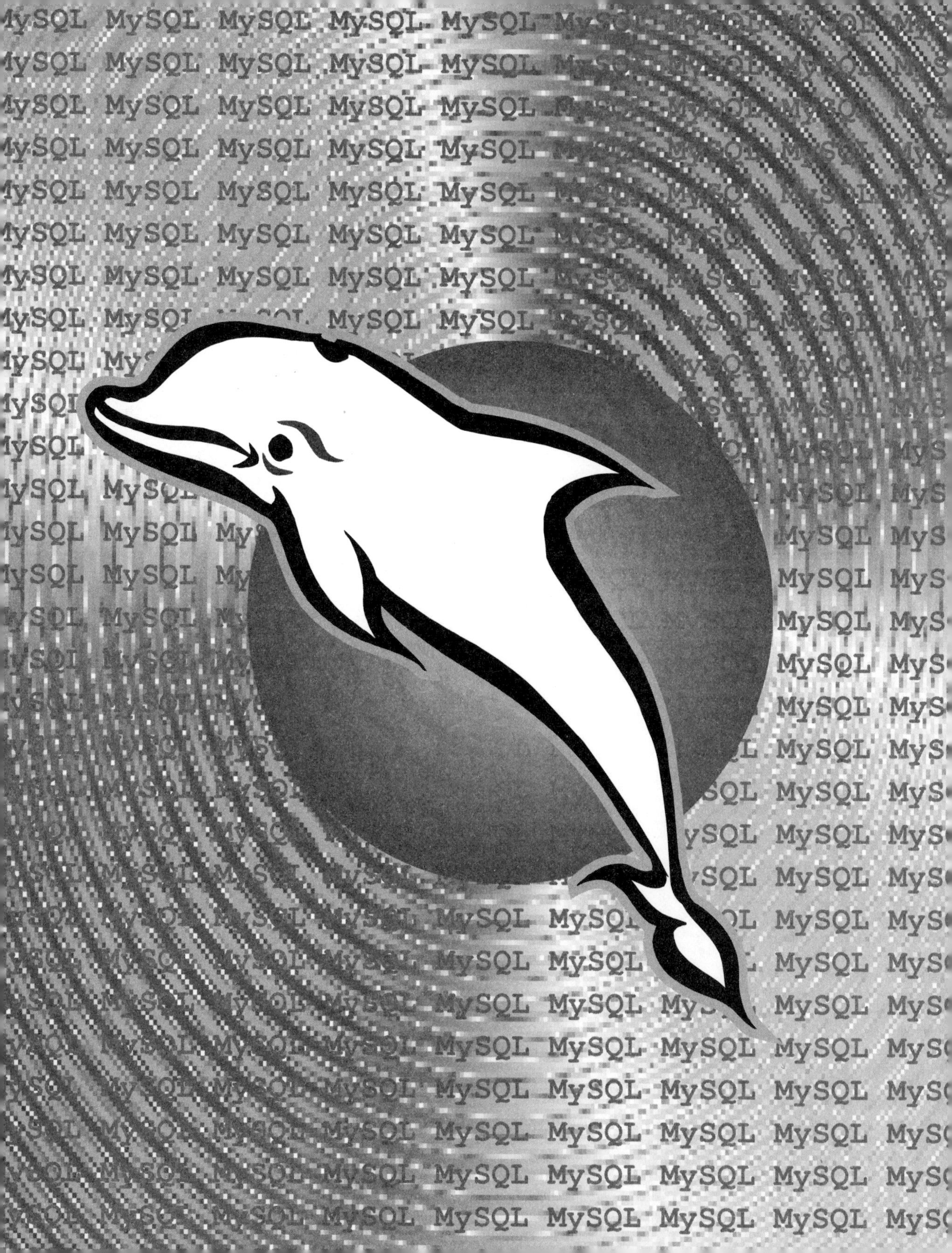
MySQL

Accessing Your Data

So far in this book, our encounters with SQL have been rather informal. We have seen some statements that retrieve data in various ways, and we also saw in the previous chapter some SQL for creating and populating tables. By now you should have MySQL up and running. In the next chapter we will see some of the GUI clients you can use, but for now we will be using the command line tool, mysql, to access the database.

In this chapter we are going to have a look at SQL, starting with the SELECT statement. In fact, most of this chapter is devoted to learning the SELECT statement. Your first impression might be that a whole chapter on one part of SQL is perhaps a bit excessive, but the SELECT statement is right at the heart of the SQL language and once you understand SELECT you really have done the hard part of learning SQL.

We will also see, in later chapters, how we can update and delete data, and further extend our understanding of SELECT to other statements for manipulating data. SQL is not case-sensitive, however MySQL unusually does make table names case-sensitive on operating systems that implement proper support for case-sensitive file names. In practice this means that on Linux and UNIX variants table names will be case-sensitive but on Microsoft Windows including Windows 2000, table names are not case-sensitive.

On operating systems where table names are not case-sensitive they are always stored in lower-case. Data stored in SQL databases is of course case-sensitive, so the character string 'Newtown' is different from the character string 'newtown' on all operating systems.

We will be using the command line tool mysql in this chapter, but you should be able to try all of the examples in this chapter from any GUI tool that allows you to type SQL directly to the MySQL database engine.

In this chapter, we'll look at:

❑   Using the mysql command line tool

❑   Simple SELECT statements

- ❏ Overriding column names
- ❏ Controlling the order of rows
- ❏ Suppressing duplicates
- ❏ Performing calculations
- ❏ Choosing the rows
- ❏ More complex conditions
- ❏ Pattern matching
- ❏ Checking dates and time
- ❏ Multiple table joins
- ❏ Aliasing table names

Throughout this chapter we will be using the sample database, bmsimple, we designed in Chapter 2, *Relational Database Principles*, which we then created and populated in Chapter 3, *Installing and Getting Started with MySQL*.

Using the mysql Command Line Tool

Assuming you have followed the instructions in Chapter 3, by now you should have a database called bmsimple accessible by your normal login prompt.

> **You should always create a new user with a password for accessing the MySQL server. Never rely on the default root user and always ensure that the default root user password has been changed.**

To start the mysql client program as user 'rick', prompting for a password and accessing the bmsimple database on a local Linux or UNIX machine, enter:

```
$ mysql -u rick -p bmsimple;
```

On Windows the options are the same but the program is called mysql.exe.

After entering the correct password you should see something like this:

```
$ mysql -u rick -p bmsimple
Enter password: ******
Reading table information for completion of table and column names
You can turn off this feature to get a quicker startup with -A

Welcome to the MySQL monitor. Commands end with ; or \g.
Your MySQL connection id is 5 to server version: X.Y.Z-Max
```

```
Type 'help;' or '\h' for help. Type '\c' to clear the buffer.

mysql>
```

To avoid providing parameters each time mysql is invoked, you can store some default parameters in a file ~/.my.cnf (Linux/UNIX), or my.ini (Windows), or C:\winnt\my.ini (Windows NT). The file is in the standard Windows.ini format. The mysql client program will read the section starting [client]. As an example, here is the my.ini file the author is using so his mysql client program executing on a Windows machine connects directly to his MySQL server on his local Linux machine:

```
[client]
user=rick
password=secret
database=bmsimple
host=192.168.100.101
```

The host can be specified here as either an IP address or as a machine name. On Windows we suggest you use the WinMySQLAdmin tool for maintaining the initialization file.

To check if you have the tables created, enter SHOW TABLES and press return. You should see output similar to this:

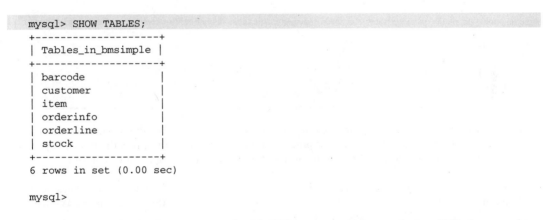

```
mysql> SHOW TABLES;
+--------------------+
| Tables_in_bmsimple |
+--------------------+
| barcode            |
| customer           |
| item               |
| orderinfo          |
| orderline          |
| stock              |
+--------------------+
6 rows in set (0.00 sec)

mysql>
```

We can also inspect the database structure for MySQL servers running on the local Windows machine using WinMySQLAdmin:

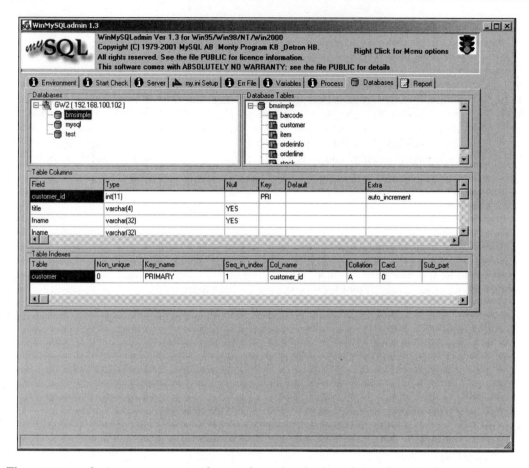

There are some basic mysql commands; it is always handy if you know them. To know more mysql commands refer to Appendix D. After typing a command, remember to press the return key. You can also use the arrow keys to recall previous lines and move about editing them if required.

In addition, the MySQL server command SHOW is very useful. This takes a variety of parameters, depending on what you want to display. For now we will just look at the main options. We will meet the full set in Chapter 5, *MySQL Graphical Tools*:

Command	Description
SHOW COLUMNS FROM *tablename*	Shows columns and their attributes from a table
DESCRIBE *tablename*	
SHOW DATABASES	Shows the databases present
SHOW STATUS	Gives you basic information about your server
SHOW TABLES	Lists the tables in the current, or another, database

A semicolon must follow each statement to terminate the input. For example:

```
mysql> SHOW DATABASES;
+----------+
| Database |
+----------+
| bmfinal  |
| bmsimple |
| mysql    |
| test     |
+----------+
4 rows in set (0.00 sec)

mysql>
```

Now we are ready to start accessing MySQL using SQL commands. For this chapter we will stick to using the `mysql` command line tool but if you prefer to use the GUI tools, you may want to look ahead to Chapter 5 first, and then come back here to learn more about the `mysql` tool.

From here on we assume you are using the `bmsimple` database created in Chapter 3, ready with the sample data.

Simple SELECT Statements

We get data from MySQL using the `SELECT` statement as in all relational databases. It's probably the most complex statement in SQL, but it really is at the heart of using relational databases effectively.

Let's start our investigation of `SELECT` by simply asking for all the data in a particular table. We do this by using a very basic form of the `SELECT` statement specifying a `FROM` clause and a table name:

```
SELECT <comma separated list of columns> FROM <table name>
```

If we can't remember what the exact column names are or want to see all the columns, we can just use a '*' in place of the column list to select all columns from the table.

Try It Out – Selecting All Columns from a Table

We will start by fetching all the data from the `item` table:

```
SELECT * FROM item;
```

Remember that the ';' is for the benefit of the `mysql` program, to tell it you have finished typing. Strictly speaking it is not part of SQL. If you prefer, you can mark the end of SQL statements typed into `mysql` with '\g', which has exactly the same effect as the semicolon.

Remember that we write SQL keywords in uppercase to make them stand out; you may use lowercase if you prefer. Case may be important in table names depending on the operating system your server is running on. In this book we will stick to lowercase while using table names.

Once you have pressed return after the executing the command mentioned above, MySQL responds like this:

```
mysql> SELECT * FROM item;
+---------+---------------+------------+------------+
| item_id | description   | cost_price | sell_price |
+---------+---------------+------------+------------+
|       1 | Wood Puzzle   |      15.23 |      21.95 |
|       2 | Rubik Cube    |       7.45 |      11.49 |
|       3 | Linux CD      |       1.99 |       2.49 |
|       4 | Tissues       |       2.11 |       3.99 |
|       5 | Picture Frame |       7.54 |       9.95 |
|       6 | Fan Small     |       9.23 |      15.75 |
|       7 | Fan Large     |      13.36 |      19.95 |
|       8 | Toothbrush    |       0.75 |       1.45 |
|       9 | Roman Coin    |       2.34 |       2.45 |
|      10 | Carrier Bag   |       0.01 |       0.00 |
|      11 | Speakers      |      19.73 |      25.32 |
+---------+---------------+------------+------------+
11 rows in set (0.01 sec)

mysql>
```

How It Works

We simply asked MySQL for all the data from all the columns in the item table, using a '*' for the column names. MySQL gave us just that, and also neatly arranged it with column headings and a pipe '|' symbol to separate each column. It even told us how many rows we retrieved and how long it took.

If you prefer you can use the \G terminator, which outputs the data in a very different format:

```
mysql> SELECT * FROM item\G
*************************** 1. row ***************************
    item_id: 1
description: Wood Puzzle
 cost_price: 15.23
 sell_price: 21.95
*************************** 2. row ***************************
    item_id: 2
description: Rubik Cube
 cost_price: 7.45
 sell_price: 11.49
*************************** 3. row ***************************
    item_id: 3
description: Linux CD
 cost_price: 1.99
 sell_price: 2.49
*************************** 4. row ***************************
    item_id: 4
description: Tissues
 cost_price: 2.11
 sell_price: 3.99
...
```

For brevity we are not showing all the records. This format may be more convenient if the width of data does not fit on a single screen. We will stick to the more conventional column output in this book.

The SELECT statement works, but suppose we didn't want all the columns? In general, you should only ask MySQL, or indeed any relational database, to retrieve the data that you actually want. Each column of each row retrieved adds a little extra work. Remember, we would want to keep things neat and efficient.

You will also find that, once you start having SQL embedded in other languages (see Chapter 12, *Accessing MySQL from C and C++*), specifying the columns exactly protects you against changes to the database schema. If you use '*' then you assume the presence and order of the columns. All experienced developers know that assumptions can be very dangerous!

> **If you name all columns explicitly, you have the possibility of searching all your code to see if the column name appears. It may not be trivial to do, but it's a lot better than your customers stumbling into a bug because you removed or renamed a column in the database and missed an occurrence in the code.**

Let's start by restricting the columns we retrieve. As we saw earlier, in the general syntax we do this by specifying each column we want to retrieve, separated by a comma. If we don't want the columns in the order we specified when we created the database table, that's fine; we can specify the columns in any order we like and they will be returned in that order.

Try It Out – Selecting Named Columns in the Order We Choose

To retrieve the name of the town and last name of all our customers, we must specify the name of the columns for town and last name, and of course the table to retrieve them from. Here is the statement we need and MySQL's response:

```
mysql> SELECT town, lname FROM customer;
+-----------+---------+
| town      | lname   |
+-----------+---------+
| Hightown  | Stones  |
| Lowtown   | Stones  |
| Nicetown  | Matthew |
| Yuleville | Matthew |
| Oahenham  | Cozens  |
| Nicetown  | Matthew |
| Bingham   | Stones  |
| Bingham   | Stones  |
| Histon    | Hickman |
| Tibsville | Howard  |
| Bingham   | Jones   |
| Winersby  | Neill   |
| Oxbridge  | Hendy   |
| Welltown  | O'Neill |
| Milltown  | Hudson  |
+-----------+---------+
15 rows in set (0.00 sec)

mysql>
```

How It Works

MySQL returns all the data rows from the table we asked for, but only from the columns we specified. It also returns the column data in the order in which we specified the columns in the SELECT statement.

Overriding Column Names

You will notice that the output uses the database column name as the heading for the output. This is not very easy to read and sometimes (as we will see later in this chapter and again in Chapter 7, *Advance Data Selection*) the output column isn't an actual database column at all and hence has no name.

There is a very simple syntax for specifying the display name to use with each column, which is to add AS "<display name>" after each column in the SELECT statement. You can specify the name of all columns you select or just a few. Where you don't specify the name, MySQL just uses the column name.

For example, to change the above output to make lname be displayed as Last Name we would write:

```
SELECT town, lname AS "Last Name" FROM customer;
```

We will see an example of this in use in the next section.

Controlling the Order of Rows

So far, we have retrieved the data from the columns we wanted but the data is not always in the most suitable order for viewing. The data we have seen may look as though it is in the order we inserted it into the database, but in fact, relational databases are under no obligation to return the data to you in any particular order, unless you specifically ask for it ordered in some way.

You may remember we mentioned in Chapter 2 that unlike a spreadsheet, the order of rows in a database is unspecified. The database server is free to store rows in the most effective way, which is not usually the most natural way for viewing the data. Generally, the data will be returned in the order it is stored in the database internally. Initially, this may look to be the same order as you inserted data into the database, but as you delete rows, and insert new rows, this order may begin to look more and more random. No SQL database including MySQL is obliged to return the rows of data in a particular order, unless you specifically request it to be ordered in a particular way.

We can control the order in which data is displayed by a SELECT statement. Simply add an additional clause to the SELECT statement, ORDER BY, which specifies the order we would like the data to be returned. The syntax is:

```
SELECT <comma separated list of columns> FROM < table name>
       ORDER BY <column name> [ASC | DESC]
```

The slightly strange looking syntax at the end means that after the column name we can optionally write either ASC (short for ascending) or DESC (short for descending). By default ASC is used. The data is then returned to us ordered by the column we specified, sorted in the manner we requested.

Try It Out – Ordering the Data

In this example, we will sort the data by town and we will also override the original column name for the lname column as we saw in the last section, to make the output slightly easier to read.

Notice that since we want the data in ascending order, we can omit the ASC as that is the default. Here is the command we require and MySQL's response:

```
mysql> SELECT town, lname AS "Last Name" FROM customer ORDER BY town;
+-----------+-----------+
| town      | Last Name |
+-----------+-----------+
| Bingham   | Stones    |
| Bingham   | Stones    |
| Bingham   | Jones     |
| Hightown  | Stones    |
| Histon    | Hickman   |
| Lowtown   | Stones    |
| Milltown  | Hudson    |
| Nicetown  | Matthew   |
| Nicetown  | Matthew   |
| Oahenham  | Cozens    |
| Oxbridge  | Hendy     |
| Tibsville | Howard    |
| Welltown  | O'Neill   |
| Winersby  | Neill     |
| Yuleville | Matthew   |
+-----------+-----------+
15 rows in set (0.00 sec)

mysql>
```

How It Works

This time we made two changes to our previous statement. We added the 'AS' clause to change the name of the second column to Last Name, which makes it easier to read, and we also added an ORDER BY clause to specify the order in which data should be returned to us.

Sometimes we need to go a little further and order by more than a single column. For example, in the output above although the data is ordered by town column, there is not much order in the Last Name. We can see, for example, that Jones is listed after Stones under all the customers found in the town Bingham.

We can specify more precisely the order we would like the output to appear in, by specifying more than one column in the ORDER BY clause. If we want to, we can even specify that the order is ascending for one column and descending for other.

Try It Out – Ordering the Data Using ASC and DESC

Let's try our SELECT again, but now we will sort the town names in descending order and the last names in ascending order, where rows share the same town name. This time, we will not override the default column names.

Here is the statement we need and MySQL's response:

```
mysql> SELECT town, lname FROM customer ORDER BY town DESC, lname ASC;
+-----------+---------+
| town      | lname   |
+-----------+---------+
| Yuleville | Matthew |
| Winersby  | Neill   |
| Welltown  | O'Neill |
| Tibsville | Howard  |
| Oxbridge  | Hendy   |
| Oahenham  | Cozens  |
| Nicetown  | Matthew |
| Nicetown  | Matthew |
| Milltown  | Hudson  |
| Lowtown   | Stones  |
| Histon    | Hickman |
| Hightown  | Stones  |
| Bingham   | Jones   |
| Bingham   | Stones  |
| Bingham   | Stones  |
+-----------+---------+
15 rows in set (0.00 sec)

mysql>
```

How It Works

As you can see, the data is first ordered by town in descending order, which was the first column we specified in our ORDER BY clause. MySQL then sorts in ascending order those entries that have multiple last names for the same town. This time, although Bingham is now last in the rows retrieved, the last names of our customers in that town are ordered in an ascending order.

Usually, the columns by which you can order the output are restricted, not unreasonably, to columns you have requested in the output. MySQL does not enforce this standard restriction and will accept a column in the ORDER BY clause that is not in the selected column list. This is a non-standard SQL and we suggest that you avoid using it.

Suppressing Duplicates

You may notice that there are several rows in the last output that appear twice:

```
Nicetown | Matthew
Bingham  | Stones
```

What's going on here? If we look back at our original data, in Chapters 2 and 3, we will see that there are indeed two customers in Nicetown called Matthew, and two customers in Bingham called Stones. For reference, here is the statement we need and part of MySQL's response, where the rows show the first names as well:

```
mysql> SELECT town, fname, lname FROM customer
    -> ORDER BY town DESC, lname ASC;
...
| Nicetown | Alex    | Matthew |
| Nicetown | Neil    | Matthew |
...
| Bingham  | Richard | Stones  |
| Bingham  | Ann     | Stones  |
...
```

When mysql listed two rows for Nicetown and Matthew, and two rows for Bingham and Stones, it was quite correct. There are two customers in each of those towns with the same last names. They look the same because we have not asked for columns that distinguish the rows. The default behavior is to list all the rows, but is not always what we want.

Notice the continuation prompt, -> where the SQL has extended over more than one line.

Suppose we wanted just a list of towns where we had customers, perhaps in a much bigger scenario to determine where we should build distribution centers. Based on our knowledge so far, we might reasonably try:

```
mysql> SELECT town FROM customer ORDER BY town;
+-----------+
| town      |
+-----------+
| Bingham   |
| Bingham   |
| Bingham   |
| Hightown  |
| Histon    |
| Lowtown   |
| Milltown  |
| Nicetown  |
| Nicetown  |
| Oahenham  |
| Oxbridge  |
| Tibsville |
| Welltown  |
| Winersby  |
| Yuleville |
+-----------+
15 rows in set (0.01 sec)

mysql>
```

What we get back is correct but perhaps not what we wanted. The SQL statement has listed all the towns, once for each time a town name appeared in the customer table so some towns appear several times. This is correct, but probably not quite the listing we would like. What we actually needed was a list where each town appeared exactly once, in other words a list of distinct towns.

In SQL, you can suppress duplicate rows by adding the clause DISTINCT to the SELECT statement. The syntax is:

```
SELECT DISTINCT <comma separated list of columns> FROM < table name>
```

As with pretty much all the clauses on SELECT, you can of course combine this with other clauses such as renaming columns or specifying an order.

Try It Out – Using DISTINCT

Let's get a list of all the unique towns that appear in our customer table without duplicates. We can use the following statement to get the response we require:

```
mysql> SELECT DISTINCT town FROM customer;
+-----------+
| town      |
+-----------+
| Hightown  |
| Lowtown   |
| Nicetown  |
| Yuleville |
| Oahenham  |
| Bingham   |
| Histon    |
| Tibsville |
| Winersby  |
| Oxbridge  |
| Welltown  |
| Milltown  |
+-----------+
12 rows in set (0.00 sec)

mysql>
```

How It Works

The DISTINCT clause removes all duplicate rows. You can also use DISTINCTROW in place of DISTINCT, which has an identical effect in MySQL, but is not standard SQL.

Notice that the DISTINCT clause is not associated with a particular column. You can only suppress rows that are duplicated in all the columns you select, not suppress duplicates of a particular column. For example, if we asked:

```
SELECT DISTINCT town, fname FROM customer;
```

We would again get 15 rows because there are 15 different town and first name combinations.

A word of warning is in order here. Although it might look like a good idea to always use the DISTINCT version of SELECT, in practice this is a bad idea for two reasons. First, by using DISTINCT you are asking the server to do significantly more work in retrieving your data and checking for duplicates. Unless you know there will be duplicates that need to be removed, you shouldn't use the DISTINCT clause. The second reason is a bit more pragmatic. Occasionally, DISTINCT will mask errors in your data or SQL that would have been easy to spot if duplicate rows were displayed.

> In short, use **DISTINCT** only where you actually need it.

Performing Calculations

We can also perform simple calculations on data in the rows we retrieve before we send them to the output.

Suppose we wanted to display the cost price of items in our `item` table. We could just execute `SELECT` as shown below, which would give us output like this:

```
mysql> SELECT description, cost_price FROM item;
+---------------+------------+
| description   | cost_price |
+---------------+------------+
| Wood Puzzle   |      15.23 |
| Rubik Cube    |       7.45 |
| Linux CD      |       1.99 |
| Tissues       |       2.11 |
| Picture Frame |       7.54 |
| Fan Small     |       9.23 |
| Fan Large     |      13.36 |
| Toothbrush    |       0.75 |
| Roman Coin    |       2.34 |
| Carrier Bag   |       0.01 |
| Speakers      |      19.73 |
+---------------+------------+
11 rows in set (0.01 sec)

mysql>
```

However, suppose we wanted to see the price in cents. We can do a simple calculation in SQL, which would give us a response as shown below:

```
mysql> SELECT description, cost_price * 100 FROM item;
+---------------+------------------+
| description   | cost_price * 100 |
+---------------+------------------+
| Wood Puzzle   |          1523.00 |
| Rubik Cube    |           745.00 |
| Linux CD      |           199.00 |
| Tissues       |           211.00 |
| Picture Frame |           754.00 |
| Fan Small     |           923.00 |
| Fan Large     |          1336.00 |
| Toothbrush    |            75.00 |
| Roman Coin    |           234.00 |
| Carrier Bag   |             1.00 |
| Speakers      |          1973.00 |
+---------------+------------------+
11 rows in set (0.00 sec)

mysql>
```

It seems a little weird with the decimal points, so let's get rid of them using a trick we will see more of later.

We use the FORMAT() function to change the number of decimal places to zero, which gives us a better looking output:

```
mysql> SELECT description, FORMAT(cost_price * 100, 0) FROM item;
+---------------+-----------------------------+
| description   | FORMAT(cost_price * 100, 0) |
+---------------+-----------------------------+
| Wood Puzzle   | 1,523                       |
| Rubik Cube    | 745                         |
| Linux CD      | 199                         |
| Tissues       | 211                         |
| Picture Frame | 754                         |
| Fan Small     | 923                         |
| Fan Large     | 1,336                       |
| Toothbrush    | 75                          |
| Roman Coin    | 234                         |
| Carrier Bag   | 1                           |
| Speakers      | 1,973                       |
+---------------+-----------------------------+
11 rows in set (0.00 sec)

mysql>
```

It's not very often you will need to perform calculations on columns. They are used more when updating the database, as we will see in Chapter 7. It is handy to know however, that the ability to calculate in SQL statements exists.

Choosing the Rows

So far, in this chapter, we have always worked with either all the rows of data or at least with all the distinct rows. It's time to look at how, just as with columns, we can choose the rows we want to see. You probably won't be surprised to learn that we do this with yet another clause on the SELECT statement.

The new clause we use for restricting the rows returned is WHERE. The syntax, simplified, is:

```
SELECT <comma-separated list of columns> FROM <table name>
    WHERE <conditions>
```

There are lots of possible conditions, which can also be combined by the logical operators AND, OR, and NOT. The standard list of comparison operators is as follows:

Operator	Description
<	Less than
<=	Less than or equal to
=	Equal to
<=>	MySQL special NULL SAFE EQUAL
>=	Greater or equal to
>	Greater than
<>	Not equal to

These operators can be used on most data types including both numeric and string (and also date, though there are some special conditions when working with dates), which we will see later. The MySQL special NULL SAFE EQUAL operator considers a comparison against NULL to be false, rather than the standard SQL result of comparing a value against NULL, which has the result NULL. We will see more of this later in the chapter.

Be aware that string comparisons in MySQL, unlike standard SQL, by default are case-insensitive.

Interestingly we can also use the SELECT statement without actually retrieving any data from the database, which gives us a convenient way of experimenting with operators, like this:

```
mysql> SELECT 1=1, 1 > 3, "Hello"="hellO", 1=NULL, 1<=>NULL;
+-----+-------+-----------------+--------+----------+
| 1=1 | 1 > 3 | "Hello"="hellO" | 1=NULL | 1<=>NULL |
+-----+-------+-----------------+--------+----------+
|   1 |     0 |               1 |   NULL |        0 |
+-----+-------+-----------------+--------+----------+
1 row in set (0.00 sec)

mysql>
```

This asks – does 1 equal 1; is 1 greater than 3; are the strings "Hello" and "hellO" equal; does 1 equal NULL, and does 1 'NULL SAFE EQUAL' NULL. The answers given are yes, no, yes, NULL and no respectively (yes is showed as 1 and no is showed as 0).

To look at the use of these operators when retrieving data, let's start with a simple condition by just choosing to retrieve rows for people who live in the town Bingham. The SELECT command we need is:

```
mysql> SELECT town, lname, fname FROM customer WHERE town = 'Bingham';
+---------+--------+---------+
| town    | lname  | fname   |
+---------+--------+---------+
| Bingham | Stones | Richard |
| Bingham | Stones | Ann     |
| Bingham | Jones  | Dave    |
+---------+--------+---------+
3 rows in set (0.01 sec)

mysql>
```

That was pretty straightforward, wasn't it? Notice the single quotes round the string Bingham, which are needed to make it clear that this is a string. If we try this again with the command:

```
mysql> SELECT town, lname, fname FROM customer WHERE town = 'bingham';
```

We will get exactly the same answer, which is probably not quite what we expected. Since we expect string comparison to be case-sensitive, as in most SQL databases, this statement should return no data.

In MySQL we need to add the BINARY keyword to make string matches case-sensitive, like this:

```
mysql> SELECT town, lname, fname FROM customer
    -> WHERE BINARY town = 'bingham';
Empty set (0.00 sec)

mysql>
```

It then retrieves no rows, because the town in the database is 'Bingham', not 'bingham'.

We can have multiple conditions combined using AND, OR, and NOT with parentheses to make the expression clear. MySQL also allows us to use conditions on columns that don't appear in the list of columns we have selected. Standard SQL will not allow conditions on columns that are not selected, so you should be careful of using this MySQL feature if portability of your SQL is important to you.

Try It Out – Using Operators

Let's try a more complicated set of conditions. Suppose we want to see the names of our customers who do not have a title of 'Mr.', but do live in either Bingham or Nicetown.

The statement we need and the response is:

```
mysql> SELECT title, fname, lname, town FROM customer WHERE title <> 'Mr'
    -> AND (BINARY town = 'Bingham' OR BINARY town = 'Nicetown');
+-------+-------+---------+----------+
| title | fname | lname   | town     |
+-------+-------+---------+----------+
| Miss  | Alex  | Matthew | Nicetown |
| Mrs   | Ann   | Stones  | Bingham  |
+-------+-------+---------+----------+
2 rows in set (0.00 sec)

mysql>
```

How It Works

Although it might look a little complex at first glance, this statement is actually quite simple. The first part is just our usual SELECT, listing the columns we want to see in the output. After the WHERE keyword, we initially check that the title is not 'Mr.', then we check that the other condition is true, using AND. This second condition is that the town is either Bingham or Nicetown.

There are other points to be noticed. First we have to use parentheses to make it clear how the clauses are to be grouped. The second point is that we used the keyword BINARY to ensure case-sensitivity of string comparisons.

You should be aware that MySQL, like any relational database, is not under any obligation to process the clauses in the order you write them in the SQL statement. All that is promised is that the result will be the correct answer to the SQL query posed. Generally, relational databases have a complex optimizer, which looks at the request then calculates the 'best' way to satisfy it. Optimizers are not perfect and you will occasionally come across statements that run better when rewritten in different ways. For reasonably simple statements like this one, we can safely assume the optimizer will do a good job.

> If you want to know how MySQL will process a SQL statement, you can get it to tell you by prefixing the SQL **SELECT** statement with **EXPLAIN** when, rather than execute the statement, MySQL will tell you how the statement would be processed.

More Complex Conditions

One of the things that we frequently need to do when working with strings is to allow partial matching. For example, we may be looking for a person called Robert, but the name may have been shortened in the database to Rob, or even Bob. There are some special operations in SQL that make working with strings, either partial ones or lists of strings, easier.

The first new condition is IN, which allows us to check against a list of items, rather than using a string of OR conditions. Consider the following (we have dropped the BINARY keyword to make the SQL easier to read):

```
mysql> SELECT title, fname, lname, town FROM customer WHERE title <> 'Mr'
    -> AND (town = 'Bingham' OR town = 'Nicetown');
```

We can rewrite this as:

```
mysql> SELECT title, fname, lname, town FROM customer WHERE title <> 'Mr'
    -> AND town IN ('Bingham', 'Nicetown');
```

We will get the same result, although it's possible the output rows could be in a different order since we did not use an ORDER BY clause. There is no particular advantage in using IN here in this case, except for the simplification of the expression.

The next new condition is BETWEEN, which allows us to check a range of values by specifying the end points. Suppose we wanted to select the rows with customer_id values between 5 and 9. Rather than writing a sequence of OR conditions or an IN with many values, we can simply use BETWEEN and get the response:

```
mysql> SELECT customer_id, town, lname FROM customer
    -> WHERE customer_id BETWEEN 5 AND 9;
+-------------+----------+---------+
| customer_id | town     | lname   |
+-------------+----------+---------+
|           5 | Oahenham | Cozens  |
|           6 | Nicetown | Matthew |
|           7 | Bingham  | Stones  |
|           8 | Bingham  | Stones  |
|           9 | Histon   | Hickman |
+-------------+----------+---------+
5 rows in set (0.01 sec)

mysql>
```

It's also possible to use BETWEEN with strings, but care is needed, because the answer may not always be the same as you would expect as we will see in the next example, which shows the use of BETWEEN with strings.

Try It Out – Complex Conditions

Let's try a BETWEEN statement, comparing strings. Suppose we wanted a distinct list of all the towns that started with letters between B and N. We know that all the towns in our table start with a capital letter, so we might well write the following, to get MySQL's response:

```
mysql> SELECT DISTINCT town FROM customer WHERE town BETWEEN 'B' AND 'N';
+----------+
| town     |
+----------+
| Hightown |
| Lowtown  |
| Bingham  |
| Histon   |
| Milltown |
+----------+
5 rows in set (0.01 sec)

mysql>
```

Which, if you look at it closely, isn't what you were probably hoping for. Where is Nicetown? It certainly starts with an N but it hasn't been listed.

Why It Didn't Work

The reason this statement didn't work is that MySQL, as per the SQL92 standard, pads the string you give it with blanks, till it is the same length as the string it is checking against. So when the comparison got to Nicetown, MySQL compared N (N followed by 6 spaces) with Nicetown and because white space appears in the ASCII table before all the other letters it decided the Nicetown came after N, so it shouldn't be included in the list.

How To Make It Work

It's actually quite easy to make it work. Either we need to prevent the behavior of adding blanks to the search string by adding some 'z' characters ourselves or search using the next letter 'O' in the BETWEEN clause. Of course, if there is a town called O we will then erroneously retrieve it, so this needs care. It's generally better to use z rather than Z, because z appears after Z in the ASCII table. Thus, our SQL should have read:

```
mysql> SELECT DISTINCT town FROM customer WHERE town BETWEEN 'B' AND 'Nz';
```

Notice that we didn't add a character after the 'B'; the 'B' string being padded with blanks does work to find all towns that start with a 'B'.

If there was a town that started with the letters Nzz we would again fail to find it because we would then compare Nz against Nzz. The comparison would have been that Nzz came after Nz because the third string location in Nz would have been padded to ' ' (space), which comes before the z in the third place of the string Nzz we are comparing against.

This type of matching has rather subtle behavior and is so easy to go wrong that even experienced SQL users get caught out occasionally. For this reason, we recommend that you avoid using BETWEEN with strings.

Pattern Matching

The string comparison operations we have seen till now are fine but they don't help very much with 'real world' string pattern matching. There is, of course, a SQL condition for doing this; it's the LIKE condition.

Unfortunately, LIKE uses a different set of string comparison rules from most common programming languages but, so long as you remember the rules, it's easy enough to use. When comparing strings with LIKE, you use '%' to mean any string of characters and '_' to match a single character.

For example, to match towns beginning with the letter 'B', we would write:

```
... WHERE town LIKE 'B%'
```

To match first names that end with 'e', we would write:

```
... WHERE fname LIKE '%e';
```

To match first names that are exactly four characters long, we would use four underscore characters like this:

```
... WHERE fname LIKE '_ _ _ _';
```

We can also combine the two types in a single string if we need to.

Try It Out – Pattern Matching

Let's find all the customers who have first names that have an 'a' as the second character by writing the SELECT statement using '%' and '_' characters and MySQL's response would be:

```
mysql> SELECT fname, lname FROM customer WHERE fname LIKE '_a%';
+-------+--------+
| fname | lname  |
+-------+--------+
| Dave  | Jones  |
| Laura | Hendy  |
| David | Hudson |
+-------+--------+
3 rows in set (0.00 sec)

mysql>
```

How It Works

The first part of the pattern, '_a' matches strings that start with any single character, then have a lower case a. The second part of the pattern, '%' matches any remaining characters. If we hadn't used the trailing '%', then only strings exactly two characters long would have been matched.

Limiting the Result

In the examples we have been using so far, the number of result rows returned has always been quite small because we only have a few sample rows in our experimental database. In 'real' databases, we could easily have many thousands of rows that match the selection criteria and if we are working on our SQL, refining our statements, we almost certainly do not want to see many thousands of rows scrolling past on our screen. A few sample rows to check our logic would be quite sufficient.

MySQL has an extra clause on the SELECT statement, LIMIT, which is not part of the SQL standard, but is very useful when we want to restrict the number of rows returned.

You can use the LIMIT clause in two slightly different ways. If you append LIMIT and a number to your SELECT clause, only rows up to the number you specified will be returned, starting from the first row.

A slightly different way to use LIMIT is to specify a pair of numbers with a 'comma' between them. If you use 'LIMIT M, N' then only N rows will be returned, after M rows have been skipped.

It's easier to show it in action than to describe it. Here we only display the first five matching rows:

```
mysql> SELECT customer_id, town FROM customer LIMIT 5;
+-------------+-----------+
| customer_id | town      |
+-------------+-----------+
|           1 | Hightown  |
|           2 | Lowtown   |
|           3 | Nicetown  |
|           4 | Yuleville |
|           5 | Oahenham  |
+-------------+-----------+
5 rows in set (0.00 sec)

mysql>
```

The following command skips the first five result rows then returns the next two rows:

```
mysql> SELECT customer_id, town FROM customer LIMIT 5,2;
+-------------+----------+
| customer_id | town     |
+-------------+----------+
|           6 | Nicetown |
|           7 | Bingham  |
+-------------+----------+
2 rows in set (0.00 sec)

mysql>
```

If you want to combine LIMIT with other SELECT clauses, then you should put the LIMIT clause at the end.

Comparisons Using Other Types

There are two special cases of matching that we need to look at separately. You will remember from Chapter 2, the rather special column value NULL, which means either 'unknown' or 'not relevant'. We need to look at this separately because if a column has the value NULL, then checking it needs special care to ensure that the results are as expected.

We have already met the special <=> operator, which forced a true or false result when comparing against NULL, rather than the standard SQL NULL result.

Checking NULL Values

One thing we have not looked at in detail yet is checking to see if a column contains a NULL value. We can check if it equals a value or a string or none, but that's not sufficient. Let's do that now and experiment with NULL values:

```
mysql> CREATE TABLE testtab (tryint int);
Query OK, 0 rows affected (0.00 sec)

mysql> INSERT INTO testtab VALUES (0);
Query OK, 1 row affected (0.00 sec)

mysql> INSERT INTO testtab VALUES (1);
Query OK, 1 row affected (0.00 sec)

mysql> INSERT INTO testtab VALUES (NULL);
Query OK, 1 row affected (0.00 sec)

mysql> SELECT * FROM testtab;
+--------+
| tryint |
+--------+
|      0 |
|      1 |
|   NULL |
+--------+
3 rows in set (0.00 sec)

mysql>
```

99

We can check if the column is 0 or 1 easily enough:

```
mysql> SELECT * FROM testtab WHERE tryint = 1;
+--------+
| tryint |
+--------+
|      1 |
+--------+
1 row in set (0.00 sec)

mysql>
```

However, checking for NULL seems, at first, not to work:

```
mysql> SELECT * FROM testtab WHERE tryint = NULL;
Empty set (0.01 sec)

mysql>
```

The standard SQL syntax for checking whether a value is NULL or not is to use the IS NULL clause, like this:

```
mysql> SELECT * FROM testtab WHERE tryint IS NULL;
+--------+
| tryint |
+--------+
|   NULL |
+--------+
1 row in set (0.02 sec)

mysql>
```

Notice that we use the keyword IS rather than an '=' sign. We can also test to see if the value is something other than NULL by adding a NOT to invert the test:

```
mysql> SELECT * FROM testtab WHERE tryint IS NOT NULL;
+--------+
| tryint |
+--------+
|      0 |
|      1 |
+--------+
2 rows in set (0.00 sec)

mysql>
```

Why do we suddenly need this extra bit of syntax? What is happening here is that instead of the logic you are probably more familiar with, two-valued logic where everything is either TRUE or FALSE, we have stumbled into three-value logic, with TRUE, FALSE, and UNKNOWN.

Unfortunately, this property of NULL being 'unknown' has some other effects outside the immediate concern of checking for NULL.

Suppose we ran our SELECT statement on a table where some values of tryint were NULL:

```
SELECT * FROM testtab WHERE tryint = 1;
```

What does our tryint = 1 mean when tryint is actually NULL? We are asking the question, 'is Unknown = 1', which is interesting, because we can't claim it is FALSE, but neither can it be TRUE. So the answer must be unknown hence the rows where NULL appears are not matched. If we reversed the test and compared tryint = 0, they would still not be found because that condition would not be true either.

Look at this in action:

```
mysql> SELECT * FROM testtab WHERE tryint = 0;
+--------+
| tryint |
+--------+
|      0 |
+--------+
1 row in set (0.00 sec)

mysql> SELECT * FROM testtab WHERE tryint <> 0;
+--------+
| tryint |
+--------+
|      1 |
+--------+
1 row in set (0.00 sec)

mysql>
```

You might be tempted to wonder if our NULL value is still there. Rest assured it is:

```
mysql> SELECT * FROM testtab;
+--------+
| tryint |
+--------+
|      0 |
|      1 |
|   NULL |
+--------+
3 rows in set (0.00 sec)

mysql>
```

This can be confusing because we have apparently used two tests, with opposite conditions and still not retrieved all the rows from the table. As we saw before, MySQL has a handy syntax extension to the equality test, the <=> operator, which always considers NULL to be not equal to a known value. You should however use this operator with care for two reasons – firstly it's not standard SQL, and secondly, how would you know that just because a value was stored as NULL (that is, unknown) it does not match the particular value you are searching for? Only use the <=> operator where portability is not important and you are sure the results will be what you intended.

We can easily experiment and see how the <=> operator differs from the standard = operator using a SELECT on the command line:

```
mysql> SELECT NULL = 1, NULL <=> 1, NULL <=> 0, NULL = NULL, NULL <=> NULL;
+----------+-----------+-----------+-------------+---------------+
| NULL = 1 | NULL <=> 1 | NULL <=> 0 | NULL = NULL | NULL <=> NULL |
+----------+-----------+-----------+-------------+---------------+
|     NULL |         0 |         0 |        NULL |             1 |
+----------+-----------+-----------+-------------+---------------+
1 row in set (0.00 sec)

mysql>
```

Notice especially that NULL = NULL gives a NULL result. This is because NULL means unknown so comparing two unknown values quite logically has an unknown result.

It's important to be aware of these issues with NULL because it's all too easy to forget about NULL values. If you start getting slightly unexpected results when using conditions on a column that can have NULL values, check to see if rows where the column is NULL are the cause of your problems.

Checking Dates and Time

Although we haven't met all the MySQL data types yet, we do need to be aware of some special functions that we can use when checking dates and time.

MySQL has four basic types for handling date and time information.

Type	Description
DATE	Holds a date value, in the format YYYY-MM-DD between 1000-01-01 and 9999-21-31.
TIME	Holds a time value, in the format HH:MM:SS between -838:59:59 and 838:59:59. The rather strange range allows a reasonable amount of elapsed time processing to be handled, rather than wrapping immediately the time difference exceeds 24 or 48 hours.
DATETIME	As you might surmise, this is a combination of the DATE and TIME types, and can hold values between 1000-01-01 00:00:00 and 9999-12-31 23:59:59.
TIMESTAMP	This is a slightly special column type, used to automatically store date and time values, which can cope with a range from 1970 (the UNIX epoch) till 2037.

In addition there is a YEAR type that was introduced in more recent versions of MySQL, but we will not consider that here.

A TIMESTAMP type column will be automatically set to the current date and time whenever you:

❑   INSERT data into a row and specify no value for the TIMESTAMP column

❑   UPDATE the value of any column in the row such that it changes value

❑ Explicitly UPDATE the TIMESTAMP column to NULL

A TIMESTAMP column is often a very convenient way of providing a limited audit trail of what has been changed.

Let's look at the other DATE and TIME types in more detail.

When we write the date 1/2/1997, what do we mean? Europeans generally mean the first day of February 1997, but Americans usually mean the second day of January 1997. This is because Europeans generally read dates as DD/MM/YYYY, but Americans expect MM/DD/YYYY.

MySQL takes a simple but effective approach to this problem, which is to interpret all dates and times in the ISO-8601 standard format. This requires dates to be written YYYY-MM-DD and times HH:MM: SS. In practice you will find that MySQL will 'interpret', usually correctly, slight variations from this standard format. However, we suggest you stick exactly to the standard to ensure dates and times always work as you expect.

Date and Time Functions

MySQL has many useful functions you might need when comparing dates, or calculating differences from dates. We list the main ones below. The complete list can be found in the MySQL manual:

Function	Description
DAYOFWEEK(date)	Returns the day in the week, using Sunday as 1
DAYOFMONTH(date)	Returns the day of the month, starting from 1
DAYOFYEAR(date)	Returns the day of the year, starting from 1
MONTH(date)	Returns the month, starting from 1
DAYNAME(date)	Returns the day of the week as a string
MONTHNAME(date)	Returns the month as a string
YEAR(date)	Returns the year part
HOUR(time)	Returns the hour part
MINUTE(time)	Returns the minute part
SECOND(time)	Returns the second part
DATE_ADD(date, INTERVAL expr type)	Adds an interval to a date, where the INTERVAL expression is interpreted quite generally, for example DATE_ADD(NOW(), INTERVAL 1 MONTH));
DATE_SUB(date, INTERVAL expr type)	Subtracts an interval from a date

Table continued on following page

Function	Description
`TO_DAYS(date)`	Converts to a number of days from year 0
`FROM_DAYS(date)`	Converts from a number of days to a date
`SEC_TO_TIME(seconds)`	Converts a number of seconds to a time value
`TIME_TO_SEC(time)`	Converts a time value to a number of seconds
`DATE_FORMAT(date, format)`	Reformats a date in a general purpose way, using format strings similar to those found in C's `sprintf()` function
`CURDATE()`	Returns the current date
`CURTIME()`	Returns the current time
`NOW()`	Returns a timestamp with both date and time

As you can see, MySQL has a very rich set of functions for working with dates and times.

The format strings that are used with date format are particularly extensive. Below we reproduce the main format strings; the complete list can be found in the MySQL manual:

String	Meaning
`%M`	Month name (January...December)
`%W`	Weekday name (Sunday...Saturday)
`%D`	Day of the month with English suffix (1st, 2nd, 3rd, etc.)
`%Y`	Year, numeric, 4 digits
`%a`	Abbreviated weekday name (Sun...Sat)
`%m`	Month, numeric (01..12)
`%b`	Abbreviated month name (Jan...Dec)
`%j`	Day of year (001..366)
`%H`	Hour (00..23)
`%i`	Minutes, numeric (00..59)
`%T`	Time, 24-hour (hh:mm:ss)
`%S`	Seconds (00..59)
`%%`	A literal `%`.

Let's see some of these functions in action:

```
mysql> SELECT DAYOFWEEK('1959-12-20'), DAYOFMONTH('1960-02-19');
+-------------------------+--------------------------+
| DAYOFWEEK('1959-12-20') | DAYOFMONTH('1960-02-19') |
+-------------------------+--------------------------+
|                       1 |                       19 |
+-------------------------+--------------------------+
1 row in set (0.00 sec)

mysql> SELECT DAYOFWEEK(date_placed) FROM orderinfo
    -> WHERE date_placed IS NOT NULL;
+------------------------+
| DAYOFWEEK(date_placed) |
+------------------------+
|                      2 |
|                      6 |
|                      7 |
|                      1 |
|                      6 |
+------------------------+
5 rows in set (0.00 sec)

mysql>
```

As you can see, the functions for selecting parts of dates are easy to use.

The DATE_ADD() and DATE_SUB() functions lets us add and subtract intervals from a date or date and time, using an interval type of SECOND, MINUTE, HOUR, DAY, MONTH, YEAR or combinations of two types such as MINUTE_SECOND:

```
mysql> SELECT DATE_ADD('1986-02-28', INTERVAL 7 DAY);
+----------------------------------------+
| DATE_ADD('1986-02-28', INTERVAL 7 DAY) |
+----------------------------------------+
| 1986-03-07                             |
+----------------------------------------+
1 row in set (0.00 sec)

mysql>
```

In later versions of MySQL (from just before version 4.0) it is possible to directly add and subtract dates and times, rather than needing to use DATE_ADD() and DATE_SUB().

The last of these formatting functions, DATE_FORMAT(), works in a similar way but with a more general purpose string controlling the format:

```
mysql> SELECT DATE_FORMAT('1986-02-28', '%D %M %Y');
+---------------------------------------+
| DATE_FORMAT('1986-02-28', '%D %M %Y') |
+---------------------------------------+
| 28th February 1986                    |
+---------------------------------------+
1 row in set (0.00 sec)

mysql>
```

Hopefully by now you have seen that MySQL provides an extensive range of functions for manipulating dates and times. We have only presented the most common functions and options here; should you need some more abstruse functions, you may find that they are available. Check the MySQL manual for the comprehensive list of functions and format options.

Selection Based On Dates and Times

We can also compare dates and times using the same operators <>, <=, <, >, >=, =, that we would use with numbers. For example:

```
mysql> SELECT * FROM orderinfo WHERE date_placed >= '2000-07-21';
+-------------+-------------+-------------+--------------+----------+
| orderinfo_id | customer_id | date_placed | date_shipped | shipping |
+-------------+-------------+-------------+--------------+----------+
|           3 |          15 | 2000-09-02  | 2000-09-12   |     3.99 |
|           4 |          13 | 2000-09-03  | 2000-09-10   |     2.99 |
|           5 |           8 | 2000-07-21  | 2000-07-24   |     0.00 |
+-------------+-------------+-------------+--------------+----------+
3 rows in set (0.00 sec)

mysql>
```

Notice that we stick to the unambiguous ISO style dates.

We can also do simple calculations using dates within the SELECT statement. For example, to discover the number of days between an order being placed and shipped, we could use a query like this:

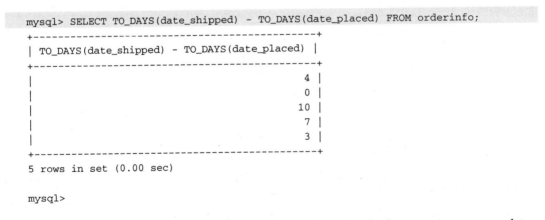

```
mysql> SELECT TO_DAYS(date_shipped) - TO_DAYS(date_placed) FROM orderinfo;
+----------------------------------------------+
| TO_DAYS(date_shipped) - TO_DAYS(date_placed) |
+----------------------------------------------+
|                                            4 |
|                                            0 |
|                                           10 |
|                                            7 |
|                                            3 |
+----------------------------------------------+
5 rows in set (0.00 sec)

mysql>
```

In newer versions of MySQL (later than version 3.23) the addition and subtraction operators on dates are directly understood so we can omit the function TO_DAYS():

```
mysql> SELECT date_shipped - date_placed FROM orderinfo;
+----------------------------+
| date_shipped - date_placed |
+----------------------------+
|                          4 |
|                          0 |
|                         10 |
|                          7 |
|                          3 |
+----------------------------+
5 rows in set (0.00 sec)

mysql>
```

Both statements return the same number of days between the two dates stored in the database in days.

Multiple Table Joins

By now you should have a good idea of how we can select data from a table, picking which columns we want, which rows we want, and how to control the order of the data. We have also seen how to handle the rather special date and time formats.

It's now time to move on to one of the most important features of SQL and indeed relational databases, relating data in one table to data in another table automatically. The good news is that it's all done with the SELECT statement, and all the good stuff you have learned so far about SELECT is just as true with many tables as it was with a single table.

Relating Two Tables

Before we look at the SQL for using many tables at the same time, let's have a quick recap on the material we saw in Chapter 2 about relating tables.

You will remember that we have a customer table, which stores details of our customers, and an orderinfo table, which stores details of the orders they have placed. This allowed us to store details of each customer only once, no matter how many orders they placed. We link the two tables together by having a common piece of data, the customer_id, stored in both tables.

If we think about this as a picture, we could imagine a row in the customer table, which has a customer_id, being related to none, one, or many rows in the orderinfo table, where the same customer_id value appears:

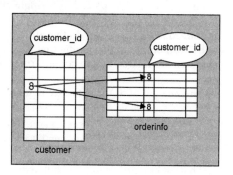

We could say that the value '8' for `customer_id` in the row in the `customer` table, relates to two rows in the `orderinfo` table, where the column `customer_id` also appears. Of course, we didn't have to have the two columns with the same name, but given that they both store the customer's ID, it would have been very confusing to give them different names.

Suppose we wanted to find all the orders that had been placed by our customer Ann Stones. Logically, what we do is look first in our `customer` table to find this customer:

```
mysql> SELECT customer_id FROM customer
    -> WHERE fname = 'Ann' AND lname = 'Stones';
+-------------+
| customer_id |
+-------------+
|           8 |
+-------------+
1 row in set (0.00 sec)

mysql>
```

Now that we know the `customer_id`, we can check for orders from this customer:

```
mysql> SELECT * FROM orderinfo WHERE customer_id = 8;
+-------------+-------------+-------------+--------------+----------+
| orderinfo_id | customer_id | date_placed | date_shipped | shipping |
+-------------+-------------+-------------+--------------+----------+
|           2 |           8 | 2000-06-23  | 2000-06-23   |     0.00 |
|           5 |           8 | 2000-07-21  | 2000-07-24   |     0.00 |
+-------------+-------------+-------------+--------------+----------+
2 rows in set (0.00 sec)

mysql>
```

This has worked, but took us two steps and we had to remember the `customer_id` between steps. If you recollect, back in Chapter 2, we told you that SQL is a declarative language, that is, you tell SQL what you want to achieve, rather than explicitly defining the steps of how to get to the solution. What we have just done is used SQL in a procedural way. We have specified two discrete steps to get to our answer, the orders placed by a single customer. Wouldn't it be more elegant to do it all in a single step?

Indeed, in SQL we can do this all in a single step by specifying that we want to know the orders placed by Ann Stones and knowing that the information is in the `customer` table and `orderinfo` table, which are related by the column `customer_id` that appears in both tables.

The new bit of SQL syntax we need to do this is an extension to the WHERE clause:

```
SELECT <column list> FROM <table list>
       WHERE <join condition> AND <row selection conditions>
```

That looks a little complex, but actually it's quite easy. Just to make our first example a little easier, let's assume we know the customer ID is '8', and just fetch the order date(s) and customer first name.

We need to specify the columns we want, the customers' first name and date the order was placed, that the two tables are related by `customer_id` column, and that we only want rows where the `customer_id` is '8'.

You will immediately realize we have a slight problem. How do we tell SQL which `customer_id` we want to use, the one in the `customer` table or the one in the `orderinfo` table? Although we are about to check that they are equal, in general this might not be the case, so how do we handle columns whose name appears in more than one table? We simply specify the column name using the extended syntax:

```
tablename.columnname
```

We can then unambiguously describe every column in our database. In general, MySQL is quite forgiving and if a column name only appears in one table in the SELECT statement, we don't have to explicitly use the table name as well. In this case, we will use `customer.fname`, even though fname would have been sufficient. This is clearly important for a newcomer to SQL as it removes ambiguity. More importantly, it is also a good design practice because if you later added a column with the same name to one of the other tables, your existing SQL would not need to change. Protecting your SQL against future changes to the database by explicit naming is a good idea. The first part of our statement therefore needs to be:

```
SELECT customer.fname, orderinfo.date_placed FROM customer, orderinfo;
```

This tells MySQL the columns and tables we wish to use.

Now we need to specify our conditions. We have two different conditions – the `customer_id` is '8', and the two tables are related or joined, using `customer_id`. Just like we saw earlier with multiple conditions, our second part would be using the keyword AND to specify multiple conditions that must all be TRUE:

```
WHERE customer.customer_id = 8
AND customer.customer_id = orderinfo.customer_id;
```

Notice that we have to tell SQL a specific `customer_id` column, using `tablename.columnname` syntax, even though in practice it would not matter which of the `customer_id` column from which table was checked against 8, since we also specify that they must have the same value.

Putting it all together, the SELECT statement we need is:

```
mysql> SELECT customer.fname, orderinfo.date_placed FROM customer, orderinfo
    -> WHERE customer.customer_id = 8
    -> AND customer.customer_id = orderinfo.customer_id;
+-------+-------------+
| fname | date_placed |
+-------+-------------+
| Ann   | 2000-06-23  |
| Ann   | 2000-07-21  |
+-------+-------------+
2 rows in set (0.01 sec)

mysql>
```

Much more elegant than multiple steps, isn't it? Perhaps more importantly, by specifying the entire problem in a single statement we allow the MySQL database engine to fully optimize the way the data is retrieved.

Now we know the principle, let's try our original question to find all the orders placed by Ann Stones, assuming we don't know the `customer_id`.

Try It Out – Relating Tables

We now only know a name, rather than a customer's ID therefore our SQL is slightly more complex. We have to specify the customer by name:

```
mysql> SELECT customer.fname, orderinfo.date_placed FROM customer, orderinfo
    -> WHERE customer.fname = 'Ann' AND customer.lname = 'Stones'
    -> AND customer.customer_id = orderinfo.customer_id;
+-------+-------------+
| fname | date_placed |
+-------+-------------+
| Ann   | 2000-06-23  |
| Ann   | 2000-07-21  |
+-------+-------------+
2 rows in set (0.00 sec)

mysql>
```

How It Works

Just as we saw in our earlier example, we specify the columns we want, (`customer.fname`, `orderinfo.date_placed`), the tables involved (`customer, orderinfo`), the selection conditions (`customer.fname = 'Ann' AND customer.lname = 'Stones'`), and how the two tables are related (`customer.customer_id = orderinfo.customer_id`).

SQL solves the rest for us. You should also notice that it doesn't matter if the customer has placed no orders, one order, or many orders as in the example, SQL is perfectly happy to execute the SQL query, provided it's valid even if there are no rows that match the condition.

Let's now look at a different example. Suppose we want to list all the products we have with their barcodes. You will remember that barcodes are held in the `barcode` table and items in the `item` table. The two tables are related by having an `item_id` column in each table. You may also remember that the reason we split this out into two tables is that many products, or items, actually have multiple barcodes.

Using our newly found expertise in joining tables, we know that we need to specify the columns and tables we want, and how they are related or joined together. Being confident, we also decide to order the result by the cost price of the item:

```
mysql> SELECT description, cost_price, barcode_ean FROM item, barcode
    -> WHERE barcode.item_id = item.item_id ORDER BY cost_price;
+---------------+------------+----------------+
| description   | cost_price | barcode_ean    |
+---------------+------------+----------------+
| Toothbrush    |       0.75 | 9473627464543  |
| Toothbrush    |       0.75 | 6241234586487  |
| Toothbrush    |       0.75 | 9473625532534  |
| Linux CD      |       1.99 | 6264537836173  |
| Linux CD      |       1.99 | 6241527746363  |
| Tissues       |       2.11 | 7465743843764  |
| Roman Coin    |       2.34 | 4587263646878  |
| Rubik Cube    |       7.45 | 6241574635234  |
| Picture Frame |       7.54 | 3453458677628  |
| Fan Small     |       9.23 | 6434564564544  |
| Fan Large     |      13.36 | 8476736836876  |
| Wood Puzzle   |      15.23 | 6241527836173  |
| Speakers      |      19.73 | 2239872376872  |
| Speakers      |      19.73 | 9879879837489  |
+---------------+------------+----------------+
14 rows in set (0.01 sec)

mysql>
```

This looks logical except several items seem to appear more than once, and we don't remember stocking two different speakers. Also, we don't remember stocking that many items. What's going on here?

Let's count the number of items we stock, using our newly found SQL skills:

```
mysql> SELECT * FROM item;
```

The result lists 11 rows. We only stocked 11 items, but our earlier query found 14 rows. Did we make a mistake?

No, all that's happened is that for some items such as Toothbrush there are many different barcodes against a single product. What happened was that the database simply repeated the information from the item table against each barcode, so that it listed all the barcodes and the item each one belonged to. This is standard SQL behavior.

You can better understand what happened here by also selecting the item_id, by adding it to the SELECT statement we used earlier, like this:

```
mysql> SELECT item.item_id, description, cost_price, barcode_ean
    -> FROM item, barcode WHERE barcode.item_id = item.item_id
    -> ORDER BY cost_price;
+---------+---------------+------------+---------------+
| item_id | description   | cost_price | barcode_ean   |
+---------+---------------+------------+---------------+
|       8 | Toothbrush    |       0.75 | 9473627464543 |
|       8 | Toothbrush    |       0.75 | 6241234586487 |
|       8 | Toothbrush    |       0.75 | 9473625532534 |
|       3 | Linux CD      |       1.99 | 6264537836173 |
|       3 | Linux CD      |       1.99 | 6241527746363 |
|       4 | Tissues       |       2.11 | 7465743843764 |
|       9 | Roman Coin    |       2.34 | 4587263646878 |
|       2 | Rubik Cube    |       7.45 | 6241574635234 |
|       5 | Picture Frame |       7.54 | 3453458677628 |
|       6 | Fan Small     |       9.23 | 6434564564544 |
|       7 | Fan Large     |      13.36 | 8476736836876 |
|       1 | Wood Puzzle   |      15.23 | 6241527836173 |
|      11 | Speakers      |      19.73 | 9879879837489 |
|      11 | Speakers      |      19.73 | 2239872376872 |
+---------+---------------+------------+---------------+
14 rows in set (0.00 sec)

mysql>
```

Notice that we have specified precisely which table item_id comes from, since it appears in the item table as well as the barcode table.

It is now clear what exactly is going on. If the data you get returned from a SELECT statement looks a little odd, it's often a good idea to add all the 'id' type columns to the SELECT statement just to see what was happening.

Aliasing Table Names

You will remember, earlier in the chapter we saw how we could change column names in the output using AS to give more descriptive names. It's also possible to alias table names, if you wish. This is handy in a few special cases where you need two names for the same table, but more frequently it is used to save on typing. You will also see it used frequently in GUI tools where it makes SQL generation a little easier.

To alias a table name, you simply put the alias name immediately after the table name in the FROM part of the SQL clause. Once you have done this, you can use the alias name rather than the real table name in the rest of the SQL statement.

It's easier to show how this works than to describe it. Suppose we had a simple SQL statement:

```
SELECT lname FROM customer;
```

As we saw earlier, you can always explicitly name the column by preceding it with the table name, like this:

```
SELECT customer.lname FROM customer;
```

If we alias the `customer` table to cu, we could instead prefix the column cu like this:

```
SELECT cu.lname FROM customer cu;
```

Notice that we have added a cu after the table name as well as prefixed the column with cu.

Using aliasing in case of a single table is not very interesting. With multiple tables it can start to be a bit more useful.

If we look back at our earlier query:

```
mysql> SELECT customer.fname, orderinfo.date_placed FROM customer, orderinfo
    -> WHERE customer.fname = 'Ann' AND customer.lname = 'Stones'
    -> AND customer.customer_id = orderinfo.customer_id;
```

With aliases for table names, we could write this as:

```
mysql> SELECT c.fname, o.date_placed FROM customer c, orderinfo o
    -> WHERE c.fname = 'Ann' AND c.lname = 'Stones'
    -> AND c.customer_id = o.customer_id;
```

Relating Three Tables

Now that we know how to relate two tables together, can we extend the idea to three or even more tables? Of course, we can. SQL is a very logical language, so if we can do something with 'N' items we can almost always do it with 'N+1' items. Of course, the more tables you include the more work the database has to do, so queries with many tables can be rather slow, especially when the tables are large.

Suppose we wanted to relate customer to actual item IDs ordered?

If you look back to our schema you will see we need to use three tables to get from customer to the actual ordered items – `customer`, `orderinfo`, and `orderline`:

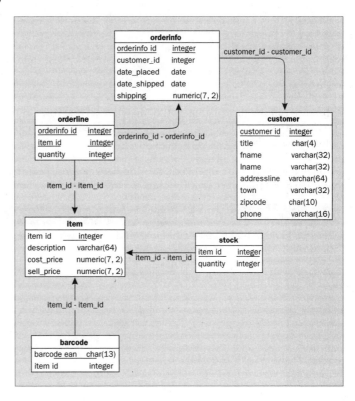

If we redraw our earlier diagram with three tables, it would look like this:

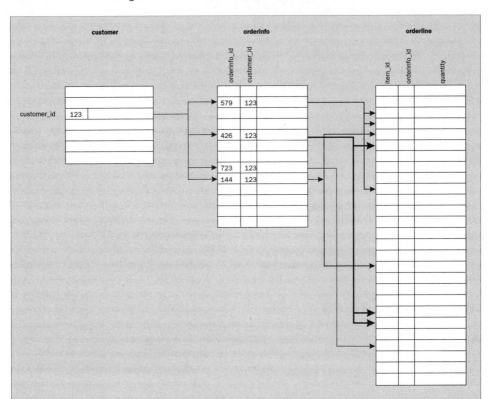

Here we can see that customer '123' matches several rows in the orderinfo table, those with orderinfo_ id of values '579', '426', '723', and '114', and each of these in turn relates to one or more rows in the orderline table.

Notice that there is no direct relationship between customer and orderline. We must use the orderinfo table since that contains the information that binds the customers to their order.

Try It Out – A Three-Table Join

Let's build ourselves a three-table join to discover what item_ids the orders from Ann Stones actually comprised.

We start with the columns we need:

```
SELECT customer.fname, customer.lname, orderinfo.date_placed, orderline.item_id,
orderline.quantity
```

Then we list the tables involved:

```
    FROM customer, orderinfo, orderline
```

Then we specify how the `customer` and `orderinfo` tables are related:

```
    WHERE customer.customer_id = orderinfo.customer_id
```

We must also specify how the `orderinfo` and `orderline` tables are related:

```
    orderinfo.orderinfo_id = orderline.orderinfo_id
```

Now our conditions:

```
    customer.fname = 'Ann' AND customer.lname = 'Stones';
```

Putting them all together, we get:

```
mysql> SELECT customer.fname, customer.lname, orderinfo.date_placed,
    -> orderline.item_id,orderline.quantity
    -> FROM customer, orderinfo, orderline
    -> WHERE customer.customer_id = orderinfo.customer_id
    -> AND orderinfo.orderinfo_id = orderline.orderinfo_id
    -> AND customer.fname = 'Ann' AND customer.lname = 'Stones';
+-------+--------+-------------+---------+----------+
| fname | lname  | date_placed | item_id | quantity |
+-------+--------+-------------+---------+----------+
| Ann   | Stones | 2000-06-23  |       1 |        1 |
| Ann   | Stones | 2000-06-23  |       4 |        2 |
| Ann   | Stones | 2000-06-23  |       7 |        2 |
| Ann   | Stones | 2000-06-23  |      10 |        1 |
| Ann   | Stones | 2000-07-21  |       1 |        1 |
| Ann   | Stones | 2000-07-21  |       3 |        1 |
+-------+--------+-------------+---------+----------+
6 rows in set (0.01 sec)

mysql>
```

Notice that whitespace outside strings is not significant to SQL so we add extra spaces and line breaks to make the SQL easier to read. The `mysql` program just waits till it sees a ';', before it tries to interpret what we have been typing.

Try It Out – A Four-Table Join

Having seen how easy it is to go from two tables to three tables, let's take our query a step further and list all the items by description that our customer Ann Stones has ordered. To do this we need to use an extra table, the `item` table to get at the item description. The rest of the query however, is pretty much as before:

```
mysql> SELECT customer.fname, customer.lname, orderinfo.date_placed,
    -> item.description, quantity
    -> FROM customer, orderinfo, orderline, item
    -> WHERE customer.customer_id = orderinfo.customer_id
```

```
    -> AND orderinfo.orderinfo_id = orderline.orderinfo_id
    -> AND orderline.item_id = item.item_id
    -> AND customer.fname = 'Ann' AND customer.lname = 'Stones';
+--------+--------+-------------+-------------+----------+
| fname  | lname  | date_placed | description | quantity |
+--------+--------+-------------+-------------+----------+
| Ann    | Stones | 2000-06-23  | Wood Puzzle |        1 |
| Ann    | Stones | 2000-06-23  | Tissues     |        2 |
| Ann    | Stones | 2000-06-23  | Fan Large   |        2 |
| Ann    | Stones | 2000-06-23  | Carrier Bag |        1 |
| Ann    | Stones | 2000-07-21  | Wood Puzzle |        1 |
| Ann    | Stones | 2000-07-21  | Linux CD    |        1 |
+--------+--------+-------------+-------------+----------+
6 rows in set (0.01 sec)

mysql>
```

How It Works

Once you have seen how three-table joins work, it's not difficult to extend the idea to more tables. We added the item description to the list of columns to be shown, the `item` table to the list of tables to select from, and we also added the information about how to relate the `item` table to the tables we already had, `orderline.item_id = item.item_id`. You will see that Wood Puzzle is listed twice since it was purchased on two different occasions.

In this `SELECT`, we have actually displayed at least one column from each of the tables we used in our join. There is really no need to do this; if we had just wanted the customer name and item description, we could have simply chosen not to retrieve the columns we didn't need.

A version retrieving fewer columns is just as valid and may be marginally more efficient than our earlier attempt:

```
mysql> SELECT customer.fname, customer.lname, item.description
    -> FROM customer, orderinfo, orderline, item
    -> WHERE customer.customer_id = orderinfo.customer_id
    -> AND orderinfo.orderinfo_id = orderline.orderinfo_id
    -> AND orderline.item_id = item.item_id
    -> AND customer.fname = 'Ann' AND customer.lname = 'Stones';
```

For our final example of SQL in this chapter, let's go back to something we learned early in the chapter: how to remove duplicate information using the `DISTINCT` keyword.

Try It Out – Adding Extra Conditions

Suppose we wanted to discover what type of items Ann Stones bought. All we want listed is the description of items purchased, ordered by the description. We don't even want to list the customer name since we know that already (we are using it to select the data). We only need to select the `item.description`, and we also need to use the `DISTINCT` option to ensure that Wood Puzzle is only listed once, even though it was bought several times:

```
mysql> SELECT DISTINCT item.description
    -> FROM customer, orderinfo, orderline, item
    -> WHERE customer.customer_id = orderinfo.customer_id
    -> AND orderinfo.orderinfo_id = orderline.orderinfo_id
    -> AND orderline.item_id = item.item_id
    -> AND customer.fname = 'Ann' AND customer.lname = 'Stones'
    -> ORDER BY item.description;
+-------------+
| description |
+-------------+
| Carrier Bag |
| Fan Large   |
| Linux CD    |
| Tissues     |
| Wood Puzzle |
+-------------+
5 rows in set (0.01 sec)

mysql>
```

How It Works

We take our earlier SQL, remove the columns we no longer need, add the DISTINCT keyword after SELECT to ensure each row only appears once, and add our ORDER BY condition after the WHERE clause.

That's one of the great things about SQL; once you have learned a feature, you can apply it in a general way. The ORDER BY, for example, works with many tables in just the same way it works with a single table.

Summary

This has been a pretty long chapter but we have learned quite a lot.

We have covered the SELECT statement in some detail, discovering how to choose columns and rows, how to order the output, and how to suppress duplicate information. We also learned a bit about the date and time types, and the many functions MySQL makes available for processing them.

We then moved on to the heart of SQL: the ability to relate tables together. After our first bit of SQL that joined a pair of tables, we saw how easy it was to extend this to three and then even to four tables. We finished off by reusing some of the knowledge we gained early in the chapter to refine our four-table selection to home in on displaying exactly the information we were searching for and removing all the extra columns and duplicate rows.

The good news is that we have now seen all the everyday features of the SELECT statement. Once you understand the SELECT statement, much of the rest of SQL is reasonably straightforward. We will be coming back to the SELECT statement in Chapter 7 to look at some more advanced features that you will need from time to time, but you will find that much of SQL you need to use in the real world has been covered in this chapter.

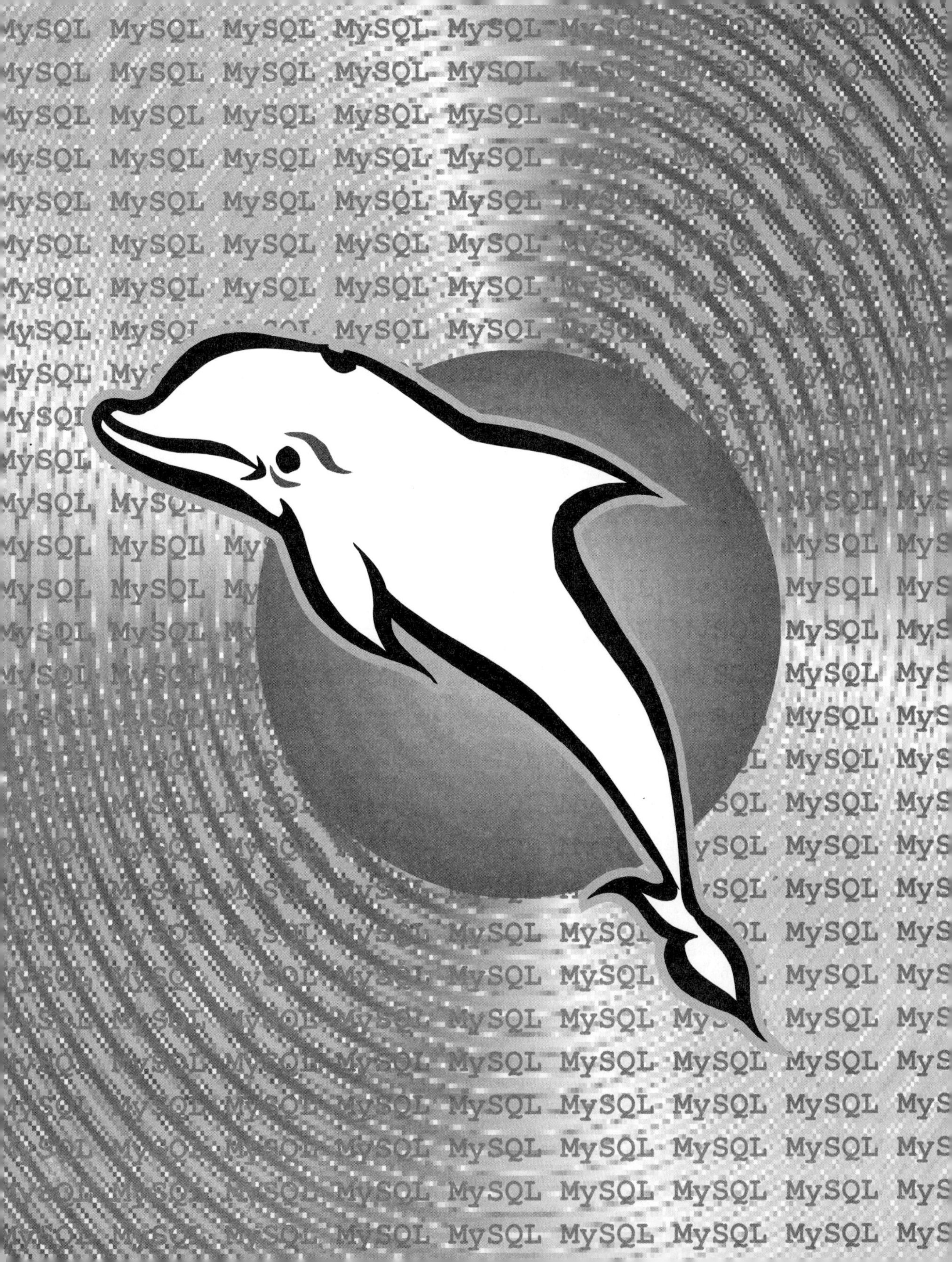

MySQL Graphical Tools

A MySQL database is generally created and administered with the command line tool mysql, which we have used in earlier chapters to get started. Command line tools, similar to mysql, are also common with commercial databases. Oracle has one such tool called SQL*PLUS, for example. While command line tools are generally complete, in the sense that they contain ways to perform all the functions that you need, they can sometimes also be a little unfriendly. On the other hand, they make no great demands, for example, in terms of graphics cards and memory.

In this chapter, we will take a look at some of the graphical tools, which are alternatives to mysql for accessing MySQL databases. Some such tools can also be used for administering databases. A special user with responsibility for managing the database performs administration tasks such as creating new users, setting permissions, and optimizing the database. We will cover administration of MySQL in some depth in Chapter 10, *MySQL Administration*, and here we will concentrate on rudimentary administration functions those general users and client application programs can perform.

We will start with a brief summary of the commands available in mysql, and as the chapter progresses, we'll look at:

mysql

KSql and KMySQL

MySQLGUI

ODBC

Microsoft Access

Microsoft Excel

mysql

We have seen in the earlier chapters that the mysql tool allows us to connect to a database, execute queries, and administer a database. It also includes creating a database, adding new tables, and entering or updating data, using SQL commands. Now let us look at this tool in detail.

Starting mysql

The command syntax for `mysql` is:

```
mysql [options] [-h host] [-u user] [-p[password]] [dbname]
```

We start `mysql` by specifying the database we wish to connect to. We may also need to know the host name of the server, and possibly the port number the database is listening on, a valid user name, and password to use for the connection. The default is to connect to MySQL on the local machine with the same user name as the current user login name.

So, to connect to a named database, for example `bmsimple`, we invoke `mysql` with a database name like this:

```
$ mysql bmsimple
```

Defaults for the user name, server host name, and listening port may be overridden by using the `-u`, `-h`, and `-P` command line options to `mysql`. If we need to give a password for the connection we can use the `-p` option, in which case we will be prompted to enter a password, or we can use `-psecret` to include the password on the command line.

```
$ mysql -h dewey -u neil -pmypassword bmsimple
```

The complete list of options for `mysql` can be seen if we invoke `mysql` with:

```
$ mysql --help
```

Defaults for the host name and password can be set by assigning values to the environment variables `MYSQL_HOST` and `MYSQL_PWD`. Since this assigning of values is inherently insecure, it is not recommended.

Commands in mysql

Once running, `mysql` will prompt for commands with a prompt that consists of the word `mysql>`. There are two different types of commands available – SQL and internal. We can issue any SQL command that MySQL supports to `mysql`, and it will execute them for us.

> **A list of all supported SQL commands can be found in Appendix C.**

Commands to `mysql` may be spread over multiple lines, and when this occurs, `mysql` will change its prompt to `->` or `">` or `'>` to indicate that more input is expected:

```
$ mysql bpsimple
...
mysql> SELECT *
```

```
        -> FROM customer
        ->;
  . . .
  $
```

To tell `mysql` that we have completed a long SQL command that might spread across multiple lines, we have to end the command with a semicolon. Note that the semicolon is not a required part of the SQL command as we have seen in Chapter 4, *Accessing your Data*. In the case above, for example, we may have wanted to add a `WHERE` clause on the next line.

Internal `mysql` commands (and some others such as `DESCRIBE`) are used to perform MySQL-specific operations not directly supported via SQL, such as executing scripts. All internal commands have both names and shortcuts that begin with a backslash.

Command History

Each command that you ask `mysql` to execute is recorded in a history. This makes it easier for the user to recall previous commands, in case they want to run them again or edit them. Use the arrow keys to scroll through the command history, and select the command you want to execute or edit. This feature, known as 'readline', must have been compiled in for your platform at build time. On UNIX and Linux the query history is preserved across `mysql` sessions; it is saved in the file `.mysql_history` in your home directory.

The current query is kept in a query buffer. You can see what is in the query buffer with \p (`print`), and you can clear it with \c. You can edit the query buffer contents on UNIX-like systems with an external editor with \e. The default editor is `vi` (on Linux and UNIX at least), but you can specify your own favorite editor by setting the `EDITOR` environment variable before starting `mysql`. The current query is executed with \g, which also clears the query buffer.

Scripting mysql

We can collect a group of `mysql` commands (both SQL and internal) in a file and use it as a simple script. The '\ .' internal command will read a set of `mysql` commands from a file. This feature is especially useful for creating and populating tables. We used it earlier to create our sample database, `bmsimple`. Here is part of the `create_tables` script file that we used in Chapter 3:

```
CREATE TABLE customer
(
    customer_id       int AUTO_INCREMENT NOT NULL PRIMARY KEY,
    title             char(4)                    ,
    fname             varchar(32)                ,
    lname             varchar(32)        NOT NULL,
    addressline       varchar(64)                ,
    town              varchar(32)                ,
    zipcode           char(10)           NOT NULL,
    phone             varchar(16)
);
```

121

```
create table item
(
    item_id            int AUTO_INCREMENT NOT NULL PRIMARY KEY,
    description        varchar(64)        NOT NULL,
    cost_price         numeric(7,2)                  ,
    sell_price         numeric(7,2)
);
```

The complete script can be found in Appendix E. We give script files an .sql extension by convention, and execute them with the \. internal command:

```
mysql> \. create_tables.sql
Query OK, 0 rows affected (0.00 sec)

Query OK, 0 rows affected (0.00 sec)

Query OK, 0 rows affected (0.00 sec)

Query OK, 0 rows affected (0.00 sec)

Query OK, 0 rows affected (0.00 sec)

Query OK, 0 rows affected (0.00 sec)

mysql>
```

Another use of script files is for simple reports. If we want to keep an eye on the expansion of our database, we could put a few commands in a script file and arrange to run it every once in a while. For example, to report the number of customers and orders taken, make a script file called report.sql that simply contains the following lines, and execute it in a mysql session:

```
use bmsimple;
select count(*) from customer;
select count(*) from orderinfo;
```

```
$ mysql bmsimple <report.sql
count(*)
15
count(*)
5
$
```

We can copy query output to a file by using either the -tee = filename command line option, or with the \T internal command from within a session.

Examining the Database

We can explore the structure of our database using a number of mysql commands. For example, the SHOW DATABASES command will list all of the databases handled by the server we are connected to, and the SHOW TABLES command lists the tables in the database we are using.

We can get a detailed description of a particular table with DESCRIBE tablename:

```
mysql> DESCRIBE customer;
+-------------+-------------+------+-----+---------+----------------+
| Field       | Type        | Null | Key | Default | Extra          |
+-------------+-------------+------+-----+---------+----------------+
| customer_id | int(11)     |      | PRI | NULL    | auto_increment |
| title       | varchar(4)  | YES  |     | NULL    |                |
| fname       | varchar(32) | YES  |     | NULL    |                |
| lname       | varchar(32) |      |     |         |                |
| addressline | varchar(64) | YES  |     | NULL    |                |
| town        | varchar(32) | YES  |     | NULL    |                |
| zipcode     | varchar(10) |      |     |         |                |
| phone       | varchar(16) | YES  |     | NULL    |                |
+-------------+-------------+------+-----+---------+----------------+
8 rows in set (0.00 sec)
```

Check out the reference tables further down in the chapter for more information on mysql internal commands, or refer to the MySQL online documentation.

Command Line Quick Reference

The mysql command line options and their meanings are reproduced in the table below:

Options	Long Name	Meaning
-?,	--help	Display help and exit.
-A,	--no-auto-rehash	No automatic rehashing. One has to use 'rehash' to get table and field completion. This gives a quicker start of mysql and disables rehashing on reconnect.
-B	--batch	Print results with a tab as separator, each row on a new line. Doesn't use history file.
	--character-sets-dir=...	Directory where character sets are located.
-C	--compress	Use compression in server/client protocol.
-D	--database=..	Database to use.
	--default-character-set=...	Set the default character set.
-e	--execute=...	Execute command and quit. (Output like with --batch).
-E	--vertical	Print the output of a query (rows) vertically.
-f	--force	Continue even if we get an SQL error.

Table continued on following page

Options	Long Name	Meaning
-g	--no-named-commands	Named commands are disabled. Use * form only, or use named commands only in the beginning of a line ending with a semicolon (;) Disable with -G.
-G	--enable-named-commands	Named commands are enabled. Opposite to -g.
-i	--ignore-space	Ignore space after function names.
-h	--host=...	Connect to host.
-H	--html	Produce HTML output.
-L	--skip-line-numbers	Don't write line number for errors.
	--no-pager	Disable pager and print to stdout.
	--no-tee	Disable outfile.
-n	--unbuffered	Flush buffer after each query.
-N	--skip-column-names	Don't write column names in results.
-O	--set-variable var=option	Give a variable a value. --help lists variables.
-o	--one-database	Only update the default database. This is useful for skipping updates to other database in the update log.
	--pager[=...]	Pager to use to display results. If you don't supply an option the default pager is taken from the environment variable PAGER. Valid pagers are less, more, cat [> filename], etc. This option does not work in batch mode.
-[password]	--password[=...]	Password to use when connecting to server If password is not given it's asked from the shell.
-P	--port=...	Port number to use for connection.
-q	--quick	Don't cache result, print it row-by-row. This may slow down the server if the output is suspended. Doesn't use history file.
-r	--raw	Write fields without conversion. Used with --batch.

Options	Long Name	Meaning
-s	--silent	Be more silent.
-S	--socket=...	Socket file to use for connection.
-t	--table	Output in table format.
-T	--debug-info	Print some debug info at exit.
	--tee=...	Append everything into outfile. Does not work in batch mode.
-u	--user=#	User for login if not current user.
-U	--safe-updates[=#] --i-am-a-dummy[=#]	Only allow UPDATE and DELETE that uses keys.
-v	--verbose	Write more. (-v -v -v gives the table output format)
-V	--version	Output version information and exit.
-w	--wait	Wait and retry if connection is down.

Internal Commands Quick Reference

The supported mysql internal commands are reproduced in the table below:

Command	Shortcut	Function
Help	\h	Display some help.
?	\?	Synonym for 'help'.
clear	\c	Clear command.
connect	\r	Reconnect to the server. Optional arguments are database name and host.
Edit	\e	Edit command with program specified by environment variable $EDITOR.
Ego	\G	Send command to MySQL server, display result vertically.
Exit	\q	Exit mysql. Same as quit.
Go	\g	Send command to MySQL server.
nopager	\n	Disable pager, print to stdout.
notee	\t	Don't write into outfile.

Table continued on following page

Command	Shortcut	Function
pager	\P	Set PAGER [to_pager]. Print the query results via PAGER.
print	\p	Print current command.
Quit	\q	Quit mysql.
rehash	\#	Rebuild completion hash.
source	\.	Execute a SQL script file. Takes a file name as an argument.
status	\s	Get status information from the server.
Tee	\T	Set outfile [to_outfile]. Append everything into given outfile.
Use	\u	Use another database. Takes database name as argument.

KSql and KMySQL

KSql is a database-independent graphical tool that runs under the 'K' desktop on Linux and other UNIX-like operating systems. Strictly speaking, KSql is the name of a forthcoming release of a program known as KMySQL, which is a database client primarily designed for MySQL. KMySQL is being developed to provide a fully usable client as an alternative to the standard text-mode client of MySQL. It uses a plug-in system to access databases and may be used to access other databases too.

According to the KSql home page you can:

Do anything you would do with the default text-mode client.

View queries result in multiple tabular views, print them or export them in HTML.

Edit your queries in a comfortable edit box with history.

Create nice forms, with a WYSIWIG editor.

Save regularly run queries and recall them with a double-click.

Create tables, and add, remove, or edit columns.

Edit the contents of your tables.

Connect to and browse any number of servers at the same time.

Use several types of SQL servers at the same time via plug-ins.

Administrate your MySQL server.

Access your forms with your browser using HTML forms and PHP.

A number of Linux distributions, for example SuSE, ship with a version of KMySQL ready to install. Source code is available at the KSql home page http://ksql.sourceforge.net together with binary packages for Linux.

Invoking the `kmysql` command within a shell under the X-Window System starts KMySQL. It requires the KDE desktop environment to be installed as it uses libraries from that product.

When we start KMySQL for the first time, we need to configure at least one server for it to connect to. We do this by selecting the Server I Add Server:

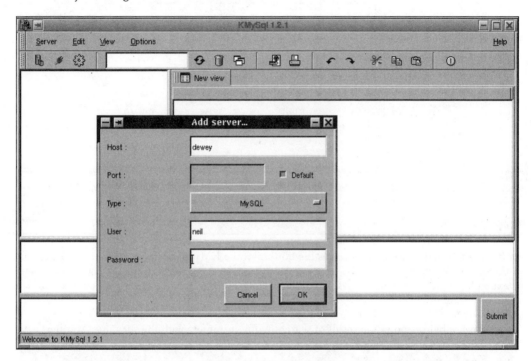

Here we enter the host to connect to, and the user name and password to use for connections to that server. KMySQL will allow simultaneous connections to a number of databases of different types. Each will appear as a top-level folder in the left-hand pane of the KMySQL window.

Table Browser

We can use KMySQL to browse our database much as we would with directories in a file system. Double-clicking on a tablename, for example `customer table`, displays the contents of that table in the view pane:

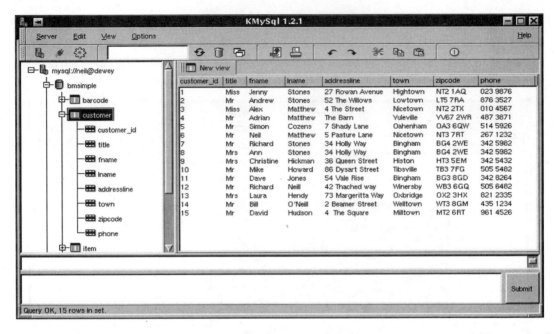

We can use the SQL entry pane towards the bottom of the KMySQL window to enter SQL commands for the database server to execute. The results are shown in the right-hand pane. This can be useful if, for example, the tables we are browsing contain many rows and we need to be selective about which records we want to view.

The screenshot below shows the result of searching for customers with the surname 'Matthew':

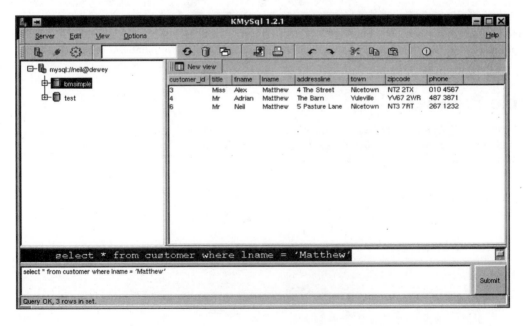

HTML Export

The View | Export HTML option of KMySQL writes an HTML file containing a table with the data displayed in the view pane:

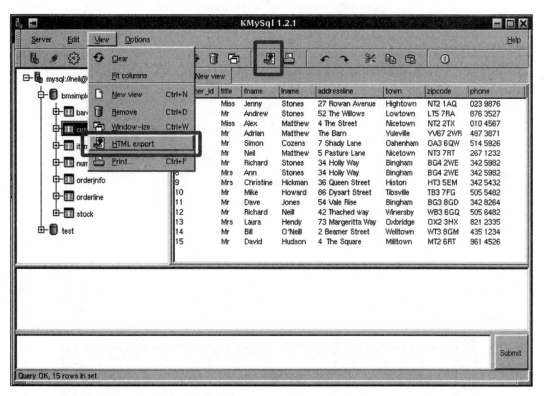

The HTML export can be very useful for preparing web pages that need to contain extracts from the database. The screenshot below shows the result of an HTML export of the previous query, as viewed in a web browser:

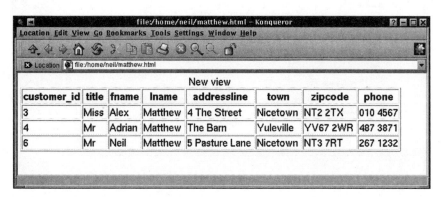

Many of the functions of KMySQL are accessed by right-clicking on an object in the left-hand explorer pane to bring up an 'object' menu. Some rudimentary server administration functions are found on the object menu for the server. The following screenshot is a partial one showing just the cascading menus:

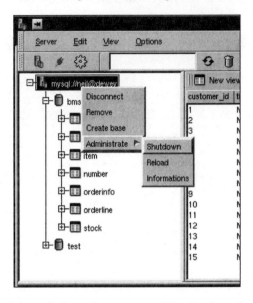

Tables may be manipulated through their object menus. We can show details about the fields in the table, and add new columns or view the contents. By selecting Edit Contents we can use KMySQL as a simple data-viewing tool:

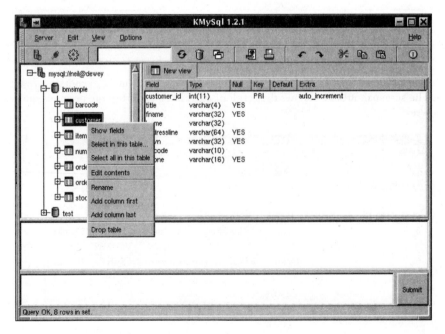

Form Designer

To facilitate data entry, KMySQL supports a form designer. Accessible from the object menu for individual databases, this tool allows you to create custom forms, containing edit-boxes, checkboxes, and drop-down lists for example. SQL may be associated with each element on the form, so that an edit-box may be pre filled with the result of a database query. A button may also be provided, to execute SQL commands; for example, an INSERT may be executed, using data from the form elements.

The screenshot on the right shows a simple form being designed for entering values into a table:

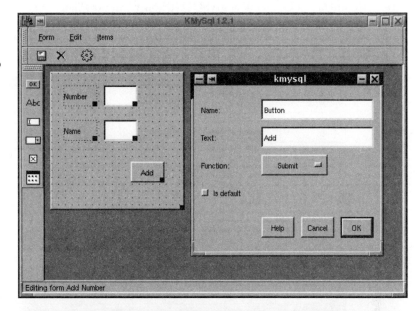

This form can be used for entering new rows into the table:

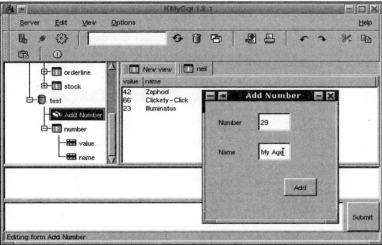

Full documentation for KMySQL (and KSql) may be found on the KSql home page.

MySQLGUI

MySQLGUI is a graphical user interface for MySQL that is available for Microsoft Windows as well as Linux and UNIX-like systems. It connects across the network to a MySQL database server that may be running on a different operating system, such as Linux, UNIX or Microsoft Windows. MySQLGUI is available on the main MySQL site, http://www.mysql.com.

Here we will take a brief look at MySQLGUI on Windows. There are no installation steps required for MySQLGUI other than unpacking the distribution .zip file into a directory. The application is started by running mysqlgui.exe. After a splash screen, and a password prompt that may be safely cancelled for now, the main client window appears:

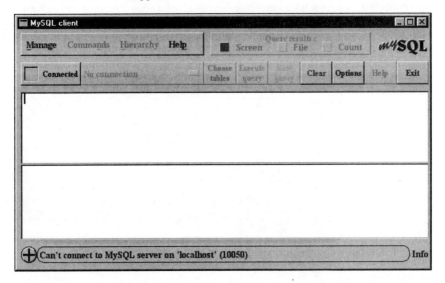

By default MySQLGUI will attempt to connect to a database server in the local computer, and prompt for the suitable password to use. To configure MySQLGUI to connect to a specific server we need to set the server options like this:

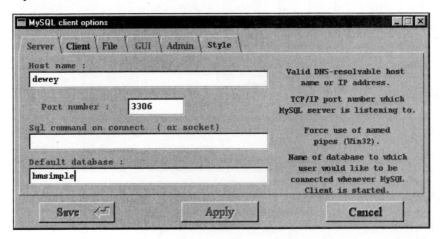

Here we need to fill in the details of the server we wish to connect to. We also need to configure a user name and password. This is done via the dialog accessed from the Client tab within the options:

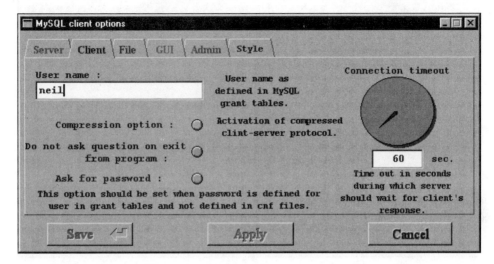

Now we are ready to connect to the database, which we can do by selecting Connect in the main client window:

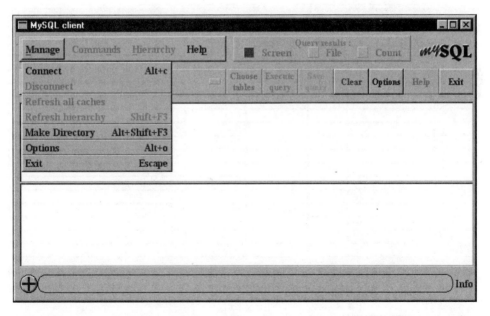

When the connection is made we are ready to execute SQL queries. We can type a query into the top pane of the main window, or select a previous query from the lower 'history' pane:

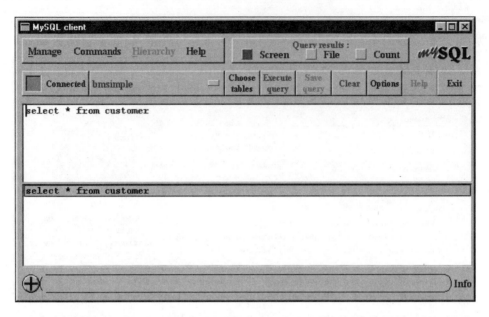

Selecting Execute Query will cause a new window to open with the results of the query displayed:

ODBC

The applications in the remainder of this chapter use the ODBC standard interface to connect to MySQL. ODBC defines a common interface for databases and is based on X/Open and ISO/IEC programming interfaces. In fact, an ODBC standard interface is not (as is often believed) limited to Microsoft Windows clients. To use ODBC on a particular client machine, you need both an application written for the ODBC interface and a driver for the particular database that you want to use.

MySQL has an ODBC driver available called MyODBC, which you can compile and install for your clients if you wish. Normally the clients will be running on different machines, and possibly under a different architecture. For example, you might have the database server on UNIX or Linux and the client applications running on Windows.

Happily, if you are using Microsoft Windows as your client, you can find a pre compiled ODBC driver at the MySQL site, http://www.mysql.com.

The files needed for download are:

myodbc-2.50.39-win95.zip (for Windows 9x/Me), or

myodbc-2.50.39-nt.zip (for Windows NT/2000)

Both of these files, or their later versions, can be found at http://www.mysql.com/downloads/api-myodbc.html.

On Microsoft Windows, ODBC drivers are made available through the ODBC Data Sources applet in Control Panel. On Windows 2000 this is found in the Administrative Tools folder of Control Panel:

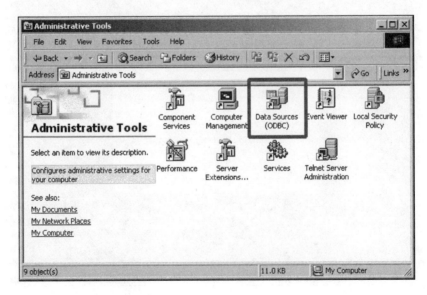

Selecting this applet shows us the installed ODBC drivers:

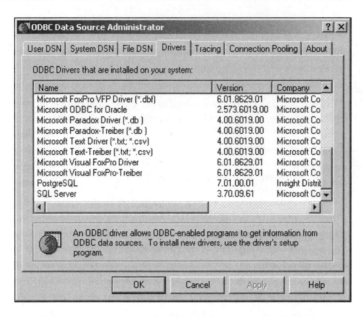

To install the MySQL ODBC driver, we have to perform two steps. Firstly, we must extract the driver files from the appropriate `.zip` file into a temporary directory. Then we must execute the setup application (`setup.exe`):

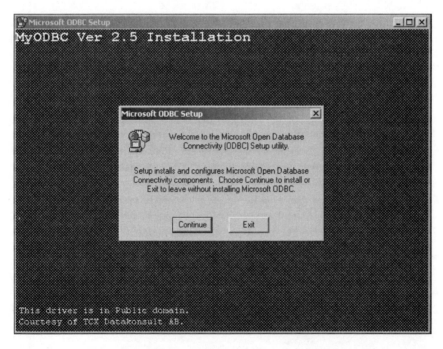

The application will lead us through the steps of installing the driver and creating an ODBC data source. In this case there is only one driver to choose from and that is MySQL:

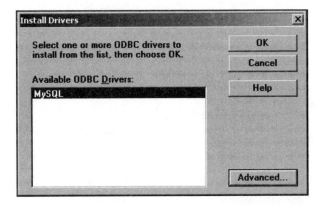

Once the driver files are copied and installed we can create a new data source using the new driver. The setup program prompts us to create a first data source as it installs. We can either create one now, or later. Additional data sources may be added by using the Control Panel later.

Let's create a data source for our bmsimple database:

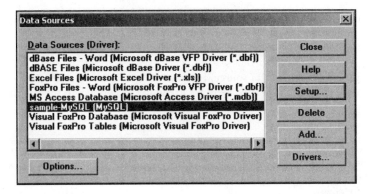

We select the MySQL driver and click on Setup to bring up the dialog for creating MySQL-specific data sources:

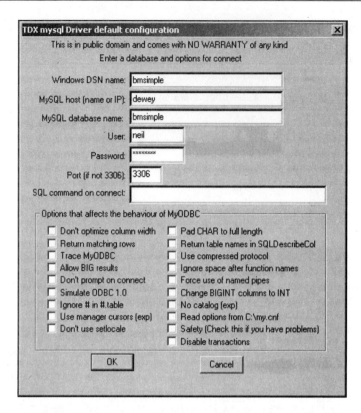

Here we enter the details for the data source. It is normally safe to leave all of the options unchecked and simply fill in the connection details. Here we are going to connect to the bmsimple database running on the machine called dewey using the user name neil.

The password we specify here must match the password that the MySQL server on dewey has recorded for neil *on the client machine*. It is not necessarily the same as the password that neil uses on dewey for logging in, or the same as the password for neil on the client.

Once we have configured the new data source, the installation is done:

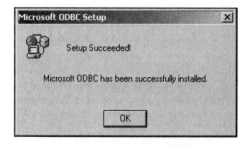

After we have performed the ODBC installation and configuration, we can confirm that we have successfully installed the driver by selecting the **Drivers** tab in the ODBC applet and noting that MySQL now appears in the list:

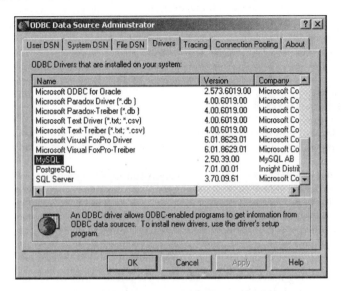

Now we will be able to use ODBC-compatible applications to connect to our MySQL databases. To make a specific database available, we have to create a data source, as we have done for our bmsimple. To add further data sources select **User DSN** in the ODBC applet to create a data source that will be available to the *current user only*. If you select **System DSN** you can create data sources that *all* users can see. Click on **Add** to begin the creation process and this will display a dialog box for selecting the type of driver the data source will use:

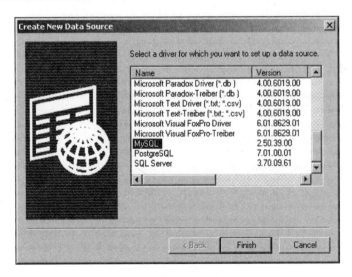

Now click on **Finish**.

We are now presented with the same dialog we saw when installing the OBDC drivers for setting up a data source and are now ready to access our MySQL database from ODBC applications.

There are many ODBC applications available, and they can be used to access MySQL databases as well as more mainstream ones, such as Oracle or Microsoft SQL Server. In the following two sections we will see how we can use two Microsoft Office applications – Microsoft Access and Microsoft Excel as graphical front-ends to our MySQL server.

Microsoft Access

Although it may seem an odd idea at first sight, we can use Microsoft Access with MySQL. Since Access is already a database system, why would we want to use MySQL to store data?

Firstly, when developing a database system, we need to consider the requirement for things such as data volumes, possibility of multiple concurrent users, security, robustness, and reliability. You may decide on MySQL because it fits better with your security model, server platforms, and data growth predictions.

Secondly, although MySQL running on a UNIX or Linux server may be the ideal environment for your data, it might not be the best or most familiar environment for your users and their applications.

There is a case for allowing users to use tools such as Access or other third-party applications to create reports or data entry forms for MySQL databases. Since MySQL has an ODBC interface this is not only possible but also remarkably easy.

Here we will look at creating an Access database that uses data stored on a remote MySQL server, and writing a simple report based on that data. We will be assuming that you are reasonably familiar with creating Access databases and applications.

Once you have established the link from Access to MySQL you can use all of the features of Access to create easy-to-use MySQL applications.

Linked Tables

Access allows you to import a table into a database in a number of different ways; one of which is by means of a **linked table**. This is a table that is represented in Access as a query. The data is retrieved from another source as and when it is needed, rather than being copied into the database. This means that when the data changes in the external database the change is also reflected in Access.

Let's create a simple Access database to update and report on the products that we are selling on our example database system. In the `bmsimple` database we have a table called `item` that records a unique identifier for each product we sell, a description of that product together with a cost price and a selling price.

In Access, we create a new blank database:

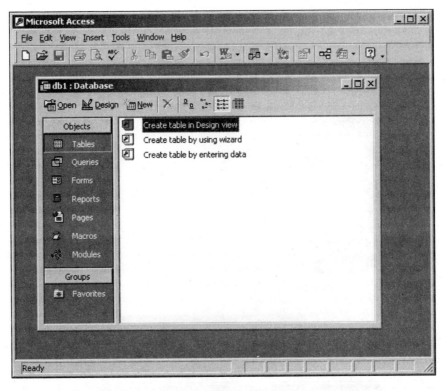

In the Tables section of the tabbed dialog box, select New to create a new table, and choose the Link Table option:

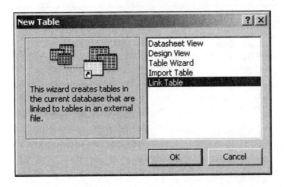

For Microsoft Access 97 use File | Get External Data | Link Tables.

In the Link dialog box that appears, choose files of type ODBC Databases:

You should then see the ODBC data source selection dialog. Select Machine Data Source and the appropriate MySQL database connection:

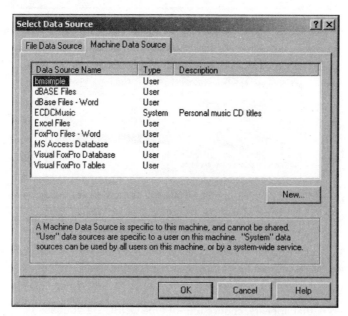

Next, we should automatically connect to the bmsimple database. If the connection fails for some reason (for example, the password we entered when we set up the data source is no longer valid), then we will be prompted to provide connection parameters again:

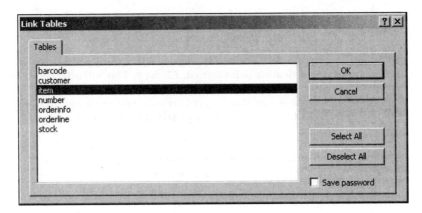

When the connection is made, we are presented with a list of available tables in the remote database. Click on item to link the item table on the remote server into our Access database:

Now we will see that the Access database has a new table also called item that we can browse just as if the data were held in Access:

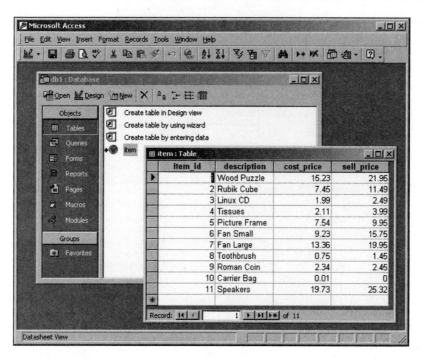

That's just about all there is to it.

> You might see slightly different screens from those shown here, depending on your versions of Windows and Access.

Data Entry

We can use the table browser in Access to examine data in the MySQL table and to add more rows.

> Microsoft Access may have some trouble mapping MySQL data types such as NUMERIC(7,2) to its own floating point format, float8. This will affect our ability to modify and delete rows. If you plan to use Access with your MySQL applications, you will need to consider using only simple types for your table columns. In particular MySQL binary objects (BLOBs) will be shown as Access OLE objects.

Here's a screenshot of an Access data entry form being used to add further items to the item table. You can use the programming features of Access to create more sophisticated data entry applications that perform validation, or prevent the modification of existing data, for example:

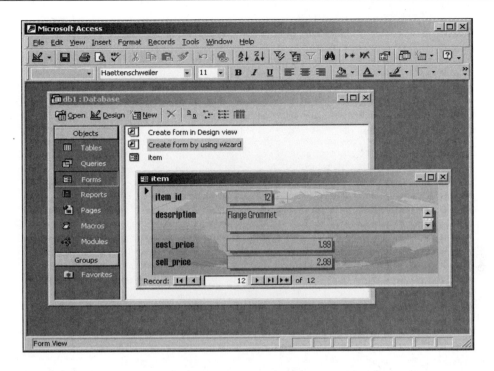

Reports

Reports are just as easy. Use the Access report designer to generate reports based on the data stored in MySQL tables just as you would from any other Access table. We can include columns in the report to answer questions about the data in the table. For example, here is an Access report that shows the price markup (that is, the difference between the sell_price and the cost_ price) that we are applying to the products in the item table:

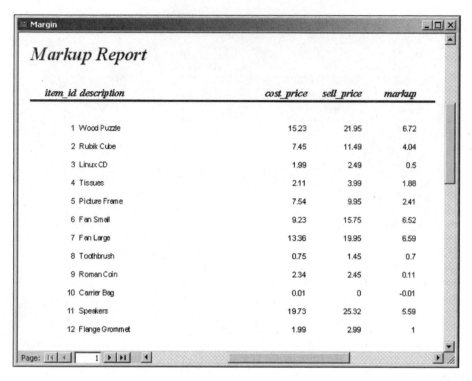

Combining Microsoft Access and MySQL increases the number of options you have for creating database applications. The scalability and reliability of MySQL combined with the familiarity and easy use of Microsoft Access may be just what you need, bearing in mind the limitations considered earlier.

Microsoft Excel

As with Microsoft Access, we can employ Microsoft Excel to add functionality to our MySQL installation. The idea is much the same as with Access; we include data in our spreadsheets that is taken from (or rather, linked to) a remote data source. When the data changes, we can refresh the spreadsheet to reflect the new data.

Once we have made a spreadsheet based on MySQL data we can use Excel's features, such as 'charting', to create graphical representations of our data.

Let's extend our `product` table example from Access to make a chart showing the *markup* we have applied to our products in the `item` table.

In a similar way as with Access, we have to tell Excel that some portion of a spreadsheet needs to be linked to an external database table. Starting from a blank spreadsheet, we choose the menu option to get external data with a new database query:

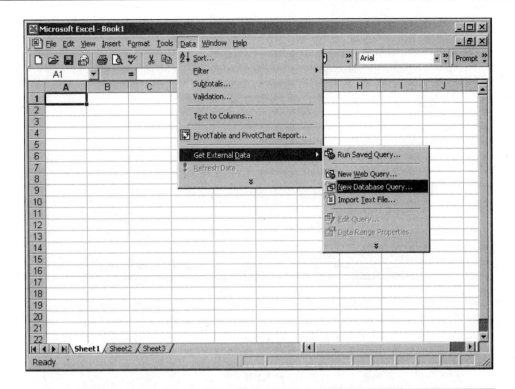

> You will need to have installed the **Microsoft Query** option for Excel to enable this functionality.

We are now presented with a familiar ODBC data source selection dialog:

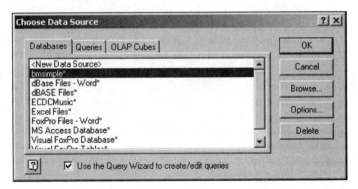

When the connection to the database is made, we can choose which table we want to use, and the columns we want to appear in the spreadsheet. Here we will select item_id, description, cost_price, and sell_price from the item table:

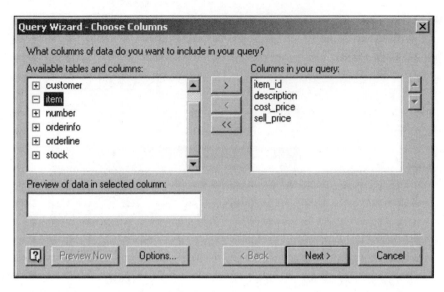

If we want to restrict the number of rows that appear in our spreadsheet we can do this by specifying selection criteria in the next dialog box. Here we select those products with a selling price greater than $2:

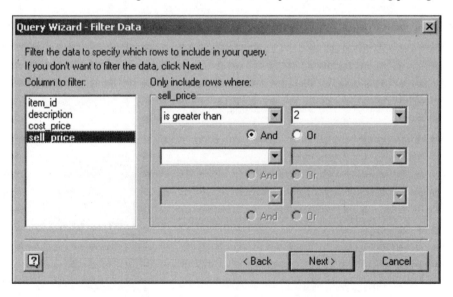

Finally, we can choose to have the data sorted by a particular column, or group of columns, in either the ascending or descending order:

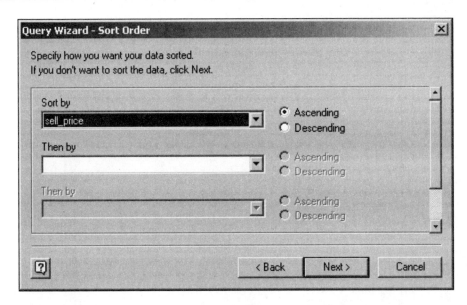

Before the data is returned to Excel, we get the chance to specify where we want it to appear in our spreadsheet. It is probably a good idea to have data from a MySQL table appear in a spreadsheet by itself. This is because we need to make sure that we cater for the number of rows increasing as the database grows. When we refresh the spreadsheet data we will need space for the data to expand into.

In this example, we simply allow the data to occupy the top-left area of the sheet:

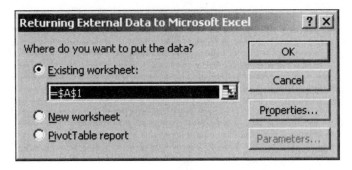

Now we can see the data present in our spreadsheet:

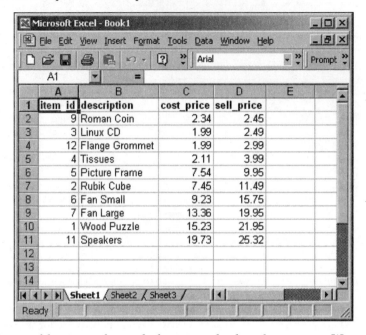

We can use this spreadsheet to perform calculations on the data if we want to. We could for example calculate the sales margin being earned from each product by setting up an additional column with an appropriate formula.

When the data changes in the database, Excel will not automatically update its version of the rows. To make sure that the data you are viewing in Excel is accurate, you must refresh the data. This is done by selecting Data | Refresh Data:

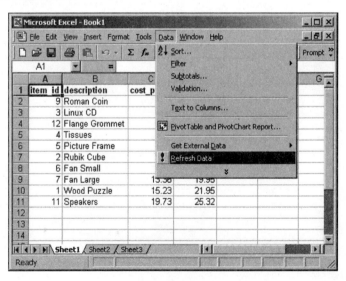

Now that we have data in our spreadsheet we can employ some of Excel's features to add value to our MySQL application. In this example, we have added a chart showing the markup on each product. It is simply built by using the Excel chart wizard and selecting the MySQL data area of the sheet as the source data for the chart:

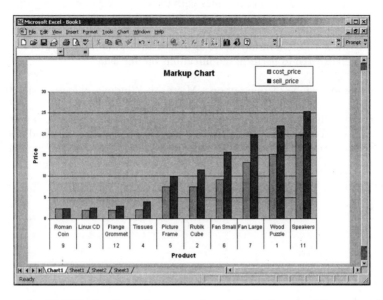

When the data in the MySQL database changes and we refresh the spreadsheet, the chart will automatically update.

Resources

A good place to start to look for tools to use with MySQL is the main MySQL site. You can also get some useful information, particularly on collection of software, both freeware and commercial. Some of the useful links are mentioned below:

http://www.mysql.com

http://www.mysql.com/portal/software/html/index.html

http://www.mysql.org

The home page for KSql (and KMySQL) is at: http://ksql.sourceforge.net

An alternative to KMySQL that is stronger for database administration is KMySQLAdmin. It is also included with some Linux distributions such as SuSE . Its homepage is at:

http://www.webeifer.de/alwin/Programs/KMySQLAdmin

The MySQL developers are currently working on MyCC, a new graphical client. For more information on this application visit the site:

http://sourceforge.net/projects/mycc

Summary

In this chapter, we have taken a look at some of the tools we have at our disposal for getting the most out of MySQL. The standard distribution comes with the command line tool `mysql` that is capable of carrying out most of the operations we need for creating and maintaining databases.

If we have the X-Window System installed, we also have the option of using graphical tools like `ksql`, `kmysql`, and `kmysqladmin` to perform modifications on our data.

Database administration can be carried out on a Microsoft Windows machine using the `MySQLGUI` tool.

We can use Microsoft Office products, including Microsoft Access and Excel, to manipulate and report on data held in a MySQL database. This allows us to combine the scalability and reliability of the MySQL system running on a UNIX or Linux platform with the ease of use of familiar tools.

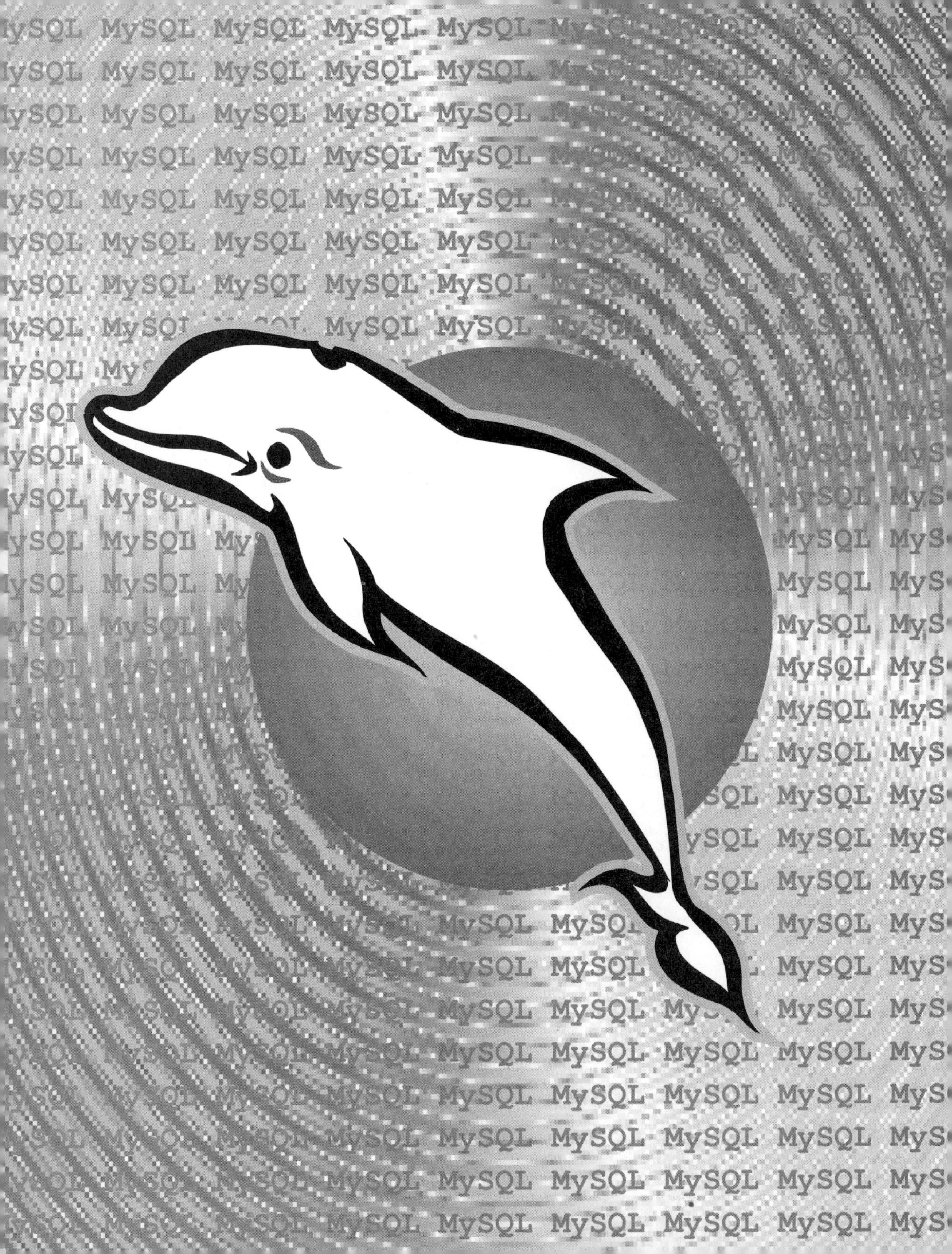

Changing Your Data

So far in this book we have looked at why a relational database – MySQL in particular – is a powerful tool for organizing and retrieving data. In the previous chapter, we looked at some of the graphical tools such as MySQL GUI, which can also be used for accessing and administering MySQL. We even looked at how to use Microsoft Access with MySQL and how to add more functionality to MySQL by using Microsoft Excel. In this chapter, we are going to see how to INSERT data into a MySQL database, UPDATE data already in the database, and finally how to DELETE data from the database.

As we work through the chapter, we will look at:

- ❑   Adding data to the database
  - ❑   The INSERT Statement
  - ❑   Inserting data into AUTO_INCREMENT columns
  - ❑   Inserting NULL values
  - ❑   The LOAD DATA command
  - ❑   Loading data using mysqlimport
  - ❑   Loading data directly from another application
- ❑   How to UPDATE data in the database
- ❑   How to DELETE data from the database

Adding Data To the Database

Surprisingly perhaps, after the complexities of the SELECT statement that we saw in Chapter 4, *Accessing your Data*, adding data into a MySQL database is quite straightforward. We add data to MySQL using the INSERT statement. We can only add data to a single table at any one time, and generally we do it one row at a time. However, more recent versions (release 4.0) of MySQL do allow multiple rows to be added with each statement, as an extension to standard SQL.

The INSERT Statement

The basic SQL `INSERT` statement has a very simple syntax:

```
INSERT INTO tablename VALUES (list of comma-separated column values);
```

We specify a list of comma-separated column values, which must be in the same order as the columns in the table. MySQL has several additional options you can use with the `INSERT` statement, and also some alternative syntax that can be used. We will see the options and alternative syntax later in the chapter.

> **Although this syntax is very appealing because of its simplicity, it is also rather dangerous. We urge you to avoid this syntax, and instead use the safer `INSERT` syntax shown later, where the column names are specified as well as the data values. We present the syntax here because you will see it in common use, but we do recommend you avoid using it.**

Try It Out – Adding Data To the Customer Table

Let's add some new rows to our `customer` table. The first thing we must do is to discover the correct column order. If we have the SQL statement used to create the table to hand, then the order of column values will simply be the same as the order in which they were listed in the `CREATE TABLE` command. If we don't have the SQL to hand, which is unfortunately all too common then we can use the `SHOW COLUMNS FROM` *tablename* command in MySQL to describe the table to us.

Suppose we wanted to have a look at the definition of the `customer` table in our database, as presented in Chapter 3, *Installing and Getting Started with MySQL*. We would then use the `SHOW COLUMNS` command to ask for its description to be shown. More details on the `SHOW COLUMNS` command can be found in Chapter 10, *MySQL Administration*. For the moment, let's look at the table definition:

```
mysql> SHOW COLUMNS FROM customer;
+-------------+-------------+------+-----+---------+----------------+
| Field       | Type        | Null | Key | Default | Extra          |
+-------------+-------------+------+-----+---------+----------------+
| customer_id | int(11)     |      | PRI | NULL    | auto_increment |
| title       | varchar(4)  | YES  |     | NULL    |                |
| fname       | varchar(32) | YES  |     | NULL    |                |
| lname       | varchar(32) |      |     |         |                |
| addressline | varchar(64) | YES  |     | NULL    |                |
| town        | varchar(32) | YES  |     | NULL    |                |
| zipcode     | varchar(10) |      |     |         |                |
| phone       | varchar(16) | YES  |     | NULL    |                |
+-------------+-------------+------+-----+---------+----------------+
8 rows in set (0.00 sec)
mysql>
```

The display shows us the column order for our `customer` table, as well as some additional details which we don't need just now.

To insert character data, we must enclose it in single quotes ('). If we need a single quote to appear in our character string, then precede it with a backslash (\). Numbers can be written as they are. For NULL values, we just write NULL or, as we shall see later in a more complex form of the INSERT statement where we explicitly list the columns, simply provide no data for that column.

Now that we know the column order, we still need one other important piece of information, as to which customer_id to use. You will remember we made customer_id a primary key, which means it must be unique, so we must use an 'id' that is not currently in use. Later in the chapter we will see how the AUTO_INCREMENT option allows us to let MySQL pick a number, but at the moment we need to pick our own value. The easiest way is to use the MAX() function that we will meet properly in Chapter 7, *Advance Data Selection*, but for now all you need to know is that it returns the highest number found in a chosen column:

```
mysql> SELECT MAX(customer_id) FROM customer;
+------------------+
| MAX(customer_id) |
+------------------+
|               15 |
+------------------+
1 row in set (0.01 sec)

mysql>
```

Now we can write our INSERT statement to add a new row to customer table, like this:

```
INSERT INTO customer VALUES(16, 'Mr', 'Gavin', 'Smyth', '23 Harlestone',
'Milltown', 'MT7 7HI', '746 3725');
```

This is what we see:

```
mysql> INSERT INTO customer VALUES(16, 'Mr', 'Gavin', 'Smyth', '23
Harlestone','Milltown', 'MT7 7HI', '746 3725');
Query OK, 1 row affected (0.00 sec)

mysql>
```

We can easily check that the data has been inserted correctly by using a SELECT statement to retrieve it, like this:

```
mysql> SELECT * FROM customer WHERE customer_id = 16;
+------------+------+------+-------+--------------+---------+---------+-------+
| customer_id| title|fname | lname | addressline  |town     | zipcode | phone |
+------------+------+------+-------+--------------+---------+---------+-------+
|          16| Mr   |Gavin | Smyth | 23 Harlestone|Milltown | MT7 7HI |7463725|
+------------+------+------+-------+--------------+---------+---------+-------+
1 row in set (0.00 sec)
mysql>
```

The display is wrapped, because of the restrictions of the page width, but you can see that the data was correctly inserted.

Suppose we wanted to insert another row where the last name was O'Rourke, then what do we do with the single quote that is already in the data?

We escape it using a single backslash (\), like this:

```
INSERT INTO customer VALUES(17, 'Mr', 'Shaun', 'O\'Rourke', '32 Sheepy Lane',
'Milltown', 'MT9 8NQ', '746 3956');
```

Notice that we use the next `customer_id` value here:

```
mysql> INSERT INTO customer VALUES(17, 'Mr', 'Shaun', 'O\'Rourke', '32 Sheepy
Lane', 'Milltown', 'MT9 8NQ', '746 3956');
Query OK, 1 row affected (0.00 sec)

mysql>
```

Let's retrieve just a couple of columns, to show how the data was inserted preserving the quote:

```
mysql> SELECT fname, lname FROM customer WHERE customer_id = 17;
+-------+----------+
| fname | lname    |
+-------+----------+
| Shaun | O'Rourke |
+-------+----------+
1 row in set (0.00 sec)

mysql>
```

How It Works

We used the `INSERT` statement to add additional data to the `customer` table, specifying column values in the same order as they were created in the table. To add a number to a column, just write the number and to add a string, enclose it in single quotes. To insert a single quote into the string, we must precede the single quote with a backslash character (\). If we ever need to insert a backslash character, then we would write a pair, like \\. Here is an example of an `INSERT` statement that inserts a backslash into the address column:

```
mysql> INSERT INTO customer VALUES(18, 'Mr', 'Jeff', 'Baggott', 'Midtown
Street A\\33', 'Milltown', 'MT9 8NQ', '746 3956');
```

Safer INSERT Statements

While you are using `INSERT` statements like we used in the above example, it is necessary to specify every single column and to get the data order exactly the same because the table column order adds an element of risk. If we rely on an assumed column order we may quite easily write an `INSERT` statement with the column data in the wrong order. This would result in our adding incorrect data to our database.

In our previous example, suppose we had erroneously exchanged the position of the `fname` and `lname` columns. The data would have been inserted successfully, because both columns are text columns, and MySQL would have been unable to detect our mistake. If we had later asked for a list of the last names of our customers, Gavin would have appeared as a valid customer last name, rather than Smyth as we intended.

Poor quality, or in this case just plain incorrect data, is a major problem in databases and we should generally take as many precautions as we can to ensure that only correct data gets included. Simple mistakes might be easy to spot in our example database with just tens of rows, but in a database with tens of thousands of rows, identifying mistakes, particularly in data with unusual names, would be very difficult indeed.

Fortunately, there is a slight variation of the `INSERT` statement, that is both easier to use, and much safer as well. This form explicitly lists the columns you wish to insert data into:

```
INSERT INTO tablename(list of column names) VALUES(list of values);
```

In this variant of the `INSERT` statement, we must list the column names and data values in the same order, which can be different from the order we used when we created the table. What we don't have to do is provide a value for every column, but only those we named. Columns not listed will get default values. Another advantage in using this variant is that we no longer need to know the order in which the columns were defined in the database. We have a nice, clear, almost 'side-by-side' list of column names and the data we are about to insert into them. We recommend you always use this form of the `INSERT` statement.

Try It Out – Inserting Values Corresponding To Column Names

Let's add another row to our database, this time explicitly naming the columns, like:

```
INSERT INTO customer(customer_id, title, fname, lname, addressline, town, zipcode,
phone) VALUES(19, 'Mrs', 'Sarah', 'Harvey', '84 Willow Way', 'Lincoln', 'LC3 7RD',
'527 3739');
```

We can also spread this command over several lines, making it easier to read and check that we have the column names and data values in the same order:

```
mysql> INSERT INTO
    -> customer(customer_id, title, lname, fname, addressline,
    -> town, zipcode, phone)
    -> VALUES(19, 'Mrs', 'Harvey', 'Sarah',  '84 Willow Way',
    -> 'Lincoln', 'LC3 7RD', '527 3739');
Query OK, 1 row affected (0.00 sec)
mysql>
```

How It Works

Notice how much easier it is to compare the names of the fields with the values being inserted into them. We deliberately swapped over the `fname` and `lname` columns, just to show that it could be done. You can use any column order you like; all that matters is that the values match the order in which you list the columns.

You will also notice the `mysql` prompt has changed to a continuation prompt on subsequent lines, and remains until we terminate the command with a semicolon.

> We strongly recommend that you always use the named column form of the `INSERT` statement, because the explicit naming of columns makes it much safer to use.

Alternative INSERT Syntax

MySQL also supports alternative syntax for inserting data into a table. The first alternative is more like the UPDATE statement we will meet later in this chapter. The syntax is:

```
INSERT INTO tablename SET column1 = value1, column2 = value2, ...
```

Using this form, we can rewrite our earlier INSERT statement like this:

```
mysql> INSERT INTO customer SET customer_id = 19, title = 'Mrs', lname =
    -> 'Harvey', fname = 'Sarah', addressline = '84 Willow Way', town
    -> = 'Lincoln', zipcode = 'LC7 7RD', phone = '527 3739';
```

Although this is not standard SQL, it does have the advantage of being easy to read.

MySQL has a second form of the INSERT statement, which is also non-standard, but executes more efficiently than the standard syntax:

```
mysql> INSERT INTO customer VALUES (1,'Miss','Jenny','Stones','27 Rowan
    -> Avenue','Hightown','NT2 1AQ','023 9876'), (2,'Mr','Andrew','Stones',
    -> '52 The Willows','Lowtown','LT5 7RA','876 3527'), (3,'Miss','Alex',
    -> 'Matthew','4 The Street','Nicetown','NT2 2TX','010 4567'), (4,'Mr',
    -> 'Adrian','Matthew','The Barn','Yuleville','YV67 2WR','487 3871'),
    -> (5,'Mr','Simon','Cozens','7 Shady Lane','Oahenham','OA3 6QW',
    -> '514 5926');
```

The backup utility, `mysqldump`, which we will meet in Chapter 10, can use this format to create `load` files.

Inserting Data into AUTO_INCREMENT Columns

At this point, it is time to confess to a minor sin we have been committing with the `customer_id` column. Up to this point in the chapter, we have not known how to insert data into some columns of a table, while leaving others alone. With the second form of the INSERT statement, using named columns, we can do this and see how it is particularly important when we are inserting data into tables with AUTO_INCREMENT type columns.

You will remember from Chapter 2, *Relational Database Principles*, that we met the rather special column option AUTO_INCREMENT, which can be applied to integer type columns, and automatically increments to give us an easy way of creating `unique_id` numbers for each row. So far in this chapter, we have been inserting data into rows, providing a value for the `customer_id` column even though it is an AUTO_INCREMENT type data field.

Let's have a look at the data in our `customer` table so far:

```
mysql> SELECT customer_id, fname, lname, addressline FROM customer;
+-------------+----------+----------+---------------------+
| customer_id | fname    | lname    | addressline         |
+-------------+----------+----------+---------------------+
|           1 | Jenny    | Stones   | 27 Rowan Avenue     |
|           2 | Andrew   | Stones   | 52 The Willows      |
|           3 | Alex     | Matthew  | 4 The Street        |
|           4 | Adrian   | Matthew  | The Barn            |
|           5 | Simon    | Cozens   | 7 Shady Lane        |
|           6 | Neil     | Matthew  | 5 Pasture Lane      |
|           7 | Richard  | Stones   | 34 Holly Way        |
|           8 | Ann      | Stones   | 34 Holly Way        |
|           9 | Christine| Hickman  | 36 Queen Street     |
|          10 | Mike     | Howard   | 86 Dysart Street    |
|          11 | Dave     | Jones    | 54 Vale Rise        |
|          12 | Richard  | Neill    | 42 Thatched way     |
|          13 | Laura    | Hendy    | 73 Margeritta Way   |
|          14 | Bill     | O'Neill  | 2 Beamer Street     |
|          15 | David    | Hudson   | 4 The Square        |
|          16 | Gavin    | Smyth    | 23 Harlestone       |
|          17 | Shaun    | O'Rourke | 32 Sheepy Lane      |
|          18 | Jeff     | Baggott  | Midtown Street A\33 |
|          19 | Sarah    | Harvey   | 84 Willow Way       |
+-------------+----------+----------+---------------------+
19 rows in set (0.01 sec)

mysql>
```

Let's now see another INSERT statement, where we try and put a duplicate entry into the `customer_id` column:

```
mysql> INSERT INTO customer SET customer_id = 19, title = 'Mrs', lname =
    -> 'Harvey', fname = 'Sarah', addressline = '84 Willow Way', town =
    -> 'Lincoln', zipcode = 'LC7 7RD', phone = '527 3739';
ERROR 1062: Duplicate entry '19' for key 1
mysql>
```

Why has MySQL rejected the INSERT? The problem is with the `customer_id` value of 19.

Look at the table definition:

```
mysql> SHOW COLUMNS FROM customer;
+-------------+-------------+------+-----+---------+----------------+
| Field       | Type        | Null | Key | Default | Extra          |
+-------------+-------------+------+-----+---------+----------------+
| customer_id | int(11)     |      | PRI | NULL    | auto_increment |
| title       | varchar(4)  | YES  |     | NULL    |                |
| fname       | varchar(32) | YES  |     | NULL    |                |
| lname       | varchar(32) |      |     |         |                |
| addressline | varchar(64) | YES  |     | NULL    |                |
| town        | varchar(32) | YES  |     | NULL    |                |
| zipcode     | varchar(10) |      |     |         |                |
| phone       | varchar(16) | YES  |     | NULL    |                |
+-------------+-------------+------+-----+---------+----------------+
8 rows in set (0.00 sec)

mysql>
```

The column `customer_id` is defined as a primary key, which means it must be unique, so quite correctly MySQL rejects the `INSERT` that tried to create two rows with a 19 stored in the `customer_id` field. The trouble is that each time we `INSERT` a row we have had to pick for ourselves a new unique number to use. This is possible, and indeed we could write code to check each time what value we should be using, but it's rather hard work and error prone.

Using the `AUTO_INCREMENT` attribute on a column gives us a much easier way – we simply `INSERT` a `NULL` value into the `AUTO_INCREMENT` column and allow MySQL to pick the next value for us. We recommend you always allow MySQL to generate values for `AUTO_INCREMENT` columns.

> **Avoid providing values for `AUTO_INCREMENT` data columns when inserting data, either use a `NULL` or do not list the column in the column list.**

In older versions of MySQL, the value MySQL provided was always one greater than the current largest value in the column. In more recent versions of MySQL the rule has changed very slightly. Now if you delete data from a table, then provided you use a `WHERE` clause, MySQL will remember the last number allocated, even if the row using it has been deleted, and allocate a new number. This behavior is described as **strictly increasing** number allocation. Let's look at what this means.

Try It Out – Allowing AUTO_INCREMENT To Pick Values

Although we have not yet met the `DELETE` statement, it's very easy to use. First let's delete the last two entries in our table:

```
mysql> DELETE FROM customer WHERE customer_id = 19 OR customer_id = 18;
Query OK, 2 rows affected (0.01 sec)

mysql>
```

Now let us reinsert the rows allowing `AUTO_INCREMENT` to pick values for us:

```
mysql> INSERT INTO customer(title, fname, lname, addressline, town, zipcode,
    -> phone) VALUES('Mr', 'Jeff', 'Baggott', 'Midtown Street A\\33',
    -> 'Milltown', 'MT9 8NQ', '746 3956');
Query OK, 1 row affected (0.00 sec)

mysql>
```

When we look at what has been inserted, we discover MySQL has picked 20 as the next `customer_id` value to use:

```
mysql> SELECT customer_id, fname, lname, addressline FROM customer
    -> WHERE customer_id >= 18;
+-------------+-------+---------+--------------------+
| customer_id | fname | lname   | addressline        |
+-------------+-------+---------+--------------------+
|          20 | Jeff  | Baggott | Midtown Street A\33 |
+-------------+-------+---------+--------------------+
1 row in set (0.00 sec)

mysql>
```

How It Works

MySQL has allocated a strictly increasing number for us. Since the table previously had an entry with the customer_id of 19, the next number it allocates is 20, even though the numbers 18 and 19 are unused.

At first sight this might seem a little odd, but in practice it's very sensible behavior, because it makes it much easier to ensure that uniqueness of id columns is maintained.

Accessing the Last AUTO_INCREMENT Value

Suppose after inserting our customer record we wanted to insert some other data in a different table that is related to that customer. We would almost certainly want to know what the customer_id of the last row we inserted was. This value is available with a function LAST_INSERT_ID() that we use like this:

```
mysql> select LAST_INSERT_ID();
+-----------------+
| last_insert_id() |
+-----------------+
|              20 |
+-----------------+
1 row in set (0.00 sec)

mysql>
```

Inserting NULL Values

We briefly mentioned, in Chapter 2, the idea of NULL values in the database. Let's look at how we can insert NULL values into the database.

If you are using the first form of the INSERT statement, where you insert data into the columns in the order they were defined when the table was created, you simply write NULL in the column value. Note that you must not use quotes; NULL is neither the same as an empty string nor any other kind of string, but a special unspecified value in SQL.

Suppose from our earlier example:

```
INSERT INTO customer VALUES(16, 'Mr', 'Gavin', 'Smyth', '23 Harlestone',
    'Milltown', 'MT7 7HI', '746 3725');
```

We assume that we do not know the first name. The table definition allows NULL in the fname column, so adding data without knowing the first name is perfectly valid. If we had written:

```
INSERT INTO customer VALUES(16, 'Mr', '', 'Smyth', '23 Harlestone',
    'Milltown', 'MT7 7HI', '746 3725');
```

This would not be what we intended, because we would have added an empty string as the first name, perhaps implying that Mr. Smyth had no first name, while what we intended was to use a NULL, because we do not know the first name.

The correct INSERT statement would have been:

```
INSERT INTO customer VALUES(16, 'Mr', NULL, 'Smyth', '23 Harlestone',
    'Milltown', 'MT7 7HI', '746 3725');
```

Notice the lack of quotes around NULL. If quotes had been used, fname would have been set to the string NULL, rather than the *value* NULL.

Using the second (safer) form of the INSERT statement, where columns are explicitly named, it is much easier to insert NULL values, where we neither list the column nor provide a value for it, like this:

```
INSERT INTO customer(title, lname, addressline, town, zipcode, phone)
    VALUES('Mr', 'Smyth', '23 Harlestone', 'Milltown', 'MT7 7HI', '746 3725');
```

Notice that the fname column is neither listed nor is a value defined for it. Alternatively we could have listed the column and then written NULL in the value list.

This will not work if we try and add a NULL value in a column that is defined as not allowing NULL values. Suppose we try to add a customer with no last name (lname) column:

```
mysql> INSERT INTO customer(title, fname, lname, addressline, town, zipcode,
    -> phone) VALUES('Ms', 'Gill', NULL, '27 Chase Avenue', 'Lowtown', 'LT5
    -> 8TQ', '876 1962');
ERROR 1048: Column 'lname' cannot be null

mysql>
```

The INSERT is rejected because we cannot put a NULL value into the lname column, as we created the database with the lname column having the attribute NOT NULL. If you look back earlier in the chapter to the SHOW COLUMNS command on the customer table, you can see that the lname column does not accept NULL values.

Be aware that trying to INSERT a NULL is different from simply failing to provide a value:

```
mysql> INSERT INTO customer(title, fname, addressline, town, zipcode, phone)
    -> VALUES('Ms', 'Gill', '27 Chase Avenue', 'Lowtown', 'LT5 8TQ', '876
    -> 1962');
Query OK, 1 row affected (0.00 sec)

mysql>
```

And retrieve the row again, by checking the last AUTO_INCREMENT value used:

```
mysql> SELECT LAST_INSERT_ID();
+-----------------+
| last_insert_id() |
+-----------------+
|              22 |
+-----------------+
1 row in set (0.00 sec)

mysql>
```

Now that we know the `customer_id`, let's fetch the row:

```
mysql> SELECT fname, lname, town FROM customer WHERE customer_id = 22;
+-------+-------+---------+
| fname | lname | town    |
+-------+-------+---------+
| Gill  |       | Lowtown |
+-------+-------+---------+
1 row in set (0.00 sec)

mysql>
```

It looks like `lname` is NULL. However, if we check more carefully we discover this is not the case:

```
mysql> SELECT fname, lname, town FROM customer WHERE customer_id = 22
    -> AND lname IS NULL;
Empty set (0.03 sec)

mysql>
```

What has happened is that we have inserted a default value for `lname`, in this case an empty string. You should note though that some databases might use a default of NULL, so you cannot rely on this behavior.

We will see in Chapter 8, *Data Definition and Manipulation*, how we can more generally define explicit default values to be used in columns when data is inserted with no value, by specifying a default value for a column. By default an empty string is used for character type columns.

The LOAD DATA Command

Although `INSERT` is the standard SQL way of adding data to a database, it is not always the most convenient.

Suppose we had a large number of rows to add to the database, but already had the actual data available, perhaps in a spreadsheet. If the only way we knew of getting data into the database was to use the `INSERT` statement, we would probably export the spreadsheet as a CSV (comma-separated variable) file. We can then use a text editor like EMACS or PFE to convert all our data into `INSERT` statements. Alternatively we might write a Perl or Python script to do the reformatting.

If we had started with data such as:

```
Miss,Jenny,Stones,27 Rowan Avenue,Hightown,NT2 1AQ,023 9876
Mr,Andrew,Stones,52 The Willows,Lowtown,LT5 7RA,876 3527
Miss,Alex,Matthew,4 The Street,Nicetown,NT2 2TX,010 4567
```

We might transform it into a series of `INSERT` statements, so it looked like this:

```
INSERT INTO customer(title, fname, lname, addressline, town, zipcode, phone)
values ('Miss','Jenny','Stones','27 Rowan Avenue','Hightown','NT2 1AQ','023
9876');
```

```
INSERT INTO customer(title, fname, lname, addressline, town, zipcode, phone)
values ('Mr','Andrew','Stones','52 The Willows','Lowtown','LT5 7RA','876 3527');

INSERT INTO customer(title, fname, lname, addressline, town, zipcode, phone)
values ('Miss','Alex','Matthew','4 The Street','Nicetown','NT2 2TX','010 4567');
```

Then save it in a text file with a .sql extension. One thing we would have to be very careful about is escaping quotes and backslashes. As we saw earlier in the chapter you must take special care of these in your data.

We could then use the source command in MySQL to execute the statements in the file. This is how the pop_all_tables.sql file works (we used this in Chapter 3 to initially populate our database).

This isn't very convenient though. It would clearly be much nicer if we could move data between flat files and the database in a more general way. There are a couple of ways of doing this in MySQL – the LOAD DATA command from inside the mysql utility, and mysqlimport, a standalone utility which acts as a front-end for the DATA IMPORT command.

Using mysqlimport, or LOAD DATA, rather than multiple INSERT statements makes it easier to set up the data ready for import, since you don't need to wrap it in INSERT statements, and it is also significantly quicker in loading.

We will look at using the LOAD DATA command first, and come back to mysqlimport later.

The LOAD DATA command has a rather complex syntax for importing data, but this does make it a very flexible way of getting data into your database. The basic syntax is:

```
LOAD DATA [LOCAL] INFILE filename INTO TABLE tablename [FIELDS [TERMINATED BY
'char'] [ENCLOSED BY 'char'] [ESCAPED BY 'char']] [LINES TERMINATED BY 'char']
[IGNORE n LINES][(column1, column2, ...)]
```

It looks a little imposing, but is quite simple to use. The sections in square braces [] are optional, so you only need to use them if required.

The first option, LOCAL, was introduced in recent versions of MySQL and means that the file is read from the local client file system, where MySQL is running, rather than the server file system where the actual database server is running. If you do not specify LOCAL then the filename given should either be an absolute path (i.e. starting with a / on Linux/UNIX systems), or be relative to the database directory.

The next set of options, those go with the FIELDS option, controls how data is delimited within the file that is being loaded. The TERMINATED BY 'char' controls how individual fields are terminated. By default this will be '\t', the tab character. The ENCLOSED BY 'char' controls characters that are stripped from the beginning and end of each field. Last, but not least, the ESCAPED BY 'char' sets the escape character that allows other special characters to be imported. By default, '\', a backslash will be used.

The LINES TERMINATED BY 'char' option specifies how lines are terminated. By default, '\n', a new line character is assumed.

The IGNORE n LINES option allows the first n lines of the imported file to be ignored, which can be very useful for skipping over a header row.

Finally the (column1, column2,...) list specifies the columns being imported. By default, a value for each column is assumed.

One thing that is very important to watch out for when inserting data directly is that the data is 'clean'. You do need to ensure that no columns are missing, there are no binary characters present, and all special data characters such as quotes and backslashes have been quoted.

Untangling several thousand rows of data that have almost been completely loaded is a slow, unreliable, and unrewarding job. It is well worth going to the effort to clean the data as much as possible *before* attempting to 'bulk load' it. It's also a good idea to take a backup of your database before doing anything major, such as loading bulk data, just in case anything goes wrong.

Well that syntax perhaps looked a little complex, but it's easy enough to use in practice.

Try It Out – Loading Data Using LOAD DATA

Suppose we had some additional customer data in a file cust.txt that looked like this:

```
Miss,Emma,Neill,21 Sheepy Lane,Hightown,NT2 1YQ,023 4245
Mr,Gavin,Neill,21 Sheepy Lane,Hightown,NT2 1YQ,023 4245
Mr,Duncan,Neill,21 Sheepy Lane,Hightown,NT2 1YQ,023 4245
```

Conveniently, there are no NULLs to worry about, so we just need to specify the comma as the column separator. To load this data, we simply execute the command:

```
mysql> LOAD DATA LOCAL INFILE 'c:/temp/cust.txt' INTO TABLE customer
    -> FIELDS TERMINATED BY ','
    -> (title, fname, lname, addressline, town, zipcode, phone);
Query OK, 3 rows affected (0.03 sec)
Records: 3  Deleted: 0  Skipped: 0  Warnings: 0

mysql>
```

Let's check what was loaded by finding the last row id used, and then selecting some sample fields:

```
mysql> SELECT LAST_INSERT_ID();
+------------------+
| last_insert_id() |
+------------------+
|               25 |
+------------------+
1 row in set (0.00 sec)

mysql> SELECT customer_id, fname, lname, town FROM customer WHERE customer_id >=
23;
+-------------+--------+-------+----------+
| customer_id | fname  | lname | town     |
+-------------+--------+-------+----------+
```

```
|            23 | Emma   | Neill | Hightown |
|            24 | Gavin  | Neill | Hightown |
|            25 | Duncan | Neill | Hightown |
+---------------+--------+-------+----------+
3 rows in set (0.00 sec)

mysql>
```

How It Works

We used the LOAD DATA command to directly load data that had been exported from a spreadsheet in CSV format into our customer table. We deliberately did not provide a customer_id column to allow MySQL to allocate unique IDs.

Loading Data Using mysqlimport

The mysqlimport utility is just a convenient front-end for the LOAD DATA command.

The syntax is:

```
mysqlimport [options] dbname filename...
```

The database name is, obviously, the name of the database where the table you want to load data with resides. There can be multiple filenames, but the primary name of each filename must be the same as the table name you want to load. So in our case, if we want to load data into the customer table, we must call the file customer.txt, or customer.ipt or something similar.

The mysqlimport utility takes a large number of options; we will only list the main ones here. For the full list consult the MySQL manual. Each option can be expressed in two ways, for example the host can be specified as '-h gw1' or '--hostname=gw1', the two forms are equivalent.

First the options that control connecting to the server:

Option	Usage	Meaning
-h hostname	--hostname=hostname	Specifies the host on which the MySQL server runs
-L	--local	Specifies that files are local
-p password	--password=password	Specifies a password
-u username	--user=username	Specifies a username

Options that control the data format, in the same way as those used by LOAD DATA:

Option	Meaning
`--columns`	A comma-separated list of columns that are to be found in the import file.
`--fields-terminated-by='char'`	Same as TERMINATED BY '*char*'
`--fields-enclosed-by='char'`	Same as ENCLOSED BY '*char*'
`--fields-escaped-by='char'`	Same as ESCAPED BY '*char*'
`--lines-terminated-by='char'`	Same as LINES TERMINATED BY '*char*'

Suppose we have some more customers to import, this time in this format:

```
Mrs   Jane   Potter   32 Queen Street   Lowtown   LT3 2YW   876 4149
Mr    Mark   Potter   32 Queen Street   Lowtown   LT3 2YW   876 4149
```

Here you will see fields are already tab separated in the file C:\Temp\customer.txt.

One oddity, which can catch you out here, is that mysqlimport will by default load options from the client section of the my.ini or my.cnf file. If that file contains an option that mysqlimport doesn't understand, you may get an error message about a parameter you didn't supply. To get round this add '--no-defaults' as the first option to mysqlimport, to prevent it from picking up default values.

We can import them from the command line (in this case a DOS prompt in Windows 2000) like this:

```
E:\mysql\bin> mysqlimport --host=192.168.100.101 --local --password=password
--user=rick  --columns=title,fname,lname,addressline,town,zipcode,phone bmsimple
C:/Temp/customer.txt
bmsimple.customer: Records: 3  Deleted: 0  Skipped: 0  Warnings: 6

E:\mysql\bin>
```

Loading Data Directly from Another Application

If we have data already in a desktop database, such as Microsoft Access, there is an even easier way to load the data into MySQL. We can simply attach the MySQL table to our Access database, via ODBC, and insert data into a MySQL table.

Often, when you are doing this, you will find that your existing data is not quite what you need, or that it needs some reworking before being inserted into its final destination table. Even if the data is in the correct format, it is often a good idea not to attempt to insert it directly into the database, but rather to first move it to a load table, and then transfer it from this load table to the real table.

Using a temporary load table is a common method in real life applications for inserting data into a database, particularly when the quality of the original data is uncertain. The data is first loaded into a load table, checked, corrected if necessary, and then moved on into the final table.

Usually, you will write a custom application to check and correct the data. Once it is ready to load into the final table though, there is a useful variant of the INSERT command that allows us to move data between tables, moving multiple rows in one command. It is the only time an INSERT statement affects multiple rows with a single statement. This is the INSERT INTO statement.

The syntax for inserting data from one table into another is:

```
INSERT INTO tablename(list of column names) SELECT normal select statement
```

Suppose we have a load table tcust that has some additional customer data to be loaded into our master customer table.

We will make our load table definition look like this:

```
CREATE TABLE tcust
(
        title               char(4)                     ,
        fname               varchar(32)                 ,
        lname               varchar(32)                 ,
        addressline         varchar(64)                 ,
        town                varchar(32)                 ,
        zipcode             char(10)                    ,
        phone               varchar(16)
);
```

Notice that there are no primary keys or constraints of any kind. It is normal when cross-loading data into a load table to make it as easy as possible to get the data into the load table. Removing the constraints makes this easier. Also notice that all the required columns are there, except the customer_id sequence number, which MySQL can create for us as we load the data in the customer table.

Suppose we have some more data to load:

```
Mr,Peter,Bradley,72 Milton Rise,Keynes,MK41 2HQ
Mr,Kevin,Carney,43 Glen Way,Lincoln,LI2 7RD,786 3454
Mr,Brian,Waters,21 Troon Rise,Lincoln,LI7 6GT,786 7243
```

We can load this into the tcust table like this (notice we need to specify the comma as field separator):

```
E:\mysql\bin> mysqlimport --host=192.168.100.101 --local --password=rick27 --
user=rick  --fields-terminated-by=, -- columns=
title,fname,lname,addressline,town,zipcode,phone bmsimple C:/Temp/tcust.txt
bmsimple.tcust: Records: 3  Deleted: 0  Skipped: 0  Warnings: 0

E:\mysql\bin>
```

Since there was no data in the phone column for Mr. Bradley, MySQL will default to setting the column to an empty string.

Once we have validated, and if necessary cleaned the data, we need to transfer it into the customer table.

Try It Out – Loading Data between Tables

The first thing we notice is that we have not yet managed to find a phone number for Mr. Bradley. This may or may not be a problem. Let's decide that for now we don't wish to load this row, but we do wish to load all the other customers. In a real world scenario of course, we may be trying to load hundreds of new customers, and it is quite probable that we will want to load groups of them as the data for each group is validated or cleaned.

The first part of the statement is quite easy to write. We will use the full syntax of INSERT, specifying precisely the columns we wish to load. This is normally the sensible choice:

```
INSERT INTO customer(title, fname, lname, addressline, town, zipcode, phone)   ...
```

Notice that we do not specify the customer_id for loading, and allow MySQL to automatically create values for us, which is always the safer way.

We now need to write the SELECT part of the statement, which will feed this INSERT statement. Remember, that we do not wish to insert Mr. Bradley yet, because his phone number is set to an empty string, as we are still trying to find it. We could, if we wanted to, load Mr. Bradley, since the phone column *will* accept NULL values. What we are doing here, is applying a slightly more stringent business rule to the data than is required by the low-level database rules. We write a SELECT statement like this:

```
SELECT title, fname, lname, addressline, town, zipcode, phone FROM tcust
    WHERE phone != "";
```

This is a perfectly valid statement. Let's test it:

```
mysql> SELECT title, fname, lname, addressline, town, zipcode, phone FROM tcust
WHERE phone != "";
+-------+-------+--------+---------------+---------+---------+-----------+
| title | fname | lname  | addressline   | town    | zipcode | phone     |
+-------+-------+--------+---------------+---------+---------+-----------+
|Mr     | Kevin | Carney | 43 Glen Way   | Lincoln | LI2 7RD | 786 3454  |
|Mr     | Brian | Waters | 21 Troon Rise | Lincoln | LI7 6GT | 786 7243  |
+-------+-------+--------+---------------+---------+---------+-----------+
2 rows in set (0.00 sec)

mysql>
```

That looks correct; it finds the rows we need, and the columns are in the same order as the INSERT statement. So we can now put the two statements together, and execute them, like this:

```
mysql> INSERT INTO customer(title, fname, lname, addressline, town, zipcode,
phone) SELECT title, fname, lname, addressline, town, zipcode, phone FROM tcust
WHERE phone != "";
Query OK, 2 rows affected (0.01 sec)
Records: 2  Duplicates: 0  Warnings: 0

mysql>
```

Notice mysql tells us that two rows have been inserted.

How It Works

We specified the columns we wanted to load in the `customer` table, and then selected the same set of data, in the same order as the `tcust` table. To allow MySQL to create unique `customer_ids` for us, we did not specify those but allow MySQL to generate them for us.

An alternative method, particularly if there is a lot of data to load, you may find it easier to add an additional column, perhaps a column `isvalid` of type `INT`, to the load table. You then load all the data into the load table, and set all the `isvalid` values to '0', using the `UPDATE` statement that we will meet more formally a little later:

```
UPDATE tcust SET isvalid = 0;
```

We have not specified a `WHERE` clause, so all rows have the `isvalid` column set to 0. We can then work on the data and for each 'good' row update, set the `isvalid` column to 1, and then load corrected data, selecting only the rows where `isvalid` is 1. Once these rows are loaded, we can remove them (we will meet the `DELETE` statement in more detail near the end of this chapter) from the `tcust` table, like this:

```
DELETE FROM tcust WHERE isvalid = 1;
```

We can then continue to work on the remaining data in the `tcust` table.

Updating Data in the Database

Now we know how to get data into the database by using `INSERT`, and how to retrieve it again, using `SELECT`. Unfortunately, data does not remain the same for very long. For example, people move house and change phone numbers in which case the date needs to be changed. We need a way of updating the data in the database. In MySQL, as in all SQL-based databases, this is done with the `UPDATE` statement. The `UPDATE` statement is remarkably simple. Its syntax is:

```
UPDATE tablename SET columnname = value WHERE condition
```

If we want to set several columns at the same time, we simply specify them as a comma-separated list, like this:

```
UPDATE customer SET town = 'Leicester', zipcode = 'LE4 2WQ'
     WHERE some condition
```

We can update as many columns simultaneously as we like, providing each column only appears once. You will notice that you can only use a single table name. This is due to the syntax of SQL. In the rare event that you need to update two separate but related tables, you must write two separate `UPDATE` statements.

Try It Out – The UPDATE Statement

Suppose we have now tracked down the phone number of `Mr. Bradley`, and want to update the data into our load table `tcust`. The first part of the `UPDATE` statement is easy:

```
UPDATE tcust SET phone = '352 3442'
```

Now we need to specify the row to update, which is simply:

```
WHERE fname = 'Peter' and lname = 'Bradley'
```

With UPDATE statements, it is always a good idea to check the WHERE clause. Let's do that now:

```
mysql> SELECT fname, lname, phone FROM tcust
    -> WHERE fname = 'Peter' AND lname = 'Bradley';
+-------+---------+---------+
| fname | lname   | phone   |
+-------+---------+---------+
| Peter | Bradley |         |
+-------+---------+---------+
1 row in set (0.00 sec)

mysql>
```

We can see that the single row we want to update is being selected, so we can go ahead and put the two halves of the statement together and execute it:

```
mysql> UPDATE tcust SET phone = '352 3442'
    -> WHERE fname = 'Peter' AND lname = 'Bradley';
Query OK, 1 row affected (0.00 sec)
Rows matched: 1  Changed: 1  Warnings: 0

mysql>
```

MySQL tells us that one row has been updated, and we could, if we wanted, re-execute our SELECT statement to check that all is well.

How It Works

We built our UPDATE statement in two stages. First, we wrote the UPDATE command part that would actually change the column value, then we wrote the WHERE clause to specify which rows to update. After testing the WHERE clause, we executed the UPDATE, which changed the row as required.

A Word of Warning

Why were we so careful to test the WHERE clause before executing the first part of the UPDATE statement? The answer is: because it is perfectly valid to have an UPDATE statement without a WHERE clause. By default, UPDATE will then update all rows in the table, which is almost never what was intended. It can also be quite hard to correct.

The tcust table contains just temporary experimental data, therefore let's just test out an UPDATE with no WHERE clause:

```
mysql> UPDATE tcust SET phone = '999 9999';
Query OK, 3 rows affected (0.00 sec)
Rows matched: 3  Changed: 3  Warnings: 0

mysql>
```

Notice that `mysql` has told us that 3 rows have been updated.

Now look at what we have:

```
mysql> SELECT fname, lname, phone FROM tcust;
+-------+---------+----------+
| fname | lname   | phone    |
+-------+---------+----------+
| Peter | Bradley | 999 9999 |
| Kevin | Carney  | 999 9999 |
| Brian | Waters  | 999 9999 |
+-------+---------+----------+
3 rows in set (0.00 sec)

mysql>
```

Almost certainly not what we wanted!

> **Always test the WHERE clause of UPDATE statements before executing them.**

If you do intend to update many rows, then rather than retrieving all the data, you can simply check how many rows you are matching using the COUNT(*) syntax, which we will meet in more detail in the next chapter. For now, all you need to know is that replacing the column names in a SELECT statement with COUNT(*) will tell you how many rows were matched, rather than returning the data in the rows. In fact, that's about all there is to the COUNT(*) statement, but it does turn out to be quite useful in practice.

As an example, here is our SELECT statement, just checking how many rows are matched by the WHERE clause:

```
mysql> SELECT count(*) from tcust
    -> WHERE fname = 'Peter' AND lname = 'Bradley';
+----------+
| count(*) |
+----------+
|        1 |
+----------+
1 row in set (0.00 sec)

mysql>
```

This tells us that the WHERE clause is sufficiently restrictive to specify a single row. Of course, with different data, even specifying both fname and lname may not be sufficient to uniquely identify a row.

Deleting Data from the Database

The last thing we need to learn about in this chapter, is deleting data from tables. Prospective customers may never actually place an order; orders get cancelled, so we often need to delete data from the database.

The normal way of deleting data is to use the DELETE statement. This has syntax similar to the UPDATE statement:

```
DELETE FROM tablename WHERE condition
```

Notice that there are no columns listed, since DELETE works on rows. If you want to remove data from a column you must use the UPDATE statement to set the value of the column to NULL, or some other appropriate value.

Now that we have copied our data for our two new customers from tcust to our live customer table, we can go ahead and delete those rows from our tcust table.

Try It Out – The DELETE Statement

Now we know just how dangerous omitting the WHERE clause in statements that change data can be. We can appreciate that accidentally deleting data is even more serious, so we will start by writing and checking our WHERE clause using a SELECT statement:

```
mysql> SELECT fname, lname FROM tcust WHERE town = 'Lincoln';
+-------+--------+
| fname | lname  |
+-------+--------+
| Kevin | Carney |
| Brian | Waters |
+-------+--------+
2 rows in set (0.00 sec)

mysql>
```

That's good – it retrieves the two rows we were expecting.

Now we can prefix the DELETE statement on the front and, after a last visual check that it looks correct, execute it:

```
mysql> DELETE FROM tcust WHERE town = 'Lincoln';
Query OK, 2 rows affected (0.00 sec)

mysql>
```

> **Deleting from the database is that easy, so be very careful!**

How It Works

We wrote, and tested, a WHERE clause to choose the rows that we wanted to delete from the database. We then executed a DELETE statement that deleted them.

Just like UPDATE and INSERT, DELETE can only work on a single table at any one time. If we ever need to manipulate related rows from more than one table we will use a **transaction**, which we will meet in Chapter 9, *Transactions and Locking*.

In the special case of wanting to delete all rows from a table, we simply don't specify a WHERE clause. In this special case, MySQL notices the lack of a WHERE clause and provides a special efficient version of the DELETE statement. The drawback of this form is that it won't tell you how many rows have been deleted, although this isn't usually particularly important. An alternative way of writing this in a more recent version of MySQL is to use the TRUNCATE statement, which is a common SQL extension.

A significant drawback of TRUNCATE is that transactions cannot 'undo' a TRUNCATE. Once the table is truncated, the data is gone forever – unless you remembered to do some backups! For this reason you should only perform TRUNCATE statements after you execute transactions.

Try It Out – The TRUNCATE Statement

Suppose we have now finished with our tcust table, and want to delete all the data in it. What we could do is drop the table, but then if we needed it again we would have to re-create it. Instead, we can TRUNCATE it to drop all the rows in the table:

```
mysql> TRUNCATE TABLE tcust;
Query OK, 0 rows affected (0.01 sec)
```

```
mysql> SELECT * FROM tcust;
Empty set (0.00 sec)

mysql>
```

All the rows are now deleted.

How It Works

TRUNCATE simply deletes all the rows from the specified table. Notice that it doesn't tell you the number of rows actually deleted, it says 0 however many rows were actually removed.

> There are two ways to delete all the rows from a table – **DELETE** without a **WHERE** clause, and **TRUNCATE**. **TRUNCATE**, although not in SQL-92, is a very common SQL statement for efficiently deleting all rows from a table.

Summary

In this chapter, we have looked at the three other parts of data manipulation, along with SELECT: the ability to add data with the INSERT command; modify data with the UPDATE command; and finally, remove data with the DELETE command.

We learned about the two forms of the INSERT command, with data explicitly included in the INSERT statement, or INSERT from data SELECTed from another table. We saw how it is safer to use the longer form of the INSERT statement, where all columns are listed, so there is less chance of mistakes. We also met INSERT's cousin command, the rather useful MySQL extension LOAD DATA and its command line cousin, mysqlimport, which allows data to be inserted into a table directly from a file.

We then learnt about these simple UPDATE and DELETE statements, and how you use them with WHERE clauses, just like the SELECT statement. We also mentioned that you should always test UPDATE and DELETE statements with WHERE clauses using a SELECT statement, as mistakes here can cause problems that are difficult to rectify.

Finally, we looked at the TRUNCATE statement, a very efficient way of deleting all rows from a table, but since it is an irrevocable deletion and not managed by transactions, it should only be used with caution.

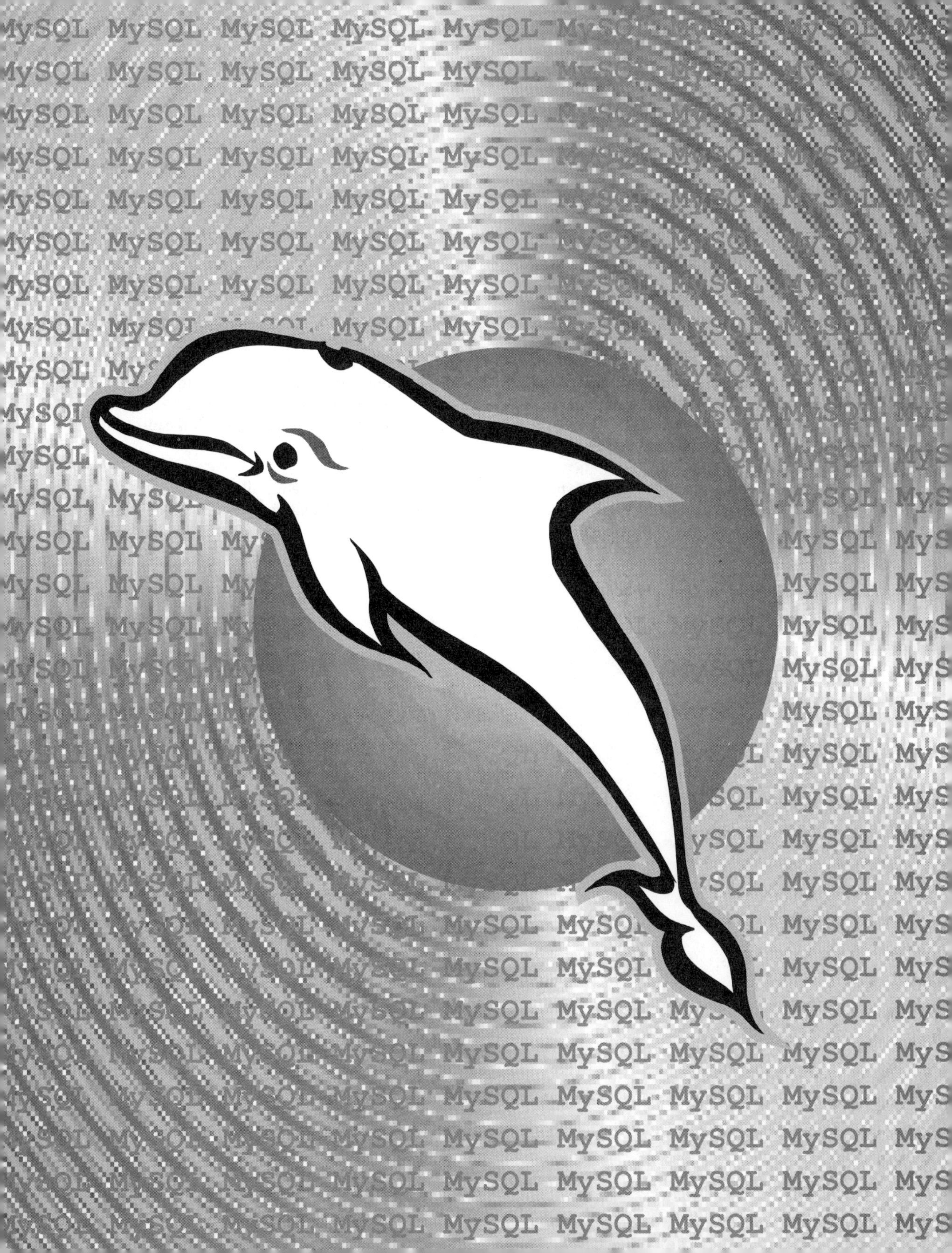
MySQL

Advanced Data Selection

In Chapter 4, *Accessing Your Data*, we looked in detail at the SELECT statement and how we can use it to retrieve data. This included selecting columns, selecting rows, and joining tables together. Subsequently in Chapter 6, *Changing your Data*, we looked at ways of adding, updating, and removing data. In this chapter we again return to the SELECT statement, this time to look at its more advanced features.

Like in other chapters, we will start with clean data in the example database. Here, we will meet some special functions called **aggregates**, which allow us to get results based on a group of rows. We will then meet some advanced **joins**, which let us control results. We will meet the very important 'outer join' that allows us to join tables together in a more flexible way than we have seen so far.

Finally, we will also meet a whole new group of queries called **subqueries**, where we use multiple SELECT statements in a single query. Unfortunately, at the time of writing, MySQL does not support subqueries, so we will present them in a theoretical way, then we will look at alternative SQL, which will allow us to get the results we need using the slightly more restrictive MySQL syntax. However, subqueries will be added to MySQL in the near future, so check the MySQL web site for the latest status.

In this chapter, we'll be looking at:

- ❑ Aggregate functions
- ❑ The UNION joins
- ❑ Self joins
- ❑ Outer joins
- ❑ Subqueries
- ❑ Replacing subqueries with alternatives

Aggregate Functions

In earlier chapters we have used a couple of special functions – the MAX() function to tell us the largest value in a column, and the COUNT(*) function to tell us the number of rows in a table. These functions belong to a small group of SQL functions called aggregates.

The important functions in this group are:

❑ COUNT(*)

❑ COUNT(column name)

❑ MIN(column name)

❑ MAX(column name)

❑ SUM(column name)

❑ AVG(column name)

They are useful and generally easy to use. We will now look at them in detail.

COUNT()

We will start by looking at COUNT(), which, as you will see from the list above, has two forms – COUNT(*) and COUNT(column name). The COUNT(*) function provides a row count for a table. It acts as a special column name in a SELECT statement. SELECT statements using any of these two aggregate functions can also use two optional clauses, which are GROUP BY and HAVING. The syntax is:

```
SELECT COUNT(*) column list FROM table name WHERE condition
       [GROUP BY column name [HAVING aggregate condition]]
```

The optional clause GROUP BY is an additional condition that can be applied to SELECT statements. It is normally useful only when an aggregate function is being used. It can also be used to provide a function similar to ORDER BY, but by working on the aggregate column. The optional HAVING clause allows us to pick out particular rows where the COUNT(*) meets some condition.

The COUNT(*) function is more efficient than retrieving the entire data set, for two reasons:

❑ No data that we don't need to see has to be retrieved from the database, or worse still, sent across a network.

❑ COUNT(*) allows the database to use its internal knowledge of the table to retrieve the answer, quite probably without actually inspecting any real data rows at all.

> **You should never retrieve data when all you need is a count of the number of rows.**

This all sounds a bit complicated, but it's actually quite easy in practice. Let's try out a very simple COUNT(*) just to get the basic idea. We will see GROUP BY in use shortly.

Try It Out – Basic Use of COUNT(*)

Suppose we wanted to know how many customers we have in our `customer` table who live in the town of Bingham. We could of course simply write a SQL query like this:

```
SELECT * FROM customer WHERE town = 'Bingham';
```

Or rather more efficiently, since it returns fewer columns, we write the SQL query like this:

```
SELECT customer_id FROM customer WHERE town = 'Bingham';
```

This will show the number of rows MySQL returns, but in a rather round about way. It also involves retrieving a lot of data we don't actually need. Suppose we had a `customer` table with many thousands of customers, with perhaps over a thousand of them living in Bingham. In such case, we would be retrieving a great deal of data that we don't need. The COUNT(*) function solves this for us, by allowing us to retrieve just a single row with the count of the number of selected rows in it. We write our SELECT statement as we normally do, but instead of selecting the actual columns we use COUNT(*) to execute this:

```
mysql> SELECT COUNT(*) FROM customer WHERE town = 'Bingham';
+----------+
| COUNT(*) |
+----------+
|        3 |
+----------+
1 row in set (0.02 sec)

mysql>
```

If we want to count all the customers, then just omit the WHERE clause:

```
mysql> SELECT COUNT(*) FROM customer;
+----------+
| COUNT(*) |
+----------+
|       15 |
+----------+
1 row in set (0.00 sec)

mysql>
```

You can see we just get a single row, with the count of customers in it. If you want to check the answer, just replace COUNT(*) with `customer_id` to show the real data.

How It Works

The function COUNT(*) allows us to retrieve a count of objects, rather than the objects themselves.

If we want to give a name to the column, we can also do that by using the AS clause we saw in the previous chapter:

181

```
mysql> SELECT COUNT(*) AS 'Total Customers' FROM customer;
+-----------------+
| Total Customers |
+-----------------+
|              15 |
+-----------------+
1 row in set (0.00 sec)

mysql>
```

GROUP BY and COUNT(*)

The answer we got in the previous section is almost what we want, but not quite. Suppose we wanted to know how many customers live in each town. We could do it by selecting all the distinct towns, and then counting how many customers we had in each town. This is a rather procedural and tedious way of solving the problem. Wouldn't it be better to have a declarative way of simply expressing the question directly in SQL? You might be tempted to try something like this:

```
SELECT COUNT(*), town FROM customer;
```

It's a reasonable guess based on what we know so far, but MySQL will produce an error message, as it is not valid SQL syntax:

```
mysql> SELECT COUNT(*), town FROM customer;
ERROR 1140: Mixing of GROUP columns (MIN(),MAX(),COUNT()...) with no GROUP columns
is illegal if there is no GROUP BY clause

mysql>
```

The additional bit of syntax you need to know to solve this problem, as the error message suggests, is the GROUP BY clause.

The GROUP BY clause tells the database that we want an aggregate function to accumulate counts for each distinct value in a specified column, or columns, and display the totals separately. It's very easy to use. You simply add a GROUP BY column name to the SELECT with a COUNT(*) function. MySQL will tell you how many of each value of your column exist in the table.

Try It Out – GROUP BY

Let's try and answer the question "how many customers live in each town?" using the GROUP BY clause.

Stage one is to write the SELECT statement to retrieve the count and column name, just like you may have guessed as before:

```
SELECT COUNT(*), town FROM customer
```

We then add the GROUP BY clause, to tell MySQL to produce a result and reset the count each time the town name changes by issuing a SQL query like this:

```
SELECT COUNT(*), town FROM customer GROUP BY town;
```

Here it is in action:

```
mysql> SELECT COUNT(*), town FROM customer GROUP BY town;
+----------+-----------+
| COUNT(*) | town      |
+----------+-----------+
|        3 | Bingham   |
|        1 | Hightown  |
|        1 | Histon    |
|        1 | Lowtown   |
|        1 | Milltown  |
|        2 | Nicetown  |
|        1 | Oahenham  |
|        1 | Oxbridge  |
|        1 | Tibsville |
|        1 | Welltown  |
|        1 | Winersby  |
|        1 | Yuleville |
+----------+-----------+
12 rows in set (0.01 sec)

mysql>
```

As you can see, we get a nice listing of towns and the number of customers in each town.

How It Works

MySQL orders the result by the column listed in the GROUP BY clause. It then keeps a running total of rows, and each time the town name changes, it writes a result row, and resets its counter to zero. This is much easier, and more efficient, than writing procedural code to loop through each town.

We can extend this idea to more than one column if we want to, providing all the columns we select are also listed in the GROUP BY. Suppose we wanted to know two pieces of information. Firstly, how many customers are in each town, and secondly, how many different last names they have. We would simply add lname to both the SELECT and GROUP BY parts of the statement:

```
mysql> SELECT count(*), lname, town FROM customer GROUP BY town, lname;
+----------+---------+-----------+
| count(*) | lname   | town      |
+----------+---------+-----------+
|        1 | Jones   | Bingham   |
|        2 | Stones  | Bingham   |
|        1 | Stones  | Hightown  |
|        1 | Hickman | Histon    |
|        1 | Stones  | Lowtown   |
|        1 | Hudson  | Milltown  |
|        2 | Matthew | Nicetown  |
|        1 | Cozens  | Oahenham  |
|        1 | Hendy   | Oxbridge  |
|        1 | Howard  | Tibsville |
|        1 | O'Neill | Welltown  |
|        1 | Neill   | Winersby  |
|        1 | Matthew | Yuleville |
+----------+---------+-----------+
13 rows in set (0.00 sec)

mysql>
```

183

Notice that the output is sorted first by `town`, then `lname`, since that is the order they are listed in the `GROUP BY` clause. Also Bingham is now listed twice, because there are customers with two different last names, 'Jones' and 'Stones' who live in Bingham.

HAVING and COUNT(*)

The last optional part of the statement is the `HAVING` clause. This clause often causes some confusion among people new to SQL, but it's not difficult to use. You just have to remember that `HAVING` is the equivalent of the `WHERE` clause, but only valid for aggregate functions. It fulfils the same purpose as `WHERE`, but with relation to `GROUP BY` clauses rather than simple column values, because it gives the appearance of selecting the separate 'pots' that the data's been grouped into. We use `HAVING` to restrict the results returned to rows where a particular aggregate condition is true, such as `COUNT(*)` is >1. We use it in just the same way as `WHERE` to restrict the rows based on the value of a column.

> Aggregates cannot be used in a **WHERE** clause; they are valid only inside the **HAVING** clause.

Let's look at an example, which should make it clear. Suppose we want to know all the towns where we have more than a single customer, we could do it using `COUNT(*)`, then visually looking for the relevant towns. That's not a sensible solution in a situation where there may be thousands of towns. Instead, we use a `HAVING` clause to restrict the answers to rows where `COUNT(*)` was greater than one, like this:

```
mysql> SELECT COUNT(*), town FROM customer GROUP BY town
    -> HAVING COUNT(*) > 1;
+----------+----------+
| COUNT(*) | town     |
+----------+----------+
|        3 | Bingham  |
|        2 | Nicetown |
+----------+----------+
2 rows in set (0.01 sec)

mysql>
```

Notice that we must still have our `GROUP BY` clause, and that it appears before the `HAVING` clause. Now that we have all the basics of `COUNT(*)`, `GROUP BY`, and `HAVING`, let's put them together in a bigger example.

Try It Out – COUNT (*), GROUP BY, and HAVING

Suppose we are thinking of setting up a delivery schedule. We want to know the last names and towns of all our customers, except that we want to exclude Lincoln (maybe it's our local town), and we are only interested in last names that occur more than once in any given town.

This is not as difficult as it might sound; we just need to build up our solution bit-by-bit. This is often a good approach with SQL. If it looks too difficult, then start by solving a simpler but similar problem, and then extend the initial solution until you solve the more complex problem. Effectively, take a problem, break it down into smaller parts, and then solve each of these.

Let's start with simply returning the data, rather than counting it:

```
mysql> SELECT lname, town FROM customer WHERE town <> 'Lincoln';
+---------+-----------+
| lname   | town      |
+---------+-----------+
| Stones  | Hightown  |
| Stones  | Lowtown   |
| Matthew | Nicetown  |
| Matthew | Yuleville |
| Cozens  | Oahenham  |
| Matthew | Nicetown  |
| Stones  | Bingham   |
| Stones  | Bingham   |
| Hickman | Histon    |
| Howard  | Tibsville |
| Jones   | Bingham   |
| Neill   | Winersby  |
| Hendy   | Oxbridge  |
| O'Neill | Welltown  |
| Hudson  | Milltown  |
+---------+-----------+
15 rows in set (0.00 sec)
mysql>
```

So far, so good. Now if we use COUNT(*) to do the counting for us, we also need to GROUP BY the lname and town:

```
mysql> SELECT COUNT(*), lname, town FROM customer WHERE town <> 'Lincoln'
    -> GROUP BY lname, town;
+----------+---------+-----------+
| COUNT(*) | lname   | town      |
+----------+---------+-----------+
|        1 | Cozens  | Oahenham  |
|        1 | Hendy   | Oxbridge  |
|        1 | Hickman | Histon    |
|        1 | Howard  | Tibsville |
|        1 | Hudson  | Milltown  |
|        1 | Jones   | Bingham   |
|        2 | Matthew | Nicetown  |
|        1 | Matthew | Yuleville |
|        1 | Neill   | Winersby  |
|        1 | O'Neill | Welltown  |
|        2 | Stones  | Bingham   |
|        1 | Stones  | Hightown  |
|        1 | Stones  | Lowtown   |
+----------+---------+-----------+
13 rows in set (0.00 sec)

mysql>
```

The last part of this exercise is to see how to use a HAVING clause to identify last names that occur more than once in any town. We can actually see the answer now by visual inspection, but we are almost at the final answer. We do this simply by adding a HAVING clause to pick out those rows with a COUNT(*) greater than one:

```
mysql> SELECT COUNT(*), lname, town FROM customer
    -> WHERE town <> 'Lincoln' GROUP BY lname, town HAVING COUNT(*) > 1;
+----------+---------+----------+
| COUNT(*) | lname   | town     |
+----------+---------+----------+
|        2 | Matthew | Nicetown |
|        2 | Stones  | Bingham  |
+----------+---------+----------+
2 rows in set (0.00 sec)

mysql>
```

As you can see, stepwise refinement of a reasonable straightforward piece of SQL has allowed us to get to our answer.

How It Works

We solved our problem in three stages:

❑   We wrote a simple SELECT statement to retrieve all the rows we were interested in.

❑   Next, we added a COUNT(*) and a GROUP BY, to count the different lname and town combinations.

❑   Finally, we added a HAVING clause to extract only those rows where the COUNT(*) was greater than one.

There is one slight problem with this approach. If we were working with a customer database containing thousands of rows, we could have had customer lists scrolling past for a very long time while we developed our query. For our sample database it was not a problem, but on a big database this iterative development approach has some other drawbacks. Fortunately, there is often an easy way to develop your queries on a sample of the data, which is by using the primary key. If we add the condition WHERE customer_id < 50 to all our queries, we could work on a sample of the first 50 customer_ids in the database. Alternatively we could use the MySQL extension, LIMIT (which we have met in Chapter 4) to restrict the number of rows returned, like this:

```
mysql> SELECT lname, town FROM customer WHERE town <> 'Lincoln' LIMIT 5;
+---------+-----------+
| lname   | town      |
+---------+-----------+
| Stones  | Hightown  |
| Stones  | Lowtown   |
| Matthew | Nicetown  |
| Matthew | Yuleville |
| Cozens  | Oahenham  |
+---------+-----------+
5 rows in set (0.01 sec)

mysql>
```

COUNT(column name)

As we mentioned earlier in this chapter, another slight variant of the COUNT(*) is to replace the '*' with a column name. The difference is that COUNT(column name) only counts occurrences in the table where the value in the specified column is not NULL.

Suppose we add some more data to our customer table, with some of the new customers having NULL telephone numbers:

```
INSERT INTO customer(title, fname, lname, addressline, town, zipcode)
        VALUES('Mr','Clive','Jones','23 Harlestone','Milltown','MT7 7HI');
INSERT INTO customer(title, fname, lname, addressline, town, zipcode, phone)
        VALUES('Mrs','Sarah','Harvey','84 Willow Way','Lincoln','LC3
        7RD','5273739');
INSERT INTO customer(title, fname, lname, addressline, town, zipcode)
        VALUES('Mr','Steve','Harvey','84 Willow Way','Lincoln','LC3 7RD');
INSERT INTO customer(title, fname, lname, addressline, town, zipcode)
        VALUES('Mr','Matthew','Harvey', '84 Willow Way','Lincoln','LC3 7RD');
```

Let's check how many customers we have for whom we don't have a phone number:

```
mysql> SELECT customer_id FROM customer WHERE phone IS NULL;
+-------------+
| customer_id |
+-------------+
|          16 |
|          18 |
|          19 |
+-------------+
3 rows in set (0.01 sec)

mysql>
```

We see that there are three customers for whom we don't have a phone number. Let's see how many customers there are in total:

```
mysql> SELECT COUNT(*) FROM customer;
+----------+
| COUNT(*) |
+----------+
|       19 |
+----------+
1 row in set (0.00 sec)

mysql>
```

Now if we count the number of customers where the phone column is not NULL, by specifying the phone column in the COUNT, hopefully there will be 16 of them:

```
mysql> SELECT COUNT(phone) FROM customer;
+--------------+
| COUNT(phone) |
+--------------+
|           16 |
+--------------+
1 row in set (0.00 sec)

mysql>
```

That's the only difference between COUNT(*) and COUNT(column name). The form with an explicit column name counts only rows where the named column is not NULL whereas the '*' form counts all rows.

The MIN() Function

Now that we understand COUNT(*) and have learned the principles of aggregate functions, we can apply the same logic to the other aggregate functions.

As you might expect, MIN() takes a column name parameter, and returns the minimum value found in that column. For numeric type columns the result would be as expected. For temporal types, such as date, it returns the earliest date from the column, which might be either in the past or future. To be on the safer side, ensure that your dates all use 4 digit years (see the example under the MAX() function in the next section).

For variable length strings, the result is slightly unexpected; it compares the strings after they have been right padded with blanks. Be wary of using MIN() or MAX() on VARCHAR type columns, the results may not always be exactly what you expect. Here are a couple of examples.

Find the smallest shipping charge we levied on an order:

```
mysql> SELECT MIN(shipping) FROM orderinfo;
+---------------+
| MIN(shipping) |
+---------------+
|          0.00 |
+---------------+
1 row in set (0.00 sec)

mysql>
```

It was, in fact, zero. Notice what happens when we try the same function on our phone column, where we know there are NULL values:

```
mysql> SELECT MIN(phone) FROM customer;
+------------+
| MIN(phone) |
+------------+
| 010 4567   |
+------------+
1 row in set (0.00 sec)

mysql>
```

Now you might perhaps have expected the answer to be NULL, or an empty string.

> Given that NULL generally means unknown, the function can not know whether the NULL value is the smallest in the table, so the MIN() function ignores NULL values. Ignoring NULL values is a feature of all the aggregate functions, except COUNT(*).

The MAX() Function

It's not going to be a surprise that the MAX() function is similar to MIN(), but in reverse, so we will not give more explanation, we will just look at some examples.

As you might expect, MAX() takes a column name parameter, and returns the maximum value found in that column. Here are some examples.

Find the largest shipping charge we levied on an order:

```
mysql> SELECT MAX(shipping) FROM orderinfo;
+---------------+
| MAX(shipping) |
+---------------+
|          3.99 |
+---------------+
1 row in set (0.00 sec)

mysql>
```

Just like in MIN(), NULL values are ignored in this case:

```
mysql> SELECT MAX(phone) FROM customer;
+------------+
| MAX(phone) |
+------------+
| 961 4526   |
+------------+
1 row in set (0.00 sec)

mysql>
```

In case of dates, the 'latest' date is returned. You do need to ensure your date or timestamp field uses four digit years for this to work properly. Adding an offset of zero using the DATE_ADD() function, which always returns a format with four digit years, can do this for us:

```
mysql> select MAX(DATE_ADD(date_placed, INTERVAL 0 DAY)) from orderinfo;
+-------------------------------------------+
| MAX(DATE_ADD(date_placed,INTERVAL 0 DAY)) |
+-------------------------------------------+
| 2000-09-03                                |
+-------------------------------------------+
1 row in set (0.01 sec)

mysql>
```

We didn't actually need the conversion in this case, since `date_placed` is already in a format with four digit years, but it does serve as an illustration.

That is pretty much all you need to know about `MAX()`, except that you can also use `GROUP BY` and `HAVING` clauses, just like with `COUNT(*)`.

The SUM() Function

The `SUM()` function takes the name of a numeric column and provides the total. Just like we saw in the case of `MIN()` and `MAX()`, `NULL` values are ignored:

```
mysql> SELECT SUM(shipping) FROM orderinfo;
+---------------+
| SUM(shipping) |
+---------------+
|          9.97 |
+---------------+
1 row in set (0.01 sec)

mysql>
```

The AVG() Function

The last aggregate function is `AVG()`, which also takes a column name and returns the average of the entries. Like `SUM()`, it also ignores `NULL` values:

```
mysql> SELECT AVG(shipping) FROM orderinfo;
+---------------+
| AVG(shipping) |
+---------------+
|      1.994000 |
+---------------+
1 row in set (0.00 sec)

mysql>
```

Note that in standard SQL it is possible to add a `DISTINCT` clause inside the aggregate function, which makes the functions look only at distinct values, ignoring duplicates. This can be useful with the `AVG()` function, but is not currently supported by MySQL.

The Union Join

We are now going to look at the way multiple SELECT statements can be combined to give us more advanced selection capabilities.

Remember the tcust table that we used as a load table in the last chapter, while adding data into our main customer table. Suppose that, in the time period between loading our tcust table with new customer data and being able to clean it and load it into our main customer table, we had been asked for a list of all the towns where we had customers with the new data. In which case, since we hadn't cleaned and loaded the customer data into the main table yet, we would not be sure of the accuracy of the new data, so any list of towns combining the two lists would not be accurate either. At any rate, in our example, perhaps all that was needed was a general indication of the geographic spread of customers, not exact data, in which case accuracy isn't so important.

We could solve this problem by selecting the town column from the customer table, saving it, and then selecting the town column from the tcust table, saving it again, and then combining the two lists. This does seem rather inelegant as we already have two tables, both with a town column.

Isn't there some way we could combine the list? As you might gather from the title of this section, there is a way, and it's called a UNION join. These joins are not very common, but in a few circumstances they are exactly what is needed to solve a problem. Also, they are also very easy to use.

The UNION join is a recent addition to MySQL, so if you are running a version before 4.0 you may find they are not supported in your current version.

Let's put some data back in our tcust table, so it looks like this:

```
mysql> SELECT fname, lname, town FROM tcust;
+-------+-----------+-------------+
| fname | lname     | town        |
+-------+-----------+-------------+
| Peter | Bradley   | Keynes      |
| Kevin | Carney    | Lincoln     |
| Brian | Waters    | Lincoln     |
| Julie | Hardcastle| Marlborough |
+-------+-----------+-------------+
4 rows in set (0.00 sec)

mysql>
```

Compare getting our list of towns from this table and our customer table.

We already know how to select the town from each table. We use a very simple pair of SELECT statements, like this:

```
SELECT town FROM tcust;
SELECT town FROM customer;
```

each of which gives us a list of towns. We combine the two using a UNION operator.

We simply use the two SELECT statements, stitched together with a UNION join:

```
mysql> SELECT town FROM tcust UNION SELECT town FROM customer;
+-------------+
| town        |
+-------------+
| Keynes      |
| Lincoln     |
| Marlborough |
| Hightown    |
| Lowtown     |
| Nicetown    |
| Yuleville   |
| Oahenham    |
| Bingham     |
| Histon      |
| Tibsville   |
| Winersby    |
| Oxbridge    |
| Welltown    |
| Milltown    |
+-------------+
15 rows in set (0.01 sec)

mysql>
```

How It Works

MySQL has taken the list of towns from both tables and combined them into a single list. Notice that it has removed all duplicates. If we wanted a list of all towns, including the duplicates, we could have written UNION ALL, like this:

```
SELECT town FROM tcust UNION ALL SELECT town FROM customer;
```

This ability to combine SELECT statements is not limited to a single column; we could have combined both the towns and zip codes:

```
SELECT town, zipcode FROM tcust UNION SELECT town, zipcode FROM customer;
```

This would have produced a list with both columns present. It would have been a longer list, because the zipcode column is included, and hence there are more unique rows to be retrieved.

When you use a UNION join, the two lists of columns you ask to be combined from the two tables must each have the same number of columns, and the chosen corresponding columns must also have compatible types. It is important to note that the columns in the two SELECT statements are combined by position, not name, so you must get the columns in the same order. Look what happens when we select different columns from the two tables:

```
mysql> SELECT title FROM tcust UNION SELECT town FROM customer;
+-------+
| title |
+-------+
| Mr    |
| Miss  |
| High  |
| Lowt  |
| Nice  |
| Yule  |
| Oahe  |
| Bing  |
| Hist  |
| Tibs  |
| Wine  |
| Oxbr  |
| Well  |
| Mill  |
| Linc  |
+-------+
15 rows in set (0.00 sec)

mysql>
```

Although the query makes little logical sense, it is quite legal. MySQL simply combines the columns and shows the result in the output.

Generally, that is all you need to know about UNION joins; they are occasionally a very handy way to combine data from two (or more) tables.

The Self Join

One very special type of join is called a **self join**, and is used where we want to use a join between columns that are in the same table. The need to use this is quite rare but occasionally it is very useful, so we will mention it briefly here.

Suppose we sell items that can be sold individually or as a set. For the sake of example, let us suppose we sell a set of chairs and table item, and also sell the table and chairs as individual items. What we would like to do is store not only the individual items, but also the relationship between them when they are sold as a single item. This is frequently called 'parts explosion'. We will meet it again later in Chapter 11, *Database Design*, when we look at what are commonly called 'recursive' relationships, or more formally 'reflexive' relationships.

Let's start by creating a table called part that can hold not only an item_id and its description, but also a second item_id, like this:

```
mysql> CREATE TABLE part (part_id INT, description VARCHAR(32),
    -> parent_part_id INT);
```

We will use the `parent_part_id` to store the component id, of which this is a component. For example, suppose we had a table and chairs set, say `item_id` 1, which was composed of chairs, say `item_id` 2, and a table, say `item_id` 3. The `INSERT` statements, when executed, would look like this:

```
mysql> INSERT INTO part(part_id, description, parent_part_id)
    -> VALUES(1, 'table and chairs', NULL);
Query OK, 1 row affected (0.00 sec)

mysql> INSERT INTO part(part_id, description, parent_part_id)
    -> VALUES(2, 'chair', 1);
Query OK, 1 row affected (0.00 sec)

mysql> INSERT INTO part(part_id, description, parent_part_id)
    -> VALUES(3, 'table', 1);
Query OK, 1 row affected (0.00 sec)

mysql>
```

Now we have stored the data, but how do we retrieve the information about what individual parts make up a particular component? We need to join the `part` table to itself.

This turns out to be quite easy. What we need to do first is alias the table names, and then write a `WHERE` clause referring to the same table, but using different names:

```
mysql> SELECT p1.description, p2.description FROM part p1, part p2
    -> WHERE p1.part_id = p2.parent_part_id;
+------------------+-------------+
| description      | description |
+------------------+-------------+
| table and chairs | chair       |
| table and chairs | table       |
+------------------+-------------+
2 rows in set (0.01 sec)

mysql>
```

This works, but is a little confusing, because we have two output columns with the same name. We can easily rectify this by renaming them using `AS`:

```
mysql> SELECT p1.description AS "Combined", p2.description AS "Parts"
    -> FROM part p1, part p2 WHERE p1.part_id = p2.parent_part_id;
+------------------+-------+
| Combined         | Parts |
+------------------+-------+
| table and chairs | chair |
| table and chairs | table |
+------------------+-------+
2 rows in set (0.00 sec)

mysql>
```

We will see self joins again in Chapter 11, when we look at how a manager/subordinate relationship can be stored in a single table.

The Outer Join

Our last major topic in this chapter is a class of joins known as **outer joins**. They are similar to more conventional joins, but use a slightly different syntax, which is why we had postponed meeting them till the end of this chapter.

Let's look at our `item` and `stock` tables:

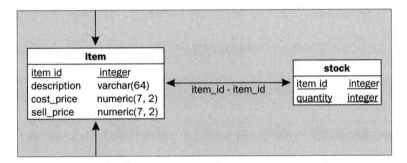

As you will remember, all the items that we might sell are held in the `item` table, but only the items we actually stock are held in the `stock` table.

Suppose we want to have a list of all items we sell, indicating the quantity we have in stock. This apparently simple request turns out to be surprisingly difficult in the SQL we know so far, though it can be done. It is quite instructive to work through a solution, so let's do it using only the SQL we know so far.

Let's try a simple `SELECT`, joining the two tables:

```
mysql> SELECT i.item_id, s.quantity FROM item i, stock s
    -> WHERE i.item_id = s.item_id;
+---------+----------+
| item_id | quantity |
+---------+----------+
|       1 |       12 |
|       2 |        2 |
|       4 |        8 |
|       5 |        3 |
|       7 |        8 |
|       8 |       18 |
|      10 |        1 |
+---------+----------+
7 rows in set (0.01 sec)

mysql>
```

It's easy to see (since we happen to know that our item_ids in the item table are sequential, with no gaps), that some item_ids are missing. The rows that are missing are those relating to items that we do not stock, hence the join between the item and stock tables fails for these rows, as the stock table has no entry for that item_id.

Suppose what we really wanted was a list of all the item_id entries, including a quantity in stock figure, even if we had no stock.

This turns out to be surprisingly difficult, though it can be done using a **subquery**. To solve this type of problem, vendors invented a type of SELECT called outer joins. Unfortunately, because it did not appear in the earlier version of the SQL standard, all the vendors invented their own solutions, with similar ideas, but different syntax.

Oracle and DB2 used a syntax where a '+' sign is used in the WHERE clause to indicate that all values of a table (the preserved table) must appear, even if the join fails. Sybase used a rather elegant syntax, using '*=' in the WHERE clause to indicate the preserved table. Both of these syntaxes are reasonably straightforward, but unfortunately different, which is not good for the portability of your SQL.

When the SQL92 standard appeared, it specified a very general-purpose way of implementing outer joins, which has a different syntax again. Vendors have been slow to implement the new standard. Sybase 11 did not support it, nor did Oracle version 8, though it was added in 2001, in version 9. PostgreSQL implemented the standard method from version 7.1 onwards, and the current version of MySQL (MySQL version 4.0) also has basic support for the standard form of outer joins, although not all of the more esoteric types of outer join are supported at the time of writing.

The SQL92 syntax for outer joins replaces the WHERE clause we are familiar with by an ON clause for joining tables, and adds the LEFT OUTER JOIN keywords.

The syntax looks like this:

```
SELECT columns FROM table1 LEFT OUTER JOIN table2
       ON table1.column = table2.column
```

The table name to the left of LEFT OUTER JOIN is always the preserved table, the one from which all rows are shown.

So now we can write our query, using this new syntax:

```
SELECT i.item_id, s.quantity FROM item i LEFT OUTER JOIN stock s
       ON i.item_id = s.item_id;
```

Let's give it a go:

```
mysql> SELECT i.item_id, s.quantity FROM item i LEFT OUTER JOIN stock s
    -> ON i.item_id = s.item_id;
+---------+----------+
| item_id | quantity |
+---------+----------+
|       1 |       12 |
|       2 |        2 |
|       3 |     NULL |
|       4 |        8 |
|       5 |        3 |
|       6 |     NULL |
|       7 |        8 |
|       8 |       18 |
|       9 |     NULL |
|      10 |        1 |
|      11 |     NULL |
+---------+----------+
11 rows in set (0.00 sec)

mysql>
```

There is also the equivalent RIGHT OUTER JOIN, not currently supported by MySQL, but in any case the LEFT OUTER JOIN is almost always the one that is used.

Try It Out – A More Complex Condition

The simple LEFT OUTER JOIN we have used till now is great as far as it goes, but how do we add more complex conditions?

Suppose that we are interested in the details of all items with a cost price greater than five, and we also want to know if we have more than two of the items in stock. This is quite a complex problem, because we want to apply one rule to the item table (that cost price is > 5.0) and a different rule to the stock table (quantity > 2), but we still want to list all rows from the item table where the condition on the item table is true, even if there is no stock at all.

What we do is combine ON conditions that work on left outer joined tables only with WHERE conditions that limit all the rows returned after the table join has been performed.

The condition on the stock table is part of the outer join. We don't want to restrict rows where there is no quantity, and so we write this as part of the ON condition:

```
ON i.item_id = s.item_id AND s.quantity > 2
```

For the item condition, which applies to all rows, we use a WHERE clause:

```
WHERE i.cost_price > 5.0;
```

Putting these conditions together, we get:

```
mysql> SELECT i.item_id, i.cost_price, s.quantity FROM item i
    -> LEFT OUTER JOIN stock s ON i.item_id = s.item_id AND s.quantity > 2
    -> WHERE i.cost_price > 5.0;
+---------+------------+----------+
| item_id | cost_price | quantity |
+---------+------------+----------+
|       1 |      15.23 |       12 |
|       2 |       7.45 |     NULL |
|       5 |       7.54 |        3 |
|       6 |       9.23 |     NULL |
|       7 |      13.36 |        8 |
|      11 |      19.73 |     NULL |
+---------+------------+----------+
6 rows in set (0.01 sec)

mysql>
```

How It Works

We use a LEFT OUTER JOIN between the item table and the stock table, so that we can select data from the item table, even if no related rows exist in the stock table. The condition stock.quantity > 2 prevents any values appearing in the quantity column unless there are at least 2 items in stock. The WHERE clause is then applied, which only allows through rows where the cost price (from the item table) is greater than five.

This is obviously a little contrived, but it does show how we can use a LEFT OUTER JOIN to display data from one table joined to a second table, even if the join can not be completed because there is no matching data in the second, or 'outer' table.

Subqueries

At the time of writing, MySQL does not support subqueries, although it is high on the 'to do' list. In this section we will cover subqueries in an introductory way and then look briefly at how you can achieve some of the same effects without using subqueries.

There is a class of SQL statements that combine two or more SELECT statements called subqueries or sometimes subselects. A subquery is where we make one (or more) of the WHERE conditions of a SELECT to be another SELECT statement. In other words, you can embed a SELECT statement inside a WHERE clause.

Suppose we want to find the items in our database that have a cost price that is higher than the average cost price of all items. We can easily do it in two queries:

```
mysql> SELECT AVG(cost_price) FROM item;
+-----------------+
| AVG(cost_price) |
+-----------------+
|        7.249091 |
+-----------------+
1 row in set (0.01 sec)

mysql> SELECT * FROM item WHERE cost_price > 7.249091;
```

```
+---------+---------------+------------+------------+
| item_id | description   | cost_price | sell_price |
+---------+---------------+------------+------------+
|       1 | Wood Puzzle   |      15.23 |      21.95 |
|       2 | Rubik Cube    |       7.45 |      11.49 |
|       5 | Picture Frame |       7.54 |       9.95 |
|       6 | Fan Small     |       9.23 |      15.75 |
|       7 | Fan Large     |      13.36 |      19.95 |
|      11 | Speakers      |      19.73 |      25.32 |
+---------+---------------+------------+------------+
6 rows in set (0.00 sec)

mysql>
```

This gets the answer we need, but is rather inelegant because we had to type the answer from the first query into the second query. What we really want to do is pass the result of the first query straight into the second query, without having to remember it and retype it. What we do is put the first query in brackets, and use it as part of a WHERE clause to the second query, like this:

```
SELECT * from ITEM WHERE cost_price > (SELECT AVG(cost_price) FROM item);
```

The result would be exactly the same as earlier, but without the intermediate step of having to remember and retype the result.

When an SQL engine sees a query like the one above, it runs the query in brackets first. After getting the answer, it then runs the outer query substituting the answer from the inner query. We can have many subqueries using various WHERE clauses if we want, though cases where we need multiple nested SELECT statements are rare.

Let's look at a more complex example. Suppose we want to know all the items where the cost price is above the average cost price, but the selling price is below the average selling price (something that probably suggests our margin is not very good, so hopefully there are not too many items that fit those criteria).

We already know how to find the average cost price – SELECT AVG(cost_price) FROM item. Finding the average selling price is similar – SELECT AVG(sell_price) FROM item.

The main query is going to be of the form:

```
SELECT * FROM item WHERE cost_price > average cost price AND sell_price < average
selling price
```

If we put these three queries together, what we get is:

```
SELECT * FROM item WHERE cost_price > (SELECT AVG(cost_price) FROM item)
        AND sell_price < (SELECT AVG(sell_price) FROM item);
```

This would be executed by first scanning the query to find that there are two queries in brackets, the subqueries. The database would then evaluate each of those subqueries independently, and then put the answers back into the appropriate part of the main query of the WHERE clause before executing it.

We could also have applied additional WHERE clauses, or ORDER BY clauses. It is perfectly valid in standard SQL to mix WHERE conditions that come from subqueries, with more conventional conditions.

199

Types of Subquery

So far we have only looked at subqueries that return a single result, as we used an aggregate function in the subquery, and these are by far the most common type of subquery. In general, subqueries can have three types of result:

❑   A single value (like those we have already seen)

❑   Zero or more rows

❑   A test for existence of something

Let's look at the second type of subquery, where several rows could be returned. Suppose we want to know what items we have in stock where the cost price is greater than ten. Now we could do this with a single SELECT statement, like this:

```
mysql> SELECT s.item_id, s.quantity FROM stock s, item i WHERE
    -> i.cost_price > 10.0 AND s.item_id = i.item_id;
+---------+----------+
| item_id | quantity |
+---------+----------+
|       1 |       12 |
|       7 |        8 |
+---------+----------+
2 rows in set (0.07 sec)

mysql>
```

Notice that we give the tables alias names (stock becomes s, item becomes i) to keep the query shorter. All we are doing is joining the two tables (s.item_id = i.item_id), while also adding a condition about the cost price in the item table (i.cost_price > 10.0).

We can also write this as a subquery, using the keyword IN to test against a list of values. What we need to do is write a query that gives us a list of item_ids where the item has a cost price less than ten:

```
SELECT item_id FROM item WHERE cost_price > 10.0;
```

We also need a query to select items from the stock table:

```
SELECT * FROM stock WHERE item_id IN list of values
```

We can then put the two queries together, like this:

```
SELECT * FROM stock WHERE item_id IN
        (SELECT item_id FROM item WHERE cost_price > 10.0;
```

This would give us the same result, but is slightly easier to read. It is quite common to be able to rewrite subqueries as joins, as we will see shortly. Just like in more conventional queries, we could negate the condition by writing NOT IN, and we could also add additional WHERE clauses and ORDER BY conditions.

Till the time MySQL supports subqueries, you have to express this selection as a join. Once MySQL does have subqueries, which type should you use - a join or a subquery? There are two things to consider – readability and performance. If it is a query that you use occasionally on small tables and it executes quickly, then use whichever form you find most readable. If it is a heavily used query on large tables, then it may be worth writing it in different ways and experimenting to discover which performs best.

You may find that the query optimizer is able to optimize both styles, so the performance is identical between the two, in which case readability automatically wins.

> Be careful in testing the performance of SQL statements. There are a lot of variables beyond your control, such as the caching of data by the operating system.

You may also find that performance is critically dependent on the data in your database, or that it varies dramatically as the number of rows in different tables change. In general, you will probably find that joins tend to execute more efficiently, but each case is different.

Correlated Subqueries

The types of subquery we have seen so far are those where we executed a query to get an answer, which we then 'plug in' to a second query. The two queries are otherwise unrelated and so are called uncorrelated subqueries. This is because there are no linked tables between the inner and outer queries. We may be using the same column from the same table in both parts of the SELECT, but they are related only by the result of the subquery being fed back into the main query's WHERE clause.

There is another group of subqueries, called **correlated subqueries** where the relationship between the two parts of the query is rather more complex. In a correlated subquery, a table in the inner SELECT will be joined to a table in the outer SELECT, hence these two queries are correlated. This is a powerful group of subqueries, which quite often cannot be rewritten as simple SELECT statements with joins.

A correlated query has the general form:

```
SELECT columnA from table1 T1 WHERE T1.columnB = (SELECT T2.columnB
        FROM table2 T2 WHERE T2.columnC = T1.columnC)
```

We have written this as some pseudo SQL to make it a little easier to explain. The important thing to notice is that the table T1, in the outer SELECT, also appears in the inner SELECT. The inner and outer queries are what are termed correlated. You will notice we have aliased the table names. This is important, as the rules for table names in correlated subqueries are rather complex, and a slight mistake can give strange results.

> We strongly suggest you always alias all tables in a correlated subquery, as this is the safest option.

When this is executed, something quite complex happens. First, a row from table T1 is retrieved for the outer SELECT, then the column T1.columnB is passed to the inner query, which then executes selecting from table T2, but using the information that is passed in. The result of this is then passed back to the outer query, which completes evaluation of the WHERE clause, before moving on to the next row.

This is shown in the diagram below:

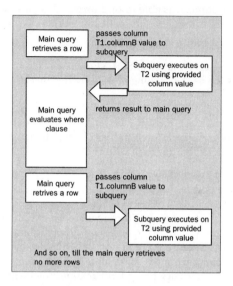

If you are thinking that this sounds a little long-winded, we agree with you. Correlated subqueries often execute inefficiently, but they can be used to solve some particularly complex problems that cannot be tackled in any other way.

On a simple database, such as the one we are using, there is little need for correlated subqueries. They can generally be rewritten in other ways and in any case, until MySQL has support for subqueries, we can't use them in our MySQL database. Suppose we want to know the date when orders were placed for customers in Bingham. Although we could, and have to if we don't have subqueries, write this (more conventionally), we will use a correlated subquery as an example, like this:

```
SELECT oi.date_placed FROM orderinfo oi WHERE oi.customer_id =
       (SELECT c.customer_id from customer c WHERE c.customer_id =
       oi.customer_id and town = 'Bingham');
```

The query would be executed by selecting a row from the orderinfo table, then executing the subquery on the customer table, using the customer_id it found, looking for rows where the customer_id from the outer query gives a row in the customer table that also has the town Bingham. If it finds one, it would pass the customer_id back to the original query, completing the WHERE clause, and, if the WHERE condition evaluates as true, include the date_placed column in the result set. The outer query then proceeds to the next row, and the sequence repeats.

Let's look at a different example. This time we will use the third type of subquery, the type we have not met yet, where the subquery tests for existence.

Suppose we want to list all the customers who have placed orders. The first part of the query is easy, we write:

```
SELECT fname, lname FROM customer c;
```

Notice that we have aliased the table name `customer` to `c`, ready for the subquery. The next part of the query needs to discover if the `customer_id` also exists in the `orderinfo` table:

```
SELECT 1 FROM orderinfo oi WHERE oi.customer_id = c.customer_id;
```

There are two very important aspects to notice here. Firstly, we have used a common 'trick'. Where we need to execute a query but don't need the results, we simply place '1' where a column name would be. This means that if any data is found, a 1 will be returned, which is an easy and efficient way of saying 'true'. This is a weird idea; let's just try it:

```
mysql> SELECT 1 FROM customer WHERE town = 'Bingham';
+---+
| 1 |
+---+
| 1 |
| 1 |
| 1 |
+---+
3 rows in set (0.08 sec)

mysql>
```

So it may look a little odd, but it does work. It is important not to use `COUNT(*)` here, because we need a result from each row where the town is Bingham, not just to know how many customers are from Bingham.

The second important thing to notice is that we use the column `customer` in this subquery, which was actually in the original `SELECT`. This is what makes it correlated. As we did earlier, we alias all the table names, ready to put the two halves together.

It's time to meet the last form of subquery, which we skipped over earlier. This subquery tests for existence using the `EXISTS` keyword in the `WHERE` clause, without needing to know what data is present.

For our query, using `EXISTS` is a good way of combining the two `SELECT` statements together, because we only want to know if the subquery returns a row. An `EXISTS` clause will normally execute more efficiently than other types of queries for join or `IN` conditions. If subqueries are available it can be worth trying them in preference to other types of join, as they may execute more efficiently.

When we put our SQL together to find customers who have ordered, we get this:

```
SELECT fname, lname FROM customer c WHERE EXISTS
    ( SELECT 1 FROM orderinfo oi WHERE oi.customer_id = c.customer_id);
```

Hopefully this will be supported in MySQL very shortly, and you will be able to try out these examples for real.

Replacing Subqueries with Alternatives

As we mentioned earlier, the version of MySQL available when we wrote this book did not have support for subqueries. It was high on the 'to do' list, so it may be worth checking the manual to see if the version you have, or the latest available on the web site, does support subqueries. If it doesn't, there are several ways around the most commonly used subqueries, which we will show here.

Our first example of a subquery is:

```
SELECT item_id from ITEM WHERE cost_price > (SELECT AVG(cost_price)
        FROM item)
```

This turns out to be one of the harder SELECT statements to rewrite. To solve this we either need to use a procedural language, which we can use to process the two queries:

```
SELECT AVG (cost_price) FROM item and
SELECT item_id from ITEM WHERE cost_price > the average cost price
```

These are processed one at a time, passing the result of the first query into the WHERE clause of the second. Alternatively, we could use two statements with a TEMPORARY table to hold the intermediate result.

A good way of doing this is to execute the MySQL syntax:

```
CREATE TABLE...SELECT...
```

This allows us to create a table, where some of the columns are automatically created and populated from a SELECT statement. We can also use the keyword TEMPORARY, so the table is automatically deleted when the session ends. We always need to have at least one column created directly so we will create a column 'x', which we will just ignore.

Let's try this out:

```
mysql> CREATE TEMPORARY TABLE someitem (x int) SELECT item_id, description FROM
item WHERE cost_price < 10;
Query OK, 8 rows affected (0.02 sec)
Records: 8  Duplicates: 0  Warnings: 0
```

If we look at the structure of the table, using DESCRIBE, we can see that it created a table with columns using the type from our SELECT statement:

```
mysql> DESCRIBE someitem;
+-------------+----------+------+-----+---------+-------+
| Field       | Type     | Null | Key | Default | Extra |
+-------------+----------+------+-----+---------+-------+
| x           | int(11)  | YES  |     | NULL    |       |
| item_id     | int(11)  |      |     | 0       |       |
| description | char(64) |      |     |         |       |
+-------------+----------+------+-----+---------+-------+
3 rows in set (0.01 sec)

mysql>
```

Let's look at the data in the table:

```
mysql> SELECT * FROM someitem;
+------+---------+---------------+
| x    | item_id | description   |
+------+---------+---------------+
| NULL |       2 | Rubik Cube    |
| NULL |       3 | Linux CD      |
| NULL |       4 | Tissues       |
| NULL |       5 | Picture Frame |
| NULL |       6 | Fan Small     |
| NULL |       8 | Toothbrush    |
| NULL |       9 | Roman Coin    |
| NULL |      10 | Carrier Bag   |
+------+---------+---------------+
8 rows in set (0.00 sec)

mysql>
```

As you can see, not only have we created a table with columns automatically picking an appropriate type for data retrieved from another table, but also we have populated it with several rows from another table. More details of this syntax can be found in the Appendix C of this book and the MySQL manual.

Now we can use this knowledge to create a table holding the average cost price that we need:

```
mysql> CREATE TEMPORARY TABLE avecostp (x int) SELECT AVG(cost_price) AS acp FROM
item;
Query OK, 1 row affected (0.01 sec)
Records: 1  Duplicates: 0  Warnings: 0
```

Notice that we use the AS clause to make sure that our column has a reasonable name. Let's just check that we have the right answer:

```
mysql> SELECT AVG(cost_price) AS acp FROM item;
+----------+
| acp      |
+----------+
| 7.249091 |
+----------+
1 row in set (0.00 sec)
```

Also the data stored in our TEMPORARY table:

```
mysql> SELECT acp from avecostp;
+----------+
| acp      |
+----------+
| 7.249091 |
+----------+
1 row in set (0.00 sec)

mysql>
```

We can now use this table as the basis for the rest of our SELECT clause, without having to ever type in the average cost price:

```
mysql> SELECT item_id, cost_price FROM item, avecostp WHERE item.cost_price >
avecostp.acp;
+---------+------------+
| item_id | cost_price |
+---------+------------+
|       1 |      15.23 |
|       2 |       7.45 |
|       5 |       7.54 |
|       6 |       9.23 |
|       7 |      13.36 |
|      11 |      19.73 |
+---------+------------+
6 rows in set (0.00 sec)

mysql>
```

In this example it would not have been overly difficult or error prone to write down then retype, or even cut and paste, the answer from one query into another. The important point here is that we can easily emulate the most common use of subqueries by using TEMPORARY tables.

Some of our other examples of subqueries are easier to replace with other forms of the SELECT statement. For example we can replace:

```
SELECT item_id, quantity FROM stock WHERE item_id IN(SELECT item_id FROM item
WHERE cost_price > 10.0);
```

With a simple join:

```
SELECT s.item_id, s.quantity FROM stock s, item i WHERE i.cost_price > 10.0 AND
s.item_id = i.item_id;
```

Do you remember our subquery to find customers who had ordered from us already? It was like this:

```
SELECT fname, lname FROM customer c WHERE EXISTS
        (SELECT 1 FROM orderinfo oi WHERE oi.customer_id = c.customer_id);
```

Rewriting this as a join is also very easy:

```
SELECT fname, lname FROM customer, orderinfo WHERE customer.customer_id =
        orderinfo.customer_id;
```

As you can see, although subqueries are important, it is often reasonably easy to avoid using them by rewriting the SQL, or by using a TEMPORARY table to achieve the same result.

Summary

We started the chapter by looking at aggregate functions that we can use in SQL to select single values from a number of rows. In particular, we met the COUNT(*) function, which you will find widely used to determine the number of rows in a table.

We then met the GROUP BY clause, which allows us to select groups of rows to apply the aggregate function to, followed by the HAVING clause, which allows us to restrict the output to rows containing particular aggregate values. We then looked briefly at the UNION join, which allows us to combine the output of two queries into a single result set. Although this is not widely used, it can occasionally be very useful.

We then took a look at subqueries, where we use the results from one query in another query. We also saw some simple examples, and touched on a much more difficult kind of query, the correlated subquery, where the same column appears in both parts of the query.

We met outer joins; a very important feature that allows us to perform joins between two tables, retrieving rows from the first table even when the join to the second table fails.

We then looked at how to rewrite queries that might have used subqueries so as to avoid them, as they are not supported in MySQL at the time of writing. We saw that, although some subqueries are hard to rewrite and we have to use TEMPORARY table, many are relatively easy to express in a different way.

In this chapter, we have covered some difficult aspects of SQL. Don't worry if some parts seem a little unclear still. One of the best ways of truly understanding SQL is to use it, and use it extensively. Get MySQL installed, install the sample database and its sample data, and experiment.

We have now covered the SELECT statement in as much detail as we will need for this book. Although it is a 'Beginning' book we have covered a wide range of SQL syntax so, should you meet some advanced SQL in existing systems, you will at least have a reasonable understanding of what is being done.

In the next chapter, we will be looking in more detail at types, creating tables, and other information that you need to build your own database.

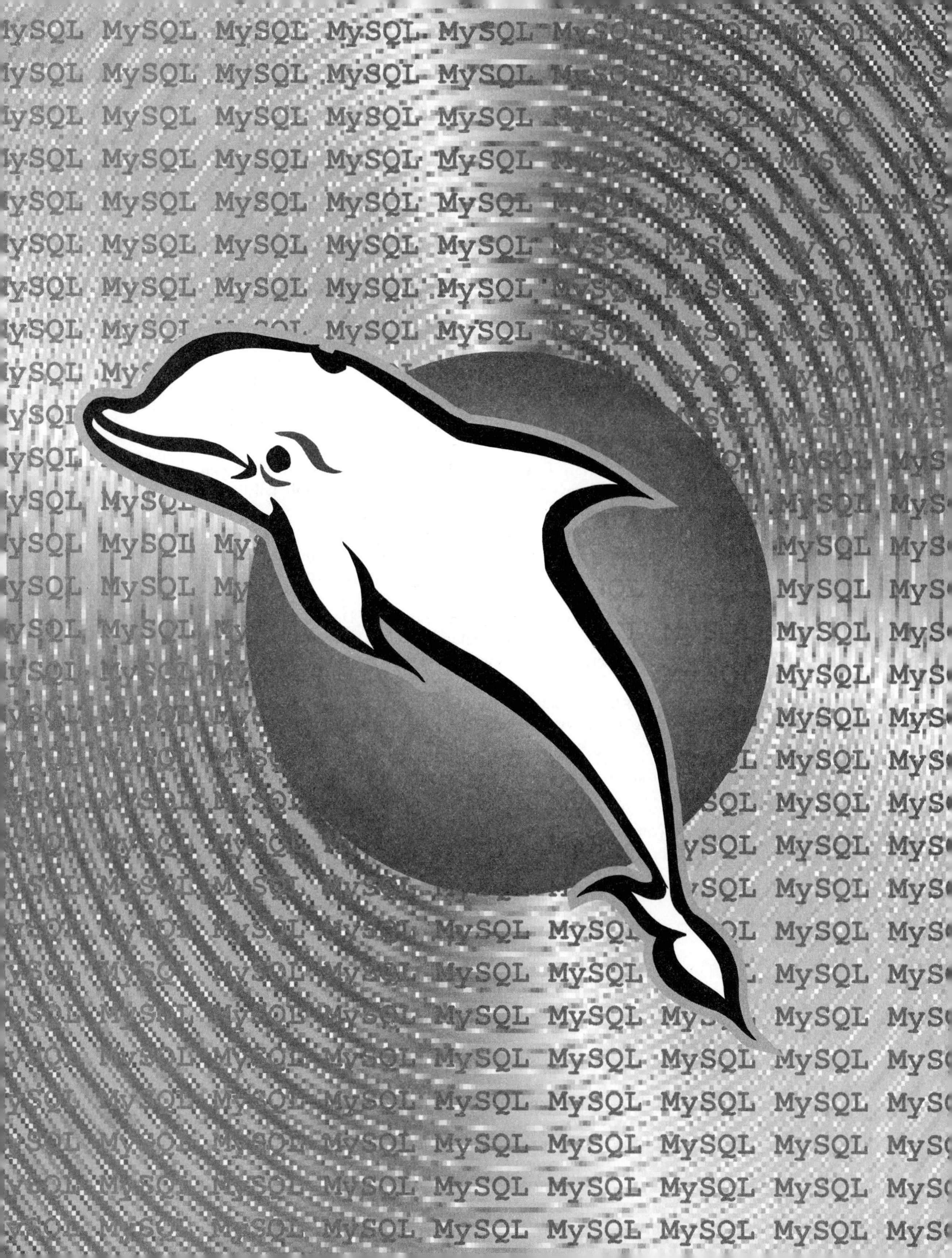
MySQL

Data Definition and Manipulation

Up until now, we have concentrated on the MySQL tools and data selection. Although we created a database early in the book, we only looked superficially at table creation and the data types available in MySQL. We kept table definitions quite simple by just using primary keys; defining a few columns that do not accept NULL values and using the AUTO_INCREMENT attribute to create columns with a unique key.

In a database, the quality of the data should always be one of our primary concerns and in this chapter we are going to look in more detail at the data types available in MySQL and how to use them. We shall be looking at the operators for manipulating data and the many functions that MySQL provides for working with data. We shall look more formally at how tables are managed and most importantly how you can use more advanced features, such as **constraints**, to significantly tighten the rules we apply when data is added to or removed from the tables in the database.

Having the database enforce very strict rules about the data at the lowest level is one of the most effective measures you can use to maintain the data in a consistent state. This is also one of the features that distinguish true databases from simple indexed files, spreadsheets, and the like.

Along the chapter, we will be looking at:

- ❑   Data types
- ❑   Operators
- ❑   Built-in functions
- ❑   Manipulating tables
- ❑   Foreign key constraints

At the time of writing, the default table type for MySQL does not support some of the more advanced features we wish to use. MySQL has a very flexible architecture, which allows us to 'plug in' alternative implementations of the underlying tables. To gain access to some of the more advanced features we will be using the InnoDB table type later in the chapter, which we have seen in Chapter 3, *Installing and Getting Started with MySQL*. More information can be found on the MySQL web site and the InnoDB web site at http://www.innodb.com.

Data Types

MySQL supports a standard set of SQL data types, and also a few esoteric types that we will mention. At the most basic level, MySQL supports these data types:

- ❑ Boolean
- ❑ Character (string)
- ❑ Number
- ❑ Temporal (time-based)
- ❑ Binary Large Object (BLOB)

Let's look at each of these in turn. For information on BLOB refer to Appendix F.

Boolean

The Boolean type is probably the simplest type. It can only store two possible values, TRUE and FALSE, and our old friend NULL, for unknown.

The type declaration for a Boolean column is simply BOOL.

Try It Out – Boolean Values

Let's create a simple table with a Boolean column and experiment with some values. As we have seen before, to create a column with a name and a type we simply give the name, some whitespace and then the type that we want to associate with the name.

We will create a table, testtype, with a variable length string and a Boolean column, insert some data and then use SELECT to display it again. Rather than experiment in our bmsimple database with our real data, we will use the test database MySQL creates when it is installed as a 'play' area.

Here is our session:

```
mysql> USE test;
Database changed
mysql> CREATE TABLE testtype ( valused VARCHAR(10), boolres BOOL );
Query OK, 0 rows affected (0.01 sec)
```

Now that we have created our table, let's experiment by adding some data:

```
mysql> INSERT INTO testtype VALUES('True' , 1);
Query OK, 1 row affected (0.00 sec)

mysql> INSERT INTO testtype VALUES('False' , 0);
Query OK, 1 row affected (0.00 sec)

mysql> INSERT INTO testtype VALUES('False' , 'F');
```

```
Query OK, 1 row affected (0.00 sec)

mysql> INSERT INTO testtype VALUES('store NULL' , NULL);
Query OK, 1 row affected (0.00 sec)

mysql>
```

Let's check that the data has been inserted:

```
mysql> SELECT * FROM testtype;
+------------+---------+
| valused    | boolres |
+------------+---------+
| True       |       1 |
| False      |       0 |
| False      |       0 |
| store NULL |    NULL |
+------------+---------+
4 rows in set (0.00 sec)

mysql>
```

How It Works

We create a table `testtype` with two columns, the first holds a string and the second holds a Boolean. We then insert data into the table, each time making the first value a string to remind us what we inserted, the second the same value, but to be stored as a Boolean value. We also inserted a NULL to show that MySQL (unlike at least one commercial database) does allow NULL to be stored in a Boolean type.

Notice that attempting to store 'F' has resulted in the value '0' being stored. MySQL will interpret any value except '1' being stored in a Boolean column as False. Be aware, this is different from several other databases, which do interpret 'T' and 'True' as a Boolean True for example.

Character

The Character data types are probably the most widely used in any database, and are divided into three subtypes:

- ❏   A single character
- ❏   Fixed length character strings
- ❏   Variable length character strings

These are standard SQL Character types but MySQL also supports several Text types. The Text types are not standard SQL types, and so should be used with caution, as they may well not be portable to other databases, should you wish to move your schema in the future. We describe the SQL standard types first, and then show the MySQL extension types in a separate table.

The SQL standard types are defined using CHAR, CHAR(N), and VARCHAR(N):

Definition	Meaning
CHAR	A single character.
CHAR(N)	A set of characters exactly N characters in length, padded with spaces. If you attempt to store a string that is too long, then the additional characters will be silently ignored. Limited to a maximum of 255 characters.
VARCHAR(N)	A set of characters up to N characters in length, no padding. Limited to a maximum of 255 characters.

MySQL has an additional attribute, BINARY that can be used after the definition. This option changes the default comparison behavior to a binary type compare, rather than the case-insensitive compare used by default when the column is named in the WHERE part of SELECT operations. We will see this in use in an example shortly.

MySQL additional types for storing longer text strings are:

Definition	Meaning
TINYTEXT	A text string of up to 255 characters, similar to VARCHAR(255).
MEDIUMTEXT	A text string of up to 65535 characters.
LONGTEXT	A text string of up to $2^{32} - 1$ characters.

Given a choice of three standard types to use for character strings, which should you pick? As always, there is no definite answer. In general, you should use the standard SQL types rather than the MySQL additional types, which is practical and will make your database structure more portable.

If you know that your database is always going to be run on MySQL, MEDIUMTEXT can be a good choice since it is easy to use and doesn't force you into anything except the most general maximum length decisions. The downside is that MEDIUMTEXT is not a standard type, so if there is a chance that you will one day need to port your database to something other than MySQL, it is best avoided. Other databases also offer alternatives to the SQL standard, for example PostgreSQL has a TEXT type, and Oracle can store up to 4000 characters in a VARCHAR type. Generally we have avoided the various TEXT types in this book, preferring the more standard SQL type definitions.

The advantage of the VARCHAR(N) type is that it only stores as many characters as required, up to 255 characters, plus a length. On the other hand, in case of CHAR(N) type the length is fixed, so it may be slightly more efficient than the VARCHAR(N) type in some circumstances. In general, if your string is short and of known length, it is probably best to use the CHAR(N) type. Where the length varies significantly between different rows of data, choose the VARCHAR(N) type. If in doubt, use VARCHAR(N).

MySQL has a slight deviation from the standard VARCHAR behavior. The standard says that the database should store the exact number of characters provided, including spaces. This is the way VARCHAR(N) will behave in most SQL databases but MySQL will strip trailing spaces. This is rarely a problem, but some slightly non-standard behavior you should be aware of.

Just like the Boolean type, all Character type columns can also store NULL (for unknown values).

Try It Out – Character Types

First, we need to drop our `testtype` table, and then we can recreate it with some different column types:

```
mysql> DROP table testtype;
Query OK, 0 rows affected (0.00 sec)
```

Now we can create our new table:

```
mysql> CREATE TABLE testtype(
    -> singlechar CHAR,
    -> fixedchar  CHAR(13),
    -> vchar      VARCHAR(128),
    -> vcharb     VARCHAR(128) BINARY,
    -> mtext      MEDIUMTEXT
    -> );
Query OK, 0 rows affected (0.00 sec)
```

Let's insert some data:

```
mysql> INSERT INTO testtype VALUES('F', '0-349-10177-9',
    -> 'The Wasp Factory', 'The Wasp Factory',
    -> 'The extraordinary world of Frank, a very unconventional sixteen year
    -> old. A stunning masterpiece by Iain Banks.');
Query OK, 1 row affected (0.00 sec)

mysql> INSERT INTO testtype VALUES('F', '1-85723-457-X',
    -> 'Excession', 'Excession',
    -> 'A best selling SF book showing extraordinary imagination');
Query OK, 1 row affected (0.00 sec)

mysql> INSERT INTO testtype VALUES(NULL, '',
    -> 'some spaces        ', '',
    -> 'Bound to be exceptional.');
Query OK, 1 row affected (0.01 sec)

mysql>
```

Now let's see how the different column types are handled. To make the output easier to read we use the '\G' option, which displays each row on a different line:

```
mysql> SELECT fixedchar, mtext FROM testtype\G
*************************** 1. row ***************************
fixedchar: 0-349-10177-9
   mtext: The extraordinary world of Frank, a very unconventional sixteen year
old. A stunning masterpiece by Iain Banks.
*************************** 2. row ***************************
fixedchar: 1-85723-457-X
   mtext: A best selling SF book showing extraordinary imagination
```

```
*************************** 3. row ***************************
fixedchar:
    mtext: Bound to be exceptional.
3 rows in set (0.00 sec)

mysql> SELECT fixedchar, vchar, vcharb FROM testtype WHERE vchar =
    -> 'EXCESSION'\G
*************************** 1. row ***************************
fixedchar: 1-85723-457-X
    vchar: Excession
   vcharb: Excession
1 row in set (0.00 sec)

mysql> SELECT fixedchar, vchar, vcharb FROM testtype WHERE vcharb =
    -> 'EXCESSION'\G
Empty set (0.01 sec)

mysql> SELECT fixedchar, vchar, vcharb FROM testtype WHERE singlechar IS
    -> NULL\G
*************************** 1. row ***************************
fixedchar:
    vchar: some spaces
   vcharb:
1 row in set (0.01 sec)

mysql>
```

How It Works

Firstly we create a table with five columns to show the main Character types. The column singlechar holds a single character, fixedchar holds exactly 13 characters, vchar holds up to 128 characters, and vcharb holds up to 128 characters but has the additional attribute BINARY. We also created an mtext column that can store longer text strings.

We then insert some data into the table, and select the fixedchar and mtext columns for all rows to show that they function as expected. The next two SELECT statements, looking for the string 'EXCESSION', show how the VARCHAR and VARCHAR BINARY column types differ. The ordinary VARCHAR column considers the strings to match, even though a mixed case string is stored but an all uppercase string is used to test against. The option BINARY changes this behavior to the perhaps more expected, and certainly more conventional characteristics of considering strings to be equal when not only the characters are the same, but also the case is same.

Finally we select the row where we stored NULL in the fixedchar column. Notice that the vchar column, which had a large number of trailing spaces in the string we inserted has had these silently trimmed in the output.

Number

The Number types in MySQL are slightly more complex than those we have met so far, but they are not particularly difficult to understand. There are two distinct types of numbers that we can store in the database, **integers** and **floating-point**. MySQL offers some variations on the standard integer type for holding different sizes of integers as well as allowing signed and unsigned variants. Floating-point numbers also subdivide into those offering general purpose floating point values and fixed precision numbers.

By default all integer values are signed, that is, they store both positive and negative values, but by adding the suffix UNSIGNED they change to hold only unsigned numbers, but can hold a slightly larger range. For example, suppose we created a table num, like this:

```
mysql> CREATE TABLE num {
    -> sint INT,
    -> uint INT UNSIGNED
    -> };
```

The sint column is (as we will see in the table below) a 32-bit type and by default is signed. This means it can hold values from minus 2^31 up to plus $2^31 - 1$, that is, -2147483648 to 2147483647. The column uint is unsigned, so holds values from zero to $2^32 -1$, that is, 0 to 4294967295.

Generally the INT type is a good general choice.

If we show all the number types in a table, it is easier to see what the choices are:

Type	Sub-type	Description
Integer numbers	TINYINT	An eight-bit type for holding small integers.
	SMALLINT	A sixteen-bit type for holding numbers.
	MEDIUMINT	A twenty four-bit type for holding numbers.
	INT	A thirty two-bit type for holding numbers.
	BIGINT	A sixty four-bit type for holding numbers. Beware that all calculations involving BIGINT are signed, so the effective range is not quite as large as you would expect.
Floating-point numbers	FLOAT(P)	A floating-point number, with at least the precision P in bits, up to a maximum of 53 bits. When P is less than 25 then it is single precision, otherwise it is a double-precision floating-point number.
	DOUBLE(D, N)	A double-precision floating-point number that is always signed. The D defines a display width; N is the number of decimals. REAL is a synonym for DOUBLE.
	NUMERIC(P,S)	A real number with P digits, S of them after the decimal point. Unlike FLOAT, this is always an exact number, but less efficient to work with than ordinary floating point numbers.
	DECIMAL(P,S)	Synonym for NUMERIC.

The split of the two types into integer and floating-point numbers is easy enough to understand but what might be less obvious is the purpose of the NUMERIC type.

Floating-point numbers are stored in scientific notation, with a **mantissa** and an **exponent**. With the NUMERIC type, you get to specify both the precision and the exact number of digits stored when performing calculations. You can also specify the number of digits held after the decimal point. The actual decimal point location comes free. This is usually the type you need to use if your calculations involve exact amounts, such as monetary values.

> A common mistake is to think that **NUMERIC**(5, 2) can store a number, such as 12345.12. This is not correct. The total number of digits stored is only five, so a declaration **NUMERIC**(5, 2) can only store numbers between 0.01 and 999.99.

MySQL is not terribly good at catching mistakes when trying to insert values into a column that can't hold them, so you need to watch out for this, or you will find the data stored isn't quite what you intended.

Try It Out – Number Types

First, we need to drop our `testtype` table, and then recreate it with some different column types:

```
mysql> DROP TABLE testtype;
Query OK, 0 rows affected (0.00 sec)

mysql> CREATE TABLE testtype (
    -> asmallint    SMALLINT,
    -> anint        INT,
    -> ausint       INT UNSIGNED,
    -> afloat       FLOAT(2),
    -> anumeric     NUMERIC(5,2)
    -> );
Query OK, 0 rows affected (0.01 sec)

mysql> INSERT INTO testtype VALUES(2, 2, 2, 2.0, 2.0);
Query OK, 1 row affected (0.00 sec)

mysql> INSERT INTO testtype VALUES(-100, -100.00, -100, 123.456789,
    -> 123.456789);
Query OK, 1 row affected (0.00 sec)

mysql> INSERT INTO testtype VALUES(300, 300, 300, 123456789, 123456789);
Query OK, 1 row affected (0.00 sec)

mysql> INSERT INTO testtype VALUES(100000, 100000, 100000,
    -> -123456789, -123456789);
Query OK, 1 row affected (0.00 sec)

mysql> SELECT * FROM testtype;
+-----------+--------+--------+---------------+----------+
| asmallint | anint  | ausint | afloat        | anumeric |
+-----------+--------+--------+---------------+----------+
|         2 |      2 |      2 |             2 |     2.00 |
|      -100 |   -100 |      0 |       123.457 |   123.46 |
|       300 |    300 |    300 |   1.23457e+008 |  9999.99 |
|     32767 | 100000 | 100000 |  -1.23457e+008 |  -999.99 |
+-----------+--------+--------+---------------+----------+
4 rows in set (0.00 sec)

mysql>
```

How It Works

What we have done here is create a table with a small integer column, a normal integer column, an unsigned integer, a floating-point number, and a numeric number with a precision of 5 and a scale of 2.

By looking at the INSERT statements and the actual data that was stored we can see several things:

❑ Attempting to store a negative number in an unsigned column results in 0 being stored.

❑ Attempting to store a number that is too large to be stored simply results in storage of the largest possible number with the same sign that can be held.

❑ Attempting to store a floating point number in an integer field simply stores the integer part of the number.

This behavior does mean that you need to watch out for mistakes caused by using the wrong type, as MySQL will not catch them for you.

Temporal

We looked at Temporal types (types that store time-related information) earlier in Chapter 4, *Accessing Your Data*, when we saw how to control date formats.

MySQL has a range of types relating to date and time, but we will confine ourselves to the standard SQL-92 types, plus the common additional type DATETIME:

Definition	Meaning
DATE	Stores date information. The earliest date accepted is Jan 1st 1000, the latest date accepted is December 31st 9999.
TIME	Stores time information. The range accepted is -838:59:59 to 838:59:59.
TIMESTAMP	Stores a date and time. The earliest time that can be stored is the January 1st 1970, the start of the UNIX epoch, and the latest time stored is the year 2037. See Appendix B for more information. The TIMESTAMP value is special, in that by attempting to insert a NULL into a TIMESTAMP column the current date and time is stored. This can be very useful for building audit trails of which rows have been updated since a particular point in time.
DATETIME	Can store values from January 1st 1000, till the last second of the year 9999.

We have already considered date and time in some detail in Chapter 4, so we will not look at them further in this chapter.

Operators

We have already seen and used some simple operators in SELECT statements. Now we shall look at these operators in detail.

We use an (=) operator to limit a selection to rows that obey a condition:

```
mysql> use bmsimple;
Database changed
mysql> SELECT town FROM customer WHERE lname = 'Jones';
+---------+
| town    |
+---------+
| Bingham |
+---------+
1 row in set (0.00 sec)

mysql>
```

We can also do numerical comparisons, for example:

```
mysql> SELECT * FROM item WHERE cost_price > 8.0;
+---------+-------------+------------+------------+
| item_id | description | cost_price | sell_price |
+---------+-------------+------------+------------+
|       1 | Wood Puzzle |      15.23 |      21.95 |
|       6 | Fan Small   |       9.23 |      15.75 |
|       7 | Fan Large   |      13.36 |      19.95 |
|      11 | Speakers    |      19.73 |      25.32 |
+---------+-------------+------------+------------+
4 rows in set (0.00 sec)

mysql>
```

Here the greater than (>) operator is applied between the cost_price attribute and 8.0, so SELECT returns only those rows where the cost price is greater than 8.0.

We can go further and include other attributes and operators to create more complex conditions, with parentheses to specify the order in which we want them evaluated:

```
mysql> SELECT description, sell_price FROM item
    -> WHERE (sell_price*100)%100 = 99;

+-------------+------------+
| description | sell_price |
+-------------+------------+
| Tissues     |       3.99 |
+-------------+------------+
1 row in set (0.00 sec)

mysql>
```

Here, we have used the multiplication (*) operator in conjunction with the modulo (%) operator to list the items that have a selling price that ends in 99¢. Let's have a look at the different operators you can use in MySQL, and how they work together.

Operator Precedence and Associativity

Many of the MySQL operators look and act like the normal arithmetic operators that you will find in many programming languages. The operators have a precedence hard-coded into the **parser** that determines the order in which operators are executed in compound expressions. As usual, the precedence can be overridden using parentheses.

Remember that MySQL allows the use of operators and functions outside WHERE clauses of the SELECT statement.

Let's try a simple test of operator precedence:

```
mysql> SELECT 1 + 2 * 3;
+-----------+
| 1 + 2 * 3 |
+-----------+
|         7 |
+-----------+
1 row in set (0.05 sec)

mysql> SELECT (1 + 2) * 3 AS "Answer";
+--------+
| Answer |
+--------+
|      9 |
+--------+
1 row in set (0.02 sec)

mysql>
```

Here we can see that the result of the expression '1+2*3' is reported as '7', displayed as an unnamed column. In the second example, the operator precedence is overridden using parentheses and the result column is named, using AS, to be the string 'Answer'.

Although some of the operators behave exactly as you might expect if you have programmed in C or any other programming language, some of the operator precedence may just catch you out. As in C, the Boolean operators have a lower precedence than arithmetic operators, so parentheses are often required to get the desired operator execution order. If in doubt, make the order explicit with parentheses.

MySQL operators also display associativity, either right or left, which determines the order in which operators of the same precedence are evaluated. Arithmetic operators, such as addition and subtraction are left associative so that '1+2-3' evaluates as if it had been written '(1+2)-3'. Others, such as the Boolean equality operator, are right associative so that 'x = y = z' is evaluated as 'x = (y = z)'. In general, the arithmetic operators 'do the right thing' for type conversions.

The table below lists the lexical precedence (in descending order) of the most common MySQL operators:

Operator	Meaning
BINARY	Makes string comparisons (case-sensitive)
NOT !	Inverts a logic test
-	Unary minus
* / %	Multiply, divide and modulo
+ -	Plus and minus
<< >>	Left shift and right shift
&	Bitwise and
|	Bitwise or
< <= = <=> <> >= > IN LIKE	Less than, less than or equal, equal, NULL safe equal, not equal, greater than or equal, greater than, check for inclusion in a list and string comparison with meta characters
BETWEEN	Range test
AND &&	Logical and
OR ||	Logical or

String Comparison with LIKE and REGEXP

We have already discovered that we need to use the keyword BINARY to make string comparisons case-sensitive, and we can do this either by adding the qualifier BINARY after the column type or by using the BINARY keyword in the WHERE clause of our SELECT statement.

We also saw the use of LIKE in Chapter 4 for matching strings. We now come back briefly to LIKE, before moving on to the more extensive pattern matching available using the MySQL REGEXP operator.

You will remember that LIKE uses '_' to match a single character, and '%' to match a sequence of characters. As before, you need to add the BINARY keyword if you want case-sensitive matching:

For example:

```
mysql> SELECT lname from customer WHERE lname LIKE "H%";
+---------+
| lname   |
+---------+
| Hickman |
| Howard  |
| Hendy   |
| Hudson  |
+---------+
4 rows in set (0.00 sec)
```

All the names that start with 'H' are matched.

Now see the same example using 'h':

```
mysql> SELECT lname from customer WHERE lname LIKE "h%";
+---------+
| lname   |
+---------+
| Hickman |
| Howard  |
| Hendy   |
| Hudson  |
+---------+
4 rows in set (0.00 sec)
```

We get the same result. We did not use the BINARY version, so the match was case-insensitive.

Using the BINARY version, we get:

```
mysql> SELECT lname from customer WHERE lname LIKE BINARY "h%";
Empty set (0.00 sec)
```

Nothing is returned, because there are no names starting with a lower case 'h'.

An 'H' followed by 5 underscore(_) characters matches names that start with an H and are of exactly 6 characters long:

```
mysql> SELECT lname from customer WHERE lname LIKE BINARY "H_____";
+--------+
| lname  |
+--------+
| Howard |
| Hudson |
+--------+
2 rows in set (0.00 sec)
```

You can use the '%' and '_' characters anywhere in the string:

```
mysql> SELECT lname from customer WHERE lname LIKE BINARY "%s";
+--------+
| lname  |
+--------+
| Stones |
| Stones |
| Cozens |
| Stones |
| Stones |
| Jones  |
+--------+
6 rows in set (0.00 sec)
```

221

Using NOT inverts the test:

```
mysql> SELECT lname from customer WHERE lname NOT LIKE BINARY "%s";
+---------+
| lname   |
+---------+
| Matthew |
| Matthew |
| Matthew |
| Hickman |
| Howard  |
| Neill   |
| Hendy   |
| O'Neill |
| Hudson  |
+---------+
9 rows in set (0.00 sec)

mysql>
```

As you can see, LIKE is quite a useful operation but there are times when you want more powerful matching, and MySQL provides a regular expression matching operation REGEXP. Those who are familiar with UNIX style regular expressions will be right at home, because MySQL uses the same character sequences. Here we present the more common expressions; consult the MySQL manual for the complete set:

Character sequence	Explanation
^	Ties the following sequence to the start of the string, so '^a' means that the string must start with an 'a'.
$	Ties the preceding sequence to the end of the string, so 's$' means that the string must end with an 's'.
.	Match any single character.
[xyz]	Match any character appearing in the brackets, so '[abc]' matches any of 'a', 'b' or 'c'. Ranges can be specified with a dash, so to match 'a' through 'h' inclusive, we would write '[a-h]'.
[^xyz]	As above, except the test is inverted, so it matches any character not appearing between the brackets.
x*	Match zero or more occurrences of the string.
x+	Match one or more occurrences of the string.
(xyz)	Group a set of characters together.

Regular expressions look complex but in practice are reasonably easy to use, so let's jump in and see them in use.

Try It Out – REGEXP

We will use our sample database, bmsimple, and experiment matching string in the last name column of the customer table.

```
mysql> SELECT lname from customer WHERE BINARY lname REGEXP "^S.*";
+--------+
| lname  |
+--------+
| Stones |
| Stones |
| Stones |
| Stones |
+--------+
4 rows in set (0.00 sec)
```

```
mysql> SELECT lname from customer WHERE BINARY lname REGEXP ".*on.*";
+--------+
| lname  |
+--------+
| Stones |
| Stones |
| Stones |
| Stones |
| Jones  |
| Hudson |
+--------+
6 rows in set (0.00 sec)
```

```
mysql> SELECT lname from customer WHERE BINARY lname REGEXP ".*on.+";
+--------+
| lname  |
+--------+
| Stones |
| Stones |
| Stones |
| Stones |
| Jones  |
+--------+
5 rows in set (0.00 sec)
```

```
mysql>
```

```
mysql> SELECT lname from customer WHERE BINARY lname REGEXP ".*[on].*";
+---------+
| lname   |
+---------+
| Stones  |
| Stones  |
| Cozens  |
| Stones  |
| Stones  |
| Hickman |
| Howard  |
| Jones   |
| Hendy   |
| Hudson  |
+---------+
10 rows in set (0.00 sec)
```

```
mysql> SELECT lname from customer WHERE BINARY lname REGEXP "^[^SJ]";
+---------+
| lname   |
+---------+
| Matthew |
| Matthew |
| Cozens  |
| Matthew |
| Hickman |
| Howard  |
| Neill   |
| Hendy   |
| O'Neill |
| Hudson  |
+---------+
10 rows in set (0.00 sec)

mysql>
```

How It Works

We start with the expression '^S.*' which matches any string that starts with a 'S' and then contains any other characters. The expression '.*on.*' means any string that has 'on' in it. We then match using '.*on.+' which means that there is at least one character after the string 'on', so that 'Hudson' no longer matches. Finally we use '.*[on].*' which means any string that has either an 'o' or a 'n' in it.

Notice how the square brackets change the meaning from the earlier '.*on.*'. In all the matches we add the BINARY keyword, so that the match is case-sensitive.

Finally we use '^[^SJ]' which matches any last names that do not start with a 'S' or a 'J'.

Converting Between Types

From time to time, we will discover that we need to convert between data types. In general, you should be very wary of this for two reasons. Firstly, if you discover that you need to do a type conversion this may indicate that there may be a mistake in your choice of database column types, and secondly MySQL (unlike most SQL databases, which have a CAST function for type conversion) likes to do type conversions automatically for you and thus you can get occasional surprises.

Generally it is safer to try and maintain some control over what conversions are being performed, and there are a couple of ways of doing this in MySQL.

Converting To Numbers

If you use a numeric operator, such as (+) for addition, then MySQL knows that the result must be numeric, so attempts to convert both operands to numbers before doing the conversion. Let's see a few examples of this in action.

Using two numbers and adding them together not surprisingly results in a numeric addition being performed:

```
mysql> SELECT 4 + 4;
+-------+
| 4 + 4 |
+-------+
|     8 |
+-------+
1 row in set (0.00 sec)
```

When we put the two numbers in quotes they become strings, but are then converted back to numbers because of the (+) operator:

```
mysql> SELECT '4' + '4';
+-----------+
| '4' + '4' |
+-----------+
|         8 |
+-----------+
1 row in set (0.00 sec)
```

Adding a string and a number together gives the result:

```
mysql> SELECT 'Hello' + 4;
+-------------+
| 'Hello' + 4 |
+-------------+
|           4 |
+-------------+
1 row in set (0.00 sec)
```

> **A warning that sometimes MySQL will silently do surprising things without generating any warning messages!**

Converting To Strings

Use the CONCAT() function, which will convert its arguments to strings and always return a string.

```
mysql> SELECT CONCAT('4', '4');
+------------------+
| CONCAT('4', '4') |
+------------------+
| 44               |
+------------------+
1 row in set (0.01 sec)
```

Now the strings are combined using the CONCAT() function, rather than added using the (+) operator.

Magic Variables

Occasionally, we want to store some information in the database that relates to the date or time in some way, perhaps to implement an audit trail. MySQL has some special variables for doing this:

❑   CURRENT_DATE

❑   CURRENT_TIME

❑   CURRENT_TIMESTAMP

You can use these just like column names or you can SELECT them without a table name at all:

```
mysql> SELECT item_id, quantity, CURRENT_TIMESTAMP FROM stock;
+---------+----------+---------------------+
| item_id | quantity | CURRENT_TIMESTAMP   |
+---------+----------+---------------------+
|       1 |       12 | 2001-10-28 17:33:44 |
|       2 |        2 | 2001-10-28 17:33:44 |
|       4 |        8 | 2001-10-28 17:33:44 |
|       5 |        3 | 2001-10-28 17:33:44 |
|       7 |        8 | 2001-10-28 17:33:44 |
|       8 |       18 | 2001-10-28 17:33:44 |
|      10 |        1 | 2001-10-28 17:33:44 |
+---------+----------+---------------------+
7 rows in set (0.03 sec)
```

These magic variables can also be used in INSERT and UPDATE statements such as this:

```
INSERT INTO orderinfo(orderinfo_id, customer_id, date_placed, date_shipped,
            shipping) VALUES (11, 8, CURRENT_DATE, NULL, 0.0);
```

Built-in Functions

MySQL boasts a very long list of built-in functions that we can use in SELECT expressions.

Here's the list of the categories of these functions:

❑   Comparison functions

❑   Numeric functions

❑   String Handling functions

❑   Date and Time functions

We cannot possibly hope to cover all of the available functions in this chapter, but we will take a peek at a few of the more useful ones. We have already come across a few of the standard ones, such as the aggregate functions in earlier chapters. We will not repeat those here. For more information, seek out the MySQL Manual.

Comparison Functions

Function	Meaning
IF(exp1, expr2, expr3)	If expr1 is TRUE and not NULL, then return expr2, else return expr3.
IFNULL(expr1, expr2)	If expr1 is NULL then return expr2, else return expr1.
ISNULL(expr1)	Return TRUE if expr1 is NULL.
STRCMP(str1, str2)	Return '0' (FALSE) if the strings are the same, NULL if either string is NULL, else '-1' if the first argument is smaller, or '1' otherwise. Do notice the slightly unexpected return result, where equality looks like a 'FALSE' result, but if you process the result as a Boolean, then both '-1' and '1' will appear as 'TRUE' results. The behavior of this function on strings that differ only in case is partly dependent on the version and configuration of MySQL that you are using. The safest solution is to type in SELECT STRCMP('foo', 'FOO'); if the answer is '0' then you have case-insensitive comparisons, otherwise STRCMP() is using case-sensitive comparisons. If used on a column declared as a BINARY character type, then the comparison will always be case sensitive.

Numeric Functions

Function	Meaning
ABS(x)	Absolute value
CEILING(x)	Return the smallest integer which is not less than 'x'
COS(x)	Return the cosine of 'x', where 'x' is in radians
DEGREES(r)	Converts angular measures from radians to degrees
RADIANS(d)	Converts angular measures from degrees to radians
EXP(x)	Natural antilogarithm, raise x to a power
FLOOR(x)	Return the largest integer not greater than x

Table continued on following page

Function	Meaning
LOG(x)	Natural logarithm
LOG10(x)	Logarithm to base 10
MOD(x,y)	Remainder after dividing 'x' by 'y', the same as 'x%y'
PI()	Returns
POW(x,y)	Raises 'x' to the power of 'y'
RAND()	Returns a random number between 0.0 and just less than 1.0
ROUND(x)	Round to nearest whole number
ROUND(x,d)	Round to specified number of decimal places, 'd'
SIN(x)	Returns the sine of 'x', where 'x' is in radians
SQRT(x)	Square root
TAN(x)	Returns the tangent of 'x', where 'x' is in radians
TRUNCATE(x,d)	Truncate 'x' to specified number of decimal places, 'd'

String Handling Functions

Function	Meaning
ASCII(x)	Returns the ASCII code of the first character in the string 'x', or '0' if the string has zero length or is NULL.
CHAR(x, y, ...)	Returns a string that is the concatenation of a sequence of numeric arguments when each is converted to an ASCII code.
CONCAT(x, y, ...)	Returns a string, which is the concatenation of the argument strings, or NULL if any of the argument strings is NULL.
FORMAT(x, y)	Formats the number 'x' to a string with 'y' decimal places.
INSTR(x, y)	Returns the position of substring 'y' in the string 'x'.
LEFT(x, y)	Returns the leftmost 'y' characters from string 'x'.
LENGTH(x)	Returns the length of the string 'x'.
LOWER(x)	Returns the string 'x' converted to lower-case.
MID(x, p, l)	Returns l character starting from position 'p' from string 'x'. The first character is considered to be in position 1.
RIGHT(x, y)	Returns the rightmost 'y' characters from string 'x'.

Function	Meaning
RTRIM(x)	Removes trailing spaces from the string 'x'.
SOUNDEX(x)	Returns a string, which shows that two strings that sound almost the same should have identical soundex strings. MySQL returns an arbitrary length string, although standard soundex strings are only 4 characters long.
SUBSTR(x, p, l)	Returns a string starting from position 'p' in string 'x', being at most l characters long. If l is omitted then all characters from position 'p' to the end of the string are returned.
TRIM(x)	Trims both leading and trailing spaces from the string 'x'.
UPPER(s)	Converts a string to upper-case.

There are a few less commonly used string manipulation functions. See the MySQL manual for the complete list.

Try It Out – Functions

Well those were quite a lot of functions; let's try some of them out:

```
mysql> SELECT STRCMP('foo', 'foo');
+----------------------+
| STRCMP('foo', 'foo') |
+----------------------+
|                    0 |
+----------------------+
1 row in set (0.00 sec)

mysql> SELECT STRCMP('foo', 'FOO');
+----------------------+
| STRCMP('foo', 'FOO') |
+----------------------+
|                    0 |
+----------------------+
1 row in set (0.00 sec)

mysql> SELECT STRCMP('foo', BINARY 'FOO');
+-----------------------------+
| STRCMP('foo', BINARY 'FOO') |
+-----------------------------+
|                           1 |
+-----------------------------+
1 row in set (0.00 sec)

mysql> SELECT STRCMP('foo', 'bar');
+----------------------+
| STRCMP('foo', 'bar') |
```

```
+----------------------+
|                    1 |
+----------------------+
1 row in set (0.00 sec)

mysql> SELECT CEILING(2.2), FLOOR(2.4), ROUND(2.2);
+--------------+------------+------------+
| CEILING(2.2) | FLOOR(2.4) | ROUND(2.2) |
+--------------+------------+------------+
|            3 |          2 |          2 |
+--------------+------------+------------+
1 row in set (0.00 sec)

mysql> SELECT description, MID(description, 2, 6), UPPER(description)
    -> FROM item WHERE item_id = 6;
+-------------+------------------------+--------------------+
| description | MID(description, 2, 6) | UPPER(description) |
+-------------+------------------------+--------------------+
| Fan Small   | an Sma                 | FAN SMALL          |
+-------------+------------------------+--------------------+
1 row in set (0.00 sec)

mysql> SELECT ASCII('A'), CHAR(65, 66, 67), CONCAT('Hello', 0x20, 0x57,
    -> 'orld');
+------------+------------------+------------------------------------+
| ASCII('A') | CHAR(65, 66, 67) | CONCAT('Hello', 0x20, 0x57, 'orld') |
+------------+------------------+------------------------------------+
|         65 | ABC              | Hello World                        |
+------------+------------------+------------------------------------+
1 row in set (0.01 sec)
```

How It Works

We start off with STRCMP() and see that like most MySQL operations it considers strings to be the same even if they differ in case, unless we use the BINARY operator. You may find that your version and configuration of MySQL returned 1 in which case you are getting case-sensitive comparisons. We then look at FLOOR(), CEILING(), and ROUND() before experimenting with some string functions.

Date and Time Functions

MySQL has a very extensive range of functions for manipulating dates and times. The Date and Time functions were covered in Chapter 4, and we will not repeat them here.

Manipulating Tables

Now that we know about MySQL data types, we can use them to create tables. We have already seen the CREATE TABLE SQL command in Chapter 3, which we used to create tables in our example database bmsimple, but we will cover it more formally here. We will also learn about additional features, such as temporary tables, altering tables after creation, and deleting tables when they are no longer required.

Creating Tables

The basic syntax for creating tables is:

```
CREATE [TEMPORARY] TABLE table-name (
    { column-name type [ column-constraint ] [,…] }
    [ CONSTRAINT table-constraint ]
) [ table-options ]
```

Although this syntax looks a little complex, it is actually quite straightforward. The first line simply says that you create tables by using CREATE TABLE, followed by the name of the table and an opening parenthesis. We will come back to TEMPORARY shortly. After that, you list the column name, its type and an optional column constraint, which we will also meet shortly. You can essentially have as many columns as you need in your table, each one separated by a comma. The optional column constraint allows us to specify additional rules for the column, and we have already seen the most common example, NOT NULL.

After the list of columns there is an optional table-level constraint, which allows us to write additional table-level rules that must be obeyed by the data in the table.

Last but not the least, come some table options, which have some interesting uses that are generally unique to MySQL.

We strongly advise to always store the commands you use for creating your database in a script and always use that script for creating your database. If you need to change the database design, it is much easier and more reliable to modify the script, than to recreate the database, or try and recall the commands you used initially. You will find that the effort of initially creating a script and keeping it up to date pays you back many, many times over.

MySQL does have a handy feature if you do lose your script though. The command SHOW CREATE TABLE tablename will write out the commands you need to create your table again, which is almost as good as having your original script. You can also use the utility mysqldump, which will write SQL to create and populate your tables. We will meet this in Chapter 10, *MySQL Administration*.

Column Constraints

We have already seen plenty of basic table creation commands in this chapter; therefore let's skip straight on to looking at the common column constraints you might need to use. It is common to have columns in your table where certain rules apply. We have seen some simple ones already, such as ensuring that a customer's last name is NOT NULL. Sometimes, we want to impose rules that govern the data in a slightly more complex manner, such as ensuring that a pay rate column will have a default value if one isn't provided or ensuring that columns are unique.

Applying constraints to columns allows us to perform these checks at the lowest level of our complete application – the database. As a rule of thumb, enforcing them at the database level is a good technique, since it is independent of the application, so any application bugs that might allow illegal values to slip through will be caught by the database. It is also often easier to apply the rule by writing a definition when a table is created, rather than writing application logic code, quite probably in many different places, to enforce the rule.

These are the principal constraints that you will find useful, although there are more advanced constraints, which you can find in the MySQL online documentation:

Definition	Meaning
NOT NULL	The column cannot have a NULL value stored in it.
PRIMARY KEY	Each table may only have a single column marked PRIMARY KEY, and the column must also be marked NOT NULL. We will see a little later in the chapter, that if you need to create a composite primary key (a primary key that comprises more than one column), you have to use a table-level constraint, rather than the column-level constraints we are discussing here.
DEFAULT value	Provides a default value when inserting data, so if no value is given the default will be used instead.
CHECK (condition)	As of MySQL 4.0 this is not functional, but the syntax is accepted for compatibility with the standard. Once this feature has been implemented you will be able to check a condition when inserting or updating data. For example you could add the clause CHECK(payscale < 42) to a column called 'payscale', and the database would check that you never insert data that would violate this rule.
AUTO_INCREMENT	We have already met this special attribute, which causes a column value to increment automatically as data is inserted.
REFERENCES	See the section *Foreign Key Constraints* near the end of this chapter.

Apart from REFERENCES, which we will cover in more detail later in the chapter, these are all quite simple to understand. Except from the special case of PRIMARY KEY, you can have as many columns with as many constraints as you need.

Try It Out – Column Constraints

The easiest way of understanding column constraints is simply to see them in action. Let's create a table in the test database we used earlier, and use it to experiment with some constraints:

```
mysql> use test;
Database changed
mysql> CREATE TABLE testcolcons (
    -> colnotnull INT NOT NULL,
    -> colprikey INT NOT NULL PRIMARY KEY,
    -> coldefault INT DEFAULT 42
    -> );
Query OK, 0 rows affected (0.01 sec)
```

Now that we have created a table with a variety of constraints on the columns, we can try inserting some data, and see how the constraints work in practice:

```
mysql> INSERT INTO testcolcons(colnotnull, colprikey, coldefault)
    -> VALUES(1, 1, 1);
Query OK, 1 row affected (0.01 sec)
```

This shows that our basic table is accepting data:

```
mysql> INSERT INTO testcolcons(colnotnull, colprikey, coldefault)
    -> VALUES(2, 2, NULL);
Query OK, 1 row affected (0.00 sec)
```

We are allowed to insert NULL into the column `coldefault`:

```
mysql> INSERT INTO testcolcons(colnotnull, colprikey, coldefault)
    -> VALUES(NULL, 3, NULL);
ERROR 1048: Column 'colnotnull' cannot be null
```

However, we cannot insert a NULL into `colnotnul`, since we specified a constraint that prevented this:

```
mysql> INSERT INTO testcolcons(colnotnull, colprikey, coldefault)
    -> VALUES(3, 2, NULL);
ERROR 1062: Duplicate entry '2' for key 1
```

We cannot insert the value '2' into the column `colprikey`, because a row with that value in that column already exists:

```
mysql> INSERT INTO testcolcons(colnotnull, colprikey)
    -> VALUES(3, 3);
Query OK, 1 row affected (0.00 sec)
```

We insert a row without providing any data for the `coldefault` column. We will see in a moment that this is different from providing a NULL value. Let's have a look at the data that was stored:

```
mysql> SELECT * FROM testcolcons;
+------------+-----------+------------+
| colnotnull | colprikey | coldefault |
+------------+-----------+------------+
|          1 |         1 |          1 |
|          2 |         2 |       NULL |
|          3 |         3 |         42 |
+------------+-----------+------------+
3 rows in set (0.00 sec)

mysql>
```

Notice that when we provide a NULL value to `coldefault`, the NULL is stored, but when in the last INSERT we provided no value at all, the default value of 42 is used:

```
mysql> UPDATE testcolcons SET colprikey = 2 WHERE colnotnull = 3;
ERROR 1062: Duplicate entry '2' for key 1
```

Finally we see that MySQL also prevents us from changing data in a column if that change would violate a constraint.

If we ever want to check the constraints on a table, we can always use DESCRIBE to show them, like this:

```
mysql> DESCRIBE testcolcons;
+------------+---------+------+-----+---------+-------+
| Field      | Type    | Null | Key | Default | Extra |
+------------+---------+------+-----+---------+-------+
| colnotnull | int(11) |      |     | 0       |       |
| colprikey  | int(11) |      | PRI | 0       |       |
| coldefault | int(11) | YES  |     | 42      |       |
+------------+---------+------+-----+---------+-------+
3 rows in set (0.00 sec)

mysql>
```

How It Works

MySQL allows you to specify constraints against columns when you create a table. You can't control the order in which constraints are checked, so if you try and change data in a way that would violate more than one constraint, there is no way of being sure in advance which error message you would receive. That said, constraints are a very powerful way of helping to maintain the quality of your data and we recommend you use them.

You can also use transactions, which we will be meeting in Chapter 9, *Transactions and Locking*, to ensure that all or none of a set of changes is made to the database.

Table Constraints

Table constraints are very similar to column constraints but as the name suggests, apply to the table, rather than an individual column. Occasionally, we need to specify constraints, such as a primary key, at table-level rather than at column-level. For example, we saw in our orderline table we needed to use two columns, orderinfo_id and item_id, together as a composite key to identify a row, since only the combination of columns has to be unique.

MySQL supports a very complex set of table-level constraints. Here we will only look at the most commonly needed options:

Name	Description
UNIQUE(column list)	The value stored in the columns must be different from that stored in all other rows of this column. This differs from PRIMARY KEY in that NULL values are allowed.
PRIMARY KEY(column list)	Effectively a combination of NOT NULL and UNIQUE. Each table may only have a single PRIMARY KEY constraint, either as a table constraint or as a column constraint. Declaring a column as a primary key automatically creates an INDEX for the column.

Name	Description
INDEX(column list)	Creates an INDEX on the columns given. This is a good idea if you know that a table is quite large and a lot of searching will be done on the table against a particular column that is not a primary key. For example, in our customer database the barcode table also stores the item_id to which the bar code relates. It's probable that this table will be quite large, and we may search using the item_id frequently. This is a case where we might add an INDEX to speed the search.

Beware of adding indexes to all your columns; adding an INDEX adds storage overhead, and can also significantly degrade the performance when rows are inserted or deleted. Generally you should not add INDEXes to your tables unless you know you have a performance problem, and then you should examine your application to identify the key column or columns where indexes will offer the most benefit. Unlike other table constraints, an INDEX is not strictly speaking a constraint, and MySQL does not allow INDEXes to be given names. You can show the indexes on a table using SHOW INDEX FROM (tablename) statement. We will see some examples of INDEX being used in the section *Foreign Key Constraints* near the end of this chapter. |
| REFERENCES | See the section *Foreign Key Constraints* near the end of this chapter. |

As you can see table constraints bear more than a passing resemblance to the column-level constraints.

The differences are:

❑ Table-level constraints are listed after all the columns.

❑ They take comma-separated lists of column names, so a table-level constraint can refer to more than one column.

Let's dive straight in and give table-level constraints a go.

Try It Out – Table-Level Constraints

First, we create a table ttconst with some constraints:

```
mysql> CREATE TABLE ttconst (
    -> mykey1 INT,
    -> mykey2 INT NOT NULL,
    -> mystring varchar(15) NOT NULL,
```

235

```
    -> CONSTRAINT cs1 UNIQUE(mykey1),
    -> CONSTRAINT cs2 PRIMARY KEY(mykey2, mystring)
    -> );
Query OK, 0 rows affected (0.00 sec)

mysql>
```

Notice we can name the constraint, though we don't have to. We can omit the names `cs1` and `cs2` if we want:

```
mysql> INSERT INTO ttconst VALUES( 1, 2, "Amy Jones");
Query OK, 1 row affected (0.00 sec)
```

```
mysql> INSERT INTO ttconst VALUES( 1, 2, "Dave Jones");
ERROR 1062: Duplicate entry '1' for key 2
```

The `INSERT` fails because we try and insert a duplicate value in `mykey1`, which violates the constraint `cs1`:

```
mysql> INSERT INTO ttconst VALUES( 2, 2, "Dave Jones");
Query OK, 1 row affected (0.00 sec)
```

It is OK to have a duplicate in `mykey2`, because the constraint `cs2` only requires that the columns `mykey2` and `mystring` are unique once they are combined:

```
mysql> INSERT INTO ttconst VALUES( 3, 2, "Amy Jones");
ERROR 1062: Duplicate entry '2-Amy Jones' for key 1
```

If we try and duplicate both values, MySQL catches the violation and rejects the data. The error message tells us the part of the data that is causing the rejection.

How It Works

As you can see, table-level constraints are very similar to their column-level equivalents. In general, it is better to use a column-level constraint if that is all that is required. Sometimes you need table-level constraints, for example, when we created our `bmsimple` database. Many people prefer to use only table-level constraints, rather than mix the two types, for the sake of consistency.

Creating Tables Using SELECT

One useful feature that was added to MySQL version 3.23 was the ability to create a table as the result of a `SELECT` statement, using the syntax:

```
CREATE TABLE newtable SELECT columnlist FROM existingtable
              [ WHERE condition ]
```

This will create a copy of the table, including any data that matches the condition. If you want all the data, simply omit the WHERE clause. If you want none of the data, make the WHERE clause always fail, for example 'WHERE 1 = 0'. Be aware that although this copies simple column constraint like NOT NULL, more complex constraints such as a primary key are not created.

This syntax is very easy to use, so let's jump straight in with an example.

Try It Out – Creating a Table Using SELECT

Suppose we want a subset of our customer data stored in a table containing the first name, last name, and zip code of customers who live in Bingham or Nicetown. With the syntax above, this is very easy to do in a single step:

```
mysql> use bmsimple;
Database changed
mysql> CREATE TABLE c2 SELECT fname, lname, zipcode FROM customer
    -> WHERE (town ='Bingham') OR (town = 'Nicetown');
Query OK, 5 rows affected (0.00 sec)
Records: 5  Duplicates: 0  Warnings: 0

mysql> DESCRIBE c2;
+---------+----------+------+-----+---------+-------+
| Field   | Type     | Null | Key | Default | Extra |
+---------+----------+------+-----+---------+-------+
| fname   | char(32) | YES  |     | NULL    |       |
| lname   | char(32) |      |     |         |       |
| zipcode | char(10) |      |     |         |       |
+---------+----------+------+-----+---------+-------+
3 rows in set (0.00 sec)

mysql> SELECT * FROM c2;
+---------+---------+---------+
| fname   | lname   | zipcode |
+---------+---------+---------+
| Alex    | Matthew | NT2 2TX |
| Neil    | Matthew | NT3 7RT |
| Richard | Stones  | BG4 2WE |
| Ann     | Stones  | BG4 2WE |
| Dave    | Jones   | BG3 8GD |
+---------+---------+---------+
5 rows in set (0.00 sec)

mysql>
```

How It Works

We start by using the CREATE TABLE statement, providing a SELECT clause from our existing customer table, with a WHERE clause to select only those customers we want in our new table, which we have called c2.

We then use the DESCRIBE() function to show the structure of our new table. You can see that not only have the columns been created with the right types and sizes, but also the attributes, such as permitting fname to be NULL but not lname or zipcode, have also been carried across into our new table.

Finally we use SELECT to show that the appropriate rows have been copied across into our new table.

The MySQL Table Types

It's now time to move on to the last part of the MySQL CREATE TABLE command – the optional 'TYPE=' part at the end. This relates to a feature pretty much unique to MySQL – the ability to mix and match different table implementations 'behind the scenes' of the SQL-based front end.

Setting the Table Type

There are two ways of setting the table type, by appending TYPE = tabletype to the end of the CREATE TABLE command, like this:

```
mysql> use test
Database changed
mysql> CREATE TABLE fred (
    -> fi INT
    -> ) TYPE = MYISAM;
Query OK, 0 rows affected (0.07 sec)
```

This allows us control over the table implementation on a table-by-table basis, which is occasionally useful. The preferred way of setting the default table type as we saw in Chapter 3, is by using a setting in the [mysqld] section of the my.cnf configuration file:

```
default-table-type=tabletype
```

This sets the table type for all subsequently created tables, unless they have a 'TYPE =' after the CREATE TABLE command which overrides the default.

As we shall see in a moment, if you change your mind all is not lost. You can still use the ALTER TABLE command to change the type after the table has been created.

MySQL Table Types

There are various table types, indeed the list of available table types changes over time, so here we will consider only the most important ones. As always, check the documentation for the latest information:

Table Type	Transaction safe	Details
HEAP	No	This is a special type of 'in memory' tables. They store the data in memory and hence are extremely quick, providing the amount of data you store in them is reasonable and you don't fill significant amounts of your physical memory with database tables. There are two other downsides. Firstly they are only ever visible to the client that created them; secondly they are automatically deleted when the MySQL server terminates. If what you need is a small amount of fast but temporary local table space, the HEAP type is generally ideal.

Table Type	Transaction safe	Details
ISAM	No	This is the original format used by MySQL. It has largely been replaced by the MyISAM format and is not recommended for new databases.
MyISAM	No	This a newer format that became the default table type from version 3.23 of MySQL. It has several advantages over the older ISAM format, notably machine-independent storage, support for very large tables, and is generally more flexible in the way indexes can be used. It retains the high performance that the ISAM table implementation gave to MySQL, and is still its best-known feature.
MERGE	No	This is a rather specialized table type that allows you to combine several other tables into a single logical table. This is handy for very large data-sets, but MERGE tables have some restrictions and are not intended for more general use. The manual contains more details.
BDB	Yes	This is often referred to as the BerkeleyDB table type and is an implementation from SleepyCat software (http://www.sleepycat.com/). Many UNIX users will be familiar with the Berkeley database system, to which this is closely related. The big advantage of BDB tables is that they support transactions, about which we will be learning more in Chapter 9, *Transactions and Locking*. At the time of writing, support for BDB tables is very new and they are not supported on all architectures on which MySQL runs. Consult the online documentation for the current state of support for BDB tables.
InnoDB	Yes	This is another external table implementation that has been added to MySQL as a back-end table type. The implementation is from Innobase Oy Inc. who can be found at http://www.innodb.com, where there is an extensive online manual. InnoDB tables require an entry in the my.cnf file to be used by default, as we saw in the Chapter 3, but once running they offer significant benefits in two areas. Firstly, they offer excellent support for transactions and we will be using InnoDB tables to show this in Chapter 9. Secondly, they also implement the foreign key constraints we will be seeing later in this chapter. If you need to use transactions or foreign key constraints, we recommend you look at the InnoDB table types. The additional effort in configuring them can be handsomely repaid with the feature-rich environment they bring. We will see more about configuring InnoDB tables in Chapter 10.

We neither have the space, nor is it appropriate in this book to go into any greater depths of the MySQL table types. Generally you should choose MyISAM for pure speed or InnoDB for features. Of course the situation may change as MySQL develops, so you should always check back for the latest online documentation about the table types available.

One thing we would recommend is being consistent, especially within a database. Decide what table implementation is most suitable and use that table implementation type for all the tables, with perhaps the exception of some temporary tables that you might wish to implement as Heap type for performance reasons.

Altering Tables

Unfortunately, life is complicated, and no matter how carefully you gather requirements and implement your database, the day will come when you need to alter the design of a table.

We saw a solution to solve this by using INSERT INTO in Chapter 6, *Changing Your Data*, where the data is gathered by selecting data from an existing table. We could do it in the following steps:

❑ Create a new working table with an identical structure to the existing table.

❑ Use INSERT INTO to populate the working table with data identical to the original table.

❑ Delete the existing table.

❑ Recreate the table with the same name, but with the changes we need.

❑ Use INSERT INTO again to populate the altered table from the working table.

❑ Delete the working table.

That is clearly a great deal of work, especially if the table contains a lot of data, if all we wanted to do is add a column to a table. MySQL follows the SQL standard, which has an ALTER TABLE command allowing columns to be added and deleted from a table 'in situ', while the table contains data. With MySQL you can also change the column declaration that is its type, though there are limits as to what can be changed while data is present in the table. We can also add and remove primary keys. The ALTER TABLE syntax has some additional variations for managing indexes; for details of those consult the manual.

You can also rename a column, preserving its data, and rename the whole table too.

The syntax is simple:

```
ALTER TABLE table-name ADD COLUMN column-name column-type
            [ FIRST | AFTER column name ]
ALTER TABLE table-name DROP COLUMN column-name
ALTER TABLE table-name CHANGE COLUMN column-name new-name new-type
ALTER TABLE old-table-name RENAME AS new-table-name
ALTER TABLE ADD PRIMARY KEY (column-list)
ALTER TABLE DROP PRIMARY KEY
```

Columns that are added to a table with existing data will have Null stored as their value for the existing rows.

Try It Out – Alter Table

Let's try these commands out using the table c2 we created a few moments ago. This is what the table structure is currently:

```
mysql> DESCRIBE c2;
+---------+----------+------+-----+---------+-------+
| Field   | Type     | Null | Key | Default | Extra |
+---------+----------+------+-----+---------+-------+
| fname   | char(32) | YES  |     | NULL    |       |
| lname   | char(32) |      |     |         |       |
| zipcode | char(10) |      |     |         |       |
+---------+----------+------+-----+---------+-------+
3 rows in set (0.01 sec)
```

Now let's add a `last_contact` column, of type Date, after the `zipcode`:

```
mysql> ALTER TABLE c2 ADD COLUMN last_contact date AFTER zipcode;
Query OK, 5 rows affected (0.03 sec)
Records: 5  Duplicates: 0  Warnings: 0
```

Now we change the `zipcode` column from a fixed `char` field to a longer variable length field. Notice that we have not specified NOT NULL. Thus the table can now have NULL values in the `zipcode` column:

```
mysql> ALTER TABLE c2 CHANGE COLUMN zipcode zipcode2 char(15);
Query OK, 5 rows affected (0.02 sec)
Records: 5  Duplicates: 0  Warnings: 0
```

Let's have a look at our table definition now:

```
mysql> DESCRIBE c2;
+--------------+----------+------+-----+---------+-------+
| Field        | Type     | Null | Key | Default | Extra |
+--------------+----------+------+-----+---------+-------+
| fname        | char(32) | YES  |     | NULL    |       |
| lname        | char(32) |      |     |         |       |
| zipcode2     | char(15) | YES  |     | NULL    |       |
| last_contact | date     | YES  |     | NULL    |       |
+--------------+----------+------+-----+---------+-------+
4 rows in set (0.00 sec)
```

We can check the data has been preserved:

```
mysql> SELECT * FROM c2;
+---------+---------+----------+--------------+
| fname   | lname   | zipcode2 | last_contact |
+---------+---------+----------+--------------+
| Alex    | Matthew | NT2 2TX  | NULL         |
| Neil    | Matthew | NT3 7RT  | NULL         |
| Richard | Stones  | BG4 2WE  | NULL         |
| Ann     | Stones  | BG4 2WE  | NULL         |
| Dave    | Jones   | BG3 8GD  | NULL         |
+---------+---------+----------+--------------+
5 rows in set (0.00 sec)
```

We can see that the combination of fname and lname is unique, and maybe we think it would be good, in this case, to make those columns a primary key. Before we can do this we have to change the fname column to give it the attribute NOT NULL, because, as you will remember, columns being used as primary keys must be declared not to hold NULL values.

You might think that because the table does have some NULL values in the current data this would be good enough, but to ensure no NULLs *ever* appear you must change the column type definition.

So let's go ahead and do that, then we can create our primary key:

```
mysql> ALTER TABLE c2 CHANGE COLUMN fname fname char(32) NOT NULL;
Query OK, 5 rows affected (0.03 sec)
Records: 5  Duplicates: 0  Warnings: 0

mysql> ALTER TABLE c2 ADD PRIMARY KEY (fname, lname);
Query OK, 5 rows affected (0.03 sec)
Records: 5  Duplicates: 0  Warnings: 0

mysql> DESCRIBE c2;
```

Field	Type	Null	Key	Default	Extra
fname	char(32)		PRI		
lname	char(32)		PRI		
zipcode2	char(15)	YES		NULL	
last_contact	date	YES		NULL	

```
4 rows in set (0.01 sec)

mysql>
```

How It Works

We have taken the c2 table we created earlier, changed the definition of some columns, added an additional column and even created a new primary key. The ALTER TABLE command in MySQL is a very powerful tool, that can help you adjust your table definitions as requirements change, without the need to unload and reload your data. The power of ALTER TABLE is not a reason to skimp on the design stage. Time invested in the design of your database is almost always time well spent.

If you ever have to use the ALTER TABLE command, do be sure to retest your application to ensure you have not caused problems to appear.

Deleting Tables

Deleting a table is very simple:

```
DROP TABLE table-name
```

> **Presto! Your table has disappeared, along with any data that was in it. A command to be used with caution!**

Temporary Tables

All the SQL we have seen so far has managed to achieve our desired result in a single, albeit occasionally complex, SELECT statement. Usually this is a good practice because you will remember we said that SQL is a declarative language. If you define what you want to achieve, SQL finds the best way of getting the result for you. Sometimes it is just not possible or convenient to do everything in a single SELECT statement and some temporary results need to be held somewhere.

Usually, the temporary storage you need is a table, so you can store many rows. Of course, you could always create a table, do your processing and then delete the table again. This entails a risk, as the intermediate tables will occasionally fail to get deleted, either because your application has a bug or due to simple forgetfulness from an inattentive user. The net result is stray tables, usually with strange names, left around in your database. Unfortunately, it is not always clear which tables are intended to be just intermediate worktables and can be deleted, and which are currently in use.

SQL has a very simple solution to this problem, the idea of **temporary tables**. When you create the table, rather than use CREATE TABLE, you use CREATE TEMPORARY TABLE. The table is created for you in the usual way, except that when your session ends and your connection to the database gets terminated, the temporary table is automatically deleted for you. Let's see this in action, using a MySQL session on a MS Windows machine:

```
mysql> use bmsimple;
Database changed

mysql> CREATE TEMPORARY TABLE foobar (
    -> x INT
    -> );
Query OK, 0 rows affected (0.02 sec)

mysql> INSERT INTO foobar VALUES(42);
Query OK, 1 row affected (0.00 sec)

mysql> SELECT * FROM foobar;
+------+
| x    |
+------+
|   42 |
+------+
1 row in set (0.01 sec)

mysql> exit
Bye

C:\>\mysql\bin\mysql
Welcome to the MySQL monitor.  Commands end with ; or \g.

Type 'help;' or '\h' for help. Type '\c' to clear the buffer.

mysql> use bmsimple;
Database changed
mysql> SELECT * FROM foobar;
ERROR 1146: Table 'bmsimple.foobar' doesn't exist
mysql>
```

As you can see, the foobar table was automatically deleted when the session ended.

Foreign Key Constraints

We now come to one of the most important kinds of constraints, called **foreign key constraints**.

When we drew our diagram of a sample `bmsimple` database, we had tables with data that joined, or were related, to other tables. Here is the relationship diagram from Chapter 2, *Relational Database Principles*, again, as a reminder:

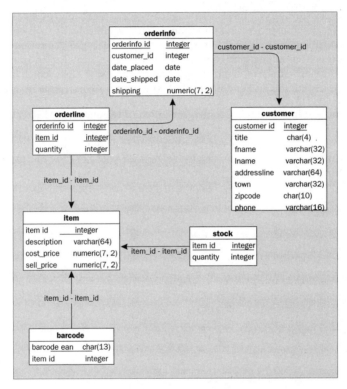

You will remember how columns in one table relate to columns in another. For example, the `customer_id` in the `orderinfo` table relates to the `customer_id` in the `customer` table. So, given an `orderinfo_id`, we can use the `customer_id` from the same row to discover the name and address of the customer to which the order relates. We learned that the `customer_id` is a primary key in the `customer` table; that is it uniquely identifies a single row in the `customer` table.

We can now learn another important piece of terminology – the `customer_id` in the `orderinfo` table is a **foreign key**. What we mean by foreign key is that although `customer_id` in the `orderinfo` table is not a primary key in that table, the column it joins to in the `customer` table is unique. Notice that there is no reverse relationship; no column in the `customer` table is a unique key of any other table that it joins with. Hence we say that the `customer` table has no foreign keys.

When we declare a foreign key constraint, MySQL will check that the column in the particular table being referenced is declared such that it must be unique. It is very common for the column referenced by a foreign key to be the primary key in the other table.

At the time of writing, MySQL does not check foreign key constraints on tables that use the normal default table type of `MyISAM`, even though the syntax is accepted. Although this makes the data access quicker, it does relax the amount of control you have at the database level over the relationships of the data that is stored. In our view, for all but reasonably lightweight databases there is significant value in implementing foreign key constraints, but the decision is of course up to the individuals when they design and implement the database. If you want to ensure foreign key constraints are implemented at the database level, we suggest you implement all your tables as `InnoDB` type, and use a minimum MySQL version of 4.0. The behavior may change in versions after MySQL 4.0, and support for checking foreign key constraints be added to the `MyISAM` type. Please check the documentation for the version of MySQL you are currently using and consider an update if necessary.

It is possible for a table to have more than one foreign key. If we look at the `orderline` table, we see that `orderinfo_id` is a foreign key, since it joins with the `orderinfo_id` in the `orderinfo` table, which is a primary key in the `orderinfo` table, and `item_id` is also a foreign key, because it joins with `item_id` in the `item` table that is a primary key in the `item` table.

In the `item` table we discover that the `item_id` is both a primary key in the `item` table, since it uniquely identifies a row, and a foreign key in the `stock` table. It is perfectly acceptable for a single column to be both a primary and foreign key, and implies a (usually optional) one-to-one relationship between rows in the two tables.

Although we don't have any examples in our sample database, it is also possible for a pair of columns, as a combined entity, to be a foreign key, just as the `orderinfo_id` and `item_id` together form a primary key in the `orderline` table.

These relationships are absolutely crucial to our database. If we have a row in our `orderinfo` table where the `customer_id` doesn't match a `customer_id` row in the `customer` table then it is a major problem. We have an order and no idea of the customer who placed the order. Although we can use application logic to enforce our relationship rules, as we said with the column and table constraints we met earlier, it is much safer, and often easier, to declare them as database rules.

You will not be surprised to learn that it is possible to declare such foreign key relationships as constraints on columns and tables, much like the constraints we have already met. This is done when tables are created, as part of the `CREATE TABLE` command, using the `REFERENCES` type of constraint that we skipped over earlier in the chapter.

We are now going to move on from our `bmsimple` database, and create a `bmfinal` database that implements foreign key constraints, to enforce data integrity.

Declaring Foreign Key Constraints

The basic syntax for declaring a column to be a foreign key in another table is very simple and comes after all the columns have been declared:

```
[CONSTRAINT [arbitrary-name]] FOREIGN KEY(column-list) REFERENCES foreign-table-
name(column-list-in-foreign-table)
```

To use foreign key constraints in MySQL with InnoDB tables, there are a couple of additional restrictions you must meet. Firstly the column to which you refer (the REFERENCES column), must either be a primary key or have an INDEX created on it. Secondly the column in the table to which you are applying the constraint, must be either a primary key or have an INDEX created on it.

> One thing to be aware of is the error messages for foreign key constraints from the InnoDB table implementation. Currently they are numeric only and a little obscure. Error 1000010 tells you that you tried to insert data, but there is no corresponding data in the table your foreign key references. Error 1000011 tells you that the deletion of data failed because other tables have foreign key references to the data. Error 1000012 tells you it could not create the table because there was an error in the foreign key constraints you specified. This is usually related to a missing INDEX or PRIMARY KEY definition.

To define a foreign key constraint on the customer_id column in the orderinfo table, relating it to the customer table, we must make three changes to our table definition. Firstly we must add an INDEX on the customer_id column in the orderinfo table; secondly we add a REFERENCES keyword along with the name of the table and column. Last but not least, we can declare the table type as InnoDB by adding 'TYPE = InnoDB', although we do not have to do this if we set the default table type (in my.cnf) to InnoDB.

> We strongly urge you to ensure that any particular database in which you wish to use InnoDB tables uses exclusively InnoDB tables, wherever feasible. The best way of doing this is to set the default table type to InnoDB (add a line default-table-type=innodb to the [mysqld] section of my.cnf), then create the database you wish to use, and then create all the tables. To double-check that you have InnoDB tables, use the command SHOW TABLE STATUS which should show the table type as InnoDB.

We show the syntax with the type declaration here for completeness, but we urge you to avoid using it wherever possible.

```
CREATE TABLE orderinfo
(
    orderinfo_id      int AUTO_INCREMENT NOT NULL PRIMARY KEY,
    customer_id       integer            NOT NULL,
    date_placed       date               NOT NULL,
    date_shipped      date                          ,
    shipping          numeric(7,2)                  ,
    INDEX (customer_id),
    CONSTRAINT orderinfo_customer_id_fk FOREIGN KEY(customer_id)
    REFERENCES customer(customer_id)
) TYPE = InnoDB;
```

We have named the constraint as orderinfo_customer_id_fk. We do not have to make any changes to the customer table, because the column we reference in the customer table, customer_id, is already a primary key in that table. We will see the effect of REFERENCES constraint very shortly.

Although the SQL standard allows you to declare foreign key constraints at the column level, we suggest that you declare them at the table level, along with PRIMARY KEY constraints. You cannot use a column constraint when multiple columns in the current table are involved in the relationship, so in such cases, you have to write it as a table-level constraint.

We start by creating a new database and recreating the tables as they were before:

```
mysql> CREATE DATABASE bmfinal;
Query OK, 1 row affected (0.00 sec)

mysql> use bmfinal;
Database changed
```

Now we re-execute our script for creating the tables:

```
mysql> \. create_tables.sql
Query OK, 0 rows affected (0.00 sec)

Query OK, 0 rows affected (0.01 sec)

Query OK, 0 rows affected (0.00 sec)

Query OK, 0 rows affected (0.01 sec)

Query OK, 0 rows affected (0.00 sec)

Query OK, 0 rows affected (0.01 sec)

mysql>
```

If we drop and recreate the orderinfo table then populate it again, we will be able to see the effect of our new constraint:

```
mysql> DROP TABLE orderinfo;
Query OK, 0 rows affected (0.01 sec)

mysql> CREATE TABLE orderinfo (
    -> orderinfo_id      integer AUTO_INCREMENT NOT NULL PRIMARY KEY,
    -> customer_id       integer                NOT NULL,
    -> date_placed       date                   NOT NULL,
    -> date_shipped      date,
    -> shipping          numeric(7,2),
    -> INDEX (customer_id),
    -> CONSTRAINT orderinfo_customer_id_fk FOREIGN KEY(customer_id)
    -> REFERENCES customer(customer_id)
    -> );
Query OK, 0 rows affected (0.00 sec)

mysql>
```

Now we can repopulate database tables from our SQL script:

```
mysql> \. pop_all_tables.sql
Query OK, 1 row affected (0.00 sec)

Query OK, 1 row affected (0.00 sec)
```

So now we are almost back to where we started, with one very important difference – the orderinfo table has a foreign key constraint, which says that rows in the orderinfo table have the customer_id column referring to the customer_id column in the customer table. This should mean that we cannot delete rows from the customer table if the row is being referenced by a column in the orderinfo table.

Try It Out – Foreign Key Constraints

We will start by checking to see what customer_ids we have in the orderinfo table:

```
mysql> SELECT orderinfo_id, customer_id FROM orderinfo;
+--------------+-------------+
| orderinfo_id | customer_id |
+--------------+-------------+
|            1 |           3 |
|            2 |           8 |
|            5 |           8 |
|            4 |          13 |
|            3 |          15 |
+--------------+-------------+
5 rows in set (0.00 sec)

mysql>
```

We now know that there are five rows in orderinfo that have customer_ids that refer to customers in the customer table and that the customers referred to have ids 3, 8, 13 and 15. There are only four customers referred to, because the row with orderinfo_ids 2 and 5 both refer to the same customer.

Now let's try and delete the row from the customer table with customer_id 3:

```
mysql> DELETE FROM customer WHERE customer_id = 3;
ERROR 1030: Got error 1000011 from table handler

mysql>
```

MySQL, in the guise of the InnoDB table handler, prevents us from deleting the row. It will still allow us to delete rows from the customer table that are not referenced:

```
mysql> DELETE FROM customer WHERE customer_id = 4;
Query OK, 1 row affected (0.00 sec)

mysql>
```

How It Works

Behind the scenes, the InnoDB table handler for these MySQL tables adds some additional checking; that no row we try to delete from the customer table is being referred to by a row in any different table, in this case the orderinfo table.

Any attempts to violate the rule result in the command being rejected and the data left unchanged. Of course, we can still delete a customer, but we have to ensure they have no orders first.

MySQL also checks that we don't try and INSERT rows into the orderinfo table that refer to non-existent customers:

```
mysql> INSERT INTO orderinfo(customer_id, date_placed, shipping) VALUES(250, '07-
25-2000', 0.00);
ERROR 1030: Got error 1000010 from table handler

mysql>
```

It is important to realize that we have taken a big step forward here. We are ensuring that the relationships between tables are enforced by the database. Referential integrity is enforced – it is no longer possible to have rows in orderinfo referring to non-existent customers.

We can now update our create_tables.sql script to add foreign key constraints to all the tables that refer to other tables, that is, orderinfo, orderline, stock, and barcode. Notice that we do not use the 'TYPE = INNODB' syntax; rather we assume that the default table type has been set in my.cnf.

The only slightly complex one is orderline, where the orderinfo_id column refers to the orderinfo table, and the item_id column refers to the item table. This is not a problem; we simply specify two constraints, one for each column such as this:

```
CREATE TABLE orderline
(
    orderinfo_id        integer            NOT NULL,
    item_id             integer            NOT NULL,
    quantity            integer            NOT NULL,
    PRIMARY KEY(orderinfo_id, item_id),
    INDEX(item_id),
    CONSTRAINT orderline_orderinfo_id_fk FOREIGN KEY (orderinfo_id) REFERENCES
orderinfo(orderinfo_id),
    CONSTRAINT orderline_item_id_fk FOREIGN KEY (item_id) REFERENCES item(item_id)
);
```

For reference, here are the other table definitions, with foreign key constraints, and where necessary, INDEXes also added. Unchanged table definitions are not listed (you will find relevant information in Appendix E):

```
CREATE TABLE orderinfo
(
    orderinfo_id           int AUTO_INCREMENT NOT NULL PRIMARY KEY,
```

```
        customer_id             integer                 NOT NULL,
        date_placed             date                    NOT NULL,
        date_shipped            date                                ,
        shipping                numeric(7,2),
        INDEX (customer_id),
        CONSTRAINT orderinfo_customer_id_fk FOREIGN KEY(customer_id) REFERENCES
customer(customer_id)
);
```

```
CREATE TABLE stock
(
    item_id             integer AUTO_INCREMENT NOT NULL PRIMARY KEY,
    quantity            integer                 NOT NULL,
    CONSTRAINT stock_item_id_fk FOREIGN KEY(item_id) REFERENCES item(item_id)
);
```

```
CREATE TABLE barcode
(
    barcode_ean         char(13)        NOT NULL PRIMARY KEY,
    item_id             integer         NOT NULL,
    INDEX(item_id),
    CONSTRAINT barcode_item_id_fk FOREIGN KEY(item_id) REFERENCES item(item_id)
);
```

These can be found in the bmfinal code bundle that can be downloaded from the Wrox web site (www.wrox.com).

When you use this database, you will also find that you must populate the tables in an order that fulfills the foreign key constraints; you can no longer populate the orderinfo table before populating the customer table for the orders to reference.

The order that we suggest is:

- ❏ customer
- ❏ item
- ❏ orderinfo
- ❏ orderline
- ❏ stock
- ❏ barcode

This is the order used in the provided pop_all_tables.sql script, available on the Wrox web site.

Foreign Key Constraint Options

We can take these referential integrity checks using foreign key constraints one step further. Since this is an advanced topic, we will only be touching on the details. More information can be found in the online documentation, particularly the InnoDB manual (http://www.innodb.com/ibman.html) and various advanced SQL books.

It might be that we get into a situation where we have entries in the orderinfo table referring to the customer table, but we need to update the customer_id. As it stands, we can't easily do this, because if we attempt to change the customer_id the foreign key constraint in orderinfo will prevent it, since the rule says that the customer_id stored in each orderinfo row must always refer to a customer_id entry in the customer table.

We can't change the customer_id in the orderinfo table, because the entry in the customer table doesn't exist yet, and we can't change the entry in the customer table, because the orderinfo table is referring it to.

Deferrable

The SQL standard allows two ways out of this. The first is to add the keyword DEFERRABLE at the end of the foreign key constraint. This changes the way foreign key constraints are enforced. Normally, SQL databases will check that foreign key constraints are met before any change is allowed to the database. If you use the DEFERRABLE keyword, then the database will allow foreign key constraints to be violated, but only inside a transaction. As we will see in the next chapter, a transaction is a group of SQL commands that must either be completely executed, or it must appear as though none of them were executed. Hence, we could start a transaction, update the customer_id in the customer table, update the related customer_ids in the orderinfo table and commit the transaction; and this would be permitted if the constraint was marked DEFERRABLE. All it will check is that the constraints are met when the transaction ends.

Summary

This chapter has presented quite a wide-ranging discussion. We started by looking more formally at the data types supported by MySQL, especially the common SQL standard types but also mentioning some of MySQL's additional types, such as TINYTEXT.

We then looked at how you can manipulate column data, in particular converting columns between types, and adding and removing columns for existing tables without losing any data (in other words, data integrity or referential integrity) currently stored in the table.

We then moved on to look at a very important topic, that of constraints. We saw that there are two effective ways of defining constraints, those against a single column and those at a table level. We saw how even simple constraints can help us to enforce the integrity of data at the database level.

Our final topic dealt with one of the most important types of constraints, foreign keys, which allow us to define formally in the database how different tables relate to each other. Most importantly, it allows us to enforce these rules, for example ensuring that we can never delete a customer where an order relating to him exists in a different table.

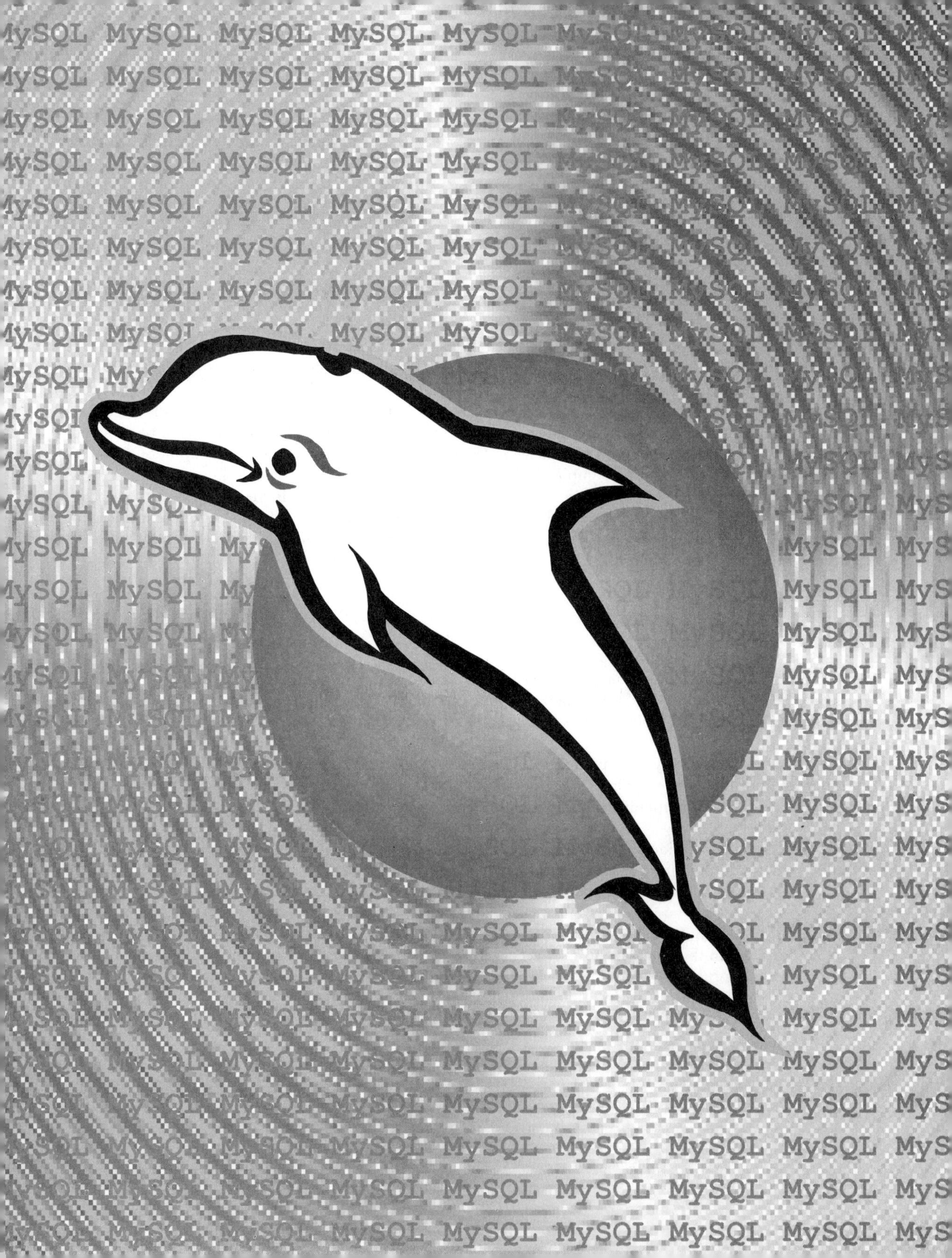
MySQL

Transactions and Locking

So far in this book we have avoided any in-depth discussion of the multi-user aspects of MySQL, assuming the idealized view that like any relational database MySQL hides the details of supporting multiple concurrent users. We have assumed that MySQL simply provides an efficient multi-user database server that behaves as if all the simultaneous users have exclusive access, and that each user appears to be independent of the others.

One positive aspect of MySQL is that, for many purposes, particularly with smaller and lightly loaded databases that are mainly accessed for reading, this idealized view is almost achieved in practice. However, though MySQL is capable, it cannot perform magic. Achieving the isolation of each user from any others requires work behind the scenes, and sometimes from the end user as well. We cannot avoid having the real world intrude on our idealized view that users can behave as though they have exclusive access to the database server.

In this chapter, we will be looking less at the technical details of how MySQL achieves its isolation of different users, and more at the practicalities of what this means for developers and users of the database. We will start with general introduction to transactions and how we measure the degree of isolation of each user from all others. We will then move on to look at the more practical aspects of using MySQL in a multi-user environment. While doing this, we will consider both the cases where the default table type of MyISAM is used, and where the table type is changed to one of the transaction-safe equivalents; by way of example we will be using InnoDB.

In this chapter, we will be looking at:

- ❑ What are transactions?
- ❑ The ACID rules
- ❑ Transactions with a single user
- ❑ Transaction with multiple users
- ❑ MySQL and Transactions
- ❑ Deadlocks

What Are Transactions?

The first topic we need to discuss is how updates are made to a database. We have said that wherever possible we should write the changes made to the database as a single declarative SQL statement. In real-world applications, however, there soon comes a point at which you need to make several changes to a database that cannot be expressed in a single SQL statement. You need either all of these changes to occur or none of them to occur, if there is a problem with any part of the group of changes.

The classic example is that of transferring money between two bank accounts, perhaps represented in different tables in a database, where you need one account to be debited and the other credited. If you debit one account and fail to credit the second for some reason, you must return the money to the first account or (preferably) behave as though it was never debited in the first place. No bank could remain in business if it 'lost' money even occasionally when transferring it between accounts.

In databases based on ANSI SQL, this is achieved with what are termed **transactions**.

> **A transaction is a logical unit of work that must not be subdivided.**

What do we mean by a logical unit of work? It is simply a set of logical changes to the database, where either all occur or none must occur, just like the example mentioned earlier of the transferring of money between accounts.

> At the time of writing, the default table type for MySQL is `MyISAM`, which does not provide full automatic support for transactions, though this is expected to be added in a future release. At present, under `MyISAM`, individual SQL statements are isolated, but not groups of statements.

If full transaction support is important to us then there are several things we can do to get around this problem with `MyISAM` tables, as we will see later in this chapter. Alternatively, we could use a transaction-safe table type, such as `InnoDB` or `DBD`.

We will start by looking how ANSI SQL defines transactions and the isolation between users, and come back to the more practical aspects of transactions in MySQL later in the chapter.

In standard SQL, transactions are controlled by three key phrases:

❑ `BEGIN WORK` starts a transaction.

❑ `COMMIT` says that all the elements of the transaction are complete, and should now be made persistent and accessible to all concurrent and subsequent transactions.

❑ `ROLLBACK` says that the transaction is to be abandoned, and all changes made to data by that SQL transaction must be cancelled. The database should appear to all users as though none of the changes made since the previous `BEGIN WORK`, have occurred.

The SQL standard does not define the BEGIN WORK SQL phrase; it defines transactions as starting automatically (hence the phrase would be redundant). However, it is a very common extension in many of the present relational databases, and in fact a requirement in some cases. With MySQL it is normal to use the BEGIN WORK phrase or just BEGIN, which are equivalent. It only has an effect on transaction-safe tables, like InnoDB and DBD table types, and even then only if AUTOCOMMIT mode is set to off. We will learn more about AUTOCOMMIT mode later in the chapter.

Some databases accept or even expect the word 'WORK' after COMMIT and ROLLBACK. The word WORK has no effect in MySQL and is not currently supported by it. In many relational databases the phrases COMMIT and COMMIT WORK carry identical meaning; in MySQL however, COMMIT WORK is invalid. The same holds true for ROLLBACK and ROLLBACK WORK. In short, the valid commands for MySQL are COMMIT and ROLLBACK.

A second aspect of transactions is that any transaction in the database is isolated from other transactions occurring at the same time. In an ideal world, each transaction would behave as though it had exclusive access. Unfortunately, as we will see later in this chapter, when we look at isolation levels, the practicalities of achieving good performance mean that often some compromises have to be made.

Let's look at a different (and hopefully fictitious!) example of where a transaction is needed. Suppose you are trying to book an airline ticket online. You check the flight you want and discover a ticket is available. Although you do not know, it is the very last ticket on that flight. While you are typing in your credit card details another customer with an account at the airline makes the same check for tickets. You have not yet purchased your ticket; they see a free seat and book it, while you are still typing in your credit card details. You now click on submit to buy 'your' ticket, and because the system knew there was a seat available when you started the transaction, it incorrectly assumes a seat is still available, and debits your card.

You log off, confident your seat has been booked, and perhaps even check that your credit card has been debited. However, the reality is that you purchased a non-existent ticket. At the instant your transaction was processed, there were no free seats.

The logic executed by your booking may have looked a little like this:

Check if seats are available.
If yes, offer seat to customer.
If customer accepts offer, ask for credit card number.
Authorize credit card transaction with bank.
Debit card.
Assign seat.
Reduce the number of free seats available by the number purchased.

Such a sequence of events is perfectly valid if only a single customer ever uses the system at any one time. The trouble only occurred because we had two customers, and what actually happened was this:

Customer 1 (with credit card)	Customer 2 (with account)	Free seats on plane
Check if seats available		1
	Check if seats available	1
If yes, offer seat to customer		1
	If yes, offer seat to customer	1
If customer accepts offer, ask for credit card or account number		1
	If customer accepts offer, ask for credit card or account number	1
Provides credit card number	Provides account number	1
Authorize credit card transaction with bank		1
	Check account is valid	1
	Update account with new transaction	1
Debit card	Assign seat	1
Assign seat	Reduce the number of free seats available by the number purchased	0
Reduce the number of free seats available by the number purchased		-1

We could improve things considerably by rechecking that a seat was available closer to the point at which we take the money, but however late we do the check, it's inevitable that the 'check a seat is available' step is separated from the 'take money' step, even if only by a tiny amount of time.

We could go to the opposite extreme to solve the problem, allowing only one person to access the ticket booking system at any one time, but the performance would be terrible, and customers would go elsewhere. Alternatively, we could write our application code using a semaphore (a value in a designated place in operating system storage that each process can check and then change) or a similar technique such as synchronized code sections, to manage access to critical sections of code inside the application. This would require every application that accessed the database to use the same semaphore, which is a much less effective and logical way to tackle the problem.

It's most unlikely that any airline would have a so simplistic system that basic errors in ticket booking occurred, but it does illustrate the principle. An alternative strategy is to 'lock' the table that holds the number of seats each time an availability check is being converted into a booking. This is better than allowing only one person to access the database, but still hurts performance if we lock all the data in the table, rather than just those relating to seats on the flight we wish to book.

In application terms, what we have is a critical section of code; a small section of code that needs exclusive access to some data. As we have seen already, it is often easy to use a database to solve problems than writing application logic. In database terms, what we have here is a transaction. The set of data manipulations from checking the seat availability through to debiting the account or card and assigning the seat: all must happen as a single unit of work. Rather than isolating the update using a critical code section, we can isolate the transactions using exclusive access to the critical section of data, so the critical data elements can only be accessed by a single application at any instant of time.

The ACID Rules

ACID is a frequently used mnemonic to describe the properties a transaction must have which are:

- ❑ **Atomic**: A transaction, even though it is a group of actions, must happen as a single unit. A transaction must happen exactly once, with no subsets. In our banking example, the moving of money between accounts must be atomic. The debit of one account and the credit of the other must both happen as though it were a single action, even if several consecutive SQL statements are required.

- ❑ **Consistent**: At the end of a transaction, the system must be left in a consistent state. We touched on this in Chapter 8, *Data Definition and Manipulation*, when we saw that we could declare a constraint as deferrable. In other words, the constraint should only be checked at the end of a transaction. In our banking example, at the end of a transaction, all the accounts must add up to the correct amount.

- ❑ **Isolated**: It means that each transaction, no matter how many are currently in progress in a database, must appear to be independent of all the others. In our airline example, transactions processing two concurrent customers must behave as though each has exclusive use of the database. In practice, we know this cannot be true if we are to have sensible performance on multi-user databases. Indeed, this turns out to be one of the places where the practicalities of the real world impinge most severely on our ideal database behavior. We will come back to the topic of isolating transactions a little later in the chapter.

- ❑ **Durable**: Once a transaction has completed, it must stay completed. Once money has been successfully transferred between accounts it must stay transferred, even if the power supply fails and the machine running the database has an uncontrolled power-down. In most relational databases, this is achieved using a transaction logfile. The way the transaction logfile works is essentially simple. As a transaction executes, not only are the changes written to the database, but also to a logfile. Once a transaction completes, a marker is written to say the transaction has finished, and the logfile data is forced to permanent storage, so it is secure even if the database server crashes.

  If the database server dies for some reason in the middle of a transaction, then as the server restarts, it is able to automatically ensure that completed transactions are correctly reflected in the database (by what is termed 'rolling forward' any transactions that exist in the transaction log, but did not get written to the database). The database does not show the changes from transaction, which were still in progress when the server went down. Transaction durability happens without user intervention, so we need not consider it further.

Transactions with Single Users

Before we look at the more complex aspects of transactions and how they behave with multiple concurrent users of the database, we need to have a look at how they behave when employed by a single user.

Even in this rather simplistic way of working, there are real advantages to using transactions. The big benefit of transactions is that they allow us to execute several SQL statements and then to undo the work we have done at a later stage, if we so decide. While using a transaction, the application does not need to worry about storing the changes made to the database and how to undo them. It can simply ask the database engine to undo a whole batch of changes in one go.

Logically, the sequence is:

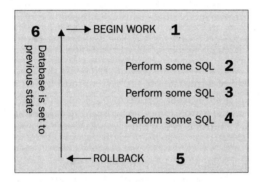

If you decide that all your changes to the database are valid at step 5, and you wish to apply them to the database so they become permanent, then all you do is replace the ROLLBACK statement with a COMMIT statement:

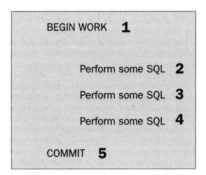

After step 5, the changes to the database are committed and can be considered permanent, so they will not be lost by power failures, disk crashes, or application errors.

In order to perform this function of 'undoing' work, databases that support transactions maintain an internal transaction log, which records all the changes that are being made to the database, along with enough additional data for the transaction to be undone. Obviously, this file could get very large very quickly.

Once a COMMIT statement is issued for a transaction, the database knows that it is no longer required to store the 'undo' information, since the database change is now irrevocable (at least automatically). The application could of course execute additional code to give the effect of undoing the changes.

Transactions with Multiple Users

Before we look at how transactions need to work for multiple concurrent users and how they are isolated from each other, we need to return to our ACID rules and look more specifically at what we mean by the I part of ACID – Isolation.

ANSI Isolation Levels

As we said, one of the most difficult implementation aspects of relational databases is isolation of different users for updates to the database. Achieving isolation in itself is not difficult. Simply allowing a single connection to the database, with only a single transaction in progress at any one time, will ensure you have complete isolation between different transactions. The difficulty occurs in achieving practical isolation without significantly damaging multi-user performance.

True isolation is extremely difficult to achieve without serious performance degradation, so the SQL standard defines different levels of isolation that databases can implement. Usually a relational database will implement at least one of these levels by default, and often allow users to specify at least one other isolation level to use.

Before we can understand the standard isolation levels, we need to tackle some more terminology.

Undesirable Phenomena

The ANSI/ISO SQL standard defines isolation levels in terms of the undesirable phenomena that can arise in multi-user databases when transactions interfere with one another.

Dirty Read

A dirty read occurs when some SQL in a transaction reads data that has been changed by another transaction, but the transaction changing the data has not yet committed its block of work.

As we discussed earlier, a transaction is a logical unit or block of work that must be atomic. Either all the elements of a transaction must occur or none of them. Until a transaction has been committed, there is always the possibility that it will fail or be abandoned with a ROLLBACK statement. Therefore, no other users of the database should see this changed data before a COMMIT.

We can illustrate this by considering what two different transactions might see as the fname of the customer with customer_id 15. This is theoretical since MySQL's MyISAM tables do not support transactions, and the InnoDB table implementation that does support transactions never allows dirty reads.

Transaction 1	Data seen by 1	What a dirty read in other transactions would see	What other transactions would see if dirty reads did not occur
BEGIN WORK			
	David	David	David
UPDATE customer SET fname='Dave'			
WHERE customer_id = 15;			
	Dave	Dave	David
COMMIT			
	Dave	Dave	Dave
BEGIN WORK			
UPDATE customer SET fname = 'David' WHERE customer_id = 15;			Dave
	David	David	Dave
ROLLBACK			
	Dave	Dave	Dave

Notice how a dirty read has permitted other transactions to 'see' data that is not yet committed to the database. This means they can see changes that are later discarded, because of the ROLLBACK command.

> **MySQL's InnoDB tables never permit dirty reads.**

Unrepeatable Reads

An unrepeatable read is very similar to a dirty read, but has a more restrictive definition.

An unrepeatable read occurs where a transaction reads a set of data, then later rereads the data, and discovers it has changed. This is much less serious than a dirty read, but not quite ideal. Let's look at what this might look like:

Transaction 1	Data seen by 1	What an unrepeatable read in other transactions would see	What other transactions would see if unrepeatable read did not occur
BEGIN WORK			
	David	David	David
UPDATE customer SET fname = 'Dave' WHERE customer_id = 15;			
	Dave	David	David
COMMIT			
	Dave	Dave	David
		COMMIT	COMMIT
		BEGIN WORK	BEGIN WORK
SELECT fname FROM customer WHERE customer_id = 15;		Dave	Dave

Notice the unrepeatable read means that a transaction can 'see' changes committed by other transactions, even though the reading transaction has not itself committed. If unrepeatable reads are prevented, then other transactions do not see changes made to the database until they themselves have committed changes.

Phantom Reads

This is quite similar to the unrepeatable read problem, but occurs when a new row is added to a table while a different transaction is updating the table, and the new row should have been updated, but isn't.

Suppose we had two transactions updating the item table. The first is adding 1 dollar to the selling price of all items; the second is adding a new item:

Transaction 1	Transaction 2
BEGIN WORK	BEGIN WORK
UPDATE item SET sell_price = sell_price + 1;	
	INSERT INTO item(….) VALUES(…);
COMMIT	
	COMMIT

What should the `sell_price` of the item added by Transaction 2 be? The `INSERT` started before the `UPDATE` was committed, so we might reasonably expect it to be greater by one than the price we inserted. If a phantom read occurs however, the new record that appears after Transaction 1 determines which rows to `UPDATE`, and the price of the new item does not get incremented.

Phantom reads are very rare, difficult to demonstrate, and rarely cause problems in real life, so generally you do not need to worry about them.

Lost Updates

Lost updates are slightly different from the previous three cases, and are more related to the way applications are written than to the way databases function. A lost update occurs when two different changes are written to the database, and the second update causes the first to be lost.

Suppose two users are using a screen-based application, which updates the `item` table:

User 1	Data seen by 1	User 2	Data seen by 2
Attempting to change the selling price from `21.95` to `22.55`		Attempting to change the cost price from `15.23` to `16.00`	
`BEGIN WORK`		`BEGIN WORK`	
`SELECT cost_price, sell_price from item WHERE item_id = 1;`	`15.23, 21.95`	`SELECT cost_price, sell_price from item WHERE item_id = 1;`	`15.23, 21.95`
`UPDATE item SET cost_price = 15.23, sell_price = 22.55 WHERE item_id = 1;`			
	`15.23, 22.55`		
`COMMIT`			
			`15.23, 22.55`
		`UPDATE item SET cost_price = 16.00, sell_price = 21.95 WHERE item_id = 1;`	
	`15.23, 22.55`		`16.00, 21.95`
		`COMMIT`	
	`16.00, 21.95`		`16.00, 21.95`

The sell_price change made by User 1 has been lost, not because there was a database error, but because User 2 read the sell_price, then 'kept it' for a while, and wrote it back to the database, destroying the change that User 1 had made. The database has quite correctly isolated the two sets of changes, but the application has still lost data.

There are several ways round this problem and which is the most appropriate will depend on individual applications. As a first step, applications should take care to keep transactions as short as possible, never holding them in progress for longer than is absolutely necessary. As a second step, applications should only ever write back data that they have changed. These two steps will prevent many occurrences of lost updates, including the mistake demonstrated above.

Of course, it is possible for both users to have been trying to update the sell_price, in which case a change would still have been lost. A more comprehensive way to prevent lost updates is to encode the value you are trying to change in the UPDATE statement:

User 1	Data seen by 1	User 2	Data seen by 2
Attempting to change the selling price from 21.95 to 22.55		Attempting to change the selling price from 21.95 to 22.99	
BEGIN WORK		BEGIN WORK	
Read sell_price where item_id = 1	21.95	Read sell_price where item_id = 1	21.95
UPDATE item SET sell_price = 22.55 WHERE item_id = 1 and sell_price = 21.95;			
	22.55		21.95
COMMIT			
			22.55
		UPDATE item SET sell_price = 21.95 WHERE item_id = 1 and sell_price = 21.95;	
		Update fails with row not found, since the sell_price has been changed	

Although this is not a perfect cure since it only works if the first transaction COMMITs before the second UPDATE is run, it does reduce the risks of losing updates significantly. We will meet this again later in the chapter when discussing the use of non-transaction-safe tables in MySQL.

ANSI/ISO definitions

Using our new terminology, we are now in a position to understand the way ANSI/ISO defined the different isolation levels a database may use. Each ANSI/ISO level is a combination of the first three types of undesirable behavior that we listed above:

ANSI/ISO isolation level definition	Dirty Read	Unrepeatable Read	Phantom
Read uncommitted	Possible	Possible	Possible
Read committed	Not Possible	Possible	Possible
Repeatable read	Not Possible	Not Possible	Possible
Serializable	Not Possible	Not Possible	Not Possible

You can see that as the isolation level moves from 'Read uncommitted' through 'Read committed' and 'Repeatable read' to the ultimate 'Serializable', the types of undesirable behavior that might occur decrease in number.

In ANSI/ISO relational databases, the isolation level is set using the SET TRANSACTION ISOLATION LEVEL command. MySQL accepts the syntax, but generally it has no effect. We will see later how we can use an alternative syntax that can be applied to the end of the SELECT statement to set the levels. Alternatively we can simply lock the table, which we will also see in use later in this chapter.

If multiple tables are involved in the transaction, then standard transactions will take care of this automatically for you. On the other hand, if you are using table locks you need to be careful to lock all the tables you require before you start any updates, or you may get to a situation partly through your set of changes where you try and lock a table only to discover it is already locked by another user.

Transaction Limitations

There are a few things you need to be careful of with transactions.

Firstly, you cannot nest transactions. A few databases have the concept of save points which are in the SQL standard, where you can set a marker part of the way through a transaction, and roll back as far as a save point, rather than the whole transaction. MySQL does not currently support this feature (nor indeed do many commercial databases). Some databases silently accept several BEGIN WORK statements. MySQL does something slightly different, in that it considers a BEGIN WORK an implicit COMMIT, followed by a BEGIN WORK, which you may find confusing, since this allows you to accidentally commit transactions. The best policy is never to attempt to nest BEGIN WORK statements.

Secondly, it is advisable to keep transactions small. Databases have to do a lot of work to ensure that transactions from different users are kept separate. A consequence of this is that the parts of a database involved in a transaction frequently need to become locked and so inaccessible by other users, to ensure that different users' transactions are kept separate. Transactions also normally involve recording all the changes in a transaction log, and the size of this depends on the number of statements involved in each transaction.

A long running transaction usually prevents other users from accessing data involved in the transaction until it is completed or cancelled. Consider an application that started a transaction when a person sat down to work on his terminal in the morning, and left the transaction running all day while others made various changes to the database. Supposing he committed the data only when he signed off at the end of the day, the performance of the database and the ability of other users to access the data would be severely affected in such a scenario.

You should also avoid having a transaction in progress when any user dialogue is required, in case the user does not respond promptly. It is advisable to collect all the information required from the user first, and then process the information in a transaction unhindered by unpredictable user responses.

A COMMIT statement usually executes quite rapidly, since it generally has very little work to perform. Rolling back transactions however normally involves at least as much work for the database as performing them initially, and frequently more. Therefore, if you start a transaction, and it takes 5 minutes to execute all the SQL, and then you decide to do a ROLLBACK to cancel it all, don't expect the ROLLBACK to be instantaneous. It could easily take longer than 5 minutes to undo all the changes.

MySQL and Transactions

Up until now in this chapter, we have been looking mostly at the theory of transactions and the SQL standard. Now it's time to look at some MySQL specifics. There are two distinct cases to look at – the behavior of MySQL when using the default table type of MyISAM, and the behavior when using a transaction-safe table type, such as InnoDB.

MySQL with MyISAM Tables

The MyISAM tables do not support transactions; rather they trade this functionality for speed. Individual statements are still considered transactions, so if you execute a statement to update several rows, you can be sure that particular statement will execute independently of statements other users are executing, but you cannot group a number of statements together as a transaction.

This doesn't mean that you should not use the MyISAM tables. Many applications do not need anything but the most basic ability to protect users from each other, perhaps because these applications are being used almost exclusively for read access, and as we will see in the next section, there are ways of ensuring that writes are independent of each other.

Emulating Transactions with Explicit Locking

When you have a situation where an application database is running on MyISAM or other non-transaction-safe table types, and needs to protect itself from other applications updating data, it can do this by locking tables explicitly. The command to lock a table is:

```
LOCK TABLES tablename [ READ | WRITE ]
```

If you need to lock more than one table in various combinations of modes, you can do this in one statement providing a list of tables and lock types, like this:

```
LOCK TABLES customer READ, orderinfo WRITE, orderline WRITE;
```

This will lock the `customer` table in 'read' mode, and the `orderinfo` and `orderline` tables in 'write' mode. Tables are unlocked with an UNLOCK command:

```
UNLOCK TABLES
```

Notice that you do not provide a list of tables to the UNLOCK command; it will always unlock all the tables currently locked.

When you lock a table for READ, this indicates that you, the client, wish to read this table without allowing other clients to change the data. In this case, there is no reason other clients should not read the table you are reading. In effect, other clients are allowed to read a table locked for reading, but they may not write to it.

When you lock a table for WRITE, this indicates that you wish to update the data in the table, and other clients should not be able to read or write to the table. In other words, you require exclusive access to the table. The client that does the locking can still read tables locked for writing, it is other clients that are blocked (hopefully briefly) until the table becomes available.

Try It Out – Locking

In order to see locking in action, we need two clients accessing the same tables. We will use client A to do the locking, and see how that affects the behavior of client B:

Client A	Client B

mysql> LOCK TABLES customer
      READ, orderinfo WRITE,
      orderline WRITE;
Query OK, 0 rows affected (0.00 sec)	

	mysql> SELECT fname, lname FROM
	      customer WHERE
	      customer_id = 1;
	+-------+--------+
	| fname | lname |
	+-------+--------+
	| Jenny | Stones |
	+-------+--------+
	1 row in set (0.01 sec)

Client A	Client B

mysql> SELECT item_id FROM
    orderline WHERE
    orderinfo_id = 2;	

```
+---------+
| item_id |
+---------+
|       1 |
|       4 |
|       7 |
|      10 |
+---------+
4 rows in set (0.00 sec)
```

	mysql> SELECT item_id FROM
	    orderline WHERE
	    orderinfo_id = 3;

mysql> UNLOCK TABLES; Query OK, 0 rows affected (0.00 sec)	(Session pauses)

```
                                    +---------+
                                    | item_id |
                                    +---------+
                                    |       1 |
                                    |       2 |
                                    +---------+
                                    2 rows in set (28.07 sec)
```

How It Works

We start with client A locking the customer table in read mode, and the orderline and orderinfo tables in write mode. Client B then reads the customer table, which is allowed because it was only locked in read mode. Next, client A reads the orderline table, which is allowed because client A did the locking. When client B attempts to read the orderline table, the session pauses because the table is locked; the program is waiting for the lock to be removed. In the next step client A unlocks the tables, which then allows the client B to continue, reading the table requested.

As you can see, the behavior of table locking is straightforward to understand. Providing the number of occasions when you need exclusive access to tables is very low, perhaps because access by most clients is for read mode only, table locks are a simple and effective solution to the problem. Note that the behavior of table locks varies slightly depending on the version of MySQL and the table type being used. You may find that your setup behaves slightly different from this, possibly requiring all locks to be made in a single statement.

Writing Update Safe Code

Another partial solution to the problem of updates is to combine the update of a row with a check that the row has not been changed. In many ways this could be regarded as good practice and often SQL generators will write code to achieve this by default.

Suppose we have an employee table that contains salary data, and we wish to increase the salary of an employee called Matthew Harvey. What we could do is:

❑   Find the employee_id and current salary.

❑   Calculate the new salary in application code.

❑   Update the table using the employee_id as a key.

In pseudocode we could write:

```
SELECT employee_id, current_salary FROM employee WHERE fname = 'Matthew' and lname
= 'Harvey'.

new_salary = current_salary + 700;

UPDATE employee SET current_salary =  $new_salary WHERE employee_id = 53;
```

This code is susceptible to other changes being made to the table between the first stage of finding the employee_id, and the third stage of updating the salary. There are two ways we can improve this:

First Method – Convert the Update into a Single Statement

We did not have to write this as multiple statements. We could have written a single UPDATE statement like this:

```
UPDATE employee SET current_salary = current_salary + 700
        WHERE fname = 'Matthew' AND lname = 'Harvey';
```

This single statement replaces the previous three statements. Since all single statements are executed in an atomic way, now there is no danger of another client altering the salary and one of the changes being lost. A useful side-effect is that this single statement will be much more efficient to execute than the two SQL statements required in the initial version. You should of course check that a single row is matched, and you do not have two employees with the same name!

Second Method – Check the Column Values

Sometimes we are not able to rewrite multiple statements in a single statement, perhaps because the calculation is too complex or user interaction is involved. In this case, we rewrite the UPDATE statement to check that another client did not change the value we wanted to change (salary, in the example at hand) while we were performing the intermediate steps. We saw this earlier when we looked at the 'lost update' problem. We would replace the UPDATE statement in the above example with one written like this, where we have used the '$' symbol to indicate a value being passed by an application program:

```
UPDATE employee SET current_salary = $new_value WHERE employee_id = 53
        AND current_salary = $old_salary;
```

By writing the UPDATE statement to check that current_salary stored in the database is the number expected as well as identifying the employee we require to update by their 'id', we ensure that the UPDATE will fail if the salary has been changed while we were calculating the new value.

Like our first improvement, writing updates like this is often considered good practice. It makes for more resilient applications.

MySQL with InnoDB Tables

At the time of writing, two table implementations are available for MySQL that provide support for transactions, InnoDB and DBD. In this book, we will be using the InnoDB table type.

By default, InnoDB tables provide repeatable read behavior, but we can adjust this behavior if required. However, before we can explore transactions with InnoDB tables, we need to digress briefly into setting the AUTOCOMMIT mode in MySQL.

Autocommit Mode

By default, MySQL operates in what it calls AUTOCOMMIT mode. In this mode, each SQL statement is considered a transaction in its own right, and the changes are committed to the database as though we executed a COMMIT statement after every SQL statement. We used this fact earlier in the book, before we knew about transactions, when we were happily making changes to our database without a BEGIN WORK or COMMIT statement to be seen.

This default mode of AUTOCOMMIT ON is sometimes referred to as **chained mode** or **implicit transaction mode**. In other databases, each SQL statement that can modify data acts as though it was a complete transaction in its own right. This is great for experimentation on the command line, but not so good for real applications, where we want to have access to transactions with explicit COMMIT or ROLLBACK statements.

There is no standard way of changing the mode. MySQL uses a SET statement:

```
SET AUTOCOMMIT = [ 0 | 1 ]
```

In other SQL servers the command may be different, for example SET CHAINED in Sybase, or SET IMPLICIT_TRANSACTIONS for Microsoft SQL Server. If you are using PostgreSQL, all you need to do is issue the command BEGIN WORK, and PostgreSQL automatically switches into a mode where following commands are grouped in a transaction, until you issue a COMMIT or ROLLBACK statement.

When a SET AUTOCOMMIT = 0 statement is executed, MySQL expects the user to issue explicit COMMIT statements to save changes to the database. If you set AUTOCOMMIT mode to 0, and forget to COMMIT your work before closing the session, MySQL will automatically ROLLBACK all your changes and they will be lost.

When a SET AUTOCOMMIT = 1 statement is executed, MySQL will COMMIT any outstanding transactions, and then return to its default behavior of considering each statement as a transaction in its own right. Be aware that, when AUTOCOMMIT mode is set to 0, issuing a BEGIN WORK statement will automatically perform a COMMIT WORK before starting a new transaction. This is different from most other databases. If you are ever unsure if you are in a transaction or not, you can always issue a ROLLBACK statement. It will succeed even if there is no work to ROLLBACK.

Note that the COMMIT and ROLLBACK statements always report 0 rows changed. This is just the way it is; it does not imply that no changes have been committed or rolled back.

The SQL standard considers all SQL statements to occur in a transaction with the transaction starting automatically on the first SQL statement and continuing until a COMMIT or ROLLBACK is encountered. Thus, standard SQL does not define a BEGIN WORK command. The MySQL way of performing transactions, with an explicit BEGIN WORK, is quite common.

The rest of this chapter assumes that you have set the default table type to InnoDB when the tables were created, by adding default-table-type=innodb to the configuration file as mentioned in Chapter 8, and further in Chapter 10, *MySQL Administration*.

Try It Out – Transactions

Let's try a very simple transaction, where we change a single row in a table, to change a name from David to Dave, and then use the ROLLBACK SQL statement to cancel the change:

```
mysql> SET AUTOCOMMIT = 0;
Query OK, 0 rows affected (0.00 sec)

mysql> BEGIN WORK;
Query OK, 0 rows affected (0.00 sec)

mysql> SELECT fname FROM customer WHERE customer_id = 15;
+-------+
| fname |
+-------+
| David |
+-------+
1 row in set (0.00 sec)

mysql> UPDATE customer SET fname = 'Dave' WHERE customer_id = 15;
Query OK, 1 row affected (0.00 sec)
Rows matched: 1  Changed: 1  Warnings: 0
```

```
mysql> SELECT fname FROM customer WHERE customer_id = 15;
+-------+
| fname |
+-------+
| Dave  |
+-------+
1 row in set (0.00 sec)

mysql> ROLLBACK;
Query OK, 0 rows affected (0.00 sec)

mysql> SELECT fname FROM customer WHERE customer_id = 15;
+-------+
| fname |
+-------+
| David |
+-------+
1 row in set (0.00 sec)

mysql> UPDATE customer SET fname = 'Dave' WHERE customer_id = 15;
Query OK, 0 rows affected (0.08 sec)
Rows matched: 1  Changed: 0  Warnings: 0

mysql> COMMIT;
Query OK, 0 rows affected (0.00 sec)

mysql> SELECT fname FROM customer WHERE customer_id = 15;
+-------+
| fname |
+-------+
| Dave  |
+-------+
1 row in set (0.01 sec)

mysql> ROLLBACK;
Query OK, 0 rows affected (0.00 sec)

mysql> SELECT fname FROM customer WHERE customer_id = 15;
+-------+
| fname |
+-------+
| Dave  |
+-------+
1 row in set (0.00 sec)

mysql>
```

How It Works

We must start by turning off AUTOCOMMIT mode, using the SET AUTOCOMMIT = 0 statement. We then start a transaction by using the BEGIN WORK command. We make a change to the database, updating the fname column of the row where the customer_id is 15. When we do a SELECT on this row, it shows the data has changed. We then call ROLLBACK. MySQL uses its internal transaction log to undo the changes since BEGIN WORK was executed, so next time we SELECT the row with customer_id as 15, our change has been backed out.

When we make the change again, and this time COMMIT it to the database, a subsequent ROLLBACK no longer undoes the change.

Transactions are not just limited to a single table or simple updates to data. Here is a more complex example, involving both an UPDATE and an INSERT INTO, on different tables, showing that ROLLBACK undoes both these changes in a single step:

```
mysql> BEGIN;
Query OK, 0 rows affected (0.00 sec)

mysql> INSERT INTO customer(title, fname, lname, addressline,
            town, zipcode, phone) VALUES('Mr', 'Matthew', 'Harvey',
            '23 Millbank Road', 'Nicetown', 'NT1 1EE', '267 4323');
Query OK, 1 row affected (0.00 sec)

mysql> UPDATE item SET sell_price = 99.99 WHERE item_id = 2;
Query OK, 1 row affected (0.00 sec)
Rows matched: 1  Changed: 1  Warnings: 0

mysql> ROLLBACK;
Query OK, 0 rows affected (0.00 sec)

mysql> SELECT fname, lname FROM customer WHERE lname = 'Harvey';
Empty set (0.00 sec)

mysql> SELECT * FROM item WHERE item_id = 2;
+---------+-------------+------------+------------+
| item_id | description | cost_price | sell_price |
+---------+-------------+------------+------------+
|       2 | Rubik Cube  |       7.45 |      11.49 |
+---------+-------------+------------+------------+
1 row in set (0.00 sec)

mysql>
```

The data added as a result of the INSERT statement has been removed, and the UPDATE to the item table reversed.

Row Locking

InnoDB table implementation allows locking by the client. It further allows locking at row level rather than the whole table.

```
SELECT ... FOR UPDATE
```

This will cause an exclusive (or write) lock to be set on the selected rows, until either a COMMIT or ROLLBACK statement is executed.

Try It Out – Explicit Row Level Locking

As before, we need two clients to see this working, and must set AUTOCOMMIT mode to 0 before we start:

Client A	Client B
Mysql> SELECT 0 FROM customer WHERE customer_id = 15 FOR UPDATE; +---+ | 0 | +---+ | 0 | +---+ 1 row in set (0.01 sec)	
	mysql> UPDATE customer SET fname = 'Annie' WHERE customer_id = 8; Query OK, 1 row affected (0.00 sec) Rows matched: 1 Changed: 1 Warnings: 0
	mysql> UPDATE customer SET fname = 'Dave' WHERE customer_id = 15;
Mysql> COMMIT; Query OK, 0 rows affected (0.00 sec)	
	Query OK, 1 row affected (9.44 sec) Rows matched: 1 Changed: 1 Warnings: 0
	mysql> COMMIT; Query OK, 0 rows affected (0.00 sec)

How It Works

Client A starts by locking the row in the customer table where the customer_id is 15, using a SELECT... FOR UPDATE statement. Notice that we select a 0, rather than any read data. We could have selected any or all columns from the row(s) if we had wanted, but we don't have to. Client B then updates a different row in the customer table, showing that the whole table is not locked. When client B attempts to UPDATE the locked row, the client waits because the row is locked. Not until client A executes a COMMIT, which releases all the locks that client holds, is client B able to proceed with the UPDATE. Finally client B also COMMITs the change.

In our example, we selected a single row which was locked. We could have selected as many rows as needed (indeed we could have selected the whole table for update by omitting the WHERE clause, which would have locked all rows). Generally you should lock the minimum number of rows required, to allow other users access to the remaining rows. There is no need to actually update rows that you have locked for update – they are simply locked in case you need to update them until you execute a COMMIT or ROLLBACK statement.

When locking rows for update, you need to balance several conflicting requirements. Firstly, you want to lock as few rows as possible since other clients cannot read locked rows. Secondly, you want to lock rows for as short a time as possible, since the longer rows are locked, the longer other clients trying to access the rows have to wait. Finally, you need to ensure that you have locked all the rows you need, so that other clients that come along are not able to lock rows that you will need later in your transaction.

The last of these requirements is important for avoiding **deadlock** situations, which is the final topic of this chapter.

Deadlocks

A deadlock happens when two different applications try and change the same data at the same time, but in a different order:

Session 1	Session 2
UPDATE row 8	
	UPDATE row 15
UPDATE row 15	
	UPDATE row 8

At this point, both sessions are blocked, since each is waiting for the other to release a lock on a table.

Try It Out – Deadlocks

Start two MySQL sessions, and try the following sequence of commands:

Session 1	Session 2
mysql> BEGIN WORK	
	mysql> BEGIN WORK
mysql> UPDATE customer SET addressline = '3 Wilton Ave' WHERE customer_id = 8;	
Query OK, 1 row affected (0.00 sec)	
Rows matched: 1 Changed: 1 Warnings: 0	
	mysql> UPDATE customer SET fname = 'Dave' WHERE customer_id = 15;
	Query OK, 0 rows affected (0.00 sec)
	Rows matched: 1 Changed: 0 Warnings: 0

Session 1	Session 2
```mysql> UPDATE customer SET addressline = '17 Millplace' WHERE customer_id = 15;```	
	```mysql> UPDATE customer SET fname = 'Ann' WHERE customer_id = 8;``` Query OK, 1 row affected (11.72 sec) Rows matched: 1 Changed: 1 Warnings: 0

You will find that both sessions block, and then after a short pause something similar to the following will happen in one of the sessions:

```
ERROR 1213: Deadlock found when trying to get lock; Try restarting transaction
```

The other session will continue. The session that had the deadlock message has been rolled back, and the changes lost. The other session can continue and execute a COMMIT statement to make the database changes permanent. (In versions of MySQL prior to version 4 you may find both sessions get aborted).

MySQL has detected a deadlock situation; both sessions are blocked, waiting for the other, and neither can progress.

How It Works

Session 1 first locked row 8, then Session 2 came along and locked row 15. Session 1 then tries to update row 15, but can't proceed, because Session 2 has locked that row. When session 2 tries to update row 8, it can't do so because Session 1 has already locked that row. After a very short interval, MySQL's deadlock detection code detected that a deadlock was occurring, as both sessions were waiting for each other. It then automatically cancelled the transaction in one of the sessions.

There is no way to know in advance which of the sessions will be killed by MySQL. Applications can, and should, take steps to avoid deadlocks. The simplest technique is the one we suggested earlier – keep your transactions as short as possible. The fewer the rows and tables involved in a transaction and the shorter the time the locks have to be held for, the less will be the chance of a conflict occurring.

The other technique is almost as simple; try and make application code always process tables and rows in the same order. In our example, if both sessions had tried to update the rows in the same order there would not have been a problem, since Session 1 would have been able to update both its rows and complete.

It's also possible to write code that tries sessions again when a deadlock occurs, but it is always better to try and design your application so that it doesn't occur in the first place.

Summary

In this chapter we have been looking at transactions and locking. We have seen how transactions are useful, even in single-user databases, by allowing us to group SQL commands together in a single atomic unit, which either happens or is abandoned.

We then moved on to look at how transactions work in a multi-user environment. We learned about the database rules described by the ACID acronym, and then saw what the ANSI standard terms undesirable phenomena mean, and how different levels of transaction consistency are defined by eliminating different types of undesirable behavior. We discussed briefly how eliminating undesirable features also caused performance degradation, and the need to strike a balance between 'ideal' behavior and improving performance.

We then moved on to look at some specific MySQL behavior, both with the non-transaction-safe MyISAM tables, and also the transaction-safe InnoDB tables. We saw how even with the MyISAM tables, there are several measures that applications can take to ensure that they behave correctly, even when other clients may be updating the data.

Finally, we looked at deadlocks, and saw how MySQL prevents sessions from waiting forever for the release of locks that can never occur.

Although transactions and locking are not always the most interesting of topics, a general understanding of how they work is very important for writing solid applications. This enables you to not only to ensure that your applications perform correctly, but also that they interact in the database in a way that minimizes the performance implications and get the best out of the multi-user capabilities of MySQL.

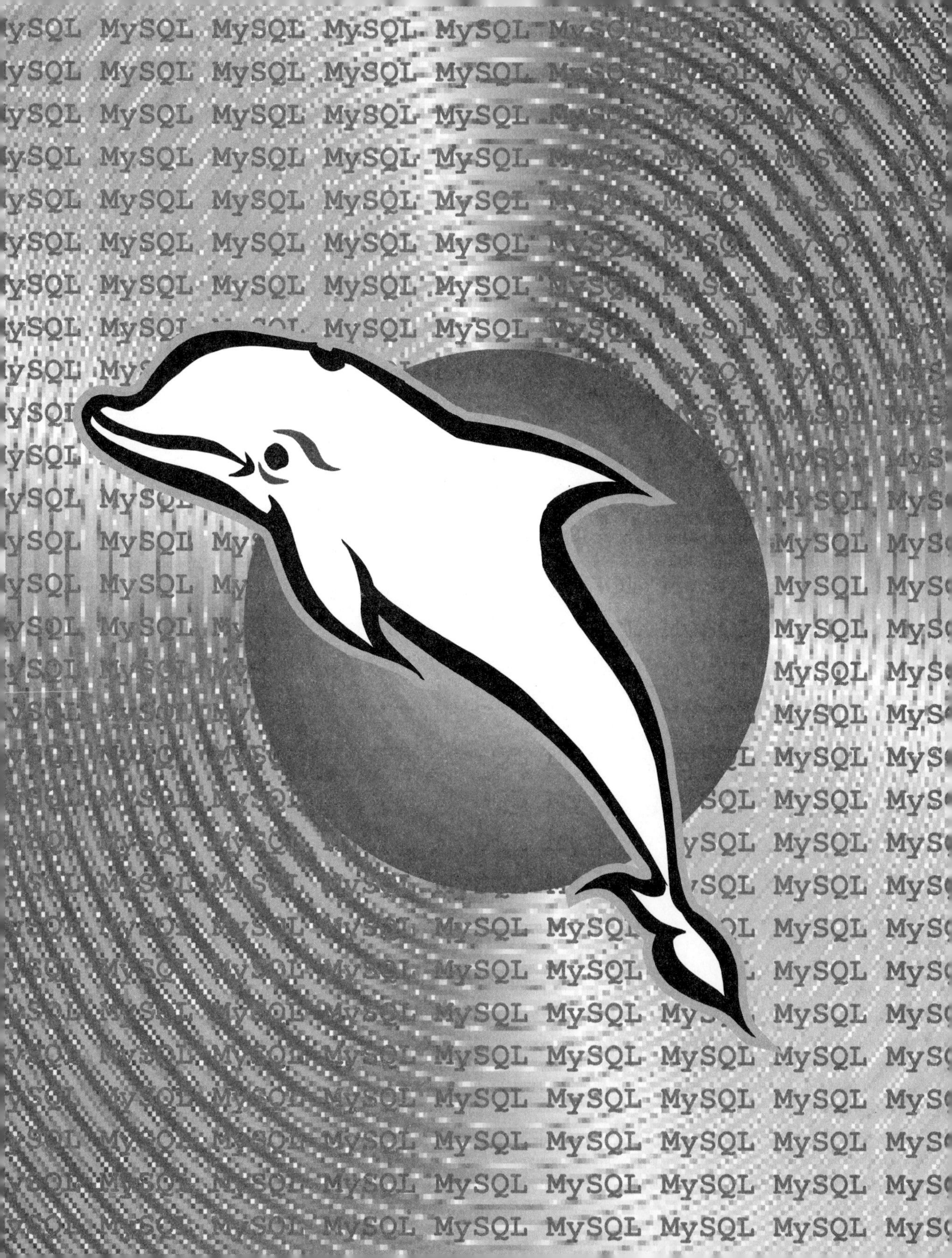

MySQL Administration

In this chapter we will be looking at our MySQL installation and how to manage it. We saw how to install MySQL in Chapter 3, *Installing and Getting Started with MySQL*, but only looked superficially at configuring the server.

In this chapter, we will be looking at:

- ❑ Starting and stopping database server
- ❑ Configuring users
- ❑ Managing user access and privileges
- ❑ Control files
- ❑ Backing up your data

We will be keeping the information reasonably straightforward. Administering a database is a significant undertaking, and in this chapter we shall cover only the basics of MySQL administration.

Starting and Stopping Database Server

Remember that behind the client program you use to access the database, there are a number of server processes running that manage the actual data. Before the client program can access the data, these server processes must be started, as we have seen in Chapter 3, *Installing and Getting Started with MySQL*, and when you shut down your machine, you must ensure that they are terminated gracefully. The server processes then have a chance to cleanly close the database files and flush any outstanding changes. If you fail to allow them to close down gracefully, you run a serious risk of corrupting your database.

> **One of the most important things to do with your MySQL server is to always ensure that it has a clean shutdown.**

The quickest way of testing if the local server is up and running is to use the `mysqladmin` command with the well-known network test option, `ping`. For example:

```
[rick@gw1 rick]$ mysqladmin ping
mysqld is alive
[rick@gw1 rick]$
```

For a more comprehensive report, use the `version` command in place of `ping`, which will tell you the version of the server you are running, how long it has been running, and provide various other pieces of information.

Now we know how to discover if our server is running; it's time to look at the mechanics of running it. The way to manage the starting and stopping of the server depends on which operating system you are using. We will look first at Microsoft Windows, and then at the more generic Linux or UNIX method.

Windows

If you are running your MySQL server on Windows, there is a good chance that after the MySQL 'install' and a machine 'restart' the server will already be running and will be automatically shut down when Windows terminates, without your needing to do anything at all. This is because on Windows NT, 2000, and XP the default installation adds MySQL as a standard Windows service. You can see this by opening the Services control under control panel (the exact location depends on the version of Windows you are running). If you look down at the list of services, you should see MySQL with an automatic startup. Here is what it looks like on Windows 2000:

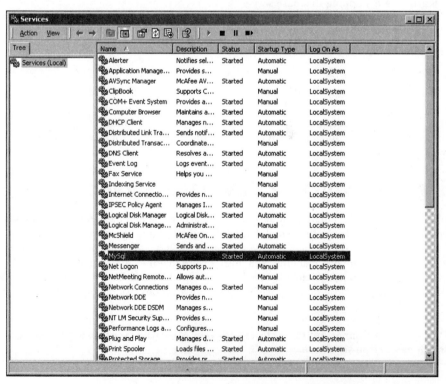

This means that the basics of stopping and starting are taken care of rather neatly.

The `WinMySQLadmin` program that you will find in the `bin` directory of your MySQL installation provides a rather higher-level control interface. It also provides a nice user-friendly way to control your server. On starting up this program, you will initially find that, after a brief flash of showing the start of the program, very little happens. If you look closely, you should find a small set of traffic lights appearing in the system tray, hopefully with a green light, which shows that the MySQL server is running. If you right-click on the traffic lights and select Show me, the full user interface of `WinMySQLadmin` will open, which looks like this:

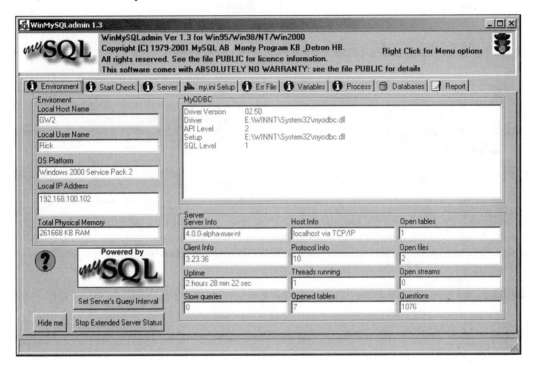

This shows some basic information about the platform and version of the server that is running. Explore the tabs and you will find a lot of useful and detailed information about the status and configuration of the server. For example, if you go to the Report tab and create a report, you will see a wealth of information about your server. This can be particularly useful if the server is not behaving as you expect.

Also very useful is the Databases tab, which lets you view the details of your databases, the tables in them, and even the definitions of the columns. In the following screenshot, we are looking at the definition of the `customer` table in the `bmsimple` database:

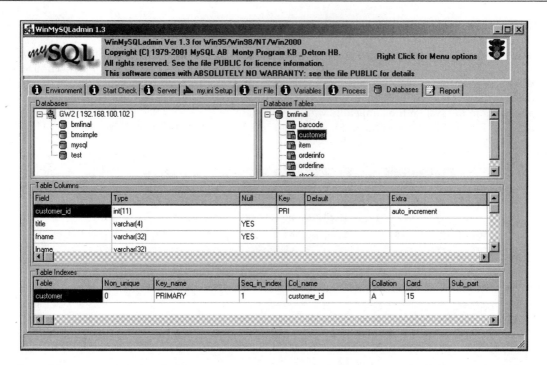

One additional, and slightly hidden piece of functionality is exposed by right-clicking on the traffic lights, which pops up a menu. The options in this menu allow you to manually start and stop the service, and also, once the service is stopped, remove MySQL as a service.

Linux

Under Linux and UNIX machines, the way the MySQL server is controlled is slightly different. This depends on whether you installed from source or from a prepackaged solution, such as RPMs for Red Hat or SuSE Linux.

Installation from a prebuilt set of binaries presents the easiest method of control. If you have done this, you will almost certainly find included in the 'install' a script to add MySQL to the startup and shutdown scripts. The exact location of these scripts depends on your distribution. If you are using Red Hat, then look in /etc/rc.d/init.d for a mysql script.

Generally, a Linux system will execute in a defined 'runlevel', which is normally 3 for command line multi-user and networking, or 5 for graphical logins. The default is set in the file /etc/inittab on most systems. When the system enters or leaves a runlevel, a set of scripts specific to that runlevel are executed. These normally reside in /etc/rc.d/rcN.d, where N is the runlevel. These scripts are normally the only symbolic links from scripts in the directory /etc/rc.d/init.d. They are named with an 'S' for scripts that run to start a runlevel, and with a number to indicate the order in which they run.

A full discussion on Linux runlevels and scripts is beyond the scope of this book. For more information see the man page for init, the HOWTO documentation, or refer to a Linux administration book such as *Linux System Administration* by Marcel Gangé, Addison-Wesley (ISBN 0-201-71934-7), or *Professional Linux Deployment* from Wrox Press (ISBN 1-861002-87-4).

The easiest way to control the runlevels in which the MySQL daemon is running is to use a graphical tool. On Red Hat 7.2, for example, you would use the Serviceconf program, which may be found under the start menu in Programs | System | Serviceconf under GNOME, or Red Hat | System | Serviceconf under KDE. If you start the program, you will see that it displays a list of services, with a checkbox for each service running in the selected runlevel. It also helpfully displays the current runlevel, which will normally be 3 if you use a command prompt login or 5 if you use a graphical login.

Here is a screenshot of Service Configuration showing a system in runlevel 3 with MySQL set to run in this particular runlevel:

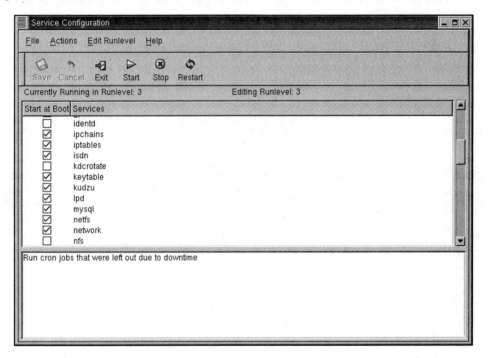

To confirm that MySQL is running, simply type ps -el | grep mysqld at a command prompt, and you should see a number of mysqld programs executing.

If you installed from source you need to do slightly more work. The first place to look is under the bin directory of your installation, where you should find a mysql_start_stop script. This is a good starting place for your control script, and generally is sufficient.

Put a copy of this script in the standard startup script location, (/etc/rc.d/init.d for Red Hat), and then use your preferred tool to configure the startup script to run in the required runlevel. You could use one of the graphical tools mentioned earlier. If you prefer a command line tool then use chkconfig, which is a handy command for manipulating the runlevels at which services are executed.

To add a `mysql` script to execute in runlevel 3, for example, copy the script to the standard location, such as `/etc/rc.d/init.d`, then use `chkconfig --level 3 mysql on` to ensure that the `mysql` service is run when the system is in runlevel 3. See the `chkconfig` manual page for more details.

Of course, you can always manually start and stop the server if you prefer, but going to the effort of automating does remove the risk of forgetting to stop the server before shutting down the machine.

Server Versions

On Linux, if you install from prepackaged binaries, you may be given a choice of packages to install. Usually there is a 'standard server package', and an optional 'max' package that you can choose to install as well. Generally the 'max' package is required if you want to use `InnoDB` or `BDB` files in addition to the standard `MyISAM` files. Unless your Linux system is a rather minimal configuration, this is generally desirable. So we would recommend installing the 'max' additional package in addition to the 'standard server package'.

If you are building from source, then on Linux you specify the type of server options you require during the configure stage, as we saw in Chapter 3. From MySQL version 4.0 and later, the default is to include support for `InnoDB` tables. After running `configure`, `make`, and `make install`, the appropriate server binary will be installed.

On Windows, things are not quite so simple where generally different versions of the server are shipped, and you pick up the one to execute. But this can be done in the `WinMySQLadmin` tool from the my.ini Setup tab:

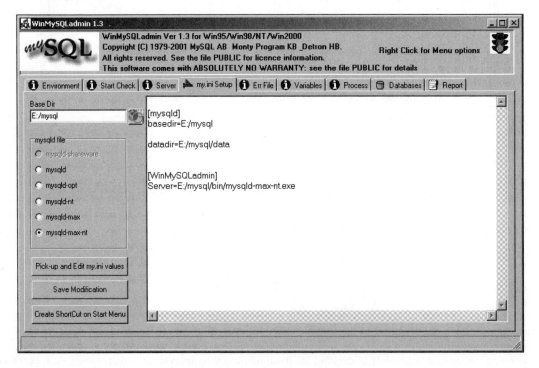

Notice the choice of servers on the left-hand side. In order to change between server versions you must:

- ❑ Select the new server type you require
- ❑ Shutdown the service
- ❑ Remove the service
- ❑ Install the service
- ❑ Start the service

Alternatively, you can do this from the command line by executing the old program with --remove and then the new one with --install to make a new binary into the default MySQL service. See the manual for more details on this process. In general, we would suggest using the mysqld-max-NT version of the server, as selected here.

You should run the 'max' or 'max-nt' version of the server if you want to use the InnoDB tables that we have been using to investigate transactions and foreign key constraints, which we have seen in Chapter 9, *Transactions and Locking*.

Adding and Removing Databases

The adding and removing of databases is quite simple. To create a database we use:

```
CREATE DATABASE dbname;
```

To remove a database we use:

```
DROP DATABASE dbname;
```

That is really about all there is to know, provided the user you used to connect to the database has appropriate permissions, which is our next topic.

Configuring Users

Now that we have dealt with the vital issue of automatically starting the database server, and, perhaps more importantly, terminating gracefully when the machine shuts down, it's time to look at configuring users.

The Administrator Login – Root

When MySQL is installed on Windows or from Linux binaries, or Linux source, two logins will be created for you – a default administrator login and an anonymous login. The administrator login name by default will be root but be aware this is not related to the Linux login of the same name. By default, this root user can login with no password and has complete control over the database, so one of your first tasks should be to set a password for this privileged account.

There are several ways to set a user's password. We will cover two – first via the `mysqladmin` utility, and second by directly updating the user data in the database.

Using `mysqladmin`, setting a `root` (administrator) password is very easy:

```
mysqladmin --user=root password new-secret-password
```

For example:

```
[rick@gw1 bmysql]$ mysqladmin --user=root password secret
[rick@gw1 bmysql]$
```

Once the password has been set, you can still use `mysqladmin` to change the password, but you must supply the current password by using the option `--password=old-password`.

The way the default logins are created, which we will look at in a moment, means there are usually two entries for each login – one for local logins and one relating to networking. Generally, the `mysqladmin` command only sets the password for the current method of logging in, which may not make the machine as secure as you would hope. For this reason, we recommend one of the other routes, which involve logging in to the database.

If you have not yet set a `root` password, you can log in as the administrator like this:

```
[rick@gw1 rick]$ mysql --user=root
Welcome to the MySQL monitor.  Commands end with ; or \g.
Your MySQL connection id is 2 to server version: 4.0.0-alpha

Type 'help;' or '\h' for help. Type '\c' to clear the buffer.

mysql>
```

If you used `mysqladmin` to set a password, then you need to supply a password, either by adding a `--password | password` parameter, or perhaps better (so no one can sneak a look) by using `-p` which asks MySQL to prompt for a password:

```
[rick@gw1 rick]$ mysql --user=root -p
Enter password: ********
Welcome to the MySQL monitor.  Commands end with ; or \g.
Your MySQL connection id is 3 to server version: 4.0.0-alpha

Type 'help;' or '\h' for help. Type '\c' to clear the buffer.

mysql>
```

Since we are now connected to the database server as the administrator, we have rights to all commands on all databases. Next, we select the `mysql` database, which holds the system tables including those used for checking connection privileges:

```
mysql> use mysql
Reading table information for completion of table and column names
You can turn off this feature to get a quicker startup with -A

Database changed
mysql>
```

It's now time to set a password for the `root` user, which we do by updating the `user` table:

```
mysql> UPDATE user SET password=PASSWORD('secret-password')
    -> WHERE user='root';
Query OK, 2 rows affected (0.14 sec)
Rows matched: 2  Changed: 2  Warnings: 0

mysql>
```

This is just a standard `UPDATE` statement, apart from a call to a function `PASSWORD()`. This statement takes the new password (a string, in our case) that we provide, and encrypts it. Notice that two rows were updated; we will see why, shortly. This encrypted result is then stored in the `user` table. Using this method we can set the password for any user since as the administrator we have complete control over the `user` table.

To make this effective, we must also execute the `FLUSH PRIVILEGES` command:

```
mysql> FLUSH PRIVILEGES;
Query OK, 0 rows affected (0.00 sec)
mysql>
```

This makes MySQL reload its internal copies of the privilege settings.

Now let's have a look at part of the `user` table, to see what updated information the server has:

```
mysql> SELECT user, host, password FROM user;
+-------+-----------+------------------+
| user  | host      | password         |
+-------+-----------+------------------+
| root  | localhost | 2ebc8c8c17adf6ed |
| root  | gw1       | 2ebc8c8c17adf6ed |
|       | localhost |                  |
|       | gw1       |                  |
+-------+-----------+------------------+
4 rows in set (0.01 sec)

mysql>
```

As you can see, the `root` user has a password set, but there are two entries for the user `root`, both having the same encrypted password. What's happening here? (Ignore the entries with no user name; we will be dealing with them in a moment!)

The answer has all to do with networking. A login to `mysql` is specific to a local machine, or a machine on the network, or a group of machines connected via a network. Here the machine is actually `gw1` but when `mysql` was installed, an additional login has been created for the machine `localhost` (a pseudonym for the local machine). On some machines you may see '127.0.0.1' rather than `localhost`, which is the IP address always associated with the local machine. It's perfectly possible to create users who have login rights only when they are using the local machine, but are denied access from other machines to which the server may be connected.

> Ensuring that the `root` user can only logon to `mysql` when logged into the server machine is probably a good choice as it reduces the risk of unauthorized users gaining access to your database server.

Recovering from a Lost Administrator Password

It is possible for the administrator password to get eliminated from the server, either by data corruption or plain human error!

Fortunately, there are several ways of recovering from the situation. If you are logged in as the `root` user already there is no problem at all. Simply change to the `mysql` database, and insert a row for user `root`, host `localhost`, no password, and `Y` in all the other columns. You can then set the `root` password as mentioned above, using:

```
UPDATE user SET password=PASSWORD('secret-password') WHERE user='root'
```

If you are not already logged in as `root`, there are still things you can do to recover. Whichever login method you have chosen, you first have to stop the server running. On a Windows machine you hopefully have the `WinMySQLadmin` tool running, and this can be used to shut down the service, or else you need to talk to a person who has local administrator rights on the machine and can manually stop the `mysql` service. On Linux you need `root` privileges to execute the shutdown script.

Now let's look at recovering the administrator rights. The best way is to start the server process by hand, with a special parameter `--skip-grant-tables`. This will tell the server to ignore the `permissions` table, and will allow you to connect as `root` without supplying a password. You will need to supply other parameters, such as the `data` directory. For example, after an install from source, with `mysql` in `/usr/local/mysql`, the command we would use on a Linux machine is:

```
/usr/local/mysql/bin/mysqld_safe --skip-grant-tables --
datadir=/usr/local/mysql/var --pid-file=/usr/local/mysql/var/gw1.pid
```

On Windows, the equivalent is to execute the server program directly from a command prompt, like this:

```
mysqld-nt --standalone --skip-grant-tables
```

If you installed from source on a Linux machine, then there is an alternative (though not generally recommended) method of recovery. During the install, you will have run a script called `mysql_install_db`. This script installed the privilege tables and rerunning it will recreate the default tables. This may result in the loss of the users that you might have created since installing the database.

> We recommend you stick to the `skip-grant-tables` option wherever possible.

By this point you should be able to start up the normal `mysql` client program and connect as `root` without supplying a password, so you can re-issue the earlier commands we saw for setting the `root` password. You should now shut down the server and restart it normally, then set a `root` password at the earliest opportunity.

Deleting Default Users

The current version of MySQL ships with a default user who can connect from the local machine, and use any database that starts with the word 'test'. Although this is quite handy for people setting up MySQL for the first time to test that users other than `root` can connect, it is always a risk to have default logins created during installation left live once the server has entered production.

For this reason we suggest deleting the default user as soon as you are sure that you have the database running satisfactorily. To do this, connect to the database as `root` and *very carefully* do this:

```
mysql> use mysql;
Reading table information for completion of table and column names
You can turn off this feature to get a quicker startup with -A

Database changed
mysql> DELETE FROM user WHERE user = '';
Query OK, 2 rows affected (0.00 sec)
```

Be very careful. If you get the DELETE command wrong, you could delete yourself from the database. Check that no more than two rows are deleted. If you do accidentally delete yourself, then leave the login alone, and skip forward in this chapter till you get to the example of creating a new administrator login, and do that immediately! You might first wish to run a SELECT FROM user WHERE user = '' command.

To make sure all is well, select some data from the `user` table, and check that your `root` user still exists on `localhost`, like this:

```
mysql> SELECT user, host FROM user where user = 'root';
+------+-----------+
| user | host      |
+------+-----------+
| root | gw1       |
| root | localhost |
+------+-----------+
2 rows in set (0.00 sec)

mysql>
```

There should be at least one row, with `root` and `localhost` present. If all is well, you can now ask MySQL to reload its privileges:

```
mysql> FLUSH PRIVILEGES;
Query OK, 0 rows affected (0.00 sec)

mysql>
```

At this point, the default user has been removed.

Managing User Access and Privileges

Now that we have secured the root login, we can look at creating ordinary users giving them permissions, and when necessary, deleting them again.

Creating Users

On older versions of MySQL a utility mysqlaccess was used to create new users on a MySQL database. This is still available, but we recommend using the newer GRANT system that came into use around version 3.2.1. This uses the GRANT command from the mysql command line tool, which is a method of managing users that we will cover here. There are slight differences between versions 3.2.1 and 4.0 of MySQL when using the GRANT command. Particularly with version 3.2.1, you must explicitly grant permissions to users to access the entire database (simply granting access to specific tables will not automatically grant access to the entire database). On the other hand, in version 4.0, granting permissions to a user to access one or more tables in a database will allow access to the entire database. The behavior in version 4 is detailed here. The GRANT command has a simple syntax, but a large number of options:

```
GRANT privilege [(column-list)] ON db-or-tables TO username
      [INDENTIFIED BY 'secret-password'] [WITH GRANT OPTION]
```

We will look at the options for the GRANT command and also see how they are used in practice. Let's look at the first option in the command, which is privilege. The list of keywords for this option is rather long, but not overly complex:

Keyword	Meaning
ALL	This allows the user all the privileges listed below.
ALL PRIVILEGES	The same as specifying ALL.
ALTER	Allows the user to use the ALTER table command.
CREATE	Allows the user to create databases and tables.
DELETE	Allows the user to delete data from tables.
DROP	Allows the user to drop tables and databases.
FILE	Allows the user to access files on the server.
INDEX	Allows the user to manage INDEXes.

Keyword	Meaning
INSERT	Allows the user to insert data into tables.
PROCESS	Allows the user to view server process information.
REFERENCES	This is a reserved phrase, but currently has no effect.
RELOAD	Allows the user to use the reload command, which makes the server re-read the GRANT tables in the MySQL database.
SELECT	Allows the user to select data from a table.
SHUTDOWN	Allows the user to shut down the database.
UPDATE	Allows the user to update existing data in a table.
USAGE	Allows the user no privileges at all. This allows you to create a user, without giving them permissions to do anything.

The next part of the GRANT command is an optional column list that determines on which columns the privilege being granted applies. This is generally useful only if you are listing a specific database table in the next section, db-or-tables, of the GRANT command, but does allow you very fine-grained control over what parts of a database users can see. We will see an example of listing specific columns when we try out the GRANT command in practice later in the chapter.

Next in the command comes the db-or-tables part. This allows us to specify one of three levels of access using the syntax databasename.tablename, with '*' acting as a pattern match. For example:

Access Level	Meaning
database or table entry	The scope of the privilege being granted.
.	All tables in all databases, including the right to create new databases.
bmsimple.*	All tables in the bmsimple database, including the right to create the database with the specified name.
bmsimple.customer	The customer table in the bmsimple database.

The next option in the command is the username. We hinted earlier that we could allow different privileges to different users depending on the machine they were using. This part of the GRANT command is where we do it, and also the part that fills in the host part of the user table in the mysql database we saw earlier.

The username is made up of three parts – a login name, an '@' symbol, and a host specifier. If we wish to grant permissions for a user only when they are currently logged into the machine on which the server is running, we use localhost as the host specifier. If we wanted to allow them access from any host, we would use the host specifier '%' (notice the single quotes). It is very important to specify the host in single quotes, or you will not grant the privilege you intended.

We can also specify any machine in a domain, for example, we could give the login Deborah access from any machine in the 'docbox.co.uk' domain, but not from other machines, by specifying the user deborah@'%.docbox.co.uk'. It's also possible to grant access by specifying IP address and subnet, for example, deborah@'192.168.100.%', which allows access from any machine in the class 'C' subnet 192.168.100.

The next part, [IDENTIFIED BY 'secret-password'], is optional and used when creating a new user; it specifies the password for that user. If you grant privileges for a user who doesn't exist, and don't specify an IDENTIFIED BY option then you will create the user with no password, which is almost certainly not a good idea.

The final part of the command, [WITH GRANT OPTION], is also optional and, if present, allows the user to 'pass on' the newly granted privilege to the other users. This can be useful in larger groups when the database administrator might want to devolve some responsibility for managing particular databases to other users, but should be used with care.

The GRANT command is cumulative, so you can use multiple GRANT commands to gradually add privileges to a user. Remember you need to execute FLUSH PRIVILEGES before GRANT commands take effect.

Try It Out – The GRANT Command

Let's start by creating a user Deborah, who only has permission to connect from a machine in the domain 'docbox.co.uk', and can only access tables in the bmsimple database:

```
mysql> GRANT ALL ON bmsimple.* TO deborah@'%.docbox.co.uk'
    -> IDENTIFIED BY 'secret';
Query OK, 0 rows affected (0.00 sec)

mysql>
```

Notice that we put quotes round the host part of the user, since we have included a '%' symbol to match any machine in the docbox.co.uk domain. Since we have granted ALL permission, Deborah can do pretty much anything she likes to tables in that database, including creating new tables. If we had wanted to allow connection from any machine that can access the server across a network, we would have used:

```
GRANT ALL ON bmsimple.* TO deborah@'% ' IDENTIFIED BY 'secret'
```

If we wanted to allow the user Deborah to also connect from the machine where the server is running, we would have to GRANT permissions for that separately, using the host localhost like this:

```
mysql> GRANT ALL ON bmsimple.* TO deborah@localhost IDENTIFIED BY 'secret';
Query OK, 0 rows affected (0.00 sec)

mysql>
```

This would have resulted in two rows in the mysql.user table, which we can check like this:

```
mysql> SELECT user, host, password FROM user where user = 'deborah';
+---------+----------------+------------------+
| user    | host           | password         |
+---------+----------------+------------------+
| deborah | localhost      | 428567f408994404 |
| deborah | %.docbox.co.uk | 428567f408994404 |
+---------+----------------+------------------+
2 rows in set (0.00 sec)

mysql>
```

For our next example, let's create a user `manager1` with very restricted privileges. Suppose `manager1` is able to retrieve only certain columns from the `customer` table from the `bmsimple` database. Also, suppose that `manager1` is only allowed access from the local machine. We use the permission `SELECT`, which only allows retrieval of information. We restrict the columns to specific named columns, and we only do the `GRANT` on a specific table to the `bmsimple` database. Even these limited privileges are only allowed when `manager1` is connected as a local user:

```
mysql> GRANT SELECT (title, fname, lname) ON bmsimple.customer TO
manager1@localhost IDENTIFIED BY 'foo';
Query OK, 0 rows affected (0.00 sec)

mysql>
```

Let's just test that our restrictions are working properly:

```
[rick@gw1 rick]$ mysql --user=manager1 -p
Enter password:
Welcome to the MySQL monitor.  Commands end with ; or \g.

Type 'help;' or '\h' for help. Type '\c' to clear the buffer.

mysql> use mysql;
ERROR 1044: Access denied for user: 'manager1@localhost' to database 'mysql'
mysql> use bmsimple;
Reading table information for completion of table and column names
You can turn off this feature to get a quicker startup with -A

Database changed
mysql>
```

So the user `manager1` does appear only able to connect to the `bmsimple` database. But you will clearly see that there are no permissions on the `item` table that this user is permitted to manage:

```
mysql> SELECT * FROM item;
ERROR 1142: select command denied to user: 'manager1@localhost' for table 'item'

mysql>
```

Now let's try `SELECT` on the `customer` table. Notice the error message has changed, this time the problem isn't that the user is allowed no access to the table at all, just that '*' implies some columns to which access isn't allowed:

```
mysql> SELECT * FROM customer;
ERROR 1143: select command denied to user: 'manager1@localhost' for column
'customer_id' in table 'customer'
```

So we did successfully grant permissions for retrieval of those fields to this user. Let's try some other things on the `customer` table:

```
mysql> SELECT title, fname, lname FROM customer WHERE lname = 'Jones';
+-------+-------+-------+
| title | fname | lname |
+-------+-------+-------+
| Mr    | Dave  | Jones |
+-------+-------+-------+
1 row in set (0.00 sec)

mysql>
```

Notice that we can't even select fields we are allowed to see, if we specify a condition (WHERE `customer_id` = 7) that requires access to a column we do not have permissions to see:

```
mysql> SELECT title, fname, lname FROM customer WHERE customer_id = 7;
ERROR 1143: select command denied to user: 'manager1@localhost' for column
'customer_id' in table 'customer'
```

Finally, we see that the user does not have permissions to add new data to the `customer` table:

```
mysql> INSERT INTO customer VALUES(NULL, 'Mr', 'Matthew', 'Harvey', '1 the drive',
'Slowtown', 'ST1 4GH', '0121-232343');
ERROR 1142: insert command denied to user: 'manager1@localhost' for table
'customer'
mysql>
```

Let's finish by creating a new user, who has all the privileges of the `root` user, including the right to grant privileges to the other users. We will allow this user to connect only if he is using the local machine.

We need, as usual, to do this when connected as the `root` user:

```
mysql> GRANT ALL ON *.* to admin247@localhost IDENTIFIED BY 'password2' WITH GRANT
OPTION;
Query OK, 0 rows affected (0.00 sec)

mysql>
```

This gives us a second administrative user, called `admin247`, with the same privileges as the original `root` user. This is obviously dangerous, but you might want to do this if you were then going to delete the original `root` user. This would make it much harder for someone to attempt to break into your server, because now, instead of assuming the administrative user is `root` and just having to guess the password for that user, they also have to guess what the new administrative user name is.

How It Works

The GRANT command manipulates data in the various tables in the mysql database. The actual data that is used is beyond the scope of this book; however, it is useful to select the user, host, and password from the user table in the mysql database, which gives you an easy-to-read list of who is able to connect, and from which machines.

Removing Rights from Users

Removing rights from users is done with the REVOKE command, which has a similar syntax to the GRANT command:

```
REVOKE privilege [(column-list)] ON db-or-tables FROM username
```

The options are all but identical to the GRANT command, so we can list explicit columns, and revoke privileges at the database or table level. Once you have done a REVOKE, you must use:

```
FLUSH PRIVILEGES;
```

This gets MySQL to reload its permission tables so that the REVOKE takes effect.

You can see the permissions a user has by using the command:

```
SHOW GRANTS FOR username;
```

For example:

```
mysql> SHOW GRANTS FOR rick;
+-----------------------------------------------------------------------------+
| Grants for rick@%                                                           |
+-----------------------------------------------------------------------------+
| GRANT USAGE ON *.* TO 'rick'@'%' IDENTIFIED BY PASSWORD '36a9b73838e6cbd9'  |
| GRANT ALL PRIVILEGES ON bmsimple.* TO 'rick'@'%'                            |
+-----------------------------------------------------------------------------+
2 rows in set (0.00 sec)

mysql>
```

For this to work, the current user must have access permissions on the mysql database.

Try It Out – Revoking Privileges

Let's start as the root user by creating a user manager2 with permissions on the item table:

```
mysql> GRANT SELECT ON bmsimple.item TO manager2@localhost;
Query OK, 0 rows affected (0.01 sec)

mysql>
```

Now, connected as `manager2`, let's check that we can access the `item` table:

```
mysql> SELECT * FROM item;
+---------+---------------+------------+------------+
| item_id | description   | cost_price | sell_price |
+---------+---------------+------------+------------+
|       1 | Wood Puzzle   |      15.23 |      21.95 |
|       2 | Rubik Cube    |       7.45 |      11.49 |
|       3 | Linux CD      |       1.99 |       2.49 |
|       4 | Tissues       |       2.11 |       3.99 |
|       5 | Picture Frame |       7.54 |       9.95 |
|       6 | Fan Small     |       9.23 |      15.75 |
|       7 | Fan Large     |      13.36 |      19.95 |
|       8 | Toothbrush    |       0.75 |       1.45 |
|       9 | Roman Coin    |       2.34 |       2.45 |
|      10 | Carrier Bag   |       0.01 |       0.00 |
|      11 | Speakers      |      19.73 |      25.32 |
+---------+---------------+------------+------------+
11 rows in set (0.01 sec)

mysql>
```

As the `root` user, again we revoke the privilege by:

```
mysql> REVOKE SELECT ON bmsimple.item FROM manager2@localhost;
Query OK, 0 rows affected (0.00 sec)

mysql> FLUSH PRIVILEGES;
Query OK, 0 rows affected (0.01 sec)

mysql>
```

And the next time `manager2` tries to access the `item` table:

```
mysql> SELECT * FROM item;
ERROR 1142: select command denied to user: 'manager2@localhost' for table
'item'mysql>

mysql>
```

How It works

The `REVOKE` command removes entries from the tables in the `mysql` database that give permissions.

> A word of warning – always check that you have successfully revoked permissions. At the time of writing, the **GRANT** and **REVOKE** implementations are reasonably new to MySQL. Also be aware that the default user, which is generally created by MySQL, can give away some permissions in unexpected ways.

If you ever want to completely remove permissions from a user, and effectively remove that user from the database forever, then you can manually remove the user from the `mysql.user` table like this:

```
DELETE FROM user WHERE user='person to delete forever';
```

It's probably wise to do a `SELECT` first, just to check! Do be very careful if you ever do this, because this does not remove all the permissions the user had, it simply prevents them from connecting to the database again. Old permissions are left around, and if the user is ever recreated on the database, you could find that the old permissions are activated and the user has more privilege than you intended.

Server Logs

Occasionally, things go wrong. Suppose we want to have a look in the server logs to see if we can determine what went wrong. Generally, MySQL writes a logfile called `<machinename>.err`, which includes the startup and shutdown information. Its exact location will depend on your setup. On a source install for Linux, on our machine `gw1`, for example, the file is to be found in `/usr/local/mysql/var/gw1.err`, and contains entries such as:

```
011209 08:12:10  mysqld started
011209  8:12:12  InnoDB: Started
/usr/local/mysql/libexec/mysqld: ready for connections
011209  8:27:58  /usr/local/mysql/libexec/mysqld: Normal shutdown

011209  8:27:58  InnoDB: Starting shutdown...
011209  8:27:58  InnoDB: Shutdown completed
011209  8:27:59  /usr/local/mysql/libexec/mysqld: Shutdown Complete

011209 08:27:59  mysqld ended

011209 08:28:07  mysqld started
011209  8:28:08  InnoDB: Started
/usr/local/mysql/libexec/mysqld: ready for connections
```

On Windows the entries are much the same, but the file is usually called `mysql.err` and is found in the `data` directory under the MySQL installation directory.

Control Files

MySQL has some files that allow us to set default configuration options for the server. These files also allow us to set at a user level some default parameters for `mysql` and other utilities that are provided with MySQL. The locations and names vary between Linux and Windows, as does the detailed syntax, but in general the information contained, and the options allowed are almost identical. Using configuration files it is possible to set default for both the server and, for Linux, the individual users.

Server Defaults

The server defaults are configured by the following files:

File Name	Contents
/etc/my.cnf	Linux (and UNIX) global configuration options.
C:\my.cnf	Windows global configuration options.
<Windows directory>\my.ini	Alternative or subsidiary Windows global configuration options.

Be aware that on Windows 2000 and later, the .cnf extension is usually associated with Speeddial, so you may find the extension hidden, and the icon associated with the file a little unusual. On Windows, if you use both a C:\my.cnf file and my.ini in the Windows system directory then both will be read, with entries in the my.ini file overriding the my.cnf file. WinMySQLadmin has a shortcut for editing the my.ini file.

For Windows you can generally use whichever location you find most convenient, except if your installation of MySQL is in a location other than C:\mysql, when you must provide a C:\my.cnf file to configure some critical locations.

Initial Configuration Files

When MySQL is installed, a sample configuration file is put in <MySQL installation dir>\my-example.cnf, and for Linux source installs a set of sample files can be found in <src directory>/support_files. There are sample files for small, medium, and large settings. If you are not sure which files to use, we suggest you start by copying the my-medium.cnf to /etc/my.cnf, as that gives you a reasonable set of initial values.

The format of the file is a fairly conventional Windows .ini format:

Option	Meaning
#	Introduces a comment line
[group]	Introduces a group of options
Option	Sets the option
option=value	Sets the option to a specific value
set-variable=variable-name =value-to-give	Sets a variable to a given value

Going through all the possible options is not appropriate here. Generally you will find that the default values should not be changed, but we will go through the settings you are most likely to want, or need, to understand or change.

The first section of the file is normally for clients, and contains something similar to:

```
[client]
#password=my_password
port=3306
```

This sets the default port, on which clients connect to the server. We recommend you do not change this number! You can also set a default password for clients, but that is generally not very secure, so we suggest you do not uncomment that line.

The next section is typical for the server configuration, and is rather more complex. It is the group mysqld:

```
# The MySQL server
[mysqld]
port=3306
#socket=MySQL
skip-locking
default-character-set=latin1
set-variable = key_buffer=16M
set-variable = max_allowed_packet=1M
set-variable = thread_stack=128K
set-variable = flush_time=1800
```

This first part of the mysqld group sets the port on which the server listens, the default character set, and some configuration parameters. We suggest you should not change any of these settings.

The next part sets the installation location:

```
# Uncomment the following rows if you move the MySQL distribution to another
# location
basedir = e:/mysql/
datadir = e:/mysql/data/
```

This section is essential on Windows if your server is not installed in the default C:\mysql directory. In a default file, the two basedir and datadir lines are commented out, but here we see how they need to be set (for example) if your MySQL server has been installed in E:\mysql.

There is then a large section for configuring InnoDB tables, which we will return to later in the chapter. However, if you are sure you do not wish to use InnoDB tables, or you are running on a low configuration machine, you may find it helpful to uncomment the skip-innodb line as shown below, as this will significantly reduce the footprint your server is using:

```
# Uncomment the following row if you are using a Max server and you don't want the
# InnoDb tables
#skip-innobd
```

There are some further sections in the file, which you should not need to change.

Client Defaults

Client defaults should normally be put in the `<Windows system directory>\my.ini` file on Windows, or in a `.my.cnf` file in the home directory on Linux. Remember that on Linux (and UNIX), filenames starting with a dot are hidden by default. It is possible to put client defaults into the global file, but this is generally not a good idea. The `mysql` program and almost all of the other binary programs that ship with MySQL use all default parameters provided in the `[client]` section of these files. These parameters are read after the `C:\my.cnf` or `/etc/my.cnf` files, so you can override client defaults by specifying a different value in the local file.

The file specification is identical to that for the global file; only the type of default you store needs to be different. The most useful information to store is client default information, which controls how clients connect to the server. As an example, here is a client section that will cause clients to automatically connect to the MySQL server running on the machine gw1. You can log in as `rick` with a password of `secret`, and then select the database `bmsimple`:

```
[client]
user=rick
password
database=bmsimple
host=gw1
```

Notice the password line just states `password` with no '=' or value. We would not want to store the actual password in the file (though we could have written a line such as password=secret) but we do need to tell `mysql` that it should prompt for a password. If we omit the password line, what we get is:

```
E:\mysql\bin> mysql
ERROR 1045: Access denied for user: 'rick@gw1' (Using password: NO)

E:\mysql\bin>
```

This is because `mysql` assumes no password is required. If the password line is included, `mysql` prompts for a password.

What is happening behind the scenes is that the client 'sees' all the values prefixed with '--' like normal options.

Suppressing Defaults

Although it's very useful to be able to set default values in `my.ini` or `~/.my.cnf` files, there are times when they get in the way and we wish to temporarily ignore the defaults provided. You can also see a problem occasionally if you specify some less common defaults, like `--xml` with `mysql`, for example, in the default file, and then discover that some programs, like `mysqldump` for example, do not understand that particular default. What you see is rather confusing, in that you invoke a program without specifying any parameters, and yet you get a usage message saying the parameters are wrong.

What has happened is that all the `mysql...` programs see all parameters, so if a particular program does not understand that parameter then you get an error. The solution to this is to use the `--no-defaults` parameter, which stops the client programs from picking up any parameters from the `my.ini` or `~/.my.cnf` files.

For example, by leaving alone the default my.ini file, which specified a default connection to a Linux server, we can also invoke mysql to talk to a local server, by turning off the default parameters and providing our own:

```
E:\mysql\bin> mysql --no-defaults --user=rick --password
Enter password: ******
Welcome to the MySQL monitor.  Commands end with ; or \g.
Your MySQL connection id is 12 to server version: 4.0.0-alpha-max-nt

Type 'help;' or '\h' for help. Type '\c' to clear the buffer.

mysql>
```

InnoDB Files

In some of the earlier sections of this book we have been using the InnoDB table type that, in some circumstances, such as support for transactions and foreign key constraints, currently offers advantages over the default MyISAM table type.

To start using InnoDB table types, you must first ensure you have a binary that supports them, as we saw earlier in the chapter. Secondly, you must either create InnoDB type tables by adding a TYPE=InnoDB clause to your CREATE TABLE commands, or, preferably, set a default table type.

To set the default table type to InnoDB you need to edit the [mysqld] section of your C:\my.cnf (Windows) or /etc/my.cnf (Linux) file and add a line:

```
default-table-type=innodb
```

This will make all subsequently created tables use the InnoDB table handler.

There are two other options in the [mysqld] section you should also check. You must ensure that basedir= and datadir= are correctly set to point to existing directories. If these are wrong then the server process can hang when trying to start.

There are a large number of other configuration parameters relevant to InnoDB in the [mysqld] section of the configuration file, many of which you should leave as the default values. If you fetch the Linux sources, there are a number of sample configuration files which provide excellent starting points for tuning your configuration. Here we describe only the main options. For a definitive list and more information, we suggest you consult the InnoDB manual, which you can find at http://www.innodb.com/ibman.html. In general, InnoDB will default to reasonable behavior so, unless you are sure, it's best to stick to a preconfigured option file or allow default values.

This is a brief explanation of the 'medium' configuration file from the Linux support files, along with the suggested values. Windows installations come with their own, similar, default configuration values:

Option	Meaning
`innodb_data_file_path = ibdata1:400M`	This sets the name and size of a file that `InnoDB` will use for holding data. It will be stored in the directory specified by `innodb_data_home_dir` and have a size of 400M. In `InnoDB` all tables are held in a single file which can not be extended, though additional data files can be added. If you have a reasonable idea of the final size of your data you should try and ensure your initial data file is sufficient in size to hold it.
`innodb_data_home_dir = /usr/local/mysql/var/`	This sets the path to the location where `InnoDB` files will be stored. On Windows you would use Windows path formats such as `innodb_data_home_dir = c:\ibdata`.
`innodb_log_group_home_dir = /usr/local/mysql/var/`	This sets the path to the location where `InnoDB` will store database logfiles. On Windows use a Windows path format.
`innodb_log_arch_dir = /usr/local/mysql/var/`	The location where archived log files will be stored. On Windows use a Windows path format.
`set-variable = innodb_mirrored_log_groups=1`	This should always be 1.
`set-variable = innodb_log_files_in_group=3`	Number of log files to use. Three is the recommended number.
`set-variable = innodb_log_file_size=5M`	The size of logfiles. This should be at least 1M, but the larger the file the better performance will tend to be, at the expense of slower restarts should the server terminate unexpectedly.
`set-variable = innodb_log_buffer_size=8M`	How much transaction data can be buffered before it is written to disk. This should never exceed (`innodb_log_files_in_group` * `innodb_log_file_size`) /2, and unless you expect very large and long-running transactions smaller values will be more than sufficient.
`innodb_flush_log_at_trx_commit=1`	Leave set to 1.
`innodb_log_archive=0`	Leave set to 0.
`set-variable = innodb_buffer_pool_size=16M`	Controls the amount of in-memory buffering that is performed. This should never be greater than 80% of the actual physical memory, even on a machine dedicated to running MySQL. On shared machines much lower values are appropriate.

Option	Meaning
`set-variable = innodb_additional_mem_pool_size=2M`	The memory used to store data dictionary information. On very complex databases with a large number of tables you may need to increase this number.
`set-variable = innodb_file_io_threads=4`	Leave set to 4.
`set-variable = innodb_lock_wait_timeout=50`	The timeout `InnoDB` uses when detecting deadlocks. Should not need to be changed.

The first time you start your server after configuring `InnoDB` tables, you may notice a delay, which may be of quite some time, while the initial data files are created.

Recovering from a Problem

Sometimes you are faced with problems like data corruption. If you are using `InnoDB` table types then generally the server will recover automatically if this is possible. If you are using `MyISAM` tables, then recovery is not always automatic, but you can use the `myisamchk` utility to manually repair tables and also provide some internal information about the tables. You should not run this repair utility unless you have a problem, except with the parameter `-d` to describe the table. The database server must be stopped before running this utility. Since it is a standalone utility, it does not operate through the server but directly on the table structures. This also means that you must tell the utility the path to the file it is to repair.

You normally run this utility in the database `data` directory, which is normally `<mysql directory>/data/<name of database>`. The main option you will normally require is `-r` to recover a table, plus you must supply a table name or `'*.MYI'` to fix all tables. Here is an example of `myisamchk` on Windows, looking at the `customer` table of the `bmsimple` database:

```
E:\mysql\data\bmsimple>..\..\bin\myisamchk -d customer.MYI
MyISAM file:        customer.MYI
Record format:      Packed
Character set:      latin1 (8)
Data records:       15   Deleted blocks:
Recordlength:       195

table description:
Key Start Len Index    Type
1   2     4   unique   long

E:\mysql\data\bmsimple>
```

There is an equivalent utility, `isamchk`, for the older `ISAM` file types. More details and options can be found in the MySQL manual.

A better option is to use the `REPAIR TABLE` command from the `mysql` prompt. This command takes a table name, or comma-separated list of table names, and attempts to repair them in the same way `myisamchk` would:

```
mysql> REPAIR TABLE customer, item;
+------------------+--------+----------+----------+
| Table            | Op     | Msg_type | Msg_text |
+------------------+--------+----------+----------+
| bmsimple.customer | repair | status   | OK       |
| bmsimple.item     | repair | status   | OK       |
+------------------+--------+----------+----------+
2 rows in set (0.03 sec)

mysql>
```

Exploring Your Databases

There are several ways of getting information about your setup, most of which we have used by this point in the book. We list them again here, as a handy reference for administrators. Except for the `mysqladmin` commands, all these are internal to the `mysql` client program, so you must be logged on to the database to execute them:

Command	Usage
`mysqladmin ping`	Quick check that the database server is running.
`mysqladmin version`	Tells you the server type, uptime, and some other status information.
`STATUS;`	Shows the current user, database, and some server information.
`SHOW DATABASES;`	Lists the databases present on the current server.
`SHOW TABLES FROM dbname;`	Lists the tables in the database `dbname`.
`SHOW TABLE STATUS FROM dbname;`	Show details about the tables in a database, including the type, number of rows, and the time it was created.
`SHOW TABLES;`	Lists the tables in the current database.
`SHOW COLUMNS FROM tablename;`	Shows information about the table `tablename`.
`DESCRIBE tablename;`	Same as `'SHOW COLMNS FROM tablename'`.
`SHOW CREATE TABLE tablename;`	Shows the SQL required for creating the table `tablename`.

Backing Up Your Data

If data is important then you should be taking backups and data stored in MySQL is no exception.

For `MyISAM` tables it is possible to back up your data by simply shutting down the database server, making a copy of all the files in the appropriate database directory, and restarting the server. For `InnoDB` tables, things are more complex, but this basic method is still possible:

- ❑ Shut down the server
- ❑ Copy the `<database name>\*`.frm files to backup
- ❑ Copy the InnoDB data files to backup
- ❑ Copy the InnoDB log files to backup
- ❑ Restart the server

Although backing up in this way is possible, and indeed efficient, we don't recommend it. A much better method is to use the `mysqldump` utility, which proves a much friendlier backup format, and also creates backups that are portable between different machines, even Windows and Linux.

The `mysqldump` utility is a standalone program, which takes a number of arguments and writes out a set of SQL instructions that can be used as a source for `mysql` to recreate a database. You will remember that `mysql` can read SQL scripts using source `<script name>` or `\. <script name>`. You do need to be careful with this utility if your table data contains unusual characters. It is possible for `mysqldump` to create a script that you have to manually edit before you can use it to recreate your database.

The syntax of `mysqldump` is:

```
mysqldump [OPTIONS] database | --all-databases [tables]
```

Normally you would provide a single database name and allow `mysqldump` to dump all the tables, but by specifying a table name you can restrict the dump to a single table. As an alternative you can use `--all-databases` option, which dumps all tables in all databases. Note that on versions of MySQL prior to 4, the table type was not saved by `mysqldump`, so if you had manually set the table type to something other than the default, this information is not dumped. From MySQL version 4, `mysqldump` always generates a `TYPE =` statement for table creation.

The number of options is considerable; here we list only the main ones. For a full list see the MySQL manual:

Option	Meaning
`--complete-insert`	Write complete `INSERT` statements.
`--compress`	Use compression.
`--extended-insert`	Use the new `INSERT` syntax, which will be quicker to restore but is not standard SQL.
`--add-drop-table`	Add a 'drop table' before each create.
`--no-data`	Don't back up any data, just the table structure.
`--result-file=`	Write the output to the specified file. The manual recommends you always use this option with MS-DOS based operating systems, as it avoids problems with line termination characters. If this parameter is not given the output is written to the standard output.

In addition, it takes the normal `--host`, `--password` and `--user` parameters, and will read these from the appropriate default configuration file.

Try It Out – Backing Up a Database

The `mysqldump` utility is very easy to use; there is no excuse for not backing up your data!

Let's try out `mysqldump` to back up our `bmfinal` database, writing complete `INSERT` statements, including SQL to drop tables if they already exist, and writing the output to the `bmfinal.backup` file:

```
E:\mysql\data\bmsimple> mysqldump --complete-insert --add-drop-table
   --result-file=bmfinal.backup bmfinal
```

```
E:\mysql\data\bmsimple>
```

How It Works

If we look at part of the resulting file, we can see we have a complete script for generating our database, just like we used earlier in the book to kickstart our database:

```
-- MySQL dump 8.17
--
-- Host: localhost    Database: bmfinal
--------------------------------------------------------
-- Server version4.0.0-max-nt


--
-- Table structure for table 'barcode'
--

DROP TABLE IF EXISTS barcode;
CREATE TABLE barcode (
    barcode_ean char(13) NOT NULL default '',
    item_id int(11) NOT NULL default '0',
    PRIMARY KEY  (barcode_ean),
    KEY item_id (item_id)
) TYPE=InnoDB;


--
-- Dumping data for table 'barcode'
--


insert into barcode (barcode_ean, item_id) VALUES ('6241527836173',1);
insert into barcode (barcode_ean, item_id) VALUES ('6241574635234',2);
insert into barcode (barcode_ean, item_id) VALUES ('6241527746363',3);
insert into barcode (barcode_ean, item_id) VALUES ('6264537836173',3);
insert into barcode (barcode_ean, item_id) VALUES ('7465743843764',4);
insert into barcode (barcode_ean, item_id) VALUES ('3453458677628',5);
insert into barcode (barcode_ean, item_id) VALUES ('6434564564544',6);
insert into barcode (barcode_ean, item_id) VALUES ('8476736836876',7);
```

```
insert into barcode (barcode_ean, item_id) VALUES ('6241234586487',8);
insert into barcode (barcode_ean, item_id) VALUES ('9473625532534',8);
insert into barcode (barcode_ean, item_id) VALUES ('9473627464543',8);
insert into barcode (barcode_ean, item_id) VALUES ('4587263646878',9);
insert into barcode (barcode_ean, item_id) VALUES ('2239872376872',11);
insert into barcode (barcode_ean, item_id) VALUES ('9879879837489',11);


--
-- Table structure for table 'customer'
--

DROP TABLE IF EXISTS customer;
CREATE TABLE customer (
   customer_id int(11) NOT NULL auto_increment,
   title varchar(4) default NULL,
   fname varchar(32) default NULL,
   lname varchar(32) NOT NULL default '',
   addressline varchar(64) default NULL,
   town varchar(32) default NULL,
   zipcode varchar(10) NOT NULL default '',
   phone varchar(16) default NULL,
   PRIMARY KEY  (customer_id)
) TYPE=InnoDB;


--
-- Dumping data for table 'customer'
--

INSERT INTO customer (customer_id, title, fname, lname, addressline, town,
zipcode, phone) VALUES (1,'Miss','Jenny','Stones','27 Rowan
Avenue','Hightown','NT2 1AQ','023 9876');
```

There are a couple of things to notice here. Firstly, there are DROP TABLE IF EXISTS statements added to the script, so if you apply this script to an existing database that has some of the tables, they will be dropped and then recreated. Secondly, because we provided a named database, although the database name appears in the comments section (lines started with --) it does not appear in the actual SQL script, so we could use this to create a copy of the bmfinal database under a different name, perhaps for development purposes.

Summary

In this chapter we have looked at four main topics. We started with the basics of getting our server running and, more importantly, ensuring that when the system is shut down, the server terminates in a controlled manner to protect our data.

We then looked at the configuration files that, although having similar formats, live in different locations for Linux and Windows. We saw how we can configure the server in the global configuration file, and also how we can preset some default options for client programs, to save us typing the same options to client programs over and over again.

We then looked at the GRANT and REVOKE commands, which allow us to control which users have access to specified elements of data in our server. We saw that by using these commands, we can exercise quite fine-grained control over which particular user can perform different types of access. We also looked at the default users that MySQL installations create, and suggested that, if required, you may wish to remove these default users for databases that hold production data, but carefully.

We looked briefly at the myisamchk utility and CHECK TABLE syntax, which can be used to recover damaged MyISAM tables.

Last, but certainly not least, we looked at the mysqldump utility that provides a way of backing up our server.

In this chapter, we have only had the space to touch on the main points of administering a MySQL server. Once you are happy with the basics we urge you to read the MySQL manual for more information and a more in-depth discussion of the topics presented here.

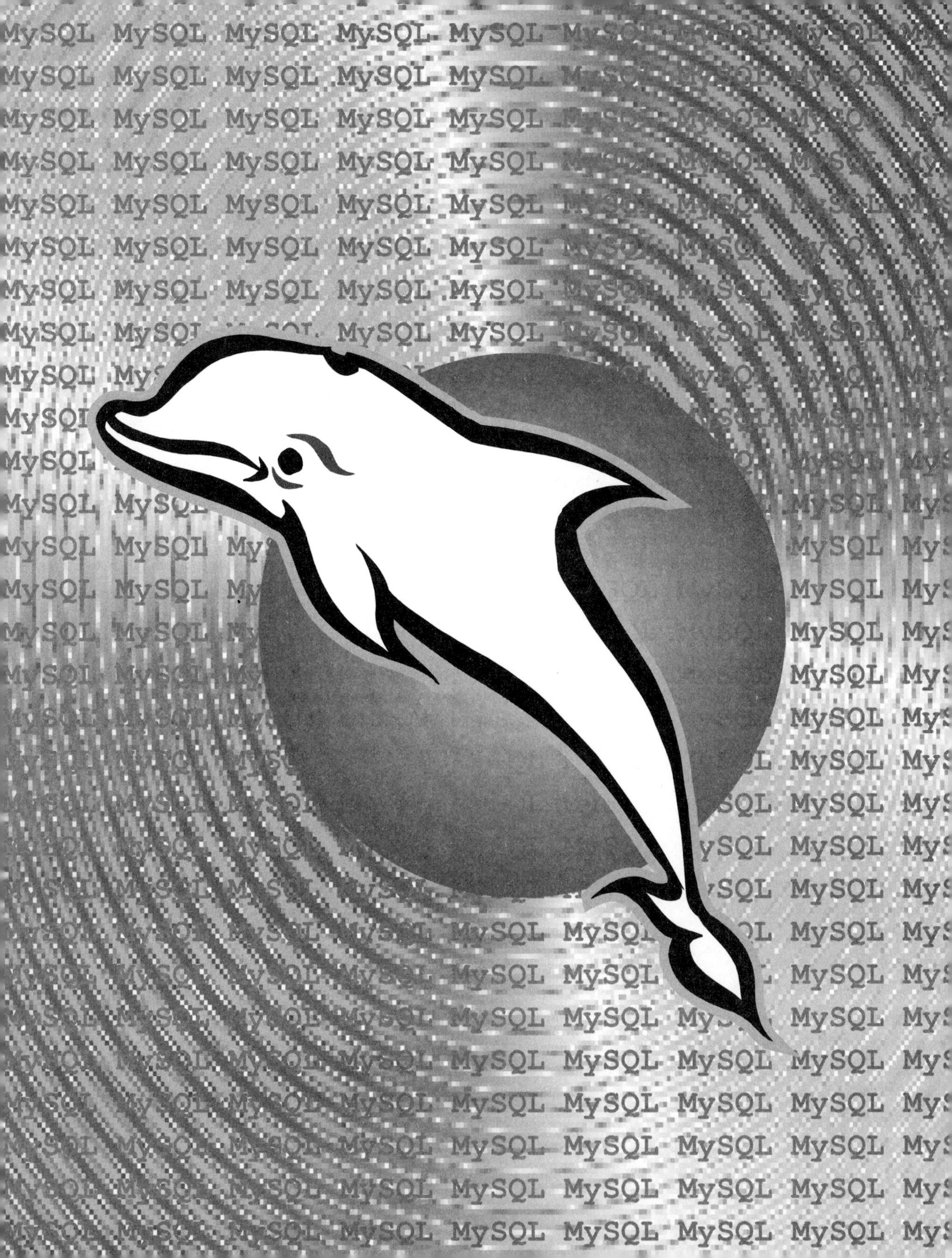
MySQL

Database Design

So far in this book we have been working with our database schema for our simple customer/orders/products data, but we have taken the design of the tables and columns for granted. Now that we understand more about the capabilities of relational databases, we are in a position to backtrack a little and look at the very important aspect of databases that is designing the database structure, more formally known as a database schema.

When researching this chapter we asked a friend with excellent database design skills, honed over several years, what he thought was the most important aspect of database design. The simple answer was 'practice'. Unfortunately we can't provide a substitute for practice, but we will explain the basics in this chapter. Also, we'll work through how the design in our example database was arrived at, and provide some pointers to other books and URLs so you can go and gain the experience from a solid base of understanding.

In this chapter, we'll be looking at the following aspects of a database design:

- ❑ Understanding the problem
- ❑ What is a good database design?
- ❑ Stages in database design
- ❑ Logical design
- ❑ Converting to a physical model
- ❑ Normal forms
- ❑ Common design patterns

Understanding the Problem

The very first step in designing a database is to understand the problem. Just like designing applications, it is important to understand the problem area well, before getting immersed in any detailed design.

Is your planned system going to replace an existing system? If so, you have a head start, because whatever its failings or shortcomings, an existing system will have captured many important features required of the replacement system. Even so, the most important thing that you should do is to talk to the potential users of the system. If it's a database for your personal use, you still need to ask questions, but ask them of yourself.

If you are interviewing a group, there are some steps you can take to make the interview as productive as possible:

❑ Don't try and interview too many people at the same time. Two or three are enough.

❑ Warn people in advance what you are trying to discover and if possible send them your headline questions in advance.

❑ See if you can get a helper to jot down notes for you, so you can concentrate on understanding what the users are saying to you.

❑ Keep the interview session short, and ensure you cover a reasonable amount of breadth, even if you have to leave some minor details undecided during the actual meeting. If some items are left unresolved, ensure you assign someone to come back to you with an answer by a specified date, say in a week.

❑ Always circulate detailed minutes after the meeting, no later than the next working day, with an explicit request to return comments within a week if any points are disputed.

Actual questions will depend very much on your particular application. At initial interviews, asking users to describe the purpose of the system and its principal functions are good opening topics. Always try and avoid the 'how', and focus on the 'what'. People will often try and tell you how things are done in the current system, but you need to know 'what' is being achieved, so you can understand the purpose better.

Potential users hold the key to a good design, even if they don't know it. Even if you are creating a system for your personal use, it is worthwhile to take some time to consider precisely what you need to do, and to try and anticipate how this may change over the time.

What Is a Good Database Design?

It's important to understand what we are trying to achieve with a database design. Different features will be important in different systems. For example, you may be building a database to collect some survey data where, once the results have been extracted, there will be no further use for the database. In this case, it's probable that designing in flexibility for future expansion is not the most effective use of time. In another example you may be designing a database to act as a central repository for complex product information, perhaps holding information about the packaging, active ingredients, and batch numbers. In such a system that is likely to be key to your business, it is probably good to take trouble to try and get the design well polished before you add any data. You are also well advised to assume that there will be some additional requirements in the future, and ensure you have the flexibility to cater for them.

Let's look at the aspects of design that may need to be taken into account when designing a database.

Ability To Hold the Required Data

This is a fairly crucial requirement of all databases, since storing data is the very reason for having a database. Even this apparently universal requirement can have degrees of necessity. If we are designing a reasonably complex database that we expect to evolve over time, we should seriously consider what are the 'must have' requirements, and implement those first, putting to one side 'nice to have' requests.

Database design can evolve through a number of design iterations, just like the spiral model of application design, where the design iterates through a number of design-code-implement loops as the system evolves. However, there is quite an important difference, in that with database design getting the fundamentals correct the first time, tends to be even more important than with application design. Once the first iteration of the database is in use and storing real data, significant design changes to the core structure will generally prove difficult, time consuming, and may require design changes in applications accessing the database.

Most database designs, even very complex ones, will probably have at the most 25% of the tables in the final design as what might be termed 'key tables', tables fundamental to the design. Identifying and designing these key tables must be our first goal. The remaining tables are important, but usually peripheral to the design.

Ability To Support the Required Relationships

The design of the database should support the relationships between the tables of the data entities. It is all too easy to become so focused on the details of the data to be stored that relationships between the data items are overlooked; yet this is the key feature of relational databases. A database design that captures all the data, but neglects the relationships between data items, will tend to suffer in the long run from data integrity problems and excessive application complexity as other parts of the system attempt to make up for its design failings.

Ability To Solve the Problem

The best-designed databases are worthless if they don't solve the problem that they were created to tackle. Throughout the design process, you must stay in touch with the problem area. If possible, communicate with and explain the design to your intended users at the major design points.

Simply mailing your users your database schema will almost certainly not do. You need to sit with them and talk through the design, explaining in business terms what the design achieves. When you do this, remember the previous two points, and explain not only the data stores, but also how each major data entity can relate to other entities. If your design only allows a single local IT supports person to support a single department, you must mention such details.

It's also important, where practical, to carefully select the users you talk to. The most valuable people to talk to are usually those with the broadest experience of the problem. Unfortunately, these also tend to be most senior, and therefore often the most difficult to get access to.

Ability To Impose Data Integrity

This aspect is closely related to the earlier point about relationships. The whole purpose of a database is to store data, and the quality of that data must be very important to us. A lot of real-world data inevitably has deficiencies, uncertainties, or is based on hand-written forms that have illegible entries or missing data. These should never be the excuses for allowing any further deterioration in data quality in our database.

We should choose our data types with care and impose column constraints. We might impose additional rules in the application that loads data into the database, perhaps a special utility that checks the data before it is moved into real tables after loading into temporary tables, as we saw in Chapter 6, *Changing your Data*, when we loaded our customer data into a `tcust` table first, then transferred it to a real `customer` table once it had been checked. Of course, we must apply some common sense and be practical, but we must never invent data if some detail is missing.

If we are entering a survey into the database and some users are unable to answer some questions, then it is better to store the fact that the answer was unknown by inserting `NULL` than to enter a best guess.

Ability To Access Data Efficiency

This is a difficult aspect of database design, because, as Donald Knuth is widely quoted as saying, "Premature optimization is the root of all evil" (Structured Programming with go to Statements, Computing Surveys, December 1974, Vol. 6, No 4, p 268). Although he was referring to application design, this is just as true, perhaps even more so, with database design.

Unfortunately, in a large heavily-used database, it is sometimes necessary to do things that spoil the purity of the design in order to achieve more practical performance goals. You should always get the design right first, before you even consider any optimizations. Often there are quite simple things, such as adding an index or rewriting a query that can give dramatic performance improvements, without compromising the core design.

What you should avoid is the temptation to arbitrarily make many small changes, such as changing a `VARCHAR` type to a `CHAR` type. Generally, these are a waste of time, and just result in a poor and inconsistent database schema. You need to invest time in profiling the application first, to determine where any bottlenecks lie, and only then consider what may need changing. Even then, changing the database design itself (as opposed to less-structural changes such as adding an index or rewriting a query) should be very much a last resort.

Extensibility

People in the software business are often surprised at just how long software remains in use, usually well beyond its design lifetime. With databases, this is even more noticeable than with applications because migrating data from an old design to a new one is often a significant problem in its own right. There will always be pressure to enhance the existing database design, rather than start from scratch and then migrate the data at a later date.

Often you will find that any changes you have made to your design in the supposed interests of efficiency, make your design harder to evolve. As Alan Perlis said in one of his programming epigrams "Optimization hinders evolution" (http://www.cs.yale.edu/homes/perlis-alan/quotes.html).

Stages in Database Design

So now that we have some idea what we are trying to achieve with our database design, we can look at the steps we should take in order to achieve it. As we hinted earlier, when discussing the need to understand the problem, database design is rarely a purely technical problem. A significant aspect is to understand the needs and expectations of users, before converting those requirements into a technical design.

Gather Information

The first stage in designing a database is to gather information about what it is for. Why are we designing a database in the first place? You should be able to define in a small number of sentences, perhaps just a single sentence, your aim with the database. If you can't come up with a simple way of describing your objective, then perhaps the objective is not yet well understood or properly defined.

It is important to have a clear objective before you attempt to collect more detailed requirements. Bear this initial simple definition in mind and if, further down the track, it all seems to be getting over-complicated and suffering from 'feature bloat', then go back to basics. Once you have a clear idea of what you are trying to achieve, you can start to expand on this initial requirement.

If your new database will be replacing an existing database, then your first task should be to understand the structure of the original database, be it relational, flat file, or perhaps just a spreadsheet. Even if the existing system is badly flawed, you can still learn from it, both good things and bad. It's likely that many of the items it currently stores will also be required in the new system, and having a look at existing sample data can often give you a good feel for what real-world data looks like. Ask what the existing system does well and what it does badly, or what it does not do at all. All this will give you clues as to how the existing design needs amending.

You should write down what the system needs to do, because writing things down focuses the mind. If reports will be generated, try mocking one up for users to comment on. If it will take data that comes from existing paper-based forms, get hold of a copy, if possible with some sample data already filled in.

At this stage, you should also be thinking about relationships and business rules, and noting any specific features and requirements that are mentioned. You need to be careful to determine which rules are simply rather arbitrary 'this is the way we do things' type rules and prone to change, and which are factual rules about the nature of things, which are much less likely to change. The latter we should probably build into the design of our database, enforcing data integrity at a low level since they are fundamental and very unlikely to change.

Logical Design

Let's see now about creating a logical database design.

Determining Entities

Once we have gathered information, we should be in a position to identify the **principal entities** (the key objects that will need to appear in our database. At this point, you generally shouldn't worry too much about minor entities. You need to pick out the key objects that define the problem area. In our sample database, we would be identifying customers, orders, and products as the key objects that we need to work with.

Additional details, such as the need to track stock and worry about barcodes, are not important at this stage, nor should you worry just yet about how the different entities relate to each other.

Once you believe you have identified the major components of your database, you need to identify the attributes of those components, in a non-formal way. For example, we would probably draw up a list of our main components, with the attributes written in plain language, like this:

Customers and potential customers
Name
Address
Phone number

Orders
Products ordered
Date placed
Date delivered
Shipping information

Product information
Description
Buy price
Sell price
Barcodes
Stock on hand

In general, very generic or ambiguous terms like 'Name' are best avoided in real databases. At this stage, we are just working with plain language so for initial design purposes we will continue to use 'Name'.

Notice that we have not yet worried about how we might store an address, or about difficulties, such as the possibility that each product might have several different barcodes. We have also kept the attribute names quite general, for example 'Address' and 'Shipping information'. This helps to keep the list of attributes reasonably short and general, so we avoid focusing on the finer details too early and losing sight of the bigger picture.

At this stage, some people find it helpful to write a brief description of each entity. In our small database, this is a little superfluous, as the components are so simple, but in larger databases, particularly those dealing with more abstract ideas, this can be helpful.

If we were writing descriptions for the components of the Product information, we might have:

Product information	Description
Description	A string of characters that describe the product, including any size or volume information. Needs to cater for at least 70 characters.
Buy price	The price in dollars that we paid the supplier per item of product, excluding any delivery costs or tax.
Sell price	The price in dollars to be paid for the item when we sell it, excluding sales tax and shipping costs.
Barcodes	The EAN13 barcode.
Stock on hand	The quantity available to sell, including any corrections applied during a stocktake.

Once you have finished this stage, pause to check back to the information you gathered initially, and make sure nothing important has been missed.

Convert Entities To Tables

Now we are ready to take a more technical step, and start converting our components and attribute lists into something that will start to look like a database. Firstly, we need to pick some sensible names for our tables.

If possible, always name tables in the singular, and try to stick to a single word, even if that is slightly artificial. In our sample database, it's easy to convert our names to more succinct versions such as `customer` or `order`. So rather than Product information, we will use `item`. (To be fair, some people prefer table names to be plural. Whichever you choose, be consistent with your naming convention.)

Now we can convert our attributes into more meaningful names, and also break down some of our more general descriptions into the columns we would like to see in a database. When breaking down descriptions into column names, it's very important to ensure that each column holds just a single attribute, where an attribute is the smallest division of data we wish to work with. As we will see later in the chapter, this is essential to ensuring our database is in **first normal form**, a key design requirement for relational databases.

Let's start with our `customer` table:

customer
name
address
phone number

Consider that 'name' is reasonably easy to break down. People normally have a title of some form, such as 'Mr.', 'Miss.', or 'Dr.', so we need to have a column for this. Developers are often tempted to use a single column for name assuming that they can always break down the name later, should the last name only be required. The clue is in the word 'assuming'. Never assume.

Names are quite complex. Suppose you have a customer with a double-barrelled last name, such as 'Rose Martin', or a German last name such as 'von Neumann'. Some people might choose to enter two first names as well as a last name, such as 'Jennifer Ann Stones'. Of course there are some societies where the 'first name' is actually the family name. For our examples, we will assume for the purposes of simplicity that we only have to deal with names where the first and last names are used consistently with the family name as last name. When you have a table of data like this:

Title	Name
Miss	Jennifer Ann Stones
Dr	John von Neumann
Mr	Andrew Stones
Mr	Adrian Alan Matthew
Mr	Robert Rose Martin

It's going to be impossible to reliably extract the first and last names at a later date. If there is ever a possibility of needing to handle names with the components separated, then it is much better to capture the separate names at the point of entry, and store them separated in the database like this:

Title	Fname	Lname
Miss	Jennifer	Stones
Dr	John	von Neumann
Mr	Andrew	Stones
Mr	Adrian	Matthew
Mr	Robert	Rose Martin

Notice that we have also decided that we are not interested in middle names, or initials, and will decide as a point of principle only to ever store a single first name. Now it's possible at some point in the future to handle the components of the name separately, so we can write to Dr J von Neumann, and start the letter "Dear John..." rather than write to Dr Neumann and start the letter "Dear John von...". That sort of carelessness does not impress customers.

Our next item is 'address'. Addresses are always hard to handle in a database, because the form of address varies widely even in a single country, never mind between different countries. For example, in the United Kingdom addresses are written in the form:

20 James Road,
Great Barr,
Birmingham
M11 2BA

Another address, however, might have no house number at all:

Arden House,
Warwick Road,
Acocks Green,
Birmingham
B27 6BH

American addresses are similar:

29 S. La Salle St,
Suite 520
Chicago
Illinois
60603

In Germany and Austria, however, addresses are written very differently:

Getreidegasse 9
A-5020 Salzburg

Getreidegasse in Salzburg. Mozart was born at number 9.

Designing a standard address structure is not easy and there is no right answer. Usually, a minimum design would be to separate out a postal town, and zip code or equivalent, which is what we have done in our sample database. In real life in real applications, it is probably better to have at least three lines for an address, plus a town, zip code, state (if in the US), and if relevant a country.

If you live outside the US, a common fault you see on web forms is assuming that everyone has a State part of the address and providing a handy drop down box to select the state, or making it a mandatory field, but forgetting to allow the 'not relevant' option for the rest of the world. It can be frustrating for people outside the US trying to enter an address and discovering that State is mandatory, when in fact it is not relevant to them.

It is usually best to avoid trying to insist on a house number, as you will cause problems for people in office buildings with a name, or people who live in apartments in condominiums and have an apartment number as well as a street address number.

Another possibility is to accept an undefined number of address lines, by splitting the address lines out into a separate table. If we do this, we must remember to impose an order on the lines, so we get the address details in the correct order. Generally, designers decide that this is overkill, and splitting the address into a fixed number is sufficient. Occasionally, too much subdivision is a bad thing.

Assuming a simplified design for our address columns, we get:

customer
title
fname
lname
addressline
town
zipcode
phone

Our item (Product information) table is already very close to having its columns described:

item
description
buy price
sell price
barcodes (may be several)
stock quantity

Notice that we have postponed the problem of multiple barcodes per item for now. We will pick this up later. Our order table is similar. We have again postponed considering some issues, such as multiple products being put on the same order, and the possibility of more than one of each product being ordered at the same time. It's clear we will need to break this table down further before we can implement it in a real database:

order
items ordered
quantity of each item
date placed
date delivered
shipping information

Determine Relationships and Cardinality

At this point, we have a list of our main entities, and although possibly not a complete list, we do at least have a reasonable first pass at the main attributes for each entity. Now comes an important phase in designing our database, breaking out those attributes that can occur several times for each entity, and deciding how our different entities relate to each other. This is often referred to as **cardinality**.

Some people like to consider the relationships even before generating an attribute list. We find that listing the main attributes helps in understanding the entities, so we perform that step first. There is no definitive right or wrong way, use whichever works best for you.

Drawing Entity Relationship Diagrams

With databases, a graphical representation of the structure of the data can be extremely helpful in understanding the design. There are many different diagramming techniques and styles in use in database circles. We will use the most commonly used notations here.

At this stage, we are working on what is termed a **conceptual model**. We are not yet concerned about the finer implementation details, but more about the logical structure of our data. In a conceptual data diagram, tables are shown as boxes, with relationships between the tables shown using lines, with symbols at the end of the line indicating the type of relationship. The symbols we will be using are:

Relationship	Symbol
Zero or one	Table
Exactly one	Table
Zero or many	Table
One or many	Table

Relationships between tables are always in two directions, therefore there will always be a symbol at each end, and you 'read' the diagram towards the table you are interested in.

Suppose we had a relationship between two tables, A and B, drawn like this:

What this means is that:

❑ For each row in A there must be exactly one row in B.

❑ For each row in B there can be zero, one or many rows in A.

For example, if table A was order, and table B customer, this would say, 'For each order there must be exactly one customer. Conversely, for each customer, there can be zero, one, or many orders'.

Viewing the Example Database

Now that we have the basics of drawing table relationships, we can look at our example with customers, orders, and products. Our customer table has no multiple attributes, so we can leave it alone for now. Let's tackle our item table next, as this is reasonably straightforward.

Our only difficulty with the item table is that each item could have more than one barcode. As we discussed earlier in the book, having an unknown number of repeating columns in a database table is not possible. Suppose most items have two barcodes, but some we know have three, so we decide that an easy solution was to add three columns, barcode1, barcode2, and barcode3 to the item table.

This seems like a nice and easy solution to the problem, but it doesn't stand up to closer scrutiny. What happens when a product comes along that has four barcodes? Do we redesign our database structure to add a fourth barcode column? How many columns is 'enough'? As we saw in Chapter 2, *Relational Database Principles*, having repeated columns is very inflexible, and is almost always the wrong solution.

Another solution we might think of is to have a variable length string, and 'hide' barcodes in that string, perhaps separated by a character we know doesn't appear in barcodes. Again, this is a bad solution, because we have stored many pieces of information in the same location. As with a good spreadsheet, it's very important to ensure that each entity is stored separately, so they can be processed independently.

We need to separate out the repeating information, the barcodes, into a new table. That way, we can arrange to store an arbitrary number of barcodes for each item. While we are breaking out the barcode, we also need to consider the relationship between an item and a barcode.

Thinking from the item side first, we know that each item could have no barcodes, one barcode, or many barcodes. Thinking from the barcode end, we know that each barcode must be associated with exactly one item. A barcode on a product is always the lowest level of identifier, identifying different versions of products, such as promotional packs or overfill packs, while the core product remains the same.

We can draw this relationship like this:

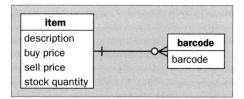

This shows that each item can have zero, one, or many barcodes, but a barcode belongs to exactly one item. You will notice that we have not identified any columns to join the two tables. This will come later. The important thing at this point is to determine relationships, not how we will express them in SQL.

Now we can move on to the `order` table, which is slightly harder to analyze. The first problem is how to represent the products that have been ordered. Often orders will consist of more than one product, so we know that we have a repeating set of information relating to orders. As before, this means that we must split out the products into a separate table. We will call our main order table `orderinfo`, and the table we split out to hold the products ordered, `orderline`, since we can imagine each row of this table corresponding to a line on a paper order.

Now we need to think about the relationship between the two. It makes no sense to have an order for nothing, or to prevent an order having multiple items on the same order, so we know that `orderinfo` to `orderline` must be a 'one-to-many' relationship. Thinking about an `orderline`, we realize that each `orderline` must relate to exactly one actual order, so the relationship between the two is that for each `orderline` entry, there must be exactly one `orderinfo` entry.
Thus, we can draw the relationship like this:

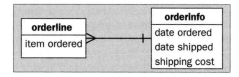

If we think about this a little longer, we can see a possible snag. When people go into a shop, they do not generally order things one at a time:

```
I'd like a coffee please
I'd like a coffee please
I'd like a donut please
I'd like a coffee please
I'd like a donut please
```

They tend to order:

```
I'd like three coffees and two donuts please
```

Currently, our design copes perfectly with the first situation, but can only cope with the second situation by converting it to the many single lines situation.

Now we might decide this is OK, but if we are going to print out an order for a large round of coffees, milk shakes, and donuts, it's going to look a bit silly to the customer if each item has a separate line. We are also making life difficult for ourselves if we do a discount on multiple items order at the same time.

For these reasons, we decided it would be better to store a quantity against each line, like this:

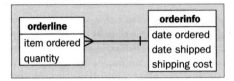

This way, we can store each type of product in an order only once, and store the quantity of the product required in a separate column.

Now we have a basic conceptual design for all our entities, it's time to relate them to each other. At the moment we have this:

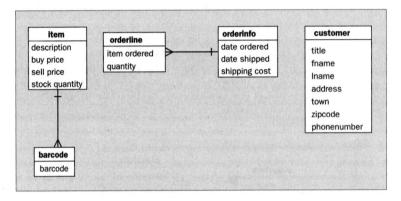

Now we can look at how the three groups relate to each other. In this simple database, it's immediately obvious that customer rows must relate to orderinfo rows. Looking at the relationship between items and orders, we can see that the relationship is not between the orderinfo and the item; it is between the orderline and the item.

How exactly do customers relate to orders? Clearly each order must relate to a single customer, and each customer could have had many orders, but could we have a customer with no orders? Although not very likely, it is possible in some situations, perhaps while a customer account is being set up, so we will allow the possibility of a customer with no orders.

Similarly, we must define the exact relationship between item and orderline. Each orderline is for an item, so this relationship is exactly one. In the opposite direction, item to orderline, any individual item could have never been ordered, or could appear on many different order lines, so the relationship is one-to-zero to many.

Adding these relationships gives us a diagram like this:

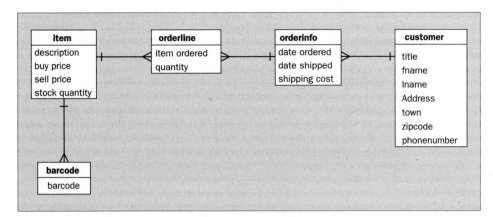

At this stage, we have what we believe to be a complete map of all the major entities and their most important attributes, broken down where we think we need to store them in individual columns, and a diagram showing the relationship between them all. We have our first conceptual database design.

At this point, it's vital that you stop and validate this initial conceptual design. A mistake at this stage will be much harder to correct later. It is a well-known tenet of software engineering that the earlier you find an error, the less it costs to fix. Some studies have suggested that the cost of correcting an error increases by a factor of 10 with each stage, as you move through the development process from requirements capture, through design, testing, and into deployment.

Invest in getting the requirements capture correct, and the initial design right. This doesn't mean you can't take an iterative approach if you prefer, you just need to get each stage right, but it is a little harder with database design, because after the first iteration, you may have significant volumes of live data in your database, and migrating this data to a later design can be challenging in its own right.

If you have identified future users of the system, this is the point at which you should go back and talk to them. Show them the diagram, and explain to them what it means, step-by-step, to check that what you have designed conforms to their expectations of the system. If your design is partially based on an existing database, go back and revisit the original, to check that you have not missed anything vital. Most users will understand basic entity relationship diagrams such as this, providing you sit with them and talk them through it. Not only does it help you validate the design, but it also makes users feel involved and consulted in the development.

Convert To a Physical Model

Now that we have a logical model of our data, which has been checked for logical correctness, we can start to move towards a physical representation of this design.

Establish Primary Keys

Our first step usually is to decide what the primary keys of each table will be. We will work through our tables, one at a time, considering them individually, and decide which piece of data in each row will make that row unique.

What we will be doing is generating **candidate keys**, possible data items that make each row uniquely identifiable and which will not change over the lifetime of the database, then picking one of the candidate keys to be the **primary key**. If we can't find any candidate keys, or think them poor candidates, we may resort to a logical primary key, which we create specially to act as a primary key. If you do find yourself having to create a special key to act as a primary key, this may be an indication that your attribute list is not complete. It's always worth revisiting your attribute list if you find there is no obvious primary key.

We will first check for a single column that will be unique, and then look for combinations that will be unique. We must also check that none of the columns in our candidate key could ever be NULL. It would make no sense to have a primary key whose value, or part of whose value, could be unknown. Indeed, SQL databases, including MySQL, enforce the restriction that primary key columns may not store NULL values.

When looking for columns to use as a primary key, we need to be aware that the shorter the field length, the more efficient searching for particular values will be and the smaller the overhead in the database will be. When we make a column a primary key, an index is constructed for that column, both to enforce the requirement that its values are unique, and also to enable the database to find values in the column efficiently. Generally, tables are searched using their primary key columns far more often than any other column, so it is important that this can be done efficiently.

You can imagine that searching a column for a description that is 200 characters long is going to be much slower than searching for a particular integer value.

Having a primary key column that has many characters also can make the index tree that has to be built very large, adding to the overheads. For these reasons, it is important that we try and choose columns with small fields as primary keys; integer values are ideal, short strings, particularly fixed length strings tolerable. Using other data types as primary key columns is best avoided.

Barcode Table

Let's look at the barcode table first, because it is nice and straightforward. We have only one column; there is only one candidate key, therefore barcode. Barcodes are unique, and generally short, therefore this candidate key makes a good primary key.

Customer Table

It's reasonably easy to see that no single column is going to give us a unique key for each row, so we move on to look at combinations of columns we might use. Let's consider some possibilities:

❑ First names and last name combined. This might be unique, but we can't be certain we will never have two customers with the same name.

❑ Last name and Zip code. This is better, but still not guaranteed to be unique, since it could just be a husband and wife, both being customers.

❑ First name, last name, and Zip code. This is probably unique, but again not a certainty. Also people change their names, for example when a woman marries. It's also rather messy to have to use three columns to get to a unique key. One is much preferable, though we will accept two.

There is no clear candidate key, so we will have to generate a logical key that is unique for each customer. To be consistent, we will always name logical keys '<table name>_id', which in this case gives us `customer_id`.

Orderinfo Table

This table has exactly the same problem as the `customer` table. There is no clear way of uniquely identifying each row, so again we will create a key, this time `orderinfo_id`.

Item Table

We could use description here, but descriptions could be quite a large text string, and long text strings do not make good keys, since they are slow to search. In any case, we cannot be certain that the descriptions will be unique. Again we will create a key, `item_id`.

Orderline Table

The `orderline` table sits between the `orderinfo` table and the `item` table. If we decide that any particular item will only appear on an order once, because we handle multiple items on the same order using a quantity column, we could consider `item` to be a candidate key. In practice, this won't work, because if two different customers order the same item it will appear in two different `orderline` rows.

We know that will we have to find some way of relating each `orderline` row to its parent order in `orderinfo`, and since there is no column present yet that can do this, we know we will have to add one. We can postpone briefly the problem of candidate keys in the `orderline` table, and come back to it in a moment.

Establish Foreign Keys

Now that we have established our primary keys for most of the tables, we can work on the mechanism we are going to use to relate our tables together. Our conceptual model has told us the way the tables relate to each other, and we have also established what uniquely identifies each row in a table. When we establish foreign keys, often all we need to do is ensure that the column we have in one table identified as a primary key, also appears in all the other tables that are directly related to that table.

After adjusting some column names to make them a little more meaningful, and changing the relationship lines to a physical model version, where we simply draw an arrow that points at the 'must exist' table, we have a diagram that looks like this:

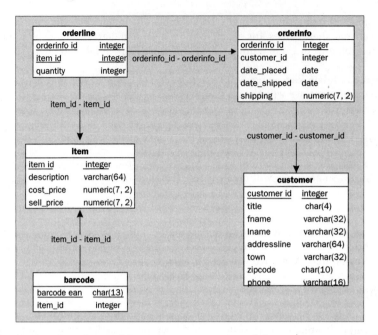

Notice how the diagram has changed from the conceptual model as we move to the physical model. Now we are showing information about how tables could join, not about the cardinality of those relationships. Notice that we have shown the primary key columns underlined.

Don't worry too much about the data types or sizes for columns yet; that will be a later step, these can be refined later, and we will revisit the type and sizes of all the columns shortly.

For now, we need to work out how to relate tables. Usually, this simply entails checking that the primary key in the 'must exist' table also exists in the table that is related to it. In this case, we needed to add `customer_id` to `orderinfo`, `orderinfo_id` to `orderline`, and `item_id` to `barcode`.

Now look at our `orderline` table:

orderline	
orderinfo id	integer
item id	integer
quantity	integer

We can see that the combination of `item_id` and `orderinfo_id` will always be unique. Adding in the extra column we need has solved our missing primary key problem.

We have one last optimization to make to our schema. We know for our particular business we have a very large number of items, but only wish to keep a few of them in stock. This means that for our `item` table, `quantity_in_stock` will almost always be zero. Now for just a single column this is unimportant, but consider the problem if we had a large amount of information for a stocked item, that was always empty for unstocked items. For example, we might store the date it arrived at the warehouse, a warehouse location, expiry dates, and batch numbers.

For the purposes of demonstration, we are going to separate out the stock information from the item information, and hold it in a separate table. Our physical design, with relationships added and primary keys underlined, now looks like this:

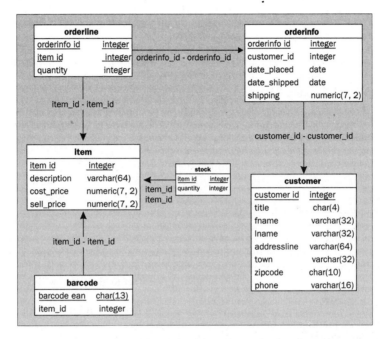

Notice we have been careful to ensure that all related columns have the same name. We didn't have to do this. We could have had a `customer_ident` in the `orderinfo` table that matched `customer_id` in the `customer` table. You will find that database designs that emphasize consistency are much easier to work with so, unless there are very good reasons indeed, we strongly urge you to try and keep column names identical for columns that are related to each other.

It's also a good idea to be very consistent in your naming. If you need an `ident` column as a primary key for a table, then stick to a naming rule, preferably one that is `<table name>_<something>`. It doesn't matter if you want to use `'id'`, `'ident'`, `'key'`, or `'pk'` as the suffix, what is important is that the naming is consistent across the database.

Establish Data Types

Now we have our tables, columns, and relationships, we can work through each table in turn adding data types to each column. At this stage, we also need to identify any columns that will need to accept NULL values, and declare the remaining columns as NOT NULL. Notice that we start from the assumption that columns should be declared NOT NULL, and look for exceptions. This is a better approach than assuming NULL is allowed, because, as we saw earlier, NULL values in columns are often hard to handle, so we should minimize their occurrence where we can.

Generally, columns to be used as primary keys or foreign keys should be set to a native data type that can be efficiently stored and processed, such as integer.

Currency is often a difficult choice. Some people prefer a MONEY type, if the database supports it; MySQL does not. You should generally avoid using a type with undefined rounding characteristics, such as a general floating point type like FLOAT(P). Fixed precision types, such as DECIMAL(P,S), are much safer for working with financial information because the rounding is defined. Some people prefer storing all values as the smallest unit, such as cents, in integer fields then dividing by 100 if a display in dollars is required.

For text strings, we have a choice of options. When we know the length of a field exactly, and it is a fixed length, such as a barcode, we will choose a CHAR(N) where N is the length we require (assuming we are sticking to EAN13 codes, which are far from the only barcodes in use, but this is a simplification we can make for the purposes of example). For other short text strings we also prefer to use fixed length strings, such as CHAR(4) for title. This is largely a matter of preference, and it would be just as valid to use a variable length type for this.

For variable length strings the standard definition defines only a VARCHAR(N) text type, where N specifies a maximum length of the string. MySQL supports this, but also supports alternatives, such as TEXT, LONGTEXT and other variants, which can be useful, but are non-standard. We value portability quite highly; therefore we will stick with the standard VARCHAR(N) type.

Again consistency is very important. Make sure all your MONEY type fields have exactly the same precision. Check that the commonly used columns such as description and name, which might well appear in several tables in your database, aren't defined differently (and thus used in different ways) in each. The fewer unique types that you need to use, the easier your database will be to work with.

Another consideration is where a column in one table references a column in a different table; the column types must be identical in both tables. We must not have customer_id as INTEGER in the customer table but store it as (for example) a VARCHAR in the orderinfo table.

Let's work through the customer table, seeing how we assign types.

The first thing to do is give a type to customer_id. It's a primary key and a column we added specially to be a primary key, so we can make it efficient by using an INTEGER type, providing we are confident that enough unique values are available. Title will be things like, Mr., Mrs., or Dr. This is always a short string of characters, therefore we make it a CHAR(4) type, though some designers prefer to always use VARCHAR to reduce the number of types being used. (Of course there are some long titles, like The Right Reverend, and His Royal Highness for example, as we have mentioned in Chapter 2, but we use a little artistic license here to demonstrate a point).

There is very little to choose between CHAR and VARCHAR in this case. VARCHAR would be a perfectly valid choice. It's perfectly possible not to know the title, so we will allow this field to store NULL values, to indicate that we do not know a title for this customer.

We then come to fname and lname, the first and second names respectively. It's unlikely these ever need to exceed 32 characters, but we know the length will be quite variable, so we make them both VARCHAR(32). We also decide that we could accept fname being a NULL (unknown), but not lname. Not knowing a customer's last name seems unreasonable.

In this database, we have chosen to keep all the address together, in a single long character array. As was discussed earlier, this is probably a little over-simplified for the real world, but addresses are always a design challenge, there is no 'right' answer.

We continue assigning types to the columns in this way; the only interesting point to note is perhaps 'phone', which we store as a character string. It is almost always a mistake to store phone numbers as numbers in a database, because it does not allow international dialing codes to be stored, for example +44 (0)116 … would be a common way of giving a UK dialing code, where the country code is 44, but if you are already in the UK you need to add a 0 before the area code. Also, storing a number with leading zeros will not work in a numeric field, and in telephone numbers leading zeros are very important.

The final type allocation for our database is shown again in this diagram:

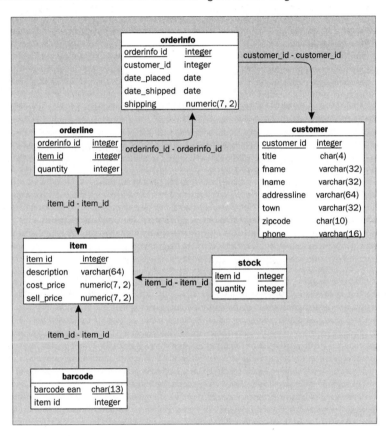

Complete Table Definitions

We now need to go back and double-check that all the information we wish to store in the database is present. All the entities should be represented, and all the attributes listed with appropriate types.

At this point, we may also decide to add some **lookup**, or **static data** tables; for example we might have a lookup table of towns. Generally, these lookup tables are unrelated to any other tables, and are simply used by the application as a convenient way of soft-coding values to offer the user. Of course we could hard code these options into our application, but generally storing them in a database, from which they can be loaded into an application at run-time, makes it much easier to add additional options. The application doesn't need to be changed; we just need to insert additional rows in our database lookup table.

If you need to reference these lookup tables from other tables, then you would normally use two columns in the lookup table, a unique key to give you an efficient way to refer to the row, and the actual data stored. On the other hand, if your lookup table is being used simply to store the value for populating a listbox, and is quite short, you may decide to just store the data. An example of this might be a survey of PCs in use in a company. You might use a lookup table to store '486', '586', '686' etc, but store the actual data entered directly in the main result table, since it is so short. If we had forgotten a value, perhaps we rashly assumed no 386-class machines were still in use, but found one in the survey, then by using a lookup table we could add the additional option in the database, and allow the application to pick up the additional option from the lookup table without changing the application.

Check the Design

By now you should have a database implemented, complete with constraints, primary keys, and column attributes such as NOT NULL. Before handing over your completed work, and celebrating a job well done, it's time to test your database again. Just because a database isn't 'code' in the conventional sense, that doesn't mean you can't test it.

Get some sample data, if possible part of the live data that will go into the database. Insert some of these sample rows. Check that attempting to insert NULL values into columns you don't think should ever be NULL results in an error. Attempt to delete data that is referenced by other data. Write some SQL to join tables together to generate the kind of data you would expect to find on reports.

Once your database has gone into production, it is difficult, although not impossible, to update your design. Anything other than the most minor change probably means stopping the system, unloading live data into text files, updating the database design, and reloading the data. Then of course there is the small matter of updating applications to accept the new table designs. This is not something you want to undertake any more than absolutely necessary. Similarly, once faulty data has been loaded into a table, you will often find it is referenced by other data, and difficult to correct or remove from the database. Time spent testing the design before it goes live is time well spent.

If possible, go back to your intended users and show them the sample data being extracted from the database, and how you can manipulate it. Even at this late stage, there is much to be gained by picking up an error, even a minor one, before the system goes live.

Normal Forms

No chapter on database design would be complete without a mention of **normal forms**, and database normalization. We have left these to the end of the chapter, since they are rather dry when presented on their own, but after the design stages we have just walked through, you should see how the final design has conformed to these rules. We will describe the first three, the most important, normal forms in a moment.

A 'normal form' is a formal definition about the way data is stored in the database. Each normal form defines different aspects of how data should be stored, and these rules are fundamental to the modeling and design of databases. Applying these rules drives your database design into a form that correctly eliminates redundant or duplicate data, and these rules have been proven over many years to be the foundations of good database designs.

What is commonly considered the origins of database normalization is a paper written by E.F.Codd in 1969, and published in "*Communications of the ACM*", Vol. 13, No. 6, June 1970. In later work, various normal forms were defined. Each normal form builds on previous rules and applies more stringent requirements on the design.

In total, there are six normal forms:

- ❑ First Normal Form
- ❑ Second Normal Form
- ❑ Third Normal form
- ❑ Boyce Codd Normal Form
- ❑ Fourth Normal Form
- ❑ Fifth Normal Form

You will be pleased to learn that only the first three forms are commonly used, and those are all that we will be looking at in this book. The formal definitions of the normal forms are very mathematical, and whilst very exact, are not very easy to understand, so we will be presenting them in a more practical and pragmatic way.

The advantage of structuring your data so that it conforms to at least the first three normal forms is that you will find it much easier to manage. Databases that are not well normalized are generally much harder to maintain, and more prone to storing invalid data.

First Normal Form

First normal form requires that each attribute in a table cannot be further subdivided, and that there are no repeating groups. For example, in our database design we separate the customer name into a title, first name, and last name. We know we may wish to use them separately and must consider them therefore as separate attributes, and store them separately.

The second part, 'no repeating groups' we saw in Chapter 2, where we looked at what happened when we tried to use a simple spreadsheet to store customers and their orders. Once a customer had more than one order, we had repeating information for that customer, and our spreadsheet no longer had the same number of rows in all columns. The same problem will occur with products that have more than one barcode; we need to store repeating information against each item.

If we had decided earlier to hold both first names in the fname column of our customer table, this would have violated first normal form, because the column fname would actually be holding 'first names' which are clearly divisible entities. Sometimes you have to take a pragmatic approach and argue that, providing you are confident you will never need to consider different first names separately, they are for the purposes of the design a single entity. Alternatively, we could decide only to ever store a single first name, which is an equally valid approach and the one taken here.

Another example of violating first normal form that is seen worryingly frequently is to store in a single column a character string where different character positions have different meanings. For example, characters 1-3 tell you the warehouse, 4-11 the bay, and 12 the shelf number. These are a clear violation of first normal form, since we do need to consider subdivisions of the column separately. In practice, they also turn out to be very hard to manage, and should always be considered a design fault, not a judicious stretching of the first normal form rule.

Second Normal Form

Second normal form says that no information in a row must depend on only part of the primary key. Suppose in our `orderline` table we had stored the date that the order was placed in this table:

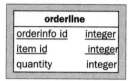

You will remember that our primary key for `orderline` is a composite of `orderinfo_id` and `item_id`. The date the order was placed depends only on the `orderinfo` information, not on the item ordered, so this would have violated second normal form. Sometimes you may find you are storing data that looks as though it may violate second normal form, but in practice it does not.

Suppose we changed our prices frequently. Customers would rightly expect to pay the price shown on the day they ordered, not on the day it was shipped. In order to do this, we would have to store the sell price in the `orderline` table to store the price in operation on the day the order was placed. This would not violate second normal form, because the price stored in the `orderline` table would depend on both the item and the actual order.

Third Normal Form

Third normal form is very similar to second normal form, but more general. It says that no information in a column that is not the primary key can depend on anything except the primary key. This is often stated, as "Non-key values must depend upon 'The key, the whole key and nothing but the key'". Suppose in our `customer` table we had stored a customer's age and date of birth.

This would violate third normal form, because the customer's age depends on their date of birth, a non-key column, as well as the actual customer, which is given by `customer_id`, the primary key.

Although putting your database into third normal form (that is to say making its structure conform to all the first three normalization rules) is almost always the preferred solution, there are occasions when it's necessary to break the rules. This is called denormalizing the database, and is occasionally necessary to improve performance. You should always design a fully normalized database first, and only denormalize if you know that you have a serious problem with performance.

Common Problem Patterns

In database design, there are a number of common problem patterns that occur over and over again, and it's useful to recognize these, because generally they can be solved in the same way. Before we conclude this chapter, we will look briefly at three standard problems that have standard solutions.

Many-to-Many

Consider two entities, which seem to have a many-to-many relationship between them. It is never correct or indeed possible to implement a many-to-many table relationship in the physical database, so you need to break the relationship.

The solution is almost always to insert an additional table, a link table, between the two tables that apparently have a many-to-many relationship. Suppose we had two tables, author, and book. Each author could have written many books, and each book, like this one, could have had contributions from more than one author. How do we represent this in a physical database?

The solution is to insert a table in between the other two tables, which normally contains the primary key of each of the other tables. In this case, we create a new table, bookauthor, which has a composite primary key, where each component is the primary key of one of the other tables:

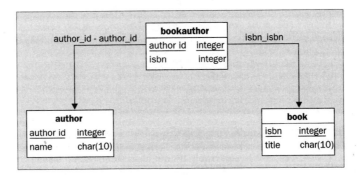

Now each author can appear in the author table exactly once, but have many entries in the bookauthor table, one for each book they have written. Each book appears exactly once in the book table, but can appear in the bookauthor table more than once, if there was more than one author. Each individual entry in the bookauthor table is however unique, the combination of book and author only ever occurs once.

Hierarchy

Another frequent pattern is a hierarchy. This can appear in many different guises. Suppose we have many shops, and each shop is in a geographic area, and in turn geographical areas are grouped into larger areas known as groups. It might be tempting to store it like this, where each shop stores the area and region in which it resides:

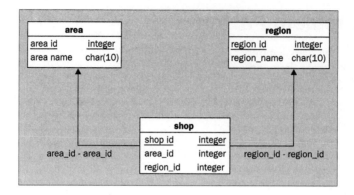

Although this might work, it's not ideal because once we know the area, we also know the region, and so storing both the area and region in the shop table is violating third normal form. The region stored in the shop table depends on the area, which is not the primary key for the shop table:

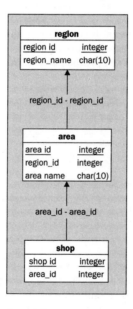

The design correctly shows the hierarchy of shop in area in region.

Recursive Relationships

Our last pattern is not quite as common as the other two, but occurs frequently in a couple of situations, representing the hierarchy of staff in a company, and 'parts explosion', where parts in an item table are themselves composed of other parts from the same table. This type of relationships, where the source and destination are the same, are called recursive relationships, or more formally, reflexive relationships.

Let us consider the staff example. All staff, from the most junior to senior managers, have many attributes in common, such as name, employee number, salary, grades, and addresses, therefore it seems logical to have a single table that is common to all members of staff to store those details. How do we then store the hierarchy of management, particularly as different areas of the company may have a different number of levels of management to be represented?

The answer is a recursive relationship, where each entry for a member of staff in the person table stores a manager_id, to record the person who is their manager. The clever bit is that the managers' information is stored in the same person table, generating a recursive relationship. So to find a person's manager, we pick up their manager_id, and look back in the same table for it to appear as an emp_id. We have stored a complex relationship, with an arbitrary number of levels in a simple one-table structure:

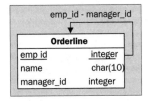

Suppose we wanted to represent a hierarchy like this:

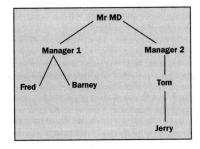

We would insert rows like this:

```
test=# INSERT INTO person(emp_id, name, manager_id) VALUES(1, 'Mr MD',
            NULL);
test=# INSERT INTO person(emp_id, name, manager_id) VALUES(2, 'Manager1',
            1);
test=# INSERT INTO person(emp_id, name, manager_id) VALUES(3, 'Manager2',
            1);
test=# INSERT INTO person(emp_id, name, manager_id) VALUES(4, 'Fred', 2);
test=# INSERT INTO person(emp_id, name, manager_id) VALUES(5, 'Barney', 2);
test=# INSERT INTO persón(emp_id, name, manager_id) VALUES(6, 'Tom', 3);
test=# INSERT INTO person(emp_id, name, manager_id) VALUES(7, 'Jerry', 6);
```

Notice that the first number, emp_id is unique, but the second number is the emp_id of the manager next up the hierarchy. For example, Tom has an emp_id of 6, but a manager_id of 3, the emp_id of Manager 2, since this is his manager.

This is fine until we need to extract data from this hierarchy. That is, when we need to join the `person` table to itself, we use a **self join**. To do this we need to alias the table names, as we saw earlier, and we can write the SQL like this:

```
mysql> SELECT n1.name AS "Manager", n2.name AS "Subordinate" FROM person n1,
    -> person n2 WHERE n1.emp_id = n2.manager_id;
```

We are creating two alternative names for the `person` table, n1 and n2, and then we can join the `emp_id` column to the `manager_id` column. We also name our columns, using `AS`, to make the output more meaningful.

This gives us a complete list of the hierarchy in our `person` table:

```
   Manager  | Subordinate
------------+-------------
Mr  MD      | Manager1
Mr  MD      | Manager2
Manager1    | Fred
Manager1    | Barney
Manager2    | Tom
Tom         | Jerry
(6 rows)
```

Resources

A couple of good books and a web site that deal with design issues are:

❏ *Database Design for Mere Mortals*, by Michael J. Hernandez. This book is from Addison-Wesley (ISBN 0-201-69471-9). This covers the topic of obtaining design information, documenting it, and database design in far more detail than we have space to cover here.

❏ *The Practical SQL handbook*, by Judith S. Bowman, Sandra L. Emerson, and Marcy Darnovsky. This book is from Addison-Wesley (ISBN 0-201-44787-8). This book has a short, but well written, section on database design and normalization.

❏ The web site www.palslib.com/Fundamentals/Database_Design.html has useful documentation on database design especially the sections: Fundamentals, SQL, and MySQL.

Summary

In this chapter, we have taken an all too brief look at database design, from capturing requirements, through generating a conceptual design and finally converting the conceptual design into a physical database design or schema. Along the way, we covered selecting candidate keys, primary keys, and foreign keys.

We also looked at choosing data types for our columns, and talked about the importance of consistency in database design.

We briefly mentioned normal forms, an important foundation of good design with relational databases. Finally, we looked at three common problem patterns that appear in database design, and how they are conventionally solved.

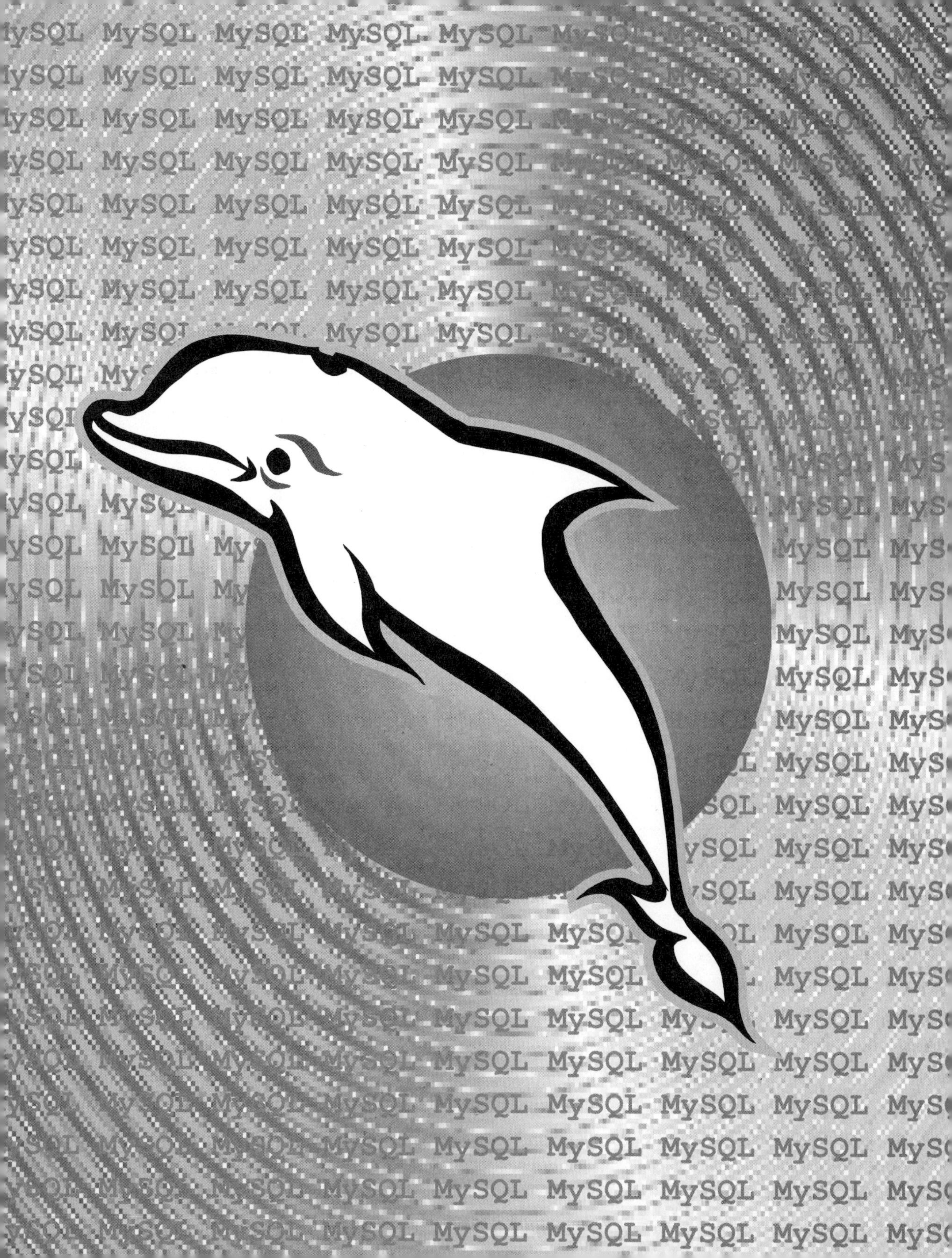

Accessing MySQL from C and C++

In this chapter, we will look at ways to create our own client applications for MySQL. Up until now, we have mostly used either command line tools such as mysql that are part of the MySQL distribution, or graphical tools such as mysqlgui that have been developed specifically for MySQL. Other tools such as Sun StarOffice, Microsoft Excel, and Microsoft Access can also be used to view and update data via ODBC links, and to create applications. However if we want complete control over our client applications, then we have to develop such applications on our own. That's where the MySQL client library libmysqlclient comes in.

In this chapter we will cover:

❑ Making database connections from C

❑ Executing SQL with libmysqlclient

❑ Transactions

❑ Living without cursors

❑ Introduction to MySQL with C++

Recall that a MySQL system is built around a client-server model. Client programs, such as mysql and mysqlgui could run on one machine, maybe a desktop PC running Windows, and the MySQL server itself could run on a UNIX or Linux or even a Windows server. The client programs send requests across a network to the server. These messages are effectively just the same as the SELECT or other SQL statements that we have used in MySQL. The server sends back result sets that the client then displays.

Messages that are conveyed between MySQL clients and the MySQL server are formatted and then transported according to a particular protocol. The client-server protocol makes sure that appropriate action is taken, should messages get lost or damaged, and it ensures that results are always delivered completely. It can also cope, to a degree, with client and server version mismatches. Clients developed to work with one version of MySQL should be compatible with later versions without too many problems.

Routines for sending and receiving these messages are included in the libmysqlclient library. To write a client application, all we have to do is use these routines and link our application with the library. We are going to assume some knowledge of the C programming language. So if you are unfamiliar with C, you might want to explore some of the following resources first:

❑   *Beginning C* by Ivor Horton, Wrox Press (ISBN 1-861001-14-2)

❑   *The C Programming Language* by Brian W. Kernighan and Dennis M. Ritchie, Prentice Hall (ISBN 0-131103-62-8)

Using the libmysqlclient Library

The functions provided by the libmysqlclient library fall into three distinct categories:

❑   Connecting to a database and managing the connection

❑   Executing SQL statements

❑   Reading the result sets obtained from queries

As with many products that have grown and evolved over many releases, there is often more than one way of doing the same thing in libmysqlclient. Here we will concentrate on the most common methods and provide hints concerning alternatives and where they might be useful.

To create MySQL client applications with libmysqlclient you will need:

❑   A 'C' compiler. We recommend GNU's gcc 2.95

❑   The MySQL library and header files

If you have installed MySQL from source code, you will have everything you need. If you have installed from a binary distribution, such as the RPM files available for Linux, you will need to have installed the -devel package.

All MySQL client applications that use the libmysqlclient library must include the appropriate header file which defines the functions libmysqlclient provides, and link with the correct library, which contains the code for those functions.

Client applications must include the header file mysql.h. This header file provides definitions of the MySQL API functions and hides the internal of MySQL that may well change between releases. Additional header files that are also provided with the MySQL distribution include definitions of the internal structures that libmysqlclient uses, but it is not recommended that they be used in normal client applications as they may change in future releases of MySQL.

The header files are normally installed in a directory of their own, a subdirectory of one of the standard locations for include files, typically /usr/include/mysql. We need to direct the C compiler to this directory so that it can find the header files using the -I option.

The libmysqlclient library will similarly be installed in a lib directory specifically for MySQL, typically /usr/lib/mysql. To incorporate the libmysqlclient functions in your application, you need to link with that library. The simplest way is to tell the compiler to link with -lmysqlclient, and specify the MySQL library directory as a place to look for libraries by using the -L option.

A typical libmysqlclient program has this structure:

```
#include <mysql.h>
main()
{
    /* Connect to a MySQL database */
    LOOP:
    /* Execute SQL statement */
    /* Read query results */

    /* Disconnect from database */
}
```

The program would be compiled and linked into an executable program by using a command line similar to this:

```
$ gcc -o program program.c -I/usr/include/mysql -L/usr/lib/mysql
     -lmysqlclient
```

Some versions of the MySQL client library are compiled with support for compression, to minimize the data that is transferred between server and client applications. In this case we need to link with the compression library (libz) too by adding -lz option to the command line for compiling the client program. Be sure to try this option if you see an error message such as:

```
/usr/lib/mysql/libmysqlclient.a(my_compress.o): In function 'my_uncompress':
my_compress.o(.text+0x9a): undefined reference to `uncompress'
/usr/lib/mysql/libmysqlclient.a(my_compress.o): In function `my_compress_alloc':
my_compress.o(.text+0x12a): undefined reference to `compress'
collect2: ld returned 1 exit status
```

If you are using a system that contains MySQL as an optional package (and you have installed it), you may find that the libmysqlclient library is installed in a location that the compiler searches by default, so you need to only specify the include directory option like this:

```
$ gcc -o program program.c -I/usr/include/mysql -lmysqlclient -lz
```

Other systems may place the include files and libraries in different places, such as subdirectories of /usr/local/mysql. We'll see later that using a Makefile can make building MySQL applications a little easier.

Database Connections

In general, a MySQL client application may connect to one or more databases as it runs. In fact, we can connect to many databases managed by many different servers all at the same time if we need to. The `libmysqlclient` library provides functions to create and maintain these connections.

When we connect to a MySQL database on a server, `libmysqlclient` returns a handle to that database connection. This is represented by an internal structure defined in the header file as `MYSQL` and we can think of it as an analog to a file structure. Many of the `libmysqlclient` functions require a `MYSQL` pointer argument to identify the particular database connection we want to operate on, in much the same way that the standard I/O library in C uses a `FILE` pointer.

Unlike a `FILE` pointer, a `MYSQL` structure needs to be initialized before it can be used to connect to a MySQL database. We can do this with `mysql_init()`:

```
MYSQL *mysql_init(MYSQL *mysql);
```

A call to `mysql_init()` will prepare a `MYSQL` structure for making a database connection. It always returns the address of the newly prepared structure:

```
MYSQL mysql;
MYSQL *ptr = mysql_init(&mysql);
```

Alternatively, we can ask `mysql_init()` to allocate a new `MYSQL` structure dynamically. In this case, the memory used for the new structure will be automatically freed when we close the associated database connection with `mysql_close()`:

```
MYSQL *ptr = mysql_init(NULL);
```

We pass `NULL` as the parameter to `mysql_init()` to request a new structure. The return result will be either the address of the new structure or `NULL` if there was insufficient memory to allocate a new `MYSQL` structure.

We will create a new database connection using `mysql_real_connect()`:

```
MYSQL *mysql_real_connect( MYSQL *conn, char *host,
                           char *user, char *password,
                           char *dbname,
                           unsigned int port, char *socketname,
                           unsigned int flags);
```

> The MySQL C API has a long history, and some of the odd function names reflect this. Some functions come in two flavors, 'standard' and 'real'. In some cases the standard function masks some complexity of the 'real' function – such as the need to handle byte-counted strings. In other cases, as with `mysql_connect()` the standard function has been deprecated, and should not be used.

The `mysql_real_connect()` function normally returns the same connection descriptor passed as the first parameter. The return result will be NULL if for some reason the database connection failed. The other arguments to `mysql_real_connect()` specify which database to connect to, and the method to be used. The arguments and their meaning are given in the table below:

Option	Meaning	Notes
host	Name or address of the server to connect to.	Use NULL or 'localhost' for the local machine – in which case the connection will be made with Unix sockets or named pipes in place of TCP/IP sockets if available.
user	MySQL user name to use when connecting.	If set to NULL, defaults to current login name. Must be set for ODBC connections from Windows.
password	Password for the specified user.	Use NULL for no password.
dbname	Name of the database to connect to.	Use NULL to connect without specifying a particular database.
port	TCP/IP port to connect to on the server.	Use 0 for the default MySQL port, or override with a non-zero value.
socketname	Unix socket or named pipe to use for local connection.	Use NULL for default behavior.
flags	Connection options.	Use 0 for default behavior.

To connect to the `bmsimple` database on the machine `dewey`, as the current user with no password, we would use a call like this:

```
mysql_real_connect(conn, "dewey", NULL, NULL, "bmsimple", 0, NULL, 0);
```

The `host` parameter names the server we want to connect to. The `mysql_real_connect()` call will result in a name lookup to determine the IP address of the server, so that the connection can be made. Usually, this is done by using DNS, the Domain Naming Service, and can take a short while to complete. If you already know the IP address of the server, you can use the `host` parameter to specify the address and thus avoid any delay while a name lookup takes place. The format of the `host` value is **a dotted quad**. The normal way of writing an IP address is four byte values separated by dots:

```
mysql_real_connect(conn, "192.168.0.22", NULL, NULL, "bmsimple", 0, NULL, 0);
```

If `host` is set to NULL then `mysql_real_connect()` will try to connect to the local machine. By default, a MySQL server will listen for client connections on TCP port 3306. If you need to connect to a server listening on a non-default port number you can specify this with the `port` parameter.

When connecting to a server on a local machine MySQL will use a UNIX domain socket rather than a TCP/IP network connection. The default is set when MySQL is installed, and is often `/tmp/mysql.sock`. The `socketname` parameter can be used to override this default.

The `flags` parameter is used to control several aspects of the connection. Refer to the MySQL online documentation for more details.

Some of the default parameters used in the call to `mysql_real_connect()` can also be overridden by using environment variables when the client program is run, as shown in the table below:

Variable	Usage
$MYSQL_UNIX_PORT	The UNIX socket name to use for connections to `localhost`.
$MYSQL_TCP_PORT	The TCP/IP port to use.
$MYSQL_PWD	The default password. This is inherently insecure.
$MYSQL_DEBUG	Debug-trace options.

For example, we can provide or override a `socketname` for connections to the local server by arranging for the environment variable $MYSQL_UNIX_PORT to be set when our program is executed. We could code a client program to call `mysql_real_connect()` with an empty string and provide the socket name we require by environment variable as in the example below:

```
#include <mysql.h>
int main()
{
MYSQL *conn = mysql_init(NULL);
conn = mysql_real_connect(conn, "", NULL, NULL, "", 0, NULL, 0);
    ...
}
$ MYSQL_UNIX_PORT=/tmp/sock ./program
```

If a connection to the database cannot be made, `mysql_real_connect()` returns `NULL` and the error variable (which can be retrieved by `mysql_errno()`) will be set to one of the following values:

Error value	Meaning
CR_CONN_HOST_ERROR	Failed to connect to remote host
CR_CONNECTION_ERROR	Failed to connect to local host
CR_IPSOCK_ERROR	Failed to create TCP/IP socket for connection
CR_OUT_OF_MEMORY	Insufficient memory
CR_SOCKET_CREATE_ERROR	Failed to create Unix domain socket for connection
CR_UNKNOWN_HOST	Host address lookup failed
CR_VERSION_ERROR	Incompatible client/server protocol versions (rare)
CR_NAMEDPIPEOPEN_ERROR	Failed to make named pipe (on Windows)

Error value	Meaning
CR_NAMEDPIPEWAIT_ERROR	Wait on named pipe failed (on Windows)
CR_NAMEDPIPESETSTATE_ERROR	Failed to create named pipe handler (on Windows)
CR_SERVER_LOST	Timeout during connect, or server died during initialization

When we have finished with a database connection we must close it, as we would with 'open file' descriptors. We do this by passing the connection descriptor pointer to `mysql_close()`:

```
void mysql_close(MYSQL *conn);
```

A call to `mysql_close()` allows the `libmysqlclient` library to release resources being consumed by the connection, including the MYSQL connection structure if it was allocated by `mysql_init()`.

Try It Out – Connecting To the Database

We can now write possibly the shortest useful MySQL program (`connect.c`), which can be used to check whether a connection can be made to a particular database. We will use mostly default arguments to `mysql_real_connect()`, but we could consider using command-line arguments or environment variables if it was appropriate for our application:

```c
#include <stdlib.h>
#include <mysql.h>

int main()
{
    MYSQL *myconnection = mysql_init(NULL);
    if(mysql_real_connect(myconnection, NULL, NULL, NULL,
        "bmsimple", 0, NULL, 0)) {
        printf("connection made\n");
        mysql_close(myconnection);
    }
    else
        printf("connection failed\n");
        return EXIT_SUCCESS;
}
```

```
$ gcc -o connect -I/usr/include/mysql -L/usr/lib/mysql connect.c
  -lmysqlclient -lz
```

```
$ ./connect
connection made
$
```

How It Works

This program simply connects to the database `bmsimple` to check the connection and closes it by calling the function `mysql_close()`.

If an error is encountered running this program, then we may need to specify the UNIX socket name and the shared library directory and run the program again. This may happen if you have installed MySQL from source code rather than RPM packages. In this case, we need to set and export a couple of environment variables before running the program as follows:

```
LD_LIBRARY_PATH=/usr/local/mysql/lib/mysql
export LD_LIBRARY_PATH
MYSQL_UNIX_PORT=/tmp/mysql.sock
export MYSQL_UNIX_PORT
```

Set these variables to the directory containing libmysqlclient.so and the value of the socket in /etc/my.cnf respectively.

API Error Checking

Many of the API functions that we will be discussing in this chapter may fail for one reason or another. We may not be able to connect to a database because of a network problem, or because we do not have the correct access permissions.

The MySQL API provides a consistent approach to handling errors, in that it provides for all APIs an error indication very similar to the errno variable used in the standard C library.

The two functions, mysql_errno() and mysql_error(), are provided for programs to determine and display any errors that arise in the use of the API functions. The mysql_errno() function returns the error condition (as a numeric value) of the last API function called by the program for a particular connection:

```
unsigned int mysql_errno(MYSQL *conn);
```

A zero return value indicates that the most recently invoked function succeeded (and a non-zero value that it failed). The error value must be checked for one API function before any further API functions are called.

> We must always check against a zero return from **mysql_errno**, as we cannot assume that a function will cause any particular error value from **mysql_errno** when it fails.

If you need to use other MySQL header files, they are located in the same directory as mysql.h. The constants defining the values of the error variable are available in the MySQL include file errmsg.h, so that our programs can check for specific types of error if required. For example, to check if a connection failed due to lack of memory we might use:

```
#include <errmsg.h>
if(mysql_errno(connection) == CR_OUT_OF_MEMORY) {
    ...
}
```

Strings containing descriptions of the errors rather than an error number can be obtained by using `mysql_error()`:

```
char *mysql_error(MYSQL *conn);
```

An empty string (`""`) is returned by `mysql_error()` if the most recently called API succeeded.

Using a Makefile

In the earlier program, we saw the `-L` and `-I` options used to indicate the compiler, where MySQL client libraries are to be found. Always remember that these are required to compile programs using `libmysqlclient`. If you use a `Makefile` to control the compilation, you can add them to the `CFLAGS` and `LDLIBS` variables respectively.

Try It Out – Using a Makefile

Here is an extremely simple `Makefile` that can be used to compile all of the sample programs in this chapter. You can download it and the source code to the examples from the Wrox web site (http://www.wrox.com):

```
# Makefile for sample programs
# in Beginning MySQL

# Edit the base directories for your
# MySQL installation

#Installed from RPMs
INC=/usr/include/mysql
LIB=/usr/lib/mysql

#Installed from source
#INC=/usr/local/mysql/include/mysql
#LIB=/usr/local/mysql/lib/mysql

CFLAGS=-I$(INC)
LDLIBS=-L$(LIB) -lmysqlclient -lz
ALL: connect create select1 select2
all: $(ALL)
```

How It Works

Once you execute the program you can generate `Makefile`, which you can eventually use to compile all of the sample programs in this chapter. You can create a program with:

```
$ make connect
```

More Information

As mentioned earlier, you can get a readable string that describes any error that might have occurred with the last API function called, by calling the function `mysql_error()`:

```
char *mysql_error(MYSQL *conn);
```

This function returns a pointer to a descriptive string. In our `connect.c` example, we could have made our connection failure message rather more helpful, like this:

```
printf("connection failed: %s", mysql_error(myconnection));
```

If you need more information about a connection after it has been made, you can use several library functions like the following to query the state of a connection:

```
char *mysql_get_client_info();
char *mysql_get_host_info(MYSQL *conn);
char *mysql_get_server_info(MYSQL *conn);
unsigned int mysql_get_proto_info(MYSQL *conn);
char *mysql_character_set_name(MYSQL *conn);
```

These functions return strings that describe the current connection, giving information about the client library version, the server host name, the server version, the protocol version and character set in use.

Try It Out – Reporting Connection Information

We can make our connection example program more informative, and call it `connect2.c`, by adding calls to these functions when we report success:

```
#include <stdlib.h>
#include <mysql.h>

int main()
{
    MYSQL *myconnection = mysql_init(NULL);
    if(mysql_real_connect(myconnection, NULL,
        "neil", "", "", 0, NULL, 0)) {
        printf("connection made\n");
        printf("client info: %s\n", mysql_get_client_info());
        printf("  host info: %s\n", mysql_get_host_info(myconnection));
        printf("server info: %s\n", mysql_get_server_info(myconnection));
        printf(" proto info: %u\n", mysql_get_proto_info(myconnection));
        mysql_close(myconnection);
    }
    else
        printf("connection failed: %s\n", mysql_error(myconnection));
    return EXIT_SUCCESS;
}
```

When we compile and run this new version, we see some more information about the connection:

```
$ make connect2
cc -I/usr/include/mysql connect2.c -L/usr/lib/mysql -lmysqlclient -lz -o connect2
$ ./connect2
connection made
```

```
client info: 3.23.43
host info: Localhost via UNIX socket
server info: 4.0.0-alpha-log
proto info: 10
$
```

How It Works

The program calls the information functions on a successful connection and prints the results.

Managing the Server Connection

There are several client library functions that are useful for setting up particular types of connection, changing characteristics of the connection, or interacting with the server.

You can change the database that an application is connected to by using mysql_select_db:

```
int mysql_select_db(MYSQL *conn, const char *dbname);
```

The function attempts to modify the connection conn to point to the database given by dbname. It returns zero if all is well and non-zero if there has been an error or the user is not authenticated. A connection may also combine a change of database with a change of user by calling mysql_change_user:

```
my_bool mysql_change_user(MYSQL *conn, char *user, char *password, char *dbname);
```

The given user name and password are authenticated and the connection modified to access the named database. If a change of database is not required, set dbname to NULL. The return result will be zero for success and non-zero on error or authentication failure.

The current status of the server can be retrieved by a call to mysql_stat(). This function returns a string describing the server uptime and number of connections, or NULL if the connection has failed:

```
char *mysql_stat(MYSQL *conn);
```

A typical return from mysql_stat() would be:

```
Uptime: 24485  Threads: 2  Questions: 99  Slow queries: 0  Opens: 23
Flush tables: 1  Open tables: 2 Queries per second avg: 0.004
```

It is possible that, with client applications that are idle for a period of time, the server connection will close. In this situation it is useful to have the ability to check the connection, and if necessary reconnect, without relying on detecting errors on queries and retrying them after reconnecting. The mysql_ping API provides this function:

```
int mysql_ping(MYSQL *conn);
```

A zero return indicates that the server is alive and connected. A non-zero return indicates that the server connection could not be re-established.

Try It Out – Connection Ping

The program below makes a connection to the database and monitors it:

```
#include <stdlib.h>
#include <mysql.h>

int main()
{
    MYSQL *myconnection = mysql_init(NULL);
    if(mysql_real_connect(myconnection, NULL,
        "neil", "", "", 0, NULL, 0)) {
        printf("connection made\n");
        while(mysql_ping(myconnection) == 0) {
            printf("server connection OK\n");
            sleep(10);
        }
        printf("server down\n");
        mysql_close(myconnection);
    }
    else
    printf("connection failed: %s\n", mysql_error(myconnection));
    return EXIT_SUCCESS;
}
```

How It Works

The program monitors the connection by calling `mysql_ping()` every 10 seconds. Should the server stop responding, the program will quit.

When we run this program we see a sequence of connection messages, one every 10 seconds:

```
$ ./ping &
connection made
server connection OK
server connection OK
server connection OK
server connection OK
server connection OK
server connection OK
server connection OK
```

If we now shut down the MySQL server we will see the program quit:

```
$ su
# /etc/rc.d/init.d/mysql stop
Killing mysqld with pid 626
Wait for mysqld to exit..........
011204 19:06:49  mysqld ended
# exit
server down
$
```

Executing SQL with libmysqlclient

Now that we can connect to a MySQL database from within a C program, the next step is to execute SQL statements. This is quite straightforward in fact, and our interface starts with the function `mysql_query()`:

```
int mysql_query(MYSQL *conn, const char *sql_string);
```

Essentially, we pass a SQL statement to `mysql_query()`, and the server we are connected to via the non-NULL connection `conn` that executes it. The `sql_string` parameter is a NULL-terminated string containing a single SQL statement. We do not add a semicolon as we do for the `mysql` command line tool. The return result from `mysql_query()` is normally zero, a non-zero value indicates that an error has occurred.

The result of the query is communicated via a result structure, a `MYSQL_RES`. This result set will contain any data returned by the server for `SELECT` statements. We can obtain a pointer to the result set for the last query executed by calling `mysql_store_result()`:

```
MYSQL_RES *mysql_store_result(MYSQL *conn);
```

A call to `mysql_store_result()` retrieves all of the data available for the last query and copies into the client application's memory. If the query was of a type that does not return data (such as an `INSERT`), `mysql_store_result()` will return a NULL pointer. On rare occasions, `mysql_store_result()` may also return a NULL pointer if there is not enough memory to allocate a new result structure, or if the connection to the server has failed during the transfer of the result, in which case a non-zero value would be returned from `mysql_errno`.

For queries where data can be returned, even when there is no data to return, `mysql_store_result()` will return a valid non-NULL pointer to a result structure that contains no data records. This will occur, for example, for `SELECT` queries that match no rows in the database table.

If want to avoid the overhead of calling `mysql_strore_result()`, we can determine whether or not the last query could have returned data by calling `mysql_field_count()`:

```
unsigned int mysql_field_count(MYSQL *conn);
```

A call to `mysql_field_count()` returns the number of columns expected in the result set for the last query. If it is zero, no data was expected.

It can sometimes be tricky, thinking about precisely what happens when we execute a query, especially telling the difference between a failed query and one that executed correctly, but happened to be of a type where no data was expected. So it can be beneficial to use some 'boilerplate' code to deal with the execution of queries and assessing the result.

Try It Out – Query Results Status

Here's an example code fragment that uses `mysql_field_count()` to determine the precise results of a call to `mysql_query()`:

```
MYSQL *conn;
char *sql_string;
MYSQL_RES *result;
...
if(mysql_query(conn, sql_string)) {
    /* Error occurred with the query */
    printf("Query failed: %s\n", mysql_error(conn));
}
else {
if(mysql_field_count(conn)) {
    /* Data may be returned */
    result = mysql_store_result(conn);

if(result) {
    /* Process result set, may have zero or more rows */
}
else
    printf("Store result failed: %s\n", mysql_error(conn));
}
else
/* Query OK, no data expected */;
}
```

How It Works

If a query succeeds, this code uses the field count as an indicator as of whether or not data could have been returned. This tells us whether any failure to return a result set is valid or not.

As with connection structures, result objects must also be freed when you are finished with them. We can do this with mysql_free_result() – 'void mysql_free_result(MYSQL_RES *result)'.

> Note that results are not cleared automatically, even when the connection is closed, so they can be kept indefinitely if required. Any non-freed result sets will of course occupy memory in our program so it is recommended that all result sets be freed when we are finished with them.

Let's look at some simple examples of executing SQL statements. We will use a very small table in our test database as an example for trying things out. Later, we will perform some operations on our sample customer table to return larger amounts of data.

We are going to create a database table called number. In it we will store numbers and some text description of them. The table will look like this:

```
value |    name
------+-------------
 42   | The Answer
 29   | My Age
 66   | Clickety-Click
```

To create the table and insert values into it, we just need to call `mysql_query()` with an appropriate string containing the SQL query we need to execute. Our program will contain calls like this:

```
MYSQL *myconnection;
...
mysql_query(myconnection,
"CREATE TABLE number (value INTEGER, name VARCHAR(64))");
mysql_query(myconnection,
"INSERT INTO number VALUES (42, 'The Answer')");
```

We will need to take care of errors that arise. For example, if the table already exists we will get an error when we try to create it again. In the case of creating the `number` table when it already exists, `mysql_error()` will return a string that says:

```
Table 'number' already exists
```

Try It Out – Simple Queries

To make things a little easier, we will develop a function of our own called `doSQL()` to execute SQL statements, check the results, and print errors. We will add more functionality to it as we go along. Here's the first version:

```
void doSQL(MYSQL *conn, char *command)
{
    printf("%s\n", command);
    mysql_query(conn, command);
    printf("Result: %s\n", mysql_error(conn));
}
```

Now we can execute SQL queries almost as easily as we can enter commands to `mysql`. Save the following code in a file called `create.c`:

```
#include <stdlib.h>
#include <mysql.h>

void doSQL(MYSQL *conn, char *command)
{
    printf("%s\n", command);
    mysql_query(conn, command);
    printf("Result: %s\n", mysql_error(conn));
}
int main()
{
    MYSQL *conn;
    conn = mysql_init(NULL);
    if(mysql_real_connect(conn, NULL,
        "neil", "", "test", 0, NULL, 0)) {
        printf("connection made\n");
        /* doSQL(conn, "DROP TABLE number"); */
        doSQL(conn, "CREATE TABLE number (
```

```
        value INTEGER,
        name VARCHAR(64)
        )");
        doSQL(conn, "INSERT INTO number values(42, 'The Answer')");
        doSQL(conn, "INSERT INTO number values(29, 'My Age')");
        doSQL(conn, "INSERT INTO number values(29, 'Anniversary')");
        doSQL(conn, "INSERT INTO number values(66, 'Clickety-Click')");
        mysql_close(conn);
    }
    else
    printf("connection failed: %s\n", mysql_error(conn));
    return EXIT_SUCCESS;
}
```

How It Works

Here we create the number table and add some entries to it. If we rerun the program, we will see an error reported, as we cannot create the table a second time. Uncomment the DROP TABLE command to change the program into one that destroys and recreates the table each time it is run.

Of course, in production code we would not be quite so cavalier in our approach to errors. Here we have omitted to return a result from doSQL() to keep things brief and we push on regardless of failures.

When we compile and run this program, we should see the command being executed and some result strings, mostly blank:

```
$ make create
$ ./create
connection made
CREATE TABLE number (
value INTEGER,
name  VARCHAR(64)
                  )
Result:
INSERT INTO number values(42, 'The Answer')
Result:
INSERT INTO number values(29, 'My Age')
Result:
INSERT INTO number values(29, 'Anniversary')
Result:
INSERT INTO number values(66, 'Clickety-Click')
Result:
$
```

To include user-specified data into the SQL as variables, we have to create a string to pass to mysql_query() that contains the values we want. To add all single digit integers we might write:

```
for(n = 0; n < 10; n++) {
sprintf(buffer,
"INSERT INTO number VALUES(%d, 'single digit')", n);
mysql_query(conn, buffer);
}
```

If we want to update or delete rows in a table, we can use the UPDATE and DELETE commands respectively:

```
UPDATE number SET name = 'Zaphod' WHERE value = 42
DELETE FROM number WHERE value = 29
```

We can add suitable calls to mysql_query() (or doSQL()) to our program, and first change the descriptive text of the number 42 to Zaphod, and then delete both of the entries for 29. We can check the result of our changes using mysql:

```
$ mysql
mysql> use test;
Database changed
mysql> SELECT * FROM number;
value |        name
------+-----------------
66    | Clickety-Click
42    | Zaphod
mysql>
```

DELETE and UPDATE may affect more than one row in the table; therefore it is often useful to know how many rows have been changed. We can get this information by calling mysql_affected_rows():

```
my_ulonglong mysql_affected_rows(MYSQL *mysql);
```

The function mysql_affected_rows() returns the number of rows affected by the last query (an INSERT, UPDATE or DELETE).

The function mysql_info() will return a string containing information about the rows affected by some changes, including DELETE commands:

```
char *mysql_info(MYSQL *conn);
```

The format of the string returned depends upon the previous command:

```
Rows matched: x  Changed: y  Warnings: z
```

For SELECT statements we will use a different function later, although mysql_affected_rows() will also return a meaningful value for SELECTs as well.

We can simply modify doSQL() function to report the rows affected:

```
printf("#rows affected %ld\n", (long) mysql_affected_rows(result));
```

We have to be careful to distinguish between commands that validly affect no rows, and those that fail and therefore affect no rows. We must always check the result status to determine errors first, before considering the number of rows affected.

357

Transactions

Sometimes we will want to ensure that a group of SQL commands are executed as a group, so that the changes to the database are made either all together or none at all if an error occurs at some point.

As in standard SQL, we can manage this with `libmysqlclient` by using the transaction support. We simply arrange to call `mysql_query()` with SQL statements that contain `BEGIN`, `COMMIT`, and `ROLLBACK`:

```
mysql_query(conn, "BEGIN WORK");
/* make changes */
if(we changed our minds) {
    mysql_query(conn, "ROLLBACK WORK");
}
else {
    mysql_query(conn, "COMMIT WORK");
}
```

We have already discussed transactions in detail in Chapter 9, *Transactions and Locking*. For MySQL table types that support transactions such as `InnoDB`, we can use all of the facilities described there in our `libmysqlclient` programs by passing the appropriate SQL query string to `mysql_query()`.

Extracting Data from Queries

Up until now, we have only been concerned with SQL statements that have not returned any data. Now it is time to consider how to deal with data returned by calls to `mysql_query()`. That is, with the result of `SELECT` statements.

When we perform a `SELECT` with `mysql_query()` the result set will contain information about the data the query has returned. Query results can seem a little tiresome to handle, as we do not always know exactly what to expect. If we execute a `SELECT`, we do not always know in advance whether we will be returned zero, one, or several millions of rows. If we use a wildcard (*) in the `SELECT`, we do not even know what columns will be returned, or what their names are.

In general, we will want to program our application so that it selects specified columns only. That way, if the design of the database changes (perhaps when new columns are added), then a function that does not rely on the new column will still work as expected.

Sometimes (for example, if you are writing a general-purpose SQL program that is taking statements from the user and displaying results) it would be better if we could program in a general way and, with MySQL, we can. There are just a few more functions to get to know.

When `mysql_query()` executes a `SELECT` without an error, we expect to see a non-`NULL` return result from `mysql_store_result()`. The next step is to determine how many rows are present in the result set. We do this by calling `mysql_num_rows()`:

```
my_ulonglong mysql_num_rows (MYSQL_RES *result);
```

This will give us the total number of rows in our result, which may, of course, be zero.

We can retrieve the number of fields (attributes or columns) in our rows by calling `mysql_num_fields()`:

```
unsigned int mysql_num_fields(MYSQL_RES *result);
```

Fields in a result set are described by a structure called `MYSQL_FIELD`. We can gain access to an array of these structures for a particular result set by calling `mysql_fetch_fields()`:

```
MYSQL_FIELD *mysql_fetch_fields(MYSQL_RES *result);
```

The fields in the result are numbered starting from zero, and we can retrieve their details by indexing into the array. We can use the `MYSQL_FIELD` pointer as long as the result set it refers to has not been freed:

```
MYSQL_FIELD *all_fields = mysql_fetch_fields(result);
MYSQL_FIELD *third_field = &all_fields[2];
```

Alternatively, we may fetch the details for one field only, by calling index number with `mysql_fetch_field_direct()`, or we may fetch field details one at a time with `mysql_fetch_field()`:

```
MYSQL_FIELD *mysql_fetch_field_direct(MYSQL_RES *result, unsigned int index);
MYSQL_FIELD *mysql_fetch_field(MYSQL_RES *result);
```

The `mysql_fetch_field()` function returns a NULL pointer if there are no more fields.

The `MYSQL_FIELD` structure contains a large amount of information about the table column it refers to. Structure members include:

Member	Meaning
`char *name`	Name of the field (table column) as a NULL-terminated string
`char *table`	Name of the table that the column resides in
`char *def`	Default value for the field, if set my `mysql_list_fields`
`enum enum_field_types type`	The field data type (see overleaf)
`unsigned int length`	The width of the column, as given by the table definition
`unsigned int max_length`	The maximum width of this column in this result set
`unsigned int flags`	Attributes assigned to the column (see overleaf)

The value of the type member of a MYSQL_FIELD structure will be one of the following constants:

Value	Meaning
FIELD_TYPE_TINY	TINYINT field
FIELD_TYPE_SHORT	SMALLINT field
FIELD_TYPE_LONG	INTEGER field
FIELD_TYPE_INT24	MEDIUMINT field
FIELD_TYPE_LONGLONG	BIGINT field
FIELD_TYPE_DECIMAL	DECIMAL or NUMERIC field
FIELD_TYPE_FLOAT	FLOAT field
FIELD_TYPE_DOUBLE	DOUBLE or REAL field
FIELD_TYPE_TIMESTAMP	TIMESTAMP field
FIELD_TYPE_DATE	DATE field
FIELD_TYPE_TIME	TIME field
FIELD_TYPE_DATETIME	DATETIME field
FIELD_TYPE_YEAR	YEAR field
FIELD_TYPE_STRING	String (CHAR or VARCHAR) field
FIELD_TYPE_BLOB	BLOB or TEXT field (use max_length rather than length to determine the maximum length)
FIELD_TYPE_SET	SET field
FIELD_TYPE_ENUM	ENUM field
FIELD_TYPE_NULL	NULL-type field

The flags member of the MYSQL_FIELD consists of a number of bit fields defined as in the table below:

Value	Meaning
NOT_NULL_FLAG	Field can't be NULL
PRI_KEY_FLAG	Field is part of a primary key
UNIQUE_KEY_FLAG	Field is part of a unique key
MULTIPLE_KEY_FLAG	Field is part of a non-unique key
UNSIGNED_FLAG	Field has the UNSIGNED attribute

Value	Meaning
ZEROFILL_FLAG	Field has the ZEROFILL attribute
BINARY_FLAG	Field has the BINARY attribute
AUTO_INCREMENT_FLAG	Field has the AUTO_INCREMENT attribute

As an example, we can discover the name of a field, its size and whether it is set to be non-NULL with the following code snippet:

```
MYSQL_FIELD *field;
printf("name is %s\n", field ->name);
printf("size is %d\n", field -> length); /* use max_length for BLOB/TEXT */
if(field -> flags & NOT_NULL_FLAG)
printf("field cannot be NULL\n");
```

Try It Out – SELECT Results

Let's modify our doSQL() function to print out some information about the data returned from a SELECT query. Here's our next version:

```
void doSQL(MYSQL *conn, char *command)
{
   MYSQL_RES *result;
   printf("%s\n", command);
   if(mysql_query(conn, command)) {
      printf("Error: %s\n", mysql_error(conn));
      return;
   }
   result = mysql_store_result(conn);
   if(!result) {
      /* No result set returned */
      printf("#rows affected %d\n", mysql_affected_rows(conn));
   }
   else {
      int n;
      int nrows = mysql_num_rows(result);
      int nfields = mysql_num_fields(result);
      MYSQL_FIELD *field = mysql_fetch_fields(result);

      printf("number of rows returned = %d\n", nrows);
      printf("number of fields returned = %d\n", nfields);
      for(n = 0; n < nfields; n++)
         printf("%s:%d ", field[n].name, field[n].length);
      printf("\n");
      mysql_free_result(result);
   }
}
```

How It Works

Now when we execute a SELECT, we can see the characteristics of the data being returned:

```
doSQL(conn, "SELECT * FROM number WHERE value = 29");
```

The call above results in the following output:

```
SELECT * FROM number WHERE value = 29
number of rows returned = 2
number of fields returned = 2
value:11 name:64
```

Now we are ready to extract the data from the fields returned in the rows of our result set. The rows are numbered, starting from zero.

The simplest way of accessing data returned in a result set is by using a string-based representation. For each row of data in the result set we will call mysql_fetch_row() to extract an array of strings, one for each field in the returned row. The strings are counted byte strings (not necessarily always NULL-terminated), so that they can if required hold binary data. Each row is represented by a MYSQL_ROW structure:

```
MYSQL_ROW mysql_fetch_row(MYSQL_RES *result);
```

The number of fields in the row is given by mysql_num_fields() as we saw earlier. The data for each field is accessed by indexing the MYSQL_ROW structure. If row is a MYSQL_ROW structure, the field data is being pointed to by row[0], row[1] and so on. Before we can make use of the counted byte data, we need to establish the lengths of each field – *in this particular row.*

> Note: Only **BLOBS** and **TEXT** types need special care as the standard types do in fact have a **NULL** terminating their string representation. Here we are writing to be general purpose so we include the fetching of length information.

We can get the actual field lengths for the current row in a result set by calling mysql_fetch_lengths():

```
unsigned long *mysql_fetch_lengths(MYSQL_RES *result);
```

This function returns an array of byte counts for the strings used to represent the data in the fields returned for the current row.

Further rows can be extracted from the result set by calling mysql_fetch_row() repeatedly. It will return NULL when all rows have been read from the result set.

Try It Out – Column Information

Let's add some data display to our doSQL() function:

```
        void doSQL(MYSQL *conn, char *command)
        {
            MYSQL_RES *result;
            int errcode;
            printf("%s\n", command);
            if(mysql_query(conn, command)) {
                printf("Error: %s\n", mysql_error(conn));
                return;
            }
            result = mysql_store_result(conn);
            if(!result) {
                /* No result set returned */
                printf("#rows affected %d\n", mysql_affected_rows(conn));
            }
            else {
                int r, n;
                int nrows = mysql_num_rows(result);
                int nfields = mysql_num_fields(result);
                MYSQL_FIELD *field = mysql_fetch_fields(result);

                printf("number of rows returned = %d\n", nrows);
                printf("number of fields returned = %d\n", nfields);

                for(r = 0; r < nrows; r++) {
                    MYSQL_ROW row = mysql_fetch_row(result);
                    unsigned long *lengths = mysql_fetch_lengths(result);

                    for(n = 0; n < nfields; n++)

                        printf("%s:[%.*s] ", field[n].name,
                          (int) lengths[n], row[n]? row[n]: "(null)");
                    printf("\n");
                }
                mysql_free_result(result);
            }
        }
```

How It Works

Scanning the fields in each row of data returned and printing it out prints the complete result of the SELECT query.

Note that we use the field length as a variable field width for printing the field data in printf. This is a very handy trick. If we are printing a value with printf we can specify a field width that is the number of characters we wish to output. If the value requires fewer characters than this, printf will fill the remainder with spaces. The printf format "*.%s" tells printf to take the field width from the next argument, giving us a way of making the field width variable at runtime.

The output becomes:

```
SELECT * FROM number WHERE value = 29
number of rows returned = 2
number of fields returned = 2
value:[29] name:[My Age]
value:[29] name:[Anniversary]
```

> String data, such as that used in columns defined as `CHAR(n)`, is padded with spaces.
> This can give unexpected results if you are checking for a particular string value or
> comparing values for a sort. If you insert the value 'Zaphod' into a column defined as
> `CHAR(8)` you will get back `"Zaphod<space><space>"` which will not compare
> equal to `"Zaphod"` if you use the C library function `strcmp`. It is best to trim any
> trailing spaces from the retuned value before performing the comparison. This little
> problem has been known to catch out some very experienced developers.

There is one small complication that we must deal with before we go any further. The fact that our
query results are being returned to us encoded within character strings, means that we cannot readily
tell the difference between an empty string and an SQL NULL value, as both will have zero length.

Fortunately, the MySQL library provides us with an indication that we can use to determine whether a
particular value of a field in a result set row is a NULL. In this case the data pointer in the `MYSQL_ROW`
structure will be NULL, whereas a zero-length field will have a non-NULL data pointer. This is used in
`doSQL()` to print `(null)` for NULL field values.

Scanning a Result Set

In our examples so far, we have simply read each row of a result set in sequence. Sometimes we might
like to be able to jump directly to a specific row in the result set, or return to a previous point in the
scan picking up where we left off.

The MySQL client library provides functions similar to C file functions **tell**() and **seek**() for moving
around inside a result set. To jump to a specified row number within a result set we can use
`mysql_data_seek()`:

```
void mysql_data_seek(MYSQL_RES *result, unsigned long long offset);
```

The rows are numbered from 0 to `mysql_num_rows(result)-1`. Invalid offset values are ignored.
To access the last row in a result set we could write:

```
MYSQL_RES *result;
MYSQL_ROW row;
mysql_data_seek(result, mysql_num_rows(result)-1);
row = mysql_fetch_row(result);
```

We can record how far through the result set we have reached by calling `mysql_row_tell`, which will
return an offset into the result set. To reset the scan position to that saved point we call
`mysql_row_seek()`:

```
MYSQL_ROW_OFFSET mysql_row_tell(MYSQL_RES *result);
MYSQL_ROW_OFFSET mysql_row_seek(MYSQL_RES *result, MYSQL_ROW_OFFSET offset);
```

Note that MySQL uses a defined type MYSQL_ROW_OFFSET for describing the current position returned by mysql_row_tell() and the desired position for mysql_row_seek. This is not simply a row number, so you must always use mysql_row_seek (rather than mysql_data_seek) with the result of mysql_row_tell(). The function mysql_row_seek() returns the current position, before moving to the desired position.

Similarly, MySQL provides functions to help with scanning along a row within a result set. The functions mysql_field_tell() and mysql_field_seek() report and set the position within the current row that the next call to mysql_fetch_field() will retrieve.

```
MYSQL_FIELD_OFFSET mysql_field_tell(MYSQL_RES *result);
MYSQL_FIELD_OFFSET mysql_field_seek(MYSQL_RES *result, MYSQL_FIELD_OFFSET offset);
```

Passing an offset of zero to mysql_field_seek() will seek the start of the row.

Living Without Cursors

In the real world, when we are writing complete applications, we may find that we need to deal with large quantities of data. A MySQL database is capable of storing tables with very large numbers of rows in them.

When it comes to processing the results of queries that produce a large amount of data however, we are rather at the mercy of the client application and its operating environment. A desktop PC may well have trouble dealing with a million rows returned all at once in a result set from a single SELECT. A large result set can consume a great deal of memory, and, if we are running across a network, may also consume a lot of bandwidth and take a substantial time to be transferred.

What we really need to do is perform the query and deal with the results part-by-part. For example, if in our application we want to show our complete customer list, we could retrieve all of them in one go. It is smarter to fetch them, say, a page of 25 at a time and display them in our application page by page. We can do this with standard SQL by employing **cursors**. Cursors are an excellent general-purpose way of catering for a potentially large number of rows being returned by a SELECT statement. If you search for a Zip code, particularly one provided by a user, you have no idea in advance if zero, one, or many rows will be returned.

In general, you should avoid writing code that assumes either a single row or no rows are returned from a SELECT statement, unless that statement is a simple aggregate, such as SELECT COUNT(*) FROM type query, or a SELECT on a primary key where you can be guaranteed the result will always be exactly one row. If the SELECT will return more than one row in your application program, then use a cursor.

In standard SQL, cursors are implemented by DECLARE and FETCH statements. At the time of writing, MySQL does not support SQL cursors, but does have a mechanism within libmysqlclient that allows us to achieve a similar level of flexibility.

To deal with multiple rows being returned from a query, we will retrieve them one (or more) at a time using mysql_fetch_row() as before, but using a result set that does not contain all of the data available as the result of a query.

To create an application that scrolls through a collection of returned rows, pulling them from the server one at a time, we must use `mysql_use_result()` in place of `mysql_store_result()`:

```
MYSQL_RES *mysql_use_result(MYSQL *conn);
```

After we have created a result set with `mysql_use_result()` we must call `mysql_fetch_row()` repeatedly until it returns NULL. As the size of the result set is not known by the client, the functions `mysql_num_rows()` and `mysql_affected_rows()` cannot be used to determine the number of rows in the result set in advance.

> NOTE: When using `mysql_use_result()` you must continue to call `mysql_fetch_row()` until all rows are returned, otherwise any unfetched rows will be returned as data for the next executed query.

Here's a version of `doSQL()` that fetches the returned rows one at a time from the server:

```c
void doSQL(MYSQL *conn, char *command)
{
    MYSQL_RES *result;
    int errcode;
    printf("%s\n", command);
    if(mysql_query(conn, command)) {
        printf("Error: %s\n", mysql_error(conn));
        return;
    }
    result = mysql_use_result(conn);
    if(!result) {
        /* No result set returned */
        printf("#rows affected %d\n", mysql_affected_rows(conn));
    }
    else {
        int r, n;
        int nrows = 0;
        int nfields = mysql_num_fields(result);
        MYSQL_FIELD *field = mysql_fetch_fields(result);
        MYSQL_ROW row;
        printf("number of fields returned = %d\n", nfields);
        while(row = mysql_fetch_row(result)) {
            unsigned long *lengths = mysql_fetch_lengths(result);
            for(n = 0; n < nfields; n++)
                printf("%s:[%.*s] ", field[n].name,
                (int) lengths[n], row[n]? row[n]: "(null)");
            printf("\n");
            nrows++;
        }
        printf("number of rows returned = %d\n", nrows);
        mysql_free_result(result);
    }
}
```

API Summary

The table below summarizes the MySQL client library functions available in `libmysqlclient` that we have covered in this chapter:

Function	Meaning
`mysql_affected_rows()`	Returns the number of rows changed/deleted/inserted by the last UPDATE, DELETE, or INSERT query.
`mysql_change_user()`	Changes user and database on an open connection.
`mysql_character_set_name()`	Returns the name of the default character set for the connection.
`mysql_close()`	Closes a server connection.
`mysql_data_seek()`	Seeks an arbitrary row in a query result set.
`mysql_errno()`	Returns the error number for the most recently invoked MySQL function.
`mysql_error()`	Returns the error message for the most recently invoked MySQL function.
`mysql_fetch_field()`	Returns the type of the next table field.
`mysql_fetch_field_direct()`	Returns the type of a table field, given a field number.
`mysql_fetch_fields()`	Returns an array of all field structures.
`mysql_fetch_lengths()`	Returns the lengths of all columns in the current row.
`mysql_fetch_row()`	Fetches the next row from the result set.
`mysql_field_count()`	Returns the number of result columns for the most recent query.
`mysql_field_seek()`	Puts the column cursor on a specified column.
`mysql_field_tell()`	Returns the position of the field cursor used for the last `mysql_fetch_field()`.
`mysql_free_result()`	Frees memory used by a result set.
`mysql_get_client_info()`	Returns client version information.
`Mysql_get_host_info()`	Returns a string describing the connection.
`Mysql_get_proto_info()`	Returns the protocol version used by the connection.
`Mysql_get_server_info()`	Returns the server version number.
`Mysql_info()`	Returns information about the most recently executed query.

Table continued on following page

Function	Meaning
Mysql_init()	Gets or initializes a MYSQL structure.
Mysql_num_fields()	Returns the number of columns in a result set.
Mysql_num_rows()	Returns the number of rows in a result set.
Mysql_ping()	Checks whether or not the connection to the server is working, reconnecting as necessary.
Mysql_query()	Executes a SQL query specified as a null-terminated string.
Mysql_real_connect()	Connects to a MySQL server.
Mysql_row_seek()	Seeks a row in a result set, using value returned from mysql_row_tell().
Mysql_row_tell()	Returns the row cursor position.
Mysql_select_db()	Selects a database.
Mysql_stat()	Returns the server status as a string.
Mysql_store_result()	Retrieves a complete result set to the client.
Mysql_use_result()	Initiates a row-by-row result set retrieval.

Some additional APIs are available, but are deprecated. This means that they have been superceded or that there are other ways of achieving the same effect, which are considered to be preferable for new applications. Check the online manual for more details of these older functions.

In many cases, SQL statements now supported in MySQL replace these APIs. Refer to Appendix C and the on-line documentation for details of the SQL commands allowed by MySQL:

Function	Meaning
Mysql_connect()	Connects to a MySQL server. Use mysql_real_connect() instead.
Mysql_create_db()	Creates a database. Use CREATE DATABASE instead.
Mysql_drop_db()	Drops a database. Use DROP DATABASE instead.
Mysql_eof()	Determines whether or not the last row of a result set has been read. mysql_errno() or mysql_error() may be used instead.
Mysql_list_dbs()	Returns database names matching a simple regular expression. Use SHOW DATABASES [LIKE] instead.

Function	Meaning
Mysql_list_fields()	Returns field names matching a simple regular expression. Use SHOW COLUMNS FROM tbl_name instead.
Mysql_list_tables()	Returns table names matching a simple regular expression. Use SHOW TABLES [LIKE] instead.
mysql_reload()	Tells the server to reload the grant tables. Use FLUSH PRIVILEGES statement instead.

Further APIs of specialist use only can be found in the online documentation. Some of the tasks executed by these functions include debugging, dealing with special characters and shutting down the database server.

Using MySQL with C++

We have seen that MySQL is distributed with a library suitable for creating client applications in C. If we want or need to create applications using C++ we can do so, using the same API library. In this way, we would be using C++ as a "better C". Ideally, we would like to use API functions more closely aligned to features of C++ such as exceptions and the STL containers. This would allow us to use an object-oriented approach in our applications, using MySQL structures as true objects.

Here we are going to take a brief look at one of the C++ interfaces to MySQL, a library called **Mysql++**. We will assume that you have some experience with C++, the standard template library, manipulators, and exceptions. If you are not comfortable with C++ you may wish to skip this part of the book.

Much of the C++ API has a direct equivalent in the C API. Here we will not cover in depth those features that are similar to ones in the C API except to list the member functions available.

Mysql++

The Mysql++ library was originally written by Kevin Atkinson and is now maintained by Sinisa Milivojevic at MySQL. It is freely available under the terms of the GNU GPL, which allows full use of the library in applications, both free and commercial. The design aim for Mysql++ is to create a database-independent C++ API, making the working with database queries as simple a matter as working with standard library containers. At the time of writing, only MySQL support is available for the Mysql++ library.

Installing Mysql++

Installation of Mysql++ is fairly straightforward, following the same scheme as a great deal of free software today. A source 'tarball' is available on the MySQL web site for download. The latest version at the time of writing is 1.7.9. The usual incantations perform the compilation and install:

```
$ tar zxf mysql++-1.7.9.tar.gz
$ cd mysql++-1.7.9
$ ./configure
$ make
$ su
# make install
```

The default build will install the Mysql++ library and header files in subdirectories (`lib` and `include`) of `/usr/local/`. To change the location for the installation, run `configure` specifying a different directory prefix:

```
$ ./configure --with-prefix=/usr //check options using ./configure --help
```

> **The Mysql++ code is very sensitive to the way that C++ compilers handle some of the features it needs. With version 1.7.9 there are problems compiling with versions of the GNU C++ compiler (GCC) other than 2.95.2, including 2.7.x, 2.8.x, 2.96 and the EGCS versions of the compiler. There is a patch available for Mysql++ 1.7.9 that enables it to work with GCC 3.0. It is possible to compile Mysql++ for use on Microsoft Windows with Borland C++ and Microsoft Visual C++ 6.**

Once installed, you may need to make the Mysql++ shared libraries available at runtime. To do this you can set the `LD_LIBRARY_PATH` environment variable, or arrange for the Mysql++ library directory to be included in the places that your system searches for dynamic libraries. On Linux, this is done by including the directory in `/etc/ld.so.conf`. If you have chosen to use the default locations then this is not necessary, except that you will need to run `ldconfig` to update the dynamic loader's cache of library locations.

Compiling with Mysql++

Compiling a C++ program that uses Mysql++ is quite simple. All of the functions that are available are defined in one header file, `sqlplus.hh`, and implemented in one library, `libsqlplus.so`. The header and library names reflect the desire for Mysql++ to become a database-independent library in the future. In addition, we need to have the C API installed as the Mysql++ requires access to its header files, and the compression library (`libz`) must be present.

Try It Out – Connect from C++

Here is just about the simplest Mysql++ program. It connects to the MySQL server on the local machine, using the current user's login name and prints a message when it has connected:

```
#include <iostream>
#include <sqlplus.hh>

int main()
{
    try {
        Connection con("bmsimple");
```

```
        cout << "connected\n";
    }
    catch (BadQuery &er) {
        cerr << "Oops: " << er.error << endl;
    }
}
```

To compile this program we use the C++ compiler, specifying the include directory for the MySQL header files and the Mysql++ library like this:

```
$ c++ -o connectcc -I/usr/include/mysql connectcc.cc -lsqlplus
```

> You may have to specify **/usr/lib/mysql/libmysqlclient.a** with some configurations after the **-lsqlplus** .

When we run the program we see a message:

```
$ ./connectcc
connected
```

If the connection fails, we will see an error message. For example, if we misspell the name of the database as bpsimple instead of bmsimple:

```
$ ./connectcc
Oops: unknown database 'bpsimple'
```

How It Works

The program creates an object of type Connection. The constructor for this type makes the connection to the database and raises an exception if it fails. The exception, of type BadQuery, defined by Mysql++ is caught and an error message printed.

To help with building C++ applications we can create a simple Makefile, or modify the one we used for the C APIs. Here is a revised version of the Makefile suitable for building both C and C++ applications:

```
# Makefile for sample programs
# in Beginning MySQL
# Edit the base directories for your
# MySQL installation
INC=/usr/include/mysql
LIB=/usr/lib/mysql
CFLAGS=-I$(INC)
LDLIBS=-L$(LIB) -lsqlplus -lmysqlclient -lz
CPPFLAGS=-I$(INC)
ALL= connectcc connect connect2 create select1 select2
all: $(ALL)
```

371

For GNU `make` at least, all that we have had to change to add C++ support is to add the Mysql++ library to the link libraries `LDLIBS`, and set the C++ options to specify an include directory in `CPPFLAGS`. The `make` takes care of the rest:

```
$ make connectcc
g++  -I/usr/include/mysql  connectcc.cc  -L/usr/lib/mysql -lsqlplus -lmysqlclient
-lz -o connectcc
```

Note that the inclusion of additional compiler flags used for C programs is harmless for C++. Strictly speaking for C++ we do not need the arguments `-L/usr/lib/mysl`, `-lmysqlclient` or `-lz`, but it keeps the `Makefile` simpler if we treat the two languages the same.

Now that we have the C++ compiler successfully compiling Mysql++ applications and we can execute them, it is time to move on to considering the C++ APIs in a little more detail.

Connection objects

The `Connection` class provides a handle for a connection to a MySQL database. It can be used to manipulate the database and execute queries. The `Connection` class has the following constructors:

```
Connection(bool te = true)
Connection(const char *db,
const char *host = "", const char *user = "", const char *passwd = "",
bool te = true)
Connection(const char *db, const char *host, const char *user, const char *passwd,
uint port, my_bool compress = 1, unsigned int connect_timeout = 5,
bool te = true, const char *socket_name = "")
```

In the example program `connectcc.cc`, we used the third form of the constructor, allowing the optional parameters to take their default values. The constructor parameters have the same usage as those in the C API `mysql_real_connect()`. The Boolean parameter `te` (for throw exceptions) indicates whether the connection object should throw an exception when errors occur. Usually this should be set to `true` which is its default value.

The `Connection` object is able to establish a connection to the server, select an appropriate database, send queries and return results. It has a large number of member functions that echo many of the C API functions including the ability to connect to a database (if the constructor has not already done so) using `mysql_real_connect()`.

The public member functions include:

```
int affected_rows ()
operator bool () // called in conditional expressions, returns success()
string client_info ()
void close ()
bool connect (cchar *db = "", cchar *host = "", cchar *user = "", cchar
    *passwd = "")
bool connected () const // returns true if a successful connection was made
```

```
bool create_db (string db)
bool drop_db (string db)
int errnum ()
string error () // last error message
bool exec (const string &str)
ResNSel execute (const string &str)
ResNSel execute (const string &str, bool te)
st_mysql_options get_options (void) const
string host_info ()
string info ()
int insert_id ()
int kill (unsigned long pid)
bool lock ()
int ping (void)
int proto_info ()
void purge (void)
inline Query query ()
int read_options (enum mysql_option option,const char *arg)
bool real_connect (cchar *db = "", cchar *host = "", cchar *user = "", cchar
    *passwd = "",
uint port = 0, my_bool compress = 0, unsigned int connect_timeout = 60,
cchar *socket_name= "")
int refresh (unsigned int refresh_options)
bool reload ()
bool select_db (const char *db)
bool select_db (string db)
string server_info ()
bool shutdown ()
string stat ()
Result store (const string &str)
Result store (const string &str, bool te)
bool success ()  // returns true if the last query was successful
void unlock ()
ResUse use (const string &str)
ResUse use (const string &str, bool te)
```

As you can see, the C++ member functions map very closely onto the C APIs, so we have for example a `real_connect` member function that is the equivalent of `mysql_real_connect` in C.

In this chapter, we will only cover the APIs we need to connect to a database, execute queries and extract data from result sets. For further information on the Mysql++ APIs refer to the documentation distributed with the source code of the library.

Try It Out – Connection Information from C++

Here is a C++ equivalent of the `connect2` program we saw in the C API discussion. It simply prints out some information about the connection using member functions of the connection object:

```
#include <iostream>
#include <sqlplus.hh>
```

```
int main()
{
    try {
        Connection con("bmsimple");
        cout << "connected\n";
        cout << "client info: " << con.client_info() << endl;
        cout << " host info: " << con.host_info() << endl;
        cout << "server info: " << con.server_info() << endl;
        cout << " proto info: " << con.proto_info() << endl;
    }
    catch (BadQuery &er) {
        cerr << "Oops: " << er.error << endl;
    }
}
```

How It Works

This program acts in the same way as `connect2.c` we saw earlier. It connects to the database and prints information about the connection. Its output looks like this:

```
$./connect2cc
connected
client info: 3.23.43
host info: Localhost via UNIX socket
server info: 4.0.0-alpha-log
proto info: 10
$
```

Exceptions

One of the key differences between the C and C++ APIs is the ability to use exceptions in C++. Applications can be written in a slightly different way when exception support is present. We are able to separate the data flow from the control flow, in that we can write the application assuming that operations are successful, and catch any errors via exceptions in a different part of the application.

Mysql++ uses several different exceptions for handling errors:

❑   BadQuery, for connection and query errors (as we used in our first example program).

❑   BadConversion for errors converting between types.

❑   BadNullConversion for errors dealing with database NULLs, and SQLQueryNEParms for insufficient parameters in a template query.

The exception structures contain information about the error that caused the exception to be raised. The exception structures behave as if they had the following definitions:

```
struct BadQuery {
    string error;   // The error message
};

struct BadConversion {
```

```
        const char*   type_name;
        const string data;
        size_t retrieved;
        size_t actual_size;
};

class BadNullConversion {};
struct SQLQueryNEParms {
        const char* error;
};
```

> **NOTE: Mysql++ supports two distinct sets of exception objects. The one described here is the default, original, set. A new set designed to act more like standard C++ exceptions is in development and may be used if Mysql++ is recompiled. To do this, the build process is changed to use an option to the configuration program –**
> `./configure --enable-exception`.

Queries

Queries can be executed using further member functions of the `Connection` class. These are:

```
bool exec (const string &str)
ResNSel execute (const string &str)
ResNSel execute (const string &str, bool te)
Result store (const string &str)
Result store (const string &str, bool te)
ResUse use (const string &str)
ResUse use (const string &str, bool te)
```

The first member function, `exec()`, sends a query to MySQL and reports whether or not the query was successful. Further information may be obtained from other APIs, such as the number of rows affected. The `execute()` functions are used for queries that do return a result set.

The `store()` functions query the database and return a complete result set as a `Result` object (equivalent to using the `mysql_store_result()` function in the C API). The `use()` functions obtain a result set that is transferred from the server a row at a time, as with `mysql_use_result()` in the C API.

We will cover the result sets in more detail in a moment.

Try It Out – Simple Queries in C++

Here is a C++ version of a C program we used earlier that uses the simple, non-result set queries to create a table, and insert and delete rows:

```
#include <iostream>
#include <sqlplus.hh>
int main()
{
```

```
    try {
        Connection con("test");
        con.exec("DROP TABLE IF EXISTS number");
        con.exec("CREATE TABLE number (
        value INTEGER,
        name  VARCHAR(64)
                )");
        con.exec("INSERT INTO number values(42, 'The Answer')");
        con.exec("INSERT INTO number values(29, 'My Age')");
        con.exec("INSERT INTO number values(29, 'Anniversary')");
        con.exec("INSERT INTO number values(66, 'Clickety-Click')");
        con.exec("DELETE FROM number WHERE value=29");
        cout << "deleted " << con.affected_rows() << " rows" << endl;
    }
    catch (BadQuery &er) {
        cerr << "Oops: " << er.error << endl;
    }
}
```

How It Works

The program creates a database connection and then executes queries to create a table and insert rows into that table.

Result Sets

As in the C API, Mysql++ defines a result set object that we use to gain access to data returned as the result of a query. There are three different result set classes used for handling the three cases:

❑   No data expected from the query (ResNSel class)

❑   All the data returned in one result set (Result class)

❑   Data returned as required (ResUse class)

The public members of the ResNSel class include:

```
bool success;
int rows;
string info;
```

The success member indicates whether the query that produced the result set was successful (even if it did return no data). The rows member indicates the number of rows affected for updates and deletes. The info string will contain any available additional information.

The Result class is an important part of the C++ API. Not only is it a data structure that contains the returned data, it is also an STL container. This means it comes with an STL compatible iterator class and provides begin() and end() functions. Specifically, it is a random access container, so we can effectively index into the returned data rows.

The member functions for the `Result` class include:

```
void data_seek (uint offset) const
const Row fetch_row () const
int num_rows () const
const Row operator (size_type i) const
size_type rows () const
size_type size () const
```

The `data_seek()`, `fetch_row()` and `num_rows()`, functions are simply interfaces to the C APIs of the same name. Mysql++ defines a type, `size_type`, for use in accessing rows within a result set. The number of rows in a set is returned as a `size_type` by the functions `size()` and `rows()`. An individual row can be extracted from a set by indexing. The row is an object of type `Row`.

Each returned row in a result set consists of a collection of fields, as in the C API. We can extract the data from each field by using an index or, if we need to, by column name. The convenience that the C++ API has over the C API is that the data from an individual column can be automatically converted into one of the C++ basic types. With C, we had to deal with string representations of the data and perform conversions ourselves. We will see this kind of automatic conversion later.

Let's look more closely at the `Row` class and then create a program that extracts some data:

The `Row` class member functions include:

```
operator bool () const
inline size_type size () const
inline const ColData operator  (const string &s) const
const ColData operator  (int i) const
inline const ColData operator  (size_type i) const
const char * raw_data (int i) const
```

A `Row` object may be tested and will act as a `true` value if the row contains data. The number of columns present in the result set for this row is given by `size()`. The column data is returned as an object of class `ColData`, which can be converted automatically to basic types. Columns can be indexed by position or by name. The underlying character data for a column can be retrieved with the `raw_data()` function. This returns a pointer to the text returned by the database query.

The `ColData` class is essentially a 'smart' string that converts itself into base types as required. A cast to a basic type is normally all that is required. Sometimes, however, the data will not be convertible into a basic type, maybe due to application coding assuming a particular column is of a particular type. When this happens then a `BadConversion` or, in the case of `NULL` values, a `BadNullConversion` exception will be raised.

A bad conversion is defined as one in which all of the characters in the string data are not consumed in the conversion, and the remaining characters are other than whitespace, zeroes, or periods. This second condition allows decimal numbers with a zero fractional part to be converted to integers without throwing an exception, for example '1.00'.

Try It Out – Results Sets in C++

Now it is time to look at a C++ program that executes a query and displays the data that is returned:

```cpp
#include <iostream>
#include <sqlplus.hh>
int main()
{
   try {
      Connection con("bmsimple");
      Result res = con.store("SELECT * FROM customer");
      cout << res.size() << " records found" << endl;
      Result::iterator r;
      for(r = res.begin(); r != res.end(); r++) {
         const Row &row = *r;
         for(int c = 0; c < row.size(); c++)
            cout << row[c] << " ";
         cout << endl;
      }
   }
   catch (BadQuery &er) {
      cerr << "Oops: " << er.error << endl;
   }
   catch (BadConversion &er) {
      cerr << "Oops: converting [" << er.data << "] to "
         << er.type_name << endl;
   }
   catch (BadNullConversion) {
      cerr << "Oops: bad NULL conversion" << endl;
   }
}
```

How It Works

Here we make use of the fact that the `Result` object is an STL container, and use an `iterator` to scan through the rows of the set. For each row we simply print out the data. The `ColData` objects representing the columns will be printed as strings. The output we see when we run the program looks like this:

```
$ ./selectcc
15 records found
1 Miss Jenny Stones 27 Rowan Avenue Hightown NT2 1AQ 023 9876
2 Mr Andrew Stones 52 The Willows Lowtown LT5 7RA 876 3527
3 Miss Alex Matthew 4 The Street Nicetown NT2 2TX 010 4567
4 Mr Adrian Matthew The Barn Yuleville YV67 2WR 487 3871
5 Mr Simon Cozens 7 Shady Lane Oahenham OA3 6QW 514 5926
6 Mr Neil Matthew 5 Pasture Lane Nicetown NT3 7RT 267 1232
7 Mr Richard Stones 34 Holly Way Bingham BG4 2WE 342 5982
8 Mrs Ann Stones 34 Holly Way Bingham BG4 2WE 342 5982
9 Mrs Christine Hickman 36 Queen Street Histon HT3 5EM 342 5432
10 Mr Mike Howard 86 Dysart Street Tibsville TB3 7FG 505 5482
11 Mr Dave Jones 54 Vale Rise Bingham BG3 8GD 342 8264
```

```
12 Mr Richard Neill 42 Thached way Winersby WB3 6GQ 505 6482
13 Mrs Laura Hendy 73 Margeritta Way Oxbridge OX2 3HX 821 2335
14 Mr Bill O'Neill 2 Beamer Street Welltown WT3 8GM 435 1234
15 Mr David Hudson 4  The Square Milltown MT2 6RT 961 4526
```

As an alternative we could have accessed the row by index, and the columns by name, like this:

```
Connection con("bmsimple");
Result res = con.store("SELECT * FROM customer");
cout << res.size() << " records found" << endl;
for(int r = 0; r < res.size(); r++) {
   Row row = res[r];
   cout << row["customer_id"] << " "
   << row["title"] << " "
   << row["fname"] << " "
   << row["lname"] << " "
   << row["addressline"] << " "
   << row["town"] << " "
   << row["zipcode"] << " "
   << row["phone"] << endl;
}
```

This would make our code less susceptible to database design changes, but at some expense in terms of performance, as it is slower to access columns by name rather than by index.

We would recommend that you avoid problems with changes in your database by specifying the columns to be returned explicitly in the SELECT statements. Then you can be sure that the columns can be indexed by position.

Try It Out – Field Data in C++

Here is another example that shows the field data being automatically converted to C++ basic type. The program calculates the average selling price of all of the items in the database. We could, of course, do this with one SELECT:

```
#include <iostream>
#include <sqlplus.hh>
int main()
{
   try {
       Connection con("bmsimple");
       Result res = con.store("SELECT sell_price FROM item");
       cout << res.size() << " records found" << endl;
       double total = 0.0;
       for(int r = 0; r < res.size(); r++) {
           Row row = res[r];
           cout << row[0] << endl;
           total += (double)row[0];
       }
       cout << "average price is " << total/res.size() << endl;
```

```
      }
      catch (BadQuery &er) {
          cerr << "Oops: " << er.error << endl;
      }
      catch (BadConversion er) {
          cerr << "Oops: converting [" << er.data << "] to "
          << er.type_name << endl;
      }
      catch (BadNullConversion) {
          cerr << "Oops: bad NULL conversion" << endl;
      }
  }
```

How It Works

The program retrieves all of the item sell prices and adds them up to calculate an average. When we run the program we see:

```
$ ./select3cc
11 records found
21.95
11.49
2.49
3.99
9.95
15.75
19.95
1.45
2.45
0.00
25.32
average price is 10.4355
```

We can, in this instance, check the result with `mysql`:

```
mysql> SELECT sell_price FROM item;
+------------+
| sell_price |
+------------+
|      21.95 |
|      11.49 |
|       2.49 |
|       3.99 |
|       9.95 |
|      15.75 |
|      19.95 |
|       1.45 |
|       2.45 |
|       0.00 |
|      25.32 |
+------------+
```

```
11 rows in set (0.01 sec)

mysql> SELECT avg(sell_price) FROM item;
+-----------------+
| avg(sell_price) |
+-----------------+
|       10.435455 |
+-----------------+
1 row in set (0.04 sec)

mysql>
```

The ResUse object type returned by the Connection object member function use(), has additional member functions for enquiring about the names and types of fields. For more details, refer to the online Mysql++ documentation.

Query Objects

Mysql++ defines a Query object, separate from the Connection object so that queries may be created, manipulated, and executed independently, although each query object is associated with a database connection. Calling the query() member function for a Connection object creates a new Query object:

```
Connection con("bmsimple");
Query q = con.query();
```

Using the overloaded output operator sets the SQL for a query:

```
q << "SELECT sell_price FROM item";
```

You can print out the query with the preview() member function:

```
cout << q.preview () << endl;
```

Execute the query with the store() member function, which returns a result set:

```
Result res = q.store();
```

You can only preview a query before you store the results.

A Query object can be reset to its initial state, ready for another SQL string to be sent to it by calling the reset() function:

```
q.reset();
```

Template Queries

One of the most powerful uses for the `Query` object class is for constructing query templates. These are parameterized queries that can be used for substituting values into `INSERT` and `UPDATE` SQL statements.

To create a parameterized query, replace the values with place indicators %0, %1, and so on. For values that need to be quoted in the SQL that is sent to MySQL add a 'q'. For example, a parameterized query for adding new products to the `item` table of our sample database might look like this:

```
INSERT INTO item(description, cost_price, sell_price) values (%0q, %1, %2)";
```

Note that the first parameter, the description, needs to be quoted as we want to send the description as a string to the database server.

To use this template query we must create a `Query` object for it and prepare it for parameter replacement. The `parse()` member function performs this preparation:

```
Query q = con.query();
q << "INSERT INTO item(description, cost_price, sell_price) values (%0q, %1,
    %2)";
q.parse();
```

Now we can execute the query as many times as we like, substituting values for the parameters:

```
q.execute("Large Teddy Bear", 8, 9.99);
q.execute("Small Teddy Bear", 6, 7.99);
```

It is also possible to provide defaults for optional trailing parameters. Refer to the Mysql++ documentation for details.

Try It Out – Template Queries in C++

Here is a complete program to perform the update mentioned in the text above:

```
#include <iostream>
#include <sqlplus.hh>
int main()
{
    try {
        Connection con("bmsimple");
        Query q = con.query();
        q << "INSERT INTO item(description, cost_price, sell_price) "
        "values (%0q, %1, %2)";
        q.parse();
        q.execute("Large Teddy Bear", 8, 9.99);
        q.execute("Small Teddy Bear", 6, 7.99);
    }
    catch (BadQuery &er) {
        cerr << "Oops: " << er.error << endl;
    }
```

```
      catch (BadConversion &er) {
         cerr << "Oops: converting [" << er.data << "] to "
         << er.type_name << endl;
      }
      catch (BadNullConversion) {
         cerr << "Oops: bad NULL conversion" << endl;
      }
   }
```

How It Works

We insert new values for the names of items and their prices into a dynamic query that we execute to add rows to the item table in the sample database.

With template queries we can very neatly write code to update our database without having to laboriously construct long strings of SQL.

Resources

❑   Source code for the Mysql++ API is available from the MySQL web site at http://www.mysql.com/download_mysql++.html.

❑   A mailing list for discussing Mysql++ is available at mysql-plusplus@lists.mysql.com. Instructions for joining the list can be found at the Mysql++ home page at www.mysql.com.

❑   Mysql++ has many more features aimed at helping application developers use databases within C++ applications, including a mapping of database records onto C++ structures. Refer to the Mysql++ documentation for more details.

Summary

In this chapter, we have looked at creating MySQL applications in C. We will see in later chapters how other languages have interfaces to MySQL.

We have seen how the libmysqlclient library provides access to the low-level functions of MySQL, allowing us to connect to a database on a local machine or on a server across the network. We have used our example programs to make and close connections, and execute SQL statements to query, insert, or update rows in our database tables.

We have also taken a quick look at the features of the Mysql++ API for C++ and seen how to connect to a database, extract, and update data records.

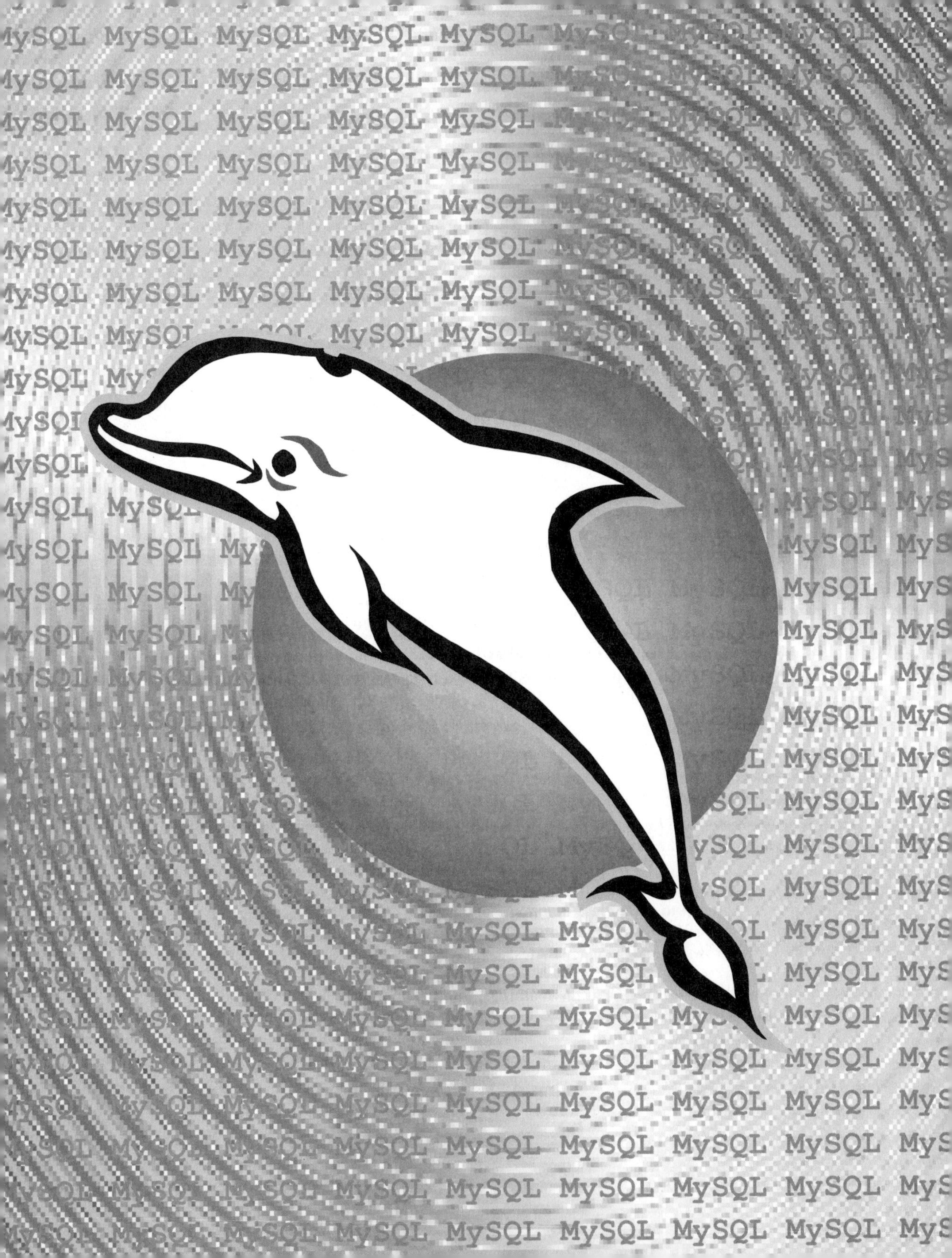
MySQL

Accessing MySQL from PHP

In this chapter, we will explore various methods for accessing MySQL from PHP. Recently, there has been a strong trend towards providing web-based interfaces to online databases. There are a number of reasons supporting this movement, including:

❑   Web browsers have become familiar interfaces for browsing data.

❑   Not every user requires an application-specific client to be installed on their machine.

❑   Web-based applications can easily be integrated into an existing web site.

❑   Web (HTML) interfaces are easily created and modified.

❑   Since web browsers exist for almost all the platforms available, a web-based application is a platform-independent application.

PHP is a server-side, cross-platform scripting language for writing web-based applications. It allows you to embed program logic in HTML pages, which enables you to serve dynamic web pages. PHP allows us to create web-based user interfaces that interact with MySQL. If you are completely unfamiliar with PHP, you might want to explore some of the following resources:

❑   The web site of PHP http://www.php.net/.

❑   *Beginning PHP 4*, by Wankyu Choi, Allan Kent, Ganesh Prasad, and Chris Ullman, with Jon Blank and Sean Cazzell, Wrox Press, (ISBN 1-861003-73-0).

Adding MySQL Support To PHP

Before you can begin developing PHP scripts that interface with a MySQL database, you will need to include MySQL support in your PHP installation. If you're not sure whether your existing PHP installation already has MySQL support, create a simple script named phpinfo.php that contains the following code:

```php
<?php
phpinfo();
?>
```

Place the file in your web server's document root. Examine the output of this script in your web browser. If MySQL support has already been included, the output will contain a section similar to the following:

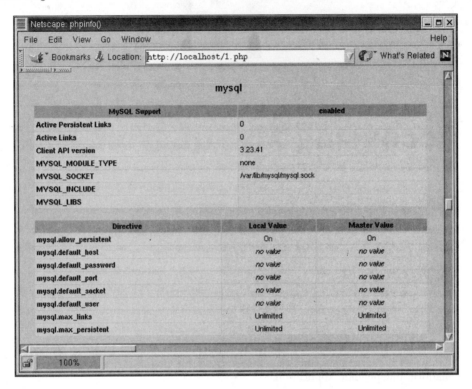

If your PHP installation already has MySQL support, you can skip ahead to the next section.

If you have the PHP source code, it is fairly easy to add MySQL support. Simply, pass the `--with-mysql` option to the `configure` script:

```
$ ./configure --with-mysql
```

You can optionally specify the directory of your MySQL installation if the `configure` script is unable to locate it by itself:

```
$ ./configure --with-mysql=/var/lib/mysql
```

Remember that you might need to pass additional options to the `configure` script depending on your build requirements. For example, to build PHP with support for MySQL, LDAP, and XML, you would use the following command line:

```
$ ./configure --with-mysql --with-imap --enable-xml
```

Refer to the PHP documentation (specifically the INSTALL document included with the PHP distribution) for additional compilation options and installation instructions. You can also find the instructions at:

http://www.php.net/manual/en/html/installation.html.

Using the PHP API for MySQL

All of the interaction with the MySQL database is performed through the PHP-MySQL extension, a comprehensive set of PHP functions for accessing MySQL. For a complete list of functions and further information about the same, refer to:

http://www.php.net/manual/ref.mysql.php.

PHP can be used to write scripts that are run from the command prompt, in a manner similar to shell scripts or Perl programs:

```
#! /usr/bin/php -q
<?php
    print("PHP from the command line is not very useful\n");
?>
```

This script can be run from the command prompt after saving it in a file and setting the appropriate execute permissions on it:

%chmod +x command_prompt.php
%./command_prompt.php
PHP from the command line is not very useful
%

However, since PHP is used almost exclusively for serving web pages, very few examples that we will consider henceforth will have to be run from the command prompt.

Here's a simple PHP script that demonstrates the basic steps involved in connecting to a database server, fetching some data from a table and displaying the result.

Try It Out – A Simple Example

```
<HTML>
<HEAD><TITLE>How many customers have we had so far</TITLE></HEAD>
<BODY BGCOLOR="FFFFFF">
<TABLE WIDTH="100%" BGCOLOR="#ffcb32">
<TR><TD>
<H2>Welcome to Beginning MySQL online</H2>
</TR></TD>
</TABLE>
<?php
$db_link = mysql_connect("localhost", "jon", "secret")
```

```
                              or die ("Could not connect to the database\n");
mysql_select_db("bmsimple") or die ("Could not select database\n");
$query = "SELECT * FROM customer";
$result_set = mysql_query($query) or die("Query failed\n");
echo "<P>We have had " . mysql_num_rows($result_set) . " patrons so far.";
mysql_close($db_link);
?>
</BODY>
</HTML>
```

How It Works

Let's examine this file step by step:

```
<HTML>
<HEAD><TITLE>How many customers have we had so far</TITLE></HEAD>
<BODY BGCOLOR="FFFFFF">
<TABLE WIDTH="100%" BGCOLOR="#ffcb32">
<TR><TD>
<H2>Welcome to Beginning MySQL online</H2>
</TR></TD>
</TABLE>
```

The first few lines aren't PHP code at all. They contain the HTML required for the header of the page that will contain our output and some introductory lines in static HTML.

```
<?php
```

This is the line where the PHP code begins. Everything that is enclosed between the <?php tag and the ?> tag is considered by the interpreter to be PHP code. There are other kinds of tags for enclosing PHP code, which we will see now.

The short-open form:

```
<?
    print("This the short-open form of the usual tags\n");
?>
```

The <SCRIPT> and the </SCRIPT> tags:

```
<SCRIPT LANGUAGE='PHP'>
    print("this style is for editors like FrontPage,
           that don't like other styles\n");
</SCRIPT>
```

ASP-style tags:

```
<%
    print("You'll like these if you use a lot of Active Server Pages\n");
%>
```

The ASP-style tags and the short-open form tags are disabled by default. To enable those, you need to make sure that the PHP initialization file contains the following lines:

```
asp_tags=on
short_open_tag=on
```

Let's continue with the example:

```
$db_link = mysql_connect("localhost", "jon", "secret")
                        or die ("Could not connect to the database\n");
mysql_select_db("bmsimple") or die ("Could not select database\n");
$query = "SELECT * FROM customer";
$result_set = mysql_query($query) or die("Query failed\n");
```

These next few lines call PHP-MySQL functions to do the following things:

❑   Connect to a MySQL database server.

❑   Select a database to work with.

❑   Select all the rows of a table into a result set.

We'll take a more detailed look at these steps later.

```
echo "<P>We have had " . mysql_num_rows($result_set) . " patrons so far.";
```

Everything that we pass to echo in the PHP code will be sent to the requesting browser as a part of a web page. So, we can directly embed HTML tags in our echo and print statements. In this line we also use a function called mysql_num_rows() that will return the number of rows in the result set that we got earlier. The '.' operator concatenates the result of the mysql_num_rows() function and the two text segments surrounded by double quotes into a single string that is echoed out to the browser.

```
mysql_close($db_link);
?>
```

Having finished the interaction with the database and having sent the output to the browser, we close the connection to the MySQL database server and end the PHP code with the ?> tag.

This is what the output will look like:

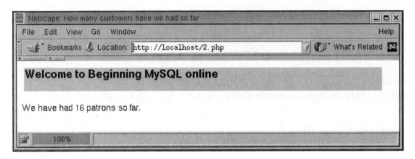

As you can see, interacting with the database from within PHP is fairly straightforward. We will now cover the various aspects of the PHP MySQL extension in more detail.

Database Connections

Before you can interact with the database server, you must first open a connection to it. Each connection is represented by a variable usually referred to as the 'link identifier'.

mysql_connect()

Database connections are opened using the mysql_connect() function. This function takes the server name, the user name and the password as three optional parameters and returns a link identifier on success.

Here's an example:

```
$db_link = mysql_connect('my.database.server:3306', 'jon', 'secret');
```

The following defaults are assumed if the arguments are not specified:

❑   The server name is assumed to be localhost:3306, where localhost is the hostname and 3306 is the port number on which the MySQL database server listens for incoming requests by default.

❑   The user name is assumed to be the name of the user that owns the server process.

❑   The password is assumed to be empty.

If you want to use PHP variables, remember to surround the parameters in double quotes instead of single quotes:

```
$server_name  = "localhost";
$user_name    = "jon";
$password     = "secret";
$db_link      = mysql_connect("$server_name", "$user_name", "$password");
```

If the connection attempt fails, the mysql_connect() function returns FALSE. Failed connection attempts can thus be detected by testing the return value:

```
<HTML>
<HEAD><TITLE>Checking if the connection works</TITLE></HEAD>
<BODY BGCOLOR="FFFFFF">
<TABLE WIDTH="100%" BGCOLOR="#ffcb32">
<TR><TD>
<H2>Welcome to Beginning MySQL online</H2>
</TR></TD>
</TABLE>
<?php
$db_link = mysql_connect('localhost', 'jon', 'secret');
if ($db_link) {
    echo 'Connection attempt succeeded.';
}
else
{
    echo 'Connection attempt failed.';
}
mysql_close($db_link);
?>
</BODY>
</HTML>
```

So far, we've kept the user name and password in a plain text file inside the document root of the web server. In a production system, this is a big security risk. The solution is to include a file that contains the connection parameters. This file should be kept outside the document root of the web server, and should have access permissions such that only the user whose UID is associated with the web server process can access it. We will use this technique later when we look at a real-world example.

Persistent Connections

A connection established using mysql_connect() is destroyed at the end of the execution of the script. This can be rather wasteful if there are a large number of clients opening and closing connections to the database for the same short queries. The time required for setting up database connections can be reduced by using persistent connections.

Persistent connections are those that stay open even after the execution of your script ends. Whenever a persistent connection is requested, and an identical connection that was opened earlier exists, it is reused; otherwise it is created. Connections are said to be identical when the hostname, the user name and the password are the same. Persistent connections are helpful if the web server being used is capable of maintaining an instance of the PHP interpreter in memory – either by loading it as a dynamically loadable module, or by loading it as a plug-in if it is a multi-threaded server.

If a multi-process server like Apache is being used, a single parent process coordinates a set of child processes that do the serving of the web pages. Now, a child process that may have to serve a page continuously for many clients does not need to reconnect to the database server for each request. The connection established the first time around will be reused.

mysql_pconnect()

To open a persistent connection to MySQL, use the mysql_pconnect() function. This function behaves exactly like the mysql_connect() function described earlier, except that it requests a persistent connection, if available.

A couple of configuration directives in the PHP initialization file affect the availability of persistent connections:

The mysql.allow_persistent flag should be set to on in order to enable persistent connections:

```
mysql.allow_persistent=on
```

The mysql.max_persistent parameter is an integer value that represents the maximum number of persistent connections that each child process may have.

```
mysql.max_persistent=10
```

You should use persistent connections with care. Overusing persistent connections could lead to a large number of idle database connections to your database. However, these connections improve efficiency when the overhead for setting up the database connection is significant.

Closing Connections

mysql_close()

Database links can be explicitly closed using the mysql_close() function:

```
mysql_close($link_identifier);
```

There are a few things that need to be pointed out here.

mysql_close() will not close persistent links. Instead, the link will just be returned to the database link-pool. The PHP4 engine ensures that all resources that are not being referred to are cleaned up, and so it automatically closes any open non-persistent database links at the end of the script's execution. Thus even though calling mysql_close() may seem largely unnecessary, it may be used for explicitly freeing resources that contains links.

If the provided link identifier is invalid, mysql_close() will return FALSE. Otherwise, mysql_close() will return TRUE upon success.

Connection Information

PHP provides a number of simple functions for retrieving information about the current database connection based on the link identifier provided as an argument. Such functions include mysql_get_client_info(), mysql_get_host_info(), mysql_get_proto_info(), and mysql_get_server_info():

Try It Out – Getting Connection Information

```html
<HTML>
<HEAD><TITLE>Getting connection information</TITLE></HEAD>
<BODY BGCOLOR="FFFFFF">
<TABLE WIDTH="100%" BGCOLOR="#ffcb32">
```

```
<TR><TD>
<H2>Welcome to Beginning MySQL online</H2>
</TR></TD>
</TABLE>
<?php
$db_link = mysql_connect("localhost", "jon", "secret")
                        or die ("Could not connect to the server\n");
print "Connected successfully\n";
mysql_select_db("bmsimple")  or die ("Could not select database\n");

echo "<h3>Connection Information</h3>";
echo "Client Info      : " . mysql_get_client_info() .          "<br>\n";
echo "Host Info        : " . mysql_get_host_info($db_link) .     "<br>\n";
echo "Protocol Info    : " . mysql_get_proto_info($db_link) .    "<br>\n";
echo "Server Info      : " . mysql_get_server_info($db_link) .   "<br>\n";

mysql_close($db_link);
?>
</BODY>
</HTML>
```

How It Works

These functions return values that describe various attributes associated with the database connection. Their return values are as follows:

Function	Return values
mysql_get_client_info()	A string representing the client library version.
mysql_get_host_info()	A string describing the kind of connection and the server host name associated with the link.
mysql_get_proto_info()	Returns the protocol version used by the link.
mysql_get_server_info()	Returns the server version used by the link

mysql_get_client_info() is the only function that does not take any argument. All the others accept a link identifier as an optional argument. If the link identifier is not specified, the last opened connection will be used. All these functions return either a string or a number upon success. Otherwise, they return FALSE.

Executing Queries

Once a connection has been established, the next step is to create a query and execute it. Queries are executed using the mysql_query() function.

mysql_query ()

The mysql_query() function sends the query string to the MySQL server and returns the result of its execution. Here's a simple example to illustrate the use of mysql_query():

```
#! /usr/local/bin/php
<?php
$db_link = mysql_connect("localhost", "jon", "password");
mysql_select_db("bmsimple");
$query = 'SELECT * FROM customer';
$result = mysql_query($query, $db_link);
mysql_close($db_link);
?>
```

How It Works

As you can see, mysql_query() requires two parameters – an active link identifier and a query string. For SELECT statements, mysql_query() returns a resource identifier that contains the result set upon successful execution of the query or FALSE on failure. We'll work with result sets in the next section. For other types of SQL statements it returns TRUE on successful execution of the query or FALSE on failure. It is prudent to test the return value of mysql_query() so that you can detect such failures. The following example includes some result checking:

```
#! /usr/local/bin/php
<?php
$db_link = mysql_connect("localhost", "jon", "password");
mysql_select_db("bmsimple");
$query = "SELECT * FROM customer";
$result = mysql_query($query, $db_link);
if ($result) {
    echo "The query executed successfully.\n";
}
else
{
    echo "The query failed with the following error:\n";
    echo mysql_error($db_link);
}
mysql_close($db_link);
?>
```

In this example, we test the return value of mysql_query(). If it is not FALSE (that is, it has a value), $result represents a result set, since the query was a SELECT statement. Otherwise, if $result is FALSE, we know that an error has occurred. We can then use the mysql_error() function to print a descriptive message for that error. We will cover error messages in more detail later in this chapter.

Working with Result Sets

Upon successful execution of a query, mysql_query() will return a result set identifier, through which we can access the result set. The result set stores the result of the query as returned by the database. For example, if a selection query were executed, the result set would contain the resulting rows.

PHP offers a number of useful functions for working with result sets. All of them take a result set identifier as an argument, so they can only be used after a query has been successfully executed. We learned how to test for successful execution in the previous section.

mysql_num_rows() And mysql_num_fields()

Now we'll start with the two simplest result functions – mysql_num_rows() and
mysql_num_fields(). Both these functions work with result sets returned by SELECT queries.

Try It Out – mysql_num_rows() and mysql_num_fields()

```
<HTML>
<HEAD>
<TITLE>Demonstration of mysql_num_rows() and mysql_num_fields()</TITLE>
</HEAD>
<BODY BGCOLOR="FFFFFF">
<TABLE WIDTH="100%" BGCOLOR="#ffcb32">
<TR><TD>
<H2>Welcome to Beginning MySQL online</H2>
</TR></TD>
</TABLE>
<H3>Demonstration of mysql_num_rows() and mysql_num_fields()</H3>
<?php
$db_link = mysql_connect("localhost", "jon", "secret");
mysql_select_db("bmsimple");
$query = "SELECT * FROM customer";
$result = mysql_query($query, $db_link);
if ($result) {
    echo "Your query executed successfully!<br>\n";
    echo "<P>mysql_num_rows tells us that we have had " .
                mysql_num_rows($result) . " happy customers so far<br>\n";

    echo "<P>And mysql_num_fields() tells us that the number of attributes
                associated with each customer in our records is: " .
                mysql_num_fields($result);
}
else
{
    echo "The query failed with the following error:<br>\n";
    echo mysql_error($db_link);
}
mysql_close($db_link);
?>

</BODY>
</HTML>
```

How It Works

mysql_num_rows() returns the number of rows in the result set while mysql_num_fields() returns
the number of fields in the result set.

mysql_affected_rows

There's also the mysql_affected_rows() function, that returns the number of rows affected by SQL
queries that do not return result sets. For example, if we were performing insertions or deletions with
our query, we wouldn't actually be retrieving any rows from the database. mysql_num_rows()
wouldn't help here since it requires a result set to work with.

`mysql_affected_rows()` works with connection link identifiers that we get from `mysql_connect()` and `mysql_pconnect()`, and not with result sets. If a link identifier is not specified, the last link opened is assumed. It returns the number of rows that were affected by INSERT, UPDATE, or DELETE statements if the previous SQL statement was executed successfully, and '-1' on failure. Here's an example where this function is used:

```php
#! /usr/bin/php
<?php
$db_link = mysql_connect("localhost", "jon", "secret");
mysql_select_db("bmsimple");

$query = "DELETE FROM item WHERE cost_price > 15.00";
$result = mysql_query($query, $db_link);

if ($result) {
    echo "The query executed successfully.<br>\n";
    echo "Number of rows deleted: " . mysql_affected_rows($db_link);
}
else
{
    echo "The query failed with the following error:<br>\n";
    echo mysql_error($db_link);
}

mysql_close($db_link);
?>
```

While doing an UPDATE, MySQL won't update columns where the new value and the old value are the same. `mysql_affected_rows()` will not include these while determining the count of affected rows. Thus, the number returned may not be equal to all the rows matched by the conditions specified in the SQL statement.

Extracting Values from Result Sets

There are a number of ways to extract values from result sets. We will start with the `mysql_result()` function.

mysql_result()

Try It Out – mysql_result()

```html
<HTML>
<HEAD>
<TITLE>Demonstration of mysql_result() - accessing fields by name</TITLE>
</HEAD>
<BODY BGCOLOR="FFFFFF">
<TABLE WIDTH="100%" BGCOLOR="#ffcb32">
<TR><TD>
<H2>Welcome to Beginning MySQL online</H2>
</TR></TD>
</TABLE>
```

```
<H3>Demonstration of mysql_result() - accessing fields by name </H3>
<?php

$db_link = mysql_connect("localhost", "jon", "secret");
mysql_select_db("bmsimple");

$query = "SELECT title, fname, lname FROM customer";
$result = mysql_query($query, $db_link);
if ($result) {
    echo "The query executed successfully.<br>";
    for ($row = 0; $row < mysql_num_rows($result); $row++) {
        $fullname = mysql_result($result, $row, 'title') . " ";
        $fullname .= mysql_result($result, $row, 'fname') . " ";
        $fullname .= mysql_result($result, $row, 'lname');
        echo "Customer: $fullname<br>\n";
    }
}
else
{
    echo "The query failed with the following error:<br>\n";
    echo mysql_error($db_link);
}
mysql_close($db_link);
?>

</BODY>
</HTML>
```

How It Works

The `mysql_result()` function is used when you want to retrieve a single value from a result set. In addition to a result set identifier, you must also specify the row and column that you want to retrieve from the result. The row is specified numerically while the field may be specified either by name or by numeric index. Numbering always starts at zero.

These methods are a bit more readable than using numeric indices, and they don't depend on the order of the fields in the result set. However, if a large number of values needs to be fetched, referring to their locations by using numeric indices would be more efficient.

Using numeric indices, the same code could also be written like this:

```
<HTML>
<HEAD>
<TITLE>Demonstration of mysql_result() - using numeric indices.</TITLE>
</HEAD>
<BODY BGCOLOR="FFFFFF">
<TABLE WIDTH="100%" BGCOLOR="#ffcb32">
<TR><TD>
<H2>Welcome to Beginning MySQL online</H2>
</TR></TD>
</TABLE>
<H3>Demonstration of mysql_result() - using numeric indices.</H3>
```

```
<?php
$db_link = mysql_connect("localhost", "jon", "secret");
mysql_select_db("bmsimple");
$query = "SELECT title, fname, lname FROM customer";
$result = mysql_query($query, $db_link);
if ($result) {
    echo "The query executed successfully.<br>\n";
    for ($row = 0; $row < mysql_num_rows($result); $row++) {
        for ($col = 0; $col < mysql_num_fields($result); $col++) {
            $fullname .= mysql_result($result, $row, $col) . " ";
        }
        echo "Customer: $fullname<br>\n";
        $fullname = "";
    }
}
else
{
    echo "The query failed with the following error:<br>\n";
    echo mysql_error($db_link);
}
mysql_close($db_link);
?>

</BODY>
</HTML>
```

Calling `mysql_result()` for getting a single field in a row isn't efficient, especially if a large number of fields have to be fetched. However, PHP also offers more advanced ways of retrieving values from result sets.

mysql_fetch_row()

Let us see an example that will make this function clear to you.

Try It Out – mysql_fetch_row()

Here we will use the previous example rewritten to use `mysql_fetch_row()`:

```
<HTML>
<HEAD>
<TITLE>Using mysql_fetch_row() to fetch information</TITLE>
</HEAD>
<BODY BGCOLOR="FFFFFF">
<TABLE WIDTH="100%" BGCOLOR="#ffcb32">
<TR><TD>
<H2>Welcome to Beginning MySQL online</H2>
</TR></TD>
</TABLE>
<H3>Using mysql_fetch_row() to fetch information</H3>
<?php
$db_link = mysql_connect("localhost", "jon", "secret");
mysql_select_db("bmsimple");
```

```
$query = "SELECT title, fname, lname FROM customer";
$result = mysql_query($query, $db_link);
if ($result) {
    echo "The query executed successfully.<br>\n";
    for ($row = 0; $row < mysql_num_rows($result); $row++) {
        $values = mysql_fetch_row($result);
        for ($col = 0; $col < count($values); $col++) {
            $fullname .= $values[$col] . " ";
        }
        echo "Customer $row: $fullname<br>\n";
        $fullname = "";
    }
}
else
{
    echo "The query failed with the following error:<br>\n";
    echo mysql_error($db_link);
}

mysql_close($db_link);
?>

</BODY>
</HTML>
```

How It Works

As you can see, using `mysql_fetch_row()` eliminates the multiple calls to `mysql_result()`. It also places the result values in an array, which can be easily manipulated using PHP's native array functions.

`mysql_fetch_row()` returns an array that corresponds to a single row in the result set that it takes as an argument. The array is indexed numerically, starting from zero. Calls to `mysql_fetch_row()` after this will return the rest of the rows, one at a time. When the last row has been reached, the next call will return FALSE.

However, in this example, we are still accessing the fields by their numeric indices. We should also be able to access each field by its name. To accomplish that, we can use the `mysql_fetch_assoc()` function.

mysql_fetch_assoc()

The following example will explain the `mysql_fetch_assoc()` function.

Try It Out – mysql_fetch_assoc()

```
<HTML>
<HEAD>
<TITLE>Using mysql_fetch_assoc() to fetch information</TITLE>
</HEAD>
<BODY BGCOLOR="FFFFFF">
<TABLE WIDTH="100%" BGCOLOR="#ffcb32">
<TR><TD>
```

```
<H2>Welcome to Beginning MySQL online</H2>
</TR></TD>
</TABLE>
<H3>Using mysql_fetch_assoc() to fetch information</H3>
<?php
$db_link = mysql_connect("localhost", "jon", "secret");
mysql_select_db("bmsimple");
$query = "SELECT title, fname, lname FROM customer";
$result = mysql_query($query, $db_link);
if ($result) {
    echo "The query executed successfully.<BR>\n";
    echo "<H3>Customer list:</H3>";
    while($values = mysql_fetch_assoc($result)) {
        $fullname = $values['title'] . " ";
        $fullname .= $values['fname'] . " ";
        $fullname .= $values['lname'];
        echo "$fullname<BR>\n";
    }
}
else
{
    echo "The query failed with the following error:<br>\n";
    echo mysql_error($db_link);
}
mysql_close($db_link);
?>
</BODY>
</HTML>
```

How It Works

`mysql_fetch_assoc()` takes a result set as an argument and returns an associative array that corresponds to a single row. The keys of the associative array are the names of the fields in the result set. Just like `mysql_fetch_row`, subsequent calls to `mysql_fetch_assoc()` will return the rest of the rows, one at a time. When the last row has been reached, the next call to `mysql_fetch_assoc()` will return `FALSE`.

This eliminates the need for iterating through the fields by using numeric indices. To access the first name of a customer record returned by `mysql_fetch_assoc()` we simply use `values['fname']`.

mysql_fetch_array()

Here's the same example once more, now using `mysql_fetch_array()`.

Try It Out – mysql_fetch_array()

```
<HTML>
<HEAD><TITLE>Demonstration of mysql_fetch_array</TITLE></HEAD>
<BODY BGCOLOR="FFFFFF">
<TABLE WIDTH="100%" BGCOLOR="#ffcb32">
<TR><TD>
<H2>Welcome to Beginning MySQL online</H2>
</TR></TD>
```

```
</TABLE>
<?php
$db_link = mysql_connect("localhost", "jon", "secret");
mysql_select_db("bmsimple");
$query = "SELECT title, fname, lname FROM customer";
$result = mysql_query($query, $db_link);
if ($result) {
    echo "The query executed successfully.<br>\n";
    echo "<H3>List of customers:</H3>";
    for ($row = 0; $row < mysql_num_rows($result); $row++) {
        $values = mysql_fetch_array($result, MYSQL_ASSOC);
        $fullname = $values['title'] . " ";
        $fullname .= $values['fname'] . " ";
        $fullname .= $values['lname'];
        echo "$fullname<br>\n";
    }
}
else
{
    echo "The query failed with the following error:<br>\n";
    echo mysql_error($db_link);
}
mysql_close($db_link);
?>

</BODY>
</HTML>
```

How It Works

The `mysql_fetch_array()` function also returns an array, but it allows us to specify whether we want that array indexed numerically, associatively (using the field names as keys) or both ways. This preference is specified by passing one of the following as the second argument to `mysql_fetch_array()`:

Argument	Meaning
MYSQL_ASSOC	Index the resulting array by field name.
MYSQL_NUM	Index the resulting array numerically.
MYSQL_BOTH	Index the resulting array both numerically and by field name.

mysql_fetch_object()

Written using `mysql_fetch_object()`, let's see what our example looks like.

Try It Out – mysql_fetch_object()

```
<HTML>
<HEAD><TITLE>Demonstrate mysql_fetch_object</TITLE></HEAD>
<BODY BGCOLOR="FFFFFF">
```

```
<TABLE WIDTH="100%" BGCOLOR="#ffcb32">
<TR><TD>
<H2>Welcome to Beginning MySQL online</H2>
</TR></TD>
</TABLE>
<?php
$db_link = mysql_connect("localhost", "jon", "secret");
mysql_select_db("bmsimple");
$query = "SELECT title, fname, lname FROM customer";
$result = mysql_query($query, $db_link);
if ($result) {
    echo "The query executed successfully.<br>\n";
    echo "<H3>List of customers:</H3>";
    for ($row = 0; $row < mysql_num_rows($result); $row++) {
        $values = mysql_fetch_object($result, MYSQL_ASSOC);
        $fullname = $values->title . " ";
        $fullname .= $values->fname . " ";
        $fullname .= $values->lname;
        echo "Customer: $fullname<br>\n";
    }
}
else
{
    echo "The query failed with the following error:<br>\n";
    echo mysql_error($db_link);
}
mysql_close($db_link);
?>

</BODY>
</HTML>
```

How It Works

PHP also allows you to fetch the result values as objects with the `mysql_fetch_object()` function.
Each field name will be represented as a property of this object. However, the fields cannot be
accessed numerically.

mysql_fetch_lengths()

Let's try the example using `mysql_fetch_lenghts()`.

Try It Out – mysql_fetch_lengths()

```
#! /usr/bin/php
<?php
$db_link = mysql_connect("localhost", "jon", "secret");
mysql_select_db("bmsimple");

$query = "SELECT * FROM customer";
$result = mysql_query($query, $db_link);
```

```
mysql_fetch_row($result);
$array = mysql_fetch_lengths($result);

print "Lengths of values in the first row of the customer table:\n ";

foreach($array as $field) {
    print "$field\t";
}
mysql_close($db_link);
?>
```

How It Works

`mysql_fetch_lengths()` returns an array containing the lengths of each field fetched by the last call to `mysql_fetch_row()`, `mysql_fetch_array()`, and `mysql_fetch_object()`. It takes the result set as an argument.

Field Information

PHP allows you to gather some information on the field values in your result set. These functions may be useful in certain circumstances, so we will cover them briefly.

mysql_fetch_field()

This function is useful for fetching certain attributes about data contained in a column of the result of a query.

Try It Out – mysql_fetch_field()

```
<HTML>
<HEAD><TITLE>Connection information</TITLE></HEAD>
<BODY BGCOLOR="FFFFFF">
<TABLE WIDTH="100%" BGCOLOR="#ffcb32">
<TR><TD>
<H2>Welcome to Beginning MySQL online</H2>
</TR></TD>
</TABLE>
<?php
$db_link = mysql_connect("localhost", "jon", "secret");
mysql_select_db("bmsimple");
$query = "SELECT * FROM customer";
$result = mysql_query($query, $db_link);
$i = 0;
echo "<H2>Information about fields in the customer table:</H2>";
while ($i < mysql_num_fields($result)) {
    echo '<TABLE BORDER=0 WRAP=256 CELLSPACING=0 CELLPADDING=0 COLS=1
    ROWS=2 BGCOLOR="#ffcb32">';
    echo '<TR><TD>';
    echo '<P STYLE="COLOR: #070568; TEXT-DECORATION: none; ">';
    echo "Information for column $i:\n";
    echo '</P>';
    echo '</TD></TR>';
    echo '<TR><TD bgcolor="white">';
```

```
    $info = mysql_fetch_field($result);
    if (!$info) {
       echo "No information available<BR>\n";
    }
    else
    {
       echo "<PRE>
       blob:          $info->blob
       max_length:    $info->max_length
       multiple_key:  $info->multiple_key
       name:          $info->name
       not_null:      $info->not_null
       numeric:       $info->numeric
       primary_key:   $info->primary_key
       table:         $info->table
       type:          $info->type
       unique_key:    $info->unique_key
       unsigned:      $info->unsigned
       zerofill:      $info->zerofill
       </PRE>";
       $i++;
    }
    echo ' </TD></TR>
    </TABLE>';
}
mysql_close($db_link);
?>
</BODY></HTML>
```

How It Works

This function also takes the offset of a field in the table as a second optional parameter. If the field offset is not specified, another call to `mysql_fetch_field()` will return data about the next field in the result set. If the call has returned information about the last field, the next call will return FALSE. This behavior can be modified by `mysql_field_seek()` as we will see later.

The object that is returned has the following properties:

Object	Properties
Name	The name of the column.
Table	The name of the table the column belongs to.
max_length	The maximum length of the column.
NOT_NULL	The value is 1 if the column cannot be NULL.
primary_key	The value is 1 if the column is a primary key.
Unique_key	The value is 1 if the column is a unique key.

Object	Properties
`multiple_key`	The value is 1 if the column is a non-unique key.
`Numeric`	The value is 1 if the column is numeric.
`BLOB`	The value is 1 if the column is a `BLOB`.
`Type`	The type of the column.
`Unsigned`	The value is 1 if the column is unsigned.
`Zerofill`	The value is 1 if the column is zero-filled.

mysql_field_seek( )

This function takes two parameters – the result of a query and a field offset. `mysql_field_seek()` has the effect of changing the location of the result pointer used by other functions like `mysql_fetch_field()`.

Try It Out – mysql_field_seek()

```
<HTML>
<HEAD><TITLE>Demonstrating mysql_field_seek()</TITLE></HEAD>
<BODY BGCOLOR="FFFFFF">
<TABLE WIDTH="100%" BGCOLOR="#ffcb32">
<TR><TD>
<H2>Welcome to Beginning MySQL online</H2>
</TR></TD>
</TABLE>
<?php
$db_link = mysql_connect("localhost", "jon", "secret");
mysql_select_db("bmsimple");

$query = "SELECT * FROM customer";
$result = mysql_query($query, $db_link);

echo "Information for the first column:<BR>\n";
$info = mysql_fetch_field($result);
if (!$info) {
    echo "No information available<BR>\n";
}
else
{
    echo "<PRE>
    name:          $info->name
    not_null:      $info->not_null
    primary_key:   $info->primary_key
    </PRE>";
}

echo "skipping over the <I>title</I> field.<BR>";
mysql_field_seek($result, 3);
```

```
    echo "<P>Information for the third column:<BR>\n";
    $info = mysql_fetch_field($result);
    if (!$info) {
        echo "No information available<BR>\n";
    }
    else
    {
        echo "<PRE>
        name:          $info->name
        not_null:      $info->not_null
        primary_key:   $info->primary_key
        </PRE>";
    }
mysql_close($db_link);
?>
</BODY>
</HTML>
```

If we call `mysql_fetch_field()` without specifying the offset of the field then the offset given to `mysql_field_seek()` in the call above it will be used.

mysql_field_flags()

This function gets the flags associated with a field in the result set. It takes two arguments – the result set and the index. The return value is a string containing a space-separated list of the flag names. Based on the version of MySQL you are using, the flag names returned will be a subset of the following:

- ❑ not_null
- ❑ primary_key
- ❑ unique_key
- ❑ multiple_key
- ❑ blob
- ❑ unsigned
- ❑ zerofill
- ❑ binary
- ❑ enum
- ❑ auto_increment
- ❑ timestamp

Here's an example that demonstrates the use of this function:

```
<HTML>
<HEAD><TITLE>Demonstrating mysql_field_flags()</TITLE></HEAD>
<BODY BGCOLOR="FFFFFF">
<TABLE WIDTH="100%" BGCOLOR="#ffcb32">
```

```
<TR><TD>
<H2>Welcome to Beginning MySQL online</H2>
</TR></TD>
</TABLE>

<?php
$db_link = mysql_connect("localhost", "jon", "secret");
mysql_select_db("bmsimple");
$query = "SELECT * FROM customer";
echo "<H2>Flags set for columns in the customer table:</H2>\n";
$result = mysql_query($query, $db_link);
$i = 0;
while ($i < mysql_num_fields($result)) {
    $description = mysql_field_flags($result, $i);
    echo "Flags for column $i: $description<BR>\n";

    $i++;
}
mysql_close($db_link);
?>
</BODY>
</HTML>
```

mysql_field_name(), mysql_field_type(), mysql_field_len()

These functions take two parameters – the result of a select query, and the offset of the column. As apparent from their names:

- ❏ `mysql_field_name()` returns the name of the specified field.

- ❏ `mysql_field_type()` returns the type of the specified field.

- ❏ `mysql_field_len()` returns the length of the specified field.

Here's an example that demonstrates the use of these functions:

```
<HTML>
<HEAD><TITLE>Fields types and length information</TITLE></HEAD>
<BODY BGCOLOR="FFFFFF">
<TABLE WIDTH="100%" BGCOLOR="#ffcb32">
<TR><TD>
<H2>Welcome to Beginning MySQL online</H2>
</TR></TD>
</TABLE>
<H2>Field types and max lengths for columns in the customer table:</H2>

<?php
$db_link = mysql_connect("localhost", "jon", "secret");
mysql_select_db("bmsimple");

$query = "SELECT * FROM customer";
$result = mysql_query($query, $db_link);
$i = 0;
```

```
echo "<TABLE CELLPADDING=10><TR>
    <TD><B>Name</B></TD>
    <TD><B>Type</B></TD>
    <TD><B>Length</B></TD>
    </TR>";

while ($i < mysql_num_fields($result)) {
    $name  = mysql_field_name($result, $i);
    $type  = mysql_field_type($result, $i);
    $length= mysql_field_len($result, $i);
    echo "<TR><TD>".$name."</TD>".
         "<TD>".$type."</TD>".
         "<TD>".$length."</TD></TR>";

    $i++;
}
echo "</TABLE>";
mysql_close($db_link);
?>
</BODY>
</HTML>
```

Freeing Result Sets

Let us now look at the function that deals with freeing the result sets.

mysql_free_result()

This function will free up the memory associated with a result set identifier:

```
$status = mysql_free_result($result);
```

`mysql_free_result()` returns TRUE on success and FALSE on failure.

PHP will automatically free up the memory taken up by result sets at the end of the script's execution. This function only needs to be called if you're worried about memory consumption in your script and you know you won't be using a particular result set again.

Error Handling

We touched on error handling very briefly in an earlier section. We will now cover it in some more detail.

Almost all functions related to MySQL return '-1' or FALSE on encountering an error condition. This makes it easy to detect error situations so that the script can exit gracefully.

If we want to do error handling ourselves, then we need to prevent the PHP error handler from doing it before us and sending error messages to the browser. The `error_reporting()` function helps us do that.

error_reporting()

This function sets the current error reporting level and returns the old level. As parameters, `error_reporting()` takes in a combination of the following named constants or their corresponding bitmasks.

Constant	Bitmask
E_ERROR	1
E_WARNING	2
E_PARSE	4
E_NOTICE	8
E_CORE_ERROR	16
E_CORE_WARNING	32
E_COMPILE_ERROR	64
E_COMIPILE_WARNING	128
E_USER_ERROR	256
E_USER_WARNING	512
E_USER_NOTICE	1024

Bitwise operators may be used for combining the various named constants or their bitmasks. For example:

```
#enable error messages of the three types given
error_reporting  (E_ERROR | E_WARNING | E_PARSE);

#enable printing of all error messages
error_reporting (E_ALL);

#disable printing of all error messages
error_reporting (~E_ALL);
```

```
<?php
error_reporting(~E_ALL);
$db_link = mysql_connect("wrong_hostname", "wrong_username", "wrong_password");
if (!$db_link) {
    header("Location: http://www.examplesite.com/custom_error_page.php");
    exit;
}
?>
<HTML>
<HEAD><TITLE>Try Connecting to a site that does not exist</TITLE></HEAD>
<BODY BGCOLOR="FFFFFF">
<TABLE WIDTH="100%" BGCOLOR="#ffcb32">
```

```
<TR><TD>
<H2>Welcome to Beginning MySQL online</H2>
</TR></TD>
</TABLE>
</BODY>
</HTML>
```

Here, we set the current error reporting level such that the PHP engine won't report any errors. In the code that follows, a failed connection attempt would cause the `header()` function to redirect the user to an error page designed by us. This is a useful method of making sure that the user does not see ugly error messages in his browser.

mysql_error()

`mysql_error()` can be used to retrieve the text of the actual error message as returned by the database server. `mysql_error()` will always return the text of the last error message generated by the server. Be sure to take that into consideration when designing your error handling and display logic.

You will find that, depending on your level of error reporting, PHP can be fairly verbose when an error occurs, often outputting several lines of errors and warnings. In a production system, the display of such messages on the user's screen is undesirable. The most direct solution is to lower the level of error reporting in PHP (controlled via the `error_reporting` configuration variable in the `php.ini`) or by using the `error_reporting()` function as demonstrated earlier.

Suppressing Errors Using the '@' Character

The second option is to suppress these error messages from PHP code per function call. To suppress all errors we use the '@' symbol as a function name prefix. For example, no errors will be output from the following code:

```php
<?php
$db_link = @mysql_connect("wrong_hostname", "wrong_username", "wrong_password");
?>
```

Without the @ symbol, this would generate an error complaining about the lack of a valid database connection (assuming your error-reporting level was high enough to cause that error to be displayed, of course).

Note that the above error could still be detected by testing the value of $db_link, though; so suppressing the error message output doesn't stop us from dealing with error situations programmatically.

Now let's look at a real-world example using what we have seen so far:

Let's look at the web interface (we have created a similar one in Chapter 14, *Accessing MySQL from Perl*), for customers to be able to give us feedback about our products. When we're done, we'll have an interface that looks like this:

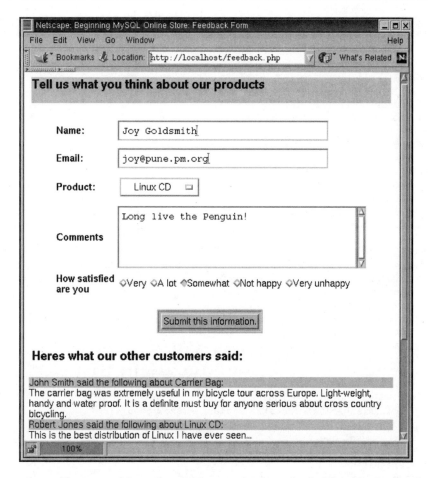

First, we need to add a new table to the `bmsimple` database for holding the feedback data. Use the following statement to create the feedback table using any of the methods you have seen so far in the book:

```
CREATE TABLE feedback (
                name          varchar(50),
                email         varchar(50),
                product       varchar(20),
                comments      varchar(255),
                sat_level     int
                );
```

Then put the following file in the document root of your web server.

Try It Out – a Real-world example

```
<HTML>
<HEAD>
<TITLE>Beginning MySQL Online Store: Feedback Form</TITLE>
</HEAD>
<BODY BGCOLOR = "FFFFFF" TEXT = "000000">
<TABLE WIDTH="100%" BGCOLOR="#ffcb32">
<TR><TD>
<H2>Tell us what you think about our products</H2>
</TD></TR>
</TABLE>

<?php
#source file not kept in the document root for connection paramters
include "/etc/connection.inc";

#connect to the database server
$db_link = mysql_connect("$hostname", "$username", "$password")
or die ("Could not connect to the server\n");
mysql_select_db("$dbname");

#if we have been asked to add a suggestion to the database
if ($suggestion_submitted == 1) {
    #insert the escaped parameters into the database
    $sql = sprintf("INSERT INTO feedback
            VALUES(\"%s\",\"%s\",\"%s\",\"%s\",\"%s\")",
            addslashes($customer_name), addslashes($client_email),
            addslashes($item_name),
            addslashes($comments), addslashes($how_good));

    $result = mysql_query($sql, $db_link);

    if (!$result) {
        echo "Cannot insert: " . mysql_error($db_link);
    }
}
?>

<FORM ACTION = "http://localhost/feedback.php" METHOD = "POST">

<INPUT NAME="suggestion_submitted" TYPE="HIDDEN" VALUE="1">

<BLOCKQUOTE>
<TABLE BORDER = "0">
<TR>
<TH ALIGN = "left">Name:</TH>
<TD><INPUT TYPE = "text" NAME = "customer_name" SIZE = "35" MAXLENGTH = "35"></TD>
</TR>

<TR>
<TH ALIGN = "left">Email:</TH>
<TD><INPUT TYPE = "text" NAME = "client_email" SIZE = "35"
```

```
      MAXLENGTH = "35"></TD>
</TR>

<TR>
<TH ALIGN = "left">Product:</TH>
<TD>
<SELECT NAME=item_name>

<?php
#get a list of all the items we have for the dropdown box
$item_list_result = mysql_query ("select description from item", $db_link);

while ($list_row = mysql_fetch_array($item_list_result)) {
   #surround each option with the necessary html and send it out

   echo "<OPTION>$list_row[0]</OPTION>\n";
}
?>

</SELECT>
</TD>
</TR>

<TR>
<TH ALIGN = "left">Comments</TH>
<TD><TEXTAREA WRAP = "virtual" NAME = "comments" ROWS = "5" COLS = "40">
</TEXTAREA></TD>
</TR>

<TR>
<TH ALIGN ="left">How satisfied are you</TH>
<TD>
<INPUT TYPE="radio" NAME="how_good" VALUE="5" CHECKED>Very</INPUT>
<INPUT TYPE="radio" NAME="how_good" VALUE="4" >A lot</INPUT>
<INPUT TYPE="radio" NAME="how_good" VALUE="3" >Somewhat</INPUT>
<INPUT TYPE="radio" NAME="how_good" VALUE="2" >Not happy</INPUT>
<INPUT TYPE="radio" NAME="how_good" VALUE="1" >Very unhappy</INPUT>
</TD>
</TR>
</TABLE>

<P>
<CENTER>
<INPUT NAME="submit_feedback" TYPE = "submit" VALUE =
            "Submit this information.">
</CENTER>
</BLOCKQUOTE>
</FORM>

<TABLE>
<TR><TD><H3>Heres what our other customers said:</H3></TD></TR>
</TABLE>
<?php
```

```
#get the suggestion data from the feedback table
$suggestion_list_result = mysql_query ("select name,product,comments from
feedback", $db_link);

while ($list_row = mysql_fetch_array($suggestion_list_result)) {
    #wrap the data with html so that it looks nice
    echo "
    <TABLE BORDER=0 WRAP=256 CELLSPACING=0 CELLPADDING=0 COLS=1 ROWS=2
    BGCOLOR='#ffcb32'>
    <TR><TD>
    <P STYLE='COLOR: #070568; TEXT-DECORATION: none;'>
    $list_row[0] said the following about $list_row[1]:
    </P>
    </TD></TR>
    <TR><TD bgcolor='white'>
    $list_row[2]
    </TD></TR>
    </TABLE>";
}
?>
</BODY>
</HTML>
```

How It Works

Now let's go through this example line by line:

```
<HTML>
<HEAD>
<TITLE>Beginning MySQL Online Store: Feedback Form</TITLE>
</HEAD>
<BODY BGCOLOR = "FFFFFF" TEXT = "000000">
<TABLE WIDTH="100%" BGCOLOR="#ffcb32">
<TR><TD>
<H2>Tell us what you think about our products</H2>
</TD></TR>
</TABLE>
```

The first few lines create the header and a table that displays what this page is about.

```
<?php
#source file not kept in the document root for connection paramters
include "/etc/connection.inc";
```

In order to keep the connection parameters from being visible to the world due to server mis-configuration, we keep them in a file called connection.inc stored outside the document root of the web server. Here are the contents of the configuration file we used:

```
<?php
$username = "jon";
$password = "secret";
$hostname = "localhost";
$dbname   = "bmsimple";
?>
```

If your operating system allows, this file should be only be readable by the user who owns the web server process.

```
#connect to the database server
$db_link = mysql_connect("$hostname", "$username", "$password")
or die ("Could not connect to the server\n");
mysql_select_db("$dbname");
```

Next, we use the parameters read in from the `connection.inc` file to connect to the database server and select the database.

```
#if we have been asked to add a suggestion to the database
if ($suggestion_submitted == 1) {
```

The variable `$suggestion_submitted` is checked to see if the feedback form has been submitted or if just the page needs to be displayed. PHP will get the value of this variable from a hidden FORM variable in this file.

```
#insert the escaped parameters into the database
$sql = sprintf("INSERT INTO feedback
        VALUES(\"%s\",\"%s\",\"%s\",\"%s\",\"%s\")",
addslashes($customer_name), addslashes($client_email), addslashes($item_name),
addslashes($comments), addslashes($how_good));
```

Similarly, PHP will also give us the values of the rest of the FORM variables as seen above. We form an SQL statement in order to insert the values that we received into the database. The `addslashes()` function takes care of the quoting issues for us, in a manner similar to the `quote()` method that we will see in Chapter 14, *Accessing MySQL through Perl*.

```
$result = mysql_query($sql, $db_link);

if (!$result) {
    echo "Cannot insert: " . mysql_error($db_link);
}
```

This segment of PHP code ends after we make sure that the INSERT has succeeded.

```
<FORM ACTION = "http://localhost/feedback.php" METHOD = "POST">

...
<TH ALIGN = "left">Product:</TH>
<TD>
```

This part of the code creates a part of the form for taking input. Note the *hidden variable* called `suggestion_submitted` that we set to '1', so that when this script is called again, this parameter will tell us if we need to insert data into the feedback database or just display the feedback page.

```
while ($list_row = mysql_fetch_array($item_list_result)) {
...
}
```

We've embedded a `while` loop that populates a dropdown box with a list of all the items present in our online store. After populating the dropdown list, we complete the form with the required HTML. The next part of the page will contain feedback given by other customers, so we fetch the feedback data from the table using a simple `SELECT` query.

```
#get the suggestion data from the feedback table
$suggestion_list_result = mysql_query ("select name,product,comments from
feedback", $db_link);
while ($list_row = mysql_fetch_array($suggestion_list_result)) {
#wrap the data with html so that it looks nice
echo "
<TABLE BORDER=0 WRAP=256 CELLSPACING=0 CELLPADDING=0 COLS=1 ROWS=2
BGCOLOR='#ffcb32'>
<TR><TD>
      <P STYLE='COLOR: #070568; TEXT-DECORATION: none;'>
      $list_row[0] said the following about $list_row[1]:
      </P>
</TD></TR>
<TR><TD bgcolor='white'>
      $list_row[2]
</TD></TR>
</TABLE>";
}
?>
</BODY>
</HTML>
```

This bit of HTML that ends the script will wrap the feedback data in a nice form like this:

Heres what our other customers said:

John Smith said the following about Carrier Bag:
The carrier bag was extremely useful in my bicycle tour across Europe. Light-weight, handy and water proof. It is a definite must buy for anyone serious about cross country bicycling.
Robert Jones said the following about Linux CD:
This is the best distribution of Linux I have ever seen...
Gregory Walters said the following about Speakers:
The speakers that I bought from the store arrived at my house in a slightly damaged package. However I am glad that the speakers themselves are first-rate and are giving me much better fidelity in the higher frequencies than my previous home-made enclosure

This example will provide you with a good starting point for building your own scripts.

Using PEAR's Database Abstraction Interface

PEAR (The **PHP Extension and Application Repository**) is an attempt to replicate the functionality of Perl's CPAN in the PHP community. To quote the official PEAR goals:

❑   To provide a consistent means for library code authors to share their code with other developers.

- ❑ To give the PHP community an infrastructure for sharing code.
- ❑ To define standards that help developers write portable and reusable code.
- ❑ To provide tools for code maintenance and distribution.

PEAR is primarily a large collection of PHP classes, which make use of PHP's object-oriented programming capabilities. Thus, you will need to become familiar with PHP's syntax for working with classes. PHP's object-oriented extensions are documented at:

http://www.php.net/manual/en/language.oop.php

More information on PEAR is available at:

http://pear.php.net/ and http://php.weblogs.com/php_pear_tutorials

PEAR's Database Abstraction Interface

PEAR has a database abstraction interface (DB) that is included with the standard PHP distribution. The advantage of using a database abstraction interface instead of calling the database's native functions directly is that the code is database-independent. Should you need to move your project to a different database, it would probably involve a major code rewrite. If you had used a database abstraction interface, however, the task would be trivial.

PEAR's DB interface also has some 'value-added' features, such as convenient access to multiple result sets and integrated error handling. All of the database interaction is handled through the DB classes and objects. This is conceptually similar to Perl's DBI interface.

The main disadvantage of a database abstraction interface is the performance overhead on the execution of your application. Once again, this is a situation where there is a trade-off between functionality, portability, and performance.

Using PEAR's DB Interface

Scripts that uses the PEAR DB interface generally do the following:

- ❑ Reference the DB.php file.
- ❑ Create a Data Source Name.
- ❑ Connect to the database using the connect() method.
- ❑ Issue SQL queries using the connection object and obtain result objects.
- ❑ Extract information from the result objects.
- ❑ Disconnect from the server.

Referencing the DB.php file

Referencing the DB.php file is necessary to start using the DB class. The following statement can do this:

```
require_once "DB.php";
```

The require_once makes sure that duplicate variable or function declarations do not break your script.

417

Creating a Data Source Name (DSN)

A DSN is a URL-style string that contains the database driver name (mysql for MySQL), the hostname where the server is running, the user name, and the password for an account with access to the database to be used, and the name of the database to be used.

The DSN syntax generally looks like:

```
mysql://user_name:password@host_name/db_name
```

Connecting To the Database

Use the connect() method of the DB class to connect to the database:

```
$dsn = "mysql://john:secret_password@localhost/bmsimple"
$link = DB::connect($dsn);
```

Persistence of Connections

A connection is non-persistent by default. If a persistent connection is required, pass the boolean value TRUE as a second argument to connect():

```
$link = DB::connect($dsn, TRUE);
```

The second parameter could also be an array of options:

```
$options = array ( "persistent" => TRUE,
                   "optimize" => "performance" );
$link = DB::connect($dsn, $options);
```

Currently the only two options supported are persistent and optimize. The value for optimize may be performance or portability.

Issuing Queries To the Database

The query method of the connection object obtained earlier can be used for passing queries to the database. This method takes the SQL query string as an argument:

```
$dsn            = "mysql://john:secret_password@localhost/bmsimple"
$link           =   DB::connect($dsn);
$query_string   = "SELECT * FROM customer";
$result         =   $link->query( $query_string );
```

Basic Error Handling

PEAR includes an integrated error-handling system. Here is some code to demonstrate error handling:

```
#! /usr/bin/php
<?php
#Import the PEAR DB interface.
```

```
require_once 'DB.php';

#Construct the DSN - Data Source Name.
$dsn = "mysql://jon:secret@localhost/bmsimple";

#Attempt to connect to the database.
$db = DB::connect($dsn);

#Check for any connection errors.
if (DB::isError($db)) {
    die ($db->getMessage());
}
else
{
    echo "Connection successful.\n";
}
?>
```

This example illustrates the use of DB::isError(), one of the basic error-handling functions. If the call to DB::connect() fails for some reason, it will return an PEAR_Error object instead of a database connection object. We can test for this case using the DB::isError() function as shown.

We can retrieve the text of the error message (in this case, the connection error generated by MySQL) using the getMessage() function.

Extracting Information from the Result Objects

Now that we have looked at how to handle errors, let's see what we can do with the results of the queries.

For Queries That Do Not Return a Result Set:

If the query is an INSERT, UPDATE or DELETE statement, the value returned on success will be a pre-defined constant DB_OK. We can also use the DB::isError() method to check for errors. After we are sure that the execution of the query has been successful, we can check for additional information that we expect to receive, such as the number of rows affected by the query.

Try It Out – Queries That Do Not Return a Result Set

```
#! /usr/bin/php

<?php
#Import the PEAR DB interface.
require_once 'DB.php';

# Database connection parameters.
$username = "jon";
$password = "secret";
$hostname = "localhost";
$dbname   = "bmsimple";

# Construct the DSN - Data Source Name.
$dsn = "mysql://$username:$password@$hostname/$dbname";
```

```
#Attempt to connect to the database.
$db = DB::connect($dsn);

#Check for any connection errors.
if (DB::isError($db)) {
    die ($db->getMessage());
}
$query_string = "insert into customer(title, fname, lname, addressline, town,
zipcode, phone) values('Mr','Joy','Goldsmith','10, Crowning
Street','Northwood','NT3 1AA','023 7870')";

$result = $db->query($query_string);
if (DB::isError($result)) {
    die ("INSERT failed ".$db->getMessage());
}
printf ("Rows inserted: %d\n", $db->affectedRows());
?>
```

For Queries That Return a Result Set

If the query is a SELECT statement, then an object that can be used to fetch the resulting data will be returned on successful execution of the query.

Try It Out – Queries That Return a Result Set

```
<HTML>
<HEAD><TITLE>How many customers have we had so far</TITLE></HEAD>
<BODY BGCOLOR="FFFFFF">
<TABLE WIDTH="100%" BGCOLOR="#ffcb32">
<TR><TD>
<H2>Welcome to Beginning MySQL online</H2>
</TR></TD>
</TABLE>
<?php

# Import the PEAR DB interface.
require_once "DB.php";

# Database connection parameters.
$username = "jon";
$password = "secret";
$hostname = "localhost";
$dbname   = "bmsimple";

# Construct the DSN - Data Source Name.
$dsn = "mysql://$username:$password@$hostname/$dbname";

# Attempt to connect to the database.
$db = DB::connect($dsn);

# Check for any connection errors.
if (DB::isError($db)) {
    die ("Connection failed. " . $db->getMessage());
}
```

```
# Execute a selection query.
$query = "SELECT title, fname, lname FROM customer";
$result = $db->query($query);

# Check for any query execution errors.
if (DB::isError($result)) {
    die ($result->getMessage());
}

# Fetch and display the query results.
echo "<H3>Customer list - using PEAR DB:</H3>";
while ($row = $result->fetchRow(DB_FETCHMODE_ASSOC)) {
    $fullname  = $row['title'] . " ";
    $fullname .= $row['fname'] . " ";
    $fullname .= $row['lname'];
echo "$fullname<BR>\n";
}

# Disconnect from the database.
$db->disconnect();
?>
</BODY>
</HTML>
```

As you can see, this code, while not using any MySQL functions directly, still follows the logic of our previous examples. It is also simple to see how the above example could easily be adapted to use another type of database (Oracle or PostgreSQL, for example). Actually, modifying the DSN for various databases would be the only change needed.

Setting Error-Handling Levels

PEAR provides a means of modifying its error handling behavior by specifying one of several error modes:

```
# Make errors fatal.
$db->setErrorHandling(PEAR_ERROR_DIE);
```

We can change PEAR's default error-handling behavior with the call to the `setErrorHandling()` method. The default error-handling mode is PEAR_ERROR_RETURN, where the error objects are returned, and the developer is responsible for taking action after examining the error object. If you don't want to check the return value of every function call, setting the error-handling behavior to PEAR_ERROR_DIE will cause PHP to exit if an error occurs. Thus, you may assume that if the script didn't die after a function call returned, the call probably succeeded.

Here's a list of the various error-handling modes:

Error Handling Mode	What it means
PEAR_ERROR_RETURN	Simply return an error object.
PEAR_ERROR_PRINT	Print the error message and continue execution.

Table continued on following page

Error Handling Mode	What it means
PEAR_ERROR_TRIGGER	Use PHP's `trigger_error()` function to raise an internal error.
PEAR_ERROR_DIE	Print the error message and abort execution.
PEAR_ERROR_CALLBACK	Use a callback function to handle the error before aborting execution.

Additional information on the PEAR_ERROR class and PEAR error handling is available at:

http://pear.php.net/manual/class.pear-error.php

Query Preparation and Execution

PEAR also includes a handle method of preparing and executing queries. This is useful when using placeholders in queries. Here's a piece of code demonstrating the `prepare()` and `execute()` methods of the DB interface:

```
<HTML>
<HEAD><TITLE>preparing and executing SQL with PEAR DB</TITLE></HEAD>
<BODY BGCOLOR="FFFFFF">
<TABLE WIDTH="100%" BGCOLOR="#ffcb32">
<TR><TD>
<H2>Welcome to Beginning MySQL online</H2>
</TR></TD>
</TABLE>
<?php

# Import the PEAR DB interface.
require_once "DB.php";

# Database connection parameters.
$username = "jon";
$password = "secret";
$hostname = "localhost";
$dbname   = "bmsimple";

# Construct the DSN - Data Source Name.
$dsn = "mysql://$username:$password@$hostname/$dbname";

# Attempt to connect to the database.
$db = DB::connect($dsn);

# Check for any connection errors.
if (DB::isError($db)) {
    die ("Connection failed. " . $db->getMessage());
}

#values to insert into placeholders
$barcode = '3000000000004';
$item_id = '40';
```

```
# Prepare our template SQL statement.
$statement = $db->prepare("INSERT INTO barcode VALUES(?, ?)");
echo "<H2>Using placeholders 'INSERT INTO barcode VALUES(?,?)':</H2>";

# Execute the statement
$db->execute($statement, array($barcode, $item_id));
echo "Inserted bar code $barcode for item $item_id<BR>";

# Disconnect from the database.
$db->disconnect();
?>
</BODY>
</HTML>
```

The call to the `prepare()` method creates an SQL template. Note the two 'wildcard' positions in the statement that are specified using question marks. The `execute()` method will replace the placeholder values in the prepared statement with those values passed to it in the second argument in array form. In the above example, this is the `array($barcode, $item_id)` argument. The placeholder values are replaced in the order these new values are specified, so it's important to get the order right when there are multiple values.

Summary

In this chapter, we examined the various ways that a MySQL database can be accessed from the PHP scripting language.

We covered the various aspects of database connections, query building and execution, result set manipulation, and error handling. We also looked at a real-world example that acts as a good starting point for you. We then introduced the PEAR database abstraction interface.

From this foundation, you should now have enough of the basic tools to begin developing your own web-based database applications using MySQL and PHP.

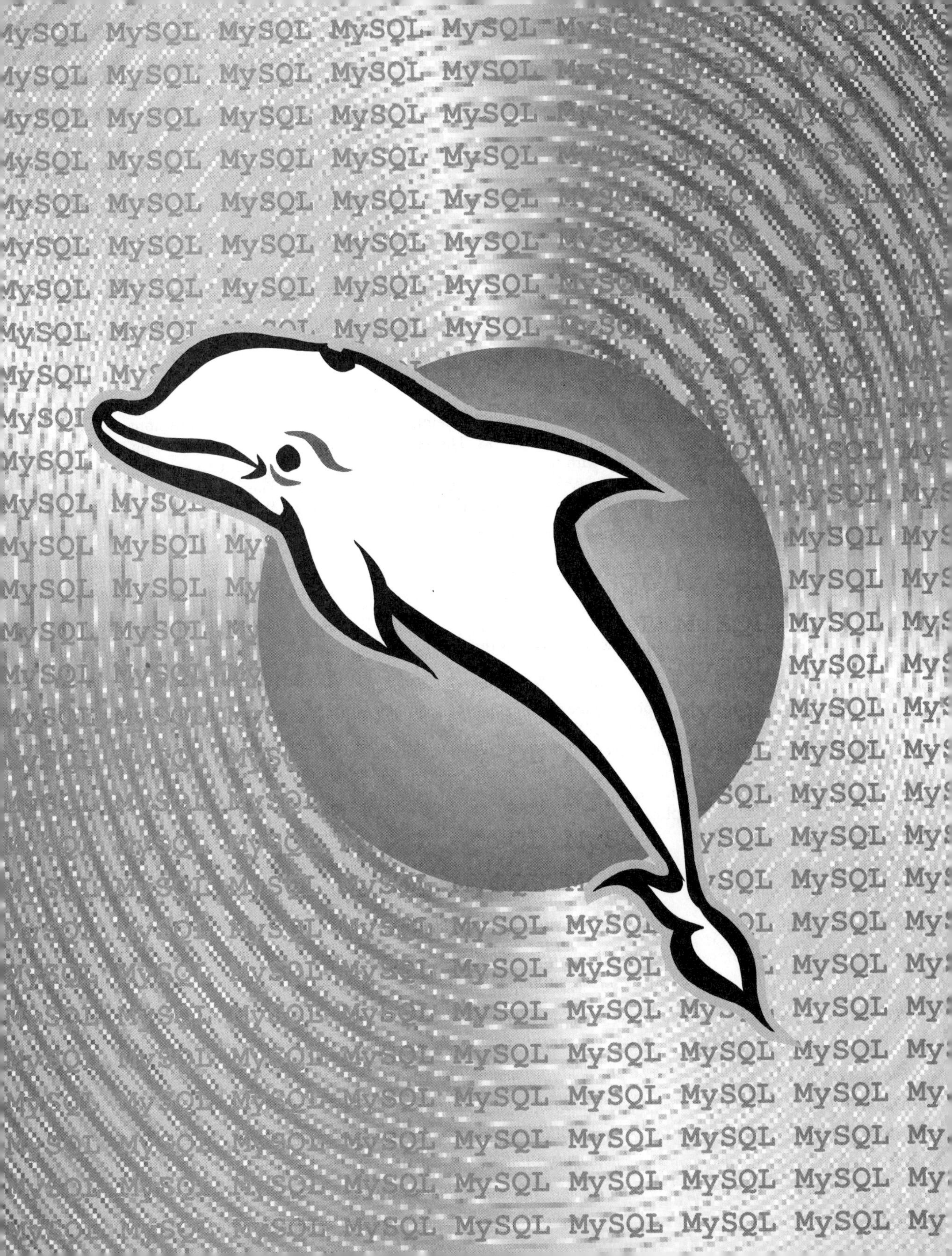

Accessing MySQL from Perl

As seen in earlier chapters, communicating with MySQL generally involves a lot of string manipulation, like converting between strings and other data types, or removing padding spaces. Perl is a language that excels at string manipulation. In this chapter we'll see how to use MySQL from Perl. In Chapter 12, *Accessing MySQL from C and C++*, we demonstrated that the `libmysqlclient` interface is powerful but it is apparent that native string representation in C is quite primitive.

For small programs written using C, the size of code dealing with strings can be significantly larger than the code that handles interaction with the database. With Perl, strings are much more sophisticated. It has built-in operations such as joining, splitting, pattern matching, and automatic conversion between data types.

There are multiple mechanisms for interacting with MySQL database servers using Perl. Some of them are listed here:

❑   The `DBI` and the `MySQL::DBD` modules

❑   ODBC

❑   The legacy `mysql.pm` module

We will not attempt to teach much Perl here, but if you are completely unfamiliar with the language, some useful starting points are:

❑   http://www.perl.org and http://www.cpan.org.

❑   *Beginning Perl* by Simon Cozens, Wrox Press, (ISBN 1-861003-14-5).

❑   *Learning Perl* by Randal L. Schwartz and Tom Christiansen, O'Reilly, (ISBN 1-56592-284-0).

> **The code in this chapter will not make use of many Perl idioms, so it should be easy to understand for most C programmers. Moreover, the discussions in this chapter are related to Linux. For other operating systems refer to the vendor documentation.**

Perl programs are just plain text files and can be created using any text editor. All programs in this chapter will follow the UNIX convention of using a first line beginning with '#!' followed by the path of the program for executing the code:

```
#!/usr/bin/perl
```

This is the line that we will be using in the text. You'll need to modify this line if the path to the Perl binary is different on your system. For example, it may be:

```
#! /usr/local/bin/perl
```

Under UNIX, a Perl program should be made executable, so that it may be run from the command prompt just by typing its name. To make a program executable, change its file mode as follows:

```
$> chmod + x program_name
```

If you are using a version of Perl that runs on Windows systems, Perl programs must be run from the command prompt as follows:

```
C:\> perl program_name
```

Otherwise, you can associate the .pl extension with perl.exe. If you save all your programs with a .pl extension, you can run them simply by typing in the program name at the command prompt:

```
C:\> program_name.pl
```

Some other things to remember are:

❑   Scalar variables (numbers or strings – Perl converts between these as required) begin with a '$' symbol.

❑   Lists (simple arrays) begin with a '@' symbol.

❑   Hashes (associative arrays) with a '%' character.

The Perl DBI

If you have done some Windows database programming, you will be familiar with ODBC, the Open Database Connectivity API, or more recent APIs such as ADO or OLE DB. Similarly, if you have used Java with databases, you will have come across JDBC. These programming interfaces are an attempt to create a layer of abstraction that unifies the mechanism for interacting with different kinds of database servers.

Perl has a similar mechanism – DBI, the **Database Interface**. As with other database-independent APIs, DBI is structured as the client API module and one or more drivers, or DBD (Database Driver) modules. You can have several different databases open at the same time, and access them via essentially the same code in your Perl programs, as illustrated opposite:

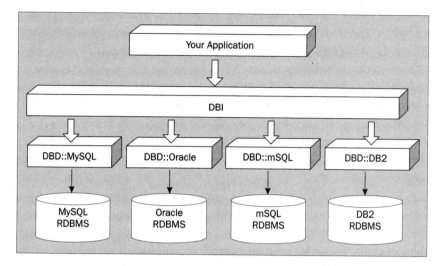

It is interesting to note that one of the available DBDs is for ODBC – a database-independent interface. Apart from the DBD::ODBC module, there is a Win32::ODBC module that could also be used to connect to MySQL. But since DBD::MySQL is available, the other modules won't be discussed further.

A useful driver that can be used with DBI is DBD::CSV. This driver emulates a database server using comma-separated value (CSV) text files, and can be useful for creating prototypes when a 'real' database server is not available.

You can find more information about DBI on its home page, http://www.symbolstone.org/technology/perl/DBI, or in *Programming the Perl DBI* by Alligator Descartes and Tim Bunce, O'Reilly, (ISBN 1-56592-699-4).

Installing DBI and the MySQL DBD

The necessary modules could be installed either from the source distributions, or by using one of the automated installation mechanisms.

If you are using the ActiveState Perl distribution with any of the Microsoft Windows platforms, the easiest way to go about installing these modules is the Perl Package Manager (PPM). After making sure that you're connected to the Internet, run PPM from the command prompt:

```
C:\> ppm
```

This will present you with a ppm prompt:

```
PPM interactive shell (2.1.5) - type 'help' for available commands.
PPM>
```

Now, install the DBI module. The Perl Package Manager will also inform you if the module has already been installed, and will give you the option of checking whether an upgrade is available:

```
PPM> install DBI
```

Now for installing the MySQL driver, type in the following at the prompt:

```
PPM> search mysql
Packages available from http://ppm.ActiveState.com/cgibin/PPM/ppmserver.pl?urn:/PPMServer
ApacheMysql [0.3   ] Initiate a persistent database connection to Mysql
DBD-Mysql   [1.2200] DBI driver for Mysql datasources
...
```

This will return a list of all the available modules that are related to MySQL. To install everything you need in order to get Perl working with MySQL from your Windows machine:

```
PPM> install DBD-Mysql
```

If you are using the CPAN exporter module, the process is pretty similar. Start the CPAN shell from the command line:

```
%perl -MCPAN -e shell
cpan>
```

Now, to install the DBI and DBD::MySQL modules, type the following commands respectively:

```
cpan> install DBI
cpan> install DBD::MySQL
```

Alternatively, you can install a 'bundle' that contains all the required modules:

```
%perl -MCPAN -e 'install Bundle::DBD::mysql'
```

This will install the following modules:

❑   DBI

❑   Data::ShowTable

❑   Mysql

❑   DBD::mysql

This has all the DBI and Non-DBI modules required to get Perl working with MySQL.

Another option is to build the modules from source. You can reach the DBD::MySQL download page by going to http://search.cpan.org/search?dist=DBD-mysql, and the DBI download page by going to http://search.cpan.org/search?dist=DBI. To check if you already have the DBI module installed on your system; try the following on the command prompt:

```
C:\WINDOWS\Desktop>perl -e "use DBI;"
Can't locate DBI.pm in @INC (@INC contains: C:/Perl/lib C:/Perl/site/lib .) at -
e line 1.
BEGIN failed--compilation aborted at -e line 1.
```

If you do not get an error message similar to the one shown above, you already have the module installed on your system.

The procedure for building these modules is the same as that for building most others, and consists of the following steps:

```
%perl Makefile.pl
%make
%make test
%make install
```

You may see some compiler warnings about unused variables during the make process. Though this is untidy, it is harmless.

Using DBI

This section mainly deals with different terminologies, query results and placeholders and binding parameters.

Terminology, Data Types and conventions

If you are a C programmer, certain analogies will help in clarifying the outline of Perl code using the DBI module. Just like we call functions in C, we invoke methods in Perl. The data is stored in structures pointed to by pointers in C. Similarly, in Perl, the data is stored in objects that we access via handles.

There are certain naming conventions that will help you when reading DBI code written by other people. It will also give your code a style similar to that of the code in the DBI documentation.

❑ $dbh contains a handle to a database object.

❑ $sth contains a handle to an SQL statement object.

❑ $fh contains a handle to a file object.

❑ $rows contains a row count.

❑   @ary contains a list of values that make up a row – returned by a query.

❑ $rc holds a Boolean return value.

❑ $rv holds an integer return value.

Let us look at a simple example that demonstrates what most programs for accessing MySQL start out as:

Try It Out – A Simple Example

```perl
#!/usr/bin/perl -w
#list_customers - print a list of all the customers

#ask the interpreter to load the DBI module
use DBI;
#force ourselves to declare the variables we're going to use
use strict;

my $dsn       = "DBI:mysql:bmsimple:localhost";    #data source name
my $user      = "jon";                             #username
my $password  = "secret";                          #password
my $dbh;                                            #database handle
my $sth;                                            #SQL query handle
my @ary;                                            #list for resulting rows

#connect to the database
$dbh = DBI->connect($dsn, $user, $password, {RaiseError => 1});

$sth = $dbh->prepare("SELECT title,fname,lname FROM customer
                      ORDER by lname");
$sth->execute();

#extract the data from the result of the query
while (@ary = $sth->fetchrow_array()) {
    print join("\t", @ary), "\n";
}

#clean up and exit
$sth->finish();
$dbh->disconnect();
exit(0);
```

How It Works

Now let us go through the file step by step:

The first line of the file gives the path of the Perl binary that will be used to run the program:

```perl
#!/usr/bin/perl
```

The next line is a comment that gives the name of the program, and a brief idea about what it does. Comments in Perl begin with a '#' symbol and carry on to the end of the line.

```perl
#list_customers - print a list of all the customers
```

The next line, 'use DBI;', tells the Perl interpreter to include the DBI module. We are not asking the Perl interpreter to load the MySQL::DBD module. Based on the parameters we give while trying to connect to the database, the correct DBD driver will be loaded by the DBI object.

430

'use strict;' is a pragma that makes Perl enforce certain good programming practices like forcing us to declare variable names before we use them. This feature is very useful for catching typographical errors, so including this in the very beginning of all your Perl programs is a good idea.

We declare all the variables and the connection parameters that we will be using:

```
my $dsn      = "DBI:mysql:bmsimple:localhost";   #data source name
my $user     = "jon";                            #username
my $password = "secret";                         #password
my $dbh;                                         #database handle
my $sth;                                         #SQL query handle
my @ary;                                         #list for resulting rows
```

After defining the code, we define the connection parameters so that we can use the connect() method to start interacting with the mysql server:

```
#connect to the database
$dbh = DBI->connect($dsn, $user, $password, {RaiseError => 1});
```

The $dsn, $user and $password parameters are optional. The following defaults are assumed:

❑   If the data source name is not specified, the value of the environment variable DBI_DSN is used as the dsn parameter.

❑   If the username is not specified in the call to connect(), the value of the environment variable DBI_USER value is utilized for the username.

❑   On Windows systems, the USER variable is used if DBI_USER is undefined.

❑   If the username is undefined or is an empty string, it defaults to 'ODBC' on Windows systems, and on UNIX variants, it defaults to the system login name.

❑   If the hostname is empty, it defaults to 'localhost'.

❑   An undefined or empty password value results in no password being sent to the MySQL server.

The data source name may have certain useful modifiers appended to it. A data source name may have more than one modifiers appended to it with each modifier preceded by a semi-colon.

You can get a complete list of modifiers from the MySQL Perl API documentation on your system or from http://www.mysql.com/doc/P/e/Perl_DBI_Class.html.

A couple of useful modifiers are mysql_read_default_file and mysql_compression.

mysql_read_default_file

To save the bother of typing the hostname, user name and password for each program you write, you may enter them in the .my.cnf file in your home directory. If you're using one of the Microsoft systems, you should enter them in the C:\my.cnf file. Also if any of these parameters change, this would reduce the number of files where you have to change them.

Here's an example configuration file:

```
[client]
host=mysql.server.name
user=jon
password=secret
```

Be sure to change those parameters to reflect the settings you are using.

Although this may save some time, it may be a security risk if the permissions on this file are not set properly. If your operating system allows, you must set the permissions to 400 or 600 so that no one else can read the file, and must store it in an area where it is not accessible through the Web if you have a web server running on the same machine.

When creating the data source name, append the `mysql_read_default_file` modifier, for Linux/UNIX variants like this:

```
my $dsn = "DBI:mysql:bmsimple;mysql_read_default_file=/home/jon/.my.cnf";
$dbh = DBI->connect($dsn);
```

and for Windows variants:

```
my $dsn = "DBI:mysql:bmsimple;mysql_read_default_file=C:\my.cnf";
$dbh = DBI->connect($dsn);
```

When the connect method is invoked with this DSN, the program will try to connect to the MySQL server running on 'mysql.server.name' as user 'jon' with the password 'secret'. You may override the parameters specified in the configuration file by explicitly specifying them in the call to the `connect()` method. This may be required if you want the user to be able to override the defaults by providing parameters on the command line.

mysql_compression

This modifier will cause communication between the client and the sever to be compressed:

```
my $dsn =
"DBI:mysql:bmsimple;mysql_read_default_file=/home/jon/.my.cnf;mysql_compression=1"
;
$dbh = DBI->connect($dsn);
```

The syntax of the connect method looks like this:

```
$dbh = DBI->connect($dsn, $uname, $pwd, \%attributes);
```

Now that we've looked at the first three parameters, let us turn our attention to the last one.

```
$dbh = DBI->connect($dsn, $user, $password, {RaiseError => 1});
```

The last parameter is a reference to an associative array that contains pairs of attributes and their values. In Perl, you can create a reference to an anonymous hash by enclosing the `'key => value'` pairs in braces.

The values in these `'key => value'` pairs will be assigned to the attributes of the database handle object that gets created by the connect statement. Let's look at a couple of useful attributes – `RaiseError` and `AutoCommit`.

RaiseError

This attribute when enabled, will cause the DBI to print an error message and end the process using the Perl function `die()`. Because it uses the `die()` function to throw an exception before exiting, you can handle the exception yourself by putting the code in an `eval` block.

AutoCommit

One important attribute of a database handle is `AutoCommit` – setting this to 1 causes DBI to treat each operation as a single transaction – as if a `commit()` had been called after each operation. Thus if you set `AutoCommit` to TRUE, and delete some rows from a table, there is no way to roll those changes back, since they have already been committed. If automatic committing has been disabled, you must insert calls to `$dbh->commit()` (or `$dbh->rollback()`) as necessary to end transactions.

The next step involves the creation of a statement handle. The `prepare()` method takes in the SQL query and returns a statement handle on success or an `undef` value on failure.

You must remember not to end the SQL query with a semi-colon as you do when interacting with the database using other clients.

The `execute()` method causes the query to be executed on the database server. `prepare` and `execute` exist as two different methods because you may want to execute the same operation several times, and the database may let you optimize access by preparing once and executing the same query multiple times. Also, the database driver may want to do some preprocessing on the query before it is sent to the database server:

```
$sth = $dbh->prepare("SELECT title,fname,lname FROM customer
                      ORDER by lname");
$sth->execute();
```

The result set may be processed after the statement has been executed. Here we do it using the `fetchrow_array()` method. This method returns the next row in the result set, as an array. After the last row has been returned, the next call returns an empty array.

Thus we iterate through all the rows in the result set and print the elements of each row on a line, separated by tabs:

```
while (@ary = $sth->fetchrow_array()) {
    print join("\t", @ary), "\n";
}
```

The `finish()` method of the statement handle frees all the temporary resources associated with the statement. This method is necessary if the entire result set hasn't been fetched – either by error or design. However, it is easier and safer to insert it after you have finished using the statement handle, instead of writing the code to determine if it is necessary or not:

```
$sth->finish();
```

After finishing the required tasks, we may disconnect from the database server and exit:

```
$dbh->disconnect();
exit(0);
```

Processing Query Results

Let's take a slightly closer look at what we can do with the results that we get after executing queries.

Queries That Do Not Return a Result Set

SQL statements containing DELETE, INSERT, UPDATE, or REPLACE do not return result sets. The results of such SQL statements are easy to process.

Let us look at an example:

Try It Out – Queries That Do Not Return a Result Set

```
#!/usr/bin/perl
#insert a customer record

#ask the interpreter to load the DBI module
use DBI;
#force ourselves to declare the variables we're going to use
use strict;

my $dsn       = "DBI:mysql:bmsimple:localhost";    #data source name
my $user      = "jon";                             #username
my $password  = "secret";                          #password
my ($dbh, $rows);                                  #database handle

#connect to the database
$dbh = DBI->connect($dsn, $user, $password);

$rows = $dbh->do("INSERT INTO customer(title, fname, lname, addressline, town,
zipcode, phone) VALUES('Mr','Slickety','Slick','10, Sloans
Street','Southwood','NT2 1AA','023 6870')");

$dbh->disconnect();
exit(0);
```

How It Works

The code contains an SQL statement that inserts a new record in the customer table. For all such statements that do not return a result set, like DELETE, INSERT, REPLACE, and UPDATE, we pass the query to the do() method. This method prepares and executes the query in a single step. It returns a count of the number of rows affected on success and an undef on failure. It is faster than the equivalent prepare() / execute() combination.

If no rows are affected, do() will return '0E0' – the value of '0' in scientific notation instead of '0'. This is done to differentiate between failure and the condition where no rows are affected.

Queries That Return a Result Set

For SQL statements like SELECT, DESCRIBE, and EXPLAIN, most of the work is done in a loop where the data is fetched from the result set after the query has been executed. There are several choices available for extracting the rows from the result set:

- ❑ fetchrow_array() returns the next row as an array of values.

- ❑ fetchrow_arrayref() returns the next row as a reference to an array of fields.

- ❑ fetchrow_hashref() returns the next row as a reference to a hash.

- ❑ fetchall_arrayref() returns all data in a structure that resembles an array of arrays.

Let us see the first example again.

fetchrow_array()

Here is an example that will demonstrate the use of the fetchrow_array() method:

```perl
#!/usr/bin/perl
#demonstrate fetchrow_array

#ask the interpreter for the DBI code
use DBI;
#force ourselves to declare the variables we're going to use
use strict;

my $dsn      = "DBI:mysql:bmsimple:localhost";    #data source name
my $user     = "root";                            #username
my $password = "timepass";                        #password
my $dbh;                                           #database handle
my $sth;                                           #SQL query handle

my ($title, $fname, $lname, $phone);

#connect to the database
$dbh = DBI->connect($dsn, $user, $password, {RaiseError => 1});

$sth = $dbh->prepare("SELECT title,fname,lname,phone FROM customer
                      ORDER by lname");
$sth->execute();

while (($title, $fname, $lname, $phone) = $sth->fetchrow_array()) {
    print "Name: $title $fname $lname \t\t\tPhone: $phone\n";
}

#clean up and exit
$sth->finish();
$dbh->disconnect();
exit(0);
```

435

Each call to `fetchrow_array()` will return an array of values that we assign to a list of scalar variables. The call to `fetchrow_array()` will return an empty list when called after the last row has been extracted.

fetchrow_arrayref()

This method is similar to `fetchrow_array()`, but it returns a reference to an array instead of returning the array itself. References in Perl are analogous to pointers in C. You can dereference the return value of this method to get the entire array using the `@{$reference_to_an_array}` construct:

```perl
#!/usr/bin/perl
#demonstrate fetchrow_arrayref
#list_customers - print a list of all the customers

#ask the interpreter for the DBI code
use DBI;
#force ourselves to declare the variables we're going to use
use strict;

my $dsn        = "DBI:mysql:bmsimple:localhost";   #data source name
my $user       = "root";                           #username
my $password   = "timepass";                       #password
my $dbh;                                            #database handle
my $sth;                                            #SQL query handle
my ($customer_entry, $ary_ref);

#connect to the database
$dbh = DBI->connect($dsn, $user, $password);

$sth = $dbh->prepare("SELECT title,fname,lname FROM customer
                      ORDER by lname");
$sth->execute();
print "Customer list\n";

while ($ary_ref = $sth->fetchrow_arrayref()) {
   $customer_entry = join " ", @{$ary_ref};
   print "$customer_entry\n";
}
#clean up and exit
$sth->finish();
$dbh->disconnect();
exit(0);
```

Another option for dereferencing the array reference is to use the `$array_reference->[$index]` construct:

```perl
...
$sth = $dbh->prepare("SELECT title,fname,lname FROM customer
                      ORDER by lname");
$sth->execute();
print "Customer list\n";
while ($ary_ref = $sth->fetchrow_arrayref()) {
```

```
    $customer_entry = "$ary_ref->[0] $ary_ref->[1] $ary_ref->[2]";
    print "$customer_entry\n";
}
...
```

After the last row has been extracted, the next call to `fetchrow_arrayref()` returns `undef`.

fetchrow_hashref()

The methods mentioned so far for fetching rows from result sets have been associated with lists. To access an element in a list, we need to know its index.

For example, when we say:

```
...
$customer_entry = "$ary_ref->[0] $ary_ref->[1] $ary_ref->[2]";
...
```

we must keep in mind that `$ary_ref->[0]` stands for the 'Title', `$ary_ref->[1]` stands for the 'First Name', and `$ary_ref->[2]` stands for the 'Last Name'.

Similarly, when we say:

```
...
while (($title, $fname, $lname, $phone) = $sth->fetchrow_array())
...
```

the order of the scalar variables on the left-hand side of the assignment must be the same as the order of the fields returned by the query.

`fetchrow_hashref()` allows us to ignore the order in which the fields are returned. It does this by returning a hash containing all the values in the next row, keyed by the field name. After all the rows have been extracted, the next call to `fetchrow_hashref()` returns an `undef`. Here's an example of how this method may be used:

```perl
#!/usr/bin/perl
#demonstrate fetchrow_hashref
#list_customers - print a list of all the customers

#ask the interpreter for the DBI code
use DBI;
#force ourselves to declare the variables we're going to use
use strict;

my $dsn      = "DBI:mysql:bmsimple:localhost";   #data source name
my $user     = "root";                           #username
my $password = "timepass";                       #password
my $dbh;                                          #database handle
```

```
my $sth;                                          #SQL query handle
my $h_ref;                                        #for a reference to the hash

my ($customer_name);

#connect to the database
$dbh = DBI->connect($dsn, $user, $password);
$sth = $dbh->prepare("SELECT phone,title,fname,lname FROM customer");
$sth->execute();
print "Customer list\n";
while ($h_ref = $sth->fetchrow_hashref()){
    $customer_name = "$$h_ref{'title'} $$h_ref{'fname'} $$h_ref{'lname'}";
    print "$customer_name Phone: $$h_ref{'phone'}\n";
}
#clean up and exit
$sth->finish();
$dbh->disconnect();
exit(0);
```

Even though it is convenient, fetchrow_hashref() is slower than the methods used for fetching rows as arrays, and should be avoided where you are looking for speed.

fetchall_arrayref()

All the methods for extracting data mentioned so far allow us to deal with a single row of values each time they are called. The data in a row is lost during the next call, unless you store it in memory. This may not be always desirable. You may face situations where you need to do multiple operations with the data in the result set, or when you want to carry out an operation that deals with the entire result set.

Consider a situation where you are an analyst in the store whose transactions are recorded in the bmsimple database that we have been using in this book, and you want to analyze the spending habits of all your customers over varying periods of time. It would be inefficient in such a situation to fetch the data from the table over and over again for each calculation and every customer.

You could iterate through the result set of your query and keep appending the rows to a growing data structure before you began your analysis. But a method that fetches the entire result set at once and stores it in a matrix-like data structure would be better than iterating through the result set. This is precisely what fetchall_arrayref() does.

It returns a reference to an array of references to arrays representing each row of the result set. Even though that sounds complicated, the members of this data structure can simply be accessed like the elements of a matrix. The following figure illustrates this data structure:

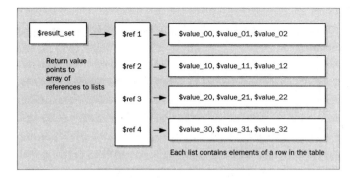

If `$result_set` contains the reference returned by `fetchall_arrayref()`, `$result_set->[0][0]` will contain the first field of the first row in the result set.

Try It Out – Using Fetchall_arrayref()

```perl
#!/usr/bin/perl
#list_customers - print a list of all the customers

use DBI;
use strict;

my $dsn       = "DBI:mysql:bmsimple:localhost";
my $user      = "jon";
my $password  = "secret";
my ($dbh, $sth, $result_set);
my @ary;
my ($row_index, $col_index, $last_row, $last_col);

$dbh = DBI->connect($dsn, $user, $password);

$sth = $dbh->prepare("SELECT title,fname,lname FROM customer
                      ORDER by lname");
$sth->execute();
#extract the data from the result of the query
$result_set = $sth->fetchall_arrayref() or die "Error extracting data\n";

$last_row = $#{$result_set};
$last_col = $#{$result_set->[$row_index]};
#iterate through the matrix in a nested loop
foreach $row_index (0..$last_row) {
   foreach $col_index (0..$last_col) {
      print "$result_set->[$row_index][$col_index]\t";
   }
   print "\n";
}

$sth->finish();
$dbh->disconnect();
exit(0);
```

How It Works

If the `fetchall_arrayref()` method is successful, `$result_set` will contain a reference to the matrix-like data structure:

```
$result_set = $sth->fetchall_arrayref() or die "Error extracting data\n"
```

Next, we get the index of last row and column in the matrix:

```
$last_row = $#{$result_set};
$last_col = $#{$result_set->[$row_index]};
```

Finally, we iterate through the entire matrix using a nested `foreach` loop.

```
foreach $row_index (0..$last_row) {
    foreach $col_index (0..$last_col) {
        print "$result_set->[$row_index][$col_index]\t";
    }
    print "\n";
}
```

Handling Data with Quote Characters

Quote characters, backslashes, or binary data in query statements may cause problems with the Perl interpreter as well as the SQL engine. For example, a small program `test.pl` containing the following lines:

```
#!/usr/bin/perl
$name = 'O'Hara';
print $name;
```

gives the error :

```
Bad name after Hara' at test.pl line 2.
```

Replacing the single quotes surrounding the name with double quotes will solve this problem:

```
$name = "O'Hara";
```

Mixing single and double quote characters won't solve all the quoting problems. A better solution would be to use the generic quote characters that Perl provides instead. For example:

```
#!/usr/bin/perl
$name = q{O'Hara};
$greeting = qq{ Greetings! Mr. $name};
print $greeting . "\n";
```

Here the `q{ string }` construct is a substitute for the single quote delimiters, and the `qq{ string }` construct is a substitute for double quote delimiters. Perl also gives you the flexibility to choose your own quote characters. Please refer to the Perl documentation for more details.

Even if we use the generic quoting mechanism in Perl to accommodate slashes, quotes and other such characters, the SQL engine will still have a problem with them. The `quote()` method of a database handle object can be used for escaping these characters before sending the query to the database server.

A small example will help illustrate this:

```perl
#!/usr/bin/perl
#list_customers - print a list of all the customers

use DBI;
use strict;

my $dsn             = "DBI:mysql:bmsimple:localhost";
my $user            = "jon";
my $password        = "secret";
my $dbh;
my ($firstname, $lastname, $rows);

$dbh             = DBI->connect($dsn, $user, $password);
$lastname        = $dbh->quote("O'Connell");
$firstname       = $dbh->quote('Mac');

$rows    = $dbh->do(qq{ INSERT INTO
customer(title,fname,lname,addressline,town,zipcode,phone) VALUES
('Mr',$firstname, $lastname, '10,Sloans Street','Eastwood','NT2 3AA','013 8870')
});

print "Number of rows affected: $rows\n";
$dbh->disconnect();
exit(0);
```

Note that, when passing `$firstname` and `$lastname` to the `'do()'` statement, we do not add the surrounding quotes; the `quote()` method inserts them for us.

Placeholders and Binding Parameters

We said earlier that DBI splits operations into a preparation stage and an execution step, so that you could execute the same query multiple times. Consider a situation where you need to insert a large number of item records in your inventory. Let's assume that the items to be inserted are present in a hash where the item id is the key, and the quantity of the item is its value. You would think of doing something like this:

```perl
#!/usr/bin/perl
#demonstrate placeholders

#ask the interpreter to load the DBI module
use DBI;
#force ourselves to declare the variables we're going to use
use strict;

my $dsn        = "DBI:mysql:bmsimple:localhost";    #data source name
```

```perl
my $user       = "jon";                        #username
my $password   = "secret";                     #password
my $dbh;                                        #database handle
my $sth;                                        #SQL query handle
my %new_stock = ( "17" => "2",
                  "18" => "1",
                  "19" => "12" );

my ($quantity, $item_id);
#connect to the database
$dbh = DBI->connect($dsn, $user, $password);

while( ($item_id, $quantity) = each (%new_stock)) {
    $dbh->do( qq{INSERT INTO stock VALUES("$item_id", "$quantity") });
}

#clean up and exit
$dbh->disconnect();
exit(0);
```

The `do()` method will end up calling `prepare()` and `execute()` for each item in `%new_stock`. Since the SQL query remains the same for each item, we need to prepare it only once and execute it multiple times. Placeholders can help us here:

```perl
#!/usr/bin/perl
#demonstrate placeholders

#ask the interpreter to load the DBI module
use DBI;
#force ourselves to declare the variables we're going to use
use strict;

my $dsn        = "DBI:mysql:bmsimple:localhost";   #data source name
my $user       = "jon";                            #username
my $password   = "secret";                         #password
my $dbh;                                            #database handle
my $sth;                                            #SQL query handle
my %new_stock = ( "17", "2",
                  "18", "1",
                  "19", "12" );

my ($quantity, $item_id);
#connect to the database
$dbh = DBI->connect($dsn, $user, $password);

$sth = $dbh->prepare( qq{ INSERT INTO stock VALUES(?,?)});
while( ($item_id, $quantity) = each (%new_stock)) {
    $sth->execute("$item_id", "$quantity");
}

#clean up and exit
$dbh->disconnect();
exit(0);
```

The question marks in the SQL query above are the placeholders. You may have multiple placeholders, but you must pass a parameter for each one of them to the execute() method.

Another way of associating the variables $item_id and $quantity with the placeholders in the SQL query is to bind them with the bind_param() method:

```perl
#!/usr/bin/perl
#demonstrate bind_param
#ask the interpreter for the DBI code
use DBI;
#force ourselves to declare the variables we're going to use
use strict;

my $dsn      = "DBI:mysql:bmsimple:localhost";    #data source name
my $user     = "root";                            #username
my $password = "timepass";                        #password
my $dbh;                                           #database handle
my $sth;                                           #SQL query handle

my %new_stock = ( "50", "2",
                  "51", "1",
                  "52", "12");

my ($quantity, $item_id);
#connect to the database
$dbh = DBI->connect($dsn, $user, $password, {RaiseError => 1});

$sth = $dbh->prepare( qq{ INSERT INTO stock VALUES(?,?)} );
$sth->bind_param(1, $item_id);
$sth->bind_param(2, $quantity);
while( ($item_id, $quantity) = each (%new_stock)) {
    $sth->execute();
    print "Inserted item $item_id ===> Quantity: $quantity\n";
}

#clean up and exit
$dbh->disconnect();
exit(0);
```

The first parameter to bind_param() is the index of the parameter in the SQL statement. The second parameter is the value to be associated with the parameter.

The values of columns in the result set may also be bound to variables.

Try It Out – Binding Output Columns To Variables

```perl
#!/usr/bin/perl
#list_customers - print a list of all the customers

use DBI;
use strict;
```

```
my $dsn          = "DBI:mysql:bmsimple:localhost";
my $user         = "jon";
my $password     = "secret";
my ($dbh, $sth);

my ($title, $first_name, $last_name);

$dbh = DBI->connect($dsn, $user, $password);

$sth = $dbh->prepare("SELECT title,fname,lname FROM customer");
$sth->execute();

#bind perl variables to output column
$sth->bind_col(1, \$title);
$sth->bind_col(2, \$first_name);
$sth->bind_col(3, \$last_name);
#fetch data from the result set
while ($sth->fetch()) {
    print "$title $first_name $last_name\n";
}

$sth->finish();
$dbh->disconnect();
exit(0);
```

How It Works

We bind the columns of the result set to the variables $title, $first_name, and $last_name. The bind_col() method takes the index of the column to associate, and a reference to the variable to associate it with. We then iterate through the result set using the fetch() method – a method that does the same thing as a fetchrow_array(). While iterating, the values of the variables bound to the columns are automatically updated with the data fetched from the result set.

Using bind_col() is faster than assigning the output of fetchrow_array() to a list, since the use of references eliminates the copying of data.

If the number of columns in the result set is large, the code will have a lot of bind_col() calls. There is a method called bind_columns that behaves similarly but only needs the names of all the variables to associate the columns with. The binding of all the columns with the variables specified happens in just one method. If we used bind_columns instead of bind_col, this is what the previous example would look like:

```
#!/usr/bin/perl
#list_customers - print a list of all the customers

use DBI;
use strict;

my $dsn          = "DBI:mysql:bmsimple:localhost";
my $user         = "jon";
```

```
my $password      = "secret";
my ($dbh, $sth);

my ($title, $first_name, $last_name);

$dbh = DBI->connect($dsn, $user, $password);

$sth = $dbh->prepare("SELECT title,fname,lname FROM customer");
$sth->execute();

#bind perl variables to output column
$sth->bind_columns(\$title, \$first_name, \$last_name);
#fetch data from the result set
while ($sth->fetch()) {
    print "$title $first_name $last_name\n";
}

$sth->finish();
$dbh->disconnect();
exit(0);
```

Debugging Your DBI code

If you want a behind-the-scenes view of your data on its way through the DBI code, the tracing mechanism that DBI provides you with will help you do just that. It is extremely useful in situations where it is otherwise difficult to find the root of a problem, or when you want to make sure that your data is being sent to the database server in exactly the format that you want.

DBI gives us a method called trace() that controls the tracking and logging of information from the point when it is called in our code. The tracing level controls the amount of information that it generates and logs. There are several tracing levels – from 0, which disables all logging, to 9, which will log information that is probably too low-level or simply too much in volume to be very helpful.

The trace method may be used in three different ways:

Passing the tracing level as an argument:

```
DBI->trace(4);
```

This will set a tracing level of 4, and the messages will be redirected to the STDERR filehandle. This can also be achieved by setting the value of an environment variable called DBI_TRACE to '4'.

Or passing the tracing level and the log file name as arguments like this:

```
DBI->trace(2, "dbi-error.log");
```

This will set a tracing level of 2, and the messages will be logged to a file called dbi-error.log. If that file doesn't exist it will be created, and if it does then the messages will be appended to it. This can also be done by setting the DBI_TRACE variable to '2=dbi-error.log', or simply 'dbi-error.log' since 2 is the default logging level.

The third way is without any argument:

```
DBI->trace();
```

This will set the tracing level to the default value 2, and the messages will be sent to STDERR.

Try It Out – Using the trace( ) method

```perl
#!/usr/bin/perl -w
#list_customers - print a list of all the customers

#ask the interpreter to load the DBI module
use DBI;
#force ourselves to declare the variables we're going to use
use strict;

#enable tracing to a file called dbi-error.log & set the tracing level to 4
DBI->trace(4, "dbi-error.log");

my $dsn      = "DBI:mysql:bmsimple:localhost";   #data source name
my $user     = "jon";                            #username
my $password = "secret";                         #password
my $dbh;                                         #database handle
my $sth;                                         #SQL statement handle
my @ary;                                         #list for resulting rows
#connect to the database
$dbh = DBI->connect($dsn, $user, $password);

#deliberately insert an invalid SQL statement in order to experiment with
#the trace() method
$sth = $dbh->prepare("SELECT title,fname,lname FROM invalid-table
                      ORDER by lname");
$sth->execute();

while (@ary = $sth->fetchrow_array()) {
    print join("\t", @ary), "\n";
}

#clean up and exit
$sth->finish();
$dbh->disconnect();
exit(0);
```

How It Works

This example should fail because of the non-existent table name that we have used in the SQL query. A file called dbi-error.log will be created in the directory from where the program was run. This file will contain a lot of information since the tracing level was set to 4.

Here is the section of the `dbi-error.log` file that shows us what went wrong in the code:

```
dbd_st_execute -2 rows
 !! ERROR: 1064 'You have an error in your SQL syntax near '-table
ORDER by lname' at line 1'
 <- execute= undef at trace.pl line 27.
 -> fetchrow_array for DBD::mysql::st (DBI::st=HASH(0x81b7100)~0x80f6370)
 -> dbd_st_fetch for 080ff580, chopblanks 0
 ERROR EVENT 19 'fetch() without execute()' on DBI::st=HASH(0x80f6370)
 fetch() without execute() error 19 recorded: fetch() without execute()
 !! ERROR: 19 'fetch() without execute()'
 <- fetchrow_array= ( ) [0 items] at trace.pl line 29.
```

DBI also provides the ability to associate a trace with an individual statement or database handle. Since this was a trivial piece of code, it was easy to locate the problem in the log file. To avoid getting lost in huge log files when working with real life programs, this facility helps us track the problem faster. In the same example, if we knew that the problem was with the SQL query, then we could have written the code like this:

```perl
#!/usr/bin/perl -w
#list_customers - print a list of all the customers

#ask the interpreter to load the DBI module
use DBI;
#force ourselves to declare the variables we're going to use
use strict;
my $dsn      = "DBI:mysql:bmsimple:localhost";    #data source name
my $user     = "jon";                             #username
my $password = "secret";                          #password
my $dbh;                                          #database handle
my $sth;                                          #SQL statement handle
my @ary;                                          #list for resulting rows
#connect to the database
$dbh = DBI->connect($dsn, $user, $password);

#deliberately insert an invalid SQL statement in order to experiment with
#the trace() method
$sth = $dbh->prepare("SELECT title,fname,lname FROM invalid-table
                      ORDER by lname");

#enable tracing to a file called select-query.trace & set the tracing level #to 2.
$sth->trace(2, "select-query.trace");

$sth->execute();

while (@ary = $sth->fetchrow_array())
{
        print join("\t", @ary), "\n";
}

#clean up and exit
$sth->finish();
$dbh->disconnect();
exit(0);
```

Since we assumed that the problem was with the SQL query, we reduced the amount of irrelevant information logged by doing the following:

❑   We started tracing just before the query got executed.

❑   We used the `trace()` method associated with the statement handle in order to log messages only related to that particular statement.

Experiment with the various tracing levels and ways of invoking the `trace()` method and observe the output sent to the log files in order to gain familiarity with using this troubleshooting technique.

Database Handle attributes

We mentioned the `RaiseError` and `AutoCommit` attributes earlier. The other attributes include:

❑   `PrintError` – this attribute is similar to `RaiseError`. The difference between the two is that `PrintError` doesn't cause the process to die. It fills `$DBI::errstr` with the error message and also sends the message out to `stderr`. Like `RaiseError`, this attribute can be useful for quick and dirty testing by developers, but it doesn't print very helpful error messages for the users of the system.

❑   `Name` – this method contains the name of the database that we have connected to. The name is the same as what we pass to the `connect()` method.

❑   `ChopBlanks` – Setting this attribute will cause trailing spaces from data stored in `CHAR` type fields to be truncated when returned by `SELECT` queries. This attribute is disabled by default.

There are some other attributes that are less commonly used. See the `DBI` and `MySQL::DBD` documentation for details.

Statement Handle attributes

Here are some statement handle attributes and what they contain:

Attributes	Meaning
`NUM_OF_FIELDS`	Number of fields returned in a query.
`NUM_OF_PARAMS`	Number of placeholders.
`NAME`	Reference to an array containing the names of the columns.
`NAME_lc`	As `NAME`, but always returns lowercase.
`NAME_uc`	As `NAME`, but always returns uppercase.
`NULLABLE`	Reference to an array containing flags indicating if each column can contain `NULL` values.
`Statement`	The string used to create the statement.
`TYPE`	Reference to an array indicating the type of each column.

Note that most 'statement handle' attributes are read-only. Since, depending on the database, some may not be available until the query has been prepared and executed, it is best to examine them only after `execute()` has been called.

We have only scratched the surface of DBI, there is much more information in the online documentation, or you can refer the *Programming the Perl DBI* book by Alligator Descartes and Tim Bunce, O'Reilly, ISBN 1-56592-699-4. One extra thing worth mentioning is the DBI shell, dbish. This is similar to mysql but, as with DBI itself, is database independent.

Using the Perl DBI with CGI

Perl is often called the 'glue of the Internet'. Due to the ease with which Perl can be learned, it has become the most popular language for server-side data processing on the web. Hence, it is only natural that this is one of the most frequently used applications of the Perl DBI.

Let us look at a simple example that demonstrates the use of DBI in code that uses the Common Gateway Interface. Let's create a web interface for customers to be able to give us feedback about our products. First, we need to add a new table to the bmsimple database for holding the feedback data.

Try It Out – Creating a Table for Storing Feedback Data

```perl
#!/usr/bin/perl
#create the table for storing feedback data

#ask the interpreter to load the DBI module
use DBI;
#force ourselves to declare the variables we're going to use
use strict;

my $dsn        = "DBI:mysql:bmsimple:localhost";    #data source name
my $user       = "jon";                             #username
my $password   = "secret";                          #password
my $dbh;                                             #database handle


#connect to the database
$dbh = DBI->connect($dsn, $user, $password);


$dbh->do(qq{
        CREATE TABLE feedback
            (
                name        VARCHAR(50),
                email       VARCHAR(50),
                product     VARCHAR(20),
                comments    VARCHAR(255),
                sat_level   INT
            )

    }
);
$dbh->disconnect();
exit(0);
```

How It Works

This is the simple `do()` method that we have seen before. We're passing it an SQL statement that creates a table called `feedback`. This table contains five fields:

- ❏ `name` – for storing the name of the customer.

- ❏ `email` – for storing the email ID of the customer.

- ❏ `product` – for storing the name of the product for which the feedback is being given.

- ❏ `comments` – for storing the feedback text.

- ❏ `sat_level` – for storing the customer satisfaction level on a scale of 1 to 5.

Now that the table has been created, let us create the web interface. This is what it'll look like once we're done with it:

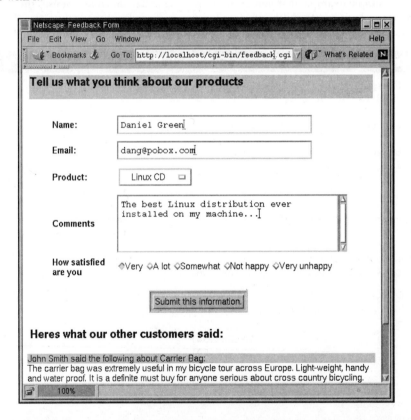

Try It Out - The Web Interface

Before you start with the code:

- ❏ Make sure that you have a web server installed.

❑ The web server should be configured to handle CGI programs. We've used the Apache web server that also comes bundled with the RedHat 7.2 distribution to test this example. However, any server that supports CGI should do.

❑ If you are using the Apache server installed from the RedHat 7.2 distribution, the cgi-bin directory is /var/www/cgi-bin. This is the directory where the CGI code that follows should go.

❑ Ensure that the database server can be reached from the machine on which the web server is running.

❑ Make sure that you have 'bmsimple.cnf' file in the location '/etc' (refer to the 'How It Works' after the code).

Save the following code in a file feedback.cgi, and move it to your cgi-bin directory:

```perl
#!/usr/bin/perl -wT

use strict;

use DBI;
use CGI;

#useful for debugging - send failure messages to the browser
use CGI::Carp qw(fatalsToBrowser);

use vars qw($DBH $CGI);

$DBH =
DBI->connect("DBI:mysql:bmsimple;mysql_read_default_file=/etc/bmsimple.cnf")
    or die "Cannot connect: " . $DBI::errstr;

$CGI = new CGI();

if ($CGI->param( "submit_feedback" ) ) {
   add_feedback_to_database( $CGI, $DBH );
}
else {
   display_suggestion_page( $CGI, $DBH );
}

sub add_feedback_to_database {
   my $cgi = shift;
   my $dbh = shift;
   my ($suggestion_text,$customer_name,$email,$item_name,
      $satisfaction_val, $field_list, $value_list, $sql);

   $suggestion_text    = $cgi->param("comments");
   $customer_name      = $cgi->param("customer_name");
   $email              = $cgi->param("client_email");
   $item_name          = $cgi->param("item_name");
   $satisfaction_val   = $cgi->param("how_good");
```

```
    #prepare the query for inserting feedback data
    $field_list = "('name','email','product','comments','sat_level')";
    $value_list = qq{
        "$customer_name","$email","$item_name",
        "$suggestion_text","$satisfaction_val"
    };

    $sql = qq{ INSERT INTO feedback VALUES($value_list)};
    $dbh->do($sql) or die "Cannot insert: " . $dbh->errstr();

    #after the data has been inserted, refresh the page
    display_suggestion_page($cgi, $dbh);

} # end of add_feedback_to_database

sub display_suggestion_page {

    my $cgi = shift;
    my $dbh = shift;

    my ( $option_val, $OPTION_STRING, $sth, $CUSTOMER_FEEDBACK,
        $comments, $name, $product);

    #create a string that contains the list of items
    #each item name should be put within <OPTION> and
    #</OPTION> tags.
    $sth = $dbh->prepare("select description from item");
    $sth->execute();

    while ( ($option_val) = $sth->fetchrow_array()) {
        $OPTION_STRING ="<OPTION>$option_val</OPTION>\n";
    }
    $sth->finish();

    $sth = $dbh->prepare("select name,product,comments from feedback");
    $sth->execute();

    #create a string that contains all the feedback
    #received so far.
    while ( ($name,$product,$comments) = $sth->fetchrow_array()) {
        $CUSTOMER_FEEDBACK = qq{

            <TABLE BORDER=0 WRAP=256 CELLSPACING=0 CELLPADDING=0 COLS=1
            ROWS=2 BGCOLOR="#ffcb32">
            <TR><TD>

            <P STYLE="COLOR: #070568; TEXT-DECORATION: none; ">
            $name said the following about $product:
            </P>
            </TD></TR>
            <TR><TD bgcolor="white">
            $comments
```

```
        </TD></TR>
        </TABLE>
    }
}

#print out the page
print "Content-type: text/html\n\n";
print << "END_OF_HTML";
<HTML>
<HEAD>
<TITLE>Feedback Form</TITLE>
</HEAD>
<BODY BGCOLOR = "FFFFFF" TEXT = "000000">
<TABLE WIDTH="100%" BGCOLOR="#ffcb32">
<TR><TD>
<H2>Tell us what you think about our products</H2>
</TD></TR>
</TABLE>
<FORM ACTION = "http://localhost/cgi-bin/feedback.cgi" METHOD = "POST">

<BLOCKQUOTE>

<TABLE BORDER = "0">

<TR>
<TH ALIGN = "left">Name:</TH>
<TD>
<INPUT TYPE = "text" NAME = "customer_name" SIZE = "35" MAXLENGTH = "35">
</TD>
</TR>

<TR>
<TH ALIGN = "left">Email:</TH>
<TD>
<INPUT TYPE = "text" NAME = "client_email" SIZE = "35" MAXLENGTH = "35">
</TD>
</TR>

<TR>
<TH ALIGN = "left">Product:</TH>
<TD>
<SELECT NAME=item_name>
$OPTION_STRING
</SELECT>
</TD>
</TR>

<TR>
<TH ALIGN = "left">Comments</TH>
<TD>
<TEXTAREA WRAP = "virtual" NAME = "comments" ROWS = "5" COLS = "40">
</TEXTAREA>
```

453

```
        </TD>
        </TR>

        <TR>
        <TH ALIGN ="left">How satisfied are you</TH>
        <TD>
        <INPUT TYPE="radio" NAME="how_good" VALUE="5" CHECKED>Very</INPUT>
        <INPUT TYPE="radio" NAME="how_good" VALUE="4" >A lot</INPUT>
        <INPUT TYPE="radio" NAME="how_good" VALUE="3" >Somewhat</INPUT>
        <INPUT TYPE="radio" NAME="how_good" VALUE="2" >Not happy</INPUT>
        <INPUT TYPE="radio" NAME="how_good" VALUE="1" >Very unhappy</INPUT>
        </TD>
        </TR>
        </TABLE>

        <P>

        <CENTER>
        <INPUT NAME="submit_feedback" TYPE = "submit" VALUE = "Submit this
        information.">
        </CENTER>

        </BLOCKQUOTE>
        </FORM>

        <TABLE>
        <TR><TD><H3>Here's what our other customers said:</H3></TD></TR>
        </TABLE>

        $CUSTOMER_FEEDBACK

        </BODY>
        </HTML>
        END_OF_HTML
}
```

How It Works

This script combines the use of the DBI and the CGI.pm modules. CGI.pm is a large module, and its creator Lincoln Stein has written a full book on using it – *Official Guide To Programming with CGI.pm*, published by John Wiley and Sons, 1998. However, in this example, we've used CGI.pm only for parsing input from HTML forms. Let's look at the code step-by-step:

```
use CGI::Carp qw(fatalsToBrowser);
```

In addition to the DBI and CGI.pm modules, we also use CGI::Carp. This line traps all fatal calls and passes the failure messages to the browser. You will find this extremely helpful during the debugging process.

```
$DBH =
DBI->connect("DBI:mysql:bmsimple;mysql_read_default_file=/etc/bmsimple.cnf")
        or die "Cannot connect: " . $DBI::errstr;
```

Since we are connecting to the database server from a web server, certain things must be done differently:

- ❏ You should take care to see that your `cgi-bin` directory is outside the web server's 'DocumentRoot'. This is necessary to prevent people from scanning your CGI code for security holes.

- ❏ Keeping user names and passwords in the CGI code is dangerous anyway, so we keep them in a separate file – `/etc/bmsimple.cnf`. If the `httpd` process runs with the credentials of the user 'apache', the 'apache' user must have ownership of `/etc/bmsimple.cnf`. Here's a sample `bmsimple.cnf` file:

```
[client]
host=mysql.server.name
user=jon
password=secret
```

- ❏ We then use the `mysql_read_default_file` modifier in the data source name in order to read in the connection parameters.

```
$CGI = new CGI();
```

The next step is the creation of a CGI object.

```
if ($CGI->param( "submit_feedback" ) ) {
    add_feedback_to_database( $CGI, $DBH );
}
else {
    display_suggestion_page( $CGI, $DBH );
}
```

These lines contain the flow of the entire script. If the feedback has been submitted, then we call the `add_feedback_to_database()` method, otherwise we just display the page using the `display_suggestion_page()` method. Both the methods require the CGI object and the database handle as parameters. We've used the `param()` method of the CGI object to determine the value of the `submit_feedback` parameter.

Now let's take a look at how `add_feedback_to_database()` works:

```
my $cgi = shift;
my $dbh = shift;
my ($suggestion_text,$customer_name,$email,$item_name,
$satisfaction_val, $field_list, $value_list, $sql);
```

We read in the arguments and declare the variables we'll be using. The arguments are shifted out of the '@_' array using the `shift` function.

```
$suggestion_text   = $cgi->param("comments");
$customer_name     = $cgi->param("customer_name");
$email             = $cgi->param("client_email");
$item_name         = $cgi->param("item_name");
$satisfaction_val  = $cgi->param("how_good");
```

Next we read in all the parameters that have come in from the HTML form.

```
#prepare the query for inserting feedback data
$value_list = qq{
            "$customer_name","$email","$item_name",
            "$suggestion_text","$satisfaction_val"
            };

$sql = qq{ INSERT INTO feedback VALUES($value_list)};
$dbh->do($sql) or die "Cannot insert: " . $dbh->errstr();
```

We create and execute an SQL statement for inserting the data that we've just read into the feedback table.

```
display_suggestion_page($cgi, $dbh);
```

Now that we've finished inserting the data into the database, we call the display_suggestion_page() method to display the updated page.

Next, let's look at the display_suggestion_page() method in order to complete our discussion of this example:

```
my $cgi = shift;
my $dbh = shift;

my ($option_val, $OPTION_STRING, $sth, $CUSTOMER_FEEDBACK,
    $comments, $name, $product);
```

In a manner similar to the add_feedback_to_database() method, we read in the arguments the method was called with and declare the variables we will need.

```
$sth = $dbh->prepare("SELECT description FROM item");
$sth->execute();

while ( ($option_val) = $sth->fetchrow_array()) {
   $OPTION_STRING .="<OPTION>$option_val</OPTION>\n";
}
$sth->finish();
```

To display a drop-down list containing all our product names, we pull out the names from the item table. Each name is surrounded by <option> and </option> tags and appended to a string.

```
$sth = $dbh->prepare("select name,product,comments from feedback");
$sth->execute();

#create a string that contains all the feedback
#received so far.
while ( ($name,$product,$comments) = $sth->fetchrow_array()) {
   $CUSTOMER_FEEDBACK .= qq{
   <TABLE BORDER=0 WRAP=256 CELLSPACING=0 CELLPADDING=0 COLS=1
   ROWS=2 BGCOLOR="#ffcb32">
   <TR><TD>
   <P STYLE="COLOR: #070568; TEXT-DECORATION: none; ">
   $name said the following about $product:
   </P>
   </TD></TR>
   <TR><TD bgcolor="white">
   $comments
   </TD></TR>
   </TABLE>
}
```

Next we fetch data from the feedback table and append it to a string after surrounding it with HTML to make it look like this:

Heres what our other customers said:

John Smith said the following about Carrier Bag:
The carrier bag was extremely useful in my bicycle tour across Europe. Light-weight, handy and water proof. It is a definite must buy for anyone serious about cross country bicycling.
Robert Jones said the following about Linux CD:
This is the best distribution of Linux I have ever seen...
Gregory Walters said the following about Speakers:
The speakers that I bought from the store arrived at my house in a slightly damaged package. However I am glad that the speakers themselves are first-rate and are giving me much better fidelity in the higher frequencies than my previous home-made enclosure

```
#print out the page
print "Content-type: text/html\n\n";
```

This line sends out the header of the HTML page that we are about to send to the browser. Here, one thing about writing CGI code that makes life easy is that whatever you print to the standard output gets sent to the browser.

```
print << "END_OF_HTML";
```

We use the 'here document' syntax of quoting our HTML for sending it to the browser. The rest of the HTML for displaying the page follows in here.

Let's consider only a couple of sections of the HTML:

```
<TR>
<TH ALIGN = "left">Product:</TH>
<TD>
<SELECT NAME=item_name>
    $OPTION_STRING
</SELECT>
</TD>
</TR>
```

This is where we're using the `$OPTION_STRING` variable that we created earlier. This string contains a list of all the products in our `item` table, surrounded by `<option>` and `</option>` tags.

```
<TABLE>
<TR><TD><H3>Here's what our other customers said:</H3></TD></TR>
</TABLE>

$CUSTOMER_FEEDBACK

</BODY>
</HTML>
```

This is where we put in the `$CUSTOMER_FEEDBACK` string that contains the data that we pulled out from the feedback table.

```
END_OF_HTML
```

This line acts as the delimiter. All HTML code till this line gets sent to the browser.

Even though we've not bothered about things like error checking or dealing with arbitrary input in this example, it'll serve as a good starting point for any web-based development you intend to do using Perl and MySQL.

Using DBIx::Easy

If you browse the database sections of CPAN, you will notice a number of DBIx modules. These are miscellaneous modules that enhance various aspects of DBI programming. One of these modules – DBIx::Easy (home page http://www.linuxia.de/DBIx/Easy/), is a simplified interface to DBI. DBIx::Easy supports only a limited subset of DBDs, but fortunately MySQL is one of them.

This module makes some database operations look different from what we have seen so far. Here's some simple Perl code that uses DBIx::Easy, to demonstrate some of its features:

```
#!/usr/bin/perl -w

use DBIx::Easy;
use strict;

sub myErrorHandler
```

```
{
    my( $statement, $err, $msg ) = @_;
    die"Oops, \"$statement\" failed ($err) - $msg";
}

# we have to specify the DB type and the dbname explicitly
my $conn = new DBIx::Easy("mysql", "bmsimple");

$conn->install_handler(\&myErrorHandler);

#process() is similar to a do()
$conn->process("CREATE TABLE number(value INT(11), name CHAR(30))");

#the statement that follows can also be read as:
#insert into table name('name','value') values ('John','42')
$conn->insert("number", name => "John",      value => 42);
$conn->insert("number", name => "Harry",     value => 23);
$conn->insert("number", name => "Timothy",   value => 23);
$conn->insert("number", name => "Mary",      value => 22);
$conn->insert("number", name => "Thomas",    value => 42);

#returns a reference to a hash of names and values where value = 23
my $numbers = $conn->makemap("number", "name", "value", "value = 23");

print "The following names have the value '23' associated with them\n";
foreach my $name (keys(%$numbers)) {
    print $name, " has value ", $$numbers{$name}, "\n";
}

#for all fields where the value = 42, the 'name' field will be updated
#so that it contains the string "Zaphod"
$conn->update("number", "value = 42", name => "Zaphod");
print "for all fields where the value = 42, the 'name' field will be updated so
that it contains the string 'Zaphod'.verify this manually...\n";

#all entries with value = 23 will be deleted.
$conn->process("DELETE FROM number WHERE value = 23");
print "All entries where the value = 23 will be deleted, verify this
manually...\n";
```

> **There could be a problem with the above code in case you are running it on Windows. Check your configuration in such cases. It works perfectly fine on a Linux machine, so do all the other code examples used in this chapter.**

Now, this looks quite a bit different from the earlier code. This is because the methods that DBIx::Easy provides us with are called process, insert, update, and makemap (query).

Before we get to those, notice how the error handler is installed: instead of testing each function for success or failure (which, admittedly, we have not been particularly rigorous about in earlier examples), we can rely on the handler being called on any error. In this case, all it does is abort the program with an error message, but you may provide something more sophisticated in your own programs.

The process(), insert(), and update() methods should be fairly obvious, but makemap deserves some explanation. This function takes the name of a table, two column names, and an optional where clause:

```
$conn->makemap($table, $keycol, $valuecol, $where)
```

This effectively executes the query:

```
SELECT $keycol, $valuecol FROM $table WHERE $where
```

and the results are inserted into a hash as if by the following code fragment:

```
while(my ($key, $value) = $sth->fetchrow_array) {
    $map{$key} = $value;
}
```

Since a hash can map each key onto only one value, multiple mappings in the source table will be lost. For example, if the table contained two rows (A, B) and (A, C), only one of those will appear in the resultant hash since the earlier one returned from the database will be overwritten by the later one. Another limitation is that only two columns can be processed at a time, unlike a general query that can return any specified number of columns. Note that this is not the same as the hash returned by the fetchrow_hashref function in DBI; fetchrow_hashref() returns a single row, with the key being the field name and the value being the data in the field.

Summary

We have examined a number of ways of accessing MySQL databases from Perl, letting us use its powerful string manipulation capabilities to avoid the task of writing C code to do the same thing. Although, as with everything else in the Perl universe, there are numerous ways to use databases with Perl, we concentrated on what is probably the most important of them all as far as MySQL programming is concerned, the database-independent layer, DBI. Within the scope of DBI, we have the option of easily using other database backends with the same client code. We have also seen an example of DBI in action in a web environment. Finally we looked at DBIx::Easy, a module that simplifies our programming job.

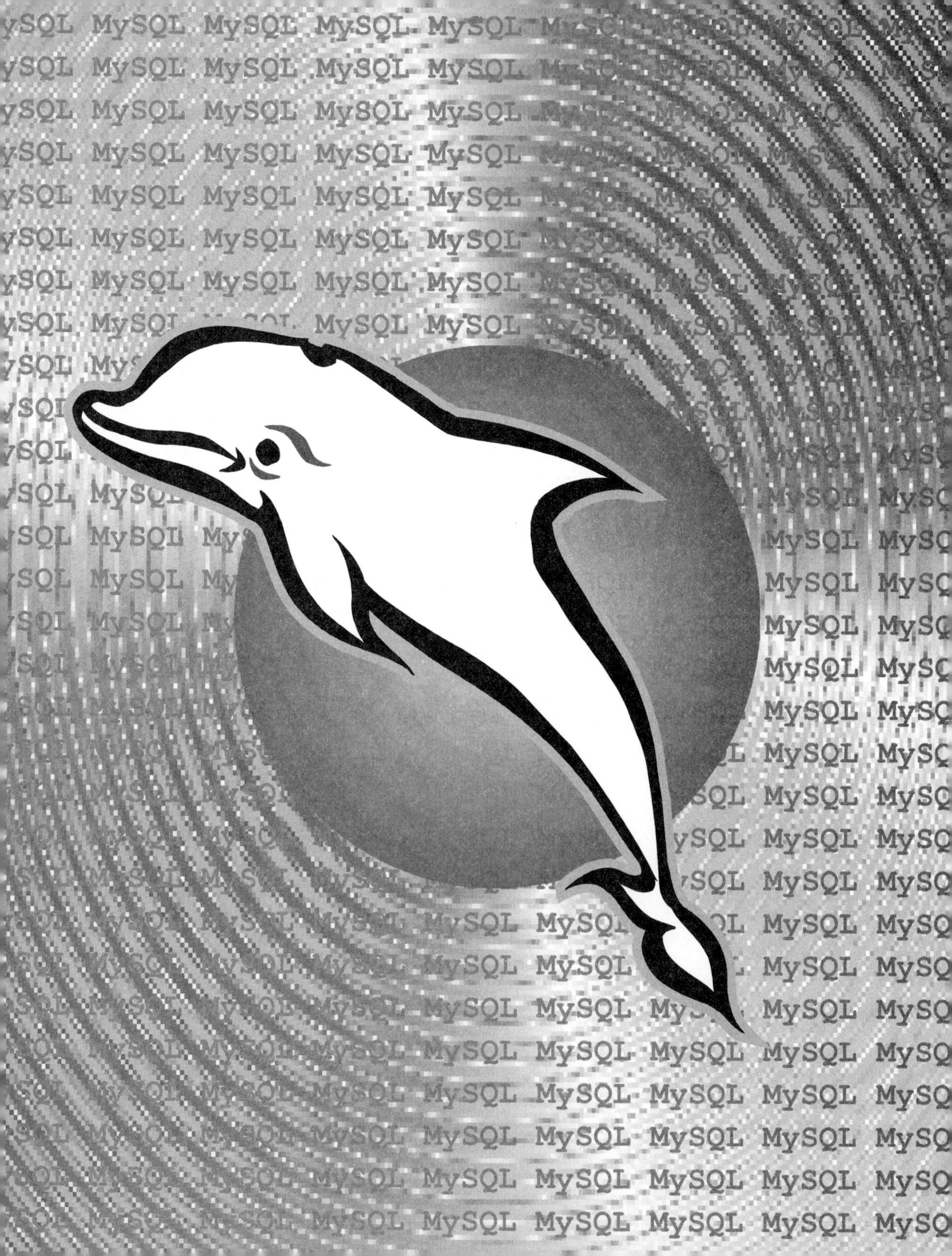
MySQL

15

Accessing MySQL from Java

Java has evolved as one of the most powerful platforms for developing enterprise application over the last five years because of its support for platform independence, rich set of APIs, and an overwhelming amount of industry support. Since the advent of Java, APIs have been developed for accessing external resources from Java language programs. JDBC (Java Database Connectivity) has been the standard used by Java language programs for accessing relational databases since the advent of Java as one of the most powerful platforms for enterprise application development.

In this chapter we will cover the JDBC API in detail and learn how Java language programs can use JDBC for accessing relational data residing in MySQL databases. We are going to assume some knowledge of the Java programming language. If you are unfamiliar with Java, you might want to explore some of the following resources first:

❑ *Beginning Java 2* by Ivor Horton, Wrox Press (ISBN-81-7366-154-5). This book explains fully this object-oriented programming language.

❑ *Thinking in Java* by Bruce Eckel, Prentice Hall (ISBN-0-13-027363-5). This is also a very good resource for understanding Java.

We will mainly look at:

❑ An overview of JDBC

❑ JDBC drivers

❑ Building the MySQL JDBC driver

❑ Creating JDBC connections

❑ Querying database and result set meta data

❑ Retrieving result sets from MySQL databases

❑ Use of JDBC statements for issuing various DDL and DML statements

❑ Use of JDBC prepared statements for issuing precompiled SQL statements

❑   Use of JDBC callable statements for executing stored procedures

❑   Batch updates

❑   A brief overview of the new features mentioned in the JDBC 3.0 API

In the end, we will conclude the chapter by building a GUI-based Java application accessing MySQL database.

JDBC Overview

JDBC is a standard API that can be used by programs written in Java for accessing external resource managers, mainly relational databases, in a resource manager-independent manner. This means a Java application written using standard JDBC classes and interfaces is portable across databases from different RDBMS vendors if it uses only standard ANSI-compliant SQL. The JDBC API consists of the core JDBC API and the extension API.

The core API mainly defines the standard interfaces for:

❑   Creating a connection to the database

❑   Creating statements

❑   Accessing result sets

❑   Querying database and result set meta data

The core classes and interfaces are defined in the `java.sql` package and are available with the Java 2 Platform Standard Edition (J2SE).

The extension API defines more sophisticated interfaces for handling XA resources, distributed transactions, pooled connections, and connection factories. XA resources are used for handling distributed transactions and two-phase commits, where a single transaction may need to span multiple databases and connections. These classes and interfaces belong to the `javax.sql` package and are available with the Java 2 Platform Enterprise Edition (J2EE).

We will concentrate on the JDBC core API here.

JDBC Drivers

The JDBC API only defines interfaces for the objects used for performing various database-related tasks like opening and closing connections, executing SQL statements, and retrieving the results. It doesn't provide the implementation classes for these interfaces. However, portable Java language programs need not be aware of the implementation classes and should only use the standard interfaces. As good object-oriented programmers, we all write our programs to interfaces and not implementations.

Either the resource manager vendor or a third party provides the implementation classes for the standard JDBC interface. These software implementations are called **JDBC drivers**. JDBC drivers transform the standard JDBC calls to the external resource manager specific API calls. The diagram below depicts how a database client written in Java accesses an external resource manager using the JDBC API and the JDBC driver:

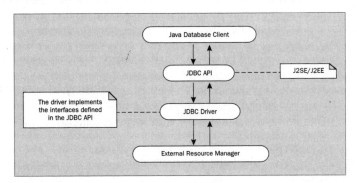

Depending on the mechanism of implementation, JDBC drivers are broadly classified into four types.

Type 1 – JDBC-ODBC Bridge

JDBC drivers implement the JDBC API on top of ODBC (Open Database Connectivity). These drivers are not generally portable because of the dependency on native libraries. These drivers translate the JDBC calls to ODBC calls and ODBC sends the request to the external data source using native library calls. The JDBC-ODBC driver that comes with the software distribution for J2SE is an example of type 1 driver.

Type 2 – Native-API / Partly Java Driver

Type 2 drivers are written in a mixture of Java and native code. They use vendor specific native API for accessing the data source. These drivers transform the JDBC calls to vendor specific calls using the vendor's native library. These drivers are also not portable like type 1 drivers because of the dependency on native code.

Type 3 – Net-protocol / All Java Driver

Type 3 drivers use an intermediate middleware server for accessing the external data sources. The calls to the middleware server are database independent. But the middleware server makes vendor specific native calls for accessing the data source. In this case the driver is purely written in Java.

Type 4 – Native-protocol / All Java Driver

Type 4 drivers again, are written in pure Java and they implement the JDBC interfaces and translate the JDBC-specific calls to vendor-specific data access calls. They implement the data transfer and network protocol for the target resource manager. This is the reason why most of the leading database vendors provide Type 4 drivers for accessing their database servers.

Building the MySQL JDBC Driver

There are many open source freeware JDBC drivers available for accessing MySQL from Java applications. One of the most commonly used is the MM.MySQL, which is the most popularly used Type 4 driver that is available under the GNU library general public license. Another Type 4 JDBC driver that is available on free license for private use may be downloaded from http://www.users.voicenet.com/~zellert/tjFM/.

In this section we will see how to build this MySQL JDBC driver. The steps to follow are:

❏   The latest version of the driver is 2.0.7 and may be downloaded by accessing the URL http://mmmysql.sourceforge.net.

❏   The downloaded .jar file is called mm.mysql-2.0.7-you-must-unjar-me.jar, which is the current relevant version.

❏   Unpack the .jar file with the following command:

```
jar xf mm.mysql-2.0.7-you-must-unjar-me.jar
```

❏   This will create the following directory structure:

```
mm.mysql - 2.0.7\build.xml
mm.mysql - 2.0.7\mm.sql - 2.0.7 -bin.jar
mm.mysql - 2.0.7\lib
mm.mysql - 2.0.7\org
mm.mysql - 2.0.7\testsuit
```

❏   The build.xml file contains the build scripts, if you are building the driver from the source files. The build script uses the ANT build tool from the Apache Software Foundation. You can find more information about the ANT build tool from http://www.apache.org.

❏   The .jar file is the precompiled and prebuilt JDBC driver.

❏   The lib directory contains the files required for building the driver from source files.

❏   The org directory contains the source and class files that implement the JDBC interfaces. These class files are included in the .jar file. Instead of having the .jar file in the classpath, you may have this directory in the classpath.

❏   The testsuite directory contains the sample files that use the JDBC driver for accessing MySQL databases.

DriverManager and Driver

The java.sql package defines an interface called java.sql.Driver that needs to be implemented by all the JDBC drivers. In addition to this, a class called java.sql.DriverManager that acts as the interface to the database clients needs to be implemented as well. It performs tasks like connecting to external resource managers and setting log streams.

When a JDBC client requests the `DriverManager` to make a connection to the external resource manager, it delegates the task to an appropriate driver class implemented by the JDBC driver provided either by the resource manager vendor or a third party. In this section, we will discuss in detail the roles of `java.sql.DriverManager` and `java.sql.Driver` in JDBC API.

java.sql.DriverManager

The primary task of the class `DriverManager` is to manage the various JDBC drivers registered. In the section on `java.sql.Driver` we will see how JDBC drivers register themselves with the `DriverManager`. The section also provides methods for:

❑   Getting connection to databases

❑   Managing JDBC logs

❑   Setting login timeout

Managing Drivers

We will start with the `java.sql.Driver` interface:

```
public static void registerDriver(Driver driver) throws SQLException
```

This method is normally used by the implementation classes of the interface `java.sql.Driver`, provided by the JDBC drivers, to register themselves with the `DriverManager`. This method throws an instance of `java.sql.SQLException` if a database error occurs. `DriverManager` uses registered drivers for delegating database connection requests.

```
public static void deregisterDriver(Driver driver) throws SQLException
```

This method is used for deregistering a driver that is already registered with the `DriverManager`.

```
public static Enumeration getDrivers()
```

This method returns an enumeration of all the drivers currently registered with the `DriverManager`.

```
public static Driver getDriver(String url) throws SQLException
```

This method is used for getting the driver registered with the `DriverManager` corresponding to the passed JDBC URL. This method throws an instance of `SQLException` if a database access error occurs. JDBC URLs are used for uniquely identifying the resource manager type and resource manager location. This means that even though a JDBC driver can handle any number of connections identified by different JDBC URLs, the basic URL format including the protocol and subprotocol is specific to the driver used. JDBC clients specify the JDBC URL when they request a connection.

The `DriverManager` can find a driver that matches the requested URL from the list of registered drivers and delegates the connection request to that driver if it finds a match. JDBC URLs normally take the following format:

```
<protocol>:<sub-protocol>:<resource>
```

The protocol is always JDBS and the subprotocol and resource depends on the type of resource manager you use. The URL for MySQL is in the format:

```
jdbc:mysql://[hostname][:port]/[dbname][?param1=value1][&param2=value2]...
```

Here `host` is the host address on which `mysqld` is running and `database` is the name of the database to which the client wishes to connect. The optional parameters that are supported by the URL are listed in the table below. These values may also be passed to the driver manager method for getting the connection using a properties object.

Parameter	Description	Default
User	The user to connect as	None
password	The password to use when connecting	None
autoReconnect	Should the driver attempt to reconnect if the connection dies?	False
maxReconnects	If `autoReconnect` is enabled, how many times should the driver attempt to reconnect?	3
initialTimeout	If `autoReconnect` is enabled, the initial time to wait between reconnect attempts (seconds)	2
maxRows	The maximum number of rows to return (0 means return all rows)	0
useUnicode	Should the driver use Unicode character encoding when handling strings? (True/False)	False
characterEncoding	If `useUnicode` is true, what character encoding should the driver use when dealing with strings?	None
relaxAutocommit	If the version of MySQL the driver connects to do not support transactions, allow calls to `COMMIT`, `ROLLBACK` and `setAutoCommit`?	False
capitalizeTypeNames	Capitalize type names in Database Meta Data	False

Please note that these parameters may also be specified using a `properties` object when the connection is created as described in the next section.

Managing Connections

This section discusses the methods provided by the `DriverManager` class for managing connections to databases.

```
public static Connection getConnection(String url) throws SQLException
```

This method gets a connection to the database specified by the JDBC URL. The class `java.sql.Connection` is covered in detail in a later section. This method throws an instance of `SQLException` if a database access error occurs.

```
public static Connection getConnection(String url,String user,String
                password) throws SQLException
```

This method gets a connection to the database specified by the JDBC URL using the specified user name and password. This method throws an instance of `SQLException` if a database access error occurs.

```
public static Connection getConnection(String url,Properties info)
                throws SQLException
```

This method gets a connection to the database specified by the JDBC URL. The instance of the class `java.util.Properties` is used for specifying the custom properties defined in the last section. This method throws an instance of `SQLException` if a database access error occurs.

Managing JDBC Logging

This section discusses the methods provided by the `DriverManager` class for managing JDBC logs:

```
public static PrintWriter getLogWriter()
```

This method gets a handle to an instance of the class `java.io.PrintWriter` to which the logging and tracing information are written. This method throws an instance of `SQLException` if a database access error occurs.

```
public static void setLogWriter(PrintWriter writer)
```

This method sets the `PrintWriter` to which all the log information is written by the `DriverManager` and all the registered drivers.

```
public static void println(String message) throws SQLException
```

This method writes the message to the current log stream.

Managing Login Timeouts

This section discusses the methods provided by the `DriverManager` class for managing logins.

```
public static int getLoginTimeout()
```

This method gets the maximum time in seconds the `DriverManager` would wait for getting a connection.

```
public static void setLogWriter(PrintWriter writer)
```

This method sets the `PrintWriter` for logging the JDBC calls.

java.sql.Driver

This interface defines the methods that need to be implemented by all JDBC drivers. The driver implementation classes are required to have static initialization code to register them with the current `DriverManager`, so that the `DriverManager` has the driver in the list of registered drivers and can delegate a connection request to an appropriate driver class depending on the JDBC URL specified. If you take a look at the source code for the class `org.gjt.mm.mysql.Driver`, which is the driver implementation for MySQL used in this chapter (in the `org/mm/mysql/` folder of the MySQL JDBC installation directory), you will find the following code snippet:

```
static {
    try {
        java.sql.DriverManager.registerDriver(new Driver());
    } catch (SQLException e) {
        e.printStackTrace();
    }
}
```

Whenever the class loader loads the class `org.gjt.mm.mysql.Driver`, it registers itself with the `DriverManager`. Hence the JDBC client needs to load the class definition of the driver they wish to use so that the `DriverManager` can use it for obtaining database connections. One obvious way of doing this is using the static `forName` method on the class `java.lang.Class` as shown below:

```
try {
    Class.forName("org.gjt.mm.mysql.Driver");
}catch(ClassNotFoundException e) {
    //Handle exception
}
```

This will throw a `ClassNotFoundException` if the class `org.gjt.mm.mysql.Driver` is not found in the classpath. Hence you need to make sure that the `mm.mysql-2.0.7-bin.jar` file which contains the required classes is available in the classpath. The sequence diagram shown below depicts a typical JDBC client getting a connection to a MySQL database called `bmsimple` running locally using the user name 'meeraj' and the password 'waheeda'. (The user name and password shown below are specific to the database running on the author's system). You may create users with appropriate passwords that can be used for obtaining a connection.

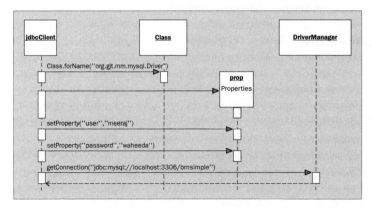

The code snippet below corresponds to the sequence of events depicted in the diagram shown above:

```
try {

    //Load the JDBC driver
    Class.forName("org.gjt.mm.mysql.Driver");

    //Create a properties object with user name and password
    Properties prop = new Properties();
    prop.setProperty("user","meeraj");
    prop.setProperty("password","waheeda");

    //Set the JDBC URL
    String url = "jdbc:mysql://localhost:3306/bmsimple";

    //Get the connection
    Connection con = DriverManager.getConnection(url,prop);

} catch(ClassNotFoundException e) {
    //Handle exception
} catch(SQLException e) {
    //Handle exception
}
```

Now we will have a look at the methods defined by the interface `java.sql.Driver`.

```
public boolean acceptsURL(String url) throws SQLException
```

This method returns `true` if the driver implementation class can open a connection to the specified URL. The implementation classes normally return `true` if they can recognize the subprotocol specified in the JDBC URL. This method throws an instance of `SQLException` if a database access error occurs.

```
public Connection connect(String url,Properties info) throws SQLException
```

This method returns a connection to the specified URL using the properties defined in the argument `info`. The `DriverManager` normally calls this method when it receives connection requests from JDBC clients. This method throws an instance of `SQLException` if a database access error occurs.

```
public int getMajorVersion()
```

This method returns the major revision number of the driver.

```
public int getMinorVersion()
```

This method returns the minor revision number of the driver.

```
public boolean jdbcCompliant()
```

This method returns `true` if the driver is JDBC-compliant. A fully compliant JDBC driver should conform strictly to the JDBC API and SQL 92 Entry Level. The various standards and specifications related to SQL may be found at http://www.opengroup.org. If it doesn't then this method should return `false`.

Connections

The interface `java.sql.Connection` defines the methods required for a persistent connection to the database. The JDBC driver vendor implements this interface. A database 'vendor neutral' client never uses the implementation class and will always use only the interface. This interface defines methods for the following tasks:

❑ Create statements, prepared statements, and callable statements. The JDBC clients use different types of statements for issuing SQL statements to the database. Statements are discussed in later sections.

❑ For getting and setting auto-commit mode.

❑ Getting **meta** information about the database.

❑ Committing and rolling back transactions.

In this section, we will cover the various methods defined in the interface `java.sql.Connection` in detail.

Creating Statements

The interface `java.sql.Connection` defines a set of methods for creating database statements. Database statements are used for sending SQL statements to the database.

```
public Statement createStatement() throws SQLException
```

This method is used for creating instances of the interface `java.sql.Statement`. This interface can be used for sending SQL statements to the database. The interface `java.sql.Statement` is normally used for sending SQL statements that don't take any arguments. This method throws an instance of `SQLException` if a database access error occurs.

```
public Statement createStatement(int resType, int resConcurrency)
        throws SQLException
```

This is the same as the previous method but it lets the JDBC clients specify the result set type and result set concurrency. Result sets are used for retrieving the results back to the client from the database. We will discuss them further later in the chapter. The result set type identifies the direction in which the result set can be traversed whereas concurrency defines how multiple threads can access the result set simultaneously.

```
public PreparedStatement prepareStatement(String sql) throws SQLException
```

This method is used for creating instances of the interface `java.sql.PreparedStatement`. The interface `java.sql.PreparedStatement` is normally used for sending SQL statements that take any arguments. `PreparedStatement` can precompile and store SQL statements. This method throws an instance of `SQLException` if a database access error occurs. The SQL statements passed to `prepared statements` can use parameter placeholders using `'?'` for sending `IN` parameters.

```
public PreparedStatement prepareStatement (String sql,int resType,
        int resConcurrency) throws SQLException
```

This is the same as the previous method, but it lets the JDBC clients specify the result set type and result set concurrency.

```
public CallableStatement prepareCall(String sql) throws SQLException
```

This method is used for creating instances of the interface `java.sql.CallableStatement`. The interface `java.sql.CallableStatement` is normally used for sending calls to the database's stored procedures that take `IN` and `OUT` parameters. This method throws an instance of `SQLException` if a database access error occurs. The stored procedure calls, passed to prepared statements, can use parameter placeholders using `'?'` for specifying both `IN` and `OUT` parameters.

```
public CallableStatement prepareCall (String sql,int resType, int resConcurrency)
throws SQLException
```

This is the same as the previous method, but it lets the JDBC clients specify the result set type and result set concurrency.

Handling Transactions

The connection interface defines a set of methods for handling database transactions.

```
public void setAutoCommit(boolean autoCommit) throws SQLException
```

This method sets the auto-commit mode. If set to `true`, SQL statements are automatically committed, otherwise the clients need to issue an explicit `commit`. This method throws an instance of `SQLException` if a database access error occurs.

```
public boolean getAutoCommit() throws SQLException
```

This method gets the current auto-commit mode. This method throws an instance of `SQLException` if a database access error occurs.

```
public void commit() throws SQLException
```

This method commits the current transaction associated with the connection. This method throws an instance of `SQLException` if a database access error occurs. Please note that this works only with database management systems that support transactions, and standard MySQL doesn't support transactions.

```
public void rollback() throws SQLException
```

This method rolls back the current transaction associated with the connection. This method throws an instance of SQLException if a database access error occurs.

```
public int getTransactionIsolation() throws SQLException
```

This method gets the current transaction isolation level. Transaction isolation level, discussed in Chapter 9, *Transactions and Locking*, dictates whether dirty reads, repeatable reads, and phantom reads can be performed or not. This method throws an instance of SQLException if a database access error occurs.

```
public void getTransactionIsolation(int level) throws SQLException
```

This method sets the transaction isolation level. It throws an instance of SQLException if a database access error occurs.

Database Meta data

The connection interface provides a method to get the database meta data.

```
public DatabaseMetaData getMetaData() throws SQLException
```

This method returns an instance of a class that implements java.sql.DatabaseMetaData interface. This method throws an instance of SQLException if a database access error occurs. This interface provides 149 methods of querying different information about the database. Please refer to the Java documentation for a complete listing of these methods. The documentation may be downloaded from http://www.javasoft.com.

Retrieving MySQL Meta data

In this section we will write an example to fetch a very small subset of the MySQL meta data. The class will first load the MySQL JDBC driver and get a connection to the database called bmsimple running on localhost. Then it obtains a handle to the database meta data from the connection and prints the following information:

❑ Database product name

❑ Database product version

❑ Driver major version

❑ Driver minor version

❑ Driver name

❑ Driver version

❑ JDBC URL

❑ Transaction support

❑ Information on whether MySQL uses local files to store tables

The source for the class is listed below. Save this into `MySQLMetaData.java`:

```java
import java.sql.Connection;
import java.sql.DatabaseMetaData;
import java.sql.DriverManager;

public class MySQLMetaData {

    public static void main(String args[]) throws Exception {

        Class.forName("org.gjt.mm.mysql.Driver");
        String url = "jdbc:mysql://localhost:3306/bmsimple";

        Connection con = DriverManager.getConnection(url);
        DatabaseMetaData dbmd = con.getMetaData();

        System.out.print("Database Product Name : ");
        System.out.println(dbmd.getDatabaseProductName());

        System.out.print("Database Product Version : ");
        System.out.println(dbmd.getDatabaseProductVersion());

        System.out.print("Driver Major Version : ");
        System.out.println(dbmd.getDriverMajorVersion());

        System.out.print("Driver Minor Version : ");
        System.out.println(dbmd.getDriverMinorVersion());

        System.out.print("Driver Name : ");
        System.out.println(dbmd.getDriverName());

        System.out.print("Driver Version : ");
        System.out.println(dbmd.getDriverVersion());

        System.out.print("JDBC URL : ");
        System.out.println(dbmd.getURL());

        System.out.print("Supports Transactions : ");
        System.out.println(dbmd.supportsTransactions());

        System.out.print("Uses Local Files : ");
        System.out.println(dbmd.usesLocalFiles());

        con.close();
    }
}
```

How It Works

First of all, you have to compile the class with the following command:

```
javac MySQLMetaData.java
```

Invoke the Java interpreter on the class with the `mm.mysql-2.0.7-bin.jar` file in the classpath. Alternatively you may use the `-cp` or `-classpath` command line switch to specify the `jar` file when you invoke the JVM:

475

```
Java MySQLMetaData
```

This will produce the following output depending on the version of MySQL you are running. Please make sure that you have the mm.mysql-2.0.7-bin.jar file in your system classpath when you invoke the JVM:

```
Database Product Name : MySQL
Database Product Version : 3.23.37 -debug
Driver Major Version : 2
Driver Minor Version : 0
Driver Name : Mark Matthews' MySQL Driver
Driver Version : 2.0.7
JDBC URL : jdbc:mysql://localhost:3306/bmsimple
Supports Transactions : true
Uses Local Files : false
```

The database meta data interface can be used to get a lot more information than this. For example, which SQL features are supported or getting catalog and tablenames. Please refer to the Java documentation for more details.

JDBC Result Sets

A JDBC result set represents a two dimensional array of data produced as a result of executing SQL SELECT statements against databases using JDBC statements. JDBC statements are covered in detail in the next section. JDBC result sets are represented by the interface java.sql.ResultSet. The JDBC vendor provides the implementation class for this interface.

Result Set Types and Concurrency

Executing appropriate methods against JDBC statement objects creates objects of type java.sql.ResultSet. As we have already seen in the section on connections, when we create statement objects we can specify the type and scroll sensitivity of the result sets that may be created by those statement objects. In this section, we will have a look at result set types and scroll sensitivity in detail.

Type

Result sets can be of one of the following types:

❑ TYPE_FORWARD_ONLY: Forward-only result sets can be traversed only in the forward direction. This means once you move the current cursor pointer to the nth row you can't move back to $(n-1)^{th}$ row. Please note that even though this option is a bit restrictive, it is the most efficient one as well.

❑ TYPE_SCROLL_INSENSITIVE: This type of result set objects is scrollable and not sensitive to changes made by other threads.

❑ TYPE_SCROLL_SENSITIVE: This type of result set objects is scrollable and sensitive to changes made by other threads.

The interface defines a method to get the result set type. The type can be set only when the statements are created using connection objects as explained in the previous section:

```
public int getType() throws SQLException
```

Concurrency

Results sets can have of one of the two following concurrency types:

- ❏ CONCUR_READ_ONLY: Concurrent read-only result sets are not updateable. Non-updateable result sets are more efficient and faster to access.

- ❏ CONCUR_UPDATEABLE: Concurrent updateable result sets are updateable.

The interface defines a method to get the result set type. The type can be set only when the statements are created using connection objects as explained in the previous section:

```
public int getConcurrency() throws SQLException
```

Traversing Result Sets

The interface `java.sql.ResultSet` defines various methods for traversing the result sets, manipulating the cursor position, and accessing `fetch direction`. In this section, we will have a look at these methods in detail.

Scrolling Result Sets

Let us have a look at the methods available for scrolling result sets.

```
public boolean next() throws SQLException
```

This method moves the current cursor pointer to the next row and returns `true` if there are more rows, otherwise it returns `false`. A `boolean` value `false` is returned when the cursor is at the last row in the result set. An instance of `SQLException` is thrown if a database access error occurs.

```
public boolean first() throws SQLException
```

This method moves the current cursor pointer to the first row and returns `true` if the cursor is on the first row, otherwise it returns `false`. This method cannot be executed against a forward-only cursor. An instance of `SQLException` is thrown if a database access error occurs.

```
public boolean last() throws SQLException
```

This method moves the current cursor pointer to the last row and returns `true` if the cursor is on the last row, otherwise `false`. This method cannot be executed against a forward-only cursor. An instance of `SQLException` is thrown if a database access error occurs.

```
public boolean absolute(int rows) throws SQLException
```

This method moves the current cursor pointer forward or backward from the start or end of the result set to the row specified by the argument. The cursor is moved forward from the start if the value of rows is positive, and it is moved backwards from the end if the value of rows is negative. An instance of SQLException is thrown if a database access error occurs.

```
public boolean relative(int row) throws SQLException
```

This method moves the current cursor pointer forward or backward from the current position to the row specified by the argument. The cursor is moved forward if the value of rows is positive, and it is moved backwards if the value of rows is negative. An instance of SQLException is thrown if a database access error occurs.

```
public boolean previous() throws SQLException
```

This method moves the current cursor pointer to the previous row. This method cannot be executed against a forward-only cursor. An instance of SQLException is thrown if a database access error occurs.

```
public void beforeFirst() throws SQLException
```

This method moves the cursor to the start of the result set, before the first row. An instance of SQLException is thrown if a database access error occurs.

```
public boolean afterLast() throws SQLException
```

This method moves the cursor to the end of the result set, after the last row. An instance of SQLException is thrown if a database access error occurs.

Querying the Cursor Position

In this section, we will see the different methods available for querying the cursor position.

```
public boolean isBeforeFirst() throws SQLException
```

Returns true if the cursor position is before the first row. An instance of SQLException is thrown if a database access error occurs.

```
public boolean isAfterLast() throws SQLException
```

Returns true if the cursor position is after the last row. An instance of SQLException is thrown if a database access error occurs.

```
public boolean isFirst() throws SQLException
```

Returns true if the cursor position is at the first row. An instance of SQLException is thrown if a database access error occurs.

```
public void isLast() throws SQLException
```

Returns true if the cursor position is at the last row. An instance of SQLException is thrown if a database access error occurs.

Fetch Direction and Size

Now we will have a look at the methods for manipulating the 'fetch direction' and size. These methods give a hint to the driver as to the direction and the size the rows will be fetched so that it can fetch records from the database accordingly.

```
public int getFetchDirection() throws SQLException
```

It returns the current fetch direction. An instance of SQLException is thrown if a database access error occurs. The JDBC API defines three fetch directions:

❑   FETCH_FORWARD

❑   FETCH_REVERSE

❑   FETCH_UNKNOWN

```
public void setFetchDirection(int direction) throws SQLException
```

This method sets the fetch direction. An instance of SQLException is thrown if a database access error occurs or a fetch direction other than FETCH_FORWARD to a forward-only result set.

```
public int getFetchSize() throws SQLException
```

It gets the current 'fetch size'. An instance of SQLException is thrown if a database access error occurs.

```
public void setFetchsize(int size) throws SQLException
```

This method gives a hint to the driver on the fetch size in rows. An instance of SQLException is thrown if a database access error occurs.

Accessing Result Set Data

The interface defines methods for getting data from the current row in the result set. The data can be retrieved as appropriate data types. These methods take the general format – getXXX(int col); where XXX can be one of the different types like int, short or string, and col is the column number in the current row from which data is to be fetched. Column numbers start from 1. Alternatively, you can specify the column names as well. Regardless of the data type, all columns can be fetched as a string. All these methods throw an instance of SQLException if a database error occurs.

The table overleaf shows some of the data access methods, and those that are missing can be extrapolated from the methods already described by referring to the JavaDoc:

Method Name	Purpose

`public boolean getBoolean(int i)`
 	
`public boolean getBoolean(String colName)`
	Gets the data in the specified column as a boolean.

`public int getInt(int i)`
 	
`public int getInt(String col)`
	Gets the data in the specified column as an integer.

`public String getString(int i)`
 	
`public String getString(String col)`
	Gets the data in the specified column as a string.

Updatable Result Sets

The result sets, which one can update, are created from statements that we created by specifying the result set concurrency as CONCUR_UPDATEABLE. The data in such result sets can be modified, and rows can be added and removed. In this section we will have a look at the methods available for modifying the state of result set.

Deleting Data

The interface defines a method for deleting the current row from the result set as well as the database.

```
public void deleteRow() throws SQLException
```

This method deletes the current row from the result set and from the database. However you cannot call this method when the cursor is on insert row. Insert row is explained in the section, *Inserting Data*. An instance of SQLException is thrown if a database access error occurs.

```
public boolean rowDeleted() throws SQLException
```

This method checks whether the current row has been deleted. An instance of SQLException is thrown if a database access error occurs.

Updating Data

The result set interface defines a set of updateXXX methods for updating the data in the current row of the result set. However, these methods don't update the underlying data in the database. The table below lists a few of these methods and the rest can be extrapolated by referring to the JavaDoc:

Method Name	Purpose

`public void updateBoolean(int i, boolean x)`
 	
`public void updateBoolean(String col, boolean x)`
	Sets the data in the specified column to the specified boolean value.

Method Name	Purpose

`public void updateInt(int i, int x)`
 	
`public void updateInt(String col,int x)`
	Sets the data in the specified column to the specified int value.

`public void updateString(int i, String x)`
 	
`public void updateString(String col, String x)`
	Sets the data in the specified column to the specified string value.

```
public void updateRow() throws SQLException
```

This method can be called to update the underlying database with the data changed using the updateXXX methods. An instance of SQLException is thrown if a database access error occurs.

```
public void refreshRow() throws SQLException
```

This method refreshes the current row with the most recent data from the database. An instance of SQLException is thrown if a database access error occurs.

```
public void cancelRowUpdates() throws SQLException
```

This method cancels the updates made to the current row. An instance of SQLException is thrown if a database access error occurs.

```
public boolean rowUpdated() throws SQLException
```

This method checks whether the current row has been updated. An instance of SQLException is thrown if a database access error occurs.

Inserting Data

Result sets have a special row called **insert row** for adding data to the underlying database. The cursor can be moved to the insert row by using the following method:

```
public boolean moveToInsertRow() throws SQLException
```

From the insert row the cursor can be moved back to the previous row using the following method. This method throws an instance of SQLException if a database access error occurs or if the result set is not updateable:

```
public boolean moveToCurrentRow() throws SQLException
```

Once the cursor is on the insert row, appropriate updateXXX methods can be called to set the data for the new row. After this, the following method can be called to create the new record in the database:

```
public boolean insertRow() throws SQLException
```

An instance of SQLException is thrown if a database access error occurs or if the cursor is not on insert row.

Other Relevant Methods

This section explains the other relevant methods available with the interface java.sql.ResultSet.

```
public void close() throws SQLException
```

This method releases the database and JDBC resources. An instance of SQLException is thrown if a database access error occurs. Please note that the garbage collector doesn't free up the database resources when the connection object goes out of scope.

```
public ResultSetMetaData getMetaData() throws SQLException
```

This method gets the result set meta data as an instance of a class that implements the interface java.sql.ResultSetMetaData. This interface defines a host of methods for accessing the result set meta data including:

❑   Catalog names

❑   Column class name

❑   Column count

❑   Column display size

❑   Column labels

❑   Column types

❑   Column type name

Please refer to the JavaDoc for a complete listing.

JDBC Statements

JDBC API defines three types of statements for sending SQL statements to the database:

❑   Statements: Statements are generally used for sending SQL statements that don't take any arguments from the Java code. The methods required for statement objects are defined by the interface java.sql.Statement. The JDBC driver provider provides the implementation class for this interface.

❑   Prepared Statements: Prepared statements are generally used for sending precompiled SQL statements that take IN arguments. IN arguments are basically arguments passed into SQL commands or stored procedures whereas OUT arguments are arguments passed out from SQL stored procedures. The methods required for prepared statement objects are defined in the interface java.sql.PreparedStatement. This interface extends the java.sql.Statement.

❑   Callable Statements: Callable statements are generally used for making calls to database stored procedures and can take both IN and OUT arguments. The methods required for prepared statement objects are defined in the interface java.sql.CallableStatement. This interface extends the java.sql.PreparedStatement.

Statements

The interface java.sql.Statement is normally used for sending SQL statements that don't have IN or OUT parameters. The JDBC driver vendor provides the implementation class for this interface. The common methods required by the different JDBC statements are defined in this interface. The methods defined by java.sql.Statement can be broadly categorized as follows:

❑   Executing SQL statements

❑   Querying results and result sets

❑   Handling SQL batches

❑   Other miscellaneous methods

Executing SQL Statements

The interface java.sql.Statement defines methods for executing different SQL statements like SELECT, UPDATE, INSERT, DELETE, and CREATE.

```
public ResultSet executeQuery(String sql) throws SQLException
```

This method can be used for sending a SELECT statement to the database and getting back the result. An instance of SQLException is thrown if a database error occurs. An example code snippet is shown below:

```
Connection con = null;
try {
   con = DriverManager.getConnection(url,prop);
   Statement stmt = con.createStatement();
   ResultSet res = stmt.executeQuery("select * from MyTable");
} catch(SQLException e) {
   //Handle exception
} finally {
   if(con != null) con.close();
}
public boolean execute(String sql) throws SQLException
```

This method can be used for sending an SQL statement that may fetch multiple result sets like a stored procedure. This returns true if the next result is a result set object. An instance of SQLException is thrown if a database error occurs.

```
public int executeUpdate(String sql) throws SQLException
```

This method can be used for sending SQL statements that don't return result sets, like INSERT, UPDATE, and DELETE statements as well as data definition language statements. This returns the number of rows affected by the SQL statement. An instance of SQLException is thrown if a database error occurs.

Querying Results and Result Sets

The statement interface defines various methods for getting information about the result of executing an SQL statement.

```
public ResultSet getResultSet() throws SQLException
```

Although executing an SQL statement can create multiple result sets, a statement object can have only one result set open at a time. This is possible when the executed SQL statement is a stored procedure that generates multiple result sets. This method returns the current result set associated with the statement object. This method returns NULL if there is no more result set available or the next result is an update count generated by executing an UPDATE, INSERT or DELETE statement. An instance of SQLException is thrown if a database error occurs.

```
public int getUpdateCount() throws SQLException
```

This method returns the update count for the last executed UPDATE, INSERT, or DELETE statement. This method returns -1 when no more update count is available or the next result is a result set generated by executing a SELECT statement. An instance of SQLException is thrown if a database error occurs.

```
public boolean getMoreResults() throws SQLException
```

This gets the statement object's next result set. This method returns false when there is no more result set available or the next result is an update count. This method closes the current result set. An instance of SQLException is thrown if a database error occurs.

Methods are also provided for performing the following 'get' or 'set' tasks:

❑ The result set concurrency with which the statement was created

❑ The result set fetch direction

❑ fetch size.

Handling SQL Batches

The statement interface also provides methods for sending a batch of SQL statements to the database.

```
public void addBatch(String sql) throws SQLException
```

This method adds the specified SQL to the current batch. Generally the SQL statements are UPDATE, INSERT or DELETE. An instance of SQLException is thrown if a database error occurs.

```
public void clearBatch() throws SQLException
```

This method clears the current batch. An instance of SQLException is thrown if a database error occurs.

```
public int[] executeBatch() throws SQLException
```

This method executes the current batch and returns an array of updated counts. An instance of SQLException is thrown if a database error occurs.

Miscellaneous Methods

Miscellaneous methods include methods for:

❑ Getting and setting query time out

❑ Closing the statement to release resources (Please note that it is not a good practice to leave unused statements open as this may cause memory leaks in the application.)

❑ Getting and setting escape processing

❑ Getting and clearing SQL warnings

❑ Getting and setting cursor names (Please note that at the time of writing MySQL doesn't support cursors.)

An Example JDBC Client

In this section we will be using all the JDBC concepts we have learned. We will be writing a JDBC client that will perform the following tasks:

❑ Gets a connection to the database

❑ Creates a statement object

❑ Inserts two records into the customer table

❑ Selects those records back from the database

❑ Deletes those records

❑ Closes the connection

Try It Out – Sample JDBC Client

First, we need to import the relevant classes, like this:

```
import java.sql.Connection;
import java.sql.Statement;
import java.sql.ResultSet;
import java.sql.DriverManager;

public class StatementClient {

    public static void main(String args[]) throws Exception {
```

Load the JDBC driver and get a connection. Create a statement from the connection:

```
        Class.forName("org.gjt.mm.mysql.Driver");
        String url = "jdbc:mysql://localhost:3306/bmsimple";

        Connection con = DriverManager.getConnection(url);

        Statement stmt = con.createStatement();
```

Add two SQL statements for inserting records into the `customer` table into a batch:

```
System.out.println("Inserting records");
stmt.executeUpdate(
    "insert into customer(title,fname," +
    "lname,addressline,town,zipcode,phone) values " +
    "('Mr','Fred','Flintstone','31 Bramble Avenue'," +
    "'London','NT2 1AQ','023 9876')");
stmt.executeUpdate ("insert into customer(title,fname," +
    "lname,addressline,town,zipcode,phone) values " +
    "('Mr','Barney','Rubble','22 Ramsons Avenue'," +
    "'London','PWD LS1','111 2313')");
```

Execute the batch:

```
System.out.println("Records Inserted");
System.out.println();
```

Select the records from the `customer` table and print the contents to the standard output:

```
System.out.println("Selecting records");
String selectSQL = "select * from customer";
ResultSet res = stmt.executeQuery(selectSQL);

while(res.next()) {
    for(int i = 1;i <= res.getMetaData().getColumnCount();i++) {
        System.out.print(res.getString(i) + "\t");
    }
    System.out.println();
}
System.out.println();
```

Delete the records from the `customer` table and print the number of records deleted:

```
System.out.println("Deleting records");
String deleteSQL = "delete from customer";
System.out.println("Records deleted: " +
    stmt.executeUpdate(deleteSQL));
```

Close the result set, statement, and connection to free up resources:

```
    res.close();
    stmt.close();
    con.close();

    }

}
```

How It Works

Firstly, we will have to compile the class and run the JVM on the compiled class with the `mm.mysql-2.0.7-bin.jar` file in the classpath in the following manner:

```
java -cp StatementClient
```

This will produce the following output depending on the records in the `customer` table:

```
Inserting records
Records Inserted

Selecting records

81   Mr   Fred     Flintstone   31 Bramble Avenue   London NT2 1AQ   0239876
82   Mr   Barney   Rubble       22 Ramsons Avenue   London PWD LS1   1112313

Deleting records
Records deleted: 2
```

Please make sure that you have the `mm.mysql-2.0.7-bin.jar` file in your system classpath when you invoke the JVM.

Prepared Statements

Prepared statements are used for executing precompiled SQL statements. They are modeled in the JDBC API using the interface `java.sql.PreparedStatement`. This interface extends the interface `java.sql.Statement`. The JDBC driver vendor provides the implementation class for this interface. Prepared statements are created using the connection objects, as we have seen already. They can also be used for executing SQL statements with parameter placeholders for IN statements defined using the symbol '?'. In case you want to execute the same SQL statements more than once using different values for the IN parameters, then prepared statements are always recommended.

The methods defined in `java.sql.PreparedStatement` can be broadly classified as follows in addition to the ones already defined in the statement interface:

- ❑ Methods for executing SQL statements
- ❑ Methods for handling SQL batches
- ❑ Methods for setting the values of SQL IN parameters if the defined SQL have IN parameter placeholders

Executing SQL Statements

The interface `java.sql.PreparedStatement` defines methods for executing different SQL statements like SELECT, UPDATE, INSERT, DELETE, and CREATE. Contrary to the corresponding methods defined in the statement interface, these methods don't take the SQL statements as arguments. The SQL statements are defined when the prepared statements are created using the connection objects.

```
public ResultSet executeQuery() throws SQLException
```

This method can be used for executing the SELECT statement associated with the prepared statement and getting back the result. An instance of SQLException is thrown if a database error occurs. An example code snippet is shown below:

```
try {
    String sql = "select * from customer where fname = ? ";
    Connection con = DriverManager.getConnection(url,prop);
    PreparedStatement stmt = con.prepareStatement(sql);
    stmt.setString(1, "Fred");
    ResultSet res = stmt.executeQuery();
} catch(SQLException e) {
    //Handle exception
}
public boolean execute() throws SQLException
```

This method can be used for executing the SQL statement associated with the prepared statement. This returns true if next result is a result set object. An instance of SQLException is thrown if a database error occurs.

```
public int executeUpdate() throws SQLException
```

This method can be used for executing the SQL statement associated with the prepared statements that don't return result sets like INSERT and UPDATE. This returns the number of rows affected by the SQL statement. An instance of SQLException is thrown if a database error occurs.

Updating Data

The prepared statement interface defines a set of setXXX methods for setting the values of the IN parameters for the precompiled SQL statement defined using the symbol '?'. The parameter indexes start from 1. The set method used should be compatible with the expected SQL type. The table below lists a few of these methods, and the rest can be extrapolated by referring to the JavaDoc:

Method Name	Purpose
public void setBoolean(int index, boolean x)	Sets the IN parameter specified by the argument index to the boolean value specified by x.
public void setInt(int index, int x)	Sets the IN parameter specified by the argument index to the int value specified by x.
public void setString(int index, string x)	Sets the IN parameter specified by the argument index to the string value specified by x.

The interface also defines a method for clearing the current values of all parameters immediately:

```
public void clearParameters() throws SQLException
```

An Example using Prepared Statements

Now we will rewrite the previous example using prepared statements, and see how the same INSERT statement can be executed multiple times using different values.

Try It Out – Prepared Statements

Like we did in the earlier example, we need to import the relevant classes here as well, like this:

```
import java.sql.Connection;
import java.sql.PreparedStatement;
import java.sql.ResultSet;
import java.sql.DriverManager;

public class PraparedStatementClient {

    public static void main(String args[]) throws Exception {

        Class.forName("org.gjt.mm.mysql.Driver");
        String url = "jdbc:mysql://localhost:3306/bmsimple";

        Connection con = DriverManager.getConnection(url);

        PreparedStatement stmt;

        String insertSQL = "insert into customer(title,fname," +
            "lname,addressline,town,zipcode,phone) values " +
            "(?,?,?,?,?,?,?)";

        stmt = con.prepareStatement(insertSQL);

        System.out.println("Inserting records");

        stmt.setString(1,"Mr");
        stmt.setString(2,"Fred");
        stmt.setString(3,"Flintstone");
        stmt.setString(4,"31 Bramble Avenue");
        stmt.setString(5,"London");
        stmt.setString(6,"NT2 1AQ");
        stmt.setString(7,"023 9876");
        stmt.executeUpdate();
        stmt.clearParameters();

        stmt.setString(1,"Mr");
        stmt.setString(2,"Barney");
        stmt.setString(3,"Rubble");
        stmt.setString(4,"22 Ramsons Avenue");
        stmt.setString(5,"London");
        stmt.setString(6,"PWD LS1");
        stmt.setString(7,"111 2313");
        stmt.executeUpdate();

        System.out.println("Records Inserted");
```

```
System.out.println();

System.out.println("Selecting records");
String selectSQL = "select * from customer";
stmt = con.prepareStatement(selectSQL);
ResultSet res = stmt.executeQuery();
while(res.next()) {
    for(int i = 1;i <= res.getMetaData().getColumnCount();i++) {
        System.out.print(res.getString(i) + "\t");
    }
    System.out.println();
}
System.out.println();

System.out.println("Deleting records");
String deleteSQL = "delete from customer " +
    where town = 'London'";
stmt = con.prepareStatement(deleteSQL);
System.out.println("Records deleted: " +
    stmt.executeUpdate());

res.close();
stmt.close();
con.close();
    }
}
```

How It Works

Firstly, we will have to compile the class and run the JVM on the compiled class with the mm.mysql-2.0.7-bin.jar file in the classpath in the following manner:

```
java -cp PreparedStatementClient
```

This will produce the following output depending on the records in the customer table:

```
Inserting records
Records Inserted

Selecting records
Mr.   Fred     Flintstone      31 Bramble Avenue,London,NT2 1AQ     023 9876
Mr.   Berney   Rubble          22 Ramsons Avenue,London,PWD LS1     111 2313

Deleting records
Records deleted: 2
```

Please make sure that you have the mm.mysql-2.0.7-bin.jar file in your system classpath when you invoke the JVM.

SQL Exceptions and Warnings

The core JDBC API provides four exceptions:

- ❏ `BatchUpdateException`: This exception is thrown when an error occurs during the execution of an SQL batch. This class gives a method to get the update counts of the SQLs that were executed successfully in the batch as an array of integers.

- ❏ `DataTruncation`: This exception is thrown when the data is unexpectedly truncated during data reads or writes. The class provides methods to access the following information:
  - ❏ Number of bytes that should have been transferred
  - ❏ Number of bytes actually transferred
  - ❏ Whether the truncation occurred for a column or a parameter
  - ❏ Whether the truncation occurred on a read or a write
  - ❏ Index of the column or the parameter

- ❏ `SQLException`: This is the super class of all the other SQL exceptions. This class provides access methods for the database error code and SQL state for the error that caused this exception.

- ❏ `SQLWarning`: This subclass of `SQLException` is thrown to indicate warnings during database access.

A JDBC GUI Application

In this section, we will develop a small GUI-based JDBC application to maintain the data in the `item` table. The requirements for the application have been formulated and modeled into a 'use case' diagram shown below:

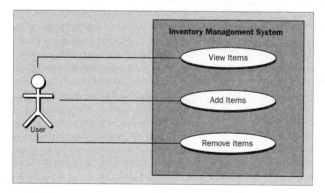

The identified use cases are:

- ❏ View the item details in a list
- ❏ Add new items
- ❏ Delete existing items

It has been decided to implement the application as a standalone Java application using the Java Swing classes. It has been further decided to list the details of existing items using a read-only list probably implemented using `JTable`, and provide a form for entering the details of a new item using a `JPanel` with required fields for entering the information. The diagram below shows the screen layout for the application:

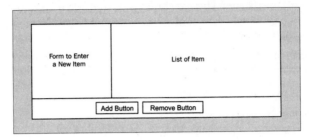

Class Diagram

After detailed analysis and design, the following classes have been identified to model the system:

❑   The main class to start the application

❑   A class to model the item entity

❑   A class to model the form for entering the details of a new item

❑   The class that contains the main methods

Item

This class models an item entity in the database:

❑   Private instance variables that correspond to the columns in the `item` table.

❑   *Accessors* and *mutators* for all the attributes.

❑   A constructor for initializing the values of the instance variables.

ItemTableModel

This class acts as a model for the `JTable` instance that displays the item information. This class implements the interface `javax.swing.table.TableModel` by extending the class `javax.swing.table.AbstractTableModel`.

❑   This class holds a collection of `Item` class instances that represent the items currently stored in the database.

❑   It implements the required callback methods used by the controller for rendering the data. Note that `JTable` and `TableModel` fit into the classic MVC pattern. MVC is the acronym for the 'Model View Controller' pattern that is widely used in object-orientated languages for writing graphical user interfaces.

❑   It provides a method to set the current list of items.

❑   A method is also provided to remove an item from the list for the specified index.

ItemPanel

This class models the form used for entering the details of a new item:

❑ Input fields are provided for entering the item details like description, cost price name and sell price.

❑ A method is provided to return an item object created from the values entered by the user.

❑ The required fields are initialized and laid out in a grid in the constructor.

❑ A method is also provided for blanking out the current values in the form.

ItemApp

This class contains the main methods like:

❑ This class has instance variables of type ItemPanel and ItemTableModel.

❑ This class extends javax.swing.Jframe.

❑ When the application starts, a connection is obtained from the database, the data is retrieved from the item table and the instance of the class ItemTableModel is populated.

❑ This object is used to initialize an instance of the JTable that displays the item info and is added to the frame.

❑ An instance of the class ItemPanel is also added to the frame.

❑ Two buttons, one for adding a new item and one for deleting the selected item from the list, are added to the frame.

❑ The class provides callback methods to handle the events when the buttons are clicked and the frame is closed. When the frame is closed the connection to the database is released.

The figure below depicts the class diagram for the system:

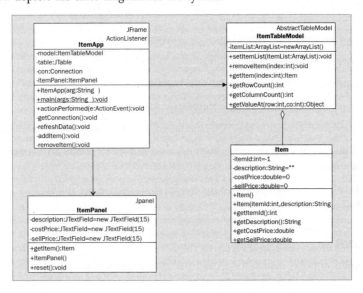

System Interaction

In this section, we will see the sequence of events instigated by the user cases associated with the system.

View Item Details

The sequence diagram below depicts the sequence of events involved in viewing the item details:

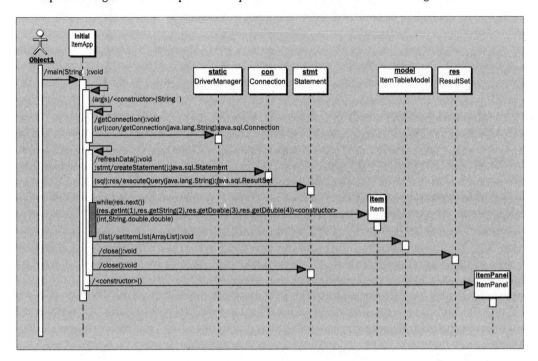

- ❑ The main class gets a connection to the database.
- ❑ An instance of the class ItemTableModel is instantiated.
- ❑ Now the private method refreshData is called.
- ❑ The connection is used to create a statement object.
- ❑ The statement object issues the SQL statement to get all the records from the item table.
- ❑ The information in each record in the result set is used to create an item object and this is added to a list.
- ❑ Finally this list is used to populate the model that will use the instance of JTable to render the data.

Adding New Item

The sequence diagram opposite depicts the sequence of events involved in adding a new item to the database:

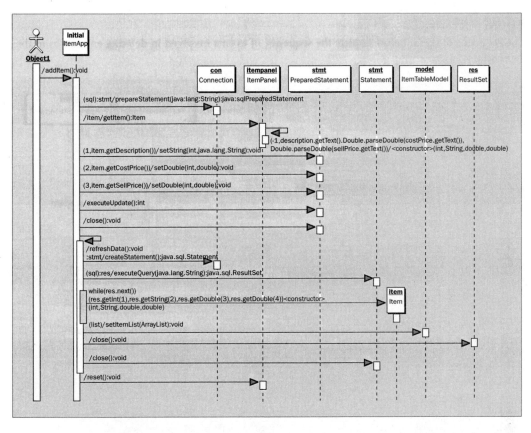

❑ The data entered by the user is retrieved from the `ItemPanel` instance encapsulated in an instance of `Item` object.

❑ A prepared statement is created using the connection.

❑ The `IN` parameters for the SQL statements are set using the data retrieved from the `Item` object.

❑ Finally the update is issued, the data in the table is refreshed and the form is reset.

Deleting Item

The sequence diagram below depicts the sequence of events involved in deleting an item from the database:

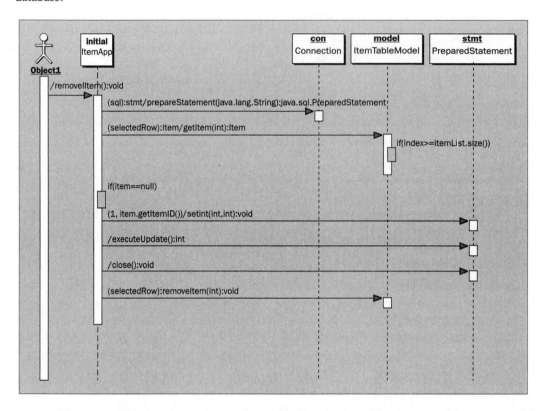

- ❑ The Item object corresponding to the selected row in the table is retrieved from the model.

- ❑ A prepared statement is created using the connection.

- ❑ The IN parameter of the SQL statement for the item id is set using the data retrieved from the Item object.

- ❑ Finally, the update is issued and the corresponding item object is removed from the model.

Try It Out – Item.java

The main class to start the application:

```
public class Item {
```

Declare the instance variables to model the database columns:

```
        private int itemId = -1;
        private String description = "";
        private double costPrice = 0;
        private double sellPrice = 0;
```

Constructor to initialize the instance variables:

```
        public Item(int itemId, String description, double costPrice,
            double sellPrice) {

            this.itemId = itemId;
            this.description = description;
            this.costPrice = costPrice;
            this.sellPrice = sellPrice;
        }
```

Access methods for the attributes:

```
        public int getItemId() {
            return itemId;
        }
        public String getDescription() {
            return description;
        }
        public double getCostPrice() {
            return costPrice;
        }
        public double getSellPrice() {
            return sellPrice;
        }
    }
```

Try It Out – ItemTableModel.java

Import the required classes:

```
    import javax.swing.table.AbstractTableModel;
    import java.util.ArrayList;
    public class ItemTableModel extends AbstractTableModel {
```

List to hold the current item entities in the database:

```
        private ArrayList itemList = new ArrayList();
```

Set the list of items. When the list is changed all the listeners are notified. This is to notify the table to redraw itself:

```
public void setItemList(ArrayList itemList) {
    this.itemList = itemList;
    fireTableDataChanged();
}
```

Remove a specific item. When the list is changed all the listeners are notified:

```
public void removeItem(int index) {
    itemList.remove(index);
    fireTableDataChanged();
}
```

Get a specific item:

```
public Item getItem(int index) {

    if(index >= itemList.size() || index < 0) {
        return null;
    }
    return (Item)itemList.get(index);
}
```

Callback method to get the number of rows to be rendered in the table:

```
public int getRowCount() {
    return itemList.size();
}
```

Callback method to get the number of columns to be rendered in the table:

```
public int getColumnCount() {
    return 3;
}
```

Callback method to get the value of the specified cell to be rendered in the table:

```
public Object getValueAt(int row,int col) {
    if(row >= itemList.size()) {
        throw new IllegalArgumentException("Invalid row");
    }
    Item item = (Item)itemList.get(row);
    switch(col) {
        case 0:
            return item.getDescription();
        case 1:
            return new Double(item.getCostPrice());
        case 2:
            return new Double(item.getSellPrice());
        default:
```

```
                    throw new IllegalArgumentException("Invalid column");
            }
        }
    }
```

Try It Out – ItemPanel.java

Import the required classes:

```
import javax.swing.JTextField;
import javax.swing.JPanel;
import javax.swing.JLabel;
import javax.swing.JOptionPane;
import javax.swing.border.TitledBorder;
import javax.swing.border.EtchedBorder;
import java.awt.GridLayout;
import java.awt.FlowLayout;
public class ItemPanel extends JPanel {
```

Instantiate the input fields for entering the details for a new item:

```
    private JTextField description = new JTextField(15);
    private JTextField costPrice = new JTextField(15);
    private JTextField sellPrice = new JTextField(15);
```

Instantiate and return an Item object using the values entered into the form fields by the user:

```
    public Item getItem() {
        try {
            return new Item(-1,
            description.getText(),
            Double.parseDouble(costPrice.getText()),
            Double.parseDouble(sellPrice.getText()));
        } catch(NumberFormatException ex) {
            JoptionPane.showMessageDialog(this, "Please enter valid data");
        }
    }
```

The constructor initializes the user interface for the form:

```
    public ItemPanel() {
```

Set the layout to a '3*1' grid:

```
        setLayout(new GridLayout(3,1));
```

Add the field for entering the description:

```
        JPanel panel1 = new JPanel();
        panel1.setLayout(new FlowLayout(FlowLayout.RIGHT));
        panel1.add(new JLabel("Description:"));
        panel1.add(description);
        add(panel1);
```

Add the field for entering the cost price:

```
        JPanel panel2 = new JPanel();
        panel2.setLayout(new FlowLayout(FlowLayout.RIGHT));
        panel2.add(new JLabel("Cost Price:"));
        panel2.add(costPrice);
        add(panel2);
```

Add the field for entering the sell price:

```
        JPanel panel3 = new JPanel();
        panel3.setLayout(new FlowLayout(FlowLayout.RIGHT));
        panel3.add(new JLabel("Sell Price:"));
        panel3.add(sellPrice);
        add(panel3);
        setBorder(new TitledBorder(new EtchedBorder(),"Add Item"));
    }
```

This method blanks out the form for entering item information:

```
    public void reset() {

        description.setText("");
        costPrice.setText("");
        sellPrice.setText("");
    }
}
```

Try It Out – ItemApp.java

Import the required classes:

```
import javax.swing.JTable;
import javax.swing.JFrame;
import javax.swing.JScrollPane;
import javax.swing.JPanel;
import javax.swing.JButton;

import java.awt.BorderLayout;

import java.awt.event.ActionEvent;
import java.awt.event.ActionListener;
import java.awt.event.WindowEvent;
import java.awt.event.WindowAdapter;

import java.util.ArrayList;

import java.sql.DriverManager;
import java.sql.Connection;
import java.sql.Statement;
import java.sql.PreparedStatement;
```

```
import java.sql.ResultSet;
import java.sql.SQLException;

public class ItemApp extends JFrame implements ActionListener {
```

An instance of the model that feeds the table that lists the item details:

```
    private ItemTableModel model;
```

Table where all item details are listed:

```
    private JTable table;
```

This is how we connect to the MySQL database:

```
    private Connection con;
```

Panel that contains the form for entering the item data:

```
    private ItemPanel itemPanel;
    public ItemApp(String[] arg) throws Exception {
        super("Inventory Management System");
```

Get a connection to the database:

```
        getConnection();
```

Create an instance of the table model and populate it with the data:

```
        model = new ItemTableModel ();
        refreshData();
```

Create the table using the model and add the table to a scroll pane. The pane is then added to the parent frame:

```
        table = new JTable(model);
        table.setAutoCreateColumnsFromModel(true);
        JScrollPane pane = new JScrollPane(table);

        getContentPane().setLayout(new BorderLayout());

        getContentPane().add(pane,BorderLayout.CENTER);
```

Add two buttons, one for adding new items and one for deleting selected items. The current class is registered as the action listener for the two buttons:

```
JPanel buttonPanel = new JPanel();
JButton newButton = new JButton("Add Item");
newButton.addActionListener(this);
buttonPanel.add(newButton);
JButton deleteButton = new JButton("Remove Item");
deleteButton.addActionListener(this);
buttonPanel.add(deleteButton);
getContentPane().add(buttonPanel,BorderLayout.SOUTH);
```

Create an instance of the item panel and add it to the frame:

```
itemPanel = new ItemPanel();
getContentPane().add(itemPanel,BorderLayout.WEST);
```

Display the frame:

```
pack();
show();
setLocation(50,50);
setSize(800,375);
setResizable(false);
validate();
```

Add an inner class that listens to the window closing events and closes the database connections:

```
addWindowListener(new WindowAdapter() {
    public void windowClosing(WindowEvent e) {
        try {
            con.close();
        } catch(SQLException ex) {
            ex.printStackTrace();
        }
        System.exit(0);
    }
});
}
public static void main(String args[]) throws Exception {
    ItemApp app = new ItemApp(args);
}
```

Callback method for listening to the button actions:

```
public void actionPerformed(ActionEvent e) {
    JButton button = (JButton)e.getSource();
    try {
```

If the button for adding items is clicked call the method to add items:

```
if("Add Item".equals(button.getText())) {
    addItem();
```

If the button for removing items is clicked call the method to remove items:

```
        }else if("Remove Item".equals(button.getText())) {
            removeItem();
        }
    }catch(SQLException ex) {
        ex.printStackTrace();
    }
    validate();
}
```

This method gets a connection to the database:

```
private void getConnection() throws Exception {
    Class.forName("org.gjt.mm.mysql.Driver");
    String url = "jdbc:mysql://localhost:3306/bmsimple";
    con = DriverManager.getConnection(url);
}
```

This method refreshes the table model data:

```
private void refreshData() throws SQLException {
    String sql = "select * from item";
    Statement stmt = con.createStatement();
    ResultSet res = stmt.executeQuery(sql);
    ArrayList list = new ArrayList();
    while(res.next()) {
        Item item = new Item(
            res.getInt(1),
            res.getString(2),
            res.getDouble(3),
            res.getDouble(4));
            list.add(item);
    }
    model.setItemList(list);
    res.close();
    stmt.close();
}
```

This method inserts a record to the database:

```
private void addItem() throws SQLException {
    String sql = "insert into item (" +
        "description,cost_price,sell_price)" +
        "values(" +
        "?,?,?)";
```

Prepare the statement:

```
PreparedStatement stmt = con.prepareStatement(sql);
Item item = itemPanel.getItem();
if(item == null) return;
```

Set the SQL IN parameters:

```
stmt.setString(1,item.getDescription());
stmt.setDouble(2,item.getCostPrice());
stmt.setDouble(3,item.getSellPrice());
```

Execute the SQL:

```
stmt.executeUpdate();
stmt.close();
```

Refresh the table:

```
refreshData();
itemPanel.reset();
}
```

This method deletes a record from the database:

```
private void removeItem() throws SQLException {
   String sql = "delete from item where item_id = ?";
   PreparedStatement stmt = con.prepareStatement(sql);
```

Get the selected item:

```
int selectedRow = table.getSelectedRow();
Item item = model.getItem(selectedRow);
if(item == null) {
   return;
}
```

Set the item id:

```
stmt.setInt(1,item.getItemId());
```

Execute the delete SQL:

```
stmt.executeUpdate();
stmt.close();
```

Remove the item from the model:

```
        model.removeItem(selectedRow);
    }
}
```

How It Works

Compile the classes using the following command:

```
javac Item*.java
```

This will produce the following class files:

- ❏ Item.class
- ❏ ItemTableModel.class
- ❏ ItemPanel.class
- ❏ ItemApp.class

Run the application using the following command:

```
java ItemApp
```

The screenshot below shows the application running. Please make sure that you have the mm.mysql-2.0.7-bin.jar file in your system classpath when you invoke the JVM.

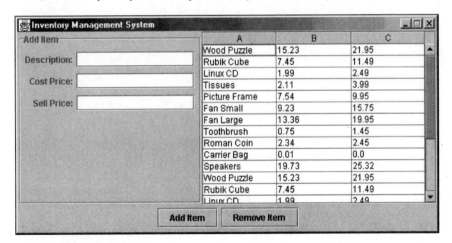

The JDBC API continues to evolve and some interesting new features will become available as vendors move to support version 3.0 of the JDBC API. New features in 3.0 include:

- ❏ Support for savepoints. Savepoints let you roll back transactions to specified locations instead of the beginning of the transaction.

- ❏ Integration of extension API with the core API and making them available with both J2EE and J2SE.

❏ Parameter meta data.

❏ Ability to have multiple result sets open simultaneously against a statement. Please note that currently only one result set may be open at a time for a statement that can produce multiple result sets.

❏ Callable statement enhancements.

Summary

In this chapter we have seen how MySQL databases can be accessed from Java language programs using JDBC. Specifically, we have covered the following in this chapter:

❏ JDBC drivers

❏ Building the MySQL JDBC driver

❏ Database connections

❏ JDBC statements

❏ Prepared statements for sending precompiled SQL

❏ JDBC result sets

❏ Database and result set meta data

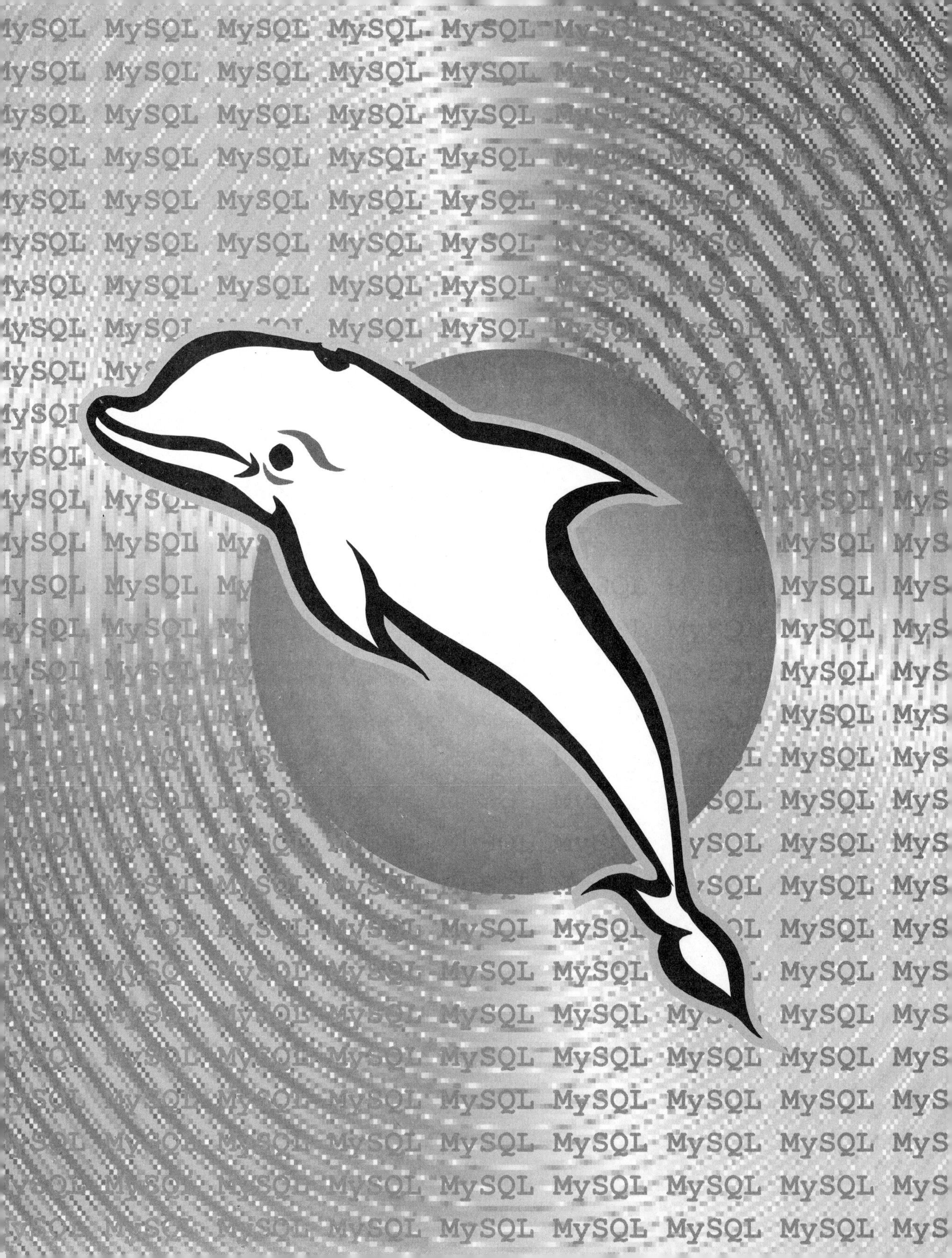
MySQL

Further Information and Resources

As you have read through this book, you will have come to appreciate that MySQL is a very capable relational database. However, it doesn't end here.

Development of MySQL has not finished; in fact it is a never-ending process and each new release brings with it additional features. In versions after 4.0.0, MySQL gains the ability to perform backups without shutting down the database. Database replication resilient to failure is a planned feature. From version 4.1 onwards, MySQL almost attains compliance with the base standard of SQL-92, including subselects and foreign key constraints. There are plans to introduce stored procedures in MySQL too. At present there is an experimental implementation of stored procedures via Perl.

We have seen that MySQL is accessible from many different programming languages, and also from remote clients across a network. The ODBC driver makes MySQL a valid choice as a backend database server, even where all the clients are Microsoft Windows-based PCs.

In this book, we have concentrated on getting MySQL up and running, but the book doesn't have the scope to investigate some of MySQL's more unusual features, particularly its ability to support multiple table types within a database or indeed all the features of all the supported table types. We have not attempted to delve into the source of MySQL, all of which is of course available for inspection and can, if you wish to, be modified for your own use. Who knows, one day maybe you will contribute to the mainstream MySQL source.

Non-Relational Storage

The relational model has been around for over 30 years now, and has proved itself to be a very powerful and flexible concept. Its sound underpinnings in mathematics have not only stood the test of time, but also the harsh realities of real-world problem solving.

There have been several challenges to the relational model through the years, most notably from object databases in the 1990s. Although there have been several attempts at pure object databases, much of the market has remained faithful to the relational model, particularly as the relational vendors like Oracle and other databases such as PostgreSQL have added features to their databases to enable them to support objects more easily.

A more recent challenge is appearing in the wake of the establishment of XML as an interchange format, from vendors who allow XML to be stored and queried in what is effectively an XML-based database. Tamino from Software AG (http://www.softwareag.com/tamino/) is an example of an XML database. Although these are very flexible, it seems to us that the relational model will adapt again, with XML interfaces added to the more traditional relational databases to enable them to interface more easily with XML. Although XML is a very flexible format, the data it conveys is almost always highly structured and amenable to storage and retrieval from a relational database. It is expected that the relational model will adapt and rise to this latest challenge.

Database Terminology

The world of databases abounds with jargons – OLTP, OLAP, Data Warehouses, Data Marts, and many others. Although often used almost as magic incantations, they are basically just different strategies for storing data, so that it is better optimized for its intended purpose.

In this book, we have been using our relational database in a very interactive way. We have considered the relational database very much a source of live data, for example, with ongoing updates as orders are added, goods shipped, and with many users simultaneously updating and accessing the data. These are **On Line Transaction Processing** (OLTP)-type characteristics.

There is another class of data, not used for interactive processing, but for after the event analysis. These are often termed **Decision Support Systems** (DSS), **Data Warehouses**, **Executive Information Systems** (EIS), and **Management Information Systems** (MIS). We will use the more technical term, **On Line Analytical Processing** (OLAP). These systems have quite different demands from the more common OLTP-type databases.

Some essential differences between OLTP and OLAP type databases are:

OLTP	OLAP
Live data, usually continuously updated	Historic data, updated at fixed times, perhaps nightly or less frequently
Used for live processing during operations	Used for analysis over a longer time frame
Usually limited to tens of gigabytes in size	Can be many terabytes in size
Usually have a limited amount of historic data	May store many years of historic data
Optimized in a relational model for efficient data updates	Optimized for data retrieval, usually in a non-relational model such as star or snowflake schemas

Our examples in this book are based around a very simple database, bmsimple, with some sample data relating to customers, customers placing orders, and items being sold. The database schema we have been using is very much an OLTP-type database. Actually it was optimized as a relational database to allow dynamic processing of orders, and very efficient storage of data.

If we had a large business that was doing well, after a while the size of the data in the database would become quite significant and performance would start to slow. Realistically, the best way of quickly improving the performance would be to simply throw away older data. We might well decide that we had no interest in customers who had not ordered from us for two years or what items we had shipped a year ago.

However, we might want to try and perform some analysis of our customers and their ordering habits, in order to improve our merchandising. We could perhaps organize a targeted marketing campaign or promotions to allow us to sell more goods.

A classic story, though perhaps an 'urban legend', is of the supermarket which discovered that sales of baby nappies and beer were linked, and that placing beer next to nappies improved sales. The reasoning was that some husbands sent shopping for nappies on the way home from work were tempted to pick up some beer at the same time, when the items were placed close together.

For this sort of analysis what we need is lots of data, probably collected over many years, and the ability to query it efficiently. We don't care if the last day's or last week's sales are not yet included, because what we are looking at is long term trends. This sort of work is done by OLAP databases. Although they can, and often are, built on conventional relational databases, the data stored in them is organized to allow it to be retrieved as efficiently as possible.

An OLAP database is often organized using a star schema, where there is a central **fact** table, and a number of **dimension** tables that are linked to it. If we were building an OLAP database for our store, we would perhaps have a central fact table that stored sales, with all the other data, such as who bought the item, when it was sold, and details of the item relegated to dimension tables:

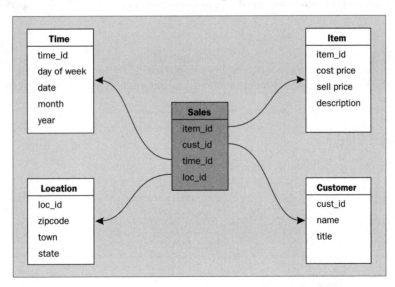

To get data into this OLAP database we would probably export the data from our normal database, and then use some custom data loading procedures to build the data in this new format.

If our business was very large, we might find that we needed to break down our OLAP database into smaller, more focused segments of data. These are often referred to as data cubes or data marts. They are smaller collections of data about specific facts organized as an OLAP database. A common flow of data in a large organization with heavy online processing needs such data marts.

Sophisticated data analysis requirements could be depicted like this:

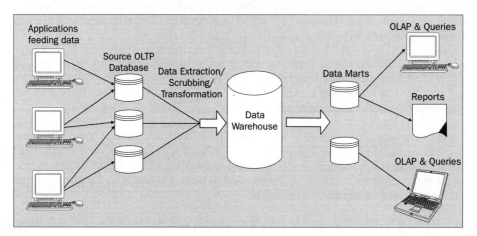

Although these OLAP databases use a very different schema design from the more normal relational schema, they are still normally implemented using relational databases. Major vendors such as Oracle and Microsoft have added features to their databases to make them easier to work with, as OLAP databases.

Resources

The long-standing nature of the relational model means that there is a good range of reference material available.

Web Resources

These of course change all the time, but some useful starting points are:

MySQL

❑   http://www.mysql.com

❑   http://www.mysql.org

❑   http://www.nusphere.com

❑   http://www.unixodbc.org

❑   http://www.devshed.com/Server_Side/MySQL

❑   http://www.weberdev.com/

PHP

- ❏ http://www.php.net
- ❏ http://www.phpbuilder.com
- ❏ http://www.phpwizard.net

Perl

- ❏ http://www.perl.com
- ❏ http://www.perl.org
- ❏ http://www.cpan.org
- ❏ http://activestate.com

Java and JDBC

- ❏ http://java.sun.com

General Tools

DeZign for databases is a database development tool using an entity relationship diagram. It visually supports the layout of the entities and relationships, and automatically generates SQL schemas for most leading databases. It supports ERDs and runs on Windows. There is an evaluation download available at:

- ❏ http://www.datanamic.com/dezign/index.html

The Toolkit for Conceptual Modeling is a collection of software tools to present conceptual models of software systems in the form of diagrams, tables, and trees. It includes ERDs, but no code generation yet, and runs on UNIX and Linux. The web site is:

- ❏ http://wwwhome.cs.utwente.nl/~tcm/

Database Design Studio (DDS) is a tool for the design of a database using an Entity Relationship Diagram. DDS runs on Windows using ODBC:

- ❏ http://www.chillisource.com/dds/

Books

There are many informative and useful books available. One may visit various sites from different publishers, who over a period of time have published many titles relating to this category.

SQL

- ❏ *MySQL* by Paul DuBois, one of the contributors to the MySQL documentation. This book is from New Riders (ISBN 0-7357-0921-1).

❑ *Database Design for Mere Mortals – A Hands-On Guide to Relational Database Design* by Michael J. Hernandez. This book is from Addison-Wesley (ISBN 0-201-69471-9). A book that concentrates on the collection of information and basic design of databases, written in a very easy-to-read style.

❑ *The Practical SQL Handbook – Using Structured Query Language* by Judith S. Bowman, Sandra L. Emerson, Marcy Darnovsky. This book is from Addison-Wesley (ISBN 0-201-44787-8). Some clear explanations of the more practical aspects of using SQL.

❑ *Mastering SQL* by Martin Gruber. This book is from Sybex (ISBN 0-7821-2538-7). A well-written guide to standard SQL.

❑ *SQL for Smarties* by Joe Celko. This book is from Morgan Kaufmann Publishers (ISBN 1-55860-576-2). An excellent book on getting the most out of the more advanced features of SQL.

❑ *Instant SQL Programming* by Joe Celko. This book is from Wrox Press (ISBN 1-874416-50-8). A straightforward guide to the SQL syntax and usage.

PHP

❑ *Professional PHP Programming* by Jesus Castagnetto, Chris Scollo, Sascha Schumann, Harish Rawat, and Deepak Veliath. This book is from Wrox Press (ISBN 1-861002-96-3). This book is about multi-tier programming with PHP, with coverage of the core PHP language and database addressing.

❑ *Beginning PHP 4* by Wankyu Choi, Chris Lea, Ganesh Prasad, Chris Ullman with Jon Blank and Sean Cazzell. This book is from Wrox Press (ISBN 1861003730). A tutorial in the PHP language, including an introduction to relational databases.

Perl

❑ *Beginning Perl* by Simon Cozens. This book is from Wrox Press (ISBN 1861003439). A tutorial in Perl on Windows and UNIX, including working with databases.

❑ *Perl Cookbook* (Third Edition), by Tom Christiansen and Nathan Torkington. This book is from O'Reilly and Associates (ISBN 0-596-00027-8). This edition of the well-known "Camel Book" has been expanded to cover Perl 5.6 and all other essentials.

❑ *Professional Perl Programming* by Peter Wainwright with Aldo Caplini, Simon Cozens, JJ Merelo-Guervos, Aalhad Saraf and Chris Nandor. This book is from Wrox Press (ISBN 1-861004-49-4). This book has an in-depth coverage of Perl 5.6, object-oriented programming, and more.

Java

❑ *Beginning Java 2* by Ivor Horton. This book is from Wrox Press (ISBN 1-861003-66-8). A book for anyone who wants to program in Java. It teaches the Java language from scratch, as well as object-oriented programming connecting to databases using JDBC and more.

❑ *Professional Java Data* by Danny Ayers, John Bell, Carl Calvert-Bettis, Thomas Bishop, Bjarki Holm, Glenn E. Mitchell, Kelly Lin Poon, Sean Rhody with Mike Bogovich, Matthew Ferris, Rick Grehan, Tony Loton, Nitin Nanda, and Mark Wilcox. This book is from Wrox Press (ISBN 1-861004-10-9). It covers information about accessing data in relational and object-oriented databases using Java.

Summary

MySQL has progressed enormously from its early days, and matured into a very capable and stable product suitable for use in many production systems, especially those that are predominately read-only. It is a very popular choice for web sites that require speedy access to data. Its support for standard SQL continues to improve with each release, as does its already strong scalability.

The open source license means that you can deploy MySQL with no client or server license costs. Coupled with the knowledge you have hopefully gained from this book, you should now be in a position to deploy a true database server in situations where license costs may have otherwise driven a less elegant solution.

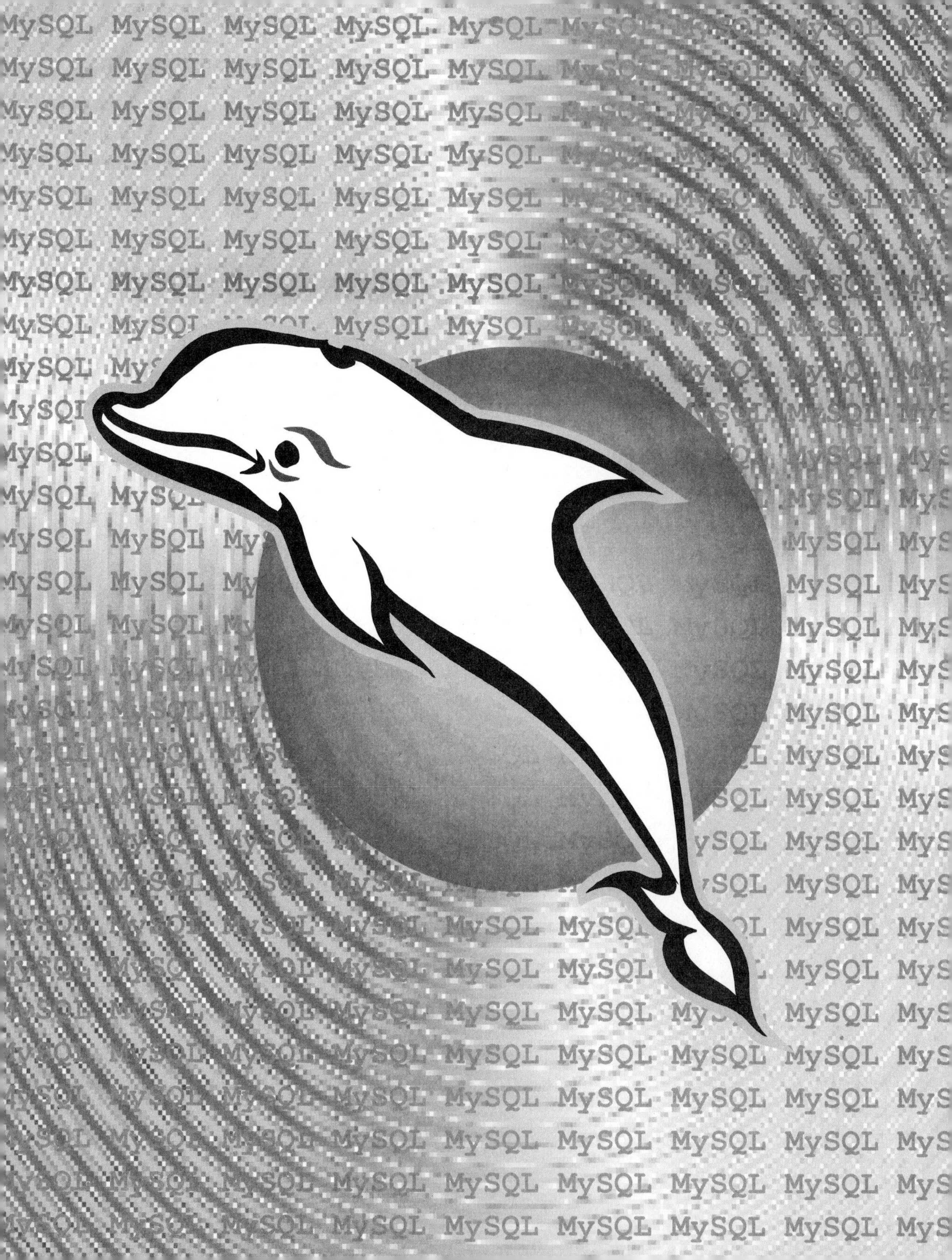
MySQL

MySQL Database Limits

When we use a database to store information, creating tables and adding rows to them, we are tempted to ignore the fact that on no platform do we have the luxury of infinite storage.

All database systems will be limited in some way, and MySQL is no exception. The amount of data that can be stored in a single column, the maximum number of columns allowed in a table and the total size of any table, all have limits, albeit in most cases quite large ones.

Recent releases of MySQL have seen most database limits relaxed, and in many cases effectively removed. Here we will mention some of the restrictions that remain as in MySQL 4.0.

For updates on limits for later versions, check out the site http://www.mysql.com.

> **The information here is derived from the MySQL online documentation and web sites of the table developers, especially `InnoDB`.**

Where a size is given as 'no limit' this means that MySQL by itself imposes no limit. The maximum size will be determined by other factors, such as the amount of available disk space or virtual memory.

Different database table types will impose different limits in some cases. Here we will mention a few variations. For example, `ISAM` tables are limited to 4GB in size, but `InnoDB` tables may be much larger.

As a limit is approached, the performance of the database will degrade. If we are, for example, manipulating very large fields consuming a large fraction of available (virtual) memory, it is likely that performance will begin to be unacceptable. Finally, MySQL will be literally unable to perform an update.

Other limits, not discussed here, may be imposed by the operating system, or network transport. For example, there are typically limits on the size of a file that can be stored on a hard disk, or the size of a query that can be made via ODBC depending on the driver. Memory limits may also be applied that would prevent very large columns, rows, or result sets from being created, transferred across a network (the operation in itself will be slow), or received by the client.

Database Size: No Limit

MySQL does not impose a limit on the total size of a database, and MySQL has been reported to handle some very large databases. At MySQL, there is a database containing 50,000,000 records. One user company reports that it is using a distributed database, with over 30 servers, containing 100,000 tables with 20,000,000,000 rows.

Due to the way that some MySQL table types arrange their data storage, you may see some performance degradation associated with databases containing many tables. MySQL will use a large number of files for storing the table data and, if the operating system does not cope well with many files in a single directory, performance may suffer.

GEMINI tables are limited to 1012 per database. This figure reduces by one for each table that has indexes defined.

Table Size: 64TB-16PB

For InnoDB tables MySQL normally stores its table data in chunks of 16k. The number of these pages is limited to a 32-bit unsigned integer (just over four billion), giving a maximum table size of 64 terabytes. The basic page size can be increased when MySQL is built, up to a maximum of 64k, thereby giving a theoretical table size limit of 256 terabytes.

Some operating systems impose a file size limit that prevents files of this size from being created, so MySQL stores table data in multiple files each 4GB or less in size. For large tables, this will result in many files and potential operating system performance degradation, as noted earlier.

The GEMINI table type has a table size limit of 16 petabytes.

Rows in a Table: 2^64

MySQL does not impose a limit on the number of rows in any table, although table type may.

InnoDB tables are limited to 2^{48} rows as a six-byte field is used to uniquely identify each row. GEMINI tables are limited to 2^{64} rows.

The MySQL manual states that there are known users of MySQL with 60,000 tables, and about 5,000,000,000 rows.

Table Indexes: 32

MySQL has a limit of 32 indexes per table. Each index may comprise 16 columns or parts of columns. The maximum length of a key is 500 bytes in MySQL 4, though recompiling from sources with different options can change this.

Of course, performance may degrade if we choose to create more and more indexes on a table with more and more columns.

Column Size: 16MB-4GB

MySQL has a limit of 4 gigabytes for the size of any one field in a table, a LONGTEXT or LONGBLOB. In practice, the limit comes from the amount of memory available for the server to manipulate the data and transfer it to the client.

GEMINI tables have a limit of 16MB per BLOB.

Columns in a Table: 1,000

The maximum number of columns that can be accommodated in a MySQL table depends on the table type and the type of the column.

InnoDB tables have a limit of 1,000 columns per table. Other table types will be constrained by the maximum size of any row in the table.

Row Size: 4GB

There is no explicit maximum size of a MySQL row. InnoDB tables are limited to 4GB per row. The size of columns and their number is limited for other table types as described above.

Other Limitations

At present, MySQL contains some other minor restrictions.

The number of characters allowed in a database, table, or column name is 64. Aliases may have up to 255 character names.

The number of characters allowed in a VARCHAR column is limited to 255 by MySQL. Some table types can already support more, typically up to 64k characters, but MySQL cannot use this feature as yet.

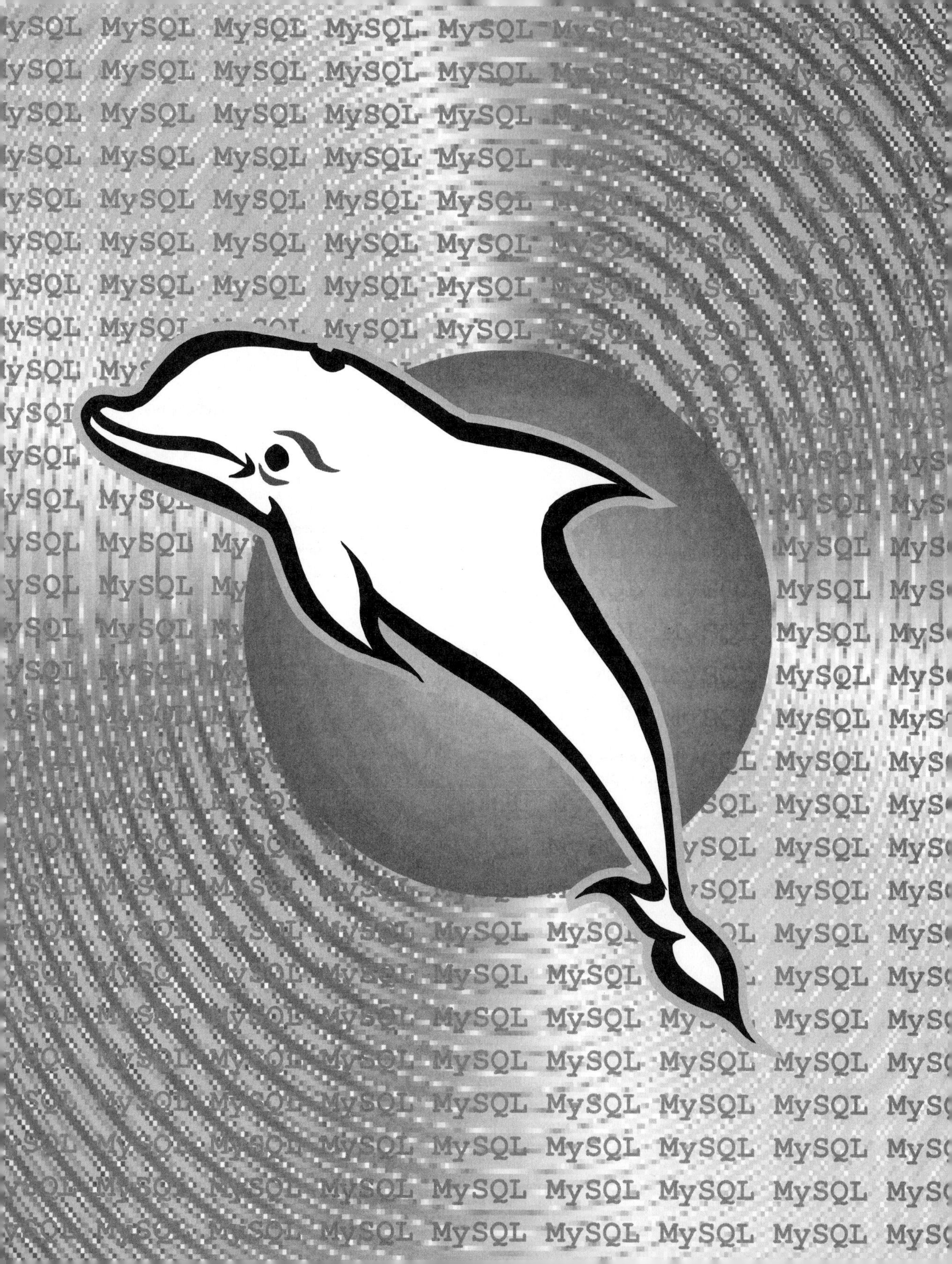
MySQL

MySQL Data Types

MySQL has a rich set of data types, which are described in the online documentation. Here we list the more useful types, ignoring some of the very specialist types and those types used only internally by MySQL.

In these tables, the standard SQL name appears first, which MySQL generally accepts, and then, any MySQL-specific alternative names.

Some types are specific to MySQL. In such cases no SQL name is given. As long as it's practical, we suggest you stick to the standard SQL types and names.

Exact Number Types

SQL Name	MySQL alternative name	Notes
	tinyint	A signed one-byte integer, which can store -128 to +127.
smallint		A signed two-byte integer, which can store -32768 to +32767.
	mediumint	A signed 3-byte integer, which can store -8388608 to +8388607.
integer, int		A signed 4-byte integer, which can store -2147483648 to +2147483647.
	bigint	A signed 8-byte integer, giving approximately 18 digits of precision.

MySQL integer column types may be declared as UNSIGNED in which case the range changes to run from zero to a maximum value roughly double the signed maximum. Adding a size in brackets can specify a maximum display width. They may also be declared ZEROFILL, which implies UNSIGNED. For example, a column type of TINYINT(2) ZEROFILL would have a range of 0 to 255 and be displayed in maximum two characters, with leading zeros.

Approximate Number Types

SQL Name	MySQL alternative name	Notes
numeric (precision, scale)		In MySQL, numeric is a synonym for decimal. In standard SQL numeric differs from decimal in that numeric must store exactly the precision specified, but decimal is free to store additional precision.
decimal (precision, scale)		A floating point number stored internally by MySQL as a string, one character per digit. The maximum range of decimal is the same as for double.
float (precision)		A floating point number with at least the given precision. If the precision requested is less than 25 (bits) a single precision float is used, otherwise for precision between 25 and 53 a double will be used with a maximum precision of 15 digits.
	float(width, decimals)	A single precision floating point with a maximum display width and number of decimal places.
real		Synonym for double in MySQL.
double precision	double(width, decimals)	A double precision floating point number. Range is approximately -1.8E+308 to -2.2E-308, 0, 2.2E-308 to 1.5E+308.

MySQL floating-point column types may not be declared as UNSIGNED. A maximum display width can be specified by adding a size in brackets. They may also be declared ZEROFILL where the default padding with spaces is replaced by padding with zeros. Unlike integer types, floating point types are signed, even if marked ZEROFILL.

Temporal Types

SQL Name	MySQL alternative name	Notes
timestamp	timestamp (width), datetime	Stores times from 1000-01-01 00:00:00 to the year 2037, with a resolution of 1 second. The width limits the number of characters retrieved, truncating from the right datetime extends the range to 9999-12-31.
	time	MySQL does not support interval. time can store an interval of time from -838:59:59 to 838:59:59 with a resolution of 1 second.
date		Stores dates from 1000-01-01 to 9999-12-31 with a resolution of 1 day. MySQL displays dates as YYYY-MM-DD.
	year	Stores a year from 1901 to 2155.
time		Stores a time from -838:59:59 to 838:59:59 with a resolution of 1 second.

Character Types

SQL Name	MySQL alternative name	Notes
char		Stores a single ASCII character.
char(n)		Stores exactly n characters, which will be padded with blanks if less characters are actually stored. MySQL trims trailing blanks when the column is retrieved. Recommended only for short strings of known length.
char varying(n)	varchar(n)	Stores a variable number of characters, up to a maximum of n characters. MySQL also trims trailing blanks when the column is stored. This is the 'standard' choice for character strings.
	tinytext, text, mediumtext, longtext	MySQL specific variants of VARCHAR, which do not require you to specify an upper limit on the number of characters. Limits are 255 for TINYTEXT, 65535 for TEXT, 16.7 million (2^24-1) for MEDIUMTEXT and 4 billion (2^32-1) for LONGTEXT.

Miscellaneous Types

SQL Name	MySQL alternative name	Notes
serial	auto_increment	In common usage SQL a serial type column is a numeric column in a table that increases each time a row is added. MySQL does not implement the `serial` type specifically. Rather an integer type column may be declared with the additional attribute `auto_increment`. When a value of 0 or NULL is inserted into such a column the value stored will be one larger than the maximum value currently in that column.
	set	A subset of up to 64 defined string values.
	enum	An enumerated type. May be set to one of a list of up to 65535 possible values.

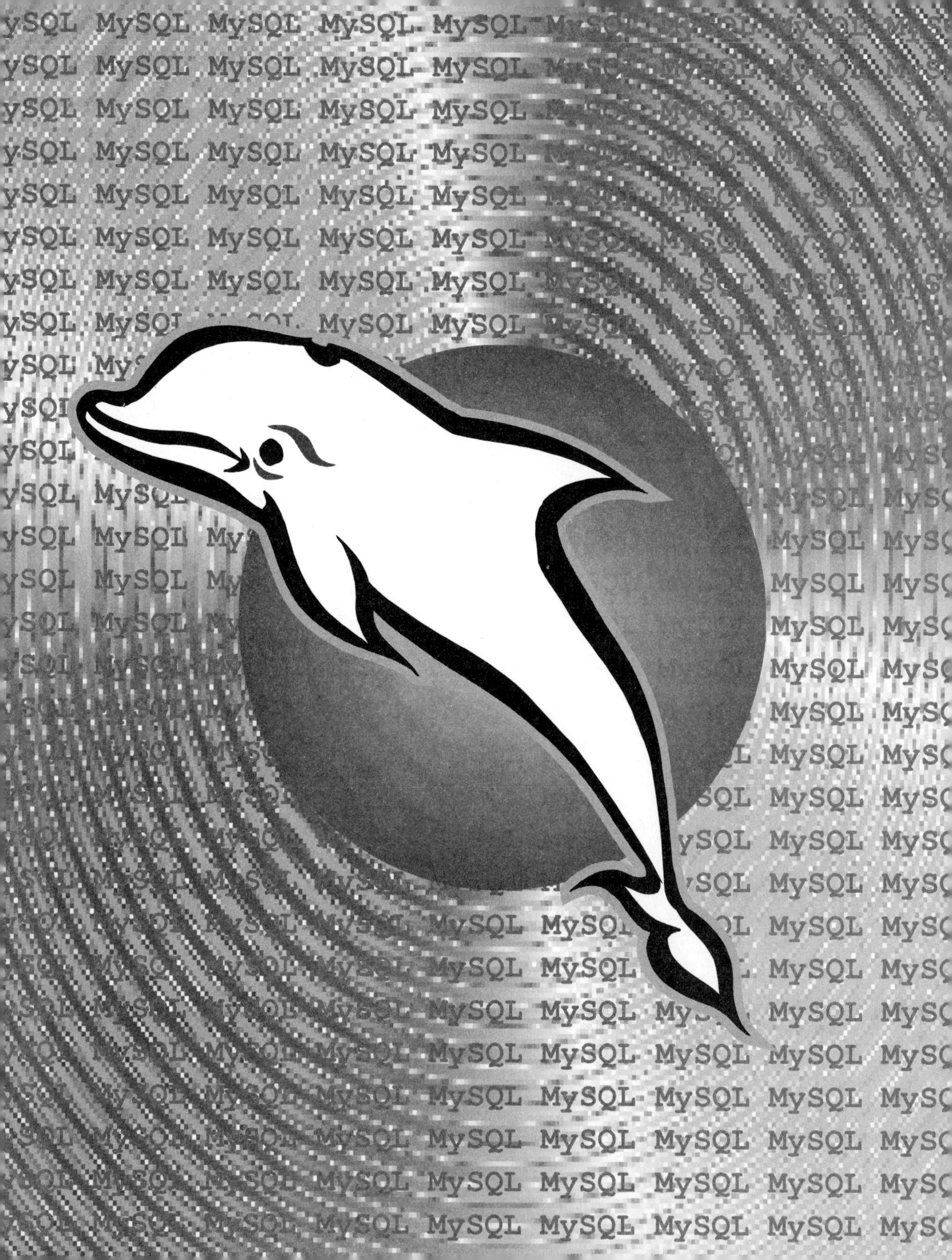
MySQL

MySQL SQL Syntax

MySQL SQL Commands

These are extracted from the MySQL manual, reproduced here for convenience:

SQL Commands used in MySQL	
ALTER TABLE	ANALYZE TABLE
BACKUP TABLE	BEGIN
CHECK TABLE	COMMIT
CREATE DATABASE	CREATE FUNCTION
CREATE INDEX	CREATE TABLE
DELETE	DESCRIBE
DROP DATABASE	DROP FUNCTION
DROP INDEX	DROP TABLE
EXPLAIN	FLUSH
GRANT	INSERT
JOIN	KILL
LOAD DATA INFILE	LOCK TABLES
OPTIMIZE TABLE	RENAME TABLE
REPAIR TABLE	REPLACE
RESTORE TABLE	REVOKE

Table continued on following page

```
SQL Commands used in MySQL

ROLLBACK                  SELECT

SET                       SET TRANSACTION

SHOW                      TRUNCATE

UNLOCK TABLES             UPDATE

USE
```

MySQL SQL Syntax

ALTER TABLE

```
ALTER [IGNORE] TABLE tbl_name alter_spec [, alter_spec ...]
```

where `alter_spec` can be:

```
        ADD [COLUMN] create_definition [FIRST | AFTER column_name]
or      ADD [COLUMN] (create_definition, create_definition,...)
or      ADD INDEX [index_name] (index_col_name,...)
or      ADD PRIMARY KEY (index_col_name,...)
or      ADD UNIQUE [index_name] (index_col_name,...)
or      ADD FULLTEXT [index_name] (index_col_name,...)
or      ADD [CONSTRAINT symbol] FOREIGN KEY index_name (index_col_name,...)
            [reference_definition]
or      ALTER [COLUMN] col_name {SET DEFAULT literal | DROP DEFAULT}
or      CHANGE [COLUMN] old_col_name create_definition
or      MODIFY [COLUMN] create_definition
or      DROP [COLUMN] col_name
or      DROP PRIMARY KEY
or      DROP INDEX index_name
or      RENAME [TO] new_tbl_name
or      ORDER BY col
or      table_options
```

Description – Modifies table properties

ANALYZE TABLE

```
ANALYZE TABLE tbl_name[,tbl_name...]
```

Description – For MyISAM and BDB table types analyzes and stores the key distribution for the named tables, used for optimizing joins. This is the equivalent of running myisamchk -a.

BACKUP TABLE

```
BACKUP TABLE tbl_name[,tbl_name...] TO '/path/to/backup/directory'
```

Description – For MyISAM tables copies the files used for the named tables to a specified directory. It copies enough to allow a restore to take place. The path should be specified using '/' on UNIX or Linux systems, but double backslashes on Windows, for example 'c:\\Temp\\temp-backup'.

BEGIN

```
SET AUTOCOMMIT=0
BEGIN [ WORK ]
```

Description – For transaction-safe table types, begins a transaction in non-autocommit mode

CHECK TABLE

```
CHECK TABLE tbl_name[,tbl_name...] [option [option...]]

option = QUICK | FAST | MEDIUM | EXTEND | CHANGED
```

Description – For MyISAM tables checks the table for errors. It's equivalent to myisamcheck -m tbl_name.

COMMIT

```
COMMIT
```

Description – Commits the current transaction.

CREATE DATABASE

```
CREATE DATABASE [IF NOT EXISTS] db_name
```

Description – Creates a new database.

CREATE FUNCTION

```
CREATE [AGGREGATE] FUNCTION function_name RETURNS {STRING|REAL|INTEGER}
    SONAME shared_library_name
```

Description – Defines a new function.

CREATE INDEX

```
CREATE [UNIQUE|FULLTEXT] INDEX index_name ON tbl_name (col_name[(length)],... )
```

Description – Invokes ALTER TABLE to construct an index.

CREATE TABLE

```
CREATE [TEMPORARY] TABLE [IF NOT EXISTS] tbl_name [(create_definition,...)]
[table_options] [select_statement]
```

where `create_definition` can be:

```
    col_name type [NOT NULL | NULL] [DEFAULT default_value] [AUTO_INCREMENT]
            [PRIMARY KEY] [reference_definition]
or  PRIMARY KEY (index_col_name,...)
or  KEY [index_name] (index_col_name,...)
or  INDEX [index_name] (index_col_name,...)
or  UNIQUE [INDEX] [index_name] (index_col_name,...)
or  FULLTEXT [INDEX] [index_name] (index_col_name,...)
or  [CONSTRAINT symbol] FOREIGN KEY index_name (index_col_name,...)
            [reference_definition]
or  CHECK (expr)
```

and column type can be:

```
    TINYINT[(length)] [UNSIGNED] [ZEROFILL]
or  SMALLINT[(length)] [UNSIGNED] [ZEROFILL]
or  MEDIUMINT[(length)] [UNSIGNED] [ZEROFILL]
or  INT[(length)] [UNSIGNED] [ZEROFILL]
or  INTEGER[(length)] [UNSIGNED] [ZEROFILL]
or  BIGINT[(length)] [UNSIGNED] [ZEROFILL]
or  REAL[(length,decimals)] [UNSIGNED] [ZEROFILL]
or  DOUBLE[(length,decimals)] [UNSIGNED] [ZEROFILL]
or  FLOAT[(length,decimals)] [UNSIGNED] [ZEROFILL]
or  DECIMAL(length,decimals) [UNSIGNED] [ZEROFILL]
or  NUMERIC(length,decimals) [UNSIGNED] [ZEROFILL]
or  CHAR(length) [BINARY]
or  VARCHAR(length) [BINARY]
or  DATE
or  TIME
or  TIMESTAMP
or  DATETIME
or  TINYBLOB
or  BLOB
or  MEDIUMBLOB
or  LONGBLOB
or  TINYTEXT
or  TEXT
or  MEDIUMTEXT
or  LONGTEXT
or  ENUM(value1,value2,value3,...)
or  SET(value1,value2,value3,...)
```

and `index_col_name` is:

```
    col_name [(length)]
```

and `reference_definition` is:

```
REFERENCES tbl_name [(index_col_name,...)]
            [MATCH FULL | MATCH PARTIAL]
            [ON DELETE reference_option]
            [ON UPDATE reference_option]
```

and `reference_option` is:

```
RESTRICT | CASCADE | SET NULL | NO ACTION | SET DEFAULT
```

`table_options` are:

```
TYPE = {BDB | HEAP | ISAM | InnoDB | MERGE | MYISAM }
or AUTO_INCREMENT = #
or AVG_ROW_LENGTH = #
or CHECKSUM = {0 | 1}
or COMMENT = "string"
or MAX_ROWS = #
or MIN_ROWS = #
or PACK_KEYS = {0 | 1}
or PASSWORD = "string"
or DELAY_KEY_WRITE = {0 | 1}
or ROW_FORMAT= { default | dynamic | fixed | compressed }
or RAID_TYPE= {1 | STRIPED | RAID0 } RAID_CHUNKS=#  RAID_CHUNKSIZE=#
or UNION = (table_name,[table_name...])
or DATA DIRECTORY="directory"
or INDEX DIRECTORY="directory"
```

and `select_statement` is:

```
[IGNORE | REPLACE] SELECT ...   (Some legal select statement)
```

Description – Creates a new table.

DELETE

```
DELETE [LOW_PRIORITY] FROM tbl_name
        [WHERE condition]
        [LIMIT rows]
```

Description – Removes rows from a table.

DESCRIBE

```
DESCRIBE tbl_name {col_name | wild}
DESC tbl_name {col_name | wild}
```

Description – Provides information about a table's columns.

DROP DATABASE

```
DROP DATABASE [IF EXISTS] db_name
```

Description – Removes an existing database.

DROP FUNCTION

```
DROP FUNCTION name
```

Description – Removes a user-defined function.

DROP INDEX

```
DROP INDEX index_name ON tbl_name
```

Description – Removes an existing index from a table.

DROP TABLE

```
DROP TABLE [IF EXISTS] tbl_name [, tbl_name,...] [RESTRICT | CASCADE]
```

Description – Removes existing tables from a database.

EXPLAIN

```
EXPLAIN tbl_name
EXPLAIN SELECT query
```

Description – Describes a table (as in DESCRIBE) or shows statement execution plan.

FLUSH

```
FLUSH flush_option [,flush_option]
```

where flush_option can be:

```
HOSTS
or LOGS
or PRIVILEGES
or TABLES
or [TABLE | TABLES] tbl_name [, tbl_name ...]
or TABLES WITH READ LOCK
or STATUS
```

Description – Clear MySQL caches.

GRANT

```
GRANT priv_type [(column_list)] [, priv_type [(column_list)] ...]
    ON {tbl_name | * | *.* | db_name.*}
    TO user_name [IDENTIFIED BY 'password']
        [, user_name [IDENTIFIED BY 'password'] ...]
    [WITH GRANT OPTION]
```

where each `priv_type` is one of:

ALL PRIVILEGES	FILE	RELOAD
ALTER	INDEX	SELECT
CREATE	INSERT	SHUTDOWN
DELETE	PROCESS	UPDATE
DROP	REFERENCES	USAGE

Description – Grants access privilege to users.

INSERT

```
    INSERT [LOW_PRIORITY | DELAYED] [IGNORE]
        [INTO] tbl_name [(col_name,...)]
        VALUES (expression,...),(...),...
or  INSERT [LOW_PRIORITY | DELAYED] [IGNORE]
        [INTO] tbl_name [(col_name,...)]
        SELECT ...
or  INSERT [LOW_PRIORITY | DELAYED] [IGNORE]
        [INTO] tbl_name
        SET col_name=expression, col_name=expression, ...
or  INSERT [LOW_PRIORITY] [IGNORE] [INTO] tbl_name
        SELECT ...
```

Description – Inserts new rows into a table.

JOIN

MySQL supports the following JOIN syntaxes for use in SELECT statements:

```
table_reference, table_reference
table_reference [CROSS] JOIN table_reference
table_reference INNER JOIN table_reference join_condition
table_reference STRAIGHT_JOIN table_reference
table_reference LEFT [OUTER] JOIN table_reference join_condition
table_reference LEFT [OUTER] JOIN table_reference
table_reference NATURAL [LEFT [OUTER]] JOIN table_reference
{ oj table_reference LEFT OUTER JOIN table_reference ON conditional_expr }
table_reference RIGHT [OUTER] JOIN table_reference join_condition
table_reference RIGHT [OUTER] JOIN table_reference
table_reference NATURAL [RIGHT [OUTER]] JOIN table_reference
```

533

where `table_reference` is:

```
table_name [[AS] alias] [USE INDEX (key_list)] [IGNORE INDEX (key_list)]
```

and `join_condition` is:

```
ON conditional_expr
or USING (column_list)
```

KILL

```
KILL thread_id
```

Description – Terminates a specified connection to the MySQL server.

LOAD DATA INFILE

```
LOAD DATA [LOW_PRIORITY | CONCURRENT] [LOCAL] INFILE 'file_name.txt'
    [REPLACE | IGNORE]
    INTO TABLE tbl_name
    [FIELDS
        [TERMINATED BY '\t']
        [[OPTIONALLY] ENCLOSED BY '']
        [ESCAPED BY '\\' ]
    ]
    [LINES TERMINATED BY '\n']
    [IGNORE number LINES]
    [(col_name,...)]
```

Description – Loads data quickly from a text file.

LOCK TABLES

```
LOCK TABLES tbl_name [AS alias] {READ | [READ LOCAL] | [LOW_PRIORITY] WRITE}
            [, tbl_name {READ | [LOW_PRIORITY] WRITE} ...]
```

Description – Requests a lock on a set of tables.

OPTIMIZE TABLE

```
OPTIMIZE TABLE tbl_name[,tbl_name]...
```

Description – Optimizes the storage of `MyISAM` and `BDB` tables.

RENAME TABLE

```
RENAME TABLE tbl_name TO new_table_name[, tbl_name2 TO new_table_name2,...]
```

Description – Renames tables. Renaming proceeds from left to right.

REPAIR TABLE

```
REPAIR TABLE tbl_name[,tbl_name...] [QUICK] [EXTENDED]
```

Description – For `MyISAM` tables attempts to recover from table corruption. It's equivalent to `myisamchk -r tbl_name`.

REPLACE

```
        REPLACE [LOW_PRIORITY | DELAYED]
            [INTO] tbl_name [(col_name,...)]
            VALUES (expression,...)
    or  REPLACE [LOW_PRIORITY | DELAYED]
            [INTO] tbl_name [(col_name,...)]
            SELECT ...
    or  REPLACE [LOW_PRIORITY | DELAYED]
            [INTO] tbl_name
            SET col_name=expression, col_name=expression,...
```

Description – As `INSERT`, but any existing rows are updated.

RESTORE TABLE

```
RESTORE TABLE tbl_name[,tbl_name...] FROM '/path/to/backup/directory'
```

Description – Restores tables backed up with `BACKUP TABLE`.

REVOKE

```
REVOKE priv_type [(column_list)] [, priv_type [(column_list)] ...]
    ON {tbl_name | * | *.* | db_name.*}
    FROM user_name [, user_name ...]
```

Description – Revokes access privilege from users.

ROLLBACK

```
ROLLBACK
```

Description – Aborts the current transaction.

SELECT

```
SELECT [STRAIGHT_JOIN] [SQL_SMALL_RESULT] [SQL_BIG_RESULT] [SQL_BUFFER_RESULT]
    [HIGH_PRIORITY]
    [DISTINCT | DISTINCTROW | ALL]
select_expression,...
[INTO {OUTFILE | DUMPFILE} 'file_name' export_options]
[FROM table_references
    [WHERE where_definition]
    [GROUP BY {unsigned_integer | col_name | formula} [ASC | DESC], ...]
```

```
[HAVING where_definition]
[ORDER BY {unsigned_integer | col_name | formula} [ASC | DESC] ,...]
[LIMIT [offset,] rows]
[PROCEDURE procedure_name]
[FOR UPDATE | LOCK IN SHARE MODE]]
```

Description – Retrieves rows from a table.

SET

```
SET [OPTION] SQL_VALUE_OPTION= value, ...
```

Description – Sets run-time parameters.

SET TRANSACTION

```
SET [GLOBAL | SESSION] TRANSACTION ISOLATION LEVEL
[READ UNCOMMITTED | READ COMMITTED | REPEATABLE READ | SERIALIZABLE]
```

Description – Sets the characteristics of the current SQL-transaction, all transactions in the session, or all transactions globally.

SHOW

```
    SHOW DATABASES [LIKE wild]
or SHOW [OPEN] TABLES [FROM db_name] [LIKE wild]
or SHOW [FULL] COLUMNS FROM tbl_name [FROM db_name] [LIKE wild]
or SHOW INDEX FROM tbl_name [FROM db_name]
or SHOW TABLE STATUS [FROM db_name] [LIKE wild]
or SHOW STATUS [LIKE wild]
or SHOW VARIABLES [LIKE wild]
or SHOW LOGS
or SHOW [FULL] PROCESSLIST
or SHOW GRANTS FOR user
or SHOW CREATE TABLE table_name
or SHOW MASTER STATUS
or SHOW MASTER LOGS
or SHOW SLAVE STATUS
```

Description – Shows run-time information.

TRUNCATE

```
TRUNCATE TABLE tbl_name
```

Description – Empties a table as if a DROP TABLE and CREATE TABLE had been executed.

UNLOCK TABLES

```
UNLOCK TABLES
```

Description – Releases all locks held by the current process.

UPDATE

```
UPDATE [LOW_PRIORITY] [IGNORE] tbl_name
    SET col_name1=expr1, [col_name2=expr2, ...]
    [WHERE where_definition]
    [ORDER BY ...]
    [LIMIT #]
```

Description – Replaces values of columns in a table.

USE

```
USE db_name
```

Description – Select a database for future queries.

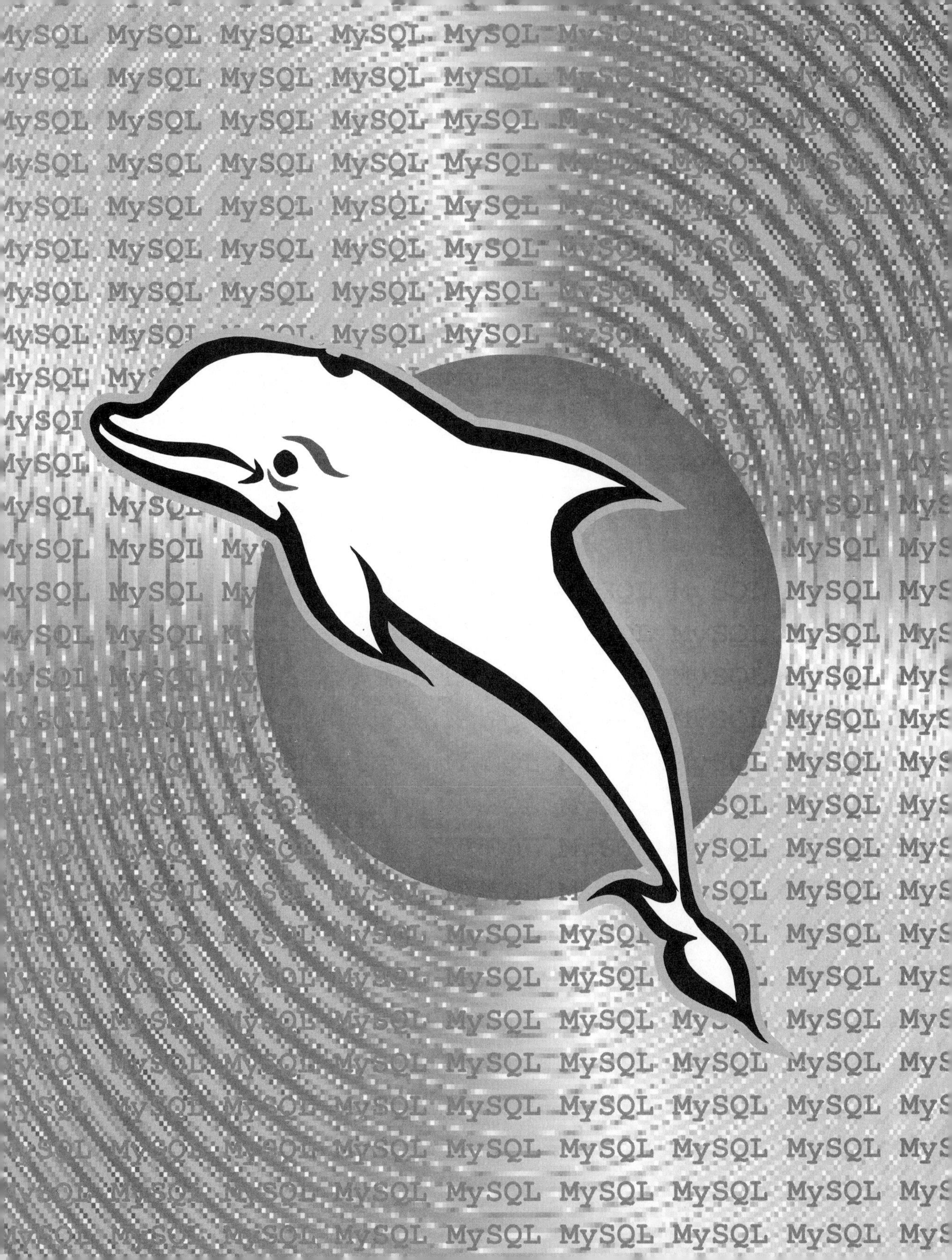

mysql Reference

mysql Command Line Options

Usage

```
mysql [options] [db_name]
```

Options

The mysql command line options are:

Options	Long Name	Meaning
-?	--help	Display help and exit.
-A	--no-auto-rehash	No automatic rehashing.
-B	--batch	Print results with each row on a new line and a tab as separator.
	--character-sets-dir=...	Set the directory where character sets are located.
-C	--compress	Use compression in server/client protocol.
-D	--database=...	Set the database to use.
	--default-character-set=...	Set the default character set.
-e	--execute=...	Execute command and quit (output like with --batch).
-E	--vertical	Print the output of a query (rows) vertically.

Table continued on following page

Options	Long Name	Meaning
-f	--force	Continue even if we get an SQL error.
-g	--no-named-commands	Named commands are disabled.
-G	--enable-named-commands	Named commands are enabled.
-i	--ignore-space	Ignore space after function names.
-h	--host=...	Connect to host.
-H	--html	Produce HTML output.
-L	--skip-line-numbers	Don't write line number for errors.
	--no-pager	Disable pager and print to stdout.
	--no-tee	Disable outfile.
-n	--unbuffered	Flush buffer after each query.
-N	--skip-column-names	Don't write column names in results.
-O	--set-variable var=option	Give a variable a value --help lists variables.
-o	--one-database	Only update the default database.
	--pager[=...]	Pager to use to display results.
-p	--password[=...]	Set password to use when connecting to server.
-P	--port=...	Port number to use for connection.
-q	--quick	Suppress cache result, print it row by row.
-r	--raw	Write fields without conversion. Used with --batch.
-s	--silent	Be more silent.
-S	--socket=...	Set socket file to use for connection.
-t	--table	Produce output in table format.
-T	--debug-info	Print some debug information at exit.
	--tee=...	Append everything into outfile.
-u	--user=#	Set user for login if not current user.
-U	--safe-updates[=# --i-am-a-dummy[=#]	Only allow UPDATE and DELETE that uses keys.
-v	--verbose	Write more (-v gives the table output format, -vv or -vvv for more verbosity).

Options	Long Name	Meaning
-V	--version	Output version information and exit.
-w	--wait	Wait and retry if connection is down.

Internal Commands

The supported internal mysql commands are:

Command	Shortcut	Function
Help	\h	Display some help.
?	\?	Synonym for `help.
Clear	\c	Clear command.
Connect	\r	Reconnect to the server. Optional arguments are database name and host.
Edit	\e	Edit command with program specified by environment variable $EDITOR.
Ego	\G	Send command to MySQL server, display result vertically.
Exit	\q	Exit mysql (same as quit).
Go	\g	Send command to MySQL server.
Nopager	\n	Disable pager, print to stdout.
Notee	\t	Don't write into outfile.
Pager	\P	Set PAGER [to_pager]. Print the query results via PAGER.
Print	\p	Print current command.
Quit	\q	Quit mysql.
Rehash	\#	Rebuild completion hash.
Source	\.	Execute a SQL script file. Takes a file name as an argument.
Status	\s	Get status information from the server.
Tee	\T	Set outfile [to_outfile].
Use	\u	Use another database. Takes database name as argument.

These sets of options and commands are taken from the MySQL online documentation.

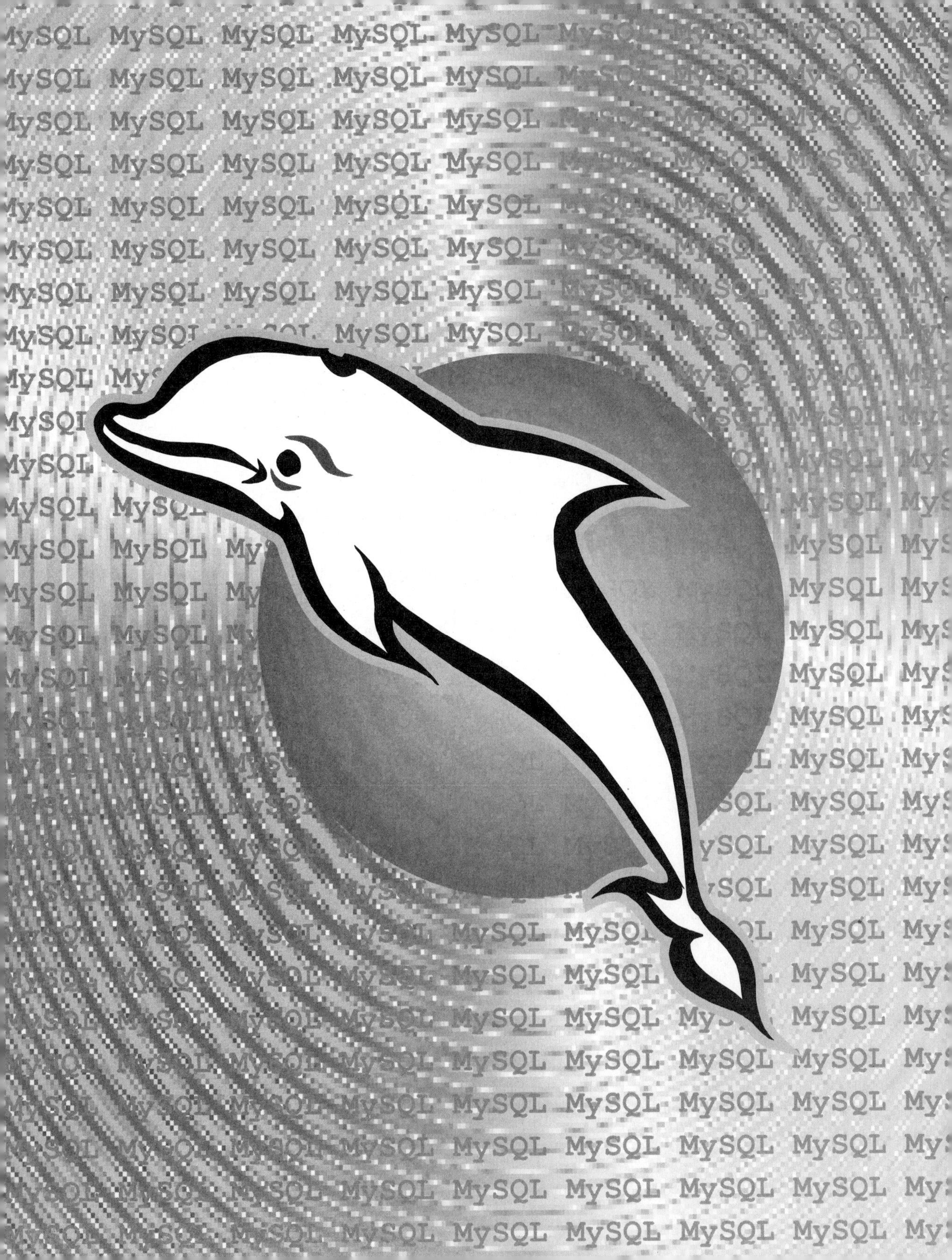
MySQL

Database Schema and Tables

The database schema used in the examples in this book is a simplified customer/orders/items database as described below:

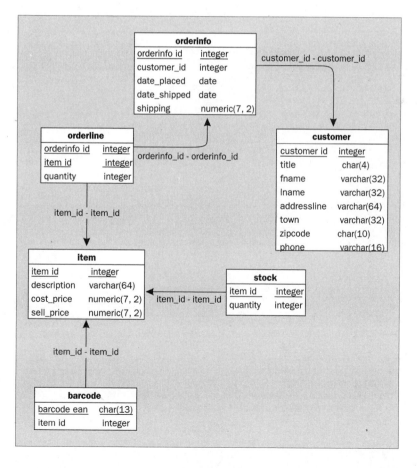

The tables need to be created in an appropriate order such that dependent tables are created first, because of the foreign key constraints. This is the same order to be followed as data is inserted into the tables. Such an order is:

❑ customer

❑ item

❑ orderinfo

❑ stock

❑ orderline

❑ barcode

The SQL to create the final version of this sample database, bmfinal, including the foreign key constraints, is:

customer table

```
create table customer
(
      customer_id         int AUTO_INCREMENT NOT NULL PRIMARY KEY,
      title               char(4)                        ,
      fname               varchar(32)                    ,
      lname               varchar(32)        NOT NULL,
      addressline         varchar(64)                    ,
      town                varchar(32)                    ,
      zipcode             char(10)           NOT NULL,
      phone               varchar(16)
) TYPE = InnoDB;
```

item table

```
create table item
(
      item_id             int AUTO_INCREMENT NOT NULL PRIMARY KEY,
      description         varchar(64)        NOT NULL,
      cost_price          numeric(7,2)                   ,
      sell_price          numeric(7,2)
) TYPE = InnoDB;
```

orderinfo table

```
create table orderinfo
(
      orderinfo_id        int AUTO_INCREMENT NOT NULL PRIMARY KEY,
      customer_id         integer            NOT NULL,
      date_placed         date               NOT NULL,
      date_shipped        date                           ,
      shipping            numeric(7,2)                   ,
      INDEX (customer_id),
      CONSTRAINT orderinfo_customer_id_fk FOREIGN KEY(customer_id)
                 REFERENCES customer(customer_id)
) TYPE = InnoDB;
```

stock table

```
create table stock
(
    item_id         integer         NOT NULL AUTO_INCREMENT PRIMARY KEY,
    quantity        integer         NOT NULL,
    CONSTRAINT stock_item_id_fk FOREIGN KEY(item_id)
            REFERENCES item(item_id)
) TYPE = InnoDB;
```

orderline table

```
create table orderline
(
    orderinfo_id    integer         NOT NULL,
    item_id         integer         NOT NULL,
    quantity        integer         NOT NULL,
    PRIMARY KEY(orderinfo_id, item_id),
    INDEX(item_id),
    CONSTRAINT orderline_orderinfo_id_fk FOREIGN KEY (orderinfo_id)
    REFERENCES orderinfo(orderinfo_id),
    CONSTRAINT orderline_item_id_fk FOREIGN KEY (item_id)
    REFERENCES item(item_id)
)   TYPE = InnoDB;
```

barcode table

```
create table barcode
(
    barcode_ean     char(13)        NOT NULL PRIMARY KEY,
    item_id         integer         NOT NULL,
    INDEX(item_id),
    CONSTRAINT barcode_item_id_fk FOREIGN KEY(item_id) REFERENCES item(item_id)
)   TYPE = InnoDB;
```

The download code bundle has the table population commands for bmfinal in an appropriate order.

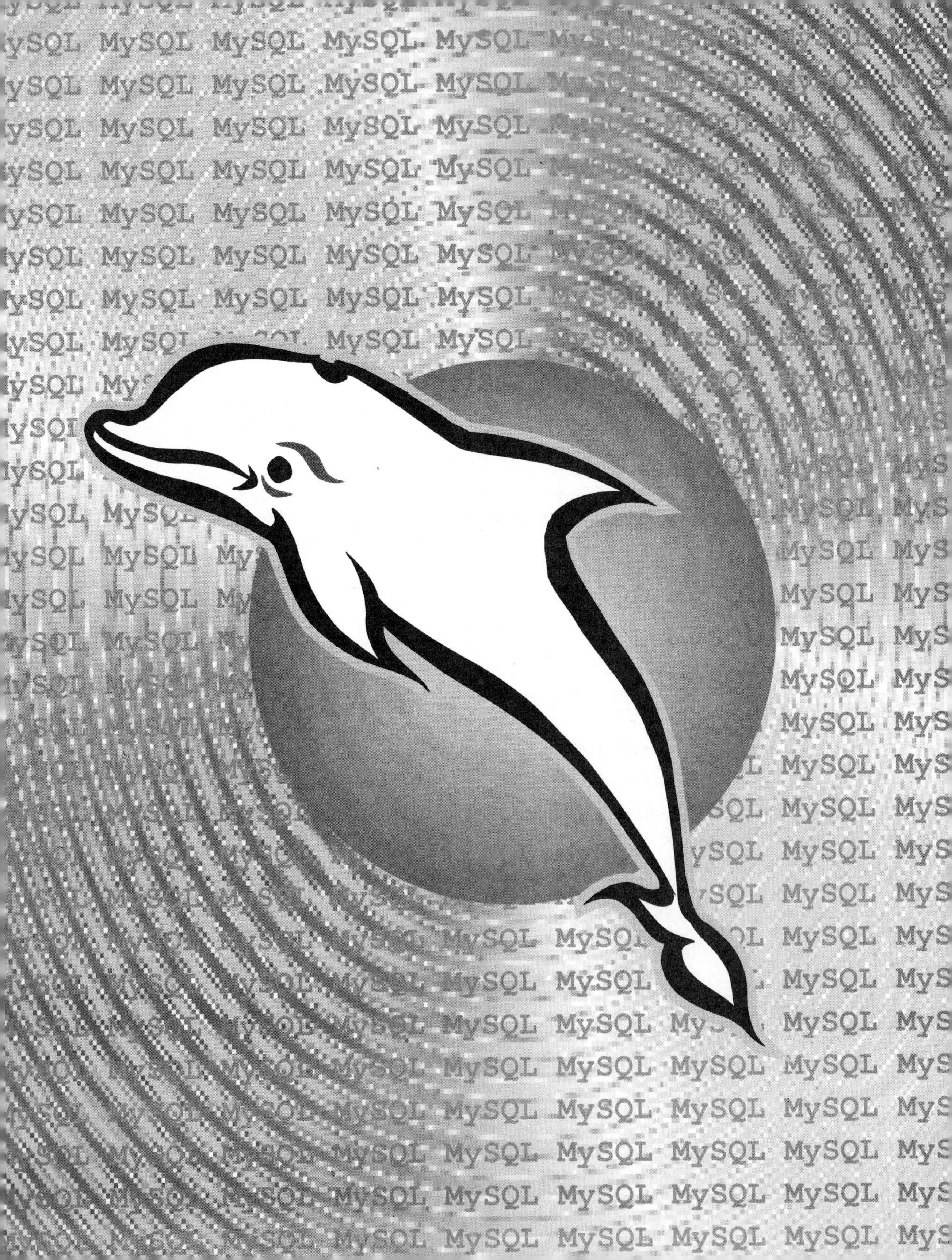
MySQL

Large Objects Support in MySQL

Traditionally, databases have been able to store data in a limited number of forms; usually as numeric values (integers, floating point, and fixed point) and text strings. Often, the size of the text data is limited. MySQL provides support for a wide variety of data types for columns in a table, including geometric objects, network addresses, and arrays.

It might be useful for us to be able to create a database application that can handle *arbitrary* unstructured data formats, for example, for images. We might want to add photographs of the products to our sample database so that our web-based interface can provide an on-line catalog.

MySQL supports an arbitrary data type, the **binary large object**, or BLOB, suitable for storing large data items. We will concentrate on these here.

> Remember, you have to be very careful while using BLOB data. If used without care, BLOBs can severely cripple the performance of your server.

BLOBs

BLOBs can be used to transfer the contents of any file into the database, and to extract an object from the database into a file. They can therefore be used to handle our product images, or any other data that we might wish to store.

MySQL supports five BLOB types:

- ❑ `tinyblob` – From 0-255 characters
- ❑ `blob` – From 0-65535 characters
- ❑ `mediumblob` – From 0-16777216 characters
- ❑ `longblob` – From 0-2147483648 characters
- ❑ `TEXT` – From 0-2147483648 characters (this is just a case-insensitive BLOB)

Note that there may be some additional constraints because of the message buffer size (a longblob field will be limited to something less than the buffer size). The message buffer defaults to 16384, but may be changed by the client. You are also constrained by available memory. You can change the buffer length when starting mysqld by use of the -O option.

For example:

```
mysqld -O max_allowed_packet=max_blob_length
```

Binary Data in BLOBs

BLOBs are the source of many problems to overcome. If you don't need them, moving from one database to another is probably not a big hassle provided you take precautions. If you need them, then be prepared for a rocky ride.

We have seen earlier that MySQL supports four different types to handle BLOBs. The difference is the maximum size of the BLOB and the number of bytes used per record. Practically, a single BLOB type should have sufficed. Oracle 8 and 9 support LOBs with either character data (CLOB) or binary data (BLOB). The difference is in the way data is translated to/from different character sets. BLOBs are never translated.

MySQL uses a string interface to BLOBs, which is simple to use. Here you insert the data as a string and also retrieve it as a string.

It is always safe to convert the file that you want to insert into the database perhaps as a BLOB. In case you wish to do so, then in that case you must escape the following characters:

- ❑   \0
- ❑   \\
- ❑   ' or ' '

MyODBC BLOB Definition

MyODBC defines BLOB values as LONGVARBINARY, and TEXT values as LONGVARCHAR. Because BLOB and TEXT values maybe extremely long, you may run up against some constraints when using them.

Using GROUP BY On a BLOB

If you want to use GROUP BY or ORDER BY on a BLOB or TEXT column, you must convert the column value into a fixed-length object. The standard way to do that is with the SUBSTRING() function. For example:

```
mysql> SELECT (comment from tbl_name), substring(comment,20) as substr ORDER BY
       substr;
```

If you don't do this, only the first max_sort_length bytes of the column are used when storing. The default value is 1024; this value can be changed using the -O option when starting the mysqld server. You can group on an expression involving BLOB or TEXT values by specifying the column position or by using an alias:

```
mysql> SELECT id, substring(blob_col,1,100) from tbl_name GROUP BY 2;
mysql> SELECT id, substring(blob_col,1,100) as b from tbl_name GROUP BY b;
```

Its type determines the maximum size of a BLOB or TEXT object. The largest value you can actually transmit between the client and server is determined by the amount of available memory and the size of the communication buffers. You can change the message buffer size, but you must do so on both the server and client ends.

> Note that a separately allocated object represents each **BLOB** and **TEXT** value internally. This is in contrast to all other column types, for which storage is allocated once per column when the table is opened.

Programming BLOBs

As you might expect, it is possible to use BLOB import and export functions from the programming languages supported by MySQL.

From C, using the `libmysqlclient` library we can use the functions `lo_import()`, `lo_export()`, and `lo_unlink()` in much the same way as above:

```
Oid lo_import(mysqlconn *conn, const char *filename);
int lo_export(mysqlconn *conn, Oid lobjId, const char *filename);
int lo_unlink(mysqlconn *conn, Oid lobjId);
```

BLOBs can be imported and exported from other languages in similar ways. For example the Tcl interface to MySQL contains the functions `mysql_lo_import()`, `mysql_lo_export()`, and `mysql_lo_unlink()`.

For finer control over large object access MySQL provides a suite of low-level functions akin to open, read, write, and friends for ordinary files:

```
int lo_open(mysqlconn *conn, Oid lobjId, int mode);
int lo_close(mysqlconn *conn, int fd);
int lo_read(mysqlconn *conn, int fd, char *buf, size_t len);
int lo_write(mysqlconn *conn, int fd, char *buf, size_t len);
int lo_lseek(mysqlconn *conn, int fd, int offset, int whence);
Oid lo_creat(mysqlconn *conn, int mode);
int lo_tell(mysqlconn *conn, int fd);
```

Refer to the online documentation for more details on these functions.

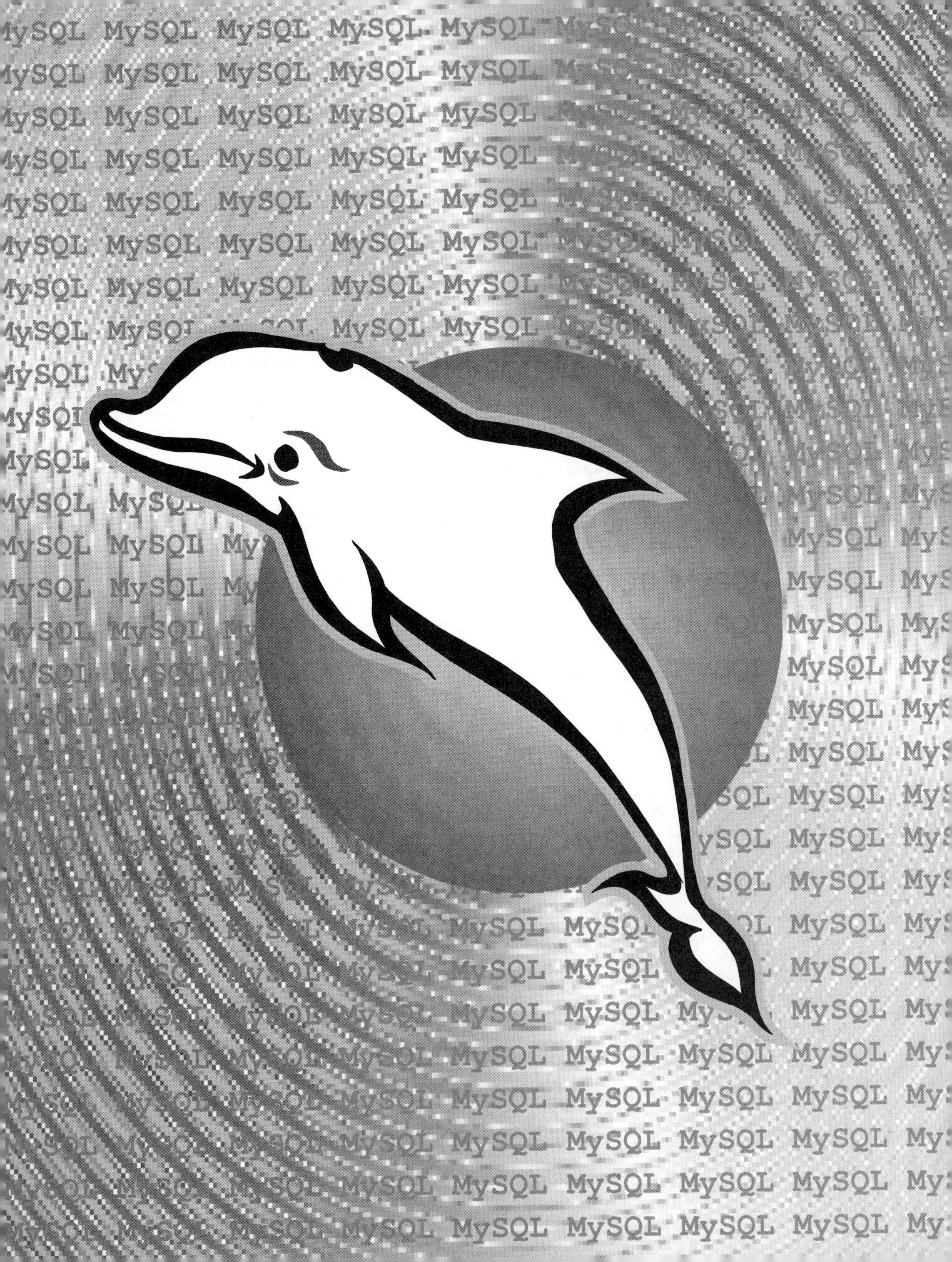

Index

A Guide to the Index

The index is arranged alphabetically in word-by-word order (that is, mysql utility would appear before mysqladmin utility), with symbols preceding the letter A. Leading symbols have been ignored in the alphabetization (thus -password option appears at p) and acronyms have been preferred to their expansions on the grounds that it's easier to guess the acronym for a phrase than to expand an unfamiliar acronym correctly. An asterisk (*) signifies variant endings.

Unmodified headings represent the main or general treatment of a topic. Thus, to find the main discussion of float data types, look under this main heading but, to retrieve every single reference to float data types, look also at the pages indexed under data types.

F

G

R

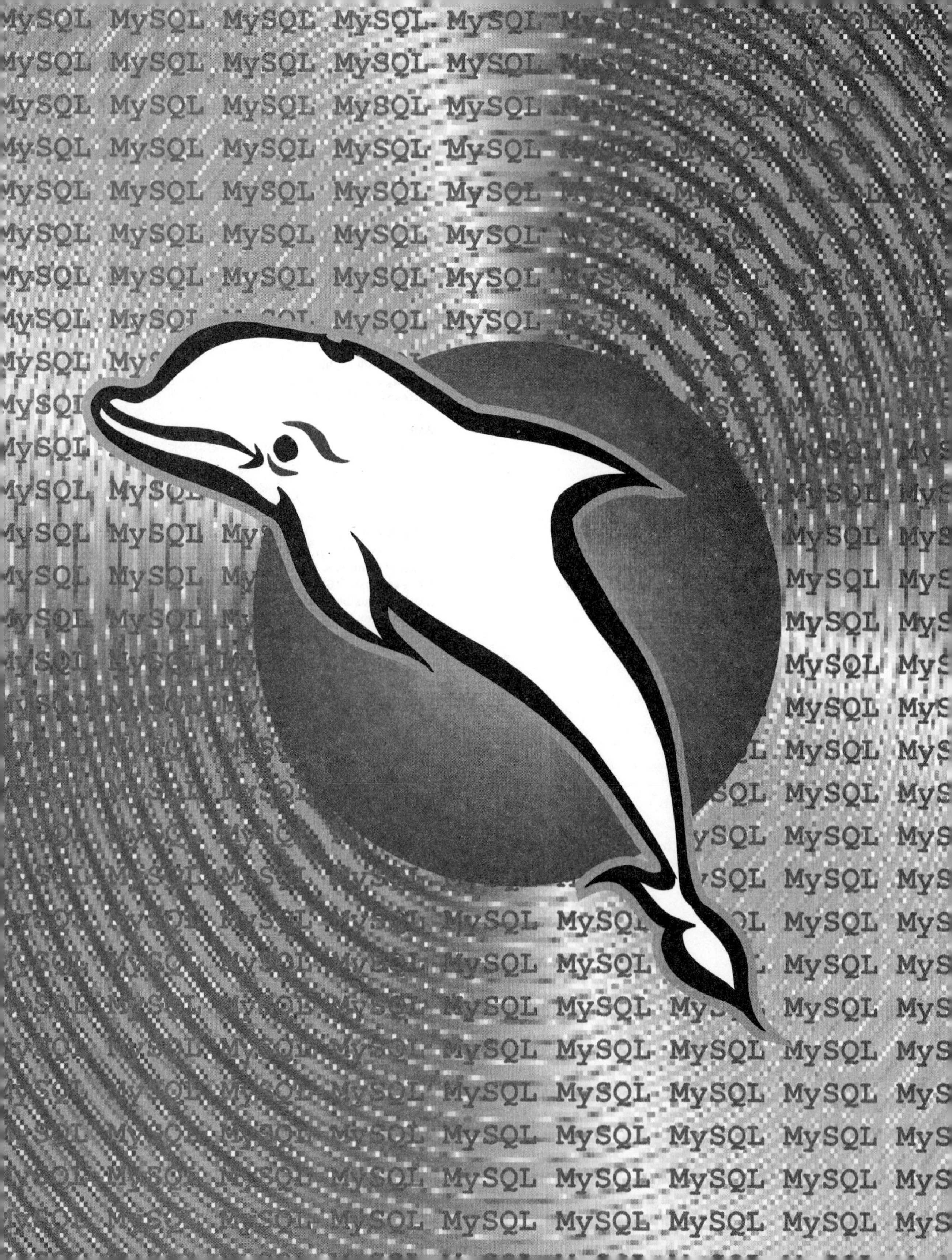
MySQL

Notes

Notes

wrox
Programmer to Programmer™

p2p.wrox.com
The programmer's resource centre

A unique free service from Wrox Press
With the aim of helping programmers to help each other

Wrox Press aims to provide timely and practical information to today's programmer. P2P is a list server offering a host of targeted mailing lists where you can share knowledge with four fellow programmers and find solutions to your problems. Whatever the level of your programming knowledge, and whatever technology you use P2P can provide you with the information you need.

ASP Support for beginners and professionals, including a resource page with hundreds of links, and a popular ASP.NET mailing list.

DATABASES For database programmers, offering support on SQL Server, mySQL, and Oracle.

MOBILE Software development for the mobile market is growing rapidly. We provide lists for the several current standards, including WAP, Windows CE, and Symbian.

JAVA A complete set of Java lists, covering beginners, professionals, and server-side programmers (including JSP, servlets and EJBs)

.NET Microsoft's new OS platform, covering topics such as ASP.NET, C#, and general .NET discussion.

VISUAL BASIC Covers all aspects of VB programming, from programming Office macros to creating components for the .NET platform.

WEB DESIGN As web page requirements become more complex, programmer's are taking a more important role in creating web sites. For these programmers, we offer lists covering technologies such as Flash, Coldfusion, and JavaScript.

XML Covering all aspects of XML, including XSLT and schemas.

OPEN SOURCE Many Open Source topics covered including PHP, Apache, Perl, Linux, Python and more.

FOREIGN LANGUAGE Several lists dedicated to Spanish and German speaking programmers, categories include. NET, Java, XML, PHP and XML

How to subscribe
Simply visit the P2P site, at http://p2p.wrox.com/

wrox

Programmer to Programmer™

Wrox writes books for you. Any suggestions, or ideas about how you want information given in your ideal book will be studied by our team. Your comments are always valued at Wrox.

Free phone in USA 800-USE-WROX
Fax (312) 893 8001

UK Tel.: (0121) 687 4100   Fax: (0121) 687 4101

Beginning Databases with MySQL – Registration Card

Name _____

Address _____

_____

_____

City _____ State/Region _____

Country _____ Postcode/Zip _____

E-Mail _____

Occupation _____

How did you hear about this book?

❏ Book review (name) _____

❏ Advertisement (name) _____

❏ Recommendation _____

❏ Catalog _____

❏ Other _____

Where did you buy this book?

❏ Bookstore (name) _____ City _____

❏ Computer store (name) _____

❏ Mail order _____

❏ Other _____

What influenced you in the purchase of this book?

❏ Cover Design ❏ Contents ❏ Other (please specify):

_____

How did you rate the overall content of this book?

❏ Excellent ❏ Good ❏ Average ❏ Poor

What did you find most useful about this book? _____

_____

What did you find least useful about this book? _____

_____

_____

Please add any additional comments. _____

_____

What other subjects will you buy a computer book on soon?

_____

What is the best computer book you have used this year?

_____

Note: This information will only be used to keep you updated about new Wrox Press titles and will not be used for any other purpose or passed to any other third party.

wrox

Programmer to Programmer™

Note: If you post the bounce back card below in the UK, please send it to:

Wrox Press Limited, Arden House, 1102 Warwick Road,
Acocks Green, Birmingham B27 6HB. UK.

Computer Book Publishers